DEVELOPING
CHILDREN'S LANGUAGE

Developing
Children's Language

WALTER T. PETTY

State University of New York
Buffalo, New York

JULIE M. JENSEN

University of Texas
Austin, Texas

ALLYN AND BACON, INC.
Boston · London · Sydney · Toronto

To the memory of
Naomi C. Chase
Harry A. Greene
Our mentors and friends

Library of Congress Cataloging in Publication Data

Petty, Walter Thomas, 1918–
  Developing children's language.

  1. Language arts (Elementary)   2. Children—
Language.   I. Jensen, Julie M., joint author.
II. Title.
LB1575.8.P46   372.6   79-24175
ISBN 0-205-06868-5

Portions of this book were previously published in *Developing Language Skills in the Elementary Schools* by Harry A. Greene and Walter T. Petty. Copyright © 1959, 1963, 1967, 1971, 1975 by Allyn and Bacon, Inc., 470 Atlantic Avenue, Boston, Massachusetts 02210.

Printed in the United States of America.

CONTENTS

v

PREFACE

Developing Children's Language underlines the importance of effective communication and implements the belief that skills, abilities, and attitudes needed
for such communication are identifiable and teachable. The child learns
language through experiences in realistic communication situations. We believe
that the school curriculum must be rich in content and activities that stimulate
genuine and extensive language expression and necessitate meaningful listening
and reading. Therefore, the language arts program we describe avoids contrived
experiences. It focuses upon developing the language proficiency of each child to
the fullest extent and doing so as efficiently as possible.

We intend the book to be comprehensive, with due recognition that the
language arts are multifaceted and interrelated in complex ways. Language
learning occurs throughout the day and results from the independent and spontaneous activity of children as well as from the formal and informal efforts of
teachers. In other words, children acquire language skills both systematically and
when opportune occasions arise.

The overall structure of the book reflects the integrative nature of the
language arts; the need for wholeness; and the importance of being able to
transfer skills, abilities, and attitudes learned in one context to another. The first
of its three parts addresses those aspects of teacher knowledge and student involvement that apply to all the language arts. Part II unifies the receptive skills of
listening and reading; Part III the productive skills of speaking and writing.
While we believe these skill pairs share important attributes, the reader must also
keep in mind the unifying features of the oral skills of listening and speaking and
the print skills of reading and writing. In general, the most meaningful language
arts experiences in the elementary classroom have no distinct skill boundaries.

In the sixteen chapters that follow:

- We are committed to teacher awareness of the scope of the language
  arts; how its facets relate to each other and to the elementary curriculum as a whole.

- We believe that good teachers possess an understanding of the nature of language and that part of this understanding about language can serve to enrich children's school experiences.
- We know that only through full awareness of the extensive language background children bring to the classroom can teachers expand their abilities in developmentally appropriate ways.
- We know that teachers must apply their knowledge of children and language in instructionally sound ways; they must be able to identify needs, design curricula, plan for instruction, evaluate, and use materials wisely.
- We want literature to permeate and enrich all aspects of teaching and learning throughout the child's day.
- We want children to be sensitive and active receivers of communication and teachers to be capable of developing children's abilities to process language for meaningful purposes, whether messages arrive through their ears or their eyes.
- We believe that a central obligation to children is the development of their skill, confidence, and versatility as speakers and writers by teachers who value and inspire individuality in self-expression.

In this book we have considered the "what," "why," "when," "how," and "how well" of language arts learning and teaching. The points of view of others appear alongside our own, because we believe that it is up to each reader to develop considered opinions after exposure to broad evidence. We discourage dependence on this book as an exclusive resource and encourage further reading by concluding each chapter with a list of references.

Our aim is to share practice as well as theory. Along with theoretical principles, therefore, we present practical examples. We believe that children's experiences must be thoughtful and cumulative—each a piece of a larger rationale. For the reader there are activities at the close of each chapter, chosen to incite action and involvement with children, with peers, with language products, with instructional decisions. They force listening, speaking, reading, and writing.

Our audience includes the beginner and the advanced student, the educator on the campus and in the field, the teacher, the librarian, the specialist, and the administrator. By sharing pertinent research and opinion, we hope to encourage our readers to develop a personal philosophical position related to language arts teaching.

To the teachers we have known and to our colleagues and students, we are grateful for many contributions made directly or indirectly to this book.

W.T.P.
J.M.J.

DEVELOPING
CHILDREN'S LANGUAGE

I

FOUNDATIONS FOR
LANGUAGE ARTS
INSTRUCTION

To silence the child's tongue is to silence his mind.—Walter Loban,
NCTE Distinguished Lecture Series

Every teacher should have a point of view—a philosophical base—for teaching the language arts. This point of view should be firmly held and articulated to others when necessary, and it should be the basis for deciding what children's needs are, what to teach, and how to teach it.

In Part I we present *our* viewpoint concerning children's language development and the teaching of the language arts, a viewpoint that is based upon research evidence, authoritative opinion, and our experiences and observations. We naturally believe that this viewpoint is sound and hope that you will give it serious consideration in founding or restructuring your own point of view.

In bringing our viewpoint into focus, we describe the language arts, discuss language and language learners, present suggestions for program and teaching organization and planning, and stress the importance of the literature program in children's language development.

1

The Language Arts

The development of the language arts occupies almost the entire school day; in reality, language is taught from the time the first child enters the classroom in the morning until the last child goes home. . . . Language is . . . a constantly used medium which can be enlarged and refined on the child's level only through experience in using it.—Ruth G. Strickland, The Language Arts in the Elementary School

Language is basic to humanity. We express our feelings and thoughts through language and stimulate actions and reactions through language. Language is basic for the acquisition of the understandings, attitudes, and ideals that are important to individuals, groups, and society in general.

Because of the fundamental importance of language in all our lives, the school program must give considerable attention to the development of each child's ability to use it as effectively as possible. This, of course, is a big task, for even a casual observer cannot help noticing both the varied uses of language in our society and the wide diversity of forms that language can take. Diverse language styles reflect variations in the culture and the individuality of each person. The function of the school is to extend children's development so that each child can communicate with maximum proficiency in a range of life situations. Thus, it is necessary to organize the school program to teach or further develop specific language skills, to foster attitudes that encourage the most effective use of language, and to build appreciation of the role of language in increasing an individual's human resources.

WHAT ARE THE LANGUAGE ARTS?

In this introductory chapter we will define the language arts and briefly discuss the elements of each of these arts and their importance both in and out of school. Because each of the language arts involves the use of language, we will also examine the interrelationships among them.

Definition of the Language Arts

The language arts are usually defined as the receptive language activities in which communication occurs by either reading or listening and the expressive language activities in which communication occurs by either speaking or writing. Although the term "language arts" is in rather widespread use to describe these activities in school programs, other terms are not uncommon. The traditional name for the part of the school program directly concerned with language is "English," and many persons continue to prefer this term. Others favor the "communicative arts"; still others use the "English language arts." Recently, there has been some tendency simply to use the term "language."

"Language arts" seems to describe best the activities of speaking, writing, listening, and reading, and it is the best label for an instructional program that focuses upon developing abilities in these language activities. "English" generally limits the content of study to writing, grammar, and literature. Some of those persons who favor "English"—and they are often secondary school teachers or persons whose experience comes primarily from secondary school programs—believe that the broader concept inherent in the terms language arts fragments and weakens the focus upon the three traditional areas of study. On the other hand, the term "English" implies to many a narrow scope that does not give adequate attention to speaking, listening, and reading. Its use may well suggest that major (and perhaps total) emphasis will be upon the study of language structure or of language and literature, to the neglect of developing all of the skills needed for effective reception and expression through language.

The label given to an aspect of the school program tends to determine what it includes. Often the label becomes the basis for planning, for selecting instructional materials, and for determining objectives. Since speaking, writing, reading, and listening are the activities that use language and since each is important to every child, as well as to society, we believe they should all receive instructional attention.

Furthermore, we do not think of the language arts as a self-contained subject in the sense that something like mathematics is. Instead, we believe that the language arts are essentially tools or skills for communicating and consequently are fundamental to learning in all subject areas.[1] To consider the language arts—even by another name—as having content for children to study apart from their experiences or apart from the information available to them in the content areas of the curriculum is to fail to recognize both the nature of the language arts and the way people learn.[2]

Elements of the Language Arts

Not everyone defines the terms "reading," "listening," "speaking," and "writing" in the same way. In particular, there is disagreement over which elements make up each aspect of the language arts. Thus, definitions may determine, to a large extent, what is taught.

Writing is sometimes referred to as "composition," but this term ignores the element of composition in speech. We must compose all discourse; that is, we must put ideas and information together in a coherent and appealing manner in order to communicate. People compose sentences as well as paragraphs and written or spoken language of greater length.

The quality of any composition reflects an individual's language and thinking abilities and knowledge of the subject of the composition. Of course, language ability and thinking ability are closely entwined. Thus, not infrequently, *thinking* is considered a fifth language art. Thinking is not only a basic element in writing and speaking, but it is also essential for both reading and listening. As with writing and speaking, thinking at the receptive end of a communication intertwines with language ability and with knowledge about the content of the message read or heard.

Writing, then, involves composition of ideas and information. It also includes the mechanical skills needed for committing ideas to print: spelling, penmanship, punctuation, and capitalization. Important, too, are the conventions and customs surrounding the appearance of written discourse for various purposes. Convention dictates acceptable form for a business letter or for footnotes in a textbook. Proofreading what we write for composition quality and accuracy and to correct errors in mechanics and conventions is yet another element of the writing process.

In *speaking*, as in writing, ideas are basic. Like writing, speaking is more than composing. It, too, involves matters of mechanics and convention associated more with *how* something is said than *what* is said, both of which are fundamen-

---

1. As we will note in the following section, some elements of the language arts do have a content of their own—literature and information about the nature of language itself, for example. However, the basic acts of reception and expression of information and thoughts require particular skills.

2. Regarding the language arts as tools, rather than as a finite subject, does not mean that some elements of them need not receive specific attention. The point is that language is used all day long, every day, and instruction in many of the skills can and should be given in the context of this use.

tal to effective expression. Refining the language children bring to school and extending its suitability to different social contexts are the tasks of the school speaking program.

Reading and *listening* entail the reception of information and ideas through language. They require similar skills for perceiving and identifying unknown words that we encounter in their graphic and oral forms. And both reading and listening require the thinking, language ability, and experience that are essential for all communication.

Like thinking, *literature* permeates a good elementary school language arts program. There is more to literature than the skill of reading, especially since we may hear it as well as read it. Literature is a special form of reading that broadens, deepens, and enriches a child's imagination. Literature requires the skills of perception and comprehension, but it also conveys attitudes and values and the emotions and ideas that it generates are frequently the basis for speaking and writing.

Dramatic activities can be as far-reaching and pleasurable for children as conventional encounters with literature. The scope of these activities ranges from informal play to story dramatization and to theater in which children are the audience. In a less conventional, but accurate, sense, "Drama does not have to be vocal, or even human; it might be a dumb show or a game among dogs. Drama is any raw phenomena as they are first being *converted* to information by some observer."[3] Thus drama is a *form* for the reception of ideas and feelings, as well as a form for expression of all kinds. In some language arts programs virtually all

---

3. James Moffett, *Teaching the Universe of Discourse* (Boston: Houghton Mifflin Co., 1968), p. 61.

listening and speaking experiences and many reading and writing activities derive from drama.

Many elementary schools include foreign languages in their language arts programs. These programs focus on hearing and speaking a foreign language. English as a second language is part of language arts programs in sections of the country where children entering school speak little or no English.

Grammar study traditionally was an element of language arts programs. However, the formal study of grammar has no relationship to language expression or reception. Hence, the subject has disappeared from good language arts programs, although some textbooks and many teachers still foster it. Gradually, grammar study is giving way to expanding children's knowledge of language through the study of word origins, dialects, word choices, and sentence reconstructions as elements of communication. Vocabulary study, for example, in a good language arts program does not mean looking up and writing down word definitions. Instead it means *using* new words in real-life speaking and writing activities.

In addition to all of the above components, a broadly conceived language arts program—one that aims to develop each child's abilities and resources as they relate to communication—must also teach children how to find specific books and other resources in a library, how to locate information in these resources, and how to use a dictionary.

To summarize, the heart of a good language arts program incorporates a wide variety of genuine communication activities. Attention to the aesthetic components of these activities as well as to skill learning will insure that the program has breadth.

Importance of the Language Arts

Developing skill in the use of language is the foundation of the school curriculum, as it has been since the establishment of schools in colonial days for the specific purpose of teaching reading and writing. The subsequent increase in school population and extension of the program to include speaking and listening has not diminished the program's importance. It continues to be the core of the curriculum despite technological changes, the expansion of knowledge, and the increasingly pluralistic nature of society.

Effective use of language is crucial to everyone's social, economic, and political well-being. Society generally recognizes this fact, as evidenced by frequent expressions of public concern that children learn to read, to spell, and to write (unfortunately there is relatively little concern for listening, speaking, dramatics, etc.). Children who have little or no difficulty with most learning may benefit from some pressure, as may children with particularly strong self-images. Others may be highly motivated by interests they develop, and in these cases the pressures have no significance. On the other hand, most children will not develop to their potential under extreme pressure and may hate and be inept with language all their lives.

If society puts too much pressure on teachers and children, much more harm than good can result. Teachers may abandon balanced programs that focus on communication for genuine purpose and ignore much that is valuable in the effort to show pupil gains on reading tests, for example. They may drop sound teaching practices in the areas of concern in ill-conceived attempts to teach the "basics." A child subjected to heavy pressures from society, the media, and the home to learn to read, for instance, may have more difficulty reading than would be the case without these pressures. Clogging children's brains with spelling rules, grammatical terminology, and handwriting drills is unjustified. Thus schools and teachers should resist pressures for doing so, even though they may stem from valid recognition that language ability is a powerful resource, an absolute necessity in many situations, and something over which people can and should have control.

INTERRELATIONSHIPS AMONG THE
LANGUAGE ARTS

The educational literature is replete with discussions of interrelationships among the language arts.[4] Much of this writing is based upon the observations and reflections about language arts teaching by various authorities, but there is an increasing amount of research that supports their contentions. The interrelationships are numerous, diverse, and, in many ways, highly intricate but they have in common the element of language itself and the fact that experience and the way an individual perceives it affects more than one aspect of language use.

In the teaching of language skills, interrelationships are of basic importance, for "language is like a rope woven of many strands, the strength of each adding to the strength of the whole."[5] A teacher who attempts to teach a child to read without recognizing the importance of listening and speaking skills and the promise of children's literature will meet with frustration. A teacher who thoughtfully recognizes the interrelationships of language skills may well discover that a reading problem really hinges upon an insufficient oral language base. Too, the teacher who is sensitive to interrelationships will not wait until confronted by a problem to put this awareness to work, but will keep the overlap in mind when teaching different skills. For instance, a lesson in letter writing will give attention

---

4. For summaries, see Elizabeth A. Thorn, *Teaching and the Language Arts* (Toronto: Gage Publishing, 1974), pp. 53–60, and Harold Newman, "Interrelationships of the Language Arts in the Classroom," in *Elementary School Language Arts: Selected Readings*, edited by Paul C. Burns and Leo M. Schell, 2d ed. (Chicago: Rand McNally and Co., 1973), pp. 19–31.

5. *Language Arts Instruction, K–6: A Handbook of Options* (Concord, Calif.: Mount Diablo Unified School District, 1973), p. 11.

to the skills of spelling, handwriting, and sentence construction, and may call for the use of listening and reading skills.

Listening and Language

An infant's first contact with language is through listening and it is the sole contact for approximately a year. The importance of listening in language development continues to be a major factor throughout life. Children come to school as listeners (proficiency varies from child to child) whose speech patterns were essentially learned by listening. Recognition of this relationship between listening and speaking points up the importance of the quality of the speech that children hear early in their lives. It is a fundamental fact to consider when attempting to make substantial changes in the way an individual speaks. Listening skills are also involved in instruction in the other aspects of language. Instruction in reading, speaking, and writing may involve speaking, and speaking and oral reading by the child call for the use of listening skills by the audience.

The relationship between listening and reading is especially close since both entail receiving messages. They exercise similar decoding subskills and both make use of many of the same attitudes, understandings, and experiences.[6] There are differences, however, particularly in the perceptive tasks required. Thus, the intricacies of relationships are greater than surface appraisal seems to indicate.

Reading and Language

The second receptive aspect of language is reading, which calls for listening, writing, and speaking both in learning and in teaching. As has been stated, the commonality of elements in reading and listening makes possible the development of skills in both while focusing on one of them. Reading performance also varies significantly with proficiency in oral language. Studies of oral language development and reading achievement, for example, have shown that children who rank high on measures of comprehension use subordination in their oral language more often than do those who rank low on these achievement measures.[7] Deficiencies in vocabulary show up in both speech performance and reading achievement (as well as in writing); by the same token, deficiency in reading ability limits the development of oral vocabulary.

What we read is frequently the substance or the point of departure for writing, and writing instruction should build upon the principle that what we write will be read by someone, even if the reader is only the author, as with a diary. The content of writing, of course, reflects the quality of thinking that goes into it, and our thinking ability bears upon success in reading and the other language arts.

One aspect of writing that has a particularly close association with reading is spelling. Attention to the form and sounds of words as they are learned in reading assists in spelling them accurately when writing.[8] It is important, however, to keep in mind that spelling is an expressive act and reading a receptive one. Thus, recognizing words is different from putting together letters to form words as required in spelling.

Speaking and Language

The linguist says that "speaking is language," but it is important to recognize the relationships between speaking, or language used in a general sense, and listening,

---

6. An excellent reference is Sara W. Lundsteen, *Listening, Its Impact at All Levels on Reading and the Other Language Arts*, NCTE/ERIC Studies in the Teaching of English (Urbana, Ill.: National Council of Teachers of English and Educational Resources Information Center, 1979).

7. Ruth G. Strickland, "The Language of Elementary School Children: Its Relationship to the Language of Reading Textbooks and the Quality of Reading of Selected Children," *Bulletin of the School of Education*, Indiana University, 38 (July 1962).

8. Gus P. Plessas and Peggy A. Dison, "Spelling Performances of Good Readers," *California Journal of Educational Research*, 16 (1965): 14–22.

reading, and writing. Preceded only by listening, speaking is a language skill that develops early in the child's life, and there is a great deal of evidence indicating that language development depends largely upon speech experiences. Of course development of vocabulary in speech is related closely to the vocabulary development that results from listening and reading. Too, delayed language development retards speaking activity. Again, many of the skills necessary for effective communication in the other language arts are essential for effective speaking.

Writing and Language

A good deal of research has pointed to a relationship between effective writing and language maturity. For example, some studies show a positive relationship between measures of language growth and such things as clause length, the number of modifications, and the number of words in the T-units (a research "substitute for sentence").[9] On the other hand, there is substantial evidence that the systematic study of the system of the language (grammar) does not result in improved writing. Yet observation alone leads to the realization that students who lack intuitive understanding of the workings of language very often write less effectively than students who have such understanding.

Writing and speaking also are obviously interrelated. While writing tends to be more formal than speech, fluency in one affects the quality of the other. In particular, children are not likely to use words in writing that go beyond their facility in speaking, a facility that is largely a reflection of language maturity.

LANGUAGE ARTS AND OTHER CURRICULAR AREAS

As has been suggested, teaching the language arts as a separate subject, without infusion of content from other fields, is bound to weaken the program. Even making literature and the study of language the content of the language arts wastes many opportunities to develop skill in reading, writing, speaking, and listening. Avoiding the use of language in other areas of the curriculum is impossible, and consciously taking the language arts into other content fields will result in more effective learning of both the content and the skills.

The integration of content areas and language skills does not mean that it is not necessary to teach these skills specifically. They should be taught directly and thoroughly, along with the related abilities and attitudes necessary for their effective use. Sometimes, in so-called "integrated programs," instruction in many of the language skills is too incidental and, hence, generally inadequate. Usually this downfall is attributable to an attempt to achieve integration by contrived and

9. Richard Braddock, "English Composition," in *Encyclopedia of Educational Research*, 4th ed., edited by Robert L. Ebel (New York: Macmillan Co., 1969), p. 452.

purposeless activities. In a good integrated program it is genuinely necessary to use most communications skills. Any inadequacy in their use, then, becomes evident, and the teacher can plan specific developmental or corrective learning activities.

The focus of this book is upon children learning to apply language well by using it in meaningful communication situations. Language ability develops to the degree that there is a genuine, real-life need to use it. Thus, the school curriculum must be rich in content and activities that stimulate genuine and extensive language expression and necessitate meaningful listening and reading.

EXERCISES FOR THOUGHT AND ACTION

1. As a chapter pretest, brainstorm in small groups all the facets that you think comprise the language arts. Arrange these elements on paper in a fashion that shows your perception of interrelationships. Make a pooled class list and reflect on why some of the language arts areas received particular attention.
2. A popularly quoted passage appears below to illustrate what language arts teaching *is not*. Extend the final paragraph based on your own elementary school experiences.

   I have taught . . . for ten years. During that time I have given assignments, among others, to a murderer, an evangelist, a pugilist, a thief and an imbecile.

   The murderer was a quiet little boy who sat on the front seat and regarded me with pale blue eyes, the evangelist, easily the most popular boy in the school, had the lead in the junior play, the pugilist lounged by the window and let loose at intervals a raucous laugh that startled even the geraniums; the thief was a gay-hearted Lothario with a song on his lips and the imbecile, a soft-eyed little animal seeking the shadows.

   The murderer awaits death in the state penitentiary, the evangelist has lain a year now in the village churchyard, the pugilist lost an eye in a brawl in Hong Kong; the thief, by standing on tiptoe, can see the windows of my room from the county jail, and the once gentle-eyed little moron beats his head against a padded wall in the state asylum.

   All of these pupils once sat in my room, sat and looked at me gravely across worn brown desks. I must have been a great help to those pupils—I taught them the rhyming scheme of the Elizabethan sonnet and how to diagram a complex sentence.[10]

3. Identify an adult whom you consider to be an effective communicator (or create your own hypothetical competent language user). What, specifically, can this individual do? Convert some of your observations into tentative goal statements for school language arts programs.
4. In the past, the skills of listening and reading were frequently referred to as

---

10. Naomi John White, "I Taught Them All," *The Clearinghouse* (November 1937), pp. 151, 192.

"passive," whereas speaking and writing were called "active." These terms are seldom used today, having been replaced, respectively, by the words "receptive" and "productive." Speculate on the reasons for this change.

5. Examine several course descriptions and instructional materials for children and adults that carry the designation "English," "language arts," or "communication." Can you accurately predict the content from these labels?

6. Is thinking a language art in your view? Why or why not? How do (1) thinking and (2) language arts relate to other curriculum areas (e.g., can a math course be a thinking course)?

7. The press, parents, and others often bill reading as the most important language art. Regardless of your personal view, build a case *against* this stand. Summarize your arguments in a letter suitable for presentation to the school board.

8. Recall your language arts experiences in elementary school. Consider both the content and your attitudes toward it. Try also to remember some of the teaching methods used. What would you draw from your own background in formulating a personal language arts teaching philosophy?

9. Together with one or a few classmates, draw up a two-column list with some school communication experiences that you consider genuine or real-life on the left side and those you regard as artificial or contrived on the right side.

10. Compose a down-to-earth, practical letter to a parent who has asked you what kinds of experiences would facilitate growth in the language arts during the prekindergarten years.

11. Some components of the language arts are clearly convergent. For example, the task in spelling is to *converge* on a single correct answer. Others are divergent, as is a response to a literary selection, which is appropriately individual and reflective of the unique experience of the reader. Think of other language arts components and attempt to place them on a convergent ⟷ divergent continuum. Finally, think about how to teach convergent language arts areas "creatively."

12. Plan a lesson demonstrating that you can integrate language arts goals with the goals of another curriculum area, such as science.

SELECTED REFERENCES

Burns, Paul C.; Alexander, J. Estill; and Davis, Arnold R., eds. *Language Arts Concepts for Elementary School Teachers.* Itasca, Ill.: F. E. Peacock Publishers, 1972.

Kean, John M., and Personke, Carl. *The Language Arts: Teaching and Learning in the Elementary School.* New York: St. Martin's Press, 1976. Chapter 13.

Kegler, Stanley B. "Language in School Programs." In *English and Reading in a Changing World*, edited by Eldonna L. Evertts, pp. 13–22. Urbana Ill.: National Council of Teachers of English, 1972.

Lewis, Michael, and Rosenblum, Leonard A., eds. *Interaction, Conversation, and the Development of Language.* New York: John Wiley and Sons, 1977.

Lundsteen, Sara W. *Listening, Its Impact at All Levels on Reading and the Other Language Arts*. NCTE/ERIC Studies in the Teaching of English. Urbana, Ill.: National Council of Teachers of English and Educational Resources Information Center, 1979.

Moffett, James and Wagner, Betty Jane. *Student-Centered Language Arts and Reading, K-13*. Boston: Houghton Mifflin Co., 1976. Chapter 2.

Muller, Herbert J. *The Uses of English*. New York: Holt, Rinehart and Winston, 1967.

Petty, Walter T., ed. *Curriculum for the Modern Elementary School*. Chicago: Rand McNally and Co., 1976. Pp. 64–87.

Squire, James R., ed. *The Teaching of English*. Seventy-sixth Yearbook of the National Society for the Study of Education, pt. 1. Chicago: University of Chicago Press, 1977.

Language

A minimum requirement for an educationally relevant approach to language is that it takes account of the child's own linguistic experience, . . . the linguistic demands that society will eventually make of him, and, in the intermediate stage, . . . the demands on language which the school is going to make and which he must meet if he is going to succeed in the classroom. —M. A. K. Halliday, "Relevant Models of Language"

This chapter focuses on the common element of the language arts, that is, language itself. The teaching of language arts must follow established linguistic principles and teachers need a good understanding of these principles. But there is a distinction between what teachers should know about language and what children need to know. It is often the case that children receive an overdose of information (and considerable misinformation) about language, whereas teachers generally suffer from a gross underdose.

WHAT IS LANGUAGE?

Surely everyone recognizes the role that language plays in listening, reading, speaking, and writing. However, it is possible that few of us understand what language actually is and what the fundamental nature of its role is. Too often we think of language in terms of grammar tests and filling in blanks rather than as the major way we transfer creativity, feelings, and thoughts to and from one another. The narrowness of this view shows a lack of understanding that has caused many language arts programs to be much less effective than they should be—to say nothing of frustrating untold numbers of children and perhaps reducing their communicative effectiveness. Recognizing the role of language in communication and in thinking helps to bring language arts programs to the highest possible levels of effectiveness.

Definition of Language

Most people would probably define language as "all the words and sentences we use as we talk with one another." Or some might say that language is used "as we communicate verbally with one another," thereby including writing as well as speaking in the definition. These are, of course, satisfactory definitions for every-day situations, but they are not sufficiently accurate to satisfy language arts researchers, linguists, and teachers of the language arts.

According to the first defining statement in Webster's *Third New International Dictionary*, language is "audible, articulate human speech as produced by the action of the tongue and adjacent vocal organs." A second statement describes language as "any means, vocal or other, of expressing or communicating feeling or thought." The first definition limits language to a human activity and to vocal sound. The second is a more inclusive definition implying that the waving of an arm or the furrowing of a brow is language. At the same time, however, it limits language to a conscious act and thus excludes the instinctive communicative acts one generally associates with animals.

An involuntary cry of pain or fear, the bark of a dog, and the wail of a hungry baby—all are audible sounds that may attract the attention of a human being within hearing range. But they are not necessarily language. If the baby wails because he or she has learned that making enough noise will get him or her food, if the dog barks because it has learned that as a result its owner will open the door and let it into the house, then these sounds may be considered means for communicating and, according to the dictionary definition, they are a kind of language.

Linguists' Definitions of Language

Linguists, the language scientists, tend to define language precisely and individually, as the following quotations show. As you will discover, though, their definitions have many features in common.

Sapir:[1] "Language is a purely human and noninstinctive method of communicating ideas, emotions, and desires by means of a system of voluntarily produced symbols. These symbols are in the first instance auditory, and they are produced by the so-called organs of speech."

Bolinger:[2] "Human language is a system of vocal-auditory communication using conventional signs composed of arbitrary patterned sound units and assembled according to set rules, interacting with the experiences of its users."

Robertson and Cassidy:[3] "Language is the vocal and audible medium of human communication."

Ornstein and Gage:[4] "A language is a structured system of vocal symbols by which a social group cooperates."

It is clear that linguists stress certain assumptions in their definitions. The most important is that "the fundamental forms of language activity are the sequences of sounds made by human lips, tongues, and vocal cords."[5] The linguist says that language is speech, which is as old as human society; writing is only about seven thousand years old. While the statement of the relative ages is a fact, writing thus being a derivative of speech, teachers and curriculum authorities should not make a fetish of saying that language is speech.[6] Certainly, language programs need to give greater attention to oral language than they traditionally have. However, we must not ignore the linguistic concerns of written expression. This is not to deny that speech is *the* language, but for school purposes, as opposed to the purposes of the linguist's studies, it is convenient to refer to oral language and to written language.

Characteristics of Language

From the foregoing linguists' definitions and the basic assumption of the oral nature of language, a number of characteristics of language emerge:[7]

---

1. Edward Sapir, "Language Defined," in *Introductory Readings on Language,* edited by Wallace L. Anderson and Norman C. Stageberg, rev. ed. (New York: Holt, Rinehart and Winston, 1967), p. 5.

2. Dwight Bolinger, "Some Traits of Language," in *Language and the Language Arts,* edited by Johanna DeStefano and Sharon Fox (Boston: Little, Brown and Co., 1974), p. 11.

3. Stuart Robertson and Frederic Cassidy, *The Development of Modern English,* 2d. ed. (Englewood Cliffs, N.J.: Prentice-Hall, 1954), p. 1.

4. Jacob Ornstein and William W. Gage, *The ABC's of Languages and Linguistics* (Philadelphia: Chilton Books, 1964), p. 3.

5. Archibald A. Hill, *Introduction to Linguistic Structures* (New York: Harcourt, Brace and World, 1958), p. 1.

6. David Reed elaborates on this subject in "A Theory of Language, Speech, and Writing," *Elementary English* (December 1965), p. 346.

7. Taken from Appendix B, *The Language Component in the Training of Teachers of English and Reading: Views and Problems,* mimeographed (Washington, D.C.: Center for Applied Linguistics and National Council of Teachers of English, 1966).

1. Language is symbolic. It is a thing of itself, quite distinct from the matter to which it relates. Such a relation is purely arbitrary and may change with time. The nature of the symbol differs in form depending on whether one is speaking or writing.

2. Language is systematic. For this reason it can be learned. For the same reason it can be described and must be described in terms of a system. Languages are universally orderly, but there is not, as was once supposed, a universal type of order to which all languages aspire.

3. Language is human. It is the most characteristic human activity, completely different in kind from the "language" of animals.

4. Language is a social instrument. Our social relationships are achieved by it and through it, on the whole, and their perpetuation is heavily dependent upon it. Social differences and language differences almost invariably go hand in hand.

5. Language is noninstinctive. It needs to be learned. The child gains control of the structure of the language in association with parents, brothers and sisters, and playmates. Much of the vocabulary, particularly that reflecting social attitudes, is acquired through the schools.

Linguists usually add the terms "arbitrary," "conventional," and "complete" to "symbolic" and point out that the attachment of words to objects or ideas represents an arbitrary act, that any designation hinges upon agreement among users, and that such attachment has been made to express every idea or feeling that the users of the language need. An illustration of the arbitrary nature of language is the symbol attached to the object we know as a dog. In French it is *le chien*, and in English it might as well be *neg* as *dog*. Since the attachment of symbols to things is arbitrary, the attachments must be learned—that is, someone who knows must tell the learner what the symbols are. The complete nature of language is shown in the fact that words and expressions are coined to take care of the language user's needs. For example, the Wichita language of the Oklahoma Indian tribe does not include *nuclear physics* or *celestial navigation*, because the speakers of Wichita have never needed these terms when using their native language.[8] Similarly, the word *acrylic* never existed in the English language until the need for it arose.

Increasingly, linguists give less stress to noninstinctiveness as a characteristic of language. The point is generally made that young children are not taught a language; they learn it by themselves.[9] That is, there is no conscious effort and application. They seem to possess an inborn faculty for learning language in general, not any one particular language.

Most persons realize that language is systematic, even though this knowledge is often unconscious. Because language components may be arranged in recurrent patterns, people presented with only part of a pattern can make predictions about the rest of it. You know, for example, that the suffix *ed* is usually added to form

---

8. Ornstein and Gage, p. 11.

9. William G. Moulton, "Language and Human Communication," in *Linguistics in School Programs*, edited by Albert H. Marckwardt (Chicago: University of Chicago Press, 1970), p. 27.

the past tense of a verb. You know that in the sentence "Bill_____s Jim an_____," the first blank requires a verb and the second a noun. Moreover, you know that not all verbs can be used in the sentence (this one must be third person singular, must end with *s*, and must be able to take both direct and indirect objects) but that words such as *gives, throws, offers,* and *takes* would fit. And you know that the noun must begin with a vowel (or silent *h*) and take an article (e.g., *apple, illustration, orange,* or *example*).

Recognizing that language is systematic does not mean that language will be the same in all contexts. A language has several varieties, corresponding, for example, with a variety of social situations. Thus, in speaking of the English language, we are referring to a kind of synthesis of common features in all of these varieties. It is the existence of these common elements which makes the many varieties of the English language understandable to all of its speakers.[10]

Still another characteristic of language—related both to its symbolic and its systematic nature—is the fact that it changes. The change in English is apparent in the following Bible verses from four versions of the "Parable of the Sower" (Mark 4:1–4):[11]

Old English text c. 1000 A.D.

1. And eft hē ongan hī aet *p*ǣre sǣ lǣ ran. And him wae s mycele menegu tō gegaderod, swā *p*ǣet hē on scip ēode, and on *p*ǣre sǣ wae s; and eall sēo menegu ymbe *p*a sǣ wae s on lande.

10. Summer Ives, "The Nature and Organization of Language," in *Language Arts Concepts for Elementary School Teachers*, edited by Paul C. Burns et al. (Itasca, Ill.: F. E. Peacock Publishers, 1972), pp. 34–41.

11. R. C. Troike, *Linguistics for English Teachers* (Austin, Tex.: Texas Education Agency, 1965), pp. 27–30.

2.   And hē hī fela on big spellum lǣ rde, and him tō cwæð on his lāre,
3.   Gehyrað Ūt ēode sē sǣ dere his sǣ d to sāwenne.
4.   And þā hē sēow, sum fēoll wið þone weg, and fugelas cōmon and hit frǣton.

Middle English text c. 1380 A.D.

1.   And eft he bigan to teche at the see; and myche puple was gaderid to hym, so that he wente in to a boot, and sat in the see, and al the puple was about to see on the loond.
2.   And he tauȝte hem in parablis many thingis. And he seide to hem in his techying,
3.   Here ȝe. Lo! A man sowynge goith out to sowe,
4.   And the while he sowith, summe seed felde aboute the weie, and briddis of heuene camen, and eeten it.

Early modern English text 1611 A.D.

1.   And he began again to teach by the sea side; and there was gathered unto him a great multitude, so that he entered into a ship and sat in the sea; and the whole multitude was by the sea on the land.
2.   And he taught them many things by parables, and said unto them in his doctrine,
3.   Hearken: Behold, there went out a sower to sow.
4.   And it came to pass, as he sowed, some fell by the way side, and the fowls of the air came and devoured it up.

Late modern English text 1953 A.D.

1.   Once more he began to teach beside the sea. But the crowd that gathered round him was greater than ever; so he got into a boat on the water and sat down there. The people all stood on the shore, facing the sea.
2.   And he taught them many things in parables. In the course of his teaching he said to them:
3.   Listen to this. Picture the sower going out to sow.
4.   It happened, as he sowed, that some of the seed fell by the path and the birds came and ate it up.

Variety in Language

There are about 2800 major languages spoken in the world today and what has been said so far about language applies to each of them. Furthermore, aside from the fact that there are many languages, a language is an entity only in a limited sense. A single language exists in numerous forms or varieties due to differences among its users, differences ranging from sex, age, ethnicity, occupation, education, income, place of residence, and specific cultural and social circumstances. Later we will discuss "standard" English and the ways in which children's language use may deviate from that standard. Yet even a little reflection about the language we encounter in the media and in our exposure to political, business, and educational leaders and other public speakers and writers, tells us that "standard" language is difficult to define. Also, if you think about the language each of us uses at home, in social settings, and in business you cannot help but recognize that language takes a variety of forms.

Recognizing and understanding the variation in language is important in language arts teaching. The absence of this appreciation will cause frustration for both the teacher and the children and will result in a less than effective language arts program.

Our English Language

The biblical verses quoted earlier reflect the influence on English of foreign invaders of the British Isles and the spread of English beyond British borders. Today, particularly, English is a polyglot language; it is rich with words contributed by other languages. The influence of Germanic and Latin languages is especially heavy, but many English words have other origins and a number of them are relatively recent additions. Consider these examples:

- Scandinavian: *saga, ski, rug, geyser*
- French: *rouge, vignette, surveillance*
- Spanish: *sombrero, guitar, corral, adobe*
- Italian: *violin, replica, ghetto, broccoli*
- Dutch: *buoy, skate, yacht, pickle*
- Hebrew: *amen, cherub, sabbath, camel*
- Persian: *caravan, bazaar, shawl*

American English is particularly adaptable and flexible. Besides adopting words from other languages, Americans readily coin words to describe new commercial products, processes, and discoveries and incorporate them in the vernacular. Many other words acquire new meaning in American English, move from slang to permanence, become abbreviated, or become part of a new compound word.

HUMAN BEHAVIOR

Most linguists stress that language is a system of human communication originating in the sound stream produced by the "organs of speech." Language is possible because everyone in a particular culture or setting agrees that certain sounds or combinations of sounds represent objects, ideas, and emotions about which they need to communicate with one another. Language is such an integral part of our everyday lives that we rarely think of it as something uniquely human.

We rarely think of the immense consequences of the invention of language: by the use of language infants become human beings; without language, becoming an adult would mean achieving only an aborted form of fulfillment.[12]

Language and Nonhumans

Observers generally believe that animal cries and actions are instinctive and do not constitute language. The close observer of nature who has watched a mother hen call her chicks under her wings at the approach of danger, a colony of ants at work, or a mother quail lure a hunter away from her nest by appearing to be crippled might question this belief. However, these behaviors are reactions to cues, as is a dog's response to a whistle, a pointing finger, or a traffic light. Even the myna bird who says, "When do we eat," while obviously vocalizing, is responding instinctively to a cue rather than consciously using language as a result of thought.

Efforts to teach language to nonhumans have occurred most intensively with chimpanzees, but because these efforts have not involved the use of oral symbols, the chimpanzees' communications do not fit our earlier definitions of language. In the late 1960s, Allan and Beatrice Gardner, psychologists at the University of Nevada, taught their chimp Washoe to use the sign language of the deaf. She learned well enough that visiting deaf people could understand her and she them. She was able to combine words into sentencelike strings, generalize from signs to real objects to pictures of objects, and invent names for new things. Dr. David Premack, of the Center for Advanced Study of Behavioral Sciences in Stanford, California, constructed several distinctively shaped and colored pieces of plastic to signify different English words. His pupil, Sarah, learned more than 130 words, which she was able to arrange in sensible sequences, and to "read" sequences assembled for her. Lana, a chimpanzee at the Yerkes Primate Research Center in Atlanta, lives with a computer console. When she pushes a series of symbol-coded buttons, her computer types out a translation of the symbols. Her attendant reads the message and composes a response, which appears for Lana on a display panel.[13] In spite of arguments to the contrary, however, the long-standing contention of linguists that humans alone possess language continues to stand.

The Uses of Language

Language, then, is the fundamental means by which humans communicate ideas and emotions. It is a vital part of every human activity. Universally humans talk,

---

12. Carl A. Lefevre, "Language and Self: Fulfillment or Trauma?" *Elementary English*, (February 1966), pp. 124–28.

13. *New York Times* News Service, "Research Showing Chimps Can Do More than Ape Human Language," *Minneapolis Tribune*, 9 June 1974.

and almost invariably they utilize some form of recorded or written expression. The Congo tribes, the Ecuadorian Indians, and residents of Los Angeles, Brooklyn, London, Moscow, Cairo, Hong Kong, and Tokyo all talk; all communicate by means of language. The language forms used depend entirely upon the culture or area in which individuals live. As soon as primitive humans began to live together, first in families and then in tribes, there was a need for some means of making their intentions and desires clear to one another. They had to warn each other of danger and to report sources of food. Probably the earliest form of communication was the use of natural signs—cries, gestures, and facial expressions—which were spontaneous responses to natural situations, and expressions of needs and emotions. From these early and surely accidental beginnings, meanings came to be refined for the signs and sounds. Vocal utterances, substituted gradually for manual signs, were found to be more effective, especially in combat and in the dark. Gradually humans recognized the need for graphic symbols (writing) to represent the natural signs. In the ages since, we have developed and refined language into a rather intricate but reasonably effective means of communication. Its development and evolution is still going on and will doubtless continue as long as our small segment of the universe survives.

The first purpose of language, then, is *communication*. Communication involves at least two persons, one to present the idea or thought by means of speaking or writing and another to receive the idea or thought by means of reading or listening. The effectiveness with which the actual communication takes place depends entirely upon the degree to which both individuals know the language and the skill with which they use it. Individuals who have a good command of language and its use for communication will be able to express their ideas and convey them to others. Likewise, if readers or listeners have an adequate command of language, they will be able to comprehend the intended meaning speedily and correctly.

Using language as a *means of releasing tensions or reacting to a specific personal incident* is a second use of language. This type of expression is very personal and may range from the ludicrous to the sublime. Thus, it may take the form of muttering under your breath or uttering an oath when you hit your thumb with a hammer or a poetic thought written simply for your own enjoyment or saying "magnificent" at the sight of the Grand Canyon.

A related use of language that is possibly the most important of all uses is *thinking*. While thinking involves the mental manipulation of meaningful symbols, not all of the symbols are language symbols. Some are mental images, such as those of the artist thinking of line and color. We do most of our thinking, though, in terms of language symbols, which means our thinking is controlled to a considerable degree by the qualities and categories of our language.[14] This fact possibly accounts for the development of language and its growth as primitive

---

14. W. Nelson Francis, "The Uses of Language," *Language Arts Concepts for Elementary School Teachers* (Itasca, Ill.: F. E. Peacock Publishers, 1972), pp. 42–46.

society became somewhat complicated. Primitive people probably had little difficulty thinking in terms of mental images when they went into the jungle to hunt for food. But living with others of their kind brought the need for rules, generalizations, laws, customs, and social mores. It is not easy to express or comprehend such abstractions as truth, honesty, love, honor, and courage by means of mental images. As civilization evolved, society became more and more complex and new concepts and experiences required the creation of new symbols to represent them. These language symbols have become the tools by which individuals form opinions or draw conclusions; they are the means by which we construct new meanings and new principles.

A fourth purpose of language is the *transmission of culture.* Many age-old ideas, opinions, deeds, and mistakes, however good or bad they may be, are accessible to us in literature. This trail exists principally because of language, although art and music, which are also forms of expression, have made contributions. *Through recorded language the accumulation of human experience is shared and conveyed to posterity.* It would be difficult to imagine what it would be like to live without being able to profit from the experiences and contributions of our ancestors recorded in history and in literature. Without language we would be isolated; we would not be able to share the thoughts and ideas of others living during the same period as ourselves. We would know nothing of history or of the marvelous literature of our own and other cultures. The preservation of the record of people's thoughts and deeds is vitally necessary to education and to the future development of people and society.

Language has no value independent of its uses. It serves people. Halliday, in emphasizing that people's learning of language is tied to their perceptions of its utility in various situations, combines the four uses described above in terms of individual circumstances of use:[15]

Instrumental: language to get things done to satisfy material needs
Regulatory: language to control the behavior, feelings, or attitudes of others
Interactional: language to establish the social status of self and others
Personal: language to express individuality, awareness of self
Heuristic: language to investigate, to learn about things
Imaginative: language to create
Representational: language to inform, describe, express

Nonlanguage Communication

Language is not a necessary prerequisite for communication to occur; that is, verbal symbols are but one means for transmitting messages. Many of the com-

15. M. A. K. Halliday, *Explorations in the Functions of Language* (London: Edward Arnold, 1973), pp. 11–16.

munication purposes that language serves can be achieved in other ways. In fact, Smith contends that language has no uses for which other means of communication are not available.[16] Primitive people, of course, believed otherwise or else they would not have invented language. To appreciate the truth of Smith's statement, consider those objects and actions that tend to be universally understood. Certain facial expressions, as well as the gestures of waving and shaking a fist convey messages that have universal meaning. Music, forms of architecture, monuments, and drama also communicate, and within certain groups of individuals, communication can take place through mathematics, rituals, forms of dress, and the like. Communication frequently occurs through the simultaneous use of many means of expression.

Communication takes place also by means of what is known as "body language." Different postures or stances convey different messages, such as anger, tension, happiness, and unhappiness. Some forms of body language are also considered masculine or feminine. In addition, we still use sounds that are not language—giggling and crying, for example—to communicate.

Besides needing to understand that they communicate to others and receive communication in many nonverbal ways, children should understand the possibilities for making oral communication more effective with gestures, facial expressions, and bodily movement. In written expression, of course, we can enhance communication by underlining words, indenting, and using other devices to call attention to particular words.

LINGUISTICS

All teachers have heard the term *linguistics*. Their definitions of it sometimes differ, however, as do their beliefs about how linguistics affects their teaching and children's learning. The fact that linguistics has penetrated most school programs reflects teacher interest in the subject and the (sometimes conflicting) efforts of commercial organizations and professional groups to include it in the curriculum. We herald the contributions of linguists to our work, but believe that what some people label as linguists is without value—even harmful—to children.

What Is Linguistics?

The most common definition of linguistics found in educational literature is "the scientific study of language," but this phrase needs explanation and extension for most persons. Postman and Weingartner suggest that "any definition of linguistics depends upon who is doing the defining."[17] Many teachers equate the term linguistics with *grammar*; others define it as the relationship of sound symbols to

---

16. Frank Smith, "The Uses of Language," *Language Arts* 54 (September 1977): 639.
17. Neil Postman and Charles Weingartner, *Linguistics, A Revolution in Teaching* (New York: Dell Publishing Co., 1966), p. 3.

graphic symbols. To many linguists a definition broadened to include studying the entire culture is most suitable. To the person on the street linguistics may mean the study of dialects or the compiling of dictionary definitions.

The Nebraska curriculum guide defines linguistics as "the study of human speech; the units, nature, structure, and modifications of language, languages, or a language, including especially such factors as phonetics, phonology, morphology, accent, syntax, semantics, general or philosophical grammar, and the relation between writing and speech."[18]

Lamb extends her "scientific study of language" with the statement: "Such study may concentrate on the sounds of language (phonology), the origin and changing meaning of words (etymology and semantics), or the arrangements of words in a meaningful context in different languages (syntax-structural or transformational grammar)."[19]

Guth says, "Linguistics is the study, according to rigorously defined methods or principles, *of language as a system.*"[20]

A particularly useful definition of linguistics is that of Postman and Weingartner: "Linguistics is a way of behaving . . . it is a way of behaving while one attempts to discover information and to acquire knowledge about language."[21] They discuss the behavior in terms of attitudes and procedures. Their emphasis is upon the inductive approach to learning, a spirit of discovery, a rejection of dogmatism, and the verifying and revising process identified with scientific study.

Linguistic Study

Linguistic study is done by linguists, though accepting the Postman and Weingartner definition means that anyone, including children in the elementary school, may undertake linguistic study if it is done in the spirit described. In a more restricted sense, however, linguistics is the study of language by language scientists—the linguists. A linguist may study any language and may specialize in a particular field of study. Linguists may study the history of a language or compare languages on such characteristics as grammar, phonology, morphology, semantics, or dialects. Linguists subscribe to different theories related to their particular interests. For example, analyses of language structure are based on widely differing theories (structural and transformational-generative are the best known). The theoretical differences lead to differences in definitions, terminology, and procedures.

Though linguists, in general, can be characterized as having certain

18. Nebraska Curriculum Development Center, *A Curriculum for English: Language Explorations for the Elementary Grades* (Lincoln: University of Nebraska Press, 1966), p. 2.

19. Pose Lamb, *Linguistics in Proper Perspective* (Columbus, O.: Charles E. Merrill Publishing Co., 1967), p. 4.

20. Hans P. Guth, *English Today and Tomorrow* (Englewood Cliffs, N.J.: Prentice-Hall, 1964), p. 25.

21. Postman and Weingartner, p. 4.

characteristic attitudes, such as being nonjudgmental about their subject and using certain common methods associated with scientific inquiry, there are several branches of linguistics, each of which has a special focus. *Historical linguists* are interested in how language began and how it grows. *Psycholinguists* ask questions about the relationship of language behavior to thought. *Linguistic geographers* explore the relationship between where people live and the way they talk. *Sociolinguists* study society and language to uncover the relationships among social class, ethnicity, and language. *Lexicographers* compile dictionaries. *Students of usage* deal with the attitudes people have toward particular words, sounds, and language structures. *Semanticists* are interested in meaning. The relationship of language to a given social situation concerns a *student of register*. All of these people are linguists.

Studying Language Structure

Of most interest in schools has been the aspect of linguistics concerned with language structure; that is, findings from the study of the system of language (and in-school study of the system) have attracted the most attention. The reason is that the traditional emphasis on the study of grammar in schools leads many teachers and others to believe that learning the findings from studies of language structure would cause pupils to write "better" and to speak "correctly." Issues regarding the teaching of grammar are discussed later in this chapter, as are matters relative to "correctness" of usage. Language learning, including the understanding young children have of the language system, will be discussed in Chapter 3. Other aspects of "the scientific study of language" and findings from such study are presented in most of the remaining chapters.

The study of language structure includes *phonology*—the study of the sounds of the language. The basic sounds, or *phonemes*, which are the smallest units of sound by which different meanings may be distinguished, are the core of this study. Most linguists identify twenty-four consonants and nine vowels as the segmental phonemes.[22] In other words, the stream of sound uttered by a human is divided into segments (phonemes) that are recognizable as significant language units. In addition, there are suprasegmental phonemes which also describe the language. These are four degrees of *stress* (loudness or softness) given to segmental phonemes, three levels of *pitch* (highness or lowness), and four *junctures* or interruptions and suspensions in the stream of sound (identified as breaks between words, e.g., "I scream" vs. "ice cream" and "nitrate" vs. "night rate").

A second area of study is *morphology*—the study of word forms. Morphology deals with the meaningful groupings of sounds, but emphasizes grammatical factors of grouping rather than meaning as we commonly think of it. *Morphemes* are described as the smallest meaningful units in language.[23] Thus, the

---

22. *A Curriculum for English*, p. 18.

23. Ornstein and Gage define morphemes as follows: "Roughly speaking, a morpheme is any of the pieces that has a function in a word" (p. 81).

word *hat* is one morpheme, but it is made up of three phonemes; *boy* is one morpheme and two phonemes; and *I* is one morpheme and one phoneme. Morphemes include word bases (or roots), prefixes, suffixes, and word-form changes or inflections. A *free morpheme* is one that may stand by itself in larger language structures, and a *bound morpheme* is one that must combine with another morpheme. The words above (boy, hat, I) are free morphemes; *pre-* and *-ness* are bound morphemes.

A third area in studying language structure concerns the forms of words. Words, of course, differ in meaning but they also differ in other characteristics. Language study based upon traditional or Latin-based grammar classified words according to their meaning (i.e., "A noun is the name of a person, place, or thing") or their function (i.e., "An adjective modifies a noun or pronoun"). Other linguists may classify words in a different way. They may speak of *form classes*—which are the traditional parts of speech in English: nouns, verbs, adjectives, and adverbs, although they are sometimes identified by the words *form class* and a number (i.e., form class I = verbs) instead of by the traditional terms. Words are classified as to form class by testing them in "slots" (The———ran fast. A———truck approached.), by determining if they will "take" certain suffixes, and by relating the stress given them to other words given like stress in sentences of the same pattern. Related to word-form classes is a fourth area of study of the language system known as *syntax* or word order. Syntax is defined as the study of the meaningful combinations of words—the study of the ways that words can be ordered or arranged significantly.[24] This study involves classification of sentences and parts of sentences. *Structural linguists* use several classification systems to categorize sentences. These include relating each sentence to certain basic patterns or sentence skeletons or to the method of expansion of a skeleton by substitution or modification. Syntax can also be studied by a *transformational-generative* approach, as does a group of linguists known as transformationalists.[25] Transformational study begins with the assumption that sentences are of two basic types: kernel sentences and transformed sentences.[26] The transformationalist has language rules that show that certain words or phrases can be grammatically moved. The approach is synthetic rather than analytic, as is the approach followed by structuralists. The transformationalist begins with the rules about the phrase structures, the possible transformations, and effects of transformations upon meaning and sound.

Teachers and Linguistics

Teachers need to be informed about the language they use and teach to children. They need to be aware of the language abilities that children possess when they

---

24. *A Curriculum for English*, p. 94.

25. A more detailed explanation of transformational grammar, as well as other grammars, is given later in this chapter.

26. Paul M. Roberts, *English Sentences*, teacher's manual (New York: Harcourt, Brace and World, 1962).

enter school and the best ways to draw forth and develop these abilities. To acquire this awareness, they should have a reasonable amount of knowledge about the findings of linguists in the several specialized areas of study. They do not need to be linguists nor must they do many of the things linguists do. They must, however, be good observers of language.

Teachers should develop appreciation of language and its all-around usefulness, but they should not attempt to teach children all that they know about language and how it works. One source expresses this concern in the following way:[27]

> It is easy to get carried away briefly, fascinated by internal logic of a well-articulated system or impressed by the weight of its scholarship, or intrigued by its refreshing "newness." It is only one step further to let it supplant the children and become the goal.

Linguistics is not the study of how to teach spelling or reading or composition. The tools and techniques of linguistic science are not intended for the classroom. The knowledge derived by linguistic study, however, should be assimilated and used "to shed new light upon the problems that arise wherever language is concerned."[28] That is, teachers must learn about linguistic findings and use this knowledge in teaching children. A knowledge of linguistics should lead to the following insights:[29]

1.   Language is a creative activity of each person.
2.   Language patterns are well learned by the time a child is five or six.
3.   A child usually knows and uses all the basic structures.
4.   Language habits, once learned, change slowly.
5.   Speech is the language; writing reflects the speech.
6.   The writing system or code of English is alphabetic and has certain inadequacies.
7.   Language is continually changing; it has a history.
8.   Language varies with the age, socioeconomic group, and geographical region of the speaker. These variations are *dialects*.
9.   Replacing the concept of "correctness" is a concept of alternatives in pronunciation, word choice, phrasing, and construction.
10. Every language has its own grammar. English grammar is not Latin grammar.
11. People speak their native language, to a degree, in unique ways. The variations spoken are each individual's *idiolect*.

---

27. *Linguistics in the Elementary Classroom* (Los Angeles: Los Angeles County Superintendent of Schools Office, 1965), p. 36.

28. Charles C. Fries, "Advances in Linguistics," *Linguistics—Current Issues* (Champaign, Ill.: National Council of Teachers of English, 1961), p. 37.

29. *Linguistics in the Elementary Classroom*, pp. 3–4.

The elementary teacher who understands these concepts can find opportunities throughout each school day to use them. The applications should usually be informal and spontaneous and always directed at helping children to appreciate, understand, and use their language better.

Beyond the informal, spontaneous teaching about language, of course, a teacher may teach much about language specifically and directly with a program directed (1) toward showing children that English is primarily a word-order language, that the structure of English syntax is often of the utmost importance; (2) toward giving children an understanding of the sound (phonology) of the language, of its music; (3) toward giving them an understanding of the language's historical dimensions (where our vocabulary came from, etc.) and of the evolution of its spelling system, both of which are important not only to spelling but also to reading; and (4) toward giving them an understanding of the extent to which punctuation is a written representation of the suprasegmental features of spoken discourse.[30]

DIALECTS, USAGE, AND GRAMMAR

A major concern in school programs has always been teaching children to speak and write "correctly." Today this concern is still very much present, but many persons substitute "acceptably" for "correctly" in recognition of the difficulty of defining "correctly" due to the difference in standards for various speaking and writing tasks. This change is probably not as agreeable to parents as it is to teachers, partly because they lack the teacher's understanding of many facts about language. Confusion also arises from differences in terminology.

It is the purpose of this section to define the terms that are relevant to teaching about language, to present evidence concerning the value of and need to teach some things about language—as well as the lack of value or need for some traditional lessons—and to discuss briefly the several grammars about which teachers should be somewhat informed.

Misconceptions and Definitions

Misconceptions about correctness in language usage and about teaching it in language arts and English programs have led to "millions (billions? trillions?) of child-hours spent writing *was* or *were* in blanks; a feeling of inferiority in millions of persons because they have been made to believe that their English is not good; a contrasting snobbishness in many others because they are convinced that they are among the elite who use good English; a belief that 'right' and 'wrong' are absolute terms in language, as they may be in mathematics; a hatred of English on

---

30. Ibid., p. *xxii*.

the part of those who have difficulty in making their language conform to the teacher's expectations."[31] Misconceptions about the teaching of grammar and usage have also led to the labeling of words, the diagramming of sentences, frustration on the part of students and teachers, and a failure to appreciate the values that might be gained from studying language history, dialectology, semantics, and other areas of linguistics.

In the everyday language of the community and school, the term "grammar" is used to refer to the way people speak and write and includes their choice of words, their construction of sentences and phrases, and even their punctuation and capitalization abilities. The term "usage" is less frequently used and when it is, it is used synonymously with grammar. "Dialect" is not a new word in general parlance, but its use has been largely confined to describing how "quaint old people in out-of-the-way places" talk.[32]

Teachers should not confuse these terms because their meanings are different, and confusion leads to poor teaching practices. *Grammar* is the description of a language. *Usage*, according to *Webster's Third New International Dictionary*, is "the way in which words and phrases are actually used (as in a particular form or sense) generally or among a community or group of persons: customary use of language." Grammar is based upon usage; the way people use a language is what the grammar of that language describes. Dialect is also related to usage. A *dialect* may be defined as "a collection of usages (including not only words and phrases but also pronunciations) characteristic of a certain individual or group."[33]

Usages change to reflect changes in meanings of words, the introduction of new words and expressions, and the acceptability or nonacceptability of particular words and phrases to different groups at a given time. Dialects reflect similar changes, although pronunciations tend to linger for a more extended period. Grammar, of course, also changes as it seeks to describe the language used. The fact that language does change has always been difficult for some teachers to accept; yet acceptance is necessary to understand the terms "grammar," "usage," and "dialect" and to provide effectively instruction about language.

Dialectology

Historically a major area of interest to linguists has been the geography of language—dialect differences by region and changes related to the movements of

---

31. J. N. Hook, Paul H. Jacobs, and Raymond D. Crisp, *What Every English Teacher Should Know* (Champaign, Ill.: National Council of Teachers of English, 1970), p. 3.

32. Raven I. McDavid, Jr., "The Sociology of Language," in *Linguistics in School Programs*, edited by Albert H. Marckwardt (Chicago: University of Chicago Press, 1970), p. 94.

33. Hook et al., p. 11.

people. This area of study is known as *dialectology*.[34] Today, it is primarily the *sociolinguists* who study social, racial, and ethnic differences as they relate to language usage. These linguists also investigate people's attitudes toward variations in their language. They do not make judgments as to what is "right" or "wrong" but simply report the attitudes of people in differing circumstances about certain words and expressions. Their investigations of usage are closely akin to traditional dialect studies in that they seek pronunciation, syntax, and vocabulary commonalities related to economic, racial, and social groups; to urban and rural regions; and to modern-day migrations of people. In quite recent times, many linguists studying dialects have shown concern for learning problems and the relation of a dialect to widespread or standard usage. Most Americans do not think that they speak a dialect.[35] Depending upon where you live, you may think that someone who comes from the South or Brooklyn or the Midwest or Boston speaks a dialect. You may consider speakers of dialects quaint, conceited, uncultivated, parochial, or any number of other things, but you noticed them by the way they speak. Clearly, most people recognize dialect differences and this recognition usually brings forth feelings or attitudes toward their speakers. Many people regard a dialect as "a corrupt form of language"[36]—an attitude and lack of understanding that is particularly significant in dealing with the problems of children's speaking and writing. Shuy says that there are at least three degrees of understanding of what constitutes a dialect.[37] The first of these is the one used in general parlance. The second is an awareness that we all speak a dialect of some sort. And the third is realizing that social layers exist within regional dialect areas. The third degree of understanding is important to concerned teachers. That is, they must realize that well-educated, partly educated, and uneducated people all may speak a particular dialect, but they speak different varieties of that dialect.

The speakers of a particular dialect may differ from speakers of other dialects by certain pronunciations they use, by the meanings they attached to some words, by particular word choices, and by grammatical forms. Most people know that identical objects or conditions have different names in different parts of the country:

- Pop, soda, soft drink, soda pop, tonic
- Corn-on-the-cob, sweet corn, roasting ears
- Green beans, snap beans, string beans
- Taxi, cab, hack
- Bag, poke, sack, toot

34. H. Rex Wilson, "The Geography of Language," in *Linguistics in School Programs*, edited by Albert H. Marckwardt (Chicago: University of Chicago Press, 1970), pp. 64–84.

35. Roger W. Shuy, *Discovering American Dialects* (Champaign, Ill.: National Council of Teachers of English, 1967). This work is the basis for much of the discussion in this section.

36. Jean Malmstrom, "Dialects—Updated," *Florida FL Reporter* 7 (Spring/Summer 1969): 47.

37. Shuy, p. 3.

- Faucet, hydrant, spicket, spigot, tap
- Turnpike, toll road, freeway, thruway, expressway

Differences in pronunciation show up, for example, between the Midwesterner's "park the car" and the New Englander's "pahk the cah." Other words whose pronunciations differ noticeably from one region to another are *creek*, *roof*, *wash*, *stomach*, *this*, *orange*, *hog*, and *greasy*.

In spite of some opinion to the contrary, pronunciation differences tend to correspond more to regions than to education or social class. To a lesser extent, the same is true for vocabulary differences. That is, the speakers of all varieties of a particular dialect generally pronounce many words in the same way (for example, midwestern or southern speakers of all education groups will say "ah'll")[38] and use words that have the same meaning (e.g., speakers in some sections of the South may call a small stream a "bayou," while midwesterners will use "creek"). Thus, as far as children's language goes, many of their pronunciations merely reflect the dialect of their native regions—a fact that teachers often do not but should recognize. The same is true of particular expressions, but of course, their vocabulary will be limited by the experiences they have had.

In contrast to differences in pronunciation and vocabulary, differences in grammar are generally indices of dialects spoken by the socially and educationally disadvantaged. The following indicate the principal types of grammatical differences.[39]

1. Absence of inflectional endings for noun plurals, noun genitives, third-singular present indicative, past tense, present participle, and past participle
2. Analogical forms, such as *hisself* and *theirselves* and the absolute genitives *ourn*, *yourn*, *hisn*, *hern*, and *theirn*
3. Double comparatives and superlatives, such as *more prettier* and *most lovingest*
4. Omission of the connective *be* with predicate nouns, predicate adjectives, present and past participles
5. *Be* as a finite verb
6. Differences in the principal parts of verbs, such as *growed*, *drawed*, *taken* as a past tense, *rid* as the past participle of *ride*, and *clum* or *clim* as the past tense or past participle of *climb*

There are other usages that generally do not reflect a lower social class or lack of education. For example, some people use *dived* as the past tense of the verb *dive*, while others use *dove*. Some people may say *this is as far as I go*; others will

---

38. Shuy, p. 60.
39. McDavid, pp. 96–97.

say *this is all the farther I go.* In each case, the usage is "standard"—that is, used by educated people.

Usage: Some Issues

As discussed previously, differences in the language children use are attributable to differences in their experiences. Regional dialects became established by immigration routes, patterns of population shifts, and geographical barriers. Similarly, dialects that reflect social class result from such factors as poverty, a lack of educational opportunity, and immobility due to ethnicity and prejudice.[40]

At one time, language usage was classified by levels—formal, standard, colloquial, and illiterate—but linguists found that this method of classification resulted in impreciseness, in a failure to recognize language change, and in negative effects on many individuals whose language they classified in the lower status categories. Many of the same problems exist with the more recently applied labels of "standard" and "nonstandard," though their use continues. Gradually there has been a movement toward using the term "dialect" in referring to differences in usage, without attaching "correct," "incorrect," "good," or "bad" to any of them. However, teachers cannot escape the fact that language changes and that usages are associated with particular social or economic groups or with particular occasions. There is a standard language (with variations) used in books. There is a generally standard language for public communication (the school, television and radio, etc.). Teachers have the obligation to make children sensitive to and appreciative of the factors that influence usage changes and choices and to help them learn to make these choices as they are appropriate.

In most settings—including that of the school—there are acceptable and nonacceptable usages. In the school setting, acceptable usage is *standard* English or the prestigious dialect of the speech community. Within the acceptable dialect or standard English there is considerable variety. This variety is the source of many teaching problems because it leads to differences of opinion as to the acceptability of particular items. Standard English simply becomes impossible to define in absolute terms. Teachers are likely to be more rigid in their definitions and in their acceptance of changes in usage within a standard English framework than are many other users of standard English. Confirmation of this fact goes back a number of years to a study of 300 randomly sampled members of the National

---

40. Some linguists believe that black speakers of nonstandard English speak a common dialect that is not particularly related to social class or to geographical region. Not all students of language share this belief, but in a sense it relates to the fact that many persons of a particular immigrant stock (Polish, for instance) have common features in their dialects, regardless of where they live or the social class to which they belong. For further discussion, see William A. Stewart, "Continuity and Change in American Negro Dialects," *Florida FL Reporter* 6 (Spring 1968).

Council of Teachers of English, who rated the acceptability in formal or informal speech and formal and informal writing of the following usage examples:[41]

1. The split infinitive
2. The case of the noun or pronoun before the gerund
3. Seven items of agreement between subject and verb and pronoun and antecedent
4. *One . . . he*
5. *. . . is when*
6. *These kind*
7. *Data is . . .*
8. Preposition at end of a sentence
9. *Either* of three
10. *Shortest* of two
11. Dangling participle (not an absurd one)
12. *Myself* used in the nominative
13. Between you and I
14. *Who* are you waiting for?
15. Drive *slow*
16. As if he *was*
17. It is *me*
18. Aren't I . . .
19. Jones was younger than *him*
20. *Building's* roof
21. After discussing the heroine, most of the young women expressed no desire to be *her*
22. It looks *like* it will rain
23. The boy felt *badly*
24. *Can* in the sense of permission
25. Very *nice* people
26. *Fixed* in the sense of repaired
27. *Different than*
28. *Awful* colds
29. New York is *further* east then Chicago
30. Try *and* finish
31. *Due to* in the sense of "because of"
32. Has *proven*
33. *Raised* instead of *reared*
34. Americans *have got* to make democracy work

41. Thurston Womack, "Teachers' Attitudes Toward Current Usage," *English Journal* 48 (April 1959): 186–90.

35. Some students do not know *if* they can . . .
36. Divided *between* three
37. The reason . . . was *because* . . .
38. The students *enthused* about . . .
39. The state *hung* the murderers
40. The old man *laid* down on his bed . . .
41. . . . *cannot help but* . . .
42. The swimmers *dove* into the pool
43. The soldiers fulfilled the *dying wish* of the commander

An item-by-item comparison of the teachers' views with published information in such sources as *Current English Usage*,[42] *Facts About Current English Usage*,[43] the "Current English Forum" in the *English Journal* or *College English*, and *Webster's New Collegiate Dictionary* revealed that, in general, the majority of teachers rejected most usages that published information identified as acceptable.[44]

Resistance to change and to accepting usage items that are really in widespread use as standard is still evident. Johnson, in a fairly recent study of the opinions of one hundred high school English teachers regarding five usage items, as well as their own use of these items, found condemnation of the items, "even though published studies of the usage of educated people have established their reputability."[45] He found that "67 per cent of the teachers opposed the use of *reason . . . is because* in speech, while 88 per cent opposed its use in writing"; that "79 per cent of the teachers were opposed to the use of *everybody . . . their* in speech and 95 per cent opposed its use in writing"; that 78 percent rejected the use of *myself* as an objective pronoun in speech and 96 percent disapproved of this usage in writing; that 26 percent judged the use of *will* to refer to the future in the first person as unacceptable and 42 percent thought it unacceptable in writing; and that 69 percent disapproved of *who* as an object pronoun in speech and 90 percent disapproved of its use in writing. Johnson also discovered that "ninety four out of the one hundred teachers used at least one of the 'incorrect' expressions which they themselves disapproved of and which they said they would 'correct' in the oral or written language of their students."

---

42. Sterling A. Leonard, *Current English Usage*, English Monograph No. 1, National Council of Teachers of English (Chicago: National Council of Teachers of English, 1932).

43. Albert H. Marckwardt and Fred G. Walcott, *Facts About Current English Usage*, English Monograph No. 7, National Council of Teachers of English (New York: D. Appleton-Century Co. 1938).

44. Published information clearly supports all but two of the usages (*between you and I* and intransitive *laid*).

45. Robert Spencer Johnson, "A Comparison of English Teachers' Own Usage with Their Attitudes Toward Usage" (Ph.D. dissertation, Columbia University, 1968), p. 154.

Grammar and Grammars

The teaching of grammar in elementary schools has been the subject of much controversy for many years. This controversy has continued in spite of an accumulation of research evidence showing that the teaching of grammar does not improve oral and written expression. Grammar teaching continues in many schools because of tradition and the slowness of teaching to change but also because the introduction of new grammars has held out hope for those who believe that a transfer will take place between the conscious knowledge of how language works and the habits of speaking and writing. On the other hand, the new terminology and better knowledge of facts about language have brought about changes at some schools in both teaching procedures and what is taught.

Because of the changes in content and practices now being advocated, further definition of grammar seems necessary. In the first place, a definition of grammar is apparently dependent, to a large extent, upon the identity and the purpose of the one defining it. Grammar is variously defined in dictionaries—the college edition of *Webster's New World Dictionary* lists six different meanings. The first two are the ones most commonly used by language scholars—that is, grammar is "that part of the study of language which deals with the forms and structure of words (morphology) and with their customary arrangement in phrases and sentences (syntax)," or it is actually "the system of word structures and word arrangements of a given language at a given time." For the educated person who is not a language expert, one of two additional meanings might come more readily to mind: grammar is "a system of rules for speaking and writing a given language, based on the study of its grammar (as a system) or on some rules." This meaning is closer to our earlier definition of usage than it is to the other definitions. The definition that grammar is the system of word structures and word arrangements of a given language is the meaning to keep in mind for the remaining discussion.

In addition to the variety of definitions of grammar and the distinction between grammar and usage, several adjectives that are frequently attached to the word "grammar" may compound the definition problem. These adjectives give us *traditional* grammar, *functional* grammar, *structural* grammar, *generative* grammar, and *transformational* grammar.

The term *traditional grammar* refers to that description of the English language that is based upon the rules of Latin grammar; this is the type of grammar that most American adults who are over thirty were taught in elementary and secondary schools.

The rules and generalizations concerning the English language that may be most useful in influencing choices of usage comprise *functional grammar;* for example, the rule that the subject of a sentence agrees with its verb in number and person is an item of functional grammar. This term came into use in the early middle years of the twentieth century as language experts became convinced that a thorough knowledge of the principles of grammar does not necessarily bring about fluency—or even correctness—in speaking and writing. It should be emphasized that the adjective "functional" refers to methodology rather than to a description of the language. In other words, it is not parallel in meaning to "traditional," "structural," or "generative" but may utilize any of these systems for describing the language in the effort to teach children to *use* the language effectively.

The term *structural grammar* came into use in the 1950s, though it was not new (scholars had been working on this idea since the late nineteenth century). This term means the description of the language based on the way it is used rather than on the rules of Latin grammar; it was the structural linguists who first recognized that, while all languages have system, not all languages have the same system, so they set about describing the English language in terms of its own system.

More recently, a fourth term has come into use, *generative grammar*—more frequently called *transformational-generative* or simply *transformational*—based upon a theoretical model or description of the way language works rather than upon a sample from the language, as is the case with structural grammar. The principal identifying characteristic is a belief in the ability of speakers to produce infinite numbers of sentences that they have not heard before. That is, given a few basic sentence patterns, individuals can generate virtually endless variations of these patterns by moving, substituting, and/or adding parts.

Grammar Teaching in Schools

The teaching of grammar developed following the rise of a wealthy middle class of merchants in the eighteenth century. Aspiring to social prominence, these newly wealthy families employed tutors to help them gain refinement of diction and usage. These tutors knew that English had no rules, no authority upon which spelling, style, or usage could be based. Thus, they based their judgments of correctness and elegance upon the system of grammar they knew best—that of Latin. It is not surprising that this should have happened. Latin was the language of learning, since it was the language of the Church, which had preserved and perpetuated learning throughout the Middle Ages; and it was also the ancestor of French, which was considered to be the most elegant of languages because it had once been the official tongue of the English court. Therefore, since the eighteenth century was an age of elegance and formality, its scholars set about formulating rules for the use of the English language based upon Latin grammatical structure, usage found in formal literary works, and language that had traditionally been considered learned and elegant. Their work deserves much credit, but it also had weaknesses. First, while recognizing that language has a system, they erroneously presupposed that all languages have the same system. Second, they failed to realize that language is a living, growing, changing thing; therefore, being true products of their century, they attempted to *prescribe* what correct usage should be, rather than to *describe* what it was even in their own day.

This formalized approach to the study of language became the rule. With the recognition of composition as a school subject about the middle of the nineteenth century, grammar continued to occupy a prominent position in the language curriculum. Because Latin and the other formal and disciplinary subjects still actively dominated the curriculum, it was natural to consider composition and language instruction a content subject, rather than a skill subject, with the study of grammar as its chief content. Instructional emphasis in the English classroom was devoted almost entirely to learning the tenses of verbs and the cases of nouns, diagramming and analyzing sentences, and memorizing rules. What little opportunity for oral or written expression the pupils enjoyed was in the form of memorized orations or declamations and the writing of formal themes.

As English-speaking nations became even more industrialized and as education became more widespread, the ability to speak and write effectively became increasingly an economic necessity rather than a social nicety. At about the same time (near the turn of the present century) interest in the psychology of learning developed and generated research into the results of the grammar teaching that was being done. Other experimentation with learning begun at this time showed that we learn by doing, rather than from development of certain mental faculties—the prevailing learning theory of the period. The assumption had been made that the study of grammar—as well as Latin, mathematics, etc.—provided mental discipline and developed the power to think in an orderly and logical fashion. Specifically, it was assumed that the study of grammar would transfer directly to individuals' abilities to express themselves verbally; that is, the ability to define and identify nouns, verbs, participles, conjunctive adverbs, and so on, and to diagram a sentence correctly would ensure fluency and correctness in writing and speaking. Contrary to these assumptions, psychological experiments suggested that to learn to speak clearly and acceptably, experience in speaking was necessary; that people learned to write not by analyzing sentences and memorizing rules but by writing and rewriting their own sentences.

At about the time that scientific study of learning was beginning, scholars also began to study language scientifically. First to appear were historical and comparative linguistics, and as scholars studied the history and development of languages, a number of important truths began to emerge. Of particular value to those interested in the teaching of the English language were these: (1) while there are families of languages, each has its own system, and the system of English is not the system of Latin; and (2) language is not static but changing. As long ago as 1891, the English grammarian Henry Sweet wrote that teachers generally fail to realize "how unsettled grammar still is,"[46] and in 1894, Otto Jesperson proposed the thesis that change in language is improvement, not corruption.[47]

Leonard Bloomfield's *Language*, published in 1933, gave some impetus to

46. James Sledd, "Grammar or Gramaye?" *English Journal* 49 (May 1960): 298.
47. Commission on the English Curriculum of The National Council of Teachers of English, *The English Language Arts* (New York: Appleton-Century-Crofts, 1952), p. 275.

the linguistic movement in the United States. It was not until several decades later, however, that its impact began to strike the curriculum, largely because of the work of such men as Trager and Smith,[48] Fries,[49] and Roberts.[50] After its slow start, the study of structural grammar gained advocates with amazing speed and moved at a steady pace from the university classroom to the secondary school and finally to the elementary level. The major drawback to its use, other than its newness, as far as most teachers were concerned was the continuing dispute about terminology and explanations for various sentence constructions. Too, the teaching approach tended to be as formal—and in a good many instances more formal—as the teaching of Latin-based grammar.

Grammarians have more recently developed grammars based upon a theory about the operation of human abilities that are thought to underlie the production and recognition of sentences.[51] The theory appeared with the publication of Noam Chomsky's *Syntactic Structures* in 1957. Its basis is the belief that language capacity is a biological endowment. Thus, if there is an inborn capacity for learning language, a human should be able to use and diagnose a language to a far greater extent than might be possible simply from exposure to that language through environmental experiences.[52] Consequently, users of a language can generate expressions that are utterly new to them, expressions that they have not heard or read. The theory also asserts that the ability to learn and process language impulses is universal among human beings; all humans have this capacity for language—but not for a particular language. This would seem to mean that all languages have much similarity, though observation would lead even a novice at language study to believe otherwise. The transformationalist, however, would explain that the similarity is at the "deep structure" level rather than at the "surface structure" level that can actually be analyzed.

Grammars—descriptions of the structure of a language—which are based upon generative-transformational theory begin with a small number of sentence types (kernels) and a larger number of rules for transforming these types by substituting, reordering, and combining parts. Transformations cannot occur indiscriminately since a grammatical utterance according to observed behavior must result. The study of the English language has shown that native speakers know most of the possible transformations, although they usually are unable to verbalize their understanding—for example, they know without being told (or "discovering" anew) that the determiner goes before the noun rather than after it. In spite of this fundamental understanding, however, some teachers and some

---

48. George L. Trager and Henry Lee Smith, *An Outline of English Structure* (Norman, Okla.: Battenberg Press, 1951).

49. Charles C. Fries, *The Structure of English* (New York: Appleton-Century-Crofts, 1952).

50. Paul Roberts, *Patterns of English* (New York: Harcourt, Brace and Co., 1956); also *English Sentences*, (1962) and *English Syntax*, (1964).

51. Bowen in *Linguistics in School Programs*, p. 44.

52. Richard W. Dettering, "Language and Thinking" in *Linguistics in School Programs*, edited by Albert H. Marckwardt (Chicago: University of Chicago Press, 1970), p. 281.

writers of the language textbooks believe that by bringing this understanding to the verbal level and extending it, by studying the sentence itself and the many ways in which transformations may be applied to it, children can be led to produce in their own writing and speaking more effective and acceptable expression.

Values Attributed to Studying Grammar

As stated earlier, the study of grammar in schools was initiated on the assumption that through such study and the development of an understanding of the grammar of the language, pupils would learn to write and speak more acceptably and effectively. Neither knowledge about learning nor empirical research evidence substantiates this assumption. Some persons interested in the preservation of the teaching of grammar have discounted earlier research in light of the development of "new" grammars. Yet there is no body of evidence supporting the teaching of structural or transformational grammar as a means for improving composition and usage.[53]

It would appear that the study of grammar, whether old or new, does not produce the ability to use language well. However, it is evident that many teachers and publishers are seizing upon one of the new grammars as *the* solution to language-teaching problems. It is probable that most linguists do not intend this interpretation, yet often their statements lead to the inference that such transfer does indeed take place. Roberts, for example, stated that "a student motivated to improve his writing will find a conscious understanding of the syntax an obvious help."[54] and further, that "a knowledge of the grammar will bear not only on the writing the student does but also on the reading he does."[55] Such statements may well be used to support the teaching of a grammar as formalized as any of a century ago.[56] Teachers would do well to keep in mind the following principles, stated in the *Handbook of Research on Teaching* prepared by the American Educational Research Association:[57]

1.   There are more efficient methods of securing *immediate* improvement in the writing of pupils, both in sentence structure and usage, than systematic grammatical instruction.

53. Roy C. O'Donnell, "Does Research in Linguistics Have Practical Applications?" *English Journal* 59 (March 1970): 410–12.

54. Paul Roberts, *English Syntax*, teacher's ed. (New York: Harcourt, Brace and World, 1964), p. 2.

55. Paul Roberts, "Linguistics and the Teaching of Composition," *English Journal* 52 (May 1963): 335.

56. See the criticism of such formal study by Wayne A. O'Neil, "Paul Roberts' Rules of Order: The Misuses of Linguistics in the Classroom," *Urban Review* 12 (June 1968).

57. N. L. Gage, ed., *Handbook of Research on Teaching* (Chicago: Rand McNally and Co., 1963), p. 981.

2.   Improvement of usage appears to be more effectively achieved through practice of desirable forms than through memorization of rules.

Actually, few linguists have ever claimed a transfer of knowledge of grammar to fluency in writing or speaking, although some pseudolinguists have. It is true, however, that some linguists earlier implied that transfer would take place. Roberts, for example, in the article previously quoted, went on to say:[58]

> It is not to be expected that study of the grammar, no matter how good a grammar it is or how carefully it is taught, will effect any enormous improvement in writing. Probably the improvement will be small and hard to demonstrate and for the large number of students who lack the motivation or the capacity to learn to write, it will be nonexistent. But even these students can learn the grammar, and it is valuable for them to do so. For grammar is the heart of the humanities, and like other humane studies its ultimate justification is that it informs the mind and teaches its own uses.

In other words, some linguists (to the extent that this statement is representative) accept the premise that certain things are valuable to know in and for themselves. If, in the words of Pope, "the proper study of mankind is man," then surely our language is also a proper study. The truth of such a statement would seem irrefutable. This point of view seems to be increasingly advanced as contentions about how study of a new grammar will improve speaking and writing are less often heard. As one writer points out:[59]

> Perhaps some of us have had unrealistic expectations of what linguistics should do. A knowledge of linguistics should reasonably be expected to have one major result, i.e., an enlightened understanding of how our language system works. If this is true, then the criterion for evaluating the merits of instruction in generative grammar, or structural grammar, or traditional grammar should be simply, "How well does it enable the student to understand how language works?" This question may be a very different one from that of how well it aids a student in writing, or speaking, or reading. It may very well be that the latter question is not a fair question at all.

Another value often proposed as a reason for the study of grammar is that this knowledge is needed for later schooling. Secondary teachers of English have historically complained that the pupils who come to them are unable to identify the parts of speech or to tell a subject from a predicate. Such complaints frequently exaggerate the supposed deficiencies and often result from (1) a lack of understanding of the functional teaching that has been done—which, for example, would have been directed at helping children choose the best verb or the proper tense and person; (2) a failure to recognize the role of the elementary school in the total program; and (3) perhaps a mistaken belief in the theory of transfer, along with ignorance of research. Certainly one of the goals of the elementary

---

58. Roberts, "Linguistics," p. 335.
59. O'Donnell, p. 411.

school is to prepare its pupils for the secondary school, just as preparing its students for college work is a function of the high school. Again, every teacher should carefully reexamine the goals of the total language arts program. Are these goals centered around the learning of grammar or are they centered around the acquisition of the skills of communication in both its expressive and receptive aspects?

Until quite recently, one of the reasons given for the teaching of grammar in the elementary schools was to prepare pupils for the study of foreign languages in the secondary school. Some foreign language teachers vociferously asserted the necessity for a thorough understanding of grammatical principles as a preparation for the study of French, Spanish, or any other language taught in the secondary school. In the past two decades, however, foreign language instruction not only has moved into the elementary school in many areas, but also has converted almost universally to the use of the oral-aural method of teaching. Presumably designers of foreign language programs have recognized the truth that experimental psychology has long been proclaiming: language skill is learned through language use.

The Research Evidence

As early as 1906, research reported that the written compositions and literature interpretations of pupils in the seventh and eighth grades who had had no training in formal grammar were as effective as the work of students who had had two years of drill on formal grammar.[60] A few years later, Briggs conducted a carefully controlled teaching experiment designed to reveal the extent of the transfer of grammatical skills to language abilities of seventh-grade pupils. He concluded that "these particular children after the amount of formal grammar that they had, do not, as measured by the means employed, show in any of the abilities tested improvement that may be attributed to their training in formal grammar."[61] This research offered conclusive proof of the failure of a formal approach to grammar study to transfer to such readily identifiable language skills as the ability to state a definition, to apply a definition, or to correct errors.

In the next several decades a number of studies corroborated the early findings. Two of these studies were done by Kraus[62] in 1957 and by Harris[63] in 1960–62. The latter is of particular interest since it avoided two criticisms often

60. Franklin S. Hoyt, "Studies in English Grammar," *Teachers College Record* 7 (November 1906): 467–500.

61. Thomas H. Briggs, "Formal English Grammar as a Discipline," *Teachers College Record* 14 (September 1913): 251–343.

62. Silvy Kraus, "A Comparison of Three Methods of Teaching Sentence Structure," *English Journal* 46 (May 1957): 275–81.

63. Roland J. Harris, "An Experimental Inquiry into the Functions and Value of Formal Grammar in the Teaching of English, with Special Reference to the Teaching of Correct Written English to Children Aged Twelve to Fourteen" (Ph.D. dissertation, University of London, 1962).

leveled at such studies: that results are based on objective test measures rather than actual writing and that they are conducted over too short a period. Harris carefully validated his criteria in a pilot study, then conducted his experiment over a two-year period and based results on frequency counts of actual writing done by the pupils before and after the two-year period. One group learned traditional grammar, while the other studied grammar only in connection with needs demonstrated in their own writing. Results of the study significantly favored the second group.

The use of graphic analysis or sentence diagramming for many years was a favorite device of upper-grade teachers; its justification was that it illustrated the relationships among the various parts of the sentence and helped children to understand these relationships better. Two different studies led to the conclusion that while diagramming is easy to teach and is readily learned, it has very slight value insofar as production of sentence mastery is concerned. Barnett, for example, demonstrated that children could learn to diagram sentences rapidly and correctly, but the skills thus acquired did not contribute in any significant degree to an improvement in the pupils' language usage or in their abilities to read and comprehend sentences.[64] Stewart also examined this problem in a comprehensive investigation involving carefully selected and balanced classes in twenty different school systems.[65] Again the children in the experimental group demonstrated that they could be taught to diagram, but those in the control group showed slightly more improvement in sentence construction than did those who learned diagramming.

Fortunately, these traditional diagrams have disappeared from textbooks, though some teachers still assert the method's efficacy. But there is some suspicion that the patterning of sentences, the use of formulas for performing transformations, and the drawing of lines from one sentence part to another, which appear in some recently published textbooks, are substitutes for diagramming.

Recent research on the influence of studying either a structural or a transformational grammar on speaking and writing has been sparse and divided as to results.[66] Research in the upper grades and high school level to determine whether students can learn the concepts of these grammars for the most part has not considered the use of such learning.[67] Some research attention has been given to transformational-grammar-based sentence-combining actitivies and has shown

---

64. W. W. Barnett, "A Study of the Effects of Sentence Diagramming on English Correctness and Silent Reading Ability" (Master's thesis, University of Iowa, 1942).

65. J. Reece Stewart, "The Effect of Diagramming on Certain Skills in English Composition" (Ph.D. dissertation, University of Iowa, 1941).

66. John W. Stewig and Pose Lamb, "Elementary Pupils' Knowledge of the Structure of American English and the Relationship of Such Knowledge to the Ability to Use Language Effectively in Composition," *Research in the Teaching of English* 7 (Winter 1973): 326.

67. Nathan S. Blount, "Research on Teaching Literature, Language and Composition," in *Second Handbook of Research on Teaching*, edited by Robert M. W. Travers (Chicago: Rand McNally College Publishing Co., 1973), p. 1081.

positive results in students' writing in the sense that they started using more mature sentence structures.[68] The present situation, however, is summarized in this statement by Lundsteen:[69]

> At this time of writing, there is no evidence anywhere that the study of grammar (whatever kind it is) fosters correctness and syntactic maturity in a fashion superior to far less time-consuming, more joyous, informal, creative, and naturalistic procedures.

LANGUAGE STUDY IN THE ELEMENTARY SCHOOL

Some elementary school teachers still teach formal grammar, with a focus on definitions, terminology, and rules that destroys interest in and appreciation for language. Teachers who are less rigid about content and course structure nevertheless may not be capitalizing on what children know and on the fact that language is the core of all school programs. Fortunately, some teachers do recognize the role of language in all areas of life and use this understanding to help children increase their appreciation and use of language.

What Language Study and How Much?

Because of the rise in importance of linguistics, language study in many schools has undergone some changes. These changes require some fundamental decisions. To what extent should the elementary school language arts program teach children to be "junior" linguists? Should they learn the terminology of the professional linguist? Must they have a conscious understanding of the system of the language?

Many persons believe that suggestions in textbooks and curriculum guides that emphasize linguistic analysis would lead to a formal program having little appeal for elementary school children—one that would increase neither understanding and appreciation of language nor proficiency in its use. Others believe that understanding, appreciation, and proficiency require formal or "disciplined" study. Too often, though, these persons' views reflect their own experience and their appreciation of a body of knowledge and its organization rather than children's needs, interests, and ways of learning.

Furthermore, what is the relative value of teaching linguistics in the elementary school, compared to other elements in the curriculum? Few linguists attach utility (in the sense of improvement in the child's speaking or writing) to the study of linguistics. O'Donnell, for example, believes that "teaching the student a linguistic principle or concept and expecting automatic improvement in com-

---

68. Ibid, p. 1086.
69. Sara W. Lundsteen, *Children Learn to Communicate* (Englewood Cliffs, N. J.: Prentice-Hall, 1976), p. 395.

munication skills" is impractical.[70] Perhaps people who prepare materials for children's use—linguists included—hope for such improvement, but there appears to be no research evidence to support it.

Linguists generally stress the humanistic value of linguistics and favor broadening traditional grammar study to a more comprehensive *language* study.[71] The teacher in the elementary classroom, of course, must help children to use language as effectively as possible to convey their ideas and thoughts and to receive the thoughts of others. Elementary teachers, as well as administrators, parents, and textbook writers, must decide how much time to devote to instruction in different content areas and, relative to children's interests and needs, what they can teach successfully. Many linguists, too, recognize the need to design curricula on the basis of needs, interests, and the results of research. One prominent linguist has stated:[72]

> The linguistic tail should not try to wag the educational dog. That is, linguists—as well as other devotees of linguistics—should be aware of the fact that linguistic factors are only one of the many considerations that have to be taken into account in the educational process. Needless to say, psychological, sociological, and just plain human factors, not to mention economic and political considerations, play a significant role in education. In this broader context the linguistic variables turn out to be important, but not necessarily primary.

This linguist also advises educators that answers to linguistic questions rarely appear in textbooks, that "linguistics has developed very few 'findings' that everyone in the profession would unquestioningly accept as definitive." But, he says, a fruitful way of bringing linguistics into the curriculum is to consider (linguists and educators together) the question: "What are the skill developments involved in the language arts, and what aspects of linguistics relate to the different skills that language arts curricula attempt to develop?"

As we stated earlier, much in linguistics undoubtedly is applicable in many areas of the language arts, especially if we accept the broad definition of linguistics. Perhaps the major value of the linguistic movement to this point has been its effect upon teachers. Surely some teachers have a more relaxed attitude toward "correctness" of usage, acceptance of language change is greater, and greater awareness of the system of the language has developed. Teachers are also realizing that a great deal of linguistics has always been part of the language arts curriculum. For example, morphology includes what teachers have called *word building;* teachers have taught children rhythm and intonation in reading and

---

70. O'Donnell, pp. 410–12.

71. For example, see H. A. Gleason, Jr., *Linguistics and English Grammar* (New York: Holt, Rinehart and Winston, 1965), pp. 476–77. He cautions, however, that a "wooden and prescriptive" teaching of grammar will not lead to the results he hopes for with respect to learning to compose.

72. Paul L. Garvin, "Linguistics and the Language Arts," mimeographed paper prepared for the Linguistic Institute at the State University of New York at Buffalo, 1971.

choral speaking; sound and symbol relationships have been part of reading and spelling instruction; children have written dictionaries and have "looked up" interesting words; and they have learned the meanings of affixes and how they work.

Grammar and the Teacher

A considerable amount of grammar teaching continues in elementary schools, largely because of its inclusion in textbooks and lingering tradition. And of course, confusion about what is usage and what is grammar helps to perpetuate old habits. This is not to say that teachers should abandon usage instruction, avoid the use of grammatical terminology altogether, or cease explaining usage and the conventions of punctuation and capitalization. The pitfall to avoid is giving focus to grammatical terminology and rules rather than to expression. About the role of the increased knowledge of language, one linguist has said:[73]

> We may speak about and even hope for some influence of new concepts of language in textbooks and in the classroom, but this is a far cry from the direct teaching of a hitherto unknown or neglected body of subject matter. The impact of linguistics is likely to be greater in terms of the way the teacher and the textbook writer think about language than in any specific body of procedural gimmickry.

The way teachers think about language almost certainly depends on what they know about language and effective language arts programs. If that knowledge is limited to their experiences in most elementary and secondary schools, it is highly likely that their attitudes about dialects and levels of usage and how speaking and writing are learned, for example, will reflect the prejudices and ignorance of years past. On the other hand, teachers who are informed about the research of linguists and psychologists should develop positive attitudes and understandings:

1.   They will recognize that grammar is descriptive rather than prescriptive. Therefore, they will more likely teach usage inductively rather than deductively by letting pupils learn through observation rather than through memorizing rules and helping pupils see that the language of educated people is more effective because it is more acceptable to those people, not because "the book says it is right."
2.   They will understand and communicate to students the fact that language grows and changes. They will learn to observe the language of those around them, will become more aware of what constitutes ac-

73. Marckwardt, p. 325.

ceptable usage, and will be better able to select from textbooks and other sources what is relevant to the needs of their classes.

3.   They will recognize that different varieties of usage are suitable to different places and occasions. Equally, they will understand that dialects and colloquialisms are not "substandard," and consequently, they will be able to help children who use nonstandard English.

4.   They will see language as part of human culture rather than merely a vehicle for its transmission—as a manifestation of individual (or a society's) needs, interests, aspirations, and activities. As a result, they will more likely create in children a desire to learn about words, to understand their uses, and to use them more effectively.

5.   They will know how children learn language and the relationship between language learning and child development; therefore, they will be better equipped to help children learn to use language acceptably and effectively.

The Usage Program

Selecting usage items for instruction is a major problem for teachers who desire to develop sensitivity to language and to help pupils to develop fully their intellectual capacities and ambitions through language facility. For some years language authorities have recommended emphasizing a limited number of usage items in the elementary school. Pooley has made these observations in support of limiting the number of items and suggests a basis for selection:[74]

1.   The constant repetition of a relatively small number of errors constitutes over 90 percent of the usage problem in the elementary grades.

2.   A large number of "errors" listed in textbooks and language workbooks are not errors at all, but standard colloquial English appropriate to the speech and writing of children and adults alike.

While it is not possible to dictate which items of usage to teach at particular grade levels, because the language backgrounds of children vary, there are several that commonly need instructional attention.[75] Teachers should not attempt to deal with all of them, nor should instruction in them take precedence over aspects of the language arts program that promote creativity, good composition of expression, and interest in language. Teachers should concentrate on the ones that, in their judgment, are more severe deviations from community standards.

---

74. Robert C. Pooley, *Teaching English Usage* (Urbana, Ill.: National Council of Teachers of English, 1974), p. 182.

75. See Pooley, *Teaching English Usage*; Pooley, Robert C., "Dare Schools Set a Standard in English Usage?" *English Journal* 49 (March 1960): 176–81; Marckwardt and Walcott, pp. 27–31.

ain't or *hain't*	*hadn't ought*	he *seen*
yourn, hern, ourn	he *give,* he *walk*	*them* books
hisen, theys	my brother, *he*	*this here*
youse	*her* and *me* went	*that there*
onct	there *is* four	*us* boys *went*
hisself, theirselves	there *was* four	we, you, they *was*
hair *are*	they *knowed*	with *we* girls
a orange	I, they *growed*	have *went*
have *ate*	*haven't no,* isn't *no*	have *wrote*
they *eats*	*leave* for *let*	the *mens*
was *broke*	haven't *nothing*	*learn* me a song
he *brung*	that's *mines*	*me and Mary* went
he *come*	where *it* at?	she *taken*
clumb	where is she *at?*	I *likes* him
had, have *did*	he *run*	I *drunk, drunks*
she, he *don't*	have *saw*	*can't hardly*
it *don't*	I *says*	*does* we have
didn't ought		

In the unlikely event that a teacher is fortunate enough to have a class whose members use none of these expressions, there will be other instances of lack of subject and verb agreement—or noun or noun equivalent with antecedent—that warrant attention. In addition, the class can work on idiomatic expressions. The usages selected for instructional emphasis, however, should be the ones that deviate most widely from generally accepted expression. Absent from the previous list are usages illustrated in the sentences which follow. These items should *not* receive instructional attention in the elementary school—even though some textbooks include them.

- You'd better go slow.
- Can I have a drink of water?
- It is me.
- We got home at noon.
- Everyone hand in their papers.
- Bill is taller than me.
- None of us were there.
- Who did you choose?
- He walks like he hurt himself.
- The heavy bat helped to better hit the ball.
- The reason he failed was because he tried too hard.
- I will go as soon as I'm ready.
- Will you meet Mrs. Jones and myself after the show?
- Our catch was pretty good.
- I'm tired of him complaining.

Usage teaching is discussed in Chapter 10, along with suggestions for determining which items should receive instructional attention. It is important to note, however, that usage should be part of all language arts instruction as this chapter has outlined it.

Linguistic Activities for the Classroom

All activities in which children use language are linguistic activities and, in effect, learning takes place as language is being used. Some activities are more appropriate for learning about language than others, and a perceptive teacher will recognize many opportunities for worthwhile linguistic study; for example, questions about words that come up in spelling, during oral reports, in talking about topics of interest and in planning writing activities offer endless possibilities for further study. An unusual spelling, the way compounds are formed, which adjectives are most descriptive, whether a word in the news came from another country, the way inflected forms of words change meaning, and the frequency of occurrence of some words are items that come up informally and provide genuine occasions for teaching about language. The following suggestions are a sampling of activities and situations that present teaching opportunities. We will add to this list in later chapters.

1. In the primary grades, playing with words—rhyming, onomatopoeia, new word uses—is interesting and presents opportunities to teach about distinctive speech sounds, pitch, and stress.
2. At all grade levels you can call attention to rising and falling inflections in speech and when the students read aloud.
3. Changing sentence structure without changing meaning or to clarify meaning are good topics for discussion and written exercises. For example: The ball game is after school/After school there is a ball game/The game after school is a ball game. This can be an entertaining way to teach word order, word meanings, and clarity of expression.
4. In the intermediate grades students can begin studying language history by searching for the origins of words met in literature, discovering sources of words incorporated into English, researching English words that have passed from use, and tracing changes in meaning and spelling.
5. The study of dialects is particularly appealing to the middle and upper grades. Content should include differences in pronunciations, meanings, and familiar expressions; observation and comparison of dialects in literature (for example, *Brighty of the Grand Canyon*, Paul Bunyan and Mike Fink tales, Lois Lenski's books, *Sweet Pea* by Krementz, Steptoe's *Stevie*, and Walter's *Lilie of Watts*); and regional dialects.
6. Dialect study can lead to projects in which children note differences in

the language used for different purposes—playground, club meetings, parties, school, conversations with adults.

7. In composition teaching, basic activities include rearranging information in sentences, adding phrases and clauses for greater clarity, and eliminating unnecessary words and phrases in sentences. You can bring in sentence patterning, language system, and functional learning of linguistic terminology as needed.

A cautionary word: there is a genuine possibility that linguistic activities and linguistic study can become too formalized. To guard against this problem, apply the test suggested by one distinguished language authority and answer these questions: "What does this task mean to these children now? Are the children really involved? Are they setting up goals and digging in?"[76] As the author of this text suggests, "Much dead wood could be removed from curricula by such screening."

EXERCISES FOR THOUGHT AND ACTION

1. Examine trade books for children on the subject of language. Examples are:

    •   Asimov, Isaac. *Words on the Map*. Boston: Houghton Mifflin Co., 1962.
    •   Folsom, Franklyn. *The Language Book*. New York: Grosset and Dunlap, 1963.
    •   Gallant, Roy. *Man Must Speak*. New York: Random House, 1969.
    •   Laird, Helen and Charlton. *The Tree of Language*. Cleveland: World Publishing Co., 1957.
    •   Ludovici, L. J. *Origins of Language*. New York: G. Putnam's Sons, 1965.
    •   Minteer, Catherine. *Words and What They Do to You*. Evanston, Ill.: Row Peterson and Co., 1953.
    •   O'Neill, Mary. *Words, Words, Words*. New York: Doubleday, 1966.
    •   Stewart, George. *Names on the Land*. Boston: Houghton Mifflin, 1951.

    Develop one limited lesson based on the nature, history, or characteristics of language.

2. Examine several language arts textbooks for elementary children and language arts curriculum guides for elementary teachers. How do the objectives and content address knowledge about the nature of language?

3. Formulate a lesson objective and a series of instructional activities derived from the samples of Old, Middle, Early Modern, and Modern English in this

---

76. Alvina Treut Burrows, "The Pursuit of Excellence in the Language Arts," *Effective Language Arts Practices in the Elementary School: Selected Readings*, ed. Harold Newman, (New York: John Wiley and Sons, Inc., 1972), p. 6.

chapter (e.g., if you photocopied the passages and shuffled them, you could ask children to arrange them chronologically and explain the resulting sequence).

4. Consider the amount and type of formal grammar study in your classroom. How do you reconcile pressures favoring this instruction (e.g., standardized tests covering grammatical terminology, public pressure) with opposing forces (e.g., research evidence, time limitations)? Write a letter to parents explaining your views, reasons, and resulting policies.

5. Read "Students' Right to Their Own Language," a position statement of the Conference on College Composition and Communication, National Council of Teachers of English, Spring 1974. Where do you stand? How does your classroom behavior reflect your attitude toward nonstandard English and its speakers?

6. (a) Listen to recordings of American regional dialects (e.g., "Americans Speaking" and "Our Changing Language," both distributed by the National Council of Teachers of English). Contrast the pronunciation of *car, fire, greasy, dog, creek, laugh,* and so on across dialects.
   (b) Obtain newspapers from another English-speaking country (a library and an international airport are two places to locate them). Note differences in syntax, vocabulary, and spelling.
   (c) Write several lesson objectives that these materials would help to achieve.

7. Trace the history of your name in the *Oxford English Dictionary.* Then look up the origins of these words: *gumbo, yam, chigger, voodoo, flabbergast, cab, grovel, potato, canoe,* and *barbeque.* What other kinds of information does the *Oxford* contain? Does it include these words: *cuckooish, spit, muck, dicky-bird?* Why? How could you use the *Oxford* in the elementary classroom?

Cabbies wanna talk bedda' to de public[77]

NEW YORK (AP)—Thoiteen cabbies got da foist verse (voice) lessons of dere lives Toosday in a' attempt to help dem talk better wid da ridin' public.

The voice and diction class, conducted by Jerry Cammarata, who himself has a slight lisp, was held in Nathan's Famous Restaurant, a favorite Times Square eatery for the city's cabbies and sponsor of the lecture.

Cammarata told the drivers they could sound like David Niven or "at least like Paul Newman," if they had "better synergistic motor movement of the buccal cavity (da mouth)."

"Duz dat mean we gonna talk better?" one driver asked aloud as his classmates smiled.

Herbert Mendelowitz of Queens, who has been operating a hack for 18 years,

---

77. Associated Press, "Cabbies Wanna Talk Bedda' to de Public," *Austin (Texas) American-Statement* 9 April 1977.

said he came to the class "cause people got an idea that we all sound like dey did in the twunnies and thoities ('20s and '30s)."

He said some passengers even think cabbies don't got no culture.

"One day dis couple gets in the cab an—cause I like opera and classical music—dey hear it on the radio and start tryin' to guess the sing-ger," he recalled.

"When I told dem who it was, the womin says, what does he know about opera?"

8. What is your reaction to the cabbies' attitudes toward their own speech? What effect are speech lessons likely to have on characteristics of cabbie speech? What impact might their new speech have on stereotypes of cabbies?

9.   'Twas brillig, and the slithy toves
                                  Did gyre and gimble in the wabe:
                              All mimsy were the borogoves,
                                  And the mome raths outgrabe.

(a) What gyred and gimbled?
(b) Where were the toves?
(c) How were the borogoves?
(d) What did the mome raths do?
(e) What principle(s) of language discussed in this chapter enabled you to answer these questions from the opening stanza of "Jabberwocky," from *Through the Looking-Glass* by Lewis Carroll.

10. The French think language can be legislated.[78] A bill passed by the French Parliament prohibits use of foreign words in all advertisements and work contracts. The aim is to stop the "corruption" of French with English, Russian, and German words. Do you think government edicts can stop or alter the course of language change? For example, can anyone prevent the people of France from using the terms "le after-shave" or "le hot-dog"? Does language change represent degradation or enrichment?

11. Ask a group of children whether they have ever made up a secret code and why (probably to exclude other children from their club). Design with them a small set of oral, written, or gestural symbols for use in classroom communication. Relate this activity to the symbolic nature of the English language.

12. In 1929, work began on the "Linguistic Atlas of the United States," for the purpose of collecting data on the pronunciation, grammar, usage, and lexicon of speakers from eight regions of this country. Take a look at Harold B. Allen's *Linguistic Atlas of the Upper Midwest.* Why is it important for language arts teachers to know whether people in a particular region use *pail* or *bucket, dove* or *dived, sick to, at, from, with,* or *in one's stomach?*

---

78. Camden, John, "Franglais dismays French," *Christian Science Monitor* News Service, 1976.

SELECTED REFERENCES

Brook, G. L. *A History of the English Language.* New York: W. W. Norton and Co., 1958.

Carroll, John B. *The Study of Language: A Survey of Linguistics and Related Disciplines.* Cambridge, Mass.: Harvard University Press, 1959.

Cazden, Courtney B.; John, Vera P.; and Hymes, Dell, eds. *Functions of Language in the Classroom.* New York: Teachers College Press, 1972.

DeStefano, Johanna S.; and Fox, Sharon E., eds. *Language and the Language Arts.* Boston: Little, Brown and Co., 1974.

Elgin, Suzette Haden. *What Is Linguistics?* Englewood Cliffs, N. J.: Prentice-Hall, 1973.

Halliday, M. A. K. *Explorations in the Functions of Language.* London: Edward Arnold, 1973.

Hook, J. N.; Jacobs, Paul H.; and Crisp, Raymond D. *What Every English Teacher Should Know.* Champaign, Ill.: National Council of Teachers of English, 1970.

Joos, Martin. *The Five Clocks.* New York: Harcourt, Brace and World, 1967.

King, Martha L.; Emans, Robert; and Cianciolo, Patricia J., eds. *The Language Arts in the Elementary School: A Forum for Focus.* Urbana, Ill.: National Council of Teachers of English, 1973.

Marckwardt, Albert H., ed. *Linguistics in School Programs.* The 1969 yearbook of the National Society for the Study of Education, Part II. Chicago: The University of Chicago Press, 1970.

Pooley, Robert C. *The Teaching of English Usage.* Urbana, Ill.: National Council of Teachers of English, 1974.

Reed, Carroll E., ed. *The Learning of Language.* New York: Appleton-Century-Crofts, 1971.

Savage, John F., ed. *Linguistics for Teachers: Selected Readings.* Chicago: Science Research Associates, 1973.

Shuy, Roger. *Discovering American Dialects.* Urbana, Ill.: National Council of Teachers of English, 1967.

Sledd, James. *A Short Introduction to English Grammar.* Chicago: Scott, Foresman and Co., 1959.

3

The Language Learner

*Language learning is a lifelong process. . . . The child who enters
school at the usual starting age has still far to go before his competence approaches that of adults. John B. Carroll, in* The Learning
of Language

Teacher interest in the process of acquisition and development of language in
early childhood is spreading, largely because of the overdue recognition that
language is a major medium of learning, that children are wondrously skilled in
its use, and that clues to all learning may be present in the knowledge of how
language is learned. This chapter includes a brief overview of how children learn
language from birth through the elementary school years. This information is
basic for teachers who want to develop language arts programs that grow from
and extend the experiences and abilities children bring to elementary schools. A
look at the untutored, natural, and highly successful growth of language before
school entry is the foundation for an examination of school learning activities. In
addition, we will discuss factors that may alter the course of natural language
growth.

A third part of this chapter focuses on a beginning language arts program
that takes into account the nature of language learning and factors impinging on
it. In this section, we will establish the framework for helping children become
skilled at listening and reading for information and enjoyment as well as at speaking and writing to share their ideas and feelings.

CHILDREN'S LANGUAGE DEVELOPMENT

Most children learn to talk without much difficulty, but how this process occurs is the subject of considerable controversy.[1] Theories of language development are continually changing as data accumulate. It appears that more researchers with more varied backgrounds are studying more children, more aspects of language and more different languages and are using more diverse methodologies. Today phonology, semantics, pragmatics, and language and cognitive development supplement the syntax studies common in the 1960s. And to add to the knowledge gained from controlled experiments, linguists and psychologists now observe spontaneous language production, often in their own children. As Brown observed:[2]

> All over the world the first sentences of small children are being as painstakingly taped, transcribed, and analyzed as if they were the last sayings of great sages. Which is a surprising fate for the likes of "That doggie," "No more milk," and "Hit ball."

Similarities and differences in children's language development have been documented. Slobin noted the remarkable similarities in children's earliest language and in the pattern of language development.[3] His bibliography of studies on the acquisition of about forty native languages notes striking similarities even across languages.[4] Language learning appears to occur in stages although the rate at which children progress from one stage to another varies. Therefore, age is a less than adequate predictor of language development. Chukovsky documented the individuality of the language learner during a forty-year period in which he collected and analyzed anecdotes related to children's linguistic creativity. Statements like "Can't you see: I'm barefoot all over!"[5] led Chukovsky to conclude:[6]

> It seems to me that, beginning with the age of two, every child becomes for a short period of time a linguistic genius. Later, beginning with the age of five or six, this talent begins to fade.

---

1. Vera P. John and Sarah Moskovitz, "Language Acquisition and Development in Early Childhood," in *Linguistics in School Programs*, edited by Albert H. Marckwardt (Chicago: University of Chicago Press, 1970), p. 169.

2. Roger Brown, *A First Language: The Early Stages* (Cambridge, Mass.: Harvard University Press, 1973), p. 97.

3. D. I. Slobin, "Universals of Grammatical Development in Children," in *Advances in Psycholinguistics*, edited by G. B. Flores d'Arcais and W. J. M. Levelt (New York: American Elsevier, 1970).

4. C. A. Ferguson and D. I. Slobin, *Studies of Child Language Development* (New York: Holt, Rinehart and Winston, 1973).

5. K. Chukovsky, *From Two to Five*, translated by M. Morton (Berkeley: University of California Press, 1968), p. 3.

6. Ibid., p. 7.

Even detailed observations about phases of great growth and individuality in learning have not produced the key to understanding the process that educators seek. According to Dale:[7]

> The more we learn about language, the less we understand how it works. The acquisition of language is one of the major feats of child development; language acquisition is a crucial test for any theory of learning.

Theories of Language Development

The two traditional positions on the acquisition of language are the *empiricist position*, which holds that no linguistic structure is innate (language is learned entirely through experience), and the *nativist position*, which maintains that the acquisition of language is a biological tendency that is activated by experience. The nativist position is based largely on the acceptance of the viewpoint that language has universal properties; that is, all languages have common characteristics. In addition, it specifies that a child has an inborn predisposition to develop a set of structures that generate language. In order to function, the "generator" requires exposure to speech (actually to language, since "children born to deaf parents who use the sign language of the deaf apparently begin to pick up the sign language at about the same age that hearing children born to normal parents begin to talk"[8]). The nature of a child's structural development depends on the structures of the language the child hears. The extent of the mental abilities necessary to remember, to break down the language heard into units of sound and meaning, and to generalize is difficult to determine.

Lenneberg says that "the evidence suggests that the capacities for speech production and related aspects of language acquisition develop according to built-in biological schedules" and that language learning appears "within limits . . . to [be] somewhat more resistant to the impact of environmental factors" than to developmental ones.[9] Thus, nativists regard language development as being similar to the development of walking; it proceeds in response to genetically determined changes that occur as the child matures. From this point of view it follows that society's concern need not focus on a child's environment and such factors as imitation and conditioning, to the extent as is presently the case, but on physiological needs.

Other theorists and researchers believe that language development rests

---

7. Philip S. Dale, *Language Development: Structure and Function* (New York: Holt, Rinehart and Winston, 1976), p. 161.

8. Martin D. S. Braine, "The Acquisition of Language in Infant and Child," in *The Learning of Language*, edited by Carroll E. Reed (New York: Appleton-Century-Crofts, 1971), p. 69.

9. Eric H. Lenneberg, "The Biological Foundations of Language," in *Language Arts Concepts for Elementary School Teachers*, edited by Paul C. Burns et al. (Itasca, Ill.: F. E. Peacock Publishers, 1972), p. 108.

largely on the child's environment. They base their argument on studies of vocabulary development and the rates at which children produce sounds, as well as the rates at which they produce words. Studies have shown that differences in environmental conditioning of infants (as young as three months) result in differences in sound production.[10] Irwin found "that the number and frequency of sound productions differ from the age of eighteen months on, between middle and low-income children."[11] Particularly with respect to younger children, however, these differences may have developed because of the amount of attention they received during the study rather than because of the language they heard. Imitation of language, though, is fundamental to this theoretical position, as is the rewarding of imitations and attempts to imitate. The rewards vary but usually include a smile, a pat, food, and the like.

Empiricists explain the fact that children produce patterns of language they have not heard as attempts to imitate that have gone awry or simply as examples of the child's normal tendency to experiment. Clearly, imitation is a major factor in language acquisition and development, for children reared in an English-speaking environment do learn English and not some other language.

Possibly too much attention is placed on the theoretical differences of a child's acquisition of language. Certainly it is a natural process, in that we could not prevent a normal child who is exposed to language from learning it. Exposure to language is a key factor in language development, of course, but the process is not the same as learning reading, writing, and arithmetic. One linguist has stated that children "seem to possess an inborn faculty for language which, like a film, merely needs to be exposed to language to become imprinted."[12] Perhaps, but the imprinting apparently requires repeated exposure.

Undoubtedly the verbal exchange between children and their parents and others plays an important role in language development. While the language of exchanges between a young child and an adult is simpler than that in an exchange between adults—the utterances are shorter, the rate of speech is slower, fewer tenses are used, etc.—it is at a higher level than the child's own production and, therefore, provides a learning challenge.[13] On the other hand, an infant learns a great deal before even attempting speech so that the first efforts represent an attempt to apply this learning. Apparently "the child formulates hypotheses about the language about her and tests them, either by formulating utterances of her own or by attempting to comprehend new utterances."[14] Possibly the hypotheses that the child develops are parts of a structure, in the form of general learning

---

10. Harriet Rheingold, "Controlling the Infant's Exploratory Behavior," in *Determinants of Infant Behavior II*, edited by B. M. Foss (New York: John Wiley and Sons, 1963), pp. 171–78.

11. Orvis C. Irwin, "Infant Speech: The Effect of Family Occupational Status and of Age on Use of Sound Types," *Journal of Speech and Hearing Disorders* 13 (1948): 224–26.

12. William G. Moulton, "The Study of Language and Human Communication" in *Linguistics in School Programs*, p. 27.

13. Dale, p. 161.

14. Dale, p. 161.

principles or a learning set for human thinking as expressed by language. As Fodor has pointed out, it is conceivable that a "child is born with a very general capacity to learn learning principles and that it is such learned principles that the child brings to the problem of mastering his language."[15]

Learning Language Sounds

Children's development in the reception and production of speech sounds proceeds in a stepwise systematic fashion at the same time they are acquiring meaning and knowledge of language structure and use. Beginning at birth, infants use their bodies to produce sounds, even though the body parts involved have other basic functions—windpipes for breathing, tongues for swallowing. A baby's first cry evolves into a variety of vocalizations during the first month. It progresses through cooing and babbling to sounds resembling standard lexical items (words), usually around age one.[16]

Recordings of infants' vocalizations during the first few months of life reveal little system and little relationship to the language they will later speak.[17] At about sixteen weeks of age there is evidence of communication as the infant begins to respond to human sounds by turning its head and eyes in apparent search for the speaker.[18] By the time the child is six months old, cooing has changed to babbling what resemble one-syllable utterances. These sounds receive much "practice" during most of the infant's waking hours. With practice the child seems to gain control of volume, pitch, and articulation, as shown by repetition.[19]

Children's first "words" usually consist of consonant plus vowel forms. They may not be words as adults know them, but they may be so labeled because they are used consistently and seem to have some meaning for the child. A child may say "Da-da," which will cause a father's face to glow; it may fall later, when the child's experimenting leads to "Ma-ma" in a corresponding setting. The child is simply naming things—perhaps someone coming into the room is what "Da-da" means. First "words"—or syllables—are particularly important to the child, for they are basic in the development of a phonological system. They signify that the child is developing a progressively sophisticated system of contrasting phonemes. According to Meyer, "Phoneme development in general is most rapid during the first year of life; by the age of thirty months the average child possesses approx-

---

15. Jerry A. Fodor, "How to Learn to Talk: Some Simple Ways," in *The Genesis of Language*, edited by Frank Smith and George A. Miller (Cambridge, Mass.: MIT Press, 1966), p. 106.

16. Paula Menyuk, "Early Development of Receptive Language," in *Language Perspectives—Acquisition, Retardation, and Intervention*, edited by Richard L. Schiefelbusch and Lyle L. Lloyd (Baltimore: University Park Press, 1974), p. 217.

17. Lenneberg, p. 128.

18. Ruth H. Weir, *Language in the Crib* (London: Mouton and Co., 1962).

19. Walter M. MacGinitie, "Language Development," in *Encyclopedia of Educational Research*, 4th ed., edited by Robert L. Ebel (New York: Macmillan Co., 1969), p. 690.

imately 77 per cent of the total adult phoneme production."[20] In light of this rapid progression, the importance of babbling and "practice" to the child is clear; it also reflects adults' concern with language learning, because in most cultures adults tend to invest children's early sounds with meaning.

At one time it was assumed that a child's phonological system at age four was approximately the same as it would be at maturity, except possibly for some deviations that would disappear by the time the child entered school.[21] While, as Carroll states, this generalization is still useful, "it must not be interpreted as implying that the phonology of the native language is completely learned by the age of 6 or that there are no interesting individual differences among children in phonological competence or performance at this or later ages."[22] Read's studies of young children's spelling attempts show unexpected but justifiable categorization of speech sounds.[23] The categorizations explain some of the systematic deviations from conventional spelling that teachers find in the early grades; they also may indicate that phonological systems are still developing. Templin's earlier study indicated that not all children had perfected their ability to either identify or produce English speech sounds by age eight, but there is no research evidence of phonological development beyond that age.[24]

Development of Grammatical Structure

Around eighteen to twenty months of age, children begin to put words together. Studies show that young children's experiments with word order are similar to their experiments with words. Most of their early word combinations tend to follow a pattern; that is, they single out a few words for use in a particular utterance position with a variety of other words.[25] Gradually the number of these words increases and the child combines them with other single words. This type of experimentation lasts only a short time. The child who says "Chair mama" at twenty months (and who probably will also say "Chair Dada" and "See chair") is trying out word order. The child perceives that some words should come first and some others second. With respect to an adult system, their perceptions often are faulty, but they produce a system or grammar representative of the child's level of

---

20. William J. Meyer, *Developmental Psychology* (New York: Center for Applied Research in Education, 1964), p. 60.

21. S. M. Ervin and W. R. Miller, "Language Development," in *Child Psychology*, edited by H. W. Stevenson et al. (Chicago: University of Chicago Press, 1963), p. 116.

22. John B. Carroll, "Development of Native Language Skills Beyond the Early Years," in *The Learning of Language*, p. 113.

23. Charles Read, *Children's Categorization of Speech Sounds in English* (Urbana, Ill.: National Council of Teachers of English, 1975).

24. Carroll, p. 115.

25. Reed, p. 31.

maturity. Before arriving at the system of adult language, the child possibly works through a series of grammars.[26]

Thus, children learn the classes of words early (but, of course, not grammatical names) as they demonstrate by using many of their first words in different contexts. The repeated words are likely to be nouns and verbs and, less often, adjectives (all of which have semantic content). The words excluded from the experimentation process have grammatical functions that are more obvious than their semantic content. For example, here are some sentences spoken by Adam, a 28.5-month-old boy:[27]

Here, Mum.	There goes.
Here coffeepot broken, Mum.	There it is.
Want coffee, Mum.	There more block.
Salad, Mum.	There more truck.
Enough, Mum.	There my house.
Here more blocks.	Blanket in there.

Undoubtedly Adam had heard these words in sentences, although probably not in adult sentences that correspond with his. Some researchers point to this kind of inventiveness as evidence that language is not entirely learned by imitation. Brown and Bellugi include the following in their records of model sentences produced by mothers and the imitations produced by children:[28]

Model Utterance	Child's Imitation
Tank car	Tank car
Daddy's briefcase	Daddy briefcase
He's going out	He go out
That's an old-time train	Old-time train

The researchers also cite these examples of utterances that are not likely to be imitations:[29]

Two foot	You naughty are
A bags	Put on it
A scissor	Cowboy did fighting me
A this truck	Put a gas in

26. Susan M. Ervin, "Imitation and Structural Change in Children's Language," in *New Directions in the Study of Language*, edited by E. H. Lenneberg (Cambridge, Mass.: MIT Press, 1964), p. 186.

27. Selected from Roger Brown and Colin Fraser, "The Acquisition of Syntax," in *Verbal Behavior and Learning*, edited by C. N. Cofer and Barbara Musgrave (New York: McGraw-Hill Book Co., 1963).

28. Roger Brown and Ursula Bellugi, "Three Processes in the Child's Acquisition of Syntax," *Harvard Educational Review* 34 (Spring 1964): 137.

29. Ibid., p. 141.

A child's apparent awareness that word order is important may be attributable to an inborn predisposition, but it is also possible that the child has learned that order is necessary to be understood. Since word order is different for different languages, the later possibility seems more likely.

Although children apparently learn the classes of words of their native language before they learn inflectional and derivational forms, they begin early to form and test hypotheses about noun and verb endings by saying *foots, goed, mines,* and so on, without having heard them. At first they overgeneralize, but they gradually learn from the responses of others that some ways of saying things are wrong. Children usually add many irregular verb forms to their vocabularies before many regular ones and construct overgeneralizations as they discover new rules.[30] As they mature, they begin to learn how to apply the rules. This process continues until the age of 9 and perhaps even beyond.[31] After they begin school, learning continues in an orderly way although children learn at very different rates.

Semantic Development

As speakers of a language, we must be able to understand sentences and relate them to our knowledge of the world. In addition to vocabulary, we need to know *semantics,* that is, how word definitions and sentence structure determine the meaning of a sentence. Dale points out that semantic development is the least understood aspect of language acquisition.[32] One reason for this is our lack of understanding of adult semantic competence. We do not know, for example, how adults discriminate among word meanings. Ordinarily, we think of words as representing "something"—a referent. But different words (lexical items) sometimes refer to the same thing. A simple example is that one person often answers to many names—*Marj, Mom, Mrs. Cole*—and refers to herself as I or *me.* Conversely, single words frequently have more than one referent or meaning: the *bank* in which money is kept, the *bank* of a stream, to *bank* a plane. And what are the referents for *and, but, if,* and *is*? Of course, some words do have single referents. A color such as *green* is specific, although there are shades of green.

Studies of vocabulary growth are neither uncommon nor new to education, but their contribution to our understanding of semantic development is limited because they typically do not explore how we combine word meanings into sentence meanings, what the relationships among word meanings are, or what a word in a child's vocabulary really means to that child.

It seems clear that young children do learn to attach words to specific

30. Courtney B. Cazden, *Language in Early Childhood Education* (Washington, D.C.: National Association for the Education of Young Children, 1972), p. 5.

31. Carol Chomsky, *The Acquisition of Syntax in Children from 5 to 10* (Cambridge, Mass.: MIT Press, 1969), p. 121.

32. Dale, p. 166.

referents (specific to the limited environment, that is). It seems equally true that they must distinguish different meanings of particular words as they are used in various contexts. This sorting out occurs at the same time children are learning how language works. Teachers are probably more aware of a child's semantic development than they are of the development of the child's grammar. Still, we know little about how semantic development occurs, in part because we have no adult model, which does exist for grammatical development, but also because semantic development is related to cognitive development. In other words, it is difficult to separate "How do children express their ideas?" from "What kinds of ideas do children have to express."[33]

Vocabulary Growth

Most children say an intelligible word during the second six months of life. Within the next few months many words follow. Lenneberg says the eighteen-month-old infant has a "definite repertoire of words—more than three, but less than fifty."[34] After speaking the first word or two, a child is likely to start naming things. As some observers have reported, "children go about the house all day long naming things (table, doggie, ball, etc.) and actions (play, see, drop, etc.).[35] By the time they are two years old, children know more than 50 words, many of which occur in two-word combinations. At age two and a half, the average child has a

33. Dale, p. 166.
34. Lenneberg, p. 129.
35. Brown and Bellugi, p. 133.

400-word vocabulary. This is the time of the most rapid increase in vocabulary, when the child vocalizes new words every day and speaks more than two words at a time. Many children this age use sentences of four or five words or more. By the time children are three years old, their vocabularies consist of approximately 1000 words.

Smith reported that the average one-year-old has a 3-word vocabulary; a year later, he or she knows 272. She also noted that the average two-year-old speaks about 80 words during an hour of free play, more than half of which are comprehensible.[36] It is important to remember, however, that generalizing about "the average" may be misleading. Some children are advanced in speech and others are slow in developing it. Some children are slow in developing speech because they have received little reinforcement or have had their needs met without having to speak.

Smith also gave estimates of the sizes of children's vocabularies at other age levels: at four, 1540 words; at five, 2072 words; at six 2562 words. Other studies have reported wide variation in size of vocabulary among first-grade children, ranging from the 2562 words reported by Smith to approximately 25,000 words. While the research procedures used in the studies reporting the larger number have been questioned, it probably is fair to say that the number of words known by a six-year-old today is larger than that Smith reported in her 1926 study.[37]

Counts or estimates of vocabulary at various stages in the school years have generally focused on the number of words children recognize by sight in reading and the number they use in writing. Dale and O'Rourke, on the other hand, studied children's meaning vocabularies. *The Living Word Vocabulary* is a record of the meanings of listed words known by children at the fourth-grade level and above (e.g., 83 percent of fourth graders understand "land along a stream" as one meaning of *bank*, 96 percent understand "where money is kept," and 85 percent understand "to save money".[38])

A major problem in measuring vocabulary size is how to count words with several meanings. Another is what method to use to collect data (e.g., by asking children to define words, by tabulating the words spoken, by tabulating the responses to stimuli, by counting the words children use in various writing or speaking situations). In addition, the sizes of one person's speaking, reading, listening, and writing vocabularies differ.

As indicated, while a considerable amount of vocabulary learning occurs during the early years of a child's life, we acquire most of our adult vocabulary during our years in school. Hence, aiding children's vocabulary growth is a major

---

36. M. E. Smith, "An Investigation of the Development of the Sentence and the Extent of Vocabulary in Young Children," *University of Iowa Studies in Child Welfare*, vol. 3, no. 5, 1926.

37. John Warren Stewig, *Exploring Language with Children*. Columbus, O.: Charles E. Merrill, 1974), p. 355.

38. Edgar Dale and Joseph O'Rourke, *The Living Word Vocabulary* (Chicago: Field Enterprises Educational Corp. 1976), p. 55.

instructional task. Teachers should focus vocabulary instruction on comprehension of multiple meanings of commonly used words as well as on acquisition of new vocabulary.

Just how teachers should teach vocabulary is not as clear as it might be. It is true that "some teaching effort causes students to learn vocabulary more successfully than does no teaching effort, [and] any attention to vocabulary development is better than none."[39] Yet the best evidence indicates that teachers need to recognize that vocabulary growth occurs as children develop their ability to use language. Teachers do need to encourage vocabulary growth whenever possible, particularly by providing an environment conducive to learning new words and meanings during genuine communicative activities. They also should avoid mechanical practices like having children look up the meanings of words in a list. None of us learns a new word or a new meaning unless we can relate it to something we already know. Furthermore, children will not retain knowledge unless they need to use what they have learned.

39. Walter T. Petty, Curtis P. Herold, and Earline Stoll, *The State of Knowledge About the Teaching of Vocabulary* (Urbana, Ill.: National Council of Teachers of English, 1968), p. 84.

Uses of Language

Ordinarily we think that the principal function of language is communication, and it is, generally. But language has many uses. For example, young children frequently speak without talking to anyone in particular. Piaget found that when children were alone and also when others were present, their speech (particularly between the ages of four and seven) was egocentric and lacked communicative intent.[40] Their talk is simply for pleasure or is thinking aloud. No communication is intended, and if an audience is present, the child apparently does not recognize it, as is the case when adults "talk to themselves." Thus, one use of language is in thinking.

The term *pragmatics* is now frequently used to mean the study of language in the contexts in which it occurs. Aside from its use in egocentric speech, language occurs in social settings. Its function in social contexts may be to get the attention of an audience; to establish rapport; or to placate, query, impress, command, clarify, caution, or threaten. Situation, speaker, topic, purpose, and listener all influence the speaker, but whatever the nature of his or her remarks, communication is the intent in the social context.[41]

Knowing how to use language is more than knowing how to construct a grammatical sentence or sequence of sentences to convey literal meaning. And it is more than knowing meanings of words. It is knowing what language is appropriate for the setting and purpose. Although research in development of pragmatic knowledge is just beginning, teachers have an obligation to help children gain this knowledge. They need to help children extend the process of identifying audiences, clarifying the purposes of particular utterances, and recognizing when they are appropriate. To do so, they must provide varied and authentic communication situations for children that demand appropriate word, phrase, and sentence choice.

FACTORS INFLUENCING LANGUAGE DEVELOPMENT

If you have ever spent time with more than one preschool child or infant, you probably noticed individual differences in language development. These differences exist because language development is a complex process that is sensitive to differences in the way children learn language, the language they learn, their personal characteristics, and the environment in which learning occurs.

In all environmental settings and all cultures, children learn language in the way we have described. They acquire the language and dialect (including the phonology, structure, and vocabulary of the dialect) of the people with whom they interact. When they enter school, this phase of their language development

40. Jean Piaget, *The Language and Thought of the Child*, translated by Marjorie Gabain (New York: World, 1955), p. 32.
41. Dale, p. 258.

will be apparent, and teachers need to be able to accommodate differences in language use attributable to it. Additional differences that we have discussed and that teachers must take into account are the rates at which children learned language and likely will continue to learn it in school, the number of words they know, fluency in speaking, and speech deviations such as stuttering.

Children have other individual differences that influence language development. Their mental abilities, physical charaoteristics, sex, home and other environmental contexts, and ethnic and economic backgrounds all have definite bearing upon their language development. We will describe each of these factors in some detail.

Intelligence

Tests designed to measure intelligence generally rely on language ability as an index of intelligence. Numerous studies have shown that relationships exist between measures of intelligence and various measures of language. For example, researchers have established positive correlations between intelligence test scores and vocabulary size, measures of articulation ability, and indices of language maturity.[42] Of course, since most tests of intelligence depend heavily on the use of language, it is difficult to determine what these correlations really indicate. Yet the magnitude of the correlation between intelligence measures and vocabulary size strongly suggests that the emphasis in intelligence tests on language does not account completely for the size of the correlations.

One theory that language abilities are relatively independent of general intellectual capacities has considerable support. One of its proponents is Lenneberg, who has stated that the developmental nature of language acquisition results in a well-developed linguistic system even by children with IQs no higher than 50.[43] Notice that his point of reference is the *system* and not vocabulary size or inclination to talk. In fact, studies of the mentally retarded have shown that whether or not a retarded person has a well-developed linguistic system, his or her language facility is generally related to the degree of retardation.

Like Lenneberg, Russian psychologist Vygotsky believes that language and conceptual skills develop independently in a child's early years, but he also sees language as a mediating factor in all learning.[44] In his view, learning takes place by means of *inner speech*, which is the process of thinking in word meanings (not talking to oneself in words and sentences).

Cumulative evidence suggests that virtually all children have knowledge of how their language works, its structure and phonology, but intelligence is a factor in the use of language. Remember, though, that talkativeness is not necessarily a

---

42. John Eisenson and Mardel Ogilvie, *Speech Correction in the Schools*, 2nd ed. (New York: Macmillan Co., 1963), p. 104.

43. Braine, p. 69.

44. L. S. Vygotsky, *Thought and Speech* (Cambridge, Mass.: MIT Press, 1962).

measure of language ability. A child who is reluctant to talk may not be dull or have poor language ability.

Sex

According to a number of studies, girls begin to talk earlier than boys and, as a result, apparently gain a head start in language development. Early vocalization is accompanied by rapid vocabulary development. Yet, in recent years tests of vocabulary, sentence comprehension, and verbal expression given to children between age two and a half and early adolescence have shown no differences attributable to sex.[45] Older adolescent girls do establish a definite pattern of superior verbal performance, which continues throughout high school and college.

Carroll points out that sex differences in verbal performance are relatively small and that "distributions of various measures of language development and skill nearly always show great overlap."[46] Recent evidence, therefore, seems to contradict the observations of elementary school teachers and others that girls do better than boys on school reading and writing tests and that language handicaps—stuttering, for instance—afflict more boys. These differences probably do not reflect actual language ability. Rather they stem from environmental factors: more female than male teachers in elementary schools, pressures on male children to achieve, possibly more frequent verbal exchange between girls and the more accessible mother, and so on. It seems likely that the current cultural and social trends will reduce these differences considerably.

Physical Condition

Language acquisition and development have several physical requirements. They include normally developed speech organs (teeth, tongue, lips, throat, and larynx) hearing organs, and neuromuscular system. In order for speech development to progress normally, all of these must function effectively. Handicaps to sight and hearing, to the ability to perform neuromuscular acts, and to sound production are likely to interfere with language development.

Language development appears to be relatively independent of motor coordination. By the time a child begins to develop finger and hand coordination, for example, he or she has usually acquired the infinitely precise and rapid movements of tongue, lips, and other organs needed for speech. Of course, motor skills and motor coordination abilities develop in set stages, but evidence that language understanding precedes its production seems to underscore the independence of language development from the stages of motor-skeletal maturation.

---

45. Dale, p. 310.
46. John B. Carroll, "Development of Native Language Skills Beyond the Early Years," in *The Learning of Language*, edited by Carroll E. Reed (New York: Appleton-Century-Crofts, 1971) p. 148.

Home and Family

The family environment of the child is the most important determinant of the quality of the language facility he or she develops. In order to acquire language facility the infant and young child need to talk, to have language exchanges with other persons, and to have experiences on which to base thoughts and language. Children who play alone or only with other children in their own homes have limited access to new ideas and concepts. If, however, they go to the park, visit the zoo, take vacation trips, travel extensively with parents, and accompany mother on a shopping expedition, they acquire a wealth of new sights and sounds and words that relate to them. Children whose parents talk with them, read to them, and generally interact with them verbally gain greatly in language development.[47] For example, studies show that eating meals together (assuming that conversation takes place) enhances a child's language facility. Even smiling at and showing warmth to young infants causes them to produce more sounds than the absence of reinforcing facial expressions or attention.[48] Reading to children is especially important because it exposes them to the structural qualities and vocabulary of the written language, which differ from those characteristics of the spoken word. Reading to children, even infants, is also a means of giving them attention, and in this way facilitating learning.

Single children generally develop language facility more slowly than do children with brothers or sisters. Slowest to develop are twins, who often associate so closely with each other that their contact with others is minimal. And because of their close association, they develop ways to communicate without having to talk. Institutionalized children, who have fewer opportunities to talk with adults than do children with parents, fall behind their peers in language development. Their progress remains retarded even through adolescence. Retarded language development has been shown to be independent of social class.[49] Not surprisingly, then, given what intuition tells us, research confirms that parents and home contribute significantly to language development.

Economic Conditions

Another major influence on children's language development is their family's economic circumstances. Numerous studies have shown relationships between language development and economic class, although the underlying causes are by no means clear and the research conclusions have many challengers. The predomi-

47. Robert D. Hess and Virginia Shipman, "Early Experiences and the Socialization of Cognitive Modes in Children," *Child Development* 36 (1965): 869–86.

48. Mollie S. Smart and Russell C. Smart, *Infants, Development and Relationships* (New York: Macmillan Co., 1973), p. 168.

49. David P. Ausubel and Edmund V. Sullivan, *Theory and Problems of Child Development*, 2nd ed. (New York: Grune and Stratton, 1970), p. 543.

nant interpretation of research data in this area is that children in middle-income (usually labeled middle-class) families exhibit a more highly developed, elaborated, or complex syntactic usage than children from low-income homes.[50] Certainly children from poverty backgrounds do not have many of the experiences that nonpoverty children usually do. Few teachers regard children from poverty or low social classes as nonverbal—in contrast to a decade or so ago—but they do recognize syntax and pronunciation differences, as well as differences in vocabulary.

Not all poor families provide similar environments to children. Some economically poor parents use standard English and talk with their children, whereas some middle-class parents pay little attention to their children's language development. Typically, however, economic strife experienced by lower-class parents and the use of "restricted" language have been associated. That is, the lower class will most often use abbreviated, nonexplicit language and focus on controlling behavior rather than on communication.[51]

Significantly, poverty may limit children's opportunities for experiences that facilitate and encourage learning. If the home environment is not conducive to language use, children may not know such concepts as *over* and *under*, which are fundamental in early instruction. They may not have verbally experienced comparing, describing, and contrasting objects. In addition, their vocabularies may contain few words related to books, crayons, pets, and experiences that underlie the content of the typical school curriculum. Thus, these children may be woefully unprepared for verbal experiences in the school classroom.

Ethnic Setting

Apparently the extent to which families encourage language development in their children differs from one ethnic group to another. In one study Jewish children demonstrated significantly greater English verbal ability than all other examined groups, followed by black, Chinese, and Puerto Ricans, in that order.[52] On measures other than verbal ones, the ranking was different. The fact that English was probably the native language of the Jewish and black participants may have affected the results. Too, Chinese and Puerto Rican families have a strong cultural identification, which encourages using Chinese or Spanish, and which may affect children's learning of English. In addition, Jewish families tend to be close-knit and child oriented.[53] In Puerto Rican families, on the other hand, children are

---

50. Davenport Plumer, "A Summary of Environmentalist Views and Some Educational Implications," in *Language and Poverty: Perspectives on a Theme*, edited by Frederick Williams (Chicago: Markham Publishing Co., 1970), p. 279.

51. Ausubel and Sullivan, p. 544.

52. Reed, p. 147.

53. John Nist, *Handicapped English* (Springfield, Ill.: Charles C. Thomas Publisher, 1974), p. 184.

passively unresponsive to verbal interactions, even to verbal task assignments by their mothers, possibly because of cultural influences.[54]

While virtually everything in a young child's environment may be a factor in language development, it is dangerous to generalize about ethnic and racial influences, especially since economic conditions may be the primary influence. Most studies of language development, home conditions, and so on of black children have focused on those in the lower socioeconomic class. On the other hand, the racial prejudice of much of the white majority population does affect the personality development of many black children, which, in turn, is a factor in their development and use of language.

Bilingualism

Attention to bilingualism is increasing in schools. Frequently the label "bilingual" is applied to children who speak (sometimes not well) Puerto Rican or Mexican Spanish, Chinese, or an Indian language and little or no American English. A metropolitan area is likely to include children from many countries who need to learn to speak, read, and write English. Thus, bilingual language development usually means learning English, while also gaining facility in the native or first language by hearing and speaking it at home.

Bilingual children encounter a number of problems with English. First, they have vocabulary difficulties; they frequently intermingle words of both languages. Their English sentences are short, often incomplete, and seldom of compound or complex forms. They make errors in inflection, verb tenses, and uses of connectives, articles, and negative forms. They also misuse idiomatic expressions because they tend to translate literally. All of these difficulties in their use of English handicap them in other schoolwork.

In addition, bilingual children have problems with pronunciation and enunciation. For example, English is one of the few languages which has both the $/\partial/$ (as in they) and the $/\theta/$ (as in thank) phonemes; therefore, children whose native language uses neither of these phonemes or only one of them need to learn how to position the tongue and lips to form these and other unfamiliar sounds and to practice using them. Furthermore, the rhythmic patterns of English sentence structure frequently cause problems.

Suggestions for teaching bilingual children appear in Chapter 4, but it is worth pointing out here that the purpose of teaching English to bilingual children is to help them learn the language. It should not be anyone's goal to erase their knowledge of their first language or to take away their cultural identities.

---

54. Mollie S. Smart and Russell C. Smart, *Preschool Children, Development and Relationships* (New York: Macmillan Co., 1973), p. 97.

LANGUAGE LEARNING IN EARLY SCHOOL SETTINGS

While much language growth occurs in infancy, children in nursery school, kindergarten, and the early primary grades are capable of taking great strides in language development. These are critical years when attitudes are formed, values learned, and habits established.

Preschool Programs

Preschool programs stem primarily from the hypothesis that children aged three to five can profit from educational experiences that only a school setting usually can provide. The objective of preschool teaching is to develop children's intellectual, emotional, social, and physical abilities. To develop intellectual powers, teachers can promote curiosity and growth of language and impart readiness for later intellectual activities. The emotional goal is to increase children's sense of security and self-respect, while the social goal is to instill concern for and responsibility toward others.

These objectives and prescribed methods of achieving them characterize practices and programs in many nursery schools. Nevertheless, increasing federal involvement in early education (e.g., Project Head Start) and the rising number of private nursery schools, day-care centers, and private and public kindergartens suggest a need to reemphasize desirable objectives and related activities.

Preschool Language Arts Objectives

Language activities provide preschoolers with a foundation for instruction in listening, reading, speaking, and writing in the school program. The activities need to be informal, to take account of differences in children's backgrounds and learning abilities, and to relate to the following objectives.

Spontaneity of expression. At the top of any list of objectives for teaching language to young children should be the development of fluency and naturalness in expression. While the desire for self-expression is instinctive in children, quite often we must encourage this trait by providing satisfying experiences that require expression. No matter how many ideas children have or how much language skill they possess, they must want to impart these ideas to others. Above all else, their experience must foster this desire. Exposing children to an abundance of experiences gives them something to talk about, the key element in the development of fluency and spontaneity in expression.

Socialization. A second objective is socialization. Each child, when entering school and continuing into the first grade at least, is in every sense of the word an "individual." Many children show little interest in listening to others, in taking turns talking, or in speaking in front of an audience. In fact, some children will have had little social contact with other children and will know little about how to behave in a group.

Young children progress through three distinct phases in the socialization process that are discernible in language: (1) *egocentric speech*, talking aloud to oneself; (2) *parallel speech*, talking at the same time as other children without giving or expecting a response; (3) *socialized speech*, talking to and responding to the talk of others. Of course, these phases overlap, but until they reach the third phase, children are not ready for instruction in many school subjects. A teacher can help children reach this phase, can guide them in learning to talk freely and easily, to listen courteously to others, and habitually to use socially accepted phrases such as "thank you" and "excuse me." Children must learn to share ideas, as well as materials, and to develop a sense of responsibility, both as individuals and as group members.

Enunciation and voice control.   A third objective is to develop the ability to enunciate words properly and to control the voice. Baby talk, lisping, stuttering, and incomplete enunciation handicap acquisition of skill and ease in speaking and language usage. Allowed to persist, they may become definite sources of embarrassment. Indistinctness and an unpleasingly high voice also impair development of ability and fluency in language. Early language programs should work toward achieving an easy, pleasant manner in speaking, good voice control—both in volume and tone—and accurate articulation and clear enunciation.

Organization of thought.   An extremely important objective is the development of skill in organizing ideas for expression. Organization is necessary to effective presentation of ideas in oral as well as written sentences and paragraphs. Early in their school experiences, children should learn to arrange pictures to tell a story. Later they should learn to order sentences to recount a story or an experience. Organization exercises should be simple and brief at first and gradually add items and details appropriate for the child's maturity.

Effective listening.   A fundamental factor in the achievement of several language arts objectives is the ability of a child to listen effectively. Problems in enunciation and voice control are often traceable to the failure to hear how we sound or how other persons sound. Before they can improve language usage, children must be able to hear accurately the correct usage. Listening is also important in reading instruction. Children not only must learn what to listen to and what to screen out as they concentrate on the printed page, but also must sharpen the skills needed to listen to and discriminate among differences in sounds. Children must learn to listen to directions, to information and ideas from other children, and to stories being read to them. They must listen to gain knowledge from virtually all communication activities.

Visual discrimination skill.   The teacher of young children must help them become skillful in focusing their attention on the visual tasks they face in learning to read and write. The visual abilities of children in early grades vary greatly, because of physical differences and because of their different backgrounds. Some children have developed habits of careful observation of details, while others have learned to react only to gross differences. Of course, a teacher cannot force physical development, but most children who have difficulty with the visual tasks called for in initial language learning activities simply need practice switching from gross visual discrimination tasks to those requiring finer judgments of shape, size, place, relationships, and arrangements.

Rhythmic movement and creativity.   Bodily movement and language expression are related—both allow us to show thoughts and feelings. Very often a child first expresses creativity through body movement. As with other abilities, young children vary in the control they have of their bodies and in the freedom and creativity they express with them. As stated above, physical development cannot

75

be speeded, but children can learn to use their bodies to the extent that their development permits. Thus attention should be given to rhythmic activities, to play which calls for bodily movement and expression. In a like manner, creative expression, by both body and voice, should also be encouraged.

Vocabulary development.   All group activities enrich children's experiences and ideas. Each new experience introduces new words and meanings to describe and explain it. Since knowledge of words and word meanings is essential in both the expressive and receptive aspects of language, vocabulary building is vital to the early language program. Therefore, program planners should design all of the children's activities to teach new vocabulary and new meanings for familiar words.

Enrichment Experiences

Having given recognition to the experiences children have had prior to coming into a school setting—experiences largely determine what they know and the habits, attitudes, emotions, and interests that make up their personalities—we cannot leave out the fact that subsequent experiences contribute to their education. Too often, educators neglect this need for "intake" in the hurry to "teach" the children. In this day of television and ease of travel, most children have had a broad range of experience. Some of their experience has been shallow, however, and children have not had similar types and amounts of experience. Children of migrant farm workers, for instance, are apt to have gone from one farm to another, bypassing urban areas and other opportunities for new experiences along the way. Teachers must be aware that differences in experience exist among children, but they must also recognize that classroom learning requires a foundation of common experience. Few children have limitless "mental bank accounts" from which to draw ideas for language programs.

Effective language programs build on a framework of communication for genuine purposes. The process of receiving ideas and information and expressing related thoughts must be continuous. There can be little "banking" of intake. Rather, opportunities for firsthand observation and participation must be numerous. Activities may involve objects, live and inanimate; trips (even if you go no further than the school yard); making plans; playing with toys and using equipment; and working and playing together in small groups. The environment should be an attractive one that fosters investigation as well as looking. Children and teacher alike should share knowledge and thoughts with each other. Most of all, however, the program should consist of much reading aloud, story telling, looking at picture books, listening to recordings—activities that convey both ideas and language.

Perception and Discrimination

All learning requires ability to perceive visual and auditory symbols accurately and to discriminate promptly and correctly among similar forms and sounds. Perception and discrimination abilities do not develop all at once. Every child entering school has developed them to some degree, but early school programs are responsible for developing them further. Here are suggestions to aid in the process:

1. Sort objects or pieces of paper according to shape (circles, squares, triangles, etc.).
2. Match pieces of paper of different shapes to outlines of shapes drawn on the chalkboard.
3. Assemble form boards or simple puzzles.
4. Sort, according to size, tagboard objects of the same shape but different size.
5. Sort pieces of paper of different colors, shapes, and sizes. Children should sort only for one characteristic (color, for instance) at first; later they can combine two, and finally all three, characteristics.
6. Match blocks or beads by size and shape.
7. Draw geometric designs shown on the board.
8. Tell in what respects objects or drawings are alike or different.
9. Discriminate between two letters of the alphabet or two words. The letters and words do not need to be named.
10. Show objects that produce different sounds when struck (glass, box, desk, etc.). Children close their eyes and try to name the object.
11. Play games that call for simple directions.
12. Have children tell whether words rhyme.
13. Pronounce pairs of words and ask children whether they begin with the same sound.
14. Listen to music and march to different rhythms.
15. Ask a child to say a word as slowly as possible, then as quickly as possible.
16. Make familiar animal sounds (cat, dog, cow, duck, rooster, pig, etc.) and ask children to name the animals.
17. Ask children to imitate sounds (airplane, train, clock, etc.).
18. Recite simple poetry and rhymes in chorus.
19. Arrange for one child or several to name and put objects on a flannel board as they are mentioned in a story that is being read or told.
20. Play games requiring different types of voices: a young child's tiny voice, a father's big, deep voice, etc.
21. Provide opportunities for dramatic play and simple puppet shows.

Expression and Vocabulary Growth

While the activities suggested in preceding sections require the use of language, as do the normal and ongoing activities of young children, it is necessary to plan experiences specifically to generate talking. Most children require very little encouragement to bring in toys and other objects from home or to talk about trips and play activities. Wise teachers use these as resources to encourage talk. Frequently "sharing" or "telling" periods accomplish this purpose, although less formality is more appropriate for less mature children.

In addition to activities based upon these largely out-of-school interests, teachers should plan many others. For example, a focus upon nature that includes continuing projects such as keeping an aquarium or terrarium, keeping indoor gardens, caring for classroom pets, keeping weather charts, and helping to plan daily activities introduces subjects that are interesting and real to children. Seasonal activities are also useful. The following are examples of activities that will lead to language exchange:

1. Noting temperature differences in sunshine and shade
2. Collecting leaves of different kinds
3. Looking at frost under a magnifying glass
4. Watching formations of flying birds
5. Feeding birds in winter
6. Collecting nuts, rocks, seeds, etc.
7. Observing results of soil erosion
8. Planning and obtaining contents for Junior Red Cross boxes
9. Making puppets to play out a story
10. Observing variations in growth of different seeds
11. Caring for a classroom pet
12. Daily observing of an ant house or a termite box
13. Feeling a variety of materials, such as velvet, fur, aluminum foil, and sand
14. Tasting substances such as berries, nuts, pickles

Activities that directly focus on words and language help to build children's vocabularies and expressional skills. For example,

1. The teacher can make a chart of pictures illustrating fruits, vegetables, furniture, animals, toys, numbers, colors, opposites, etc. The children classify, name, and describe each object.
2. Children may retell stories read by the teacher.
3. Children may play word games. For example, they may be told to walk, skip, sit, listen, and hop. Then an adverb is added and they must walk slowly, quickly, happily; sit quietly, lazily, sadly, etc.
4. Children may describe objects, each other, clothes, animals, etc.

5. Word games can also require listening and knowledge of concepts. For example, children can be directed to place an object in, on, under, beside, below, above, behind another object.

Effective Listening

Since every communicative act requires reception as well as expression, the presence of an audience of one or more persons who really want to listen to the speaker is the best possible motivation for good expression. Any audience that wants to listen has considerable ability to do so effectively, but it is possible to learn skills for improved listening (see Chapter 7). In particular, preschool children and children in beginning primary grades respond to listening games, as well as to music and sound patterns and activities that require listening to language, such as:

1. *Remembering action words:* After the children have listened to a story ask them to list certain action words that help tell the story. For example, after one story the children may recall the following words and tell what they remember about the story: bark, running, rumbling, jumped, piled, raced, fell.
2. *Summarize a story:* The teacher reads a short story to the group and asks pupils to retell the plot in one sentence. Use stories on the reading level of the group.
3. *What happens next?* Read aloud part of a story that is unfamiliar to the children and ask them to suggest what will happen next.
4. *Telling back:* Read a story to the group and ask the children to retell it in their own words.
5. *Following directions:* After dividing the group into two or three teams, the teacher gives a series of directions, perhaps three or four specific things to do. A child is then selected from each group to carry out the directions. Each child who can follow the directions accurately and in order scores one point for his or her team.
6. *Listening to conversation:* Reading aloud the conversational parts of a story may help children to listen for dialogue or for characterizations.
7. *Taping a story:* Children may record stories they have made up themselves, as the class listens and asks questions.[55]

Attention to Creative Interests

Young children love to pretend, to experiment with uses of language, and to hear and tell stories. They appreciate hearing poetry and rhymes and enjoy reciting

---

55. Selected from *Language Arts Curriculum Guide, K–6,* Jefferson County Public Schools, Lakewood, Colo., 1960.

them in unison. Their creativity is largely unhampered by societal conventions, a condition that the learning environment and activities should encourage.

It is not unusual to see young children pretending to be mothers and fathers, doctors, drivers, pilots, and the like. Children also like to pretend that they are animals, by imitating a pet dog's bark, the buzzing of a bee, the soaring of a bird. All such dramatic play is a part of growing up. It is a part of their life outside the school and will continue in school if encouraged to do so and if space and materials are provided. Both preschool and kindergarten rooms should have blocks of various sizes; play furniture, cooking utensils and equipment, and toys to represent buses and airplanes; a puppet stage with paper bag and stick puppets; and objects to use as buildings, roads, and so on.

At the first-grade level children like to choose the characters whom they will represent. Many, of course, want to be the same character, and so they must take turns, and in some cases, dramatize only part of a story or do the entire story in segments.

While dramatic play is essentially impulsive and an activity that the teacher should not direct, such play can provide a great deal of learning. Planning settings, changing settings, getting specific equipment or costumes, and considering the context of the activities are all subject to discussion by the group, including the teacher. Talking things over with children leads to dramatic play and to more talking as the children play.

Reading to and telling children stories also fosters creativity. This experience naturally leads the children themselves to tell stories that they have heard and perhaps "acted" out. Through story telling they develop the ability to recall events in proper sequence, use descriptive words and phrases, speak loudly and distinctly enough for all to hear, and avoid fragmentary and run-on sentences. In addition, they will learn to change their voices for emphasis or to express characterizations and to speak fluently and without selfconsciousness.

The creative quality of expression may appear early in the child's language development, and it will grow in extent and effectiveness with encouragement, and especially through reference to familiar personal experiences. Children relive their experiences and interpret them if they have the opportunity to express their own thoughts and feelings. Giving vent to personal feelings, Jimmie tells his fellow first-graders about George. He calls his story "The Bad Kitty":

> This cat is sort of grey and funny looking. He does silly things and gets in trouble. He's got a spool that he spins and tosses, and sometimes he sits in the big chair. One time he caught a mouse. Then what do you think he did? He ran away!
>
>   Yesterday George put his paw in his milk and spilled it. Boy, did he get into trouble!

Children's story telling and informal dramatizing introduce them to literature, but good beginning language arts programs emphasize reading good literature to children and helping them to appreciate it. Teachers should give particular attention to the reading of poetry. Children enjoy poetry and it is a valuable vehicle for helping them to use language effectively, for giving a feeling for language, and for helping them appreciate rhythm and rhyme. If carefully chosen and well read, poetry teaches children to listen carefully and appreciatively. It teaches them new words, new ways of saying things, and new ideas and feelings for self-expression.

Children love to play with words, to feel their power and rhythm, to experiment with them. Not all of these activities require group participation. One kindergartener composed this "Slide Song" and his teacher wrote it for him:

> Down, down
> Yellow and brown.
> Here comes someone down the slide!

Young children also enjoy repeating poetry in unison. Group reading or choral speaking helps to improve voice quality and clear speech. It also provides opportunities for the shy to participate without embarrassment. A teacher has to read or repeat a poem to primary children only once or twice. Allowing them to say as much as they can after each reading will help them to remember it. Children sometimes enjoy having solo parts instead of repeating the entire selection in unison.

Introduction to Written Expression

Young children experiment early with "writing." They scribble with crayons and pencils and "pretend." The first actual written expression should capitalize on this interest. The teacher can serve as scribe and the children help to decide what to write. The subject may be an upcoming or recent group activity: a trip, film, party, visit from someone, or even a story, song, or event that takes place in the classroom. Prior to a field trip, the group could discuss appropriate behavior before leaving and the teacher could write down suggestions to guide the children on the trip; if they are written, children will be more likely to remember them than if they had only talked about them. If the children are taking a trip to the dairy, they might have questions about cows, milk, and how the milk gets to the supermarket. The teacher might record their questions on chart paper:

- Where does milk come from?
- How does it get in the cartons?
- How does it get to the store?

After the trip the children will be able to draw upon the experience for talking and writing activities. In the discussion following, they should find the answers to their questions and the teacher should record this information, perhaps in story form. In addition to finding answers to the initial questions, the children will probably learn about milking machines, pasteurization, and the sterilization of containers. They will learn many new words and concepts to include in the group stories.

Children need guidance in the composition of group stories. If they are going to write about what they saw at the dairy, the teacher can usually guide the story's development with questions:

- Where did we go first?
- Where are the cows kept?
- What does the milking machine do?

At first writing, the children's responses and the story they form may not be organized well. The teacher may say, "Let's go back over this and decide which sentences we need to keep in our story and how they should be arranged." The final story should be the product of the children's thinking rather than of what the teacher wants, although good guidance and stimulation of thinking may produce a story that will please everyone, such as this one:

Our Halloween party

We had a Halloween party.
We had cookies and milk.
Mothers sent the cookies.
Thank you, Mothers.
Some visitors came.
We had fun!

Even in the very first group writing efforts, children should start learning mechanical skills. As the teacher uses a capital letter, he or she may say, "I'm making a capital letter to begin my sentence," and later ask, "How do I begin this sentence?" The same approach works with periods and other punctuation and with margins, position of title, and the spelling of words, however with less direct attention.

At times the teacher may make copies of stories for the children so that they may put their names on them and identify them as their stories. It may please the children just to hear the story read to them or to have a copy to keep.

Writing group stories on chart paper rather than on the chalkboard makes it possible to display them in the room. This practice will help to fix vocabulary, give opportunity to learn the spelling of words, and, of course, aid in reading instruction. Duplicates or copies made by the children can be kept in story booklets.

After children have had considerable experience generating group stories and other forms of written expression, they can begin to create their own pieces. For example, the children might suggest several appropriate messages for "get-well" cards to send to an absent classmate: "Get well soon"; "Come back soon"; "I miss you"; "We miss you at school"; and so on. From the suggestions that the teacher has written on the board, they may select the ones they like and write them on their cards.

Independent and individual writing is a natural and gradual outgrowth of language activities, including group composition. The children's lack of handwriting and spelling skills initially will limit individual efforts, but the teacher should encourage them nevertheless. The ability to write letters and to spell some words is enough for some children to begin writing. The first independent writing children do should be simple enough for them to complete it successfully. For example, the group could compose a story of three lines, which the teacher writes down and the children copy, and then each of them can add a fourth line to his or her own paper. For example,

Our trip

We visited the zoo.
We went on the bus.
It was fun riding that far.

Different children might add "We saw elephants and lions"; "We had fun"; "I liked the monkeys"; and so on.

Other independent writing projects include story titles, captions for pictures or charts, one word or phrase to complete a sentence, names, and numbers. The emphasis in such writing should be making children think, while minimizing the actual writing they must do.

Teachers should bear in mind the need for transition from group to independent writing (with the recognition that the length of the transition period will vary from child to child). As with group composition and story writing, children will enjoy both writing independently about their interests and the experiences they have had and making up stories, particularly if the classroom climate encourages such expression and if they receive recognition for it. They need to write answers to questions, compose short reports, and make lists, all of which they do willingly as a part of larger activities. Primary children also enjoy writing directions for various activities, keeping records of classroom events, making booklets, writing rhymes and jingles, and writing letters and notes. Interest and development of ability in writing begins in prewriting, group writing, and beginning individual writing. The activities suggested in this chapter will prepare young children to meet the writing challenges they will encounter later in their school careers (see Chapters 13 and 14).

Learning to Read: The Beginning

Learning to read is a lifelong task. In school, the rate of progress fluctuates for each child and varies from child to child. Preschool language arts programs must recognize that learning to read is a prolonged process.

At what age children should begin receiving instruction in reading has been a subject of controversy for many years. Several studies have shown that children are receptive to reading instruction earlier than the traditional first-grade age. Other studies have shown that some children are able to read beginning books when they enter the first grade, although only about 1 percent will be able to do so unless they received reading instruction in kindergarten.[56]

Virtually all children are eager to learn to read. They expect to learn and their parents expect them to learn. Although parents sometimes expect instruction in reading to begin in kindergarten or perhaps even earlier, children usually sustain their enthusiasm throughout the period of preparatory activities—unless it is extended beyond the point at which they are ready for their first formal reading instruction.

The objectives established in this chapter will prepare children to learn to read and keep their interest high. Children need spontaneity and considerable fluency in oral expression before encountering the printed word in the context of formal reading instruction. Each child must also make satisfactory social adjustment to being in a classroom, to working with other children and the teacher, to accepting direction, and to working independently on assigned tasks.

There is no sharp line of demarcation between many of the activities suggested in this chapter and initial experiences in reading. As children show signs of understanding the meaning of written symbols, teachers should introduce them to reading, at first by reading group stories, particularly the ones they have copied or added a sentence to, and then using beginning materials from the formal reading program and children's literature. In Chapters 8 and 9, we give further attention to reading and procedures to use in a developmental program.

---

56. Dolores Durkin, "Early Readers—Reflections After Six Years of Research," *The Reading Teacher* 18 (October 1964): 3–7.

EXERCISES FOR THOUGHT AND ACTION

1. List additional objectives for language arts programs in preschools and the primary grades. How would you go about achieving them?
2. Arrange to observe for fifteen minutes a planned activity for a group of nursery school or kindergarten children. Immediately afterward write what you learned about the children and your conclusions about the effectiveness of your observation.
3. Prepare a bibliography of books to read to nursery school and kindergarten children. See recent publications of the Association for Childhood Education International, American Library Association, and National Council of Teachers of English for assistance.
4. Observe groups of children of several preschool age levels. How do their interests and maturity levels differ? How are their uses of language different? What are the implications of these differences for planning language arts programs for these different age groups?
5. What advice would you give parents of an infant or very young child who asked you what they should be doing to help their child's language development?
6. Viewpoints about how children learn language change frequently as new research evidence becomes available. Report to the class any modifications of the viewpoints identified in this chapter that you discover in the most recent educational literature.
7. Record an experience dictated by one or more children. Transfer the story to chart paper.
8. The chapter mentions Read's studies of young children's spelling attempts. Examine Read's work and report examples of how children's categorizations of speech sounds influence their early spelling attempts.
9. Select, plan, and tell one of your peers a story that would be suitable for young listeners. Solicit constructive criticism.
10. Collect resources for a language arts program that includes some children for whom English is not the native language. How could you increase understanding among native English speakers of the language and culture of these children?
11. Describe steps you could take to help a shy kindergarten child to become more expressive.
12. Survey your local television schedule for programming suitable for the preschool and primary child. View several of the programs (e.g., "Sesame Street" and "Mister Rogers' Neighborhood") and prepare to discuss which ones you would recommend and for what reasons.
13. If you could enroll your three-year-old either in a preschool program that emphasizes language skills or in one that emphasizes interaction with peers and adults for the primary purpose of social and emotional development, which would you choose? Why?

14. Undertake an in-depth study of a topic pertinent to the subject of this chapter (e.g., the course of language development in the deaf or verbal behavior of children isolated from human contact).

SELECTED REFERENCES

Bar-Adon, A., and Leopold, W. F., eds. *Child Language: A Book of Readings.* Englewood Cliffs, N. J.: Prentice-Hall, 1971.

Brown Roger. *A First Language: The Early Stages.* Cambridge, Mass.: Harvard University Press, 1973.

Bumpass, Faye L. *Teaching Young Students English as a Foreign Language.* New York: American Book Co., 1963.

Cazden, Courtney B. *Child Language and Education.* New York: Holt, Rinehart and Winston, 1972.

Cazden, Courtney B., ed. *Language in Early Childhood Education.* Washington, D.C.: National Association for the Education of Young Children, 1972.

Chomsky, Carol. *The Acquisition of Syntax in Children from 5 to 10.* Cambridge, Mass.: MIT Press, Research Monograph No. 57, 1969.

Chukovsky, K. *From Two to Five.* Translated by M. Morton. Berkeley: University of California Press, 1968.

Clark, E. V. "What's in a Word? On the Child's Acquisition of Semantics in His First Language." In *Cognitive Development and the Acquisition of Language,* edited by T. E. Moore. New York: Academic Press, 1973.

Clark, Herbert, H. and Clark, Eve V. *Psychology and Language: An Introduction to Psycholinguistics.* New York: Harcourt Brace Jovanovich, 1977.

Creber, J. W. Patrick. *Lost for Words, Language and Educational Failure.* Baltimore: Penguin Books, 1972.

Cuban, Larry. *To Make a Difference, Teaching in the Inner City.* New York: Free Press, 1970.

Dale, Philip S. *Language Development, Structure and Function.* 2nd ed. New York: Holt, Rinehart and Winston, 1972.

Dawson, Mildred A., and Newman, Georgianna C. *Language Teaching in Kindergarten and the Early Primary Grades.* New York: Harcourt, Brace, and World, 1966.

Ferguson, C. A., and Slobin, D. I., eds. *Studies of Child Language Development.* New York: Holt, Rinehart and Winston, 1973.

Gordon, Ira J., ed. *Early Childhood Education,* Seventy-first Yearbook of the National Society for the Study of Education, pt. 2. Chicago: University of Chicago Press, 1972.

Gumperz, J. J., and Hymes, D. *Directions in Sociolinguistics.* New York: Holt, Rinehart and Winston, 1972.

Landreth, Catherine. *Preschool Learning and Teaching.* New York: Harper and Row, 1972.

Leeper, Sarah Hammond, *et al. Good Schools for Young Children.* 3rd ed. New York: Macmillan Co., 1974.

Lenneberg, Eric H. *The Biological Foundations of Language.* New York: John Wiley and Sons, 1967.

Loban, Walter. *Language Development: Kindergarten Through Grade Twelve.* Urbana, Ill.: National Council of Teachers of English, 1976.

Loban, Walter. *The Language of Elementary School Children.* Urbana, Ill.: National Council of Teachers of English, 1963.

McNeill, D. *The Acquisition of Language: The Study of Developmental Psycholinguistics.* New York: Harper and Row, 1970.

Piaget, Jean. *The Language and Thought of the Child.* Translated by Marjorie Gabain. New York: World, 1973.

Reed, Carroll E., ed. *The Learning of Language.* New York: Appleton-Century-Crofts, 1971.

Smart, Mollie S. and Smart, Russell C. *Infants, Development and Relationships.* New York: Macmillan Co., 1973.

Smart, Mollie S., and Smart, Russell C. *Preschool Children, Development and Relationships.* New York: Macmillan Co., 1973.

Spodek, Bernard. *Teaching in the Early Years.* Englewood Cliffs, N.J.: Prentice-Hall, 1972.

Stent, Madelon D.; Hazard, William R.; and Rivlin, Harry N. *Cultural Pluralism in Education.* New York: Appleton-Century-Crofts, 1973.

Vygotsky, L. S. *Thought and Language.* Translated by E. Hanfmann and G. Vakar. Cambridge, Mass.: MIT Press, 1962.

4

The Language Arts Teacher

The control of the class teacher is no longer judged by her ability to keep the children just where she wants them and silent until spoken to. She holds the reins by guiding the children through their spontaneous chatter towards becoming articulate. The harmonious hum of a happy workshop suggests a control within which the child's individual modes of expression can flourish. —Alice Yardley, Exploration and Language

If you read the first chapters in this book, you should understand what the language arts are and what language is and how children learn it. You should also have an idea of what teachers can do to focus their teaching on the learner. These concepts and principles are applicable not only to all of the facets of language arts discussed in this and later chapters, but also to other subjects in the curriculum. Teaching science, math, and social studies also requires identifying and providing for individual pupil needs, determining curriculum content, organizing instruction, designing basic instructional plans, evaluating, and providing useful materials.

CONSIDERING THE CHILD IN PLANNING

Children within any given school group differ in mental capacity, sex, physical size and strength, motor control, sensory acuity, skin tone, emotional stability, interests, and many other aspects of total growth and development. Teachers must accommodate all of these differences, as well as specific language differences in their teaching and planning.

Differences in Language Ability

In Chapter 3, we discussed the wide variance in language development and use. Children at all school levels differ in language sophistication. In addition, children demonstrate different degrees of language ability in different communication tasks. Some are good talkers but poor listeners; others appear to be good listeners but do not express ideas well orally. Some children fail to learn to read or write in spite of well-developed oral skills because of vision and motor problems. Others learn to read from an excellent oral language base. Still others read well but are not fluent talkers. Some children develop good handwriting skills but cannot produce effective sentences. In sum, any single child may experience quite irregular development in language skills.[1]

Teacher Identification of Pupil Needs

It is relatively easy to estimate the range of individual differences that teachers can expect to find in a classroom, but it is another matter to draw a clear, detailed picture of each child. Teachers must interpret general facts regarding individual differences in terms of concrete realities as they work with the children day by day and remember that each child is a person, an individual and not a statistic.

Evaluation and observation must be continuous in order to know the specific abilities and needs of each child. Only then can a teacher decide where to begin instruction in each aspect of the language arts for each child, how much to emphasize in each aspect, what types of materials to use, and what learning conditions to establish.

Procedures for determining individual language abilities, levels of performance, and specific deficiencies are:

1. Systematically observe and record (by tapes or notes) the speaking performance of each child, particularly noting his or her manner with the audience and the reaction of the audience to features of the speaker's efforts. In other words, evaluate the child's articulation, enunciation, physical mannerisms, and voice projection. Note the audience reaction to the speaker's use of gestures as well as to the general manner of presentation, content, and organization.

---

1. Marion Monroe, "The Child and His Language Come to School," in *Language, Reading, and the Communication Process*, edited by Carl Braun (Newark, Del.: International Reading Association, 1971), pp. 121–42.

2. Make observational notes on individual pupils at regular intervals with respect to nonstandard usage, problems in organizing expression effectively, or lack of ease in speaking.
3. Record on a checklist or inventory form the degree of skill in reading, listening, writing, or speaking situations.
4. Compile a list of instructional needs based on an examination of all types of writing products. Note mechanical errors (capitalization, punctuation, appearance) and compositional qualities (organization, clarity, coherence, interest factors).
5. Use teacher-made and standardized tests in a planned program for measuring growth and achievement in total and specific aspects of language performance.
6. Tabulate departures from standard speech that occur in children's formal and informal conversation and other language activities in the classroom and on the playground.
7. Tape-record children's speech and oral reading and analyze them. In particular, make note of common problems for class and group instructional emphasis.

Pupil Identification of Own Needs

Most children realize that everyone should know how to communicate effectively, but they often do not recognize what skills are essential to effective communication. The importance that children attach to a particular skill varies with each child, as does the degree of mastery of that skill. Getting each child to identify personal needs and goals is a major problem for the language arts teacher.

Stimulating pupils to identify their own needs—skills, abilities, and attitudes that they need to improve—is a basic motivational procedure, one that will pay rich dividends to the teacher who can do it successfully. Children should learn to use their own writing, reading, listening, and speaking efforts—in all of their classwork—as bases for judging their progress in using language effectively. This skill will enable them to work steadily on their own problems, noting their own errors, examining their own papers, and searching for ways to improve their skills. This list suggests to teachers ways in which children can identify their own needs:

1. Using a checklist, preferably one that they have helped to devise, children can record their own performance of various skills.
2. Working in pairs or in small groups, they can identify areas that need improvement by themselves or their partners.
3. Encourage children to examine samples of their own work and records of achievement and determine their needs.

4. Children should participate in group discussions of needs, efforts to meet class-established standards, and plans for learning activities.
5. Meeting with the teacher, children should discuss abilities, specific needs, and plans for improvement.
6. Children should correct their own papers and proofread and edit their own work.
7. Ask children to plot or record their test scores and compare them with the results of previous testing.
8. Children can keep charts of their own growth, such as meeting punctuation and capitalization standards.
9. Children can record in notebooks problems that need work—spelling words, new vocabulary, usage errors, and so on.

DETERMINING THE CURRICULUM

In addition to identifying the differences in language abilities of each child—and aiding each to identify his or her own strengths and weaknesses—teachers must work on developing the knowledge, attitudes, skills, and abilities that society regards as useful and valuable. Thus all programs in the curriculum must reflect acceptance of the responsibility for preparing individuals, within the limits of their ability, to meet the demands of society both as children and as adults. They should not attempt, however, to divert children from their own areas of interest or to impose unrealistic objectives.

Curriculum Content

Each child must use language to receive and express information and ideas on a daily basis and must learn to meet specific demands of communication throughout life. Consequently, the place to look for necessary skills, attitudes, knowledge, and abilities must be in life itself. For example, the vocabulary of the spelling curriculum should include words that an individual needs to use in writing, not words that are infrequently written. Logically, the place to find these words is in the actual writing of children and adults. The same may be said about almost every language arts area; an effort should be made to include in the program what society regards as useful and valuable.

Two factors tend to slow down the development of effective school programs in general, and language arts programs in particular. One is the unwillingness of many educators to discard content even though it has proved to be unsound, obsolete, and indefensible in light of either research evidence or changing needs. This kind of lethargy exists in many areas of society; in teaching, you hear "I'll teach this, and in this way, because I was taught this." A second factor is that the complexity of several areas of the language arts limits the techniques by which we can determine socially useful skills. Thus differences of opinion as to what should be taught may be reasonably legitimate.

The general difficulty is illustrated by the areas of oral and written expression. Evidence shows that although approximately 95 percent of all language activity is oral, instructional emphasis is largely on written skills. Doubtless, this imbalance primarily stems from problems encountered in oral language research and the relative ease of identifying some written language skills.

The need to make the best use of both teacher and pupil time and effort is a compelling reason for the school curriculum to provide experiences that simulate life generally and, specifically, it should force the adoption of a social utility point of view for the language arts curriculum. Thus, course content should reflect analyses of the attitudes, skills, abilities, and experiences that people encounter in life and recognition of which of these children need to learn, based on answers to questions such as:

1. How frequently is this skill (ability, etc.) needed and used in life activities?
2. How vital is this value, attitude, skill, or activity when the need for it arises?
3. How universally does this element occur in all types of life activities?
4. Does this element show evidence of meeting a permanent individual need?

Evidence is available in each area of the language arts regarding the relative values of many skills and abilities. For example, few would question that the ability to carry on an intelligent conversation with ease fills a constant need in daily activities. Surely, the demand for conversational ability is universal; we have reason to believe that it is as permanent as civilization. On the other hand, few adults need to give an oral report on a scientific or social studies subject or to prepare a detailed topical outline. Yet, in school activities, these skills may be crucial to academic success. Almost everyone is frequently obliged to write notes and friendly letters, but we rarely need to write a letter of condolence or an answer to a formal invitation. Nevertheless, we should all be able to handle each of these situations appropriately should it arise. When we do have to write a business letter, it is usually an important one, as in the case of a letter of application for employment. An error in form or a mistake in spelling might cause a potential employer to discard the application. These examples illustrate how the criterion of social utility applies to the selection or elimination of content in the language arts curriculum.

Of course, there is a danger of applying social utility standards too rigidly in curriculum development. For example, it could produce a curriculum that meets the needs of the average child but ignores the capabilities of a great many children. Using a cross-section of social needs as the basis for language arts instruction may result in inadequate preparation of some children to fulfill their social aspirations.

In addition, some children may show a need for language skills and abilities in situations that may occur very rarely in adult life. Almost invariably these needs arise out of a school-stimulated activity. The fact that they are childhood needs makes them important, particularly to the child or the children involved. Children in school take part in plays, entertainment, and other activities in which the average adult seldom participates. Children make oral and written reports on special school activities. They need to understand and be able to spell terms peculiar to a variety of subject-matter areas. Such activities have value in the school curriculum, but the particular skills they require, although useful to the school child, may have little value to the adult. On the other hand, of course, language arts skills that the child has little reason to use will be beneficial to the adult.

ORGANIZING FOR INSTRUCTION

A teacher must organize a classroom of youngsters and the subject matter that they are to learn in a way that will maximize learning as well as teaching satisfaction. This is not an easy task or one that the teacher can do alone. Class organization must follow the organizational pattern of the school. Traditionally, elementary school classrooms have been self-contained—that is, one teacher has been responsible for all teaching for a particular class—but increasingly, organizational plans call for instruction by a team of teachers. Even in the middle grades the movement of pupils from teacher to teacher is becoming more common.

Whatever the organizational plan of a school, teachers generally must organize their classrooms to conform to that plan.

Regardless of the organizational pattern, however, every teacher in an elementary school has responsibility for teaching the language arts. Teachers who are in self-contained classrooms, as well as those who are principally responsible for the language arts in departmentalized or team systems, must consider how they will organize to teach language skills and abilities, attitudes necessary for effective communication, and knowledge of language and literature. All teachers— not just those who teach the language arts directly and specifically—must organize their teaching and should also consider both the interrelationships among the language arts and the relationships of these arts to their own teaching concerns. As someone has said, "Teaching children to use their language effectively is too important to be left only to the English teacher."

Organizing Subject Matter

Education authorities generally favor relating subject areas to one another as much as possible and have designed several plans for implementing this objective. The 1973 yearbook of the National Society for the Study of Education mentions *interdisciplinary*, *child-oriented*, and *socially-oriented* curricula, all of which emphasize problems or topics rather than subject matter.[2] These are not new patterns or designs; historically, efforts have been made to institute *integration*, *unit teaching*, and *child-interest-centered* programs.

Regardless of what a program is called, the objective should be to get away from formalized and isolated teaching of subject matter, which too often ignores children's abilities, needs, and interests. In the language arts it is advisable to use a *functional* and *integrated* program. Sometimes these two words are used to identify separate programs, although the difference is generally one of degree. For example, a functional program "provides for closely relating language to work in other areas of study but sets aside some particular periods for systematic work in language," whereas in an integrated program, "language work does not appear as a separate subject, but is very closely tied into other areas of study."[3] Specifically, in the language arts, the desirable approach is to develop and maintain children's language skills in the context of their communication needs in subject-matter areas and other ongoing school activities.

This does not mean that language skills do not warrant direct instruction apart from the integrative program. Societally based objectives, the interests and needs of the children, and the teacher's own good judgment may determine that

---

2. Wilma S. Longstreet, "The School's Curriculum," in *The Elementary School in the United States*, edited by John L. Goodlad and Harold G. Shane (Chicago: University of Chicago Press, 1973), pp. 244–71.

3. Willard F. Tidyman, Charlene Weddle Smith, and Marguerite Butterfield, *Teaching the Language Arts*, 3rd ed. (New York: McGraw-Hill Book Co., 1969), p. 434.

some attitudes, knowledge, skills, and abilities do not fit naturally into integrative units. Failure to recognize a poor fit can lead either to an artificial kind of integration in which relationships are forced or to the neglect of some material that the children should learn.

This problem should be a minimal one in the language arts. All children must learn that language skills are the tools by which they receive and transmit ideas and information about their daily activities, in school and out. These activities are the content around which a successful language arts program operates. Thus, integration of the language skills with every area of the school curriculum can and should occur naturally and continuously.

Organizing the Class for Learning

Elementary school teachers should plan to teach an entire class, to work with groups within the class, and to teach and guide individual pupils. They should try to care for each child's needs while promoting maximum growth for all the children in the class. Flexibility in planning and organizing is necessary to accomplish this goal.

Together, the class can discuss topics, set goals, assign tasks to one another, and receive instruction when there are common needs. The class also serves as an audience for dramatizations, group and individual reports, stories, news items, book reports, and announcements. Certainly, and not least of all, the entire class can have fun together. Class games, songs, and dancing can all be worthwhile learning activities that are appropriate for the entire group.

There are many ways to divide a classroom of children into groups. One common procedure is to group children by assessed abilities or levels of performance. Apparently this procedure works reasonably well in some areas, such as aspects of reading, spelling, and handwriting, but it does not live up to theoretical possibilities in others. The reason is a logical one: not all aspects or factors of many abilities are easy to identify and measure. Thus, the theoretical objective of reducing the range of individual differences and simplifying instructional problems may not be realistic. And often the grouping tends to become somewhat permanent for the year, causing some social stigma and indicating a failure to recognize learning that has occurred.

Teachers can overcome many of the shortcomings of grouping with flexibility and by supplementing group activities with individual instruction. One course guide suggests that most children need opportunities to participate in three types of groups: power groups, skill groups, and social groups.[4] Although references to this idea relate generally to reading programs, it is applicable to other areas. Other groupings may center on interests, friendships, and special projects. Not to

4. *Language Arts in the Elementary School*, ESEA Title III (Greensboro, N.C.: Model Developmental Reading School, 1970), pp. 70–72.

be overlooked in planning is the fact that a group may consist of two children. In fact, pairing children for many tasks can be very beneficial.

The Allens, in discussing language experience, report that a teacher may work with a small group while other children are individually working in learning centers.[5] They suggest that in the small groups the teacher might demonstrate group games; take "dictation from one pupil while others observe and listen to the conversation about letter formation, beginning sound-symbol relationships, words that are alike, words that begin alike, and other relevant points"; and let children read and discuss books that include their own writing.

Accepting the reality of individual differences among pupils and determining the extent of these differences bring a teacher face to face with the problem of providing appropriate instruction for each pupil. Clymer and Kearney point out a number of needs to take into account in giving such instruction, although they also indicate that "no prescription can be given" for assessing and meeting individual needs.[6] They list the following objectives:

1. Know the students.
2. Recognize that not all teachers will adjust to individual differences in the same way.
3. Provide generous time allotments.
4. Plan carefully whatever is to be done in the classroom.
5. Work effectively with the group as a whole.
6. Move slowly into any type of adjustment to individual differences.
7. Accept more noise and more confusion.
8. Recognize failure and begin again.
9. Accept less than 100 percent adjustment to individual differences.
10. Recognize that adjusting to individual differences calls for plain, hard work.

Suggestions of ways to individualize instruction appear in a subsequent section of this chapter and in chapters discussing specific areas of the language arts.

Organizing the Classroom

A major task of organizing for instruction is the establishment of an environment that truly facilitates instruction and fosters maximum learning. This is not a simple matter.

Physically, the classroom should stimulate language usage and growth. Lit-

---

5. Roach Van Allen and Claryce Allen, *Language Experiences in Early Childhood* (Chicago: Encyclopaedia Britannica Press, 1969), p. 28.

6. Theodore Clymer and Nolan C. Kearney, "Curricular and Instructional Provisions for Individual Differences," in *Individualizing Instruction*, edited by Nelson B. Henry (Chicago: University of Chicago Press, 1962), p. 276.

tle will come from drabness. Wall and bulletin board displays, realia, pictures, objects to handle and talk about, room for children to move about, and work areas all contribute to more effective teaching and learning. To create an optimal classroom environment, a teacher needs support from the principal, custodian, and other adults in the school. These people must see the value of a happy, busy, and interesting classroom and foster it at every opportunity.

The principal factor in the environment, of course, is the teacher. The effective teacher is a vital person, one who is interesting and interested, sensitive and encouraging, and one who accepts each child as an important member of the group. These qualities encourage children to be confident in speaking, listening, reading, and writing. They will develop children's attitudes toward and interest in learning.

The teacher also has the key role in determining experiences and activities within the environment. What the teacher does in this role determines, to a great extent, the children's behavior and attitudes. It is most desirable that a teacher choose experiences and activities that encourage children to act and talk freely and yet provide for enough control to insure constructive listening and thinking. Classroom activities must permit expression (communication), but they must not disrupt learning.

A BASIC INSTRUCTIONAL APPROACH

The following sections outline a basic plan for teaching the language expressional skills and abilities. Although the approach focuses upon the arts of speaking and writing, reading and listening lend themselves to a similar approach—and, of course, several skills probably will come together as the plan operates. And instruction of new skills, such as handwriting, spellings of specific words, and word recognition skills in reading, will necessitate modifying the plan.

The plan calls for two types of lessons: expressional and follow-up, or correctional. *Expressional lessons* deal mainly with content—*what* is said or written rather than *how*. Expressional lessons may involve reading and listening abilities as well as writing and speaking skills. In all instances, though, the principal focus is on content. The purpose of expressional lessons is communication, usually about subject matter in various curricular areas, but in any case they emphasize the content of communication. A *follow-up* or *correctional lesson* centers on the effectiveness of expression; the focus is upon the *how*.

Expressional Lessons

As children discuss plans for a science field trip, converse about some event on the playground, write letters requesting materials for a social studies project, tell a story that they have read or heard, introduce their parents to the teacher or principal, write imaginative stories for pleasure, keep records of class activities, or respond to questions about a health unit, the opportunity is present for an expressional lesson. In this section, we will examine elements of expressional lessons, along with appropriate teaching techniques.

Learning by doing.   Teachers should not assume that children's writing and speaking will improve through discussion of the need for improvement and a program of practice exercises or activities. Nothing could be further from the truth. While practice exercises may have value if the children understand the need for them, it is contrary to good psychological practice to expect real improvement except through a program of natural and meaningful writing and speaking experience. Quoting from a United States Office of Education publication:[7]

> Children learn to write by writing. There should be opportunities for every child to write every day in ways that are purposeful. This will not be writing of a formal sort, but rather for many purposes: writing a question on the board, taking notes to answer questions on a problem, writing a letter, ordering merchandise, making an outline for a play, making a bibliography of books containing stories about dogs, writing a fanciful story, or any one of a hundred or more activities that children find interesting and useful.

A similar relationship exists between effective speaking and the opportunity to speak:[8]

> People learn to speak by speaking. To improve in speaking, a person needs directions and evaluative techniques by which he can measure his progress toward the goals which he sets for himself. One junior boy complained that his class talked about speeches, they planned speeches, and they hunted information about speeches, but often there was so little time left that only a few of the class had opportunity to give the talks they had prepared. Arranging for guided experience is perhaps the crux of the problem of helping young people to become effective in communicating through speech.

Activity planning.   Both teacher and pupils will profit from the cooperative planning of expressional activities. While the teacher may plan opportunities for these lessons and formulate purposes at first, the children ultimately should participate in the basic planning. Keep in mind that students need to understand the purpose of speaking and writing activities when they prepare for them. One sixth-grade class undertook the organization of the school's periodicals, which might otherwise have been discarded. This project illustrates the value of cooperative planning:[9]

---

7. Helen K. Mackintosh and Wilhelmina Hill, *How Children Learn to Write*, Bulletin no. 2, U.S. Department of Health, Education, and Welfare (Washington, D.C.: U.S. Government Printing Office, 1953), pp. 10–11.
8. Helen F. Olson, "Speech for All," Leaflet 1, *Speech in the English Classroom*, a portfolio published by the National Council of Teachers of English, n.d.
9. The Commission on the English Curriculum of the National Council of Teachers of English, *Language Arts for Today's Children* (New York: Appleton-Century-Crofts, 1954), pp. 285–86.

Teacher and pupils planned together from the start. The pupil's activity was directed by repeated questions: How shall we proceed? What shall we do next? What jobs need to be done and who will do them? How much time each week shall we devote to the problem?

It was decided to limit the work on the problem to three eighty-minute periods a week. The teacher's remark that some record of work and procedure would be needed as the activity broadened brought forth from the class a suggestion that they keep a diary. The pupils agreed to keep a record of the activities in which they participated on large sheets of paper attached to an easel. A guide for writing the diary entries was then set up.

Audience-reader consideration.   An important objective of every expressional lesson is keeping the audience's attention. An attentive, interested audience or an interested reader motivates the child to make his or her expression as effective as possible. To be well received, expression must be interesting, appealing, and effectively organized. Oral expression must communicate something that the audience wants to know or something in which the audience is likely to become interested. Written expression, also, must attract readers and hold their attention.

Consideration of the audience or the readers should be part of lesson planning. What is the audience like? Is the subject likely to interest them? Is the information or idea to be conveyed new? What in this expression will have appeal?

The role of models.   Children can learn about speaking by observing, listening to, and imitating others. They also learn from models of written expression. Thus, if children are to write neat letters, to give effective reports, and to tell stories well, there must be models for them to see and hear. In speaking, the teacher or a tape recording may be the model. In writing, pupils may make their own models from samples in textbooks or the entire class may work together to produce a model on the board.

Evolving standards.   The teacher and students together should establish standards for each type of expressional activity, perhaps after students have seen or heard a model or following a class discussion. The standards should be the pupils' own statements, even if they fall below the goals of the teacher or the textbook, and they should be subject to change as the need arises. If they are too low for one lesson, the children will notice and change them for similar subsequent lessons and activities. Standards should be recorded in writing, possibly by both the teacher and the pupils. First, the teacher should write them on the board, and later, he or she should put them on a chart where all can refer to them. Suggested standards may also be found in textbooks. For example, one book suggests the following storytelling guidelines:[10]

1.   Make sure you have a good story to tell.
2.   If possible, write out your story first.

---

10. Thomas Clark Pollock et al., *The Macmillan English Series 4* (New York: Macmillan Co., 1967), p. 310.

3.   Memorize one or two parts of your story.
4.   Keep in mind the purpose of your story as you tell it.
5.   Try to make the characters in your story interesting ones.
6.   Speak in a loud, clear voice.

Self-editing and group assessment.   After the expressional activity has ended, it is appropriate to compare performance to the established standards. In oral expression this step takes the form of group assessment of the speaker and what has been said, whereas in written expression the writer examines the product, perhaps with a peer or the teacher. The importance of this step in expressional lessons is that, in both spoken and written expression, "on the spot" assessment is particularly conducive to learning.

Teaching children to edit their own writing, to compare their products with the standards, takes time. Although children can learn much in a school year about evaluating their own papers, real editing skill takes several years to develop, and all teachers in a school should teach it. Criticism, on the other hand, comes rather naturally to most persons—perhaps too much so, for it often is not constructive. Children may be needlessly harsh or cruel in their comments. For this reason, expression in lessons intended particularly to develop appreciation or enjoyment should not be subjected to critical assessment by pupils. Sometimes teachers should encourage frank and friendly discussion of children's expression, but it is a better idea to focus on providing positive feedback. As least at the beginning of the school year, and at other times with younger children, the teacher should control the evaluation. The object is to develop in each child a willingness to accept an evaluation by someone else and to learn to view personal expression critically.

Follow-up Lessons

The language activity of expressional lessons determines the content of the second basic type of lesson: the follow-up lesson. Follow-up lessons focus on mastery of the knowledge, skills, and abilities required for effective communication by the individual student. Although these areas may have received attention in expressional lessons during "on the spot" assessment, the follow-up lesson allows teachers and students to concentrate on items that need the most improvement.

Evaluation and diagnosis.   By evaluating expressional lessons, the teacher can help each child to identify specific errors, bad habits, or special weaknesses (this evaluation is often simply an extension of group assessment and individual assessment). The precision of the diagnosis depends to a large degree on the nature and refinement of the evaluative instruments and procedures. In some language arts areas, including most oral expression and written composition, evaluation is largely subjective and hence teachers and students may refer to standards, models, and checklists. In areas that are generally labeled "mechanical," standardized and teacher-made tests are conventional tools for diagnosis.

Identification of individual needs.   If diagnosis and evaluation are to provide a reasonable basis for corrective instruction, they must pinpoint the needs of each pupil as closely as possible. Moreover, as suggested previously in this chapter, children must be aware of their own deficiencies and weaknesses if they are to have the motivation to remedy them. In addition, teachers should record for each pupil the particular errors, bad habits, and skills and abilities in which they need instruction. Charts like the one shown on p. 102 provide quick reference to individual and group needs. Separate charts or records should be kept for all language activities. Notations will vary with the grade and ability levels of the children.

Instructional drive.   As soon as any general weaknesses and individual weaknesses have been identified, the teacher should begin an instructional drive to correct the grossest errors. Last month's errors and even last week's occurred too far in the past to be the subject of a correctional lesson today. The attack on an error made yesterday should have begun yesterday, if at all possible. Of course, attacking all errors, habits, and weaknesses at once is impossible and detrimental to the self-concept of the child. Therefore, attend to the most common ones first. Each pupil is likely to require individual attention and instruction in something. Often classmates can help the teacher correct individual problems. For example, if teachers reproduce compositions with all defects and errors duplicated, either on the board or on transparencies to show with an overhead projector, students can help the author revise his or her work. Such a procedure should identify writing strengths and confine criticism to areas of greatest need.

This procedure, of course, requires cautious use. Begin with a composition that contains only a few errors. Some pupils may not be able to handle group correction, at least until they understand that the objective is to help rather than to criticize or find fault. An alternative is a special composition contrived by the teacher to illustrate particular errors or weaknesses. Whatever procedure the teacher chooses—and perhaps it should be varied—the key point is to identify specific weaknesses or errors for teaching attention and improvement.

Corrective practice.   When children recognize their own errors or weaknesses, they can benefit from properly designed practice exercises and activities. These should apply only to items in which they have received instruction, items in which improvement is desirable. Otherwise, they become tasks that have no relationship to purposes the pupil thinks are important. In some areas practice occurs as the pupil participates in another expressional lesson; in others, such as punctuation items, practice exercises may be useful.

WRITTEN WORK CHECKLIST

	Bill	Ernest	Jill	Margie	Sarah	Linda	Tom	Peter	Jean
Margins	✓	✓					✓		
Capital letters									
First word in sentence	✓								
Proper names	✓	✓					✓	✓	
In titles		✓				✓			
Others Organization Names			✓						
Periods									
In sentences	✓								
After abbreviations				✓					
After initials									
Others									
Commas									
In dates									
In addresses									
In a list									
Apostrophes									
In contractions									

PROVIDING FOR INDIVIDUALIZED INSTRUCTION

Because children vary in ability, skill development, level of understanding, and attitudes, they must be able to pursue independent activities in the classroom. The following sections describe numerous ways to provide for independent learning and individualized instruction.

Laboratory Programs

A laboratory program in which pupils work on their own writing or plan speaking activities is an effective type of individual instruction. While students work by themselves, the teacher moves from one to another to offer help, make suggestions, and give encouragement. The advantage of this type of instruction is that it allows students to do something that has purpose for them and permits the teacher to help solve individual problems as they come up in the course of completing a project.

The laboratory approach has many applications throughout the school day as children learn new words, choose materials and read, listen to various forms of spoken expression, and so on. It is also effective in science and social studies. One child may be taking notes for an individual assignment, another may be writing a report, a third may be listing words, other children may be conversing, and so on.

Learning Centers

Good supplements to a laboratory program are learning centers where children use or practice language skills. For example, a discussion center might allow children to sit together to make plans, review achievements, or simply talk about activities. Other centers may be for browsing and reading, writing, listening, viewing (filmstrips, slides, pictures), acting, games, puppets, skill practice, and being alone.

The movement to organize instruction on an informal pupil-centered base (modeled, in part, on British primary schools) has given great impetus to the development of learning centers. In these informal classrooms, the emphasis in the centers is upon the child as an active learner. In other words, children, for the most part, personally choose the centers in which they work and the tasks they perform.

An operating principle for all classrooms with learning centers is that the children and teacher together decide how the centers will be used. Sometimes children may be assigned to certain centers for a portion of the day. At other times they may go to centers of their own choice. If they have evaluated themselves—their own speaking, writing, listening, and reading—they will choose to go to centers in which they can further develop their skills.

Centers should not become permanent installations. The length of time that a given center remains in operation should vary from a day to several weeks or longer, depending upon how much it is used. Therefore, the teacher must carefully determine the purpose of the center and must know what is going on there. In and of itself, space set aside for a learning center will not provide individualized instruction.

Individualizing Practice

Teachers should provide specific practice in language skills that takes account of individual differences. If both teacher and pupil have identified particular instructional needs, the teacher can distribute practice materials and/or pupils can select practice exercises themselves. Teachers may also require children to use the indexes of textbooks and workbooks to locate practice material. One way to provide practice exercises is to cut up discarded language arts textbooks and workbooks and organize them according to types of exercises—the particular skills

to be practiced. The pages can be placed in envelopes or pasted on stiff paper (particularly if two copies of the textbook or workbook are available) and labeled by type. The teacher can hand out these exercises or leave the choice of exercises to pupils who know what skills they need to improve. Pupils may keep records of their use of exercises by signing the envelopes or the backs of the sheets.

To extend and modify these suggestions, teachers can make up their own practice exercises (particularly for vocabulary study, spelling, and decoding activities in reading) instead of taking pages from textbooks or workbooks. Also, games and enriching activities can be handled in the same way as study exercises. To keep pages clean, teachers can insert exercise pages in clear plastic envelopes (children can write on them with washable crayons). Furthermore, to emphasize individual evaluation, the teacher can place the answers on the envelopes or on the backs of pages so that pupils can check their own work.

Proofreading and Self-editing

Many of the weaknesses in pupils' written expression, including mechanical errors, are the result of their carelessness. To reduce carelessness teachers must teach pupils to proofread their own writing to see whether it conveys the meaning intended and to correct mechanical errors. Such teaching presupposes that the writing is purposeful and that each pupil genuinely desires to do as well as possible.

The habit of proofreading and self-editing all written work should lead children logically and directly to the discovery that by rewriting they can usually improve their work. They should understand that rewriting entails more than merely recopying the proofread original, a process that has doubtful value. Pupils will be ready for rewriting when only their best efforts will satisfy them. This is a state of mind that the teacher must help children to develop.

Encouraging Creative Efforts

Fostering creative expression permits a great deal of flexibility to meet individual instructional needs. Children who want to dramatize, present orally, or write something of their own and who want to make their expression imaginative and personal strive to do their best and turn naturally to the teacher for help with problems. Teachers may encourage children also to turn to peers for assistance in appropriate situations.

Varying Assignments

It is possible to vary the difficulty of individual assignments and yet have the entire class working on the same general topic (for example, giving reports in social studies). The following example illustrates this procedure:[11]

> All members of a class might be preparing reports for a social studies unit but the reports might be of differing degrees of difficulty. One child might be seeking information for a report on the foods the pioneers ate; another might be writing the conversation two wagon masters might have had before leaving with their wagon trains; a third might be preparing a critique of a western television show; and a fourth might be tracing routes on a map. The task of each child depends upon his interest and his ability. The child searching for names of foods may have limited reading and writing skills, so he is essentially engaged in finding words and listing them. The child writing conversation must have read extensively, and must be fairly skilled in writing. Each child's task should challenge him, however, and in order to be of value in teaching language skills, should call for the use of some of these skills—particularly those he needs most.

Using Programmed Instruction

Programmed instruction materials are available for several subject areas of the school curriculum. Commercially prepared programmed materials are available

---

11. Walter T. Petty, *The Language Arts in Elementary Schools* (Washington, D.C.: Center for Applied Research in Education, 1962), p. 8.

in the language arts areas of reading, spelling, and punctuation. They are the subject of considerable controversy, however, and it is doubtful that educators will widely accept them.

Programmed materials separate the information to be taught into fundamental units and then regroup, or *program*, it into a particular progressive order. Specific items then may be presented mechanically, as in showing one frame of a film at a time, or in a more-or-less textbooklike fashion. A programmed textbook (or series of visuals) differs from regular textbook and film materials in that the learner must finish one step (answer a question, for example) before moving on to the next. Programmed materials, unlike textbooks, are designed for individual use.

Programmed instruction can be useful in teaching particular skills because each step provides the user with immediate knowledge or immediate responses to questions and thus reinforces learning. However, because reading, listening, writing, and speaking require the integration of many skills (which, by no means, have been adequately defined), programmed materials are not likely to supplant teachers and other methods of teaching.

Choosing Special Activities

There are many activities in which individual pupils or small groups can participate. Education journals are a good source of ideas that may lend themselves to individualization in classrooms. Some suggestions are:

1. Each pupil could keep a notebook record of words that he or she has misspelled in written work and study it during free time.
2. Children who do good work could help those who are having difficulty.
3. Children who finish assignments early could make copies of work to be preserved or posted on bulletin boards.
4. Spell difficult words that pupils need in writing; that is, write words on the board that they have not studied but need in their writing.
5. Children could keep individual notebooks for doing unassigned writing of a personal nature to show to the teacher later, if they chose to do so.
6. Pupils could choose their own report topics, their own story ideas, and their own roles for dramatization.
7. Give incidental individual correction of nonstandard usage.

Other chapters suggest activities for independent learning and additional teacher's aids for individualized instruction.

INSTRUCTIONAL MATERIALS

The textbook has long been and continues to be the principal material resource in most elementary school programs in language arts, despite the availability of an abundance of multimedia materials, including filmstrips, tapes and cassettes, films, games, boxes of activity cards, and pictures. These materials may substitute for textbooks or supplement them. When used instead of a textbook, they tend to serve the same purposes as a textbook and in similar ways. Therefore, suggestions and cautions regarding the selection and use of textbooks and practice materials apply to all materials that a teacher uses.

Textbooks

For many teachers the textbook is a basic guide to program content, methods of teaching, and performance evaluation. A textbook may be a useful *guide* and *resource,* but it should not be the program for any teacher.

Today's textbook.   Textbooks have always received a good deal of attention by professional groups of teachers, by the public, and sometimes by governmental agencies. This interest reflects a general concern with educational problems and is likely to remain strong. Yet much of the commentary about textbooks—to say nothing of what we hear about education, in general—is based on opinion rather than on research. Hilton, in reviewing the history of textbooks and research regarding their function, selection, and influence, makes the following points:[12]

1. Textbooks change in response to various pressures. These include changes in educational purposes, in learning theory and practice, in subject matter, and in printing technology.
2. There is little research to support statements as to the direction and extent of textbook changes.
3. Textbooks seeking to incorporate new learning about content and methods sometimes go to extremes.
4. A textbook's influence is modified by how a teacher uses it.
5. The idea of a single textbook is increasingly giving way to one in which the textbook is used with supplemental materials, including other textbooks.
6. "Non-textbook teaching" is not necessarily good teaching.
7. Textbook selection is largely done on a subjective basis.

---

12. Ernest Hilton, "Textbooks," in *Encyclopedia of Educational Research,* 4th ed., edited by Robert L. Ebel (New York: Macmillan Co., 1969), pp. 1470–78.

Functions of the language textbook.   Although the quality of textbooks varies widely, it is not too much to expect a textbook to represent the highest level of curriculum development in the subject. In the language arts curriculum, the basic textbook should serve the following functions:

1. Reflect a defensible and modern point of view on language teaching and demonstrate its application in the instructional material presented
2. Provide a well-organized and properly graded source of the skills that bear the burden in communication
3. Present a rich, readable, and varied source of subject matter and learning activities geared to children's interests and needs, as the basis for a program in which language skills are acquired under lifelike conditions
4. Present, together with accompanying instructor's manual, teaching methods and means for motivating children
5. Provide initial fixation and maintenance practice exercises
6. Provide evaluation and corrective suggestions

Teachers should know and understand the functions of the language textbook in order to plan and develop effective instructional programs. They should consider these functions, relate them to their own viewpoints and knowledge, and learn how to use the textbook properly. The following paragraphs discuss the functions separately while emphasizing the importance of the textbook in the program and the need for most teachers to depend on it as an instructional aid.

1. Reflecting a point of view: Language texts published since 1890 reveal in striking ways how perspectives on the teaching of receptive and expressive language abilities and skills have changed from one decade to the next. In general, the trend has been away from the abstract and formal toward the functional, although at times (including the present) there have been minor but surprising reversals in this trend. Some textbooks continue to stress teaching a grammatical system and present content formally. Fortunately, others seek to develop understanding and appreciation of language in a functional manner. Still others, particularly recently published ones, attempt to satisfy everyone's ideas about what is basic by using both approaches. Nevertheless, a substantial and sustained movement away from the functional approach seems unlikely.
2. Serving as a source of content: The language arts program includes so many specific skills that only a highly trained subject matter specialist could possibly keep them all in mind. For the typical teacher, who is overloaded with many activities and pupils, the textbook provides an

organized catalog of information on the curriculum considered suitable for instruction at a particular level.

3.   Presenting suitable subject matter: Language skills do not develop economically by talking about language but develop by using language in genuine communicative activities. Textbooks should provide suggestions for worthwhile classroom activities that require the use of language, though page limitations keep textbook authors from including as much of this sort of information as they should. Nevertheless, textbooks at least should suggest the kinds of activities that permit tailoring teaching to actual need. Some textbooks contain much about the language (structure, history, and manipulation) that may serve as suitable subject matter *if the teacher approaches it functionally and in connection with ongoing classroom activities that appeal to children.* A formal approach that focuses largely on learning about language rather than on using it will do little to help a child to write or speak more effectively.

4.   Serving as a source of teaching methods: Unless a teacher has had considerable education in and experience in teaching language arts in elementary school, he or she needs a textbook that suggests ways to teach specific lessons. While the instructions in a textbook lesson are for the guidance of the pupil, often they are directed toward the teacher as well. In addition to these indirect hints on how to present a lesson, the teacher manuals prepared by most publishers usually offer instructional suggestions. These manuals are generally well written, and in many cases, they contain the benefit of the extensive knowledge and experience of successful teachers and supervisors.

5.   Providing fixation and maintenance practice: Economy of time necessitates using all available sources of material to fix skills at the time of initial learning. Many language skills require a great deal of practice and the textbook can be the source of much of it. Most textbooks in language attempt to provide exercises, practice materials, and suggestions for activities; yet, in the opinion of many teachers, few texts provide enough of them. Consequently, teachers must supplement what is available with original material or other commercial resources.

6.   Providing a source of evaluation material: The textbook should supply materials for measuring the results of the instructional program and directions for using them effectively in corrective instruction. The textbook or teachers' manual should acknowledge the importance of teacher-made tests and other evaluative instruments, as well as the role of standardized tests. In addition, there should be some attention to inventory techniques, either in the form of objective exercises or class-made standards.

Textbook Selection

Teachers should evaluate the quality of a textbook or series as objectively as possible.[13] The authors' reputations as scholars and teachers, the publisher's reputation for quality materials, the extent of use of the particular book or books, and the quality of the paper and printing are several indices of the quality of a book. Scorecards listing features of a quality textbook facilitate objective comparison. In addition, reputable publishers should make available objective evidence about their books. For example, the publisher of a reading series should be able to furnish a detailed tabulation of the exact words in the basic vocabulary, the new words introduced at each successive level in the program, and the sequence in which skills are introduced. Likewise, a spelling textbook publisher should present the facts about the source of the vocabulary comprising the spelling program. Distributions showing frequencies of appearance of practice exercises in particular areas should be sought.

The textbook selection process should consist of critically examining several competing books or series of books and evaluating them as objectively as possible in terms of teaching objectives, the children who will use them, and other available resources. Factors to keep in mind when examining textbooks for possible use in the classroom are discussed below.

Appeal to child interest.   One key factor to consider when judging the suitability and usability of a textbook for a given level is its appeal to the children who will have to study it. Most children sense the importance of a textbook. They know that adults use textbooks so they expect their books to be useful. They have every right to expect the textbook to take into account their backgrounds and experience, their values, and their interests. Inner-city children should have texts that show an understanding of their life and interests. The same is true for children who live in other environments and have had other experiences. The wide differences in children's experiences make the task of appealing to all children who may use a textbook a difficult one.

Motivation.   Another important element in a text is the manner in which it presents devices and procedures for stimulating each child to take an active personal interest in each new language activity. The child must be made to feel that her or his ideas and opinions are important. Children must be given experiences of

---

13. Scorecards or outlines of points to consider in selecting language arts textbooks appear in some professional textbooks. For example, there is an outline in Paul C. Burns and Alberta L. Lowe, *The Language Arts in Childhood Education* (Rand McNally, 1966), pp. 344–46; in the 1963 edition of Harry A. Greene and Walter T. Petty, *Developing Language Skills in the Elementary Schools* (Allyn and Bacon), a scorecard for language arts textbooks appears on pp. 446–48. In addition, the handbook by Kenneth S. Goodman et al., *Choosing Materials to Teach Reading* (Wayne State University Press, 1966) gives psychological, sociocultural, educational, linguistic, and literary principles, many of which need to be considered in selecting language arts textbooks.

such richness, novelty, and interest that they want to communicate their feelings and ideas to others.

The primary motivation for effective language use arises from well-planned activities. Group discussions to develop plans for an activity, committee meetings at which important decisions are reached, and class meetings to formulate standards of usage or personal conduct all stimulate individuals to share responsibility. To carry out this responsibility, children must organize and present their ideas, criticize and disagree tactfully, and assume leadership in areas in which they are qualified to lead. Textbooks in language should emphasize the importance of an activity program in motivating language use and in providing opportunities for effectively mastering language skills in lifelike situations.

Illustrations.   Colorful and attractive illustrations in a book make the presentation interesting and may prove to be important motivational devices. The more physical activity the illustrations demonstrate, the more children seem to like them. Children are attracted to a book with a colorful cover and like to talk about the children and activities portrayed on each page and relate them to their own lives. Of course, textbook illustrations should be instructional; that is, they should do more than simply provide color or show other children. In addition to pictures, charts and diagrams that illustrate activities or otherwise motivate children are welcome.

Linguistic considerations.   The language in a textbook should be clear and natural. Explanations should be simply written, without talking down to the child. Technical or special words must be defined and illustrated in the context in which they appear. Understandable language involves more than a simple vocabulary, however. Often it is difficult to discover just what makes the presentation in one textbook interesting and that in another boring. The answer probably lies in the individuals who do the writing. Not all authors write in a style that children like. It is not the purpose of a language arts textbook to provide light, entertaining reading, but it must have enough interesting facts, activities, and information to keep children hunting for more.

Relation to other subjects.   One very important advance in many language arts textbooks is that the instructional effort seeks to relate language to nearly all other school subjects and activities. It is in those other subjects that the real motivation for language mastery develops. Language skills become habitual through use in all school activities. Oral and written expression is just as important in science, mathematics, music, art, and social studies classes as it is in the class in which language is supposed to be the central activity.

Stimulation of personal activity.   A good language arts textbooks stimulates children to become personally active. Language structure may provide topics for class discussion, but the primary value of knowledge about language is evident in the *use* of language in personal communication. The extent to which a text stimulates the child in creative oral or written expression is one of the best measures of its quality.

Vague and unusual concepts.   A common shortcoming of instructional material in textbooks is the introduction of words and concepts that are meaningless to many children. For example, what do the expressions *several times a day*, *a high wind*, and *a few miles away*, mean? How many times is *several* times? How strong is a *high* wind? How far away is *a few miles?* In Maine, a few miles might be two; in Ohio, it might be twenty; in Texas, it might be one hundred. The child of seven or eight has sufficient difficulty comprehending concisely worded instructional material without being further confused by the introduction of vague and uncertain terms. Examination of language textbooks under consideration for adoption, therefore, should include a careful check of vocabulary suitability and frequency of occurrence of vague and ambiguous terms.

Point of view.   Authors and publishers of different language arts textbooks may have different ideas about what language skills and subject matter children should learn and how to teach them. If the textbook under consideration does not make clear its general point of view in an introductory statement, a careful check of the teachers' manual for this information is advisable. In the event that the philosophy of the school is in disagreement with the approach of the text under consideration, a reexamination of the philosophy may be in order. A further examination of the text also may be necessary.

Consistency in emphasis on child and adult values.   The language arts textbook should present a program that balances children's immediate language needs and their ultimate language needs as adults. Some books take an adult view and ignore children's present school needs. They seem to assume that the needs of all age groups are identical or that other school activities will automatically meet a child's need for language growth. Neither assumption is correct. Although children and adults have many similar needs, many others may be quite different. An effective language program adjusts instructional emphasis to the maturity of the pupils as well as to their language needs.

Recognition of individual differences.   Limitations of space usually force authors to adapt the content of the book to the abilities and interests of the large middle or average group of children at a specific level. The rather sizable group that will not be able to work as rapidly as the average pupils requires supplementary instruction, and a good textbook will provide it.

Another problem is providing for children who encounter little or no difficulty with routine activities and lessons and are frequently bored. Surely they cannot be asked to do more of the same types of exercises. Superior texts make a definite attempt to aid the teacher by providing individualized enrichment activities designed for pupils who have met all minimum and average requirements.

Use of Textbooks in the Language Program

A teacher who begins with the first page of a language arts textbook and continues page by page through the entire book fails to take into account the language abilities and needs of a particular class, to say nothing of the varied needs and abilities of individual students. Textbooks in language arts as well as in other subject areas lend themselves to a variety of instructional uses. Possibly a very capable teacher, teaching in a unique situation and having adequate resources, does not need to use a textbook. But most teachers do not have the teaching resources and some lack the education and experience to teach without a textbook. This does not mean, however, that a teacher must be a slave to the textbook and show no initiative or professional competence. It also does not mean that the language assignment from day to day should consist merely of completing a specified number of textbook pages.

Teachers should understand the possibilities for using a language textbook while recognizing that a textbook has limitations:

1. By itself, a textbook does not teach (although some learning may be achieved by reading it).
2. The context in which a textbook presents language activities is bound not to fit the needs and experiences of a particular class.
3. The practice exercises are likely to be inadequate due to space limitations and because so much language practice needs to be oral.
4. The teaching suggestions are also brief due to space limitations.
5. The evaluation aids are only suggestive and do not permit thorough assessment.

Furthermore, some textbooks do not even provide all of the aids just listed. For example, some language arts textbooks make no provision for evaluation, and some have no practice activities. Others may ignore listening, proofreading, or some other area or aspect of the language arts. Many textbooks have shortcomings that teachers using them should recognize in order to compensate for them.

Classroom activities and textbook use.   Opportunities for purposeful language use in the classroom are limitless. The teacher who has difficulty in recognizing opportunities for language teaching in all classroom activities may turn to the textbook for guidance. For example, as the children return from recess they may be discussing (or arguing about) a misunderstanding of the rules of a game they were playing. This may be the ideal time to teach them how to give directions. The children might look in their language textbooks for information on how to give directions. After reading that particular section of the book, the children can practice giving directions, setting standards, and learning special usage items.

Or perhaps many of the children regularly use the expression, "We was going." Upon hearing this usage, the teacher can suggest looking it up in the textbook. In turn, the children involved might examine the textbook's examples, practice related exercises, and perform textbook drills designed to establish a more acceptable habit of expression.

The textbook as a guide.   Teachers may use the language textbook to determine what skills, abilities, and knowledge to teach and reinforce and, particularly, to guide the sequence of their presentation. The activities of a classroom are not likely to coincide with the sequence of the textbook presentation and thus page-by-page use is inappropriate, but the activities, skills, and abilities in a textbook represent a careful selection and planning process and no teacher should ignore them. Prudent teachers painstakingly and regularly compare their language teaching program with the textbook and plan activities that will use sections of the textbook that the class has not already covered and for which a need exists.

The following example illustrates the type of textbook material that a teacher can use to supplement language teaching opportunities that occur naturally.[14]

With a partner do the following things:

1.   Choose a game that both of you like to play.
2.   Think about the rules for beginning, ending, and playing this game. Write the rules on a piece of paper. Do this by yourself.
3.   Now show each other your list of rules. Compare what you have written. Talk about any rules that either of you forgot to write down. Also talk about how you could make your rules easier to understand.
4.   Now, with your partner write a new list of rules for the same game.
5.   Draw a picture showing the game being played. Display your list of rules.

Practice Materials in the Language Program

What part should workbooks and similar practice materials play in the language arts program? To answer this question we must first consider two other broad questions. First, is there a real need for the kind of instructional practice that these materials purport to supply? Second, if this need is evident, do these materials meet that need satisfactorily?

Consideration of practice materials.   Workbooks and supplementary materials in language tend to emphasize readily identifiable, mechanical features of expression, such as punctuation, capitalization, form, and some matters of usage and thus reflect definite points of view concerning "correctness." For the teacher who believes that such skills and habits need not be practiced other than in connection with expressional activities, the practice materials have little appeal. Others, though they may agree that the functional development of these skills through oral and written expression is important, believe that supplemen-

---

14. John S. Hand et al., *Exploring in English: Experiences in Language* (Chicago: Laidlaw Brothers, Publishers, 1972), p. 227.

tary practice is not only desirable but also necessary for effective learning. For these teachers, the problem is not deciding whether or not to use practice material for certain instructional purposes, but determining which materials show the greatest promise. As suggested elsewhere, teachers ideally should assemble or produce all of the material they need for their teaching unless heavy teaching schedules and crowded classes place a severe strain on both time and energy.

Although educators widely disagree about the advantages and disadvantages of practice materials like workbooks, they agree that all learning is the result of personal and purposeful mental activity on the part of the learner and that it takes place most readily when the individual is motivated and has a clear understanding of what is expected. Most teachers agree that they have a responsibility to provide interesting situations that call forth personal and purposeful mental activities and responses on the part of their pupils. Whether a workbook, an actual communicative activity, or some other device offers the best way to attain these objectives is an open question. Unfortunately, both sides seem to base their arguments more heavily on subjective opinions than on the results of research. The argument is further clouded by the fact that the available evidence is inconclusive and often contradictory.[15]

Criticisms of workbooks fall into two general categories, one related to content and organization and the other concerned with the manner in which the material fits into the total instructional program. Years ago, Pooley attacked workbooks on the ground that children acquire habits of usage through meaningful communication activities rather than through use of exercises or teaching a grammatical system. This criticism seems equally valid today:[16]

> The workbooks in language are generally unsound in method, in that the type of practice given is the filling in of blanks and the crossing out of alternative forms. Such practice may aid the brighter pupil to discover certain distinctions in usage, but it has very slight effect in the establishing of good habits or the breaking of undesirable habits. Such practice for the slower pupil often reinforces bad habits, as he tends to supply the familiar but undesirable form, or to cross off the desired form. Above all, such practice is futile because it is silent and detached from genuine communication.

Those who favor the use of language workbooks and similar practice materials insist that this and other criticisms apply equally well to textbooks and all supplemental types of instructional materials. In a discussion dealing primarily with the value of reading workbooks, Gray set down five guidelines for authors and teachers. Carefully followed, these principles would make workbooks valuable instruments in any skill area:[17]

---

15. Miller J. Stewart, "Workbooks: Help or Hindrance?" *Elementary English* 43 (May 1966): 477–79.

16. Robert C. Pooley, *Teaching English Usage* (New York: Appleton-Century-Crofts, 1946), pp. 183–84.

17. W. S. Gray, *Basic Instruction in Reading in the Elementary and High Schools* (Chicago: University of Chicago Press, October 1948), pp. 149–51.

1. Make each exercise fit the total skill program necessary for each level.
2. Provide varying types of exercises to fit the needs and interests of the child. Then supplement the materials with teacher-made material. It will prevent boredom.
3. Never let the material become an end in itself. Practice on skills should be a means to an end. The end is to use the skill in a functional situation. . . . A transfer of learning takes place only when the teacher deliberately attempts to make it take place.
4. The material should be the basis for additional teaching. Every page should be checked so that the difficulties will be noted and removed through further teaching and practice. Every practice lesson should be a diagnostic lesson.
5. The children must be able to understand what, how, and why they are to do each thing they do. Seeing a reason facilitates a transfer of learning.

Selection and Use of Practice Materials. The following questions will help to assess the quality and appropriateness of practice materials:

1. Does this type of material support and strengthen the objectives of the program?
2. Is the content organized to help the children attain these objectives?
3. Is it interesting to the pupils?
4. Is it attractively arranged?
5. Does it supplement and enrich class activities?
6. Will the pupils gain a feeling of success in using this material?
7. Are the exercises varied and motivating?
8. Does the material utilize sound principles of learning?
9. Is the vocabulary suitable for the pupils who will use it?
10. Are the directions simple, clear, and concise enough to permit pupils to work independently?
11. Does the material provide the types of practice that most pupils need?
12. Does it provide practice material of a suitable range of difficulty?
13. Does it contain material capable of stimulating written expression in other than a mechanical manner?
14. Does it indicate that proper regard was given to research findings in the selection of content?
15. Does it provide adequate review exercises?
16. Does it stimulate self-appraisal by the pupil?
17. Does it contain suitable inventory, check, and mastery test material for pupil guidance?
18. Can a teacher score the material objectively and rapidly to allow time to prepare other learning activities for the children?
19. Is it economically priced?

In order to realize fully the advantages of these materials as instructional aids, teachers must carefully consider how to use them. As a first and general principle, it is not wise to use many different workbooks on a wide variety of subjects or to use any one workbook too often. Leaning heavily on these materials may keep a teacher from doing his or her best job of teaching. The following statements summarize concisely a number of other important principles regarding the use of practice materials:

1. Before using any supplementary practice material, teachers should determine just what they want it to accomplish and plan to use it to reach this objective. Teachers should outline each particular practice lesson with as much care as any other lesson.

2. Workbooks and other practice material require close evaluation in terms of criteria like those suggested in this chapter. Acceptability of point of view, suitability of content, adequacy of methods, physical and mechanical features, and, in particular, the ways in which the materials utilize accepted pedagogical and psychological principles all warrant attention.

3. Each workbook test or practice lesson should be checked as soon as possible; preferably, the children should check their own work. The children should always know exactly what errors they made and why they are errors so that they can correct them.

4. Practice exercises may help pupils to acquire necessary new skills. A pretesting program consisting of informal, teacher-designed tests or objective inventory tests, like the ones that accompany many workbooks, provides a practical and economical means of identifying children who need further practice and the areas in which they are deficient.

5. Since abilities and needs vary markedly within every class, there is no justification for assigning the same practice or workbook lesson to the entire class unless all of the students clearly need it.

6. Teachers cannot expect children to gain adequate and permanent mastery of a skill from a single lesson, so they must carefully choose and properly schedule practice to produce effectively the desired results.

7. The assignment of a carefully chosen practice exercise does not conclude the teacher's responsibility. It is up to the teacher to motivate students to use the material and to follow up what they have practiced.

8. A frank explanation, discussion, and demonstration of an easy sample lesson may convey to students the potential values of practice materials. The best way to sustain the interest of children whose records indicate that they need considerable practice is to provide a variety of types of practice, to insure that the practice materials are as functional as possible relative to needs, and to stay abreast of each child's progress.

9. In addition to basic exercises, the better practice materials include inventory devices, checklists and tests to measure progress, guide sheets for further practice, mastery tests, explanatory materials for teachers and pupils, suggestions for follow-up activities, progress charts, record

blanks, and other features. Teacher and pupils alike should become familiar with all of these elements and use them whenever appropriate.

10. In attempting to individualize workbook assignments in language arts classes, teachers certainly will encounter a number of problems in classroom management. Many of these problems are predictable, and taking time to develop a systematic plan to handle administrative details is most worthwhile. Any competent teacher can devise an efficient system for administering inventory tests, carrying out diagnostic procedures, individualizing assignments, checking and recording test scores and results, and handling the physical materials of the program. Unless the teacher coordinates all of these tasks, workbooks are likely to degenerate into merely another set of instruments in the regimentation of instruction.

EVALUATION IN THE INSTRUCTIONAL PROGRAM

The purpose of evaluation is to measure the progress of an entire class and each person in it in meeting instructional goals. In this section, we will look at different types of evaluative instruments and procedures and discuss grading. In later chapters, we will consider specific evaluative techniques and materials and their uses.

Relationship of Evaluation to Instruction

"Evaluation procedures are an inherent part of the language program and . . . no attempt to separate them in order to justify the use of poor or inadequate instruments for evaluation can change that fact. Certainly the most important factor in the learning situation is the goal of the learner."[18] Evaluation is not a responsibility to treat lightly or regard as only a minor or incidental aspect of the program. It should be an integral element of the teaching process at all levels of instruction as outlined here:

1. Before starting to teach a particular aspect of the program, administer initial or inventory tests or devise other measures to determine each child's mastery of the subject. The instruments used should confront each child with situations calling for responses to the precise abilities or skills included in this aspect of the instructional program. This procedure will insure that children do not waste time on something they have already mastered and allows teachers to focus instruction on elements that each child needs to master.

18. Walter W. Cook, "Evaluation in the Language Arts Program," in *Teaching Language in the Elementary School*, edited by M. R. Trabue (Chicago: University of Chicago Press, 1944), p. 195.

2. Design the program to meet individual needs. Develop language skills through oral presentation, discussion, and demonstration in realistic and lifelike situations.

3. Follow at once with valid and properly motivated opportunities for each child to demonstrate learning. The purpose is to fix the attitudes or skills so that the responses become habitual.

4. Administer a check test that closely parallels the content of the inventory test to determine the extent of each child's improvement.

5. Analyze each check test to discover each child's remaining difficulties.

6. Reteach material that the student failed to grasp and give further practice.

7. Retest, and if necessary, reteach.

Types of Instruments and Techniques

Measuring instruments and appraisal techniques vary widely in type, structure, and function. The most commonly used are the following: oral questioning (of an individual or a group); essay tests (varying as to length of answers required); objective achievement tests (either commercially produced and standardized or teacher-made); diagnostic or analytical tests (also objective and either commercially prepared or teacher-made, but designed specifically to identify individual pupil strengths and weaknesses); and scales (sample items for comparison with pupil work). The teacher and students may design other, informal instruments and techniques, including checklists, statements of standards, models, score cards, questionnaires, attitude scales, progress charts, and conferences. Also useful in evaluation are pupil folders, teacher's logs, pupils' diaries, autobiographies, samples of work, and systematic observations of classroom performance. We will examine many of these instruments and procedures at length in later chapters. Additional information is available in measurement and evaluation textbooks.

Cautions Concerning Testing

Too often evaluation is equated with testing—and most often with standardized testing. Standardized tests are one device teachers can use to discover the results of their teaching. Usually they reflect efforts to establish valid measures; that is, their designs have tried to make them measure what they purport to measure. Many aspects of language use are difficult to measure, however. In fact, at the present time, some aspects are impossible to measure objectively, as standardized tests seek to do. A standardized test, for example, may measure a pupil's ability to choose the acceptable verb form for a sentence from two or three possible choices, but it may not measure that pupil's ability or habitual use of that verb form in oral and written expression.

Standardized tests have come under considerable criticism on the grounds that (1) they are not valid and (2) their use in judging the effectiveness of teaching can lead to mistaken conclusions. In a National Council of Teachers of English effort to review published tests, Jenkins stated that designing testing materials for a national market "may have been economically profitable, but educationally they verge on bankruptcy. The tests . . . simply do not do what they purport to do, nor what this reviewer thinks they ought to do."[19] He concludes:[20]

> The chief deficiency of the tests reviewed is that they tend to ignore the several cultures which make up society. This deficiency is serious. If education is anything, it is the understanding of and induction into one's own culture, whatever it may be. Unfortunately, these tests evidently measure understanding of only one culture.

Since we do not ordinarily construe the purpose of language tests as a means of "measuring understanding of a culture," Jenkins's earlier statement focuses more directly on the issue (even though tests designed for national use are absurd if they lead to comparisons of groups of children with diverse backgrounds). Jenkins also stated that "test writers oversimplify language in their desire and attempts to reduce it to the relatively mechanical operation of taking a standardized test. . . . A broader context is needed to measure language arts abilities than it is possible to give in most of these tests."[21]

Standardized language tests best assess abilities in spelling, punctuation, and capitalization, but as Loban points out, "These are not the true fundamentals of language."[22] Standardized tests are weakest in assessing pupils' abilities to use language "(a) to put order into experience and (b) for clarifying thought, feeling, and volition by making distinctions, modifying ideas, and controlling unity through arrangement and emphasis."[23]

Not only do standardized tests fail to measure many crucial aspects of ability in language use, but interpretation of what they do measure is frequently faulty or misused, as well. As a result, teachers often encounter pressure to insure that their students will receive higher test scores, teachers and schools are subject to unfair criticism, more formalized teaching occurs, and so on. Professional organizations, such as the National Council of Teachers of English, have acted to reduce or alleviate this pressure by publishing *Common Sense and Testing* for the public, particularly parents. This publication asserts:[24]

---

19. William A. Jenkins, "Elementary School Language Tests," in *Reviews of Selected Published Tests in English*, edited by Alfred H. Grommon (Urbana, Ill.: National Council of Teachers of English, 1976), p. 57.

20. Ibid., p. 57.

21. Ibid., pp. 52–53.

22. Walter Loban, "Language Development and Its Evaluation" in *Reviews of Selected Published Tests in English*, edited by Alfred H. Grommon (Urbana, Ill.: National Council of Teachers of English, 1976), p. 45.

23. Ibid., p. 46.

24. Task Force on Measurement and Evaluation in the Study of English, *Common Sense and Testing in English* (Urbana, Ill.: National Council of Teachers of English, 1975), pp. 31–32.

On the basis of tests that skim the surface of their learning, children and their parents are told that one child is two years above grade level and another is a year and a half behind. Whole schools are ranked and whole groups of children are branded with labels like "slow learner" or "underachiever."

Standardized achievement tests in English are usually treated as though they were the ultimate word on the ability and performance of our children; yet they give inadequate information to administrators, parents, teachers and children. . . .

Most standardized tests compare a student, a class, or a school to a national average. This comparison has many faults: it assumes that any group of students will always vary from very good to very poor, no matter what they have been taught or how well; and it insures that some do well and some poorly by asking questions of varying difficulty (some about things a student might not have studied). The questions deal with general topics in English rather than the specific topics that students in a particular school might have learned. It asks questions regardless of whether the material is even taught in that school. Nationwide or statewide tests cannot represent the specifics of a particular school's English program.

The point is not to disparage the use of standardized tests or to suggest that evaluation is not a significant part of teaching. The purpose is simply to urge interpreting and applying the results and information gained from standardized testing—or any evaluation procedure—with informed consideration of their limitations. Teachers should remember that some evaluative tools give more valid and reliable information than others. Most standardized tests are reasonably reliable, as shown by the fact that different forms of the same test usually yield closely comparable test scores. Informal evaluative procedures or instruments, in contrast, often are not reliable. They may or may not be valid. Thus, a teacher should judge any test, and any other evaluation tool, in terms of its value in assessing the learning sought by the program objectives, the curriculum content, and the teaching.

Evaluation and Grading

Teachers show more concern about grading students' performance than any other aspect of curriculum and methods. Grading is also a major concern of parents, as witnessed by the frequency with which a school district typically changes its reporting form and procedures.

Evaluation and grading are not the same thing, however. Evaluation is a major part of the teaching process, while the assigning of grades is a custom that exists, presumably, to inform parents and others of the pupil's growth and achievement. Proper recognition of this difference should reduce the number of evaluative acts that a teacher grades and increase the proper use of evaluation.

Teachers must assign grades (or somehow report a child's performance to parents, school authorities, and pupils), and it is logical to use the results of evaluation as the basis for a grade. It is not necessary, however, to grade the results of every evaluative effort, nor should a teacher believe that a grade is an adequate report to either parents or children.

A teacher, of course, must observe the reporting policies of the school and district, and in the majority of schools it is necessary to enter grades on a report card. Teachers should extend the reporting process, however, by sending home samples of children's work (with comments rather than grades), evaluative statements, and explanations of the school program. Also, conferring with parents whenever possible is very desirable.

The following are ironclad principles of reporting:

1.   Reports should be based on evidence that can be shown and understood and is as nearly objective as possible.
2.   Reports should consider the child and their effect upon him or her and his or her learning; they must be as accurate an assessment of the child's achievement or progress as possible, as personal as possible, and respectful of the feelings and personalities of all concerned.

THE PROFESSIONAL TEACHER

This chapter has presented a considerable amount of information about teaching language arts, and in the chapters that follow we will build on this base. In order to utilize effectively this information, however, a teacher must fulfill certain professional requirements and obligations, which we will examine here.

Qualifications of the Language Arts Teacher

In its 1976 publication *A Statement on the Preparation of Teachers of English and the Language Arts* the National Council of Teachers of English identified forty-three qualifications needed by language arts teachers. The intent of this statement was to inform teachers and those who prepare teachers for the classroom of the knowledge, abilities, and attitudes that enable a teacher to work effectively in a classroom with a variety of students. The NCTE qualifications appear here in the form of a checklist so that teachers may evaluate their individual professional needs.

Professionalism

There are countless routes toward developing the professional skills needed to launch a teaching career and as many ways to stay up to date on trends and research. The most common means for achieving professionalism are taking courses and reading professional publications. Recently, in a survey involving 10 percent of its membership, the National Council of Teachers of English asked: "If you could recommend a book no elementary teacher should miss, what would you

Qualifications needed by language arts teachers

Qualification	Degree of development			
	Not developed 1	2	3	Highly developed 4

KNOWLEDGE. Teachers of English need to know, and know how to draw on for their teaching, according to the needs and interests of their students:

1. processes by which children develop in their ability to acquire, understand, and use language, both oral and written, from early childhood onward;

2. the relations between students' learning of language and the social, cultural, and economic conditions within which they are reared;

3. the workings (phonological, grammatical, semantic) and uses of the language in general and of the English language in particular; and the processes of development and change in language;

4. linguistic, rhetorical, and stylistic concepts that furnish useful ways of understanding and talking about the substance, structure, development, and manner of expression in written and oral discourse;

5. the activities that make up the process of oral and written composing (these activities may differ among different students);

6. processes by which one learns to read, from initial exposure to language in early childhood, through the first stages of readiness-to-read, through more advanced stages by which the reader comes increasingly to understand and respond to details of meaning and nuances of expression;

7. an extensive body of literature in English (including literature for children and adolescents, popular literature, oral literature, nonwestern literature, and literature by women and minority groups);

8. varied ways of responding to, discussing, and understanding works of literature in all forms;

9. ways in which nonprint and nonverbal media differ from print and verbal media, and ways of discussing works in nonprint and nonverbal media;

10. ways in which nonprint and nonverbal media can supplement and extend the experiences of print and verbal media;

123

Qualifications needed by language arts teachers (continued)

Qualification	Degree of development			
	Not developed 1	2	3	Highly developed 4
11. instructional resources (including educational technology) and varied sources of information (books, magazines, newspapers, tapes, recordings, films, pictures, and other nonprint and nonverbal materials) that will help students understand—through both intellect and imagination—the subjects and issues they are studying;				
12. the uses and abuses of language in our society, particularly the ways in which language is manipulated by various interests for varied purposes;				
13. problems faced and procedures used by teachers and educational leaders in designing curricula in English for students of different ages, abilities, and linguistic backgrounds;				
14. the uses and abuses of testing procedures and other evaluative techniques for describing students' progress in the handling and understanding of language;				
15. major research studies on acquisition and growth of language in children and adults, on reading, on response to literature, on the processes of composing, and on the building of curricula for different kinds of students in different settings.				

ABILITIES: Teachers of English must be able:

16. to identify, assess, and interpret student progress in listening, reading, speaking, and writing;

17. to take appropriate steps to help students improve their skill in responding to and using language;

18. to work effectively with students of different ethnic groups, including those who do not speak English as their native language;

19. to organize groups of learners for a variety of purposes appropriate to the English classroom, e.g., discussion, creative problem-solving, composing, and commenting on compositions;

124

20. to engage both the intellect and the imagination of students in their listening, reading, speaking, and writing;

21. to ask questions (at varying levels of abstraction) that elicit facts, opinions, and judgments that are appropriate to the subject and occasion;

22. to respond specifically and constructively to student discourse;

23. to communicate to students, parents, administrators, and officials the conclusions that can be legitimately inferred from results of tests purporting to measure progress in using and understanding language;

24. to set professional goals for themselves and evaluate their progress toward them;

25. to guide students in producing discourse that satisfies their own distinctive needs;

26. to help students distinguish between effective and ineffective discourse;

27. to help students experience the connection between the experience of reading and the experience of writing;

28. to help students learn to observe and report accurately;

29. to help students distinguish among the language options (such as registers and levels of usage) open to them in various social and cultural settings;

30. to help students respond appropriately to the differing demands made on speech and writing by different contexts, audiences, and purposes;

31. to help both beginning and maturing readers apply varied techniques to improve reading comprehension;

32. to help students learn to listen effectively for information, for understanding and for pleasure;

33. to help students develop satisfying ways of responding to, and productive ways of talking about, works of literature;

34. to help students identify and weigh facts, implications, inferences, and judgments in both spoken and written discourse;

35. to help students develop the ability to respond appropriately to and create nonprint and nonverbal forms of communication, including both symbolic forms and other visual and aural forms (including film, videotape, photography, dramatic performance, song, and other art forms).

Qualifications needed by language arts teachers (continued)

Qualification	Degree of development			
	Not developed 1	2	3	Highly developed 4
ATTITUDES: Teachers of English at all levels need to reveal in their classes and in their work with individual students:				
36. a conviction that by helping students increase their power to use and respond to language both creatively and responsibly they are helping those students to grow as human beings;				
37. a respect for the individual language and dialect of each student;				
38. a willingness to respond and help students respond to work in all the different media of communication;				
39. a desire to help students become familiar with the diverse cultures and their art;				
40. a recognition that, whatever their rate of growth and progress, all children are worthy of a teacher's sympathetic attention;				
41. a sensitivity to the impact that events and developments in the world outside the school may have on themselves and their students;				
42. a flexibility in teaching strategies and a willingness to seek a match between students' needs and the teacher's objectives, methods, and materials;				
43. a commitment to continued professional growth.				

Source: From National Council of Teachers of English, *A Statement on the Preparation of Teachers of English and the Language Arts* (Urbana, Ill.: National Council of Teachers of English, 1976).

suggest?" The eight most often mentioned might serve as a guide to your future professional reading:

1. *Wishes, Lies and Dreams* by Kenneth Koch
2. *A Student-Centered Language Arts Curriculum* by James Moffett
3. *Teacher* by Sylvia Ashton Warner
4. *Understanding Reading* by Frank Smith
5. *Hooked on Books: Program and Proof* by Fader and McNeill
6. *Creative Teaching of the Language Arts in the Elementary School* by James A. Smith
7. *Experiences in Language* by Petty, Petty, and Becking
8. *Teaching As a Subversive Activity* by Postman and Weingartner

Professional reading should also include journals. *Language Arts* is the journal of the Elementary Section of the National Council of Teachers of English. Since 1924 it has served as an open forum for original contributions on all facets of language arts teaching and learning. Its largest audience consists of teachers and teacher-educators of children in the preschool through middle school years. Published eight times a year, *Language Arts* contains reviews of new children's trade books and professional materials, research applications, perspectives on language arts teaching from authors in related disciplines, and profiles of well-known authors and illustrators for children, in addition to feature articles.

The Reading Teacher, published nine times per year by the International Reading Association, is helpful in the teaching of reading. This journal and *Language Arts* are but two of the professional periodicals to which elementary school language arts teachers can turn for help in the classroom.

Affiliating with a professional organization is an easy way to share in a range of services useful to teachers. Organizations like the National Council of Teachers of English (1111 Kenyon Rd., Urbana, Ill. 61801) and the International Reading Association (800 Barksdale Road, Newark, Del. 19711) publish teaching and professional materials, hold conferences, provide consultant services (e.g., evaluation of curriculum materials), and publish a range of professional journals.

EXERCISES FOR THOUGHT AND ACTION

1. Find out who selected the language arts textbooks used in a particular school (Were they adopted at the state, city, or building level?). Ask a few teachers about the strengths and weaknesses of these books and the ways they use them in their classrooms.
2. Evaluate a commercial kit, game, or textbook designed for a single language arts area (e.g., spelling or handwriting). Use as criteria the suggestions in this chapter, your own objectives, and your knowledge of children at a selected school level.

3. Propose a procedure for selecting and adopting a series of language textbooks and related materials for a school system in which you are a teacher.

4. Take a stand on this statement: "Any instructional resource can be well used or misused. It is not the type of material itself that is inherently good or bad." (You may wish to direct your argument toward kits or workbooks.) Select one type of material and discuss ways to use it appropriately.

5. What are the chief factors that have stimulated the development of the growing number of supplemental materials other than workbooks?

6. Consult the list of "Qualifications Needed by Teachers of English" in this chapter and select five from each of the three categories (knowledge, abilities, and attitudes) that you consider to be most important. Rank each set of five in order of priority.

7. Make a well-organized and expandable file of instructional resources relating to each facet of a language arts program. (You might begin by stopping at a market for a cardboard box about twelve to fifteen inches wide, at least ten inches deep, and as long as possible.) Use the table of contents of this book to come up with labels to put on manila folders or cardboard dividers within the box. File any accumulated but unorganized resources that might be useful in language arts teaching. Resolve to develop a teacher's eye and enlarge your file.

8. Examine carefully one or more of the journals published for elementary language arts teachers. Select an article and evaluate it according to criteria you have formulated.

9. Find out what standardized language arts tests the local school administers. How are they chosen? When are they given? For what purposes? Evaluate a standardized test according to this checklist:[25]

Checklist for evaluating English tests and test uses

Name of test_____
Date when test was made and latest revision_____
Content or skill areas of English for which test is designed_____

Test Content
    Do items represent the content or skill area adequately?_____
        What parts of the area are omitted?_____
        How important is the area measured to the curriculum of the school?_____
    Does providing the correct answer require the skill or knowledge tested?
    _____
    Is the answer format an appropriate index of the skill?_____
    Is the test label accurate?_____

---

25. Task Force on Measurement and Evaluation in the Study of English, *Common Sense and Testing in English* (Urbana, Ill.: National Council of Teachers of English, 1975), pp. 29–30.

Test Format
  Are the items clear or are they ambiguous in wording?_____
  Are the items likely to be of interest to students?_____
  Are the items responsive to human diversity?_____
  Are the test instructions clear?_____
  Does the test seem to have a logic or sequence that is appropriate?_____
  Is the language of the test current?_____

Test Manual
  Does the manual describe the purpose of the test?_____
  Did teachers help construct the test?_____
  What checks of validity have been made?_____
  Are specific items related to specific objectives?_____
  If test is norm-referenced:
    What is norming population?_____
    Does it match local conditions?_____
    Is test the same form of the test used for norming?_____
    What is reliability of test?_____
      of subtests?_____
    What is standard error of measurement?_____
    How are scores reported?_____
    Are percentiles or stanines given as well as grade levels?_____
    Are there adequate warnings about misrepresentation of score reporting in the manual?_____
  If test is criterion-referenced or domain-referenced:
  Has the criterion been defined clearly?_____
  Is the criterion appropriate to the curriculum?_____
  Is the criterion appropriate to the student's level?_____
  Do the items measure the criterion?_____

Test Reporting
  Is there a clear statement of relation of test to program objectives?_____
  Is there a clear statement that teachers helped choose the test?_____
  Is there a clear statement of the limited inferences that can be drawn from the test? _____
  If a norm-referenced test:
    Is there a clear statement of relation of test scores to publisher's norms?_____
      to local norms?_____
  Is there a clear explanation of what scores mean?_____
    of the problem in interpreting grade scores?_____
    of the fact that scores provide a description of groups, not individuals?_____

10. Ask three children from the same classroom to tell you everything they do from the time they get up in the morning until the time they arrive in the classroom. Tape their remarks and describe differences in the oral language of different children. Likewise, examine several written products from one classroom. Formulate several speaking and writing goals for each child.

11. Produce a diagram of the physical setting of a classroom that might be conducive to language learning.
12. Think of a language arts goal that a learning center might advance. Design the center and describe your plan for its use.
13. Make several individual, self-correcting practice exercises (may be games) for reinforcing a specific language arts skill.
14. Choose one of the eight books from the NCTE readership poll. Read it, and convince another teacher to do likewise.
15. Have a class debate on the issue of whether Johnny and Jane can read and write as well as they once could.

SELECTED REFERENCES

Burton, W. H. *The Guidance of Learning Activities*. 3rd ed. New York: Appleton-Century-Crofts, 1962.

Garner, Wayne L. *Programmed Instruction*. New York: Center for Applied Research in Education, 1966.

Goodman, Kenneth S.; Olsen, Hans C., Jr.; Colvin, Cynthia M.; and VanderLinde, Louis F. *Choosing Materials to Teach Reading*. Detroit: Wayne State University Press, 1966.

Hennings, Dorothy Grant. *Communication in Action*. Chicago: Rand McNally College Publishing Co., 1978.

Henry, Nelson B., ed. *Individualizing Instruction*. Sixty-first Yearbook of the National Society for the Study of Education, pt. 1. Chicago: University of Chicago Press, 1962.

Hilton, Ernest. "Textbooks." In *Encyclopedia of Educational Research*, 4th ed., edited by Robert L. Ebel, pp. 1470–78. New York: Macmillan Co., 1969.

Hopkins, L. B. *Let Them Be Themselves*. New York: Citation Press, 1974.

Maloney, Henry B., ed. *Goal-making for English Teaching*. Urbana, Ill.: National Council of Teachers of English, 1973.

Popham, W. James, and Baker, Eva L. *Establishing Instructional Goals*. Englewood Cliffs, N.J.: Prentice-Hall, 1970.

Stewig, John W. *Exploring Language with Children*. Columbus, O.: Charles Merrill, 1974.

Thomas, George I., and Crescimbeni, Joseph. *Individualizing Instruction in the Elementary School*. New York: Random House, 1967.

Thomas, R. Murry, and Thomas, Shirley. *Individual Differences in the Classroom*. New York: David McKay Co., 1965.

Waskin, Yvonne. *Teacher-Pupil Planning for Better Classroom Learning*. New York: Pitman Publishing Corp., 1967.

5

Literature and Children

All that people have ever thought, done, or dreamed, lies waiting to be discovered in a book. —Charlotte S. Huck, Children's Literature in the Elementary School

There seems to be some danger that the schools are teaching children to read but, at the same time, discouraging them from ever doing so out of the classroom. Avoiding this danger hinges on many factors, but undoubtedly, it depends greatly on the effectiveness of a school's literature program, which, in turn, depends on recognition of children's needs and interests, the availability of literature, and a teacher who is knowledgeable about both.

The teaching of literature in the elementary school has been criticized from several points of view as being too structured, too incidental, too middle class, too skills oriented, and so on. The most serious criticism, however, might be that in some classrooms literature receives no attention at all and many students apparently have very little exposure to it.

In this chapter, we will discuss literature in a general sense but will focus on teaching and learning procedures. Oral interpretation of literature, writing about or being motivated by literature, and extension of listening and reading skills through literature are important elements of a language arts program and they will enter into later discussions in this book, but the teaching of literature need not have a utilitarian purpose. The enjoyment of books is a valuable outcome of the school program in and of itself, and no teacher should have to justify literature instruction as a means of improving performance in associated skills.

This chapter appears at the end of the introductory section of the book to emphasize its basic importance in the sections that follow. Literature is an all-encompassing experience. Extensive involvement with it breathes life into the total language arts program and the experience of living.

OBJECTIVES OF THE LITERATURE PROGRAM

The objectives of literature programs usually are relatively general statements, so the individual teacher can take into account the needs of particular pupils or classes when designing an instruction program to meet them. Almost invariably, these objectives revolve around four major purposes: enrichment of the individual, development of insights and understandings, transmission of culture, and development of taste in reading. Whitehead has translated these purposes into eight goals that the teacher of literature should keep in mind:[1]

1. To help the child understand himself and his present problems.
2. To provide opportunities for escape from routine.
3. To provide a focus for leisure time activities.
4. To develop an appreciation of country and American ideals.
5. To increase the child's knowledge and understanding of the problems of others.
6. To discover and develop ethical standards.
7. To utilize literature as a source for further creative endeavor.
8. To promote an appreciation of the English language.

According to Huck, the primary purpose of a literature program in the elementary school is to encourage children to discover delight in books—to give them the opportunity to experience literature, and to enter into and become involved with a book. Three other purposes she identifies are:[2]

1. To interpret literature—to grow in the ability to respond to literature through in-depth looks at the meaning of a story for one's own life.
2. To lead children gradually to an awareness of types of literature, the elements of literature, the place of classics, and the works of particular authors and illustrators.
3. To develop literary appreciation, a lifetime pattern of preference for reading quality literature.

Related to the objectives of a literature program is its overall organization. Odland reported that five approaches to the teaching of literature are prevalent in elementary schools. Briefly, these approaches are:[3]

---

1. Robert Whitehead, *Children's Literature: Strategies of Teaching*, © 1968, pp. 6–7. Reprinted by permission of Prentice-Hall, Inc., Englewood Cliffs, New Jersey.

2. Charlotte S. Huck, *Children's Literature in the Elementary School*, 3rd ed. (New York: Holt, Rinehart and Winston, 1976), pp. 708–11.

3. Norine Odland, "Planning a Literature Program for the Elementary School," *Language Arts*, April 1979, pp. 363–364.

1. A designated period of time labeled "literature," having a methodological emphasis similar to that common in secondary school and college literature classes.

2. Access to a library or media center either with or without a structured program in its use and guidance in selecting and reading books.

3. Literature as only a peripheral responsibility of the school, with virtually no teaching attention given it.

4. A supplement to content teaching in social studies, science, and other curricular areas to meet objectives related indirectly to literature.

5. A planned program having as principal objectives the enjoyment of and continued interest in reading through development of sensitivity to both literary elements and content.

Odland's survey showed that the fourth approach is the most common one, even though most authorities on children's literature advocate the fifth approach.[4]

Every teacher should have a plan to meet rather specific objectives determined with students' needs and abilities in mind. Therefore, teachers must first observe and perhaps survey children to discover their needs, interests, experiences, and abilities. Based on the results, they can plan the program.

A literature program should be child-centered, not teacher-centered. Teachers should not force preconceived standards upon the children or expect that all pupils will respond to or even read a particular story or poem because adults say it is "good." Furthermore, to achieve the primary objectives of attitude formation, insight, and understanding, teachers must avoid dictating content and, in effect, telling students what they should like and what they should gain from their reading.[5] Children need guidance and encouragement to find pleasure in reading, for, unless it is a pleasurable experience for them, they will read little besides what is required.

The Teacher and the Literature

The availability of books and the reading habits of parents undoubtedly influence how much children read and whether they continue to be interested in reading. Nevertheless, a teacher's influence is strong during the years when children are learning to read and forming reading habits. Consequently we can consider teachers to be an important element of the literature program.

Certainly teachers must like to read if they are to exert a desirable influence on children's reading habits. Teachers who do not regard reading as important enough to set aside time each day for their own reading have a limited ability to inspire a love for reading in their students. Enthusiasm is catching; studies and

---

4. Bernice E. Cullinan, *Literature for Children, Its Discipline and Content* (Dubuque, Iowa: William C. Brown Co., 1971).

5. The point of view expressed here is substantiated by research. See Bernice E. Cullinan, "Teaching Literature to Children, 1966–1972," *Elementary English*, (November 1972), pp. 1028–37.

reports of teachers' observations have shown that pupils like best those areas of the curriculum that teachers most enjoy.

A thorough knowledge of children's literature is also a significant advantage. Every teacher needs to keep up with what books are available and which ones are good. Unfortunately, one study showed that only half of the teachers in a national survey had taken a course in children's literature during the preceding eight years.[6] Obviously, taking courses is not the only way to become informed. Later in this chapter we will discuss several excellent books about children's literature and numerous listings of books recommended for various age and grade levels. School and public librarians are another valuable resource. But teachers who want to inspire a real love of reading must truly be familiar with children's books. The beginning teacher should consider it a prerequisite to spend several days in the children's section of the library getting to know what is available and compiling a list of books that seem particularly suitable for oral reading as well as for a particular grade level. And every teacher, whether new or experienced, should visit the library regularly to become familiar with new additions and discover selections that fit the needs and interests of particular children. It is a good idea to take a packet of index cards on these expeditions and make up descriptive cards for each book that you want to remember.

Animal Stories, ages 3–6

Horton Hatches the Egg
by Dr. Seuss

delightful fantasy elephant hatches egg
good for reading aloud (1 sitting)
  verse form
many pictures, large enough to show to group

                                        Norton Library

Another requirement for teaching literature is knowing the class. Many studies have told us a lot about children's interests in reading (see next section), but the concerned teacher is aware that the pupils in every class are individuals who have individual interests, individual abilities, and individual needs.

A final but equally important consideration in teaching literature is reading aloud to children, doing it well and frequently, and enjoying it. Each day's schedule should include some time for reading to children, particularly in the

---

6. Chow Loy Tom, "A National Survey of What Teachers Read to Children in the Middle Grades" (Ph.D. dissertation, Ohio State University, 1969).

Christa Armstrong and Harold Buttrick.

early school years, but reading to children should not stop there. In the upper grades, when other activities become important, the value of reading for relaxation and enjoyment needs reemphasizing. Students who read well may want to participate in oral reading activities and should certainly be encouraged to do so, but the teacher should furnish the model. All materials for reading aloud, of course, should be carefully selected and prepared. Teachers who feel they do not read well should practice—even seek help—so that the oral reading experience will be personally rewarding, as well as a happy experience for children. Reading aloud is the primary way for the teacher to communicate enthusiasm for books to children and therefore it is an essential element of daily instruction.

Children's Reading Interests

Authorities agree that any successful program aimed at encouraging children to read and improving their taste in reading materials must start at the children's level and must include a carefully planned program for broadening their interests and elevating their taste. Therefore the teacher should begin by discovering what subjects the children are interested in and providing a wide variety of materials suited to their interests and to their reading ability.

Favat believes that any attempt to alter the child-determined course of reading interests is sure to encounter difficulty and, furthermore, that at each stage of development children adapt their reading selection to satisfy current needs. He states:[7]

> Children read what they please, or more accurately, what pleases them.
> . . . Teachers and parents must come to understand that the question is not whether one kind of reading produces a more respectable.experience than another but whether it produces a more satisfying experience than another—that is, whether children find in the stories an ever-continuing fulfilling of their own needs and desires.

Obviously, each child has unique interests and abilities, but studies of children's interests have established a few guidelines to aid in the selection of reading materials.

Kindergarten and primary grades.   Children who have not learned to read or are just beginning to enjoy picture books known as "wordless books with stories."[8] These books stimulate language development, impart a "sense of reading," and serve as models for storytelling. *Look What I Can Do* by Jose Aruego, for example, provides a framework for children to tell the story in their own words. Most picture books are a natural stimulus for thinking and talking, and children can easily "read" them if the books do not require too many words to tell their stories.

Books illustrated in bold colors, rather than muted ones, appeal to young children. Pictures should be simple representations of objects, animals, and people that children can easily identify. They need not be photographic in quality, for children are perceptive and imaginative; in fact, a simple line drawing may be more meaningful than a photograph, which could show too many distracting details.

Of course, young children like many books that do contain words because they want to read. Illustrations in these books should meet qualifications similar to those for picture books. The stories themselves should provide assurance and a sense of achievement:[9]

> The youngest children in our schools, the prereaders and beginners in reading, just because they are small and inexperienced, are uncertain, insecure, and generally find themselves in the wrong. Someone is always saying, "Don't do that," or "No, you aren't old enough for that." So, of course, these young pilgrims need lots of reassurance about their place in the world, that they are loved, needed, and capable of doing things on their own.

---

7. André Favat, *Child and Tale: The Origins of Interest* (Urbana, Ill.: National Council of Teachers of English, 1977), p. 65.

8. Donald J. Bissett, "Literature in the Classroom," *Elementary English*, November 1972, p. 1016.

9. May Hill Arbuthnot, "Developing Life Values Through Reading," *Elementary English*, January 1966, p. 11.

Because children in this age group are imaginative and love stories about animals and mechanical objects, they readily identify with such characters as the *Happy Lion* in the series by Louise Fatio or Maurice Sendak's *Little Bear.* They will shiver through the winter with poor Horton as he faithfully sits on his egg, struggle courageously up the hill with *The Little Engine That Could,* and sympathize with *The Little House.* All children may find solace in a story like *Whistle for Willie,* by Ezra Jack Keats, and identify with Willie, for children have no prejudice and they all know the agony of being unable to do the things that older children and adults can do easily.

Folk tales are also popular with young children. They love talking animals and the humor and magic of traditional stories. Naturally, they equally appreciate the "little people," witches and wizards, and the giants and ogres of fairy tales. Both folk and fairy tales should be made available and read to children because they are a vital part of the literary heritage of children *and* grownups and because they pave the way for acceptance and enjoyment of the world of imaginative literature that lies ahead.

Middle grades.   By the time children reach the middle grades their interests are broader because their experience has exposed them to a larger part of the world. Informational books such as *What Tree Is It?*, *First Book of Birds*, *All About Us*, *A Great Bicycle Book*, and *The Guinness Book of World Records* help to satisfy and encourage their growing curiosity. And as they learn about other lands and other cultures in social studies, they enjoy stories about the people, customs, and literature of these lands, as well as their own country. The exciting and colorful literature about the adventures of heroes and explorers is popular with this age group and helps to introduce a new type of literature: biography. *Carry On, Mr. Bowditch* and other biographies by Jean Lee Latham, biographies of American historical heroes by James Daugherty and Clara Ingram Judson, and biography series like the "Step Up" books, the Childhood of Famous Americans, and the Landmark books appeal to children between the third- and fifth-grade levels. Animal stories remain popular with both boys and girls of this age group, and by about the fifth or sixth grade, boys and girls usually develop an interest in stories about male and female athletes.

It must not be presumed, however, that because middle-graders are interested in real people and the real world, they have lost their taste for the imaginative, and it is particularly important not to encourage their interest in realism to the point of crowding out the imaginary world. Paul Bunyan is as much a part of the story of the expanding frontier as the first railroad, and these children delight in tall tales and folk stories of all lands. Furthermore, they are quite as willing to accept Peter Pan's ability to fly through the air as they are to demand that this same delightful boy should shiver at the approach of Captain Hook and know the universal need for a mother's love and care.

Children in the middle grades also enjoy humor, and this appreciation deserves nurturing because laughter is an invaluable weapon against the tensions and cares of modern life. Mary Poppins and Henry Huggins will delight these children, as will the huge but friendly dinosaur hatched from Oliver Butterworth's *Enormous Egg*.

Upper grades.   Nearly all of the interests of the middle grades carry over into the upper elementary years. Perhaps the most significant change at this level is that boys and girls begin to prefer different kinds of books. Because they mature more rapidly, girls begin to show interest in stories with some love interest, whereas the boys' preference for sports and adventure increases. At this age, children are active and full of life, so they want plots that move rapidly; they love mystery and adventure of all kinds. At the same time, however, they are experiencing the first pains of approaching maturity, and they are well aware that the adult world is full of problems that they must soon face. They not only want but need to be exposed to stories in which people like themselves attempt to find workable solutions to realistic problems. Popular authors include Blume (*Are You There God? It's Me, Margaret*), Donovan (*I'll Get There, It Better Be Worth the Trip*), George (*Julie of the Wolves*), Armstrong (*Sounder*), Wersba (*The Dream Watcher*), Rodgers (*Freaky Friday*), L'Engle (*Wrinkle in Time*), and Cunningham (*Dorp Dead*).

Best books.   Listings of favorite books abound. To illustrate, in 1977 Odland and Beach asked Minnesota elementary school librarians to list the five most popular titles in their school library.[10] The 515 participating librarians named 434 titles. Most frequently named were the following:

Title	Number of times named
Little House Books	218
Charlotte's Web	168
Are You There God? It's Me Margaret	116
Curious George	111
Guinness Book of World Records	105
Tales of a Fourth Grade Nothing	100
Boxcar Children	89
Charlie and the Chocolate Factory	87
Encyclopedia Brown	71
Freaky Friday	71
Hardy Boys	57
Nancy Drew	56
Where the Red Fern Grows	51
Great Monsters of the Movies	48
Mouse and the Motorcycle	31

10. Norine Odland and Richard Beach, "Book Preferences of Minnesota Students Survey" (unpublished). Results for middle school/junior high and senior high are available from the authors (College of Education, Peik Hall, University of Minnesota, Minneapolis, Minn. 55455).

The Children's Literature Association, an international organization of teachers, librarians, authors, and publishers, compiled this list of ten American children's books written in the past two hundred years that have the most enduring quality:

1. *Charlotte's Web* by E. B. White
2. *Where the Wild Things Are* by Maurice Sendak
3. *Tom Sawyer* by Mark Twain
4. *Little Women* by Louisa May Alcott
5. *The Adventures of Huckleberry Finn* by Mark Twain
6. *The Little House in the Big Woods* by Laura Ingalls Wilder
7. *Johnny Tremaine* by Esther Forbes
8. *The Wizard of Oz* by Frank Baum
9. *The Little House on the Prairie* by Laura Ingalls Wilder
10. *Island of the Blue Dolphins* by Scott O'Dell and *Julie of the Wolves* by Jean George.

TECHNIQUES IN TEACHING LITERATURE

Sometimes teachers who come to the classroom fresh from college literature courses are so impressed with their newly acquired knowledge of symbolism, literary allusion, onomatopoeia, and other writing techniques that they believe such knowledge is necessary to children's appreciation of literature. Those teachers need to reexamine their instructional objectives. Seldom is the ability to analyze a piece of literature a goal of children's literature programs. The Nebraska *Curriculum for English*, for example, specifically recommends that teachers avoid this practice:[11]

> The teacher should not deliver lectures and ready-made literary analyses to elementary school children. She should not deliver the background material in the units to students but lead them when and as they can to perceive what a work is about. She should not ask children to recognize and apply the technical critical terminology of the interpretive analyses given in these sections of the units: the primary purpose of the curriculum is to create understanding.

Perhaps the temptation to analyze is rooted at least partly in the fact that this knowledge *can be tested*, whereas measuring appreciation or increased self-awareness is difficult indeed. Certainly teachers may ask "Do you know who Apollo was?" or "What do you like about the sound of this poem?" but they should remember not to spoil enjoyment with prolonged analysis and explication.

In a similar vein, teachers should beware of ruining reading pleasure by requiring students to fill out book report forms or write long reports. The purpose of

---

11. *A Curriculum for English*, Grade 5, Units 45–57 (Lincoln: University of Nebraska Press, 1966), p. xiv.

a book report is to allow students to share their reading in a way that suits the child and the book and not to prove that they actually read the books. Of course, the written report is one means of extending a reading experience and should not be eliminated, but teachers can encourage pupils to react to a book in many other ways, as we will see later.

A final caution concerns memorization. Undoubtedly, requiring children to memorize lines or poems is not as common as it once was, but many teachers still cling to this custom. No one would say that children should *never* memorize poems. In order to share a poem with other children, a child should know it well enough to read it fluently and expressively and be able to maintain eye contact with the audience. A child may even decide that he or she *wants* to memorize a poem. Similarly, a group may decide to memorize a poem they are choral-reading, but the decision should come from the group rather than from the teacher.

The teacher who truly loves words and the sound of words and who enjoys memorizing favorite phrases or poems will often communicate this feeling to pupils so that they will choose to memorize their own favorites. Sometimes memorization of favorite works comes informally and automatically in classrooms where literature is read regularly and where the children choose what they will hear; repeated requests for Gag's *Millions of Cats*, for example, brings mastery of its familiar refrain. Memorization should never be a "blanket" assignment or one that pupils look upon as a chore.

Finding Children's Interests

Much has already been said about children's interests at various age levels, and a teacher could probably build a fairly successful program around the suggestions that research has given us. Children are individuals, however, and they respond more enthusiastically if we know literature that suits their individual likes and dislikes, as well as their capabilities. A shy child may come out of her shell when the teacher takes the trouble to find a book about her special hobby, astronomy; or a reluctant seventh-grade reader may actually enjoy a book for the first time because it is about his favorite baseball hero.

Among the ways to determine the interests and needs of a particular class, perhaps the simplest is to keep a card of each child's reading level, interests, and perhaps the titles of books read during the year. To obtain information for the cards the teacher may informally talk with the children as they browse, or hold regular discussions or hand out a short questionnaire asking such questions as the following:

1. What person do you most admire?
2. What is your favorite TV program?
3. Name one book that you especially liked.

well-rounded reader

4. What to you like to do after school or on Saturdays?
5. What place in the world would you most like to visit?
6. If there were only one book in the room, what would you want it to be about?

This type of information and a good knowledge of children's literature will permit the teacher to choose new books for the classroom library or to make recommendations to the librarian. Such information is also helpful in broadening interests, challenging abilities, and raising levels of taste.

Setting up a Room Library

It is a truism that books must be available to children to encourage them to read and to benefit from reading. Every elementary classroom should have a book corner where pupils may go to browse and to read. The book corner should be bright, attractive, and comfortable so that children will take time to select the books they want to read. Books should be attractively displayed, not just filed on shelves, and they should be changed frequently so that children will not "run out" of reading matter. The library corner may also be a place to display student-crafted models, pictures, dioramas, and so on. A bulletin board would provide a place for pictures or writing by the children, colorful book jackets, announcements about new books in the school or room library, or magazine pictures attractively mounted to illustrate a particular book or group of books.

Reading Aloud by the Teacher

In addition to providing books and a place to put them, the teacher should actively participate in the children's discovery and enjoyment of books. If the teacher obviously likes to read, the children will also come to love reading. Oral reading by the teacher has been shown to increase children's language ability and to have a significant effect on their reading performance.[12] Clearly, then, no matter how full the day may seem to be, daily reading to children is a must. Teachers who share a chapter a day of a lengthy work can build anticipation for the next installment and plant enthusiasm for a particular author or type of work. Short poems and excerpts from literature are ideal fillers for spare moments in the school day. Carefully selected and presented, oral reading can enhance enjoyment and interest in independent reading.

At the kindergarten and primary levels it is common practice for a teacher to do much reading aloud. Particularly at these levels, teachers should show the pictures as they read a story and allow time for the children to examine them. After hearing a story, the children may want to look at the book and enjoy remembering the story. Later they may read it themselves or, lacking the reading skills, pretend to.

For teachers who want to practice before reading a selection aloud, a tape recorder is a real help. Distinct articulation is basic to oral reading, as are a pleasing voice tone and pitch. Conversation needs to be read naturally, and volume should be appropriate to the content of the story. Give particular attention to dialects. Most significantly, in order to read with feeling, a teacher must be very familiar with the material.

Oral reading of a book or the works of a particular author serves as a sort of "sales pitch" to build interest. It is a good way to challenge children to extend their reading abilities, to foster tastes, and to offer the opportunity to explore customs, values, and attitudes. "Selling" should not be overdone, however, for children tire of this approach. Some reading selections demand to be read aloud and shared in their entirety simply because they are delightful, beautifully written, or powerful in their message.

Teachers today can go to a variety of reliable sources for assistance in choosing what to read aloud: book lists, book reviews in journals, publishers' catalogs, textbooks on children's literature, and knowledgeable children's librarians. Still, the task of choosing falls upon the teacher, who must accommodate a particular group of children.

Whitehead suggests that teachers follow these criteria in selecting literature to read to children:[13]

---

12. See summary in Cullinan, "Teaching Literature to Children, 1966–1972."
13. Whitehead, *Children's Literature: Strategies of Teaching,* pp. 93–94.

1. Is each book quality literature? Does it contain a meaningful message, consistent characterization, a plausible plot, and superlative style? If the book is nonfiction, is the content accurate, logical, and well-written?

2. Does the book make a significant contribution to the child's world today? Does it offer him something for future use: an idea, a value, a nugget of knowledge? Does the book give enjoyment to the listener? Does it promote appreciation?

3. Does the book spark the imaginations of the children? Does it contain genuine emotion?

4. Does the book itself gain from being shared orally because of its humor, its thought-provoking qualities, its colorful phrases, or its truths? Is it a book that children could or would not be likely to read for themselves?

5. Is the book suitable to the ages and stages of development of the students? Are the children psychologically ready for it?

6. What piece of literature is most suitable to the various class groups from the standpoint of length? If the book is for preschool or first-grade children, can it be completed in one reading? Does the longer book for older children have chapters of the proper length so that natural stopping-places may be readily identified? Does the book provide natural and stimulating "launching pads" for the next reading without necessitating undue review of what has gone before?

Special days call for selections related to them. Every teacher should have readily available a supply of stories and poems for holidays and special events, such as the first snowfall. Most libraries have a special shelf for such materials, but it would be wise for the teacher to have a private collection of favorites as well. In fact, a subject file of stories and poems and where to find them will prove invaluable.

Storytelling

A discussion of the importance of storytelling and the development of children's ability in this oral skill is part of Chapter 13, but no discussion of literature would be complete without reference to it. Story telling by the teacher is closely related to the practice of reading to children. An effective teacher of literature is a good storyteller as well as a capable reader.[14]

Storytelling is also a good technique in the following situations:

1. The teacher wishes to show the pictures in a book while telling the story.
2. The illustrations in a story are not particularly appealing, and the teacher wishes to use puppets or flannelboard figures.
3. The story itself is an excellent one, but its vocabulary is too difficult for the children.
4. The story is too long for reading, but may be shortened for telling without losing meaning.
5. The story contains lengthy descriptive passages which might cause children to lose interest.

Storytelling is an act of sharing—an even more intimate one than reading to another person or to a group. It must be an enjoyable experience for both teller and listeners. Thus, teachers should not attempt to tell stories that they do not enjoy or do not know very well. Effective storytelling requires careful preparation and practice. Under no circumstances should the storyteller attempt to memorize the entire story; however, if certain words or phrases are repeated throughout the story or if specific wording is important to the denouement, the teacher should carefully learn them. But if the way in which the author tells a story is part of its charm—as it is, for example, with Thurber's delightful fables[15]—then the teacher should read it rather than telling it.

---

14. See Caroline Feller Bauer's *Handbook for Storytellers* (American Library Association, 1977) for 381 pages of ways to bring literature to children through storytelling.

15. *The Thirteen Clocks, The White Deer*, and others.

Reading Silently

Reading is perhaps the most valuable leisure-time activity for people of all ages. Therefore, the school should do everything possible to foster the reading habit and the classroom schedule should always allow time for it.

In addition to reading and telling stories to the children, every teacher should allow time each day for pupils to browse and read or, at the primary level, look at books and become accustomed to handling them. This may also be a time when children share books, but the time should not be entirely taken up by these activities. The teacher can allocate some of this time to helping pupils to select books or, by means of extending activities, to finding out more about their interests and discovering ways to encourage them to read at higher levels or in other areas.

A currently popular approach to silent reading is USSR (Uninterrupted Sustained Silent Reading). This plan establishes a quiet time each day when everyone in the classroom or in the entire school reads a book of their choice. A feature worth emphasizing here is the example of an adult reading.

Creating a "Reading Atmosphere"

All kinds of learning are more apt to occur when the atmosphere in the classroom is pleasant and free from pressure, but reading and sharing literature, in particular, require a carefully planned setting. Both teacher and pupils should anticipate these activities with pleasure. In the lower grades, for example, grouping the children in a circle around the teacher for oral reading or story telling is not only more relaxed and informal, but it also facilitates showing illustrations and other visuals. Questions and comments by the children should not be discouraged at these times, though, of course, they should not be so prolonged that the thread of the story disappears. Similarly, when children are in the library corner, the teacher should allow them to share an amusing illustration, to help each other find books, or to work together on a group report.

Working with Libraries and Librarians

Even though the classroom has its own library corner, the school library and librarian should be an integral part of the literature program. The teacher and the librarian should work together. Most librarians welcome suggestions from teachers as to what books the library might add to its collection or the number of copies of a particular book it should contain. In addition, because the librarian has many book selection aids at hand, he or she can often be an invaluable help in finding just the right book for a reluctant reader, a book about a particular subject for a hobbyist, or a selection of books for the room library.

The librarian is a person with whom children may not come into regular contact—except by arrangement—and so many children are afraid to ask for information or help in a library. Even college students frequently do not know how valuable and willing a helper librarians can be. Thus, it is worthwhile inviting the librarian to the classroom occasionally, perhaps as a guest at a special activity or to show the children new books or tell them a story. The children should go to the library, too, and become familiar with its arrangement and its resources. In the early grades, several children might go to the library with the teacher to select books for the room library; in the middle grades, the entire class should visit the library and learn where to find different kinds of books and how to use the card catalog, and of course, individuals or small groups should have open access to the library whenever they cannot find the books they want in the room library. The classroom library is not intended to supplant the school or public library, but simply to make books readily available to the pupils and encourage them to form reading habits.

Teachers can use the public library in much the same way as the school library. If there is a story hour at the local library, arrange for students to attend it regularly. The class should make a scheduled visit to the library, learn how it is arranged, become acquainted with the librarian and other staff, and obtain library cards. Getting library cards is particularly important for children who may not have access to many books at home and whose parents do not accompany them to the library. Many neighborhoods also have special children's libraries. The teacher should know about these and take the children to visit them.

If two heads are better than one, surely several working together can make a literature program vital and exciting and can entice even the most reluctant reader to find pleasure in books.

Responding to Books

Book reports have contributed their share to the destruction of children's pleasure in reading. Teachers can do much to erase attitudes created by this traditional practice—or see that children never develop them in the first place. Encouraging children to act upon what they have read, to extend it, and to share it can do much to enhance literature program objectives at every level.

First it should be said that no rule requires that every book read must be followed up in some way. If the sole purpose of response assignments is to discover whether or not a child actually read a book, if pupils are required to read a specific number of books or pages, or if the teacher urges them to compete with each other in number of books read, they will find many ways of complying without reading books. On the other hand, if a child has enjoyed a book, he or she will also enjoy *sharing* the experience, as we have pointed out often in this book.

How can a particular child share with others his or her enjoyment of a particular book? The imaginative teacher will know many answers to this question. Perhaps a young artist might illustrate a scene from a story, draw a picture or caricature of one of the characters, prepare advertising copy for the book, create a filmstrip or slide show, design a literature game, or draw a comic strip depicting one of the scenes. Another might like to draw costumes of another era or another country or perhaps even dress a doll in an appropriate costume. Other possibilities include making maps to show the locale or topography of a story's setting; mobiles; models of ships, forts, weapons, or different types of habitation; and dioramas. Even pictures cut from magazines, neatly mounted, and titled to illustrate a story not only will add variety and appeal to individual talents and interests but also will brighten up the library corner and the entire classroom. Still other creative outlets include music, cooking, movement, dance, mime, and puppetry.

Oral activities could include describing the relation to the book of one of the objects just mentioned, reading or telling about an exciting incident, describing the character one would most like to be, composing and presenting to the class a speech that one of the characters might have made in a particular situation, or, if several children have read the same book, enacting a scene from the story. Of course, the teacher should assist in preparations for these presentations and make sure that they are meaningful to the audience. For example, in speaking as one of the book's characters, a student should say something about the circumstances that preceded the speech. In addition, the teacher should plan for variety in the type of presentations the children will make. Nothing could be deadlier than several such speeches, all given on the same day. Interest will be much greater if only two or three children give oral presentations and the audience has a chance to respond after each of them. Presentations should also be complete (neither student nor teacher should build to an exciting point and then conclude by saying, "If you want to find out what happens next, read the book"), but they should not reveal the entire story so that the rest of the class has no reason to read the book. In other words, the student can relate one incident from the book in its entirety and then tell the class, "This is just one of many amusing incidents that happened to Peter in his journey." With this technique, the speaker can pique the interest of the rest of the class and that is one of the purposes for sharing.

Written responses also have a place in the literature program, although teachers should discourage the simple recounting of the plot. Children should learn early to retell a story in a few sentences because it will help them to organize their thinking about the book and prepare them for discovering the theme. Page after page of detail is both dull and purposeless. A variety of other approaches can be much more interesting, including:

1. Write a character sketch of the most admirable character (or the most unusual or least admirable).
2. What did you learn from this book that you did not already know?
3. Describe the setting of the book. What did it look like and what kind of place was it. Was it happy, gloomy, lonely, or what? Was the setting suitable for the story?
4. Did the characters in the book behave like real people? Give examples to support your answer.
5. Write a different ending that would fit the events of the story and the way the people in it behaved.
6. Write a dialogue for one of the incidents in the story as though it were a scene from a play.
7. Write a poem that shows how the book made you feel or about the setting or one of the characters.
8. Write a letter to one of the characters in which you discuss an event or situation that occurred in the story.
9. Write a portion of a diary that one of the characters might have kept. (This could be an entry for a single day or it could cover a period of time during which a particular incident occurred.)
10. Write a letter to the book's author or illustrator and explain why you liked the book.
11. Make an individual or class book of favorite words, phrases, or passages from books.
12. Produce a classroom newsletter containing book news (e.g., books

read, new acquisitions, reports of experiences with authors or illustrators, announcements of book-related community events, book
reviews, photos of ways books have been shared in the classrooms, ads
for books).

13.   Conduct a survey to find out what books students think should win
      school book awards. Report the results.

The teacher can display products of such activities on bulletin boards or
compile them in attractively covered notebooks and add them to the library corner to help children in selecting books. Or the children themselves can make a
card file to which each class member may contribute descriptions of books they
especially liked and want to recommend to other students. Cards should be at
least 5 by 8 inches in size, perhaps even larger. For uniformity, students could
follow a set format in filling out their cards. Here is an example they might use:

Name of book _____
Name of author _____
Principal characters (tell their names and who they are):

Where and when does the story take place?

What is the book about (in three sentences)?

Why did you particularly like this book?

Making these cards can be excellent preparation for writing book reviews,
which children should learn to do in the upper grades. Writing a good review is
difficult and requires careful preparation. A first step is for the teacher to
distribute copies of several reviews of different kinds of books, such as a collection
of stories, a novel, a nonfiction selection, and a book of pictures, photographs, or
maps, or make transparencies so that all pupils can see them at the same time.
Class discussion can focus on similarities and differences and students can discuss
which ones they think are best and which of the books described might be interesting to read. Following this discussion, the class could draw up a list of questions that a good review might answer, perhaps including the following:

1. What is the name of the book?
2. Who wrote it?
3. Who are the main characters? What kind of people are they?
4. What is the book about?
5. Is the author trying to prove something about people or life?
6. Does he or she succeed in this purpose? Did the author persuade you that he or she is right?
7. Are the illustrations appropriate and interesting?
8. What is the setting of the story? Is it suited to the characters and the purpose of the story?
9. Are historical information, scientific data, and so on accurate?
10. What kind of people would like this book?
11. What are the strengths and weaknesses of the book?
12. Are there any special features that make the book unusual—illustrations, language, relation of author to content, and so on?

After they have formulated their questions, the children could discuss whether all of them are suitable for every type of book; or they could pick books that most of them know and decide which questions would be appropriate to answer in a review of each. So that students could use their questions later when they are writing their own reviews, the teacher could duplicate the list and add an introduction similar to the following:

> This is a list of questions that a book review might answer. When you are ready to write a review, decide which questions are appropriate for the book you have read and arrange them in the order in which you think they should be answered. After each question, briefly note the information you think the answer should include. This is the outline for your paper; use it to write a first draft and then decide what corrections and improvements you want to make. Select a suitable title and write the final draft neatly in ink.

This plan avoids dull, stereotyped reports and teaches organization of information. Additionally, it helps pupils to see that general principles provide a framework, but that each book, like individual people, is different in some way from all others. Of course, children need assistance in learning to select the appropriate questions and the information necessary to answer them. An excellent preparation for this task is to have them select a story or book that they have read together—perhaps even a textbook—choose relevant questions and decide what information the answers should include. Working together, the class can turn this outline into a composition, which the teacher writes on the chalkboard or on a transparency. This exercise helps to teach children not to begin each section with the question it answers. Posting the best of these reviews on the bulletin board or putting them into a booklet will enable the children to use them as models.

Group Reading

If a literature program is to respond to individual needs, interests, and abilities, children must select their reading material for themselves. But they can develop insights and understandings by exchanging ideas about a common reading experience. From the very beginning, selections that the teacher reads to the class can be a springboard for discussion of ideas and ways to present them, for group composition, or for individual creative efforts on a common theme. In the middle and upper grades, groups may read the same selection. The teacher should use great care and accept student suggestions in choosing material for collective reading. Under no circumstances should a teacher use a particular selection simply because enough copies are available or plan to have a class read every selection in a literature book. Even a difficult book may be a successful choice if the pupils have a purpose for reading it, and a simple one may capture the most precocious student if its theme is captivating and its language pleasing. If class members' interests and abilities are particularly diverse, it might be wise to choose several stories with some common element that could lead to plans for group activities—perhaps a panel discussion about the ideas presented or a dramatization of one episode of a story—or group discussions of their common experience. In any case, a selection for group reading should meet these criteria:

1. Is it suitable to the interests of the group?
2. Does it have an enduring theme or purpose?
3. Does it fit the reading abilities of members of the group?
4. Can it lead to some activity that will extend the literary understanding and appreciation of the pupils who will read it?

SPECIAL CONSIDERATIONS IN TEACHING POETRY

Poetry is (or should be) a vital part of the literature program, yet too many of today's schools neglect it or teach it badly. Some teachers simply do not know how to present poetry to children; others feel it has little place in the modern world; and, unfortunately, a few spoil children's appreciation because they read poetry badly or belabor analysis of form and style.

Children love rhythm, rhyme, and the sound of words. Toddlers repeat advertising jingles they hear on TV. On the playground, older children tease each other in verse—"Mary's mad, and I am glad, and I know what will please her." They write rhymes in memory books and school yearbooks—"Roses are red, violets are blue, sugar is sweet, why aren't you?" They play games like "London Bridge Is Falling Down" or "Farmer in the Dell" and jump rope to rhythmic chants. And they respond joyously to words like "hippity-hop," "galumph," and "the great gray-green greasy Limpopo River."

In the adult world, too, poetry is at least as old as recorded history. Primitive people sang chants to the gods of nature, and the ballad was one of the earliest forms of story telling. The first great literary work in the English language, *The Canterbury Tales,* was in poetic form, and audiences still flock to watch *Hamlet* and *Othello.* Successful poetic dramas have played Broadway. Musicals such as *Hello, Dolly* have broken box office records. Television jingles have made fortunes for advertising agencies. Folk songs have become the language of protest. And throughout the ages, lovers have written rhymes of varying degrees of excellence to their sweethearts and mothers have sung lullabies and recited nursery rhymes to their children. Poetry, then, is a natural way to express emotions—and perhaps in the tension-filled world of today its value is greater than ever.

Presentation of Poetry

The examples cited above suggest one key to teaching poetry: with very few exceptions (and these works are generally unsuitable for elementary grades) poems are meant to be *heard.* So much of the quality of poetry depends on its sound, as is evident from the number of poems that have been set to music.

The teacher primarily determines whether children develop an aversion for or a love of poetry. Therefore, with poetry more than with other forms of literature, the teacher's own attitude is of utmost importance. If a teacher has had unpleasant experiences with poetry—having struggled, perhaps, to recite before a class of snickering adolescents the entire prologue to *The Canterbury Tales* in the original Middle English or failed to develop a liking for poetry—the first step is to find some poetry that you like. There are many ways to ease the search. Attending a competent performance of a Shakespearean play, for example, can erase the effects of countless hours of classroom boredom. A volume of twentieth-century poetry may amaze the reader who suffered overexposure to eighteenth-century poets, or that same reader, having survived an initial reading of Pope's *Essay on Man* by some years, may be able to appreciate Pope's wisdom and artistry after rereading it. For some, learning more about poetry may be the answer, but whatever the means of discovery, the search will be well rewarded, both for the teacher and pupils, by the addition of a new dimension to literary enjoyment. Of course, young children probably will not appreciate Shakespeare, Eliot (except for *Old Possum's Book of Practical Cats*), or Pope, but these masters may help teachers to find appreciation on a personal level so that they can pass along their enthusiasm for the form itself to children.

The next step for the teacher is to explore the world of children's poetry and assemble a store of poems suitable for many occasions. These poems not only should appeal to the teacher, but also should match the children's backgrounds.

---

16. Rose Fyleman, *Fifty-one New Nursery Rhymes* (Garden City, N.Y.: Doubleday, Doran and Co., 1932).

For example, children from the inner city will probably find little meaning in the lines "Over the river and through the woods,/To Grandmother's house we go," but these children might be surprised and delighted by Rose Fyleman's "Mice"[16] or Rachel Field's "Skyscrapers":[17]

> Do skyscrapers ever grow tired
> Of holding themselves up high?
> Do they ever shiver on frosty nights
> With their tops against the sky?
> Do they feel lonely sometimes
> Because they have grown so tall?
> Do they ever wish they could lie right down
> And never get up at all?

From areas of immediate understanding pupils will move to other interests and greater appreciation, but, as with every facet of the literature program, they must start at their level of ability and experience. Perhaps this is especially true of poetry because it is an expression of emotion and must be understood before it can be appreciated. Experience can be vicarious and literature is a vehicle for such experience, but it requires a background for understanding. Pictures, records, and movies can help to create this background, and the addition of poetry brings new depth to understanding.

If poetry is a natural outgrowth of daily experience, then children should learn about it as one of the ways in which people express their feelings, not as something in which only artists and intellectuals indulge. For example, during a lesson on Indians, the teacher will surely want to tell some of the enchanting Indian legends and introduce the children to their songs and religious chants. A cold morning when the classroom windows are frosted over is a perfect time for David McCord's "Frost Pane,"[18] perhaps accompanied by the drawing of a Nalphabet or a Nelephant. Or newly fallen snow might prompt these lines:[19]

> Last night there walked across our lawn a beast we didn't know—
> We saw his little footprints marked quite plainly in the snow.
> It might have been an ocelot, or perhaps a grizzly bear—
> We *hoped* it was a dragon, come out walking from its lair;
> We didn't want a grown-up one, all fire and scales and foam,
> But just a baby dragonlet that we could carry home;
> We'd keep him in the nursery and give him a nice name,
> And have him for a fam'ly pet, with ribbons on, quite tame.

17. Reprinted with permission of Macmillan Publishing Co., Inc., from *The Pointed People*, by Rachel Field. Copyright 1924, 1930 by Macmillan Co., Inc.

18. David McCord, *Far and Few, Rhymes of the Never Was and Always Is* (Boston: Little, Brown and Co., 1952).

19. From "The Family Dragon"—with acknowledgments to Kenneth Graham in *Little Girl and Boy Land* by Margaret Widdemer, copyright 1924 by Harcourt Brace Jovanovich, Inc.; renewed 1952, by Margaret Widdemer Schauffler. Reprinted by permission of the publishers.

Naturally, poetry does not need a special occasion. If it did, children would miss many pleasurable experiences. Neither should poetry gush forth with clocklike regularity at every possible opportunity, however. Children should come to accept poetry as a unique and delightful way to express feelings about the world and all that is in it. An ordinary day in the classroom for example, might call forth Myra Cohn Livingston's "Whispers."[20]

As we noted earlier, poetry is meant to be heard. Therefore, in addition to liking poetry and creating an atmosphere for its appreciation, the teacher must learn to read it well. Reading anything well requires practice, but a poem demands special preparation so that its sound and rhythm create the desired effect. The children, too, should be aware of the need for practice before reading poems to others, and the teacher should encourage them to read aloud often, to share favorite poems with other members of the class or to perform choral poetry readings.[21] Choral reading especially enhances appreciation because it provides opportunities to experiment with different speeds, voice levels, and intonations and to discover how much the sound of poetry contributes to meaning and enjoyment. Reading aloud, either singly or together, also helps children to recognize differences in quality among poems.

Listening to records is another way to introduce children to the pleasures of hearing poetry. The teacher should listen to poetry recordings before playing them for the class, however. Hearing poets read their own work may be instructive, but some do not read well, even from their own work, and their presentations do not always inspire appreciation; professional actors often give much better renditions. Most libraries have record collections, so teachers would be wise to listen to a library copy of a recording they are considering using before purchasing it for the school.

Although the presentation of poetry should be almost exclusively oral, visual aids can make poetry more interesting. Pictures that illustrate specific poems are appropriate for use with oral presentations, and occasionally a few lines of poetry or a short poem, whether new or already known by the children, make a nice theme for a bulletin board display. For example, a bulletin board display may honor poets whose work the children enjoy. Or perhaps different classes can join in planning a tribute to poetry or to a single poet. For instance, one school had a "David McCord Day" to honor the poet who won the first National Council of Teachers of English award for excellence in poetry for children in 1977.

No teacher should feel any compulsion to teach particular poems because they are in the suggested course of study, because they are in the anthology available to the class, or because they are reputed to be classics. There are enough "good" poems to accommodate different tastes. An invaluable asset is a file of poetry titles and their sources; alternatively, the file cards may contain the complete poems. Arranged by subject or in whatever manner is convenient, this file

20. Myra Cohn Livingston, *Whispers and Other Poems* (New York: Harcourt Brace Jovanovich, Inc., 1958).
21. Choral reading is discussed in Chapter 13.

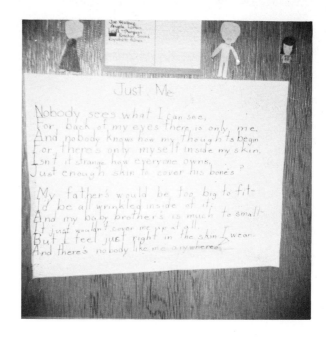

should include a generous assortment of poems suitable for holidays, the seasons of the year, and other subjects appropriate to the grade level and backgrounds of the children. Perhaps some children will want to compile poetry files of their own.

Follow-up Activities

The primary purpose of teaching poetry is to foster enjoyment and appreciation. A measure of a teacher's success will be the number of activities that develop as natural outgrowths of the program. For example, a poetry bulletin board may inspire the children to seek pictures that illustrate favorite poems. Or they may decide to make their own personal poetry scrapbooks and illustrate them with their own drawings or with pictures they cut out of magazines. And, just as pictures may be used to inspire writing, so poems may inspire drawings, which, of course, should be displayed.

  Poetry particularly kindles interest in words and ways of saying things. "In May" by Dorothy Aldis and "A Modern Dragon" by Rowena Bennett are two poems—and there are many more—that illustrate the use of metaphor in a way children can understand. Word pictures are vivid in "Fairies" by John Herndon and in "The Woodpecker" by Elizabeth Madox Roberts. John Ciardi attaches unusual meanings to *up* and *most* in "How to Tell the Top of the Hill," and "In Just" e.e. cummings introduces new words as well as entertains with "mud luscious" and "puddle wonderful." Finding poetry that uses words in novel ways seems to be a natural activity for children as they come to enjoy poetry.

155

Certainly, poetry reading inspires writing. Children will want to try writing poems themselves; even the most reluctant writer may be willing to try some verse forms. Other kinds of writing that a good poetry program may generate include stories, simple dramas, and compositions expressing personal feelings and reactions. Whatever the form, the effort should be voluntary.

Carlson suggests many enrichment or follow-up ideas, including making maps, creating games, conducting research, tape recording, and playing music.[22] Planning a "Poetry Day" for parents or for another class is another activity that children enjoy.

EVALUATION OF THE LITERATURE PROGRAM

This chapter has repeatedly emphasized that the objectives of the literature program are—and should be—most frequently stated in terms of qualities that are difficult to measure. Indeed, if being a lifelong reader is the mark of success of the elementary literature program, measurement may be impossible. This fact makes any objective evaluation of achievement in literature unrealistic. But as one writer has pointed out:[23]

> It is difficult to resist the assumption that those attributes which we can measure are the elements which we consider most important. . . . The behavorial analyst seems to assume that for an objective to be worthwhile, we must have methods of assessing progress toward these goals. Goals are derived from our needs and from our philosophies. They are not and should not be derived primarily from our measures.

If we accept this philosophy—and the objectives of the literature program—we must also accept the fact that evaluation in this area is highly subjective. Still, questions like the ones formulated by Huck (see below) may help not only in evaluation but also in the development of a literature program.[24] It is easy to see that answers to such questions are not easily arrived at.

A guide for evaluating a literature program

Availability of Books and Other Media
1. Is there a school library media center in each elementary-school building? Does it meet American Library Association standards for books and other media?

---

22. Ruth Kearney Carlson, *Literature for Children: Enrichment Ideas* (Dubuque, Iowa: William C. Brown Co., 1970).

23. Myron Atkin, "Behavioral Objectives in Curriculum Design: A Cautionary Note," in *Current Research on Instruction*, edited by Richard C. Anderson et al. (Englewood Cliffs, N.J.: Prentice-Hall, 1969), pp. 64–65.

24. From *Children's Literature in the Elementary School*, 3rd ed'n, by Charlotte S. Huck. Copyright © 1961, 1968 by Holt, Rinehart and Winston, Inc. Reprinted by permission of Holt, Rinehart and Winston and Charlotte S. Huck.

2. Is there a professionally trained librarian and adequate support staff in each building?
3. Does every classroom contain several hundred paperbacks and a changing collection of hardbacks?
4. Are reference books easily accessible to each classroom?
5. May children purchase books in a school-run paperback bookstore?
6. Do teachers encourage children to order books through various school book clubs?
7. May children take books and some media home?
8. Has the school board made some provision for keeping library media centers functioning during vacation periods?
9. Are children made aware of the program of the public library?

Time for Literature
10. Do all children have time to read books of their own choosing every day?
11. Do all teachers read to the children at least once a day?
12. Do children have time to discuss their books with an interested adult or with other children every week?
13. Are children allowed time to interpret books through art, drama, music, or writing?

Stimulating Interest
14. Do teachers show their enthusiasm for books by sharing new ones with children, reading parts of their favorite ones, discussing them, and so on?
15. Do classroom and library displays call attention to particular books?
16. Are children encouraged to set up book displays in the media center, the halls, and their classrooms?
17. Does the media specialist plan special events—such as story hours, book talks, sharing films, working with book clubs?
18. Do teachers and librarians work with parents to stimulate children's reading?
19. Are special bibliographies prepared by the librarians or groups of children on topics of special interest—such as mysteries, animal stories, science fiction, fantasy, and so on?
20. Are opportunities planned for contacts with authors and illustrators to kindle interest and enthusiasm for reading?

Balances in the Curriculum
21. Do teachers and librarians try to introduce children to a wide variety of genre and to different authors when reading aloud?
22. Do teachers share poetry as frequently as prose?
23. Do children read both fiction and nonfiction?

24. Are children exposed to new books and contemporary poems as frequently as some of the old favorites of both prose and poetry?
25. Do children have a balance of wide reading experiences with small group in-depth discussion of books?

26. Are children encouraged to keep records of their own reading?
27. Do these records go into the child's cumulative file so that the next teacher knows what he has read?
28. Do teachers give children an "Inventory on Literature" to determine their background of exposure to books?
29. Do teachers record examples of children's unsolicited responses to literature, as seen in their play, talk, art, or writing?
30. Do children seem attentive and involved, as they listen to stories? Do they have favorites which they ask to have reread?
31. Are children allowed to respond to books in a variety of ways (art, drama, writing), rather than by required book reports?
32. Is depth of understanding emphasized, rather than the number of books read?
33. Are children responding to a greater range and complexity of work?
34. Are children relating literature to their own lives?
35. Are children voluntarily reading more at school?
36. Do parents report an increase in reading at home?
37. What percentage of the children can be described as active readers? Has this percentage increased?
38. Are some children beginning to see literature as a source of life-long pleasure?

Evaluating the Professional Growth of Teachers
39. Are teachers increasing their knowledge of children's literature?
40. What percentage of the staff has taken a course in children's literature in the past five years?
41. Are some staff meetings devoted to ways of improving the use of literature in the curriculum?
42. Do teachers attend professional meetings that feature programs on children's literature?
43. Are in-service programs in literature made available on a regular basis?
44. Are such professional journals as *Language Arts* (formerly *Elementary English*), *The Horn Book*, and *Children's Literature in Education* available in every teachers' lounge?
45. Are professional books on children's literature available in each elementary school?
46. Have the teachers and librarians had a share in planning their literature programs?
47. Do teachers feel responsible not only for teaching children to read but for helping children find joy in reading?

Evaluating individual children or a class in terms of the objectives of the program is even more difficult than evaluating the program itself. Some standardized reading comprehension tests measure understanding of literature excerpts, and teachers, of course, can construct similar tests. Commercial efforts to develop literature appreciation tests have focused principally on levels beyond the elementary schools. The test "A Look at Literature," for example, is suitable for children in the fourth grade and above.[25] This test may be considered an appreciation test, but as Cooper has pointed out, it probably is only a good "measure of perceiving and interpretation."[26]

Appreciation, of course, is the key measure of an effective literature program, but the amount of reading children do is also a good clue. Teachers can usually tell which children are reading and how much. An appreciation of literature will extend learning and stimulate further literary exploration. The elementary teacher can best determine appreciation by noting how absorbed children are in what they are reading, by reading emotions on the faces as children listen, and by paying attention to their comments.

CHILDREN'S LITERATURE RESOURCES FOR TEACHERS

Hundreds of children's books are written each year and this fact alone accounts for the existence of many resources aimed toward fostering children's reading and appreciation of literature. In addition, teachers usually have an interest in good literature programs and currently national organizations and publishers seem to be placing particular emphasis on literature teaching. Thus, the resources available to teachers are so numerous that some recommendations seem appropriate.

Anthologies of Children's Literature

Several excellent anthologies and books about children's literature will help teachers to select material to read to children and to guide the children's individual reading. Many of them list sources of additional information about books.

1. May Hill Arbuthnot, *The Arbuthnot Anthology of Children's Literature* (New York: Lothrop, 1976).
2. May Hill Arbuthnot et al., eds., *Children's Books Too Good to Miss* (Bloomington: Indiana University Press, 1971).

---

25. Educational Testing Service, *A Look at Literature* (Princeton: N.J.: Educational Testing Service, 1968).
26. Charles R. Cooper, *Measuring Growth in Appreciation of Literature* (Newark, Del.: International Reading Association, 1972), p. 7.

3. Miriam Blaton Huber, *Story and Verse for Children* (New York: Macmillan Co., 1965).
4. Charlotte S. Huck, *Children's Literature in the Elementary School*, 3d ed. (New York: Holt, Rinehart and Winston, 1976).
5. Leland B. Jacobs, ed., *Using Literature with Young Children* (New York: Teachers College Press, Columbia University, 1965).
6. Edna Johnson, Carrie E. Scott, and Evelyn R. Sickels, *Anthology of Children's Literature* (Boston: Houghton Mifflin Co., 1970).
7. Nancy Larrick, *A Parent's Guide to Children's Reading* (Garden City, N.Y.: Doubleday, 1975).

Lists Published by Professional Organizations and Publishers

Many book lists are published to help teachers, parents, and librarians find the best of current titles. The most complete listing of children's books is *The Children's Catalog*, published by the H. W. Wilson Co. (950 University Avenue, New York, N.Y.) every five years and updated with annual supplements. The R. R. Bowker Co. also publishes an annual listing called *Best Books for Children* (1180 Avenue of the Americas, New York, N.Y. 10036). The American Library Association (50 E. Huron Street, Chicago, Ill. 60611) publishes *Subject Index to Books for Primary Grades*, *Subject Index to Books for Intermediate Grades*, *Subject Index to Poetry for Children and Young People*, *Subject and Title Index to Short Stories for Children*, and *Basic Book Collection for Elementary Grades*. This association also publishes book lists, as do the Association for Childhood Education International (3615 Wisconsin Avenue, N.W., Washington D.C. 20016), the Child Study Association of America (9 East 89th Street, New York, N.Y. 10028), and the Children's Book Council, Inc. (67 Irving Place, New York, N.Y. 10003). In 1977 the National Council of Teachers of English published a revised edition of *Adventuring with Books*, a topically organized and annotated list of 2500 books for prekindergarten through grade 8.

Reports and Reviews

A number of periodicals report new children's publications and review many of them:

1. *The American Library Association Bulletin* includes a section on "Notable Children's Books" in every April issue.
2. *The Booklist and Subscription Books Bulletin* is published every two weeks by the American Library Association.
3. *The Bulletin of the Center for Children's Books* is published monthly (except August) by the University of Chicago Press.

4. *Childhood Education* is published by the Association for Childhood Education International and each issue contains book reviews.
5. *The Horn Book* (Horn Book Inc., 585 Boylston Street, Boston, Mass. 05116) is published six times each year and is devoted entirely to children's literature.
6. *Instructor*, published monthly, has a section called "Books for Children."
7. *Interracial Books for Children* is published quarterly by the Council on Interracial Books for Children.
8. *Language Arts* has a monthly book review section and often has additional articles on authors, illustrators, and special books.
9. *Library Journal*, published by Bowker, is published every two weeks except in July and August, when it appears monthly.
10. *The New York Times Book Review* is a Sunday publication of book reviews that gives over special issues to children's books.
11. *Parents Magazine* (Parents Institute, 52 Vanderbilt Avenue, New York, N.Y. 02116) regularly reports on children's books.
12. *School Library Journal* is published monthly September through May by R. R. Bowker Co., (1180 Avenue of the Americas, New York, N.Y. 10036).
13. *Top of the News* is published quarterly by the American Library Association.
14. *Wilson Library Bulletin* is published monthly except July and August.

Newspapers and Magazines

Many magazines and newspapers designed for children are sources of supplementary reading material and have special appeal for some readers because they are different from books. A few of them are:

1. *Cricket Magazine* (Open Court Publishing Co., 1058 Eighth Street, LaSalle, Ill. 61301).
2. *Ebony Jr.* (Johnson Publishing Co., 820 S. Michigan Avenue, Chicago, Ill. 60605).
3. *The Electric Company Magazine* (1 Lincoln Plaza, New York, N.Y. 10023).
4. *Highlights for Children* (Highlights for Children, 2300 Fifth Avenue, West, Columbus, O.) for grades 1–6.
5. *Kids* (747 Third Ave., New York, N.Y. 10017).
6. *National Geographic World* (17th and M Streets, N.W., Washington, D.C. 20036).
7. *Ranger Rick's Nature Magazine* (National Wildlife Federation, 1412 Sixteenth St., N.W., Washington, D.C. 20036).

8.   *Sesame Street Magazine* (P. O. Box C-10, Birmingham, Ala. 34282).
9.   *Young World* (1100 Waterway Blvd., Indianapolis, Ind. 46202).

Paperback Books

Paperback books are an integral part of a literature program because they make it possible to buy a greater number of books or multiple copies of a single book. Nearly every major publisher of books for schools publishes a series of paperbacks for use in the literature program, and these add variety and vitality to the literature program. In addition, paperback book clubs are making available books to pupils themselves at little cost. Teachers, administrators, and others concerned with the literature program should make it a point to visit publishers' displays at meetings of professional organizations to try to keep up with the ever-growing number of new titles. Listings of paperbacks for children include:

1.   *Paperback Books for Children* (Scholastic Magazines, 904 Slyvan Avenue, Englewood Cliffs, N.J. 07632).
2.   *Paperback Books for Young People: An Annotated Guide to Publishers and Distributors* (American Library Association, 50 E. Huron Street, Chicago, Ill. 60611).
3.   *Paperbound Books in Print* (published monthly by R. R. Bowker Co. 1180 Avenue of the Americas, New York, N. Y. 10036).
4.   *RIF's Guide to Book Selection* (Reading Is Fundamental, Room 2407, Arts and Industries Building, Smithsonian Institute, Washington, D.C. 20560).

Book Clubs

Many children become interested in literature through the incentive of membership in a book club. Some clubs exist only for the purpose of exchanging personal books the children have. Others are primarily booksellers. Following are the names of some clubs, their addresses, and details of the age levels for which their selections are appropriate:

1.   Scholastic Book Clubs, 50 West 44th Street, New York, N.Y. 10036. Various ages.
2.   Junior Literary Guild, 277 Park Ave., New York, N.Y. 10017. Ages 5–16.
3.   Parents Magazine, Read Aloud and Easy Reading Program, 52 Vanderbilt Ave., New York, New York 10017. Ages 3–8.
4.   Weekly Reader Children's Book Club, 245 Long Hill Road, Middletown, Conn. 06457. Various ages.

5.   Young Readers Press (several clubs), Simon and Schuster, 1 West 39th
     Street, New York, N.Y. 10018.

Books for Particular Purposes

Children will develop a greater understanding of themselves and others only if
the people who select books for the literature program become more realistic in
their attempts to accomplish this goal than they have been in the past. For many
years, literature programs have included units designed to help pupils learn more
about children in other lands—and rightly so, of course—as well as stories about
the way in which individuals have met and solved personal problems. But we have
done little to help create better understanding among different groups within our
own country. The American Indian has received some attention, largely through
the social studies program, and in several stories in our literature center on the
theme of understanding people who are "different" in some way. But American
schools and American literature have developed largely in the WASP tradition.
Fortunately, however, changes are evident. Illustrations in newer books picture
children of different races, stories by and about blacks are appearing in some
quantity, and some excellent books about Jewish customs and beliefs are now
available.

Particularly noteworthy are books that emphasize similarities rather than
differences among children of different races. *Whistle for Willie*,[27] which is about
a small boy's efforts to whistle for his dog, reveals only in its illustrations that
Willie is black, and in *What Happens When You Go to the Hospital*,[28]
Karen—also black—goes to the hospital to have her tonsils removed and experiences the usual interests, fears, and pleasures of a child's first experience of
this type. Equally important are books like *The Way It Is*,[29] which portrays life in
a slum neighborhood and features photographs by fifteen black and Puerto Rican
boys. An excellent annotated bibliography of books that may help children to retain knowledge and understanding of people who live in another country or
another community or whose ethnic or cultural background is different from their
own is *Reading Ladders for Human Relations*.[30] This list or a similar one would be
a valuable addition to the library of any teacher.

Additionally, the Council on Interracial Books for Children has published a
collection of critical reviews and ratings of children's books as part of their program to promote learning materials that embody principles of cultural

---

27. Ezra Jack Keats, *Whistle for Willie* (New York: Viking Press, 1964.)
28. Arthur Shay, *What Happens When You Go to the Hospital* (New York: Reilly and Lee,
1969).
29. John Holland, ed., *The Way It Is* (New York: Harcourt, Brace and World, 1969).
30. Virginia Reid, ed., *Reading Ladders for Human Relations*, 5th ed. (Washington, D.C.:
American Council on Education, 1972).

VALUES CHECKLIST

	ART	WORDS		ART	WORDS		ART	WORDS	N.A.
anti-Racist			non-Racist			Racist omission / commission			
anti-Sexist			non-Sexist			Sexist			
anti-Elitist			non-Elitist			Elitist			
anti-Materialist			non-Materialist			Materialist			
anti-Individualist			non-Individualist			Individualist			
anti-Ageist			non-Ageist			Ageist			
anti-Conformist			non-Conformist			Conformist			
anti-Escapist			non-Escapist			Escapist			
Builds positive image of females/ minorities			Builds negative image of females/ minorities				Excellent	Good	Fair	Poor
						Literary quality			
Inspires action vs. oppression			Culturally authentic			Art quality			

N.A. stands for Not Applicable.

"Racist by omission" means that third world people could logically have been included but were not.

"Racist by commission" means that the words or the art were openly racist in some way which the book's analysis will detail.

"Non" before a negative value means that the book's impact was neutral in that regard.

"Anti" before a negative value means that the book made some positive impact.

"Inspires action against oppression" means that the book not only describes injustice but in some way encourages readers to act against injustice.

Note: The Checklist will always *follow* the analysis of the book.

pluralism.[31] This checklist, which follows an evaluation of each book, reveals the priorities of the council.

The array of resources for teachers of children's literature is varied and rich, as is the body of that literature. For teachers, the challenge is to know its range and to learn the strengths and limitations of its offerings.

---

31. Reprinted from *Human and Anti-human Values in Children's Books* by the Council on Interracial Books for Children. The council also operates the Racism and Sexism Resource Center for Educators and has a free catalog of antiracist, antisexist teaching materials. Write to the council at 1841 Broadway, New York, N.Y. 10023.

EXERCISES FOR THOUGHT AND ACTION

1. Begin a poetry index by typing favorite poems on 5" × 8" cards. Make it expandable so you can encourage children to contribute their favorites to the file, and help them to develop a categorizing scheme that will give easy access to a poem.

2. For future reference, make a categorized list of ways children can respond to a book. Consult *Adventuring with Books* (NCTE, 1977). Select one book that you like and "sell" it to a group of your peers using a method from your list.

3. Divide the class into small groups and design a classroom library/reading center. Produce a rough floor plan and a list of materials. Discuss ways to involve children in planning the center. Share your ideas with other groups.

4. Plan a five-day teaching unit for a group of your choice about an author or illustrator of children's books. Include your objectives, a summary of your research on the person, five detailed lesson plans, and a resource bibliography.

5. Consult several literature curriculum guides for program objectives, suggested content and materials, and activities. Report your findings.

6. Are you a reader? Why or why not? List ten of your favorite children's books. Why do you value each book?

7. Examine three different elementary language arts textbook series at the grade level that primarily interests you. How much literature does each include? How do the publishers or authors suggest teaching it?

8. Formulate several ways that you can be a model of enthusiasm for reading and literature appreciation. Suggest how parents can serve as positive role models.

9. Prepare a story to read orally to a small group of your peers. Ask them to tell you both what you did well and how you could improve.

10. Bring to class resources assigned to you from the categories comprising the resources section of this chapter (anthologies, book lists, book reviews, newspapers/magazines, paperback books, book clubs, and books for particular purposes). Introduce the resource briefly to the class, then display it for individual examination to create the semblance of a book fair.

11. Examine catalogs and holdings of local library/media facilities. Compile a bibliography of nonprint resources for sharing literature with children. In particular, look for recordings, films, and filmstrips produced by Weston Woods, Scholastic, Caedmon, Miller-Brody, Folkways, Viking, National Film Board of Canada, Spoken Arts, American Library Association, Coronet, and Crowell-Collier-Macmillan.

12. Plan an in-service program for teachers on the subject of children's literature. You may want to preview and include a film, such as "The Lively Art of Picture Books" or "American Songfest," both by Weston Woods. An

alternative resource is the series "Prelude: Children's Book Council Mini-Seminars on Using Books Creatively," a collection of audio-cassettes produced by the CBC (67 Irving Place, New York, N.Y. 10003).

13. Tour a school and a home. Based on your observations draw conclusions about the value placed on literature in each environment.
14. Begin a file of biographical material, pictures, and other information about children's authors and illustrators.
15. Choose a children's book that you would enjoy sharing with children. List activities that would extend the children's pleasure in that book.

SELECTED REFERENCES

Bader, Barbara. *American Picture Books from Noah's Ark to The Beast Within*. New York: Macmillan Co., 1976.

Bettelheim, Bruno. *The Uses of Enchantment*. New York: Alfred A. Knopf, 1977.

Cullinan, Bernice E., and Carmichael, Carolyn W., eds. *Literature and Young Children*. Urbana, Ill.: National Council of Teachers of English, 1977.

Hopkins, Lee Bennett. *Books Are by People: Interviews with 104 Authors and Illustrators of Books for Young Children*. Englewood Cliffs, N.J.: Citation Press, 1969.

Hopkins, Lee Bennett. *More Books by More People: Interviews with Sixty-five Authors of Books for Children*. Englewood Cliffs, N.J.: Citation Press, 1974.

Huck, Charlotte S. *Children's Literature in the Elementary School*, 3rd ed. New York: Holt, Rinehart and Winston, 1976.

Hughes, Rosalind. *Let's Enjoy Poetry*. Boston: Houghton Mifflin Co., 1966.

Johnson, Edna; Sickels, Evelyn R.; and Sayers, Frances C. *Anthology of Children's Literature*. Boston: Houghton Mifflin Co., 1970.

Karl, Jean. *From Childhood to Childhood: Children's Books and Their Creators*. New York: John Day Co., 1970.

Lamb, Pose, ed. *Literature for Children Series*. Dubuque, Iowa: Wm. C. Brown Co. Includes Dewey W. Chambers, *Storytelling and Creative Drama*, 1970; Patricia Cianciolo, *Illustrations in Children's Books*, 1970; Ruth Kearney Carlson, *Enrichment Ideas*, 1970; Margaret C. Gillespie, *History and Trends*, 1970; Virginia Witucke, *Poetry in the Elementary School*, 1970; Bernice Cullinan, *Its Discipline and Content*, 1971; and Mary Montebello, *Children's Literature in the Curriculum*, 1972.

Purves, Alan, and Beach, Richard. *Literature and the Reader: Research in Response to Literature, Reading Interests, and the Teaching of Literature*. Urbana, Ill.: National Council of Teachers of English, 1972.

Smith, Dora V. *Fifty Years of Children's Books*. Urbana, Ill.: National Council of Teachers of English, 1963.

Sutherland, Zena, and Arbuthnot, May Hill. *Children and Books*, 5th ed. Chicago: Scott, Foresman and Co., 1977.

Whitehead, Robert. *Children's Literature: Strategies of Teaching*. Englewood Cliffs, N.J.: Prentice-Hall, 1968.

II

RECEIVING LANGUAGE

There has to be a listener around for a speaker to get his point across. . . . Writing has no purpose without a reader. The receiver of a message, whether listener or reader, has to make a contribution at least as great as that of the transmitter if communication is to occur.—*Frank Smith,* Understanding Reading

The receptive language arts—listening and reading—are the subject of the four chapters in this unit. Individuals receive verbal communication by listening and reading. Both activities require the perception, identification, and interpretation of language symbols and reaction to them to achieve understanding. In this sense, reading and listening skills are essentially the same, and the two activities have much in common.

Reading receives far more attention from both children and teachers, but this fact does not mean that listening is less important. For too long a time concern about children's listening abilities has been more obvious than attempts to develop listening skills. Chapter 7 represents an effort to change this state of affairs by focusing attention on listening instruction. Chapter 6 explores the skills that listening and reading both require, and Chapters 8 and 9 emphasize reading.

The objective of these chapters is to aid teachers in developing children's abilities to derive, interpret, and apply meaning effectively to the language that they hear and read. Thus the focus is on children's language ability as it relates to both reading and listening and the skills necessary to use this knowledge.

6

Listening and Reading:
Their Relationships

Listening and reading are both receptive communication acts . . . they are alike because the individual brings to both the same experience background and employs many of the same thinking skills in each. —*Stanford E. Taylor*, Listening: What Research Says to the Teacher

Earlier in the book, we identified listening and reading as the receptive language arts. In this chapter we will examine the relationships between these two language arts, as well as the research that uncovered them and the implications of those relationships for learning and teaching. The crux of these relationships lies in the thinking that both readers and listeners must do in order to make sense of their reading and listening. The skills needed to process the messages in each mode of presentation are evidence that the two acts are similar. In addition to discussing their similarities, we will make several observations about reading and listening instruction.

LANGUAGE AND THINKING

Comprehension of spoken and written material requires the use of both language and thought. Without language and the ability to manipulate it, we would have no way of representing what we have heard or read. Thinking allows us to process

170

the ideas we receive from reading and listening and to relate them to our
storehouse of knowledge.

Few people would disagree that thinking and language are interrelated, but
we have not always had a consensus on the nature of their relationship. The noted
linguist Sapir, stressing the primary nature of language, stated "that language is
an instrument originally put to uses lower than the conceptual plane and that
thought arises as a refined interpretation of its content."[1] Taking the opposite
view, the Russian psychologist Vygotsky wrote, "The bond between thought and
words is a living process; thought is brought forth in words. The word deprived of
thought, is a dead word."[2] Regardless of the differences in these viewpoints, both
writers, significantly, recognized the interaction of language and thought.
Children certainly develop language and thinking in the same context: experience. In other words, the array of sounds, sights, smells, and other sensations
that children experience stimulate their first thoughts and their first use of
language.

As we discussed in Chapter 3, very young infants learn about their environment in nonverbal ways, through direct interaction, touching, tasting, and
manipulating. As they mature, their sensations fuse or become organized into
awareness patterns or perceptions to which they react. At first these perceptions
are not attached to language. The spoon and the jar of baby food have meaning
for an infant without mother saying, "It's time to eat," or "Are you hungry?" As
the child matures, however, most perceptions become concepts that are
represented symbolically: language is attached to them. This representation
begins when the child associates a particular language utterance with
characteristics of the context in which he or she has heard it. For instance, after
repeatedly hearing the word "Mommy," the child becomes aware that a particular person is present when he hears it. Still the child does not know if this person is "Mommy" or something else in the environment is. Thus the child must go
through a sorting out, or delimiting, of the term to make the accurate association.
This process continues usually until the child learns that by approximating the
sound of "Mommy," he or she can attract attention from this particular person.

Once a child has attached some meaning to a word, however incomplete it
is, he or she will use that meaning accordingly. The word becomes part of his or
her language and its meaning enters a storehouse of knowledge.

PROCESSING OF LANGUAGE RECEIVED

The thinking/language manipulation that occurs as young children attach meaning to words is a process that continues throughout life. This activity occurs, of

1. Quoted in Carl A. Lefevre, "A Multidisciplinary Approach to Language and to Reading: Some
Projections," in *The Psycholinguistic Nature of the Reading Process*, edited by Kenneth S. Goodman
(Detroit: Wayne State University Press, 1973), p. 294.
2. Ibid., p. 295.

course, in the mind of the receiver—listener or reader—and, in its first phase, it is a reaction to units of language in a message. Because of the knowledge we have about how language operates and because of the structured and systematic nature of language, including the high degree of redundancy in it, we do not need to take in every letter or phoneme, word or phrase to receive a message.[3] Instead, as listeners or readers, we sample the total language of the message. Accepting the validity of the sampling process certainly does not mean that instruction in reading and listening skills can be minimal. How much sampling is necessary and the rapidity with which it occurs depends on the language ability of the receiver and his or her relationship to the content of the message. The language ability of the receiver particularly includes knowledge of the language structures in which that message is presented. When children are beginning to develop proficiency in reading, for example, they are unfamiliar with the written form of language, sometimes with its structures, and possibly the context of the message they want to read. Consequently, they require many more sampling cues than they will need later. Similarly, listeners must follow messages more closely (sample more extensively) if the language "sounds unnatural" to them, or if they have difficulty relating what they hear to something they already know.

The second processing activity is reconstructing the meaning of a message from the partial cues or fragments received. Again, the effectiveness of this reconstruction depends on the experience and language ability of the receiver. Differences in individual experiences are reflected in language abilities as well as in the storehouse of meanings at our disposal. Therefore the receiver's reconstruction is never totally that which the writer or speaker intended. The closer the experiences of the receiver parallel those of the transmitter, if language abilities also match, the closer the receiver's reconstruction will be.

RELATIONSHIPS REPORTED FROM RESEARCH

The relationships between listening and reading have been the focus of much research. Of particular interest has been the relationship that emerges from studies of achievement test scores. For example, in a comparatively early study of this relationship, Plessas reported correlation coefficients ranging from .27 to .80 for listening test scores and measures of achievement obtained through reading tests.[4] Lundsteen reported a correlation of .52 between critical listening and

---

3. References to the theory and research that is the basis for this description of language processing may be found in Laurence Walker, "Comparative Study of Selected Reading and Listening Processes, in *Insights into Why and How to Read*, edited by Robert T. Williams (Newark, Del.: International Reading Association, 1976), pp. 39–46.

4. Gus P. Plessas, "Reading Abilities and Intelligence Factors of Children Having High and Low Auditing Ability," Ph.D. dissertation, University of California, 1957.

reading achievement at the fifth-grade level.[5] Several years later, in a discussion of research related to reading and listening comparisons, Devine reported that researchers correlating scores from standardized tests of reading and listening had cited coefficients of .74, .76, .77, and .82.[6] Researchers appear to have accepted a strong correlation for tests of reading and listening comprehension and, in general, no longer report coefficients. The few who do report them support the findings of the earlier studies.[7]

In the context of correlational studies, Devine and others have questioned what the listening tests measure. Devine suggests that they measure verbal comprehension rather than skills specific to listening.[8] Of course, aside from measurement of word identification or decoding ability, the same might be said about reading tests.

Another debated issue that has received research attention is whether reading or listening is the principal source of learning. Hampleman, who compared the listening and reading comprehension of fourth-grade and sixth-grade pupils, found that listening comprehension was superior to reading comprehension at both grade levels.[9] He also reported that sixth-grade pupils were superior to fourth-grade pupils in both listening and reading ability and that boys scored higher than girls in listening comprehension of difficult material. In a more recent study, Breiter confirmed the higher listening scores among boys and also reported that sixth-grade children of above-average intelligence learned more by reading than by listening.[10] Hampleman earlier had suggested investigating specifically what kinds of subject matter are most suitable for auditory presentation; on an informal level, teachers can pursue this investigation without waiting for published reports.

Several researchers since Hampleman have found that some persons are better adapted to learning by visual means than auditory means and vice versa. Therefore Hampleman's contention that listening is more conducive to learning difficult material may not always be true.[11] After studying second-, third-, and fourth-grade children's comprehension of material of the same readability level presented by the two modes, Swain reported that "both methods of learning need

5. Sara Lundsteen, "Teaching Abilities in Critical Listening in the Fifth and Sixth Grades." Ph.D. dissertation, University of California, 1963.

6. Thomas G. Devine, "Reading and Listening: New Research Findings," *Elementary English* 45 (March 1968): 346–48.

7. For example, Paul Shafer ("An Analysis of the Effects of Listening, Reading, and Critical Thinking Abilities of Eleventh Grade Students," Ph.D. dissertation, University of Southern Mississippi, 1971) found a coefficient of .80 on listening and reading measures.

8. Devine, p. 348.

9. Richard S. Hampleman, "Comparison of Listening and Reading Comprehension Ability of Fourth and Sixth Grade Pupils," *Elementary English* 35 (January 1958): 49–51.

10. Joan C. Breiter, "Reading or Listening: A Comparison of Techniques of Instruction in Elementary Social Studies," *The Alberta Journal of Educational Research*, (June 1975), p. 21.

11. Robert J. Kibler, II, "The Impact of Message Style and Channel in Communications," Ph.D. dissertation, Ohio State University, 1962.

to be used in lower elementary classrooms . . . [and that] which one is used with each child depends upon the relationship of reading ability and the readability level of the article."[12]

Another aspect of the relationship—and the one often considered the most important for teachers—concerns the improvement of reading by teaching listening and the improvement of listening by teaching reading. Research regarding this relationship has produced conflicting findings, the majority of such studies have indicated that listening instruction may enhance reading instruction, particularly at the first-grade level.[13] Variations in these findings may be due to dissimilarities in the tasks involved in the two types of lessons, as well as dissimilarities between the lessons and the test materials.[14] Also, the short-term duration of some experiments undoubtedly made possible greater variation. For the most part, too, the effort in the experiments was to improve reading skills by teaching listening, rather than the other way around, so that generalizations about the transfer of skills may be based largely on research that had a single focus.

SKILLS COMMON TO READING AND LISTENING

Reading and listening require the application of similar skills in order to process information. In both reading and listening, no single sound or letter—not even a word—is the unit of comprehension, although we may sample the cues any of them provide. Essentially, comprehension occurs because we understand the structure (the grammatical pattern) of the language heard or read and can relate the content to our experience. Rapid and accurate perception of language is the first step in skilled listening and skilled reading. Perception presents no particular problem if we know the words and can hear or see them without interference. On the other hand, an unfamiliar word may force us to attend to individual sounds, letters, and words in order to comprehend the larger language units. Thus, in both reading and listening, we must know how to determine the meanings of unknown words as well as larger units of expression.

The beginning reader knows virtually no words in their graphic form and has to learn to interpret the meanings of graphic symbols. Basically, the reader learns to associate (by being told, relating to pictures, etc.) what he or she sees with spoken words. In other words, the reader develops an ability to perceive words quickly and acquires a sight vocabulary that permits him or her to recognize these graphic forms in other contexts. This sight vocabulary grows as a

---

12. James E. Swain, "Is Listening Really More Effective for Learning in the Early Grades," *Elementary English* 51 (November/December 1974): 1110–13.

13. Estoy Reddin, "Informal Listening Instruction and Reading Improvement," *The Reading Teacher* 22 (May 1969): 742–45.

14. Sara W. Lundsteen, *Listening, Its Impact at All Levels on Reading and the Other Language Arts* (Urbana, Ill.: National Council of Teachers of English/Educational Resources Information Center Clearinghouse on Reading and Communication Skills, 1979), p. 4.

child learns skills that aid in adding to it, reads more often and increasingly infers the meanings of new words, and generally matures in terms of language experiences. Skills for adding words to the sight vocabulary include making sound associations (phonics), making visual associations (structural analysis), and deriving meaning from the context in which unknown words appear (see Chapter 9 for a discussion of these skills).

Learning to listen is a similar task. Although children develop rather large aural or listening vocabularies at an early age, they need to be able to determine the meanings of unfamiliar words in an aural context. Unfortunately, however, this process is more difficult than interpreting unknown words in print. A listener cannot stop the listening activity in order to analyze a sequence of sounds, and ordinarily it is not possible to "go back" and relisten. Still, a listener can construct meanings from the context, from clues in the speaker's facial expressions or gestures, and from the organization of the message. Moreover, speech includes more redundancies than written language does; a speaker tends to say the same thing in different ways much more often than the writer does. Nevertheless the listening vocabulary grows in many of the same ways as the sight vocabulary (repetition of a word in several contexts, being told, etc.).

Both reading and listening also require paying attention to signals—punctuation marks in reading and pauses and intonation in listening. The reader, furthermore, must attend to other conventions—spelling, indentations, and other ways of setting off particular points or ideas (numbering of statements or poetry forms, for instance). On the other hand, the listener must notice voice inflections (tone, volume, rhythm) as well as gestures and other visual cues. Both listener and reader need to be alert for signals that certain words provide ("on the other hand," "first," "moreover," "last," etc.).

In addition to these parallel skills, a host of comprehension skills are common to both listening and reading. While these may be regarded by some persons as thinking skills—or even thinking behaviors—ability to use them effectively requires that they be taught to children.[15] They include the ability to determine the main idea; to perceive details accurately; to follow directions; to understand denotative and connotative meanings; to select information pertinent to a specific topic; to follow the sequence of a plot, explanation, or argument; to recognize relationships of cause and effect, time, space, and place; to understand figurative and idiomatic language; and to distinguish among fact, fiction, and fancy.

The extent to which an individual has mastered the above skills reflects overall language ability. Other skills are closely related to the degree of attention the receiver gives the material. If we are only passively attentive in either listening or reading, we are likely to miss clues to understanding. Inadequate language ability and experience will cause a person to be unaware of the significance of such things as figurative language and differences between fact and fancy. Both listeners and readers should also be able to determine the author's or speaker's purpose and organization, make inferences from the context, form sensory images, detect bias and prejudice, separate the relevant from the irrelevant in the context, and arrive at a conclusion or course of action based on what they have heard or read.

DIFFERENCES BETWEEN LISTENING AND READING

The similarities between listening and reading should by now be obvious to the reader, but it is equally obvious that these receptive acts are also different. First of all, oral language symbols are different from written language. In addition, noise that prevents or masks hearing interferes with listening. According to Carroll, "The listener must have a continuous set to listen and understand," and this set is susceptible to physical and psychological factors other than noise. Some of these factors—extraneous thoughts entering the mind or fatigue, for example—may also affect reading, but the reader can stop, rest, or continue with less than desirable alertness and review the material later.[16] Thus, while a reader also may become fatigued or notice his or her mind wandering and possibly suffer blurred vision as a result, he or she does not have to sustain the same level of attentiveness that a listener does, so this type of interference is not as bothersome. Simply put, listeners' reception is largely in the speaker's control, whereas readers control their reception.

Another difference between reading and listening is that much spoken

---

15. Lundsteen, "Listening," p. 61.
16. John B. Carroll, "Development of Native Language Skills Beyond the Early Years," in *The Learning of Language*, edited by Carroll E. Reed (New York: Appleton-Century-Crofts, 1971), p. 127.

language (but not all, of course) differs in form and vocabulary from written language. As mentioned earlier, there are more redundancies in spoken messages, which also tend to be much less formal than almost all written language. Speech also reflects social, ethnic, and regional dialects, but written work seldom does (except for some vocabulary choices). You may have heard that "Writing is speech written down," but it really is much more than that. Few people write the way they talk.

The spoken language that we hear most often is spontaneous speech, which has a less varied vocabulary and fewer subordinate elements than does writing.[17] It is also characterized by mazes, false starts, repetition, and sentence fragments.[18] The effect of these characteristics, which may be considered deficiencies as well as extraneous cues, may be to obscure the message by confusing the listener and interfering with the sampling process. This problem is most likely to occur when listening to a recorded speech, however. When the listener can see the speaker, the setting and the extralinguistic signals of the speaker's gestures and facial expressions contribute visual cues that compensate, to some extent, for deficiencies of speech. Of course, too many of these characteristics—particularly repetition— may distract the listener from important elements of the message.

Evidently listeners tend to reproduce these features of speech in their own speaking or writing. Asked to relate what they have heard, listeners often use more words, looser constructions, and more repetition than people who are asked to reproduce something they have read.[19] Readers' reproductions tend to correspond more closely to the intended meaning, so perhaps the more formal written language influences readers in cue selection and meaning reconstruction.[20]

The point of delineating these differences between reading and listening is to emphasize further that generalizations about the transfer of skills from one activity to the other (which we believe is possible if properly planned and taught) does not mean that listening and reading need not receive separate instructional attention.

AN OVERVIEW OF READING AND LISTENING INSTRUCTION

Acceptance of the relationship between listening and reading suggests that we look for common objectives and methods for teaching them. Effective listening and reading instruction requires a certain amount of preparation, which may in-

---

17. Laurence Walker, "Comprehending Writing and Spontaneous Speech," *Reading Research Quarterly* 11 (1975–76): 146.

18. Walter Loban, *Language Development: Kindergarten Through Grade Twelve* (Urbana, Ill.: National Council of Teachers of English, 1976), p. 58.

19. Milton W. Horowitz and Alan Berkowitz, "Listening and Reading, Speaking and Writing: An Experimental Investigation of Differential Acquisition and Reproduction of Memory," *Perceptual and Motor Skills* 1967 (No. 24): 207–15.

20. Walker, p. 164.

clude vocabulary enrichment sufficient to the tasks, fostering interest in language activities, and the development of the ability to follow and remember a short sequence of ideas. These teaching tasks may not be easy to accomplish because of the great variation in children's backgrounds and abilities. Nor is it possible for a teacher to assume that because children enter school with considerable experience in listening, they are better prepared for classroom listening activities than for reading.

At the individual and group levels, listening and reading skills flourish in a relaxed, meaningful setting, in which the ideas and the language of the material are at least partly familiar. Also, reception by each method is more effective when its purpose is clear and receivers know what that purpose is. In general, the purpose of reading and listening can be functional or appreciative or both; one does not preclude the other. Generally, though, in functional reading and listening, the task is to find facts, get a general idea, follow directions, or put the material to work in some way, whereas in appreciative reading and listening, the goal is to enjoy a selection for its own sake, as in reading a story for its humor or listening to a poem for its expressive words.

Readers and listeners similarly have several operational levels depending on their purposes, which range from passive recognition to active, creative use of materials and ideas (see Chapter 7). This range of operational levels suggests numerous techniques for developing skills conducive to effective learning through either listening or reading.

As a final note, teachers should capitalize on the similarities of reading and listening, but they should not divert instructional attention toward either or both of them at the expense of a unified focus on teaching language arts skills in genuine communication situations.

EXERCISES FOR THOUGHT AND ACTION

1. While reading and listening are considered the receptive language arts and are frequently paired together in discussions, what case could you make for pairing listening and speaking? Reading and writing?
2. Ask teacher friends whether they perceive the good listeners in their classes to be good readers as well.
3. Based on your own observations, do you believe good readers are also always good listeners? If you believe that they are not, how do you account for the variation?
4. Correlations between listening and reading are based on tests of listening ability and of reading ability. What do you suspect may be a major weakness of such studies?
5. This chapter suggested several instructional guidelines for both listening and reading. One of these was "fostering interest in language activities." What does this phrase mean? What would you do at a grade level of your choice to foster interest in language activities?

6.   Based on your observations and experience, do you think teachers emphasize similarities in reading and listening in teaching one or the other? Explain your answer.

7.   What research evidence indicates that transfer of skills in listening to reading may occur? Is there evidence of transfer the other way? Does careful program planning increase skill transfer? What sort of "careful planning " is necessary?

8.   Oral language that is read is generally considered to be more difficult to understand than if it is spoken. If this statement is true how would you account for the phenomenon?

SELECTED REFERENCES

Barker, Larry L. *Listening Behavior.* Englewood Cliffs, N.J.: Prentice-Hall, 1971.

Duckworth, Eleanor. "The Language and Thought of Piaget: And Some Comments on Learning to Spell." In *A Forum for Focus,* edited by Martha L. King, Robert Emans, and Patricia J. Cianciolo, pp. 15–31. Urbana, Ill.: National Council of Teachers of English, 1973.

Duker, Sam. "Listening." In *Encyclopedia of Educational Research,* 4th ed., edited by Robert L. Ebel, pp. 747–52. New York: Macmillan Co., 1969.

Lundsteen, Sara W. *Listening, Its Impact at All Levels on Reading and the Other Language Arts.* Urbana, Ill.: National Council of Teachers of English/Educational Resources Information Center Clearinghouse on Reading and Communication Skills, 1979.

Menyuk, Paula. *The Acquisition and Development of Language.* Englewood Cliffs, N.J.: Prentice-Hall, 1971.

Ruddell, Robert B. *Reading-language Instruction: Innovative Practices.* Englewood Cliffs, N.J.: Prentice-Hall, 1974. Chapter 11.

Singer, Harry, and Ruddell, Robert B., eds. *Theoretical Models and Processes of Reading.* Newark, Del.: International Reading Association, 1976.

Thorn, Elizabeth A. *Teaching the Language Arts.* Toronto: Gage Educational Publishing, 1974. Chapters 2 and 4.

Williams, Robert T., ed. *Insights into Why and How to Read.* Newark, Del.: International Reading Association, 1976.

7

Listening Instruction

—What's new in listening? It's a completely different world from the one in which I grew up. . . . Today we must find out what they listen to, what they listen for, whether several levels of listening can go on at a time, and provide the time and climate in which ideas can be explored, hypotheses developed, data gathered, and conclusions drawn.—Miriam E. Wilt, A Forum for Focus

Most kindergarten or first-grade teachers will testify that children coming to school for the first time have learned a great deal through listening. They will also say that it is apparent that these children demonstrate listening skill in the communication activities in which they engage. Yet the same teachers also often say that children "don't listen" or "don't know how to listen," and as the children progress through school, other teachers echo this opinion.

Of course, young children do listen to speech and other sounds that interest them or are significant to their lives. They listen effectively if what they hear is presented well and is within their language abilities and experience. The fact that children have acquired considerable listening ability, however, does not mean that listening skills need not be part of their language arts instruction. Rather, the ability young children have in listening provides the basis for an instructional program that will develop their skills further. Thus, the teacher should strive to motivate children to listen, maintain and refine existing skills, alleviate poor habits, provide meaningful practice, and teach children to evaluate and criticize what they hear.

THE NATURE OF LISTENING

Listening involves more than just hearing or paying attention. Effective listening requires active and conscious attention to sounds in order to gain meaning from them. We may listen to an interesting speaker, to the music of a fine orchestra, or to traffic sounds as we drive. In each of these endeavors we react to what we hear.

As discussed in Chapter 6, listening and thinking are closely interrelated. Lundsteen has stated that "listening refers to the process by which spoken language is converted to meaning in the mind."[1] She then warns about defining a complex process in a sentence.

For instructional purposes, however, it is convenient to think of the listening process as having four steps: (1) hearing, (2) understanding, (3) evaluating, and (4) responding. First we *hear* a series of sounds, the actual words and sentences. Second, we *understand* the meanings of these words and sentences in the context in which we have heard them. Third, we *evaluate* the meanings and accept or reject the total communication. Finally, we *respond* to what we have heard with further thought, bodily movement, facial expression, or audible reaction.

Those four steps apply to all acts of receiving communication by auditory means, but some researchers prefer to think of the total act as having three distinguishable stages: hearing, listening, and auding.[2] From this point of view, *hearing* is the process by which we receive and modify sound waves by ear, *listening* is the process of becoming aware of the sound components and recognizing these components in sequences that have meaning, and *auding* is the process of translating the flow of sound sequences of speech into meaning. Nichols and Lewis do not use the term "auding," but they describe essentially the same process in fewer stages.[3] They say that hearing and listening obviously are not identical and should be thought of as two distinguishable phases: the receiving of sound and the interpreting of sound. The first phase (hearing) requires perceiving sounds and discriminating among them; during the second (listening) phase, we attach meaning to these sounds.

TYPES OF LISTENING

Everyone listens in different ways at different times and in different situations. An instructional program needs to take into account when different types of

---

1. Sara W. Lundsteen, *Listening, Its Impact at All Levels on Reading and the Other Language Arts* (Urbana, Ill.: National Council of Teachers of English/Educational Resources Information Center Clearinghouse on Reading and Communication Skills, 1979), p. 1.

2. Stanford E. Taylor, *What Research Says to the Teacher: Teaching Listening* (Washington, D.C.: National Education Association, April 1964), p. 1.

3. Ralph G. Nichols and Thomas R. Lewis, *Speaking and Listening* (Dubuque, Iowa: William C. Brown Co., 1965), p. 6.

listening are appropriate, as well as the nature or process of listening and the skills involved. The literature describes numerous ways of classifying types of listening: appreciational, informational, and critical;[4] attentive, purposeful, critical, and responsive;[5] passive or marginal, appreciative, attention, and analytical.[6]

Another type of classification identifies various "levels" of listening, such that a given experience involves listening at one of several levels of intensity:

1. Hearing sounds or words but not reacting beyond bare recognition that there is sound
2. Intermittent listening during which the mind wanders
3. Partial awareness, or listening only closely enough to know when it is the listener's turn to respond in some manner
4. Listening passively with little or no effort to respond
5. Listening narrowly, that is, missing significant parts but accepting what is familiar or agreeable
6. Listening and forming associations with experiences
7. Listening closely enough to determine the organization of the material heard (main idea and supporting details)
8. Listening critically, including asking for more data on statements made
9. Appreciative and creative listening with genuine intellectual and emotional response

These so-called "levels" are not as discrete as the list suggests and we should not assume that the objective of listening instruction is to "move" pupils from one level to the next. Minimal recognition of a sound stimulus is appropriate in some listening contexts, whereas nothing less than active processing followed by critical response is appropriate in others.

FACTORS AFFECTING LISTENING

As we have suggested, the interest of listeners in what they hear is of major importance in listening effectively. Apart from interest listening is also subject to several physical and environmental elements and conditions.

---

4. Ralph G. Nichols, "Ten Components of Effective Listening," *Education* 75 (January 1955): 292–302.

5. Earl J. Dias, "Three Levels of Listening," *English Journal* 36 (May 1947): 252–53.

6. Commission on the English Curriculum, National Council of Teachers of English, *Language Arts for Today's Children* (New York: Appleton-Century-Crofts, 1954), p. 80.

Listening and Hearing

Hearing is basic to listening and several factors affect how well we hear: auditory acuity, binaural hearing, auditory perception and discrimination, the masking of communication by other sounds, and auditory fatigue. Problems with any of these or a combination of two or more of them may reduce hearing effectiveness and thus listening ability.

Auditory acuity is the ability to receive sound waves of various frequencies (tones) at various intensities (levels of loudness).[7] The inability to respond to normal frequencies and intensities represents a hearing loss, which may be minor or serious. An estimated 5 to 10 percent of children have such hearing handicaps. Many of these losses are discovered through audiometer tests, which most school children receive; sometimes they are evident in a child's behavior, such as cupping the ear and leaning forward when spoken to. Teachers should closely observe children who seem to speak too loudly or too softly or who seem to have difficulty with pronunciation and articulation and difficulty with rhyming and other phonetic exercises. These children should be referred for further testing.

Binaural hearing may be related to depth perception in vision. A listener whose binaural hearing is adequate can locate a particular speaker among several people talking at once. Recent studies have shown that less capable listeners have difficulty with this task.[8] Related problems that have no physical basis, are masking and auditory fatigue. *Masking* occurs when superimposed sounds interfere with sounds that we are trying to hear. *Auditory fatigue* is a temporary hearing difficulty often caused by a monotonous tone or droning voice. Both conditions impair listening effectiveness.

The importance of normal hearing to effective listening should not be minimized, but hearing losses need not be an excuse for poor listening habits. Teachers should be careful not to confuse genuine hearing loss or masking and auditory fatigue with inattention, boredom, indifference, defiance, or even mental retardation.

Hearing and Noise

Distracting noise, particularly loud noise, affects hearing in obvious ways. Teachers should be aware of the effects of the ever-increasing noise level in our environment. While the kind of noise that most of us think of as distracting—jet airplanes, hydraulic hammers, rock music—may not be a classroom problem, most classrooms are not acoustically treated and noise may be more of a problem than we sense it to be. There is evidence that reducing the normal noise level of a

---

7. Taylor, p. 6.
8. Taylor, p. 8.

classroom enhances auditory perception.[9] Furthermore, noise affects more than hearing. Lundsteen reports that "Children . . . calmed considerably with the change from the typical noise-box classroom to the school's new sound-treated rooms."[10]

The answer to the problem of noise in the classroom is not a return to the no-talking classroom of earlier days, because growth in the use of language hinges on the occurrence of many genuine and normal communication activities. On the other hand, teachers may be able to institute quiet corners and quiet times, break up and soften classroom space (e.g., with rugs) to minimize sound reverberations, and plan around the occurrence of inevitable loud noises. Finally, teachers can help children to become intolerant of poor listening conditions so that they will take the initiative to seek better listening vantage points or change other conditions within their control.

Auditory Discrimination

Every child who can speak has considerable ability to perceive sounds and discriminate among them, but the extent of this ability apparently varies widely among children. Less than adequate ability to discriminate among individual speech sounds (phonemes) may be a source of listening difficulty (as well as of speaking and reading difficulty) and should receive instructional attention.

Some children whose hearing seems to be satisfactory are unable to perceive distinctions between similar sounds. For instance, they may confuse *bin* and *pin* or *seeing* and *ceiling*, and thus they may fail to understand fully what they hear. Such discrimination difficulties may be due to the child's level of maturity, the speaker's indistinct articulation, or the child's lack of familiarity with particular distinctions.[11] Too, inferior auditory discrimination ability may indicate a speech or hearing difficulty, and teachers should keep this possibility in mind; one study found that a number of children with some hearing loss spoke slightly inarticulately and yet their teachers had failed to detect their problems.[12]

Dialect differences also bear upon the ability of children to discriminate as teachers may expect and as they should in order to be fully functional listeners. It is difficult for many teachers to decide whether omissions, additions, distortions, and substitutions in a child's speech are signs of weak auditory discrimination or are simply features of a dialect. If the latter is the case, the teacher must learn to understand the child and to take the dialect into account in instruction. Instruc-

---

9. Linda W. Nober, "Auditory Discrimination and Classroom Noise," *Reading Teacher* 27 (December 1973): 288–91.

10. Lundsteen, p. xiv.

11. Ibid., p. 5–8.

12. Jon Eisenson and Mardel Ogilvie, *Speech Correction in the Schools* (New York: Macmillan Co., 1963), p. 190.

tional attention to auditory discrimination may be necessary if children have problems understanding what they are called upon to listen to.

Listening and Intelligence

Because any language activity—expressive or receptive—is a thinking activity, teachers can assume that there is a strong relationship between listening and intelligence. Much research supports this assumption: Ross found a correlation of .76 between listening scores and verbal intelligence scores;[13] Brown found it to be .82 at the fourth-grade level and .76 at the fifth-grade level;[14] and Anderson and Baldauf reported a coefficient of .58.[15] It is important to remember, however, that a high correlation does not mean a cause-and-effect relationship. As researchers have pointed out, the high correlations between listening and intelligence are probably somewhat spurious due to the similarities of tests used to measure listening and intelligence.[16]

Evidently, children who have above-average *nonlanguage* intelligence scores are better listeners than they are readers.[17] One study indicates that students of below-average intelligence tend to possess larger listening vocabularies than they do reading vocabularies.[18] Thus, "nonverbal" children may learn better from listening than from reading, though they are not likely to learn as effectively by either means as classmates who score higher on intelligence tests.

Attention and Concentration

Our listening effectiveness may depend largely on the attention and concentration we give to the listening act. Efforts to improve concentration have been shown to affect listening positively.[19] The degree of attention and concentration given may depend on what we are listening to, but listening habits and personality traits also have a bearing. While problems in measuring personality traits as

---

13. Ramon Ross, "A Look at Listeners," *Elementary School Journal* 64 (April 1964): 369–72.

14. Charles T. Brown, "Three Studies of the Listening of Children," *Speech Monographs* 32 (June 1965): 129–38.

15. Harold M. Anderson and Robert J. Baldauf, "A Study of a Measure of Listening," *Journal of Educational Research* 57 (December 1963): 197–200.

16. Edwin E. Vineyard and Robert B. Bailey, "Interrelationships of Reading Ability, Listening Skill, Intelligence and Scholastic Achievement," *Journal of Developmental Reading* 3 (1960): 174–78.

17. Robert O. Hall, "An Exploratory Study of Listening of Fifth Grade Pupils" (Ph.D. dissertation, University of Southern California, 1954).

18. Stanley B. Kegler, "A Comparative Study of the Size and Nature of Reading and Listening Vocabularies" (Ph.D. dissertation, University of Minnesota, 1958).

19. Ralph G. Nichols, "Factors Accounting for Differences in Comprehension of Materials Presented Orally in the Classroom" (unpublished Ph.D. dissertation, University of Iowa, 1948).

well as in testing listening skill have restricted research in listening-personality relationships, some work has been done. Nevertheless, Kelly found that selected personality traits, notably emotional stability, are characteristic of the good listener.[20] Jackson reported similar findings and suggested that an individual's adjustment may directly affect the ability to use listening skills.[21]

Tone, style, gestures, mannerisms, and rate of speech all affect attention and concentration, as do the motivation of the listener, the appeal of the content and its organization, and the listening environment (temperature, distractions, acoustics, etc.). A difference between the rate of speech and that of listening and thinking may also affect attention. The time lag permits the listener, especially the poor listener, to become distracted and lose attention. Research indicates that increasing the presentation speed of much of what we listen to would not result in comprehension loss, and in fact, training in listening to rapid speech can increase comprehension.[22]

Listening and Speaking

Performance in listening and speaking are obviously related, but the nature of the relationship has not been established by research. Some studies have positively

---

20. Charles M. Kelly, "Mental Ability and Personality Factors in Listening," *Quarterly Journal of Speech*, April 1963, pp. 152–56.

21. Ann E. Jackson, "An Investigation of the Relationship Between Listening and Selected Variables in Grades 4, 5 and 6" (Ph.D. dissertation, Arizona State University, 1966).

22. C. David Wood, "Comprehension and Compressed Speech by Elementary School Children" (Ph.D. dissertation, Indiana University, 1965).

correlated children's listening and speaking abilities. Others have reported similar relationships between the structure of children's language and listening.[23] For example, Strickland stated, "The structure of children's oral language as measured by the fluency of use of the common structural patterns was more closely related to listening comprehension than to any other variable."[24]

Some researchers have suggested that the development of an individual's listening skill "probably plays an important role in the ultimate development of his skill as a speaker in being able to order verbal behavior."[25] Others have reported that the organization of a speech or the manner in which it is delivered has no effect on comprehension.[26]

Other Factors Affecting Listening

In listening, sound identification is necessary if a message is to have meaning. Usually this process is automatic because the sound is known; it is a sound or word that the listener has heard many times and immediately recognizes. Sound identification is not automatic for new words and sounds. Unless the listener can attach some meaning to them, the communication may be lost. The principal clue listeners have for identifying unknown sounds is the total context in which they hear them, in particular that context that is adjacent to the unknown. This context may supply identification cues, but of course their value depends upon the skill of the listener, the content of the message, and factors affecting concentration. Clues to unknown sounds come also from the manner of delivery and from the mood created by both the setting and the speaker.

In general, listening effectiveness depends on the skill of the listener, but we can break down this skill into several components: the *skills* of listening. Effective listening does not just happen. It requires the identification of necessary skills, development of these skills, and practice in their use.

LISTENING SKILLS

As suggested earlier, the skills required for listening and comprehending meaning include skills that are really thinking skills. The implication is that the principal

23. Joel Stark, "An Investigation of the Relationship of the Vocal and Communicative Aspects of Speech Competency with Listening Comprehension," *Speech Monographs* 24 (June 1957): 98–99.

24. Ruth C. Strickland," The Language of Elementary School Children: Its Relationship to the Language of Reading Textbooks and the Quality of Reading of Selected Children," Bulletin of the School of Education, Indiana University, 38 (1962): 85–86.

25. Reed Lawson, "Verbal Sequencing Without Mediation," *Journal of Communication* (June 1964): 98–104.

26. David B. Orr et al. "Trainability of Listening Comprehension of Speeded Discourse," *Journal of Educational Psychology* 56 (1965): 148–56.

concern in a listening program should be the skills of sound perception and discrimination and the arrangement of these sounds to attain meaning. Thinking skills do not necessarily transfer from one means of receiving to another, however, and the transfer from expression to reception is even less. Certainly, without learning and experience, no transfer will take place.

Listening skills take many forms, depending upon the purpose of the activity. Of principal concern to us are the skills necessary for the accurate and thoughtful reception of speaking, although a program may include listening to music and to sounds for the purpose of setting the mood for creative expression. Identifying skills needed for different types and levels of listening is by no means as simple as we would like it to be. For example, Lundsteen's description and categorization of various skills is nineteen pages long and it includes various lists of skills and subskills based on work by numerous listening authorities.[27] Regardless of identification and listing problems, the essential skills may be classified into four categories: (1) perception of sounds, (2) accuracy of reception and sequencing, (3) attainment of meaning, and (4) meaning utilization.

An early study identified these listening skills:[28]

1. Word perception
    a. Recall of word meanings
    b. Deduction of meanings of unknown words
2. Comprehension of ideas
    a. Noting details
    b. Following directions
    c. Organizing into main and subordinate ideas
    d. Selecting information pertinent to a specific topic
    e. Detecting clues that show the speaker's trend of thought
3. Using ideas to build understanding
    a. Evaluating an expressed point of view or fact in relation to previous learning
    b. Making justifiable inferences

Other, similar lists of skills sometimes imply a greater number of skills or further division of basic ones. For example, the following may suggest additi͏   .i skills or subskills:

1. Listening to answer questions or to gain specific information
2. Determining the speaker's purpose and means for accomplishing it
3. Selecting items or particular content for summary or for drawing conclusions

---

27. Lundsteen, pp. 55–74.

28. Edward Pratt and Harry A. Greene, *Training Children to Listen. A Monograph for Elementary Teachers* (Evanston, Ill.: Row, Peterson and Co. 1955).

4.   Separating fact from opinion
5.   Recognizing emotional appeal in content
6.   Detecting bias, prejudice, or propaganda
7.   Responding to mood or setting of what is heard
8.   Understanding use of asides, satire, and voice inflections
9.   Creating visual images from verbal descriptions

Recent emphasis on stating teaching objectives in terms of behaviors expected has led to still other lists. Essentially, however, the principal difference between these lists and the more traditional ones lies in the way the skills are stated. For example, in a behavioral list we might see: "Having listened to a reasonably short passage, the student is able to provide the detailed examples it contains, when given the main idea" or "Having listened to a passage containing a sequence of ideas, the student is able to reproduce sequences."[29]

INSTRUCTION IN LISTENING SKILLS

Although an ever-increasing number of teachers are aware of the need to teach listening, too few know how to teach it, too few take advantage of daily opportunities for such teaching, and too few go beyond demanding silence and attention from students. The dearth of cohesive, varied, comprehensive, and sequenced instruction aids, compared to what is available for other areas of language arts instruction can be overcome by thoughtful use of existing resources. Duker has identified a large number of studies and expository articles that are helpful in making such an attempt.[30] This list covers the teaching of listening at all school levels, and the sources generally agree that listening skills are teachable and that the results are measurable.

Teachers' Listening

In planning instruction in listening for children, teachers should first give attention to their own listening. Teachers should show that they value listening by "paying attention," "showing courtesy to the speaker," and observing all the other practices that they will urge children to use. Being engrossed in telling—a practice that may not be teaching—prevents adequate listening.

One writer has suggested that teachers ask themselves the following questions:[31]

---

29. "Listening Skills Improve Reading Too!" *Reading Newsreport* 4 (October 1969): 31.
30. Sam Duker, *Listening Bibliography*, 2d ed. (Metuchen, N.J.: Scarecrow Press, 1968).
31. Sidney Trubowitz, "The Listening Teacher," *Childhood Education*, (April/May 1975), p. 322.

Do I listen more than I talk?

Have I developed a classroom atmosphere in which children feel free to express themselves?

Am I aware when I stop listening?

Do I know what gets in the way of my listening better?

Have I learned to hear the messages that are communicated underneath words and beneath facial and body expressions?

Do I listen as accurately, carefully, sensitively as I am able?

Teachers also need to be mindful of experiences that have blocked their own listening—an argument at home, a traffic jam on the way to school, confrontation by an angry parent—and to recognize that similar experiences may interfere with the listening of their pupils. And all of us value silence, so that we can think without someone talking. Children have a right to quiet periods, too.

No speaker should try to "out-shout" other speakers or to speak in such a low voice that it is impossible for listeners to hear easily. On the other hand, tone should be low enough to force listeners to stay alert in order to keep up with the speaker. It is advisable, too, to establish and reinforce classroom practices of not repeating instructions, explanations, or announcements. In addition, the speaker must make every effort to ensure that the message is so interesting that everyone will want to listen.

Basic Teaching Procedures

Lundsteen lists twenty-one tasks for the listening teacher, including providing a suitable atmosphere, planning a program for the entire year, selecting appropriate material, avoiding needless repetition of instructions, and providing feedback to children on their listening efforts.[32] Essentially, however, the first task is to make the children aware of the importance of listening. Children must learn that skillful listening is important to them in school, on the playground, and at home. They must also learn that listening is important to adults in almost every life activity. They must learn that their listening skill can be further developed, that development results from attention to habits that they can easily learn, and that effective listening will reward them with richer, more meaningful lives.

The second task is to stimulate children's sense of hearing, or auditory acuity. For example, the teacher might ask individual children to name all the sounds they can hear at a particular time, say, while sitting in a corner of the playground. Perhaps some pupils will be interested in writing a story based on the activities that the sounds suggest and reading their stories to the class. Similar exercises based on familiar situations will contribute to the development of a keen appreciation of the sense of hearing and will make children more alert to sounds they previously took for granted.

---

32. Lundsteen, pp. 118–125.

The third step is to provide opportunities for meaningful listening. A wide variety of opportunities must be introduced into the classroom if the children are to learn to adapt their listening to the purpose of the activity.[33] Thus, the program should include listening to music, poetry, stories, reports, descriptions, and so on, for the purpose of appreciation, information, or critical evaluation.

Related to the provision of opportunities is the fourth task: teaching children the specific skills for various listening purposes, with emphasis on development of the skills through specific situations and activities rather than on "paying attention." Thus the teacher must know the skills and the purposes must be clear to the pupils. The teacher must also know procedures for developing each skill.

In addition to following these steps, teachers should keep these principles in mind:

1. Considerable flexibility is needed in the activities provided, because children's listening abilities vary widely and because different types of listening are appropriate for different occasions.
2. Careful preparation for listening experiences increases the learning gained from listening. The teacher and pupils should discuss the purpose of a listening activity and make preparations related to previous experiences, new vocabulary, and the type of listening required.
3. Listening should be *for* rather than *at*. Successful listening requires a clear purpose formulated by an active receiver of communication.
4. Listening may be used as a change of pace, perhaps for relaxation or pleasure, as well as a way of getting information.
5. Children profit from formulating standards for both the speaker and the listener and from teacher attention to these in the planning, in the activity itself, and in the evaluation.

Listening Activities

Although every oral communication situation is an opportunity for developing listening skills and fostering good listening habits, an organized instructional program planned in detail and evaluated with adequate attention to objectives should be part of every classroom. An effective program will include activities for teaching skills as well as for building interest in learning to listen well and fostering good listening habits. Specific teaching activities should generally have these

---

33. Good sources of ideas for listening situations are: David H. Russell and Elizabeth F. Russell, *Listening Aids Through the Grades* (New York: Bureau of Publications, Teachers College, Columbia University, 1959); Guy Wagner, Max Hosier, and Mildred Blackman, *Listening Games* (Darien, Conn.: Teachers Publishing Corp., 1962); and Goldie Marie Gigous, *Improving Listening Skills* (Dansville, N.Y.: F. A. Owen Publishing Co., 1967).

characteristics: a clearly defined purpose, preliminary attention to unfamiliar vocabulary and ideas, and some provision for follow-up. Sometimes listening guides are helpful, but usually a better practice is to have the children formulate their own plan to achieve the purpose or purposes for listening.

Teachers should have no difficulty designing listening activities to teach one or more listening skills. The following are examples of listening activities that can be designed for specific purposes.[34] Each teacher should consider the experiences the children have had or are having in choosing content for such activities.

Listening for details.   The teacher asks the children to listen for details about what Father and Mother do and then reads the following paragraph:

> Every morning Father goes to work by bus. He usually leaves the house about seven o'clock. In rainy weather Mother drives him to the bus station on her way to work. When the bus reaches the city at seven forty-five, Father goes to the general office of his company. An elevator carries him to the eighth floor. His job sometimes takes hours of extra time, and many evenings he doesn't arrive home until nearly bedtime. Joe and Betty are disappointed when he works at night, for he frequently helps them with their lessons. And if there is time after they have finished studying, the family often plays games.

Following the reading the teacher asks questions such as these:

1.   What time does Father leave the house in the morning?
2.   What does Mother do during the day?
3.   On what floor is Father's office?
4.   How does Father help Joe and Betty when he is home early?
5.   When does the family play games?

Listening for the main idea.   The teacher writes these sentences on the board or on a transparency for an overhead projector and covers them:

1.   The burro is a very gentle animal.
2.   Children ride on their burros.
3.   The burro is a favorite pet in Mexico.
4.   The children give names to their burros.

The teacher asks the children to listen carefully to what they will hear and to think of the one thing it tells about. This paragraph is then read:

> Many children in Mexico have burros for pets. The burro is so gentle that a small child can take care of it. The children enjoy riding on their burros. Sometimes the children ride them in parades. They call their pet burros by name and talk to them just as they talk to one another. Often a boy will carry sugar in his pocket. His burro will follow him, sniffing in his pocket to get the sugar.

---

34. For additional suggestions, see Taylor and preceding footnotes in this chapter, as well as many of the recently published basal reading textbooks.

The teacher uncovers the sentences, reads them aloud, and then asks the children to write·the number of the sentence that expresses the main idea of the paragraph.

Listening to follow directions.   The teacher distributes to each pupil one sheet of lined paper and says, "Today we are going to have a game to see how well you can listen to directions. Have your pencils ready, and be sure to do exactly what my directions say. I will give each direction only once." The teacher then reads:

1. Write your first and last name in the upper right-hand corner of the paper.
2. At the left-hand margin, on every other line, write the numbers from one to ten.
3. After number 1 write the words *from, with, at.*
4. If California is south of Oregon, write the word *south.*
5. Listen to these numbers and write the largest of them 6–2–7–5–1–8–3.
6. Draw a square and put the number 3 in the lower right-hand corner of it.

The teacher can continue giving directions as long as he or she desires and the pupils are motivated to listen. Answers should be checked by the pupils.

Listening to distinguish the relevant from the irrelevant.   The teacher asks the pupils to listen to this selection and to be ready to tell which sentences are necessary to gain the meaning and which do not really relate to the remainder of the selection.

There were six boys beside the campfire. The dry sticks blazed and the heavy logs glowed with the heat. It was almost time to put the fish in the frying pan. Already they had poked the potatoes in their foil wrappings and they were softening. Jim's older brother had stayed at home. He was going to college this fall. All the boys were hungry and were anxious to eat. Bill put on more wood and Bob got the frying pan.

The teacher then asks the pupils what the selection is about and rereads the selection sentence by sentence. After reading a sentence, he or she asks the pupils to tell whether it relates to the remainder of the paragraph and why or why not.

Listening to draw inferences.   The teacher tells the pupils to listen to the following paragraph to answer some questions that require listening "between the lines."

The air was crisp and clear, but a wet snow had pelted the windows last night. I breathed deeply, glanced toward the snow-covered cars parked along the curbing and thought, "What a beautiful day." Suddenly I came down with a bump on the sidewalk.

After the teacher asks these questions, the class discusses the meaning of making inferences.

1.   Why did the speaker fall?
2.   Does the speaker live in town or in the country?
3.   About what time of day is it?

Many curriculum guides contain suggestions for listening lessons. For example, the following come from an Alameda County (California) guide.[35]

Inferring word meanings

In today's listening lesson, you will hear selections that contain an unfamiliar or unknown word. After listening to how the word is used, you will be asked to identify its meaning or tell what it is like by choosing from four definitions.

Here is an example to help you understand what to do.

Mammoths were ponderous animals. Dinosaurs were ponderous too. Such animals would leave deep footprints in the mud when they walked near waterholes because they were ponderous.

Circle the number of the word that you believe is like the word *ponderous*.

1.   plant-eating
2.   prehistoric
3.   very heavy
4.   four-footed

Identifying mood

After hearing the stories in today's listening lesson, you will again be asked to identify the feeling or mood that the writer is trying to create, such as happiness, sadness, pride, or sympathy.

Here is an example. Listen carefully to feel the mood the writer wants you to feel about the place in the story.

The winter sky was filled with grey clouds. Icy wind whistled through the trees. Birds fluffed their feathers and squirrels curled up in their warm nests. The windows of the tiny cabin by the lake were boarded over; no smoke came from its chimney.

Circle the number of the sentence that tells the way the writer wants you to feel.

1.   It is a sad place.
2.   It is a lonely place.
3.   It is a happy place.
4.   It is an exciting place.

---

35. *Listening Comprehension Skills*, Teacher's Manual, Level B (Hayward, Calif.: Alameda County School Department, 1973), p. 1/1Ba. The material is also available on tape.

Judging persuasion.

In today's listening lesson, you are going to hear selections meant to make you act in a certain way. That is what is meant by persuasion. In advertising you can hear good examples of persuasion.

Logical argument is a way of persuasion in which facts are told honestly to try to have someone act or think in a certain way.

Another kind of persuasion is by propaganda, that is, trying to make people think or act in a certain way without knowing the whole truth. People persuaded by propaganda do not hear all the reasons for thinking or acting in a certain way, and that way might not be best for them. There are several kinds of devices of propaganda. You will learn about three of them in this lesson.

One is the card-stacking device, meaning telling only the favorable facts, only good things, and not telling any others.

A second kind of propaganda is the testimonial device, meaning using a famous person's words to tell about a person, idea or thing.

A third propaganda device is repetition, meaning to repeat favorable words or slogans over and over about a person, idea or thing.

After hearing the selections in this lesson, you will be asked to decide what way of persuasion was used. Here is an example to help you to know what to do.

> Ladies and gentlemen, Rocky Passum, greatest quarterback in professional football history, uses Go-Go gasoline in all his cars. He always pulls up to the purple and green Go-Go station and says, "Fill it up with Go-Go!"

Circle the number of the words which describe the way of persuasion used in that selection.

1. Card-stacking device
2. Logical argument
3. Testimonial device
4. Repetition device

Activities like these can be developed relatively easily. Excessive use of such exercises, however, can make instruction too formalized, structured, and artificial and risks destroying children's interest in improving their skills. Relating the listening objectives to content of other areas of the curriculum or to ongoing types of activities and situations will reduce the danger of artificiality.

Other Teaching Opportunities

Every school day abounds with informal and meaningful opportunities for teaching children to be more effective listeners.[36] Converting all of these situations to listening lessons as specific as the ones suggested is not necessary or ad-

---

36. Many curriculum guides provide reminders of these opportunities. For example, see *English Language Arts: Listening and Speaking K–12* (Albany, N.Y.: State Education Department, 1969).

visable although it is generally possible. Capitalizing on spontaneous opportunities to extend or reinforce listening skills is crucial to growth in listening.

Many activities in reading skills programs can be adapted for listening instruction. For example, read a description of a scene to the children so that they can draw pictures depicting the scene. Or substitute descriptions of people; historical and contemporary figures can be used. Instead of drawing the face, the children may simply guess who the person is. A similar activity is to read a short poem or story and ask the children to guess the title or suggest an appropriate one. Ask them to give reasons for the choice. Another activity is to omit occasional words in the selection read aloud so that the children can supply the missing words or determine the meaning from the clues supplied. These activities should encourage the children to "listen on" (corresponds to "read on") in order to determine the words or the meanings.

The teacher need not do all of the reading. Pupils can listen to classmates read and try to determine the punctuation in a selection. They might also evaluate readers' performance in terms of reading with feeling, ability to "capture" the audience, intonation, and so on. Social studies and science reports provide many opportunities for instruction and practice in using context clues: synonyms, summary statements, transition words, definitional sentences, words that indicate the order of reporting, and so on.

Many times children need to listen for directions and similar types of messages. In fact, teachers may have children carry oral messages from class to class so that they can practice both listening to details and retaining information. Many directions are naturally given orally. Teachers should give directions in several parts (without repeating them). For example: "Write your last name first, then your first name, in the upper right-hand corner of your paper. Under this information write the date." If children are absent from class, ask one or more of those present to summarize and convey the assignments to the absentees. It is a good idea to follow up and make sure that no misinformation is given.

Try giving tests orally; that is, instead of writing questions on the chalkboard or preparing dittoed sheets, read the questions aloud on occasion. This method usually works better for questions requiring short answers. Better, because it allows for individual response rates, is the practice of taping tests or assignments for pupils to take or work on individually.

Tape recordings are useful in many ways. For example, the teacher can shut off a tape recording of a talk before the conclusion and ask the children to anticipate the speaker's conclusion. Such exercises should vary in difficulty and progress from the simple to the difficult. Recordings of radio and TV broadcasters and commentators provide good content for listening for fact and opinion, clarity of ideas, and the effects of good delivery.

The teacher can also prepare tape recordings that focus on particular skills or content. For instance, the material might provide signals that guide pupils to meaning. Language signals may be such phrases as "three reasons for this plan . . . ," "the following are . . . ," and "my major concern is . . . ," or transition words and phrases such as "on the other hand," "on the contrary," and "another viewpoint is." Recording different types of television programs permits practice in listening to certain language styles. For instance, travel programs use much descriptive language, sports programs use figurative and idiomatic expressions, and commercials make sensory appeals through language. Radio and TV programs employ different tones, stresses, and rates of speech in order to produce desired effects. From recordings of different programs pupils can determine the effects from the ways language is used.

There are many techniques for focusing on specific listening skills. After a child gives an oral report the teacher can ask the class various types of questions, such as "What was Jim's major point?" Oral arithmetic gives attention to sequence and to details: "Let's see if you can follow a number trail. Add 13 to 3, take away 6, multiply by 5, and divide by 2. What do you have?" Activities in which children must complete a tall tale or other story (orally or in writing) require using sequence and detail skills.

It's a good idea to have pupils keep records of the good listening habits they observe. Initially, teachers help by calling attention to and asking evaluative questions about potential observations to be recorded. Children might keep TV and radio listening logs, and the class could then discuss their own habits and standards as revealed in their logs. Another log could be a record of habits and courtesies shown in the classroom. Occasionally the teacher might want to combine individual logs on a chart or to keep a class chart.

Individualized Listening Instruction

Because children's levels of development in the various listening skills and their listening habits vary, the listening program, like all others in the language arts should be individualized. One method of accommodating individual differences is to record listening activities and lessons on cassette tapes. Commercially available recordings also present listening activities or give practice in particular skills. These tapes allow children to select the kinds of materials they most need to use and enable teachers to assign lessons on an individual basis. Subjects for children's tapes include literature selections, directions for writing activities, spelling lessons, vocabulary exercises, and specific lessons of the types suggested earlier.

Children can listen to tape recordings anywhere in the room where earphones are available or in a specially designated "listening center." The center, of course, may be set up so that several children can listen at the same time, either to separate tapes or to one that they all need to or want to hear.

LISTENING INSTRUCTION AIDS

There are many resources available to aid the development of more effective listening. The content of listening lessons and other activities may come from textbooks in various subject areas. Audiovisual materials are a source of literature selections, social studies and science content, environmental information, library skills, and so on. These materials, in addition to commercially available aids designed especially for teaching listening, may be used by pupils individually, by a group, or by the entire class.

Records and Tapes

Literature narrations, historical accounts, folktales and songs, games and activities, and social studies concepts are widely available on records and tapes. Some records exercise sound identification skills. They include *Sounds Around Us* (Scott, Foresman and Co.); *The Downtown Story, The Sounds of Camp, Sounds of Insects*, and so on (Folkways Scholastic Records); and *Let's Listen* (Ginn).

Materials related to reading and listening include *Listening Skills for Pre-Readers* and *Sounds for Young Readers* (Kimbo Records), *Listening Time* (Educational Records Sales), and *Listening Skill Builders* (Science Research Associates). Among the resources that focus directly on listening are the *Countdown for Listening* cassettes. Science Research Associates' *Listening Language Laboratories Series* is also available for grades 1–3 and 4–6 (twenty-four cassettes each).

American Landmarks records (Enrichment Teaching Materials) provide historical dramatizations that motivate listening as does *Grass Roots: An Oral History of the American People* (Visual Education Corp.). Literature records include the *Hans Christian Andersen Fairy Tales, Just So Stories, Old Possum's Book of Practical Cats, You Know Who* (Encyclopedia Britannica), *John Ciardi Reads: You Read to Me and I'll Read to you* (Spoken Arts), *Poetry Time* (Scott, Foresman and Co.), *Prose and Poetry Enrichment* (Enrichment Teaching Materials). The tape series that includes *Stories Are Fun, Open the Door*, and *Land of Make Believe* (National Tape Recording Repository) is also helpful, and Caedmon records has many literature records, among them *Hans Brinker, The Wizard of Oz, Hansi, Where the Wild Things Are*, and *The Secret Garden*. Sunburst Communications has *Tune-in: Listening and Literature Through the Magic of Old-time Radio*.

Films and Filmstrips

Most films made for children can provide worthwhile listening experiences. Companies such as BFA Educational Media, Weston Woods, Learning Corporation of America, Encyclopedia Britannica, Cornet, Stephen Bosustow Productions, and International Film Bureau can furnish many appealing films. Cornet has *Listening Skills: An Introduction; Listen Well, Learn Well*; and *Your Communication Skills: Listening*. Churchill Films has *Listening*. Some of the other available films are part of multimedia packages.

Filmstrips directed at teaching listening skills include *Look and Listen* (Filmstrip House), *How to Listen* (Society for Visual Education), and *Listening, Looking, and Feeling* (Bailey-Film Associates).

Books

The content of listening lessons can come from appealing and informative books. Most of the basal reading series provide for some listening lessons, particularly in the primary grades, and relate them to the reading skills in the text. Other books that have great appeal and develop listening abilities are Margaret Wise Brown's books for primary grades (*The City Noisy Book* and *The Winter Noisy Book*), Helen Borton's *Do You Hear What I Hear?* Paul Showers' *The Listening Walk*, Don Safier's *The Listening Book*, Benjamin Elkins's *The Loudest Noise in the World*, Alvin Tresselt's *Wake Up, City* and *Wake Up, Farm*, and Bernice W. Carlson's *Listen! And Help the Story*.

Multimedia

Increased instruction in listening has led to the commercial development of multimedia listening programs. Examples are *Listening-reading Program* (D.C. Heath); *Look, Listen and Learn* (Millikin Publishing Co.); *Sights and Sounds* (Random House); *Listen and Do* (Houghton Mifflin Co.); and *First Talking Storybook Box* (Scott, Foresman and Co.).

LISTENING EVALUATION

Now that listening instruction has gained importance, instruments for measuring listening skills are available. Few of these instruments are standardized tests, so much of the task of measuring specific skills and determining levels of achievement falls upon the teacher.[37]

Standardized Tests

Generally speaking, standardized tests do not provide dependable measures of how effectively children will listen in the normal classroom activities. To some extent, of course, this problem is typical of all tests that seek to measure achievement of particular abilities or skills. On the other hand, without standardized

---

37. O. W. Kopp, "The Evaluation of Oral Language Activities: Teaching and Learning," in *Research in Oral Language*, edited by Walter T. Petty, (Champaign, Ill.: National Council of Teachers of English, 1967).

tests and other evaluative measures, neither teachers nor children would have access to the information that they need for further teaching and learning.

One series of standardized listening tests that is appropriate for elementary school is the *Sequential Tests of Educational Progress* (the STEP test).[38] Available in graded versions for several levels (primary, and grades 4–6, 7–9, 10–12, 13–14), this test attempts simply to measure comprehension, interpretation, evaluation, and application. The teacher presents the test orally and the pupils choose one of the four optional answers to each question. Because the pupils have copies of the questions and the four options, the test involves certain elements of reading ability. This fact has provoked criticism. Critics also have pointed out that any comprehension test (reading or listening) may measure prior knowledge as well as intellectual abilities.

Graded listening tests are also part of the *Cooperative Primary Tests* (grades 1–2 and 2–3).[39] In these tests, the teacher reads words, stories, poems, and so on. The child indicates comprehension by marking illustrations.

A third standardized test is the *Durrell Listening-reading Series*, which "is designed to provide a comparison of children's reading and listening abilities."[40] The test series seeks to measure both vocabulary knowledge and comprehension ability at three levels: grades 1–3.5, 3.5–6, and 7–9. The teacher administers the tests and optional responses orally so that the pupil does no reading.

Tests like the *Illinois Test of Psycholinguistic Abilities* (ITPA) and the *Wepman Auditory Discrimination Test* (WAST) allow assessment of auditory perception, discrimination, and sequencing.[41] The increasing number of commerically published listening programs usually include listening tests. Likewise, many of the instruments designed to measure reading skills are adaptable for listening.

Unpublished Tests

Research reports are another source of listening tests, although they are not always readily available. The Duker bibliography lists sixty-five unpublished tests and *Dissertation Abstracts* and similar publications mention that tests have been developed.[42]

Curriculum guides also may contain listening tests as well as lesson and activity suggestions. One example is the *Alameda County Hackett Test of Language Comprehension Skills*, which has two levels.[43]

---

38. Educational Testing Service, Princeton, N.J., 1967.

39. Educational Testing Service, Princeton, N.J., 1967.

40. Donald D. Durrell et al. *Durrell Listening-reading Series* (New York: Harcourt, Brace and World, 1969).

41. University of Illinois Press (Urbana); Language Research Associates (Chicago).

42. Duker, *Listening Biography*.

43. *Listening Comprehension Skills*, Alameda County School Department, 1973.

Teacher-made Tests

The teacher may use a standardized listening test as a model to construct an informal test. Lists of skills like the ones in this chapter or those provided in reports of research directed at teaching listening are useful guides in this process. In addition, descriptions of listening activities may suggest test items. Among the skills that lend themselves to testing are:

1. Identification and recall of details
2. Sequence of details and other information
3. Retention of information
4. Identification of the central idea
5. Drawing inferences from supporting facts
6. Distinguishing relevant from irrelevant materials
7. Use of contextual clues to word meanings
8. Recognition of transitional elements

Pupil Self-evaluation

Involving pupils directly in evaluation is very important. Even in the primary grades children can formulate standards for listening and judge whether or not their performances meet their own standards. In the early grades, performance standards should focus upon audience behavior and should emphasize listening courteously and attentively, expressing enjoyment and appreciation, avoiding interruption, and offering constructive criticism or asking intelligent questions.

Criteria for good listening apply to any experience that involves listening. Positively stated standards follow from the teacher's request that pupils name the good listening behaviors they exhibit during a listening activity (e.g., "We saved our questions until the speaker asked for them"). To encourage growth, the teacher then asks, "What should we try to remember so that next time we will be even better listeners?" Again responses should be positive and constructive: "We should give our full attention to the speaker," not "Roger and Judy shouldn't draw pictures next time." When "next time" comes, the children should review their strengths and remind themselves of their plan for change. Some children may be able to focus on only one criterion at a time.

An effective time to involve children in developing listening standards is following an activity that has not been very successful because they did not listen well. Discussion of the standards should focus on *why* and *how* and the statements developed should reflect the children's careful analysis and thought. One source suggests the following as appropriate standards for an upper-grade group:[44]

---

44. Goldie Marie Gigous, *Improving Listening Skills* (Dansville, N.Y.: F. A. Owen Publishing Co., 1967), p. 14.

1. Hold the thread of discussion in mind.
2. Follow the main idea.
3. Recognize transitional phrases and changes of thought.
4. Take notes during a speech or report.
5. Write a brief summary.
6. Be aware of biased attitudes and comments.
7. Disagree with a speaker courteously.
8. Listen to different viewpoints in discussion.
9. Draw conclusions from a variety of ideas.

Standards should change as children mature, and they should be more specific and comprehensive at the end of the year than at the beginning. It is a good idea to write the standards on tagboard and post them. They need not remain posted all year, but the teacher can bring them out occasionally as reminders or for revision.

ADDITIONAL SUGGESTIONS FOR EVALUATING LISTENING

Pupils can keep logs of their listening activities and analyze what they have learned and which activities were most effective. This practice is helpful in evaluating many listening experiences, but it should be discontinued when pupils lose interest in it. A related idea that will help pupils to recognize the importance of being both speakers and listeners is to chart the flow of discussion. Whether the teacher or one of the students keeps the chart, the class can analyze it as they would analyze their logs and the teacher can help them to relate it to their own performances as listeners. Even more informally, pupils and the teacher may simply discuss listening in their classroom, the particular skills involved, and the effect of their listening.

All of the procedures described have assessment value, but teachers should supplement them with some kind of written record of specific listening behaviors and attainments. A checklist like the following is probably the best type of written record since it forces the pupil to react to direct questions. Most statements of standards can be effectively translated into checklists.[45]

Checking up on my listening

		Yes	No
1. Did I remember to get ready for listening?			
a.	Was I seated comfortably where I could see and hear?	_____	_____
b.	Were my eyes focused on the speaker?	_____	_____

---

45. Adapted from Kopp, pp. 114–123.

2. Was I ready to concentrate on what the speaker had to say?
    a. Was I able to push unrelated thoughts out of my mind for the time being?   _____ _____
    b. Was I ready to think about the topic and call to mind the things I already knew about it?   _____ _____
    c. Was I ready to learn more about the topic?   _____ _____
3. Was I ready for "takeoff"?
    a. Did I discover in the first few minutes where the speaker was taking me?   _____ _____
    b. Did I discover the central idea so that I could follow it through the speech?   _____ _____
4. Was I able to pick out the ideas that supported the main idea?
    a. Did I take advantage of the speaker's clues (such as "first" and "next") to help organize the ideas in my mind?   _____ _____
    b. Did I use my extra "think" time to summarize and take notes—either mentally or on paper?   _____ _____
5. After the speaker finished, did I evaluate what had been said?
    a. Did this new knowledge seem to fit with the knowledge I already had?   _____ _____
    b. Did I weigh each idea to see if I agreed with the speaker?   _____ _____
    If you marked any questions *No*, decide why you could not honestly answer them *Yes*.

The most important objective in evaluating children's listening skills is simply to do it. Every teacher must identify listening behaviors that children should exhibit. These behaviors should be the goals of the teaching program and the basis for evaluating the effectiveness of the teaching-learning situation.

EXERCISES FOR THOUGHT AND ACTION

1. Keep a log of the listening activities and the approximate amount of time you spend doing each of them in a single day. Note the types of listening you did, the skills that you used, and the interferences you encountered.
2. Assemble a file of listening activities (4 x 6 cards are good) that might be

useful in your classroom. Organize them as much as possible by types of
listening and particular skills.

3. Research the literature to learn the effects of physical conditions on listening. What are the implications of these conditions for the elementary school
classroom?

4. Examine publishers' catalogs for resources to use in teaching listening. Note
especially any that would help you to integrate listening instruction with
other areas of the curriculum. Put your findings on cards for easy reference.

5. Write a plan for one lesson on critical listening for the grade level of your
choice.

6. Spend at least an hour in an elementary school classroom observing the occasions for and types of pupil listening and teacher listening. Also record
your own impressions.

7. Prepare tape recordings of selections you can play in class to help the
children listen for main ideas, details, etc. Incorporate outlining and note
taking in this activity.

8. Survey the ways in which several teachers teach listening. Keep a record of
what they tell you and compare their responses to the suggestions in this
chapter.

9. Examine the objectives and content of a comprehensive language arts textbook series for the elementary school. What are the stated listening objectives? How have the authors implemented them?

10. Arrange to have your hearing tested on a pure tone audiometer or observe a
child being tested. Describe the procedure and your reactions.

11. Describe a classroom in which listening conditions are positive. Also
describe a home where such conditions exist.

12. Review and report on one or more listening films/tapes/records.

13. Examine one or more of the standardized tests described in this chapter.
Evaluate the test(s) as a means of measuring listening ability.

14. Illustrate your design for a listening center.

SELECTED REFERENCES

Barker, Larry L. *Listening Behavior.* Englewood Cliffs, N.J.: Prentice-Hall, 1971.
Duker, Sam. *Listening: Readings II.* Metuchen, N.J.: Scarecrow Press, 1971.
Duker, Sam. *Listening Bibliography.* Metuchen, N.J.: Scarecrow Press, 1968.
Duker, Sam. *Teaching Listening in the Elementary School.* Metuchen, N.J.: Scarecrow
Press, 1971.
Farrell, Muriel, and Flint, Shirley H. "Are They Listening?" *Childhood Education*, May
1967, pp. 528–29.
Halley, Richard D. "Some Suggestions for the Teaching of Listening," *Speech Teacher* 24
(November 1975): 386–89.
Hollingsworth, Paul M. "Let's Improve Listening Skills." *Elementary English*
(November/December 1974): 1156–57.

Horrworth, Gloria L. "Listening: A Facet of Oral Language." *Elementary English*, December 1966, pp. 856–64.

Lundsteen, Sara W. *Listening, Its Impact at All Levels on Reading and the Other Language Arts*. Urbana, Ill.: National Council of Teachers of English/Educational Resources Information Center Clearinghouse on Reading and Communication Skills, 1979.

Monaghan, R. R., and Martin, J. G. "Symbolic Interaction: Analysis of Listening." *Journal of Communication* 18 (June 1968): 127–30.

Petty, Walter T.; Petty, Dorothy C.; and Becking, Marjorie F. *Experiences in Language: Tools and Techniques for Language Arts Methods*, 2d ed. Boston: Allyn and Bacon, 1976.

Smith, James A. *Classroom Organization for the Language Arts*. Itasca, Ill.: F. E. Peacock Publishers, 1977.

Taylor, Stanford. *What Research Says to the Teacher: Teaching Listening*. Washington, D.C.: National Education Association, 1964.

Thorn, Elizabeth A. *Teaching the Language Arts: Speaking, Listening, Reading, Writing*. Toronto: Gage Educational Publishing, 1974.

Tutolo, D. J. "Teaching Critical Listening." *Language Arts* 52 (November 1975): 1108–12.

8

Reading: A Language Art

We are all of us learning to read all the time. —I. A. Richards

Reading instruction dominates the curriculum in most elementary school classrooms. It also receives more attention in the public press than any other aspect of schooling and it is the matter of greatest concern to parents of children in the elementary school. In one sense this attention and concern is justifiable: the ability to read is crucial in contemporary society. On the other hand, parental concern and media attention often cause a great deal of anxiety that serves no good purpose and causes a great deal of frustration among many teachers and children. It also seems inevitably to lead to a narrow focus on the skills needed to read and neglect of the role reading has in communication and human development.

We believe that reading is important, and that given the proper conditions virtually all children can learn to read. However, reading is but *one* of the language arts. As the authors of one reading methods book have said, "There is no such thing as an effective reading program that does not embrace *all* of the language arts—and their interrelationships."[1]

There may be a need to teach reading skills in special periods or special situations (as it is necessary to give specific instruction in other language arts

---

1. Robert A. McCracken and Marlene J. McCracken, *Reading Is Only the Tiger's Tail* (San Rafael, Calif.: Leswing Press, 1972), p. 13.

206

skills), but in general, reading instruction should be ongoing all day, every day, in the context of the other language arts and the purposes it serves. One of the over-riding messages of this book is that opportunities for teaching the language arts in meaningful ways abound throughout each day and that teachers who recognize these opportunities and know each child's needs can make the most of them. The receptive language arts of listening and reading, coupled with basic abilities of observing and thinking, enable us to acquire information and develop ideas that become ingredients in our speaking and writing. Children who express their reactions and creative extensions of the newly gained ideas and knowledge come to need and desire further reception.

READING AND LANGUAGE

Children know a great deal about their language. They show that they know how it works by their use of it, and using it reflects their understanding of the purposes it may serve. A teacher can build a successful reading instruction program by using what children already know as the foundation. In addition, a teacher must recognize that what children say and how they say it provide clues to the kinds of reading experiences from which they will learn best. Finally, learning to read does not take place suddenly—no more so than learning to talk. Without proper regard for these basic facts, a teacher may fall into the trap of teaching a mechanistic letter and word decoding approach that ignores the developmental nature of all learning and the real need for and the value of reading. Children's language ability reflects their maturity levels and the experiences they have had. It is a crucial factor in beginning reading and at subsequent levels of proficiency.

What Is Reading?

The previous paragraphs suggest a definition of reading, but in fact, a universally acceptable definition does not exist. Some teachers and a considerably larger number of parents consider vocalizing words as reading. Others would define reading as "getting meaning from print." Stauffer reports that teachers' responses to the question, "What is reading?" were usually one of these:[2]

1. Reading is a complex process.
2. Reading means to get information from the printed page.
3. Reading is the ability to pronounce and comprehend the printed word.
4. Reading is interpreting signs, letters, or symbols by assigning meanings to them.

---

2. Russell G. Stauffer, *Directing Reading Maturity as a Cognitive Process* (New York: Harper and Row, 1967), p. 5.

5.   Reading is receiving ideas and impressions from an author via the printed word.

Children's definitions are more creative. One of the authors of this book asked fifth graders, "What is reading?" and heard these answers:

1.   "Reading is where words go into your eyes and out your mouth."
2.   "Reading is a book with many, many adventures, and time and time again there are spots where you say 'I knew it.' "
3.   "Reading is when you open a book and words fall out."
4.   "Reading is when words come out of your book and into your head, so you can understand them."
5.   "Reading is like words floating across my mind."

Reading, of course, is a complex process, and it is this complexity that accounts for the variety of definitions of it. The absence of a comprehensive definition becomes apparent to anyone who tries to find one in a reading methods textbook. A number of these books do not even attempt to define reading and a greater number discuss the definition for several pages without actually giving a defining statement. There are exceptions. Wardhaugh says, "When a person reads, he is processing information."[3] (Of course, he does not say that all information processing is reading.) Spache and Spache state a fundamental fact: "Reading is obviously a multifaceted process, a process that, like a chameleon, changes its nature from one developmental stage to the next."[4] They point out that at one stage reading is largely a visual discrimination and remembering process; at another stage reading is largely recalling, interpreting, judging, and evaluating; and in both stages the success the reader achieves "is conditioned by such factors as his language development, his readiness for the school's objectives as determined by his home background, and the accuracy of his perceptual behavior in both visual and auditory discrimination." A final definition is Stauffer's: "Reading is a mental process requiring accurate word recognition, ability to call to mind particular meanings, and ability to shift or reassociate meanings—until the constructs or concepts presented are clearly grasped, critically evaluated, accepted and applied, or rejected."[5]

A teacher's understanding of the process of reading is doubtlessly much more important than a definition. Understanding of the process largely determines how he or she teaches it; therefore, if a teacher thinks that reading is pronouncing words correctly or that "meaning" comes from a printed page, it is the pupils' loss.

---

3. Ronald Wardhaugh, *Reading: A Linguistic Perspective* (New York: Harcourt, Brace and World, 1969), p. 52.

4. George D. Spache and Evelyn B. Spache, *Reading in the Elementary School*, 4th ed. (Boston: Allyn and Bacon, 1977), p. 3.

5. Stauffer, p. 16.

Value of Reading

In spite of the pressure for everyone to learn to read, it is not uncommon to hear that the need for reading is declining. Many people admit to learning virtually all that they know of current world events from television, and movie and television dramatizations of fiction are common. Children typically spend at least as much time each year watching TV as they do in the classroom.[6] And teachers well know that children remember TV commercials more easily than virtually anything in the school curriculum.

Yet at least a 1000 books are published in the United States each month and over 7500 magazines are published yearly. Undoubtedly the readers of these publications make up only a fraction of the total population—certainly less than 25 percent—but even adults who seldom read appear to value reading. Perhaps the reason is that everyone recognizes the need for communication and reading has been the major medium not only for transmitting thought, but also for building concepts; developing vocabulary; providing knowledge, pleasure, personal enrichment, and intellectual growth; aiding in understanding of personal problems and improving one's self-concept; and conveying the problems and ways of other peoples and cultures.

Reading also has the value of helping children learn to express their own thoughts and making them familiar with language patterns and ways of using language effectively. Reading stirs children's imaginations and helps to stimulate creative talents expressed through speech, writing, and dramatization.

Language Ability and Reading

The need for reading instructors to know the levels of children's language development and the nature of their experiences cannot be overemphasized. A child's performance in speaking is not always evidence of his or her language ability, but some degree of assurance and proficiency in language is essential to the child who is learning to read. Language proficiency shows not only in the ease and confidence of a child's speech but also in the ability to listen to and understand speech. Total language ability permits the child to learn to comprehend ideas formulated into sentences, to determine word meanings from the context of sentences, and to interpret ideas expressed by means of word symbols. Many of the difficulties children encounter in reading are highly related to inadequacies in using language. When the language to be read is too far removed from children's experiences, which they receive and express largely through language, problems in recognizing and understanding symbols are apt to arise.

A child's first sounds are without meaning; they are purely reflexive

---

6. George J. Becker, *Television and the Classroom Reading Program* (Newark, Del.: International Reading Association, 1973), p. 5.

responses to stimuli, but they include phonemes that later will be parts of words. Gradually, meanings become attached to various combinations or clusters of phonemes, perhaps first by the child and later by other persons in the environment (although their meanings might not correspond: to the child "da-da" may mean "This is fun," but a father interprets it to mean that the child has recognized him). As these combinations of phonemes begin to resemble words in the language a child hears from other people—"ba-ba," "ma-ma," and similar babbling—meaningful associations really begin. Thus, children learn early to associate meaning with patterns of sounds. They learn of the relationship between words and meanings. Children entering school can speak several thousand words; for many of these and other words they have some meaning attachment. For some words that they can speak they will have vague or false ideas about their meanings. This condition never changes although, of course, the number of words they speak and the meanings they know will increase. Language learning is a continuous process. We humans are always learning new words and their meanings, new meanings for words we already know, and new ways to combine words to express ideas and relate knowledge.

It is possible that a child who is proficient in language—or reasonably so—upon coming to school will not learn to read. Conceivably, too, after beginning to learn to read, a child who has considerable language ability will develop difficulties in reading. Problems associated with visual perception, emotional blocking, skill deficiencies, and so forth, may prevent reading success. On the other hand, without some proficiency in language, a child will not truly learn reading, no matter how well he or she can perceive word forms and perform other functions related to effective reading, because content will be unintelligible.

Necessary Skills for Reading

Because children's backgrounds, experiences, and maturity levels are so different, we cannot expect beginning readers to have the same skills and to have developed them equally or in a particular order. A reader may show strength in several of the reading skills that the mature reader possesses and weakness in others. In a general sense, the mature reader tends to merge the skills that children learn separately so that reading becomes a single skill. A brief description of the components of the total skill of reading follows;[7] we will elaborate in later sections of this chapter and in Chapter 9.

---

7. Adapted from John B. Carroll, "The Nature of the Reading Process," in *Reading Forum*, National Institute of Neurological Diseases and Stroke Monograph No. 11 (Washington, D.C.: U.S. Department of Health, Education, and Welfare, n.d.), pp. 5–7.

1. Skill in using the language that is to be read: Since language learning is a lifelong process, the extent of this skill, which beginners need, may, in some sense, be thought of as minimal. Usually a minimal level is some ability to speak and understand with confidence and fluency. Most important, the necessary level is knowledge of how the language works—how sentences are put together, what word order signifies, that some words name things, etc.—as demonstrated in language use. Each reader must have some skill in using language in order for the development of the composite skill of reading to continue.
2. Skill in dissecting spoken words into component sounds: Every reader needs to "sound out" words at times in order to determine meaning—although the maturing reader often merges this skill or uses it in conjunction with other skills.
3. Skill in recognizing and distinguishing different forms of letters in the alphabet (i.e., uppercase and lowercase letters, as well as different printed and handwritten forms).
4. Skill in applying the left-to-right principle by which words are spelled and put in order in continuous text: The mature reader demonstrates mastery of this skill with a minimal amount of refracted eye movement and "rereading."
5. Skill in using patterns of correspondence between letters and sounds that help in recognizing words known in speech or that help in pronouncing words that are not familiar: In a sense, this skill is a composite of several of the preceding ones; that is, skill in determining the sound values associated with letters, recognizing letters, and following a left-to-right order is necessary to learn the patterns of correspondence.
6. Skill in recognizing words by cues (total configuration, recognition of a structural element, and derivation of meaning from the context) as well as being able to use cues for pronunciation as an intermediate step in recognition.
7. Skill in apprehending the meaning of words and a "total message" in a manner analogous to apprehending meaning by listening.
8. Skill in reasoning and thinking about what is read: This skill is limited to the ability of the reader and to the experiences he or she has had. As the definitions of reading that are most comprehensive state, this skill at its highest level requires shifting and reassociating meanings until the reader grasps and reacts to the meaning in a particular context.

Some reading authorities do not consider all of the skills described as reading skills or might state them differently. Skills that our list does not include that some people might add—reading at a rate appropriate to the material, surveying or skimming material, determining the relevance of material to the purpose, and using resources—are skills in applying reading rather than in learning to read. All of these skills need instructional attention because an individual may not be able to make the greatest possible use of reading without them.

A MODERN READING PROGRAM

Reading in a modern school program is not an isolated entity; children read to gain information and ideas and for enjoyment as they learn the skills of reading. The use of reading as a learning tool thus receives emphasis from the very beginning of reading instruction. Reading is a natural part of many school activities, and a modern program encourages reading whenever possible. The reading program also takes into account the many different interests and abilities of the children in a class. Consequently today's reading programs are considerably more ambitious than one that merely "has" a child "in" a reading textbook.

Objectives of the Program

The fundamental objective for teaching reading is to develop in each child the attitudes, abilities, and skills that will enable him or her to secure information, foster and react to ideas, develop interests and tastes, and derive pleasure through reading. Instruction should focus on making all children as able and as diversified in reading as their capabilities allow. The first task is to help them acquire the skills to bring their experiences to bear upon the written symbols in order to interpret them efficiently and effectively. The second task is to develop the appreciation of reading and the skill to use it for personal growth. Success in *both* tasks is a prerequisite for achieving the fundamental objective of teaching reading, but the second task warrants special emphasis because experience has shown that schools successfully teach reading skills to most children but fail to transform these children into adults who actually read.

To accomplish the necessary tasks, a reading program should have three parts—which in a modern program are intertwined rather than built one upon another. These parts are:

1. Development of the fundamental skills of the reading process
2. Functional use of reading in learning
3. Use of reading for recreation and personal growth

The Bases of the Program

We commonly hear that there is no single best way to teach reading. For example, England's "Bullock Report," states:[8]

---

8. Alan Bullock, chair, *A Language for Life* (London: Her Majesty's Stationery Office, 1975), p. 77.

There is no one method, medium, approach, device or philosophy that holds the key to the process of learning to read. We believe that knowledge does exist to improve the teaching of reading, but that it does not lie in the triumphant discovery, or re-discovery, of a particular formula.

Nevertheless, recognizing that reading is a vital part (but only a part) of a total and interrelated program in all of the language arts does rule out some pro-cedures that have been used to teach children to read. Likewise, acceptance of particular objectives for reading instruction precludes the use of methods that are without merit in achieving these objectives. In other words, there may be no "one best way," but some procedures are not sound and some procedures are better than others.

1. A modern reading program requires conditions that facilitate reading, including an abundance of attractive reading materials in the class-room, a well-equipped and well-managed library that is easily accessi-ble to every child, attention to reading in all school activities, physical equipment that is attractive and appeals to children, and a vital in-terest in reading on the part of all teachers in the school.

2. An effective program provides for systematic skill development as needed by individual children. The program is often built around a series of textbooks that have been planned for sequential development of vocabulary and reading skills. Supplementary study guides and teacher's manuals usually provide content enrichment and practice ex-ercises, and corresponding workbooks supply additional practice and learning assessment materials. An adequate program, whether or not it has a high degree of structure and follows the content and organiza-tion of commercial materials, should foster continuity of growth in reading habits, skills, and attitudes and provide a wide variety of reading activities and materials that match children's interests and needs, including their needs in other school subjects.

3. A modern program must provide reading opportunities in the content areas of the curriculum. On an independent basis and under the teacher's guidance, students should read textbooks and trade books in content areas, as well as encyclopedias and other reference materials. In particular, learning to interpret maps, charts, tables, and graphs should be part of the program.

4. Guided literature reading, including the reading of prose and poetry by the teacher, is part of a modern reading program, as we saw in Chapter 5 and will consider again in subsequent chapters.

5. The reading program must provide time for free and voluntary reading by the children, outside of reading class without teacher guidance, of materials that interest them.

These components are basic to an effective program for teaching reading, but the most important element in instruction—other than the children, of

course—is the teacher.[9] Teachers need to understand how children learn to read and the factors that influence that learning. Smith urges teacher understanding in four areas: (1) the reading process and how children learn, (2) how language operates and the functioning of the brain, (3) the fact that in reading the brain provides more information than the print does, and (4) children learn to read by reading.[10] Put another way, in order to focus on the fundamental elements in learning to read, an effective program starts with teacher understanding of the following concepts and with incorporation of this understanding into instruction.

1. Success in learning to read derives from a background of rich experiences and the language associated with those experiences.
2. A close relationship binds instruction and growth in reading to experiences in oral language and writing.
3. Learning to read is a developmental process—a lifelong occupation—that relates to language growth and, in turn, facilitates it.

Perhaps it is true, though, as Heilman has said, that "reading problems in American schools are due less to the teachers' lack of knowledge than to their disinclination or inability to follow the sound principles of teaching which they already know."[11]

---

9. Harry Singer, in S. Jay Samuels, ed., *What Research Has to Say About Reading Instruction* (Newark, Del.: International Reading Association, 1978), p. 67, says that the hypothesis that it is the teacher and not the method or program that makes a difference in reading achievement has not yet been tested. However, he points out that the implication of this is not that a "teacher in a school could adopt any method or program of instruction and yet attain high achievement." Research has shown that some practices are better than others.

10. Adapted from Frank Smith, *Understanding Reading* (New York: Holt, Rinehart and Winston, 1978), p. v.

11. Arthur W. Heilman, *Principles and Practices of Teaching Reading* (Columbus, O.: Charles E. Merrill Books, 1961), p. 2.

214

Principles of Reading Instruction

Principles of reading instruction derive from the study of children's intellectual, physiological, and emotional growth and development. They are not infallible laws but they do provide a sound basis for teaching reading at all levels of instruction.

Arousing interest.   *The reading program must be stimulating, yet free from too much or the wrong kind of pressure.* Most children want to learn to read; they come to school eagerly and are willing to devote the time, effort, and energy necessary to learn. If the material they encounter in the reading program is interesting in content and style, their motivation to learn to read will remain high at each level of instruction. Materials—the books—do not provide all that is necessary in a stimulating reading program. The total classroom environment must be rich and vital, reading must be useful and fundamental to the total curriculum, and the teacher must be capable and understanding. Often the teacher, other forces in the school, and the parents—either together or singly—exert overt and subtle pressures on the child. Goals set beyond the child's capabilities, achievements compared with inappropriate norms, emphasis on "getting through" the material rather than on teaching, and expressions of disappointment and disapproval are sources of pressure that do not foster learning and growth.

Individualizing instruction.   *Learning to read is an individual process that calls for adjusting procedures and materials to fit each individual.* Teachers should study and teach children as individuals by accommodating differences in rate of learning, experiential background, maturity, interests, and so on. Dividing a class into three or four groups for instruction may be useful, but it will not teach children to read because it does not necessarily recognize the individuality of any child in any of the groups. The teacher must genuinely seek to meet the child's needs and expectations.

Insuring success.   *No child should experience repeated failure.* No one thrives on failure. Failure leads only to confusion and frustration. When children experience reading difficulty, they tend to avoid doing it, and the more difficulty they have, the more they will try to avoid it out of a fear of failing again. Certainly this practice may have serious personality and social consequences for children aside from preventing them from learning to read. Instead of not challenging children or avoiding the assignment of difficult tasks, however, teachers should remember that children will develop reading skills at different rates and that a reading program should offer opportunities for growth without failure.

Organizing instruction.   *The learning of new skills, attitudes, and abilities depends on previous learning.* This principle is as true in reading as in other learning. Classroom teachers, textbook authors, and other reading experts

disagree about the specificity of reading skills and the sequence in which teachers should present them. Some recognize a greater number of skills or subskills than do others and are explicit about sequence of presentation. Others have a more flexible approach to instructional sequence. Still others express little concern over the specificity of the skills and even less about teaching sequence. Differences of opinion aside, areas of agreement do exist. Obviously, for example, before children can use a dictionary properly, they must know alphabetical sequence, which they can learn only when they can recognize letters. Good teachers understand such logical needs and the appropriate learning sequence, and at the same time, they acknowledge individual variability. The important point is that teachers should organize instruction so as to reduce the hazard of neglecting essential skills or of "teaching" already acquired ones.

Deriving meaning. *Reading is a process of deriving meaning from written language.* It is not a process of deriving the exact meaning that an author intended since the meaning any reader obtains depends on language ability and the experiences that he or she brings to the reading act. Of course, if reading material is appropriate for the audience, the difference between intended meaning and meaning gained will be small, particularly if the audience has the skills to compensate for differences in language ability and experiences. Reading is not just a mechanical process of word-calling or "decoding"; simply saying words or recognizing them in silent reading does not constitute reading. Rather, reading requires the use of all of an individual's capabilities in deriving meaning from print. This is the point of reading from the beginning.

Encouraging independence. *Reading instruction must teach each child independence in reading.* Children must acquire skill in recognizing words without

216

having to consult another person, in completing tasks without continual direction, and in achieving the purposes of reading without teacher guidance. Of course, the development of such independence will occur gradually with guidance and encouragement.

Appraising progress.   *The program should include systematic and continuous diagnosis and evaluation.* The developmental nature of reading instruction makes it axiomatic that skills and abilities taught at each level should be appraised before progression to the next level. Much appraisal can be informal, by the teacher and by the child, but more formal evaluation should take place at regular intervals. Most importantly, evaluation results should guide instruction; that is, evaluation should be diagnostic and teachers should use it to determine what reteaching is necessary and what skills and abilities to teach next.

PRACTICES AND ISSUES IN THE TEACHING OF READING

As has been suggested, instruction in learning to read and guidance in the use of reading skills should spring from certain principles. Methods and approaches vary, however, and may depart in some respects from some of the principles outlined. In the following paragraphs, we will examine issues of a controversial nature, as well as practices that warrant special attention.

Pre–first-grade Reading

The question of when reading instruction should begin has no clear and simple answer. Is it "reading instruction" to help children recognize their names in print or to read them a story or to reinforce recognition of words such as *stop* on a sign, *men* and *women* on rest room doors, and names on the labels of their favorite food products? Indeed, few people agree on what constitutes instruction in reading. Never is this fact more apparent than when observing reading programs for young children. These programs vary considerably in philosophy, content, pace, and materials.

     A committee sponsored by seven national organizations issued a report on current practices in pre–first-grade reading instruction and recommended ways to improve them.[12] The committee strongly advocated giving young children sufficient opportunity to "express orally, graphically, and dramatically their feelings and responses to experiences," as well as to "interpret the language of others whether it is written, spoken, or nonverbal." Also, the report urges preparing

---

12. Interorganizational Committee, "Reading and Pre–First Grade: A Joint Statement of Concerns About Present Practices in Pre–First Grade Reading Instruction and Recommendations for Improvement," *Language Arts* 54 (April 1977): 459–61.

teachers to emphasize developmentally appropriate language experiences for young children and calls on professional organizations, colleges, and universities to support teachers in these efforts. The concerns and recommendations of the committee are these:

Concerns

1. A growing number of children are enrolled in pre-kindergarten and kindergarten classes in which highly structured pre-reading and reading programs are being used.
2. Decisions related to schooling, including the teaching of reading, are increasingly being made on economic and political bases instead of on our knowledge of young children and of how they best learn.
3. In a time of diminishing financial resources, schools often try to make "a good showing" on measures of achievement that may or may not be appropriate for the children involved. Such measures all too often dictate the content and goals of the programs.
4. In attempting to respond to pressures for high scores on widely-used measures of achievement, teachers of young children sometimes feel compelled to use materials, methods, and activities designed for older children. In so doing, they may impede the development of intellectual functions such as curiosity, critical thinking, and creative expression, and, at the same time, promote negative attitudes toward reading.
5. A need exists to provide alternative ways to teach and evaluate progress in pre-reading and reading skills.
6. Teachers of pre-first graders who are carrying out highly individualized programs without depending upon commercial readers and workbooks need help in articulating for themselves and the public *what* they are doing and *why*.

Recommendations

1. Provide reading experiences as an integrated part of the broader communication process that includes listening, speaking, and writing. A language experience approach is an example of such integration.
2. Provide for a broad range of activities both in scope and in content. Include direct experiences that offer opportunities to communicate in different settings with different persons.
3. Foster children's affective and cognitive development by providing materials, experiences, and opportunities to communicate what they know and how they feel.
4. Continually appraise how various aspects of each child's total development affects his/her reading development.
5. Use evaluative procedures that are developmentally appropriate for the children being assessed and that reflect the goals and objectives of the instructional program.
6. Insure feelings of success for all children in order to help them see themselves as persons who can enjoy exploring language and learning to read.
7. Plan flexibly in order to accommodate a variety of learning styles and ways of thinking.

8. Respect the language the child brings to school, and use it as a base for language activities.
9. Plan activities that will cause children to become active participants in the learning process rather than passive recipients of knowledge.
10. Provide opportunities for children to experiment with language and simply to have fun with it.
11. Require that pre-service and inservice teachers of young children be prepared in the teaching of reading in a way that emphasizes reading as an integral part of the language arts as well as the total curriculum.
12. Encourage developmentally appropriate language learning opportunities in the home.

The committee did not intend to focus its concerns and recommendations on materials and structured total-class programs and to ignore the differences among children in needs, interests, and experiences. It is the preschool situations which have structured formal programs for *all* children in a classroom at which the group was directing criticism. Obviously some children are ready to learn to read—and do so—before entering the first grade. Furthermore, no one should condemn the structured programs and materials themselves. The committee's criticisms of preschool reading programs may apply equally to the first grade—and beyond, with respect to some children. The issue is forcing children into situations for which they are not ready, and indeed, the dominant use of unrealistic appraisal methods combined with highly structured and narrowly conceived instructional materials may put pressure even on children who actually are ready for beginning reading instruction. Poor-quality materials and inadequate teaching are inexcusable at any level.

Reading Readiness

This discussion of reading readiness is fundamentally related to earlier statements regarding pupil differences in the development of various skills, abilities, and attitudes. Reading readiness is not an all-or-none proposition, however, nor does the term have the same meaning to all persons. Some people regard readiness (in reading or any skill area) as a stage in maturation—physical, mental, and emotional. Others define it as an expression of desire, purpose, or interest. Still others emphasize that readiness hinges largely on information and abilities gained through experience. In a longitudinal study of New Zealand children, for example, Marie Clay found that beginning readers become implicitly aware of and are able to integrate two distinct sets of concepts about print that adults tend to take for granted.[13] The first category, language concepts about print, includes (1) the child's understanding that print can be turned into speech to provide a message, (2) a knowledge that pictures aid in interpretation of the message, and (3) a

---

13. Marie Clay, *Reading: The Patterning of Complex Behavior* (Auckland, N.Z.: Heinemann Educational Books, 1972).

realization that print must be as sensible as spoken language. A second category, visual concepts about print, includes understanding that (1) print is directional, moving top to bottom and left to right, (2) a word is surrounded by white space, and (3) that concepts like "word" and "letter" are not the same.

Evidently, readiness for initial reading instruction depends generally on: (1) physical factors, such as the child's ability to see and hear words clearly; (2) mental factors, such as the ability to follow directions or to relate the sequence of events in a simple story; (3) social factors, such as the ability to work with others and to accept direction; (4) psychological factors, such as adjustment to schoolwork or apparent interest in reading; and (5) experiential factors, such as knowledge of the concepts and information that the child will meet in reading experiences.

Reading readiness simply expresses the old teaching rule that the teacher must begin at the child's level—the level of what he or she knows or can do—and build upon it. Reading readiness functions at all grade levels and in all reading activities. Children learn to read most rapidly and most successfully when all factors affecting readiness are favorable. At any stage in reading instruction, it is possible to improve and develop many of these factors. Predictably, however, views about the scope and nature of reading instruction are diverse. They range from delaying instruction until the child has matured sufficiently to cope with the symbolic nature of reading and shows an interest in print, planning opportunities for children to discover the relationships between print and oral language by sharing books and reinforcing understanding through writing activities, and isolating skills for mastery, to developing readiness systematically in such areas as personal and social adjustment, visual and auditory discrimination, language facility, habits of attention and work, eye movements, interests, and concept building through experiences.

Critics of the concept of reading readiness claim that it delays learning how to read. They have complained that some children are ready to learn to read, or perhaps may even be able to read, when they first enter school. It is true, of course, that some children already can read when they enter school. The percentage of children in the nation who know how to read when they begin school is unknown, but several studies completed in the late 1950s indicated that about 1 percent of children entering the first grade in one California city had learned to read.[14] We can speculate whether such factors as preschoolers' exposure to television shows like *Sesame Street* has affected preschool reading over the past two decades, but it is probably still safe to say that most kindergarten and first-grade teachers believe that a majority of first graders are not ready for immediate reading instruction at the start of the school year and that they benefit from a specific and highly individualized readiness program. Nevertheless, the widespread practice of spending six weeks developing "readiness" at the begin-

---

14. Dolores Durkin, "The Precocious Reader: A Study of Pre-school Reading Ability," *California Journal for Instructional Improvement* 2 (December 1959): 24–28.

ning of the year in the first grade and then instructing all of the children in beginning reading is unwarranted. Teachers and schools that follow this procedure have failed to recognize the purpose of reading readiness programs.

Perceptual and Discriminatory Development

Reading success depends considerably on visual and hearing abilities. Accurate vision is obviously important in reading, but it is equally obvious to most teachers that children, at any grade level, may have difficulty making fine visual discriminations, such as between *ch* and *th*. The relationship of the accurate perception of sounds to reading is perhaps less obvious since most reading is not done orally. The fact that reading is highly dependent on language development establishes the relationship, however.

Children entering school have developed considerable ability to see and distinguish likenesses and differences. Although they can discriminate among small items as well as large ones, they may not have had much experience in perceiving letters, combinations of letters, and combinations of words or in discriminating among them. Readiness programs typically provide practice in noting likenesses and differences among geometric figures and drawings of animals and other objects, however this kind of experience does not really develop perception and discrimination skills needed for reading. The value of perceptual training is not clear, but it appears that activities directed at visual perception and discrimination should focus primarily on words and letters.[15] Such practice does not require knowing names of either the letters or the words.

---

15. Lloyd O. Ollila, ed., *The Kindergarten Child and Reading* (Newark, Del.: International Reading Association, 1977), p. 15.

Rather, it should emphasize recognition of likenesses and differences as in the case of objects or drawings.

Auditory acuity is usually good by five years of age, but poor auditory acuity may retard reading achievement.[16] Of course, most beginning school children have the necessary acuity and most have considerable ability in auditory discrimination (since they have learned their language). Nevertheless, some children may have difficulty producing some sounds and discriminating among similar ones and they need both abilities to use auditory analysis to identify unknown written forms of words. Some children may profit from practice hearing differences in sounds in the several parts of words, hearing similar sounds, relating sounds to letters, and accurately pronouncing words that they use in their speech.

Word Recognition Skills

Children use word recognition or decoding skills to analyze unfamiliar written symbols for clues to their meaning. Essentially word recognition skills fit into two categories, structural and phonetic, although the context itself, as stated earlier, gives important clues to the meanings of unknown words. Pictures, word configuration or appearance, and dictionary pronunciations and definitions also facilitate recognition. The principal issues regarding these skills concern teaching methods and the extent to which individual children need to receive instruction in them.

Structural analysis is the recognition and use of word parts or the visual characteristics of words, in contrast to auditory characteristics. For example, a child may recognize a compound word like *football* by noting first that the word *ball* is part of it. Structural analysis also involves using knowledge of prefixes, suffixes, roots, inflectional endings, the division of words into syllables, and the effect of accent. The basis of structural analysis rests upon two fundamental facts about language: (1) a root word retains its basic meaning in derived and inflected forms and in compounds and (2) affixes to the root either have meaning themselves or add to the meaning of the root in specific ways. Thus, the addition of *s* to *boy* denotes a specific meaning; adding *un* to *like* combines the meaning of the root and the meaning of the prefix to give the meaning of the new word; and the meaning of the compound word *horseback* comes from the meanings of the words that form it.

Phonics is a tool for determining the pronunciation of an unknown graphic representation of a word. Beginning readers, in particular, may have large speaking and listening vocabularies, but they have no familiarity with the written

16. Henry P. Smith and Emerald V. Dechant, *Psychology in Teaching Reading* (Englewood Cliffs, N.J.: Prentice-Hall, 1961), pp. 137–38.

forms of these words. Of course, unless a word appears in speech, applying phonics to the written or printed form accomplishes nothing, even if the correct pronunciation ensues.

It is important to remember that children ordinarily come to school knowing several thousand words; that is, they have heard many thousands of words, have related meanings to many of them, and are able to use a large proportion of them in their own speaking. Thus, analyzing a word whose written form they may not know is often helpful because they may know the sound of it. Too, phonics may provide only an approximate pronunciation, but even from this version a reader may be able to derive the correct word, particularly if he or she uses other word recognition aids as well. For example, if a child encountered the sentence "The oar fell out of the boat" and knew every word except *oar*, phonetic analysis would provide at least a close approximation of its pronunciation. Then, whatever the child knew about oars (because he or she had seen them or had heard something about them referred to in stories), combined with the context of the sentence, should cue the correct pronunciation and the meaning of the word.

Context clues are important to a reader when used in combination with structural and phonetic clues, but also when used alone because they provide the quickest route to the meaning of an unknown word in most circumstances. For example, in the sentence "Bill climbed to the _____ of the tree" a reader would have no difficulty recognizing *top* if this were the unknown word and thus would not need to pause and use structural and phonetic clues. Of course, if the word were *apex, crown,* or *pinnacle*—though the likelihood that it would be one of these words would not be great—the context might not be enough and the readers would have to combine other clues or perhaps—because the use of such words is not common—use a dictionary. The more difficult the total context is to the reader, the less likely it is that the immediate context alone will provide adequate clues to word recognition. Using context clues properly, however, requires looking at more than the immediate context. Infrequently, readers will not recognize several words in a single sentence and will have to consult several preceding and subsequent sentences for context clues.

Teachers must remember that the skilled use of word recognition techniques is not an end in itself. The purpose of learning them is to be able to determine meaning. Pronouncing a word is effective if the child recognizes it by its sound. Knowing the meaning of a structural element may provide enough aid to determine the meaning. But gaining the meaning of a word—by any of the word recognition skills or various combinations of them—is only a necessary basic step in reading.

Good readers use word recognition clues with such versatility that they need not slow their reading by dwelling on phonic or structural analysis because they can determine the meaning of an unknown word from its context, its configuration, the construction of the sentence in which it appears, an accompanying diagram or picture, the paragraph or section heading, or some other means. Careless, unskilled, or unnecessary use of any word recognition technique can lead to the kinds of mistakes that cause loss of meaning and frustrate the reader. Skillful readers use only the most appropriate techniques, however, and use them cautiously.

The Phonics Controversy

As we pointed out in the preceding section, phonics is "the practice of using letter sounds as an aid to word recognition."[17] Phonics is and always has been very controversial. Its value rests on the assumption that there is enough consistency in the graphic representations of speech sounds that knowing these representations will help readers to identify unknown words. The crux of the controversy is how much instruction in symbol-to-sound correspondences is really helpful. Other sources of disagreement are whether some symbol-sound relationships are more useful than others, how to teach phonics, and what order or organization of phonics instruction is preferable.

Phonics enjoys tremendous popularity among many teachers as well as with the general public. Countless instructional programs stress phonics, as do the media. Many see it as the solution to *any* reading problem. Perhaps the most notable proponent of this view is Flesch, who wrote in *Why Johnny Can't Read*: "Reading means getting meaning from certain combinations of letters. Teach the child what each letter stands for and he can read."[18] Smith takes the opposite stand:[19]

> There is absolutely no evidence that teaching grammar helps a child to learn to speak, and none that drills in phonics or other non-reading activities help the development of reading. It is not difficult to argue that mastery of phonics develops only to the extent that reading proficiency is acquired, just as grammar is a meaningful and useful subject (if at all) only to those who already know how to use language . . . . Learning to read is not a matter of mastering rules. Children learn to read by reading.

Several other writers take a moderate position. Goodman stresses that fluent readers use three comprehension strategies in processing print: (1) graphophonic (written symbol/sound), (2) syntactic, and (3) semantic (meaning).[20] Artley views the role of phonics this way:[21]

---

17. Spache and Spache, p. 362.
18. Rudolph Flesch, *Why Johnny Can't Read* (New York: Harper, 1955), p. 2.
19. Frank Smith, *Psycholinguistics and Reading* (New York: Holt, Rinehart and Winston, 1973), p. 184.
20. Kenneth S. Goodman, "Behind the Eye: What Happens in Reading," in *Reading Process and Program*, edited by Kenneth S. Goodman and Olive S. Niles (Urbana, Ill.: National Council of Teachers of English, 1970), pp. 15–16.
21. A. Sterl Artley, "Phonics Revisited," *Language Arts* 54 (February 1977): 124–25.

There is no question about the fact that phonic cues are important in the identification of unfamiliar words, not as the primary means of identification, but as a support to other cue systems. If one is reading for meaning—and that is what reading is all about—one's intuitive knowledge of language, of the way words must 'fit' and make sense, is usually all that is required to enable the reader to predict what the unidentified words must be.

In addition to differences of opinion about the amount of phonics taught, the content and method of phonics teaching provoke wide disagreement. Several myths and a number of noncontroversial ideas about reading instruction also frequently factor into arguments concerning the major issues. For example, one myth has evolved from statements concerning the number of words that children must know by sight before they can use word recognition techniques, including phonics. Often instructions to teachers in basal reading series and in textbooks on reading instruction state that children need a vocabulary of 50, 75, 150, or some other number of sight words before learning phonics. Certainly, ability to recognize some words at sight is mandatory in order to use aids to word recognition (since such aids or techniques require relating an unknown word or a part of a word to a known word), but it is also true that even in beginning reading instruction such knowledge and techniques can be useful. For example, the child who can recognize at sight the words *can* and *mother* can learn that *man* begins like *mother* and rhymes with *can*. Instruction in all of the word recognition techniques described in the preceding section can begin during the initial reading lessons. Of course, children should learn them only if and as they need them.

Some researchers disapprove of phonics teaching because they say there is a lack of sound-symbol regularity in the language (many rules must have many exceptions, given that twenty-six letters must represent forty sounds). Studies have focused on the question of the utility of familiar phonics rules. Clymer, for example, examined forty-five commonly taught rules and found that only eighteen have few enough exceptions to be valid 75 percent of the time.[22] Emans found that the "two vowels go walking" rule applies to only 18 percent of the words he studied.[23] Of course, research evidence does not necessarily mean that a rule or generalization is equally useful to all readers.

Smith does not acknowledge that a reader would implement skills in addition to phonics in attempting to gain meaning or that a phonics rule might give the reader a beginning clue. Emphasizing the phenomenal number of rules required to account for the most common correspondences, Smith cites a Southwest Regional Laboratory for Educational Development study, which found that 166 rules would be necessary to account for the "spelling-to-sound" correspondences

---

22. Theodore Clymer, "The Utility of Phonic Generalizations in the Primary Grades," *Reading Teacher* 16 (1963): 252–58.

23. Robert Emans, "The Usefulness of Phonic Generalizations Above the Primary Grades," *Reading Teacher* 20 (1967): 419–25.

in 90 percent of the 6000 one- and two-syllable words in the vocabulary of children aged six to nine. Smith further states:[24]

> The rules often cannot be applied unless one is aware of the meaning and the syntactic role of the word and the way it carries stress. In other words, phonics is easy—provided one knows what a word is in the first place. . . . .[And] it is easy to show that any attempt to read by translating letters into sounds through the application and integration of phonics rules could result only in a catastrophic overloading of short-term memory. Besides, the use of spelling-to-sound rules is as absurd as clipping a lawn with nail scissors.

Given that most reading authorities, as well as classroom teachers, agree that at least some phonics teaching is essential, the question remains: how should phonics teaching occur. On this point, Spache and Spache have said, "We now know by reason of the overall results of the First-Grade Reading Studies and those extended into the second and third grades that no one system of teaching phonics is significantly better than any other, nor are reading systems based strongly on phonics superior."[25] Adams et al. suggest teaching phonics to beginning readers in a way that concentrates on patterns of letters because patterns, not individual letters, provide pronunciation clues. They further suggest that practice designed to promote rapid decoding should place unfamiliar words in sentences so that children can use spelling along with cues provided by the context.[26]

Competent readers have many cue systems to assist them in comprehending written language. Phonics, therefore, is not the most important area of reading instruction, nor does "sounding it out" constitute the most important way to derive meaning from a word that cannot be recognized at sight. Certainly, gaining understanding from graphic symbols is the purpose of reading and drills in phonic techniques should end with mastery of those principles helpful in gaining meaning. Heilman expressed this position well: "In the final analysis, the *optimum* amount of phonics instruction for every child is the *minimum* that he needs to become an independent reader."[27]

Linguistics and Reading

In recent decades, several kinds of linguists have taken an interest in reading instruction. They have proposed a variety of approaches, each of which seems to

---

24. Smith, *Psycholinguistics and Reading*, p. 186.

25. Spache and Spache, p. 361.

26. J. J. Adams, R. C. Anderson, and Dolores Durkin, "Beginning Reading: Theory and Practice," *Language Arts* 55 (January 1978): 19–25.

27. Arthur W. Heilman, *Principles and Practices of Teaching Reading* (Columbus, O.: Charles Merrill, 1972), p. 280.

have given rise to new instructional materials and/or models of the reading pro-cess. While not all phonologists, structuralists, transformationalists, and others agree on what to teach, they generally object to the following: the isolation of speech sounds, the use of a controlled or limited vocabulary in reading materials, stress on learning individual words rather than learning larger contextual units, and the unnatural language patterns present in some reading materials. Materials developed presumably on the basis of these objections, however, frequently have violated the principles these objections suggest.[28] Materials developed about a decade ago especially contradicted linguists' views, possibly, in part, because linguists at that time emphasized gaining meaning through the process of oral reading, on the grounds that the structure of language as it is voiced provided the clues necessary to meaning.

Fortunately, most linguists either have modified their positions concerning reading instruction or feel that much of what they earlier thought should be known is now common knowledge. On the other hand, an increasing number of *psycholinguists* are challenging other traditional understandings about the nature of the reading process. Psycholinguistics has its roots in transformational-generative grammar. The word itself denotes a combination of psychology and linguistics—the study of the development and nature of language combined with the study of how individuals acquire behavior and knowledge. Commenting on the extent to which psycholinguists have caught the attention and interest of educators, Smith describes them as "theorists and researchers in the scientific study of the uniquely human skills of language learning and use."[29]

Psycholinguists do not claim expertise in all aspects of reading instruction. To date, they have not directly investigated testing, motivation, persistence, and reading preferences, choices or tastes, for example. Educators probably know them best for studies of the meaning of children's oral reading errors, the rela-tionship between decoding (translating letters into sounds) and encoding, and the influence of context upon comprehension.

Psycholinguists' primary interest is how meaning is represented and recovered. Psycholinguistic literature challenges the concept of reading as word-by-word processing. In reading, as in speech, psycholinguists consider meaning to lie in a total utterance, not in separate letters or words. Psycholinguistic theory faults the assumptions that readers progress in stepwise fashion from print to speech to meaning (believing in a flow from print directly to meaning) and that the meaning of a sentence equals the sum of the meanings of each word in it. Goodman, for example, writes, "children have a driving concern for meaning from the very beginning"[30] and "the persistent search for and preoccupation with

---

28. See, for example, Spache and Spache, Chapter 4, for a discussion of this phenomenon.
29. Frank Smith, *Psycholinguistics and Reading,* p. v.
30. Kenneth S. Goodman, "What We Know About Reading," in *Findings of Research in Miscue Analysis,* edited by P. Allen and D. Watson (Urbana, Ill.: ERIC /RCS and National Council of Teachers of English, 1976), p. 6C.

meaning is more important than the particular meaning the reader arrives at."[31] Kavale and Schreiner describe the nature of psycholinguistic reading models in detail.[32] These models conceptualize skilled reading behavior as a "constructive language process where graphic, syntactic, and semantic information is processed simultaneously to achieve a reconstruction of meaning." The reconstruction process involves predicting the message of the writer, then confirming, rejecting, or modifying that prediction based on the extent to which it reduces uncertainty about the message as reading progresses.

Smith describes the following psycholinguistic themes and insights:[33]

1.   Only a small part of the information necessary for reading comprehension comes from the printed page.
2.   Comprehension must precede the identification of individual words.
3.   Reading is not decoding to spoken language.

The first and third statements, of course, are not really new insights, but they have been neglected. In 1937, Horn stated that a writer "does not really convey ideas to the reader; he merely stimulates him to construct them out of his own experience. If the concept is already in the reader's mind, the task is relatively easy."[34] And even earlier, Huey stated that "until the insidious thought of reading as word pronouncing is well worked out of our heads, it is well to place the emphasis where it really belongs, on reading as thought-getting, independent of expression."[35] A more accurate statement of the second insight or theme would be: "*Some* comprehension must precede the identification of individual words."

The point is that to obtain meaning from print readers must draw upon what they know about language and about the world. In their quest for meaning, it is unlikely that readers will be able to make "sense" of a passage by concentrating on individual letters or even on individual words. Goodman defines effective and efficient readers, for example, as "those who get meaning by using the least amount of perceptual information necessary."[36] Readers do not really recode, that is, go from a written symbol system or code to an oral one, but rather skip from print to meaning: "Research has demonstrated that readers, proficient or otherwise, cannot really be going from print to oral language and then to meaning. Very early, readers learn to do in parallel fashion with reading what they

31. Ibid., p. 58.
32. K. Kavale and R. Schreiner, "Psycholinguistic Implications for Beginning Reading Instruction," *Language Arts* 55 (January 1978): 34–35.
33. Smith, *Psycholinguistics and Reading*, p. v.
34. Ernest V. Horn, *Methods of Instruction in the Social Studies* (New York: Scribners, 1937), p. 154.
35. Edmund Burke Huey, *The Psychology and Pedagogy of Reading* (New York: Macmillan Co., 1913), p. 350.
36. Goodman, "What We Know About Reading," p. 59.

have learned to do with listening; to go from code, this time in graphic form, to meaning."[37]

Comprehension

Understanding usually comes from the ability to relate the writer's words to personal experiences, along with adequate language attached to those experiences and facility in utilizing word recognition clues. As the preceding section implied, however, there is a danger in many reading programs that too much emphasis on word recognition will retard the child's attainment of reading maturity and, in particular, may lead to inattention to reading for understanding.

Comprehension, which is the ultimate goal beyond word recognition, is a complex activity. The printed page itself contains no meaning. It is just ink on paper. Meaning comes from the mind of the reader. Thus, the problem in teaching children to read with understanding becomes one of providing many different experiences, selecting reading materials that relate to experiences they have had, and using skills that facilitate comparing the language on the printed page to their experiences.

A comprehensive reading program includes activities that will enable children to accomplish the following:

1. Get the main idea of a sentence, paragraph, or longer selection
2. Select important details
3. Follow directions
4. Determine the organization of the selection
5. Secure visual or other images from the material
6. Draw inferences
7. Anticipate meaning and predict outcomes and conclusions
8. Summarize what they have read
9. Discriminate between fact and opinion
10. Gain information from specific kinds of materials such as encyclopedias, atlases, maps, and graphs

These purposes apply not just to reading programs but to content studies as well. Reading instruction is only a foundation and cannot possibly give the amount and type of practice necessary to make a mature reader.

Not to be overlooked in teaching comprehension are concepts directly related to word meaning. Every teacher knows that it is possible for a child to recognize a word as one he or she has seen before and to say it without faltering

---

37. Ibid., p. 65.

but fail to understand clearly and correctly what it means in the setting in which it appears. The explanations of this phenomenon vary. Certainly some reading content is too abstract to convey meaning instantly. The principal reason, however, is that the teacher accepts the mere reproduction of the symbols, that is, equates saying the words with reading. Eliminating this kind of willingness requires that a teacher better understand the meaning of reading and acknowledge that students must go beyond such verbalism to read with understanding. The following procedures and similar ones should help in this effort:

1. Children require a background of experience that will help them to understand the reading they will do. To add to the experiences they have had outside of school, teachers should plan field trips; show them objects, films, pictures; play recordings; discuss their experiences and relate them to their reading; and tell children about events related to the content of their reading. Discussing the meanings of words that may be beyond the range of children's normal use and words that have uncommon meanings in the reading should not be forgotten.

2. Encourage children to raise questions regarding a selection before they read it. Also encourage questioning during and after reading; the focus should be upon *meaning* rather than on words or manner of reading.

3. Ask questions that require more than recalling facts and oral reading in response to factual questions. A question such as "What did Father do first when the car stopped?" followed by "Read the sentence that tells what he did," may be helpful in teaching scanning, providing practice in reading orally, and possibly in discovering word recognition difficulties, but the child might be able to answer it without having real understanding. Ask judgment and reasoning questions such as "What would you have done first?" "Why?"

4. Help children to recognize and interpret punctuation marks. This ability requires meaningful instruction in the use of punctuation in written expression and oral reading practice that includes attention to thought units and the relation of punctuation to reading by such units.

5. Ask children to paraphrase or tell in their own words what they have read. In order to comply, a child must grasp the meaning while reading by seeing relationships between the various parts and how they fit together for the total effect sought by the author. Related to the ability to paraphrase is understanding of the organization of sentences, paragraphs, and larger units. Make a deliberate effort to teach sentence sense and variations in sentence and paragraph order.

6. The most effective learning about a topic results from wide reading on that topic rather than from intensive "digging" in only one source. Thus, teachers should help children locate and read selectively from a range of sources on topics that interest them. Reading activities should expose pupils to figurative language, bias, and analogy.

Oral Reading

Oral reading, in contrast to silent reading, is a slow, inefficient, word-by-word process. Its indiscriminate use in the classroom can do much to develop bad reading and listening habits. It appears most indefensibly and routinely in reading instruction as "round-robin" reading, the practice of having a group silently "follow along" while its members take turns reading aloud. Oral reading, nevertheless, is a form of communication and can have a place in the classroom.

There are two types of oral reading: (1) sight reading, in which the reader has not prepared for the oral presentation; and (2) prepared oral reading for communication and/or enjoyment. The teacher uses the first type to determine a pupil's ability in recognizing words, in phrasing, and in enunciation, and to evaluate the attention given to punctuation in reading. This type of oral reading is done individually, with only the teacher for an audience. An illustration of one-to-one oral reading by a child for diagnostic purposes is "miscue analysis," a set of specific procedures for analyzing children's oral reading miscues (errors).[38] The second type of oral reading calls for preparation and is a form of true communication that is useful in proving a point in a discussion; sharing an exciting, happy, or sad part of a story; answering specific questions; reading reports, directions, announcements, and creative products; and reading in choral and dramatic situations.

Oral reading is a complex skill that demands that the reader not only recognize the words and understand the content, but also convey this understanding to an audience. Because of this complexity, silent reading (except as noted above) should always precede oral reading in order to resolve vocabulary and meaning problems prior to facing the audience. A child who stumbles through unfamiliar material feels confused and inadequate and not only fails to interpret the material to the audience but also is likely to be less interested in reading or speaking before a group again.

Oral reading has a particular place in the teaching of literature. The teacher reads orally to develop interest in reading, to develop appreciation, and to provide stimulation and excitement. Poetry should always be read aloud and the rhyme and rhythm savored and enjoyed. Many stories, too, are more effective when read aloud and accompanied by sound effects and changes in intonation and speed. Every day the teacher should spend time reading aloud something that the children will enjoy. Sometimes the selection can be above the reading level of some listeners, as long as it is not above the comprehension level. For example, few third-grade children would read *Rabbit Hill* for themselves, but they

---

38. Not only has miscue analysis been applied to instructional decision making for individual children, but a model of the reading process has also been inferred from the miscues observed in the oral reading of hundreds of children. See, for example, *Findings of Research in Miscue Analysis: Classroom Implications* edited by P. David Allen and D. W. Watson (Urbana, Ill.: ERIC/RCS and National Council of Teachers of English, 1976).

enjoy hearing it read.[39] In addition, a child might read a selection from a story that he or she has particularly enjoyed and classmates have not read. Some of the other children might decide to read the same story as a result of the presentation. It is good practice for the children to establish standards for oral reading, as they might for other oral and written language activities. One fifth-grade class developed these standards and a pupil wrote them on a chart:

When reading aloud

1. Make sure you have a good reason.
2. Prepare ahead of time.
3. Read carefully and clearly.
4. Be certain everyone hears you.
5. Pay attention to punctuation.
6. Try to read with expression.

Organizing for Instruction

Of the many ways to organize an instructional reading program, the traditional one is to divide the children into two to five groups (most commonly three), based on the children's reading levels as measured by standardized reading tests, informal appraisal of reading ability by the teacher, and knowledge about the children's previous experiences. The intent is for all of the children in a group to have approximately the same reading ability. The principal advantage of this plan is that it narrows the range of abilities that the teacher must deal with at any one time.

Nevertheless, the traditional plan has a number of limitations, which have led to the advancement of other plans for instruction. One limitation is that individual variation in ability is so great that grouping does not really solve the problem inherent in teaching widely different individuals. Another is that standardized reading tests and other means of appraisal may not reveal differences in the level of different reading abilities used by a child, but rather give only a composite picture that may not be meaningful for specific instructional purposes. Critics of the traditional plan also have argued that the stigma of being in the lower-level groups may retard growth.

Other plans for instruction include: (1) grouping on the basis of interests rather than ability and (2) grouping on the basis of social preferences. Both of these plans allow a teacher to deal with fewer children at a time, just as the traditional plan does. But both are likely to produce groups whose range of reading abilities is even greater than the ones the traditional plan would create.

An organizational plan that has received considerable attention recently is

---

39. Robert Lawson, *Rabbit Hill* (New York: Viking Press, 1944).

the individualized approach, which we will discuss at length in Chapter 9 (see section entitled "Approaches to Reading Instruction"). Briefly, this plan allows children to read materials of their own choosing at their own rate and to keep their own records. Advocates of the plan claim that it truly provides instruction for children at their own levels, that children's interest in reading is greater because they have chosen what they will read, and that it fosters self-direction, self-confidence and other positive traits. Additionally, proponents emphasize that it eliminates competition among groups, although they admit to increased competition among individual pupils. Criticism of the individualized approach centers on the possible lack of a systematic plan for teaching various reading skills. Obviously a limited supply of books, an inexperienced teacher, and a large number of pupils in some classrooms would all complicate implementation of the plan.

Teachers may decide to be eclectic, to combine features of many plans. For example, group study may facilitate instruction in a specific skill that members need to improve. Group membership remains flexible to accommodate special interests and individual problems. Instruction on an individual basis as well as in large and small groups accompanies oral reading by the teacher, free reading, and other forms of instruction in balanced language arts and literature programs.

In planning for reading instruction the teacher must recognize the purposes of such instruction, the fact that these purposes tend to be very specific from time to time, and that they change as children's reading abilities expand. Such recognition shows an awareness of the range of children's interests, needs, attitudes, and abilities. Even so, no single plan will achieve all of the purposes, recognize all of the differences, and be compatible with every teacher's personality and teaching ability. In other words, "To find one plan of class organization to be executed effectively by all teachers with all children is as difficult as finding a word to rhyme with orange."[40]

EXERCISES FOR THOUGHT AND ACTION

1. What activities or situations that occur daily or almost every day in the classroom might provide opportunities for purposeful oral reading? List them and explain how you would make oral reading part of each.
2. What is the significance of a child's early language development in learning to read? How can the teacher extend this development?
3. As a class, plan a booklet for parents of children learning to read. Decide on the most useful content and plan a format that will invite their reading.
4. Discuss or debate the following statement by Frank Smith: "Teachers have a critical function in helping children learn to read . . . . They must be trusted more because formal instructional systems—prepackaged materials and programs—must be trusted less" (*Understanding Reading*, p. 186).
5. Select three basal readers for the same level from three different publishers. Examine them carefully using criteria provided in Chapter 4. Recommend one for adoption in a local school and provide a written rationale for your choice.
6. Examine several reading methods textbooks (e.g., Spache and Spache). In a general way, compare their treatment of reading: its definition, major issues, popular approaches, and so on.
7. Write your reaction to Chapter V, "The Nature of the Perceptual Process in Reading," in *The Psychology and Pedagogy of Reading* by Edmund Burke Huey (Cambridge, Mass.: MIT Press, 1968) in terms of what you know about this process now and what Huey knew when he wrote the chapter (first published in 1908).
8. Prepare a resource file of teacher-made or commercial materials that might be useful in your reading program. The file must be expandable and well organized for easy access. Bring the file to class and share it with colleagues. Categories in the file might include: getting the main idea, selecting details, following directions, drawing inferences, summarizing, discriminating fact from opinion, and using reference materials.
9. From the statement of reading instruction principles presented in this chapter, select one principle to react to critically. Support your reaction

---

40. Emmett A. Betts, "Developing Basic Reading Skills Through Effective Class Organization," *Education* 78 (May 1958): 571.

with references to the educational literature on the teaching of reading, including reports of research in that literature.

10. If reading instruction is part of the program in a kindergarten or preschool classroom in the nearby area, arrange to observe and discuss the program with the teacher. Report what you learned.

11. Psycholinguistics is a very popular word today in the vocabulary of reading instruction. Scan the issues of one educational journal published in the past year for articles about psycholinguistics and reading. Compare the contents of relevant articles with the statements on the topic in this chapter.

12. Not all of the issues concerning reading instruction were discussed in this chapter (nor are they in the next). Investigate the literature and report to the class the substance of other issues (e.g., measurement of reading achievement, teaching children with dialects considerably divergent from standard English). Contrast different viewpoints.

13. Pre–first-grade reading instruction has a lengthy history and has been the subject of a fair amount of research. Investigate this topic and summarize your findings for the class.

14. Examine one or more of the widely advertised phonics programs for teaching reading or for supplementing basal programs. Criticize these programs on the basis of your personal experience and your reading. What do they contain that you would find useful as a teacher?

SELECTED REFERENCES

Allen, Roach Van. *Language Experiences in Communication.* Boston: Houghton Mifflin, 1976.

Durkin, Dolores. *Teaching Them to Read.* Boston: Allyn and Bacon, 1978.

Heilman, A. *Principles and Practices of Teaching Reading.* Columbus, O.: Charles Merrill, 1972.

McCracken, Robert A., and McCracken, Marlene J. *Reading Is Only the Tiger's Tail.* San Rafael, Calif.: Leswing Press, 1972.

Page, William, ed. *Help for the Reading Teacher: New Directions in Research.* Urbana, Ill.: ERIC Clearinghouse on Reading and Communication Skills, 1975.

Pearson, P. David, and Johnson, Dale D. *Teaching Reading Comprehension.* New York: Holt, Rinehart and Winston, 1978.

Smith, Frank. *Comprehension and Learning: A Conceptual Framework for Teachers.* New York: Holt, Rinehart and Winston, 1975.

Smith, Frank. *Psycholinguistics and Reading.* New York: Holt, Rinehart and Winston, 1973.

Smith, Frank. *Understanding Reading: A Psycholinguistic Analysis of Reading and Learning to Read.* 2d ed. New York: Holt, Rinehart and Winston, 1978.

Spache, George D., and Spache, Evelyn B. *Reading in the Elementary School.* 4th ed. Boston: Allyn and Bacon, 1977.

Stauffer, Russell G. *Directing the Reading-thinking Process.* New York: Harper and Row, 1975.

9

Instruction in Reading Skills

Then she went to the blackboard and printed the alphabet in enor-
mous square capitals, turned to the class and asked, "Does anybody
know what these are?"
    I suppose she chose me because she knew my name; as I read
the alphabet a faint line appeared between her eyebrows, and after
making me read most of My First Reader *and the stock-market*
quotations from The Mobile Register *aloud, she discovered that I*
was literate and looked at me with more than faint distaste. Miss
Caroline told me to tell my father not to teach me any more, it would
interfere with my reading.—Harper Lee, To Kill a Mockingbird.*

More has been said and written about teaching reading than about any of the other language arts areas or, for that matter, about any other aspect of the school curriculum. All of this attention stems from the importance of reading in school and throughout life and from the fact that some children have difficulty learning to read or never learn to read very well. Delay in learning and inability to read very well hinder successful learning in most areas of the school curriculum.

    Although concern about children who have trouble learning to read is justifiable, perhaps we should show greater concern for the fact that few of the people who do learn to read ever do more reading than is absolutely required of them. One reason for this lack of interest may be that our school reading pro-

---

* Harper Lee, *To Kill a Mockingbird* (Philadelphia: J. B. Lippincott Co.), p. 23. Copyright © 1960 by Harper Lee. Used by permission of the publisher.

grams give too little regard to the bases and principles of reading, which we discussed in Chapter 8. In this chapter we will look at various methods not only to teach children to read but also to motivate them to develop lifetime reading habits. Included in this discussion are examples of reading lessons and activities, and comments about instructional reading materials and the role of evaluation in the reading program.

APPROACHES TO READING INSTRUCTION

A wide range of methods for or approaches to instruction in reading covers the educational landscape. Some approaches are relatively new, some are old ones in new apparel, and some have been in use for many years. Differences in approaches that involve actual procedures we can rightly call differences in method, although within some approaches the emphasis given each element (e.g., phonics) or the prescribed order of skill instruction varies. For the most part, however, the differences simply involve different types of materials, different ways of grouping, or variations in the way a child progresses from one achievement level to another.

The Basal Reader Approach

The basal reader approach is the one most widely used in teaching reading and the one that has been in longest continual use in schools. The basis of the approach is the belief that the skills needed to recognize words, gain understanding from written language, and use reading as a means for learning must be organized systematically and as completely as possible, with full recognition of the relationships among the skills and the developmental nature of learning. The approach requires a set of textbooks (and usually workbooks, filmstrips, supplemental books, etc.) that present skills and vocabulary systematically and in a sequential and developmental fashion. In other words, the program or approach is in the textbooks and related materials, which include, as a fundamental part of the program, teachers' manuals containing specific directions for developing skills, vocabulary, and related attitudes and abilities; for organizing the class to provide effective instruction; and for evaluating achievement and diagnosing difficulties.

While the instructional designs of all basal reading textbooks series are not alike, they do generally provide for (1) preparational activities—introduction of new vocabulary, setting purposes for reading, and establishing experiential backgrounds; (2) directed reading of the selection; (3) introduction to and practice in the use of particular skills; (4) checking skill learning; and (5) enrichment activities—supplemental reading, related arts, and ways to provide additional background.

The Spaches say that "because of its almost universal use in America, the

basal reading program is the target of much criticism and abuse."[1] Certainly, if teachers use only these materials or if they use all of the reading experiences provided with all of the children and vary only the rates of presentation, much of the criticism is justifiable. Likewise, a program characterized by excessive vocabulary control and repetition, awkward and unchildlike sentence constructions, insistence on a set number of reading groups, and unrealistic or unappealing stories warrants criticism. Many reading authorities also argue that the materials in a basal program may furnish a crutch for uninspired teachers.

Those who advocate a basal program value its organized instructional sequence. In using basal programs, however, teachers need to be flexible in grouping pupils, use the teacher's manuals as guides rather than as prescriptions, and emphasize comprehension to a greater degree than some basal programs suggest (instead of decoding or word identification). In addition, teachers should use workbooks and ditto worksheets appropriately, assigning portions of them to individual students as their needs dictate rather than simply having all children fill in all the blanks.

In recent years textbook publishers have responded to criticisms of basal programs by eliminating rigidly graded and labeled books and by increasing the vocabulary loads in them; incorporating more mature, less repetitive, and naturally structured language; and including a variety of supplementary materials that permit a good deal of individualization in instruction. They have

---

1. George D. Spache and Evelyn B. Spache, *Reading in the Elementary School*, 4th ed. (Boston: Allyn and Bacon, 1977), p. 41.

238

also made an effort to change the suburban, middle-class flavor of the content. Content increasingly includes stories about various ethnic and racial groups in varied settings.

The Language-experience Approach

Children's experiential backgrounds and their abilities to express themselves orally should determine the content and form of their reading material, according to proponents of the language-experience approach. The basic premise of the approach is that children need to understand the relationship between speaking and writing—and thus between speaking and reading—in order to learn to read easily. Pupils write about their experiences or familiar subjects either independently or by dictating to the teacher. From the time children start school, teachers encourage them to talk about subjects that interest them. They may speak individually or join together in telling about an activity in which they participated. After the teacher has written the stories on charts, the child or group of children who "wrote" them reads them to classmates. Subsequently the teacher encourages children to write their own stories. Thus, writing receives earlier and greater emphasis in this approach than it does in some others.

Many aspects of this approach are little different from practices that responsible teachers have always used in connection with basal programs. What makes this method unique is that teachers introduce reading skills as they emerge from writing and reading. Consequently the responsibility for the program thus rests heavily on the teacher, who must understand not only the process of reading but also the role of each element in the process and its relationship to the others. Hall says that teachers who adopt this approach should demonstrate the following:[2]

1.   Acceptance of each child's language as it is
2.   Recognition of the creative nature of the approach
3.   Recognition of reading as a language activity that serves as a communication tool and requires the integration of its teaching with language instruction.

The language-experience approach is particularly useful in the beginning stages of reading instruction because young children take genuine interest in the attention it gives to their ideas and to what they say. Initial emphasis on reading as communication is crucial to the development of attitudes that pay off in later instruction. Of course, some children have difficulty talking about their experiences, but as we stressed in Chapter 8, adequate attention to oral language development will avert this problem.

---

2. Mary Anne Hall, *Teaching Reading as a Language Experience* (Columbus, O.: Charles E. Merrill Publishing Co., 1970), p. 10.

A number of writers, including Shuy, have emphasized the value of the language experience approach for disadvantaged pupils.[3] Shuy suggests that using the child's language avoids the types of sentences that these children have difficulty reading and minimizes omission of inflections, and word endings and other problems with standard English grammar. But writing experiences told in a nonstandard dialect raises the issue of spelling and possibly limits the speaker's progress toward reading and writing standard English.

Critics of the language-experience approach do not deny the value of integrating instruction of all communication skills, but they do question the assumption that a child's listening, speaking, writing, and reading vocabularies are similar and that vocabulary learning transfers readily from one skill to another. In addition, they frown on the frequently incidental nature of this approach in teaching skills and question the wisdom of using this approach alone to teach pupils who soon will have to do a considerable amount of content reading. On the other hand, proper planning by an industrious and skilled teacher who has many materials at hand should overcome such problems.

The Individualized Approach

Since children learn at different rates and in different ways, few educators would disagree with the assertion that learning is more effective and more efficient when learners are allowed to progress at their own pace and to the extent of their capacities. For this reason and because of the fact that motivation to learn is a significant factor in success, interest has been generated in recent years in an individualized approach to reading instruction. In this approach each pupil chooses his or her own reading materials. Presumably, given this freedom, the child will pursue personal interests and read extensively.

The literature supports this concept of wide reading of self-selected high quality materials. In an excellent discussion of individualized reading instruction, Stauffer states that certain skills (locating and selecting information, being resourceful, etc.) can be taught only in an individualized approach and others can be brought to highest fruition only in such a program.[4] In a related discussion focusing on the neglected goal of "making readers" (as opposed to merely teaching children how to read) Huck has stated, "I believe that children become readers only by reading many books of their own choosing and by hearing someone reading literature of quality aloud with obvious delight and enthusiasm."[5]

---

3. Roger W. Shuy, "Some Considerations for Developing Beginning Reading Materials for Ghetto Children, *Journal of Reading Behavior* 1 (Spring 1969): 33–44.

4. Russell G. Stauffer, *Directing Reading Maturity as a Cognitive Process* (New York: Harper and Row, 1969), p. 124.

5. Charlotte S. Huck, *Children's Literature in the Elementary School* (New York: Holt, Rinehart and Winston, 1976), p. viii.

And Smith says "children learn to read only by reading . . . provided children have adequate opportunity to explore and test their hypotheses in a world of meaningful print, they can and do succeed in learning to read."[6]

While teaching practices in this approach vary widely, all emphasize that the pupil and the teacher should meet at least every few days to discuss what the child has read and to check progress in skill development. As Durkin points out, however, many teachers turn these conferences into a full-scale tutoring program and spend an undue amount of time exclusively teaching reading skills.[7] In fact, the aim of the conference is to personalize instruction somewhat and to assess pupil growth.

Durkin also emphasizes that today there is "great variety in classroom practices that go under the heading of Individualized Reading Program."[8] Perhaps individualized reading is an expression of a philosophy about classroom organization and materials rather than an "approach," although descriptions of individualized reading programs by Jeannette Veatch, Lyman C. Hunt, Jr., and others are quite prescriptive.[9] Nevertheless, at the instructional level the various programs do share some characteristics. Extensive reading of varied materials is one. A second characteristic is that individualized reading programs develop skills based on a child's needs right from the start (skill activities might take place in small groups) and the teacher keeps a record of each child's progress. Good record keeping is an integral part of effective individualized programs. In some programs, the teacher initially follows a language-experience approach, whereas in others, beginning instruction comes from the first books of a basal series. In still others, teachers use simply written books from various sources to teach the first reading skills.

Some advocates of an individualized approach stress the role of technology in achieving learning objectives. By "technology" they mean programmed materials, audiovisual devices and programs, boxed kits, and computer-assisted instruction. Many of these materials permit a large degree of self-instruction and present skills sequentially. As we will see in a later section, the mechanistic aspects of this type of individualization disturb many teachers. The actual effects of technological instruction on a child's learning are difficult to determine, as are the effects of most educational materials.

Of far greater importance than technological aids to the success of this approach is making many books accessible to the children. Teachers must discover and feed children's interests. By making a large number of books available, the

6. Frank Smith, *Understanding Reading* (New York: Holt, Rinehart and Winston, 1978), p. 186.

7. Dolores Durkin, *Teaching Them to Read*, 2d ed. (Boston: Allyn and Bacon, 1974), p. 72.

8. Ibid., p. 73

9. Lyman C. Hunt, Jr., ed., *The Individualized Reading Program: A Guide for Classroom Teaching*, Proceedings of the Eleventh Annual Convention of the International Reading Association, vol. II, pt. 3 (Newark, Del.: International Reading Association, 1967).

teacher can enhance the possibility that children will increase their reading skill by selecting their own reading material (e. g., a child may continue to read books of the same difficulty level), a possibility raised by some critics of the individualized approach. The likelihood is small that all of the books about a particular subject will have the same reading level. Sharing what they have read with classmates is a good way to extend students' reading interests.

Linguistic Approaches

Some publishers advertise reading programs as "linguistic" programs. In fact, virtually all basal programs at least purport to be "linguistically oriented." This emphasis is declining somewhat in overdue recognition that *any* reading program could not be other than linguistic. In addition, the programs developed in the 1960s and early 1970s varied so greatly in their stress on "linguistic orientation" that ideas about what linguistic principles have value in reading methodology became quite confused. Linguists developed some linguistic approaches, but others were the result of attempts by educators to apply linguistic research to reading instruction. The results of linguistic research have changed the teaching of reading (although many have been misapplied), but they have not addressed all of the issues or solved all of the problems. Thus, this early statement by Goodman remains sound:[10]

> The linguist is carrying on his proper function when he advances linguistic generalizations that he believes apply to the teaching of reading. He is also performing a fitting and useful function when he criticizes the teaching of reading from his linguistic vantage point. But he is not on firm ground when he produces reading programs that are based solely on linguistic criteria.

Differences in "linguistic" approaches to reading instruction are due both to differences among linguists as to their specialties and the theoretical bases for their studies of language and to differences in interpretation of their findings and research applications by educators and the many nonlinguists who "jumped on the linguistic bandwagon." Adding to the confusion over *what principles* of linguistics apply to reading instruction is the fact that knowledge about language—how it works and how we learn it—has changed rather rapidly in recent years. Basically, though, most of the linguistic programs, particularly the ones based on commercial materials, strive to avoid various elements of conventional practice. In other words, the programs that stress a linguistic orientation often do not include the learning of whole words, learning words by sight, and using phonics and picture clues to identify words. At least they tend not to use terminology that would indicate they advocate using phonics clues, whole words,

---

10. Kenneth S. Goodman, "The Linguistics of Reading," *Elementary School Journal* 64 (April 1964): 355–61.

and so on. Generally, the theoretical base is that reading is the translation of graphic symbols into speech sounds. Some emphasize learning "regular" spelling patterns to accomplish this goal; others emphasize language patterns and oral reading. Many have departed from more-or-less typical content; that is, some have virtually no story content and others include literature selections without regard to controlling vocabulary.

In general, reading programs identified as "linguistic" do not owe their origins to individuals identified by themselves or others as psycholinguists, although some recently published basal programs indicate that they were written from a "psycholinguistic perspective." Presumably, psycholinguists helped to develop them. Many psycholinguists, such as Smith, remain critics of aspects of reading instruction,[11] although his and other psycholinguists' theories and research findings have likely affected teaching practices. For example, Goodman's suggestion that prompting and correcting oral reading errors may interfere with a child's comprehension has probably changed some practices of a fair number of teachers.

Programmed Reading Instruction

Commercial programmed instructional materials present subject matter (in reading, skills related to decoding and comprehension) in small units, each calling for a response from the pupil. Following each unit is a key that tells the child whether his or her answer is right or wrong. The objective of programmed instruction is to permit each child to learn at her or his own rate, and the basis of the programmed reading instruction is that learning to read requires learning various skills, which can be divided into small units and taught sequentially.

Proponents of programming state that pupils may or may not become involved with the content of a conventional book, but they must become involved in a program. They also stress the value of reinforcing learning at each step and the opportunity to correct mistakes immediately. Critics of programming are disturbed by its impersonal approach and question the view that effective readers are those who have mastered a series of sequentially presented skills, if indeed the theoretical base that underlies the order and content of the program can be said to exist in the first place.

There are many unanswered questions regarding all programmed instruction, and reading programs are no exception. Perhaps the careful analysis of reading skills and abilities that is necessary for the writing of programs will benefit all reading instruction. Too, recognizing differences in students' learning rates may add insight into their needs and ways of learning. On the other hand, the mechanical nature of programming is not likely to have sustained appeal for instinctively creative teachers and pupils.

---

11. Smith, *Understanding Reading.*

Other Approaches

Still other approaches that have won some acceptance with teachers use different procedures (because the underlying philosophies differ), but the characteristic that sets most of them apart is their use of different materials. For example, the Initial Teaching Alphabet approach (abbreviated "i.t.a." or "i/t/a") is a set of materials that employs a special alphabet that children are also to use in their writing. This alphabet contains forty-four symbols that look somewhat like the letters in the conventional alphabet—except that i/t/a does not use "g" and "x"—all of which are in lowercase form. The objective is to achieve a closer grapheme-phoneme correspondence than is ordinarily possible. Thus the child theoretically sees only one symbol for each sound and learns to make only one symbol, rather than both capital and lowercase (the capital letters are simply larger versions of lowercase ones). The alphabet does not allow printed variation in pronunciation, but presumably a teacher writing in i/t/a could take into account the local dialect. Results from using i/t/a have generally shown that children do learn to read early, that they do a good deal of writing, and that they can make the transition to reading conventional material. Many reading authorities, however, seem to agree with Heilman that, "Data from various studies have failed to indicate any significant superiority in reading achievement at the end of grade one which accrues from the use of i/t/a."[12]

Another program, called "Words in Color," codes forty-eight phonemes with different colors. In other words, a particular sound is always the same color even though it is represented by various letters. A third program, which is essentially a phonics approach is the "Open Court" program. Described as a "cor-related language arts program," it includes extensive alphabet drills, attention to blending of sounds, and detailed teacher's manuals with day-by-day directions for teaching spelling, punctuation, composition, oral activities, and so on.

Actually, defining an approach or method results in a great deal of ambiguity, because some characteristics of one approach tend to merge with those of one or more of the others. Various reports of reading research are likely to identify all of the approaches just described plus many other improvizations on or combinations of them.

Regardless of the name given to the approach or method that a teacher adopts, the program should meet the criteria for an effective program stated in Chapter 8 and should be compatible with the principles of reading instruction we have outlined. The real key to effective instruction in reading, then, is the teacher, rather than an approach or method itself. The teacher who understands the processes of reading and learning how to read is a far greater asset to children than an explicit approach, a prepackaged program, or a set of materials. Endorsing this view is the British team responsible for the Bullock report: "Much of the misunderstanding surrounding the debate about reading results from the lack of a

---

12. Arthur W. Heilman, *Principles and Practices of Teaching Reading*, 4th ed. (Columbus, O.: Charles E. Merrill Publishing Co., 1977), p. 115.

proper examination of what the process involves."[13] The responsibility for developing a program based on sound principles clearly belongs to the teacher.

THE READING LESSON

Knowing what to do and when to do it is essential in effective reading instruction. This kind of awareness requires a great deal of knowledge about children in general and about each individual in a classroom. Teachers also need to have knowledge about language and the way we learn it, the reading process, and the materials available for instruction. Using this knowledge in the best manner possible also calls for long-range and daily planning. Planning specific lessons will be the focus of much of this effort, but teachers should also develop a general procedure with which they will be comfortable.

Lesson Planning

Flexibility should characterize the instructional procedures and techniques used from day to day and from one particular teaching situation to another—within fundamental bases and principles, of course. Even though procedures may vary, lessons should invariably focus on reading to gain meaning and to interpret and use the ideas encountered in print. Most statements of methods include this goal, although some that overemphasize "word calling" perhaps do not give it proper attention. Procedures generally follow a fundamental instructional plan for all directed reading activities. The basic components of such a plan typically include the following:

1. Developing readiness for the reading activity
    a. By discussing experiences that relate to the content to be read.
    b. By introducing new words and new concepts and relating them to words and concepts that the children already know.
    c. By stimulating interest in what the students will read and establishing purposes for the reading.
2. Guiding the first, or survey, reading of the selection
    a. With motivating questions related to the purpose(s).
    b. By discussing the organization of the selection.
3. Rereading for specific purposes, such as
    a. Answering specific questions.
    b. Giving an oral interpretation.
    c. Finding specific words or explanations of particular concepts.
4. Developing important habits and skills
    a. Through direct instruction and practice in using word recognition techniques, comprehension skills, and so forth.

---

13. Alan Bullock, Chair., *A Language for Life* (London: Her Majesty's Stationery Office, 1975), p. 78.

      b.   Through the use of workbook and teacher-prepared materials.

      c.   Through evaluation of progress and the establishment of further instructional goals.

5.   Providing for enrichment

      a.   By following up on activities begun during reading.

      b.   By relating what children have read to interests and needs in their lives and in other curriculum areas.

      c.   By suggesting supplemental reading and other activities.

Basal reading programs and other commercial materials tend to develop points 2, 3, and 4 adequately, but they often fail to provide adequate readiness for the reading and follow-up enrichment. The principal reason for these shortcomings is that building readiness and enriching experience both require consideration of the backgrounds and needs of a particular class, whereas the other sections of the lesson deal mostly with the story or reading material itself. Also, space limitations in teacher's guides restrict the addition of enrichment ideas—other stories and poetry, games, activities, project suggestions—in the amounts desirable.

Regardless of these limitations, it is imperative that a teacher build readiness and purpose for reading—purpose, that is, other than simply reading the next story in a book. Children will go through the motions of a reading lesson without genuine motivation, but will learn little or nothing as a result. Children's interest in learning and in reading depends on how appealing and possible the task is. The introduction of information and concepts that have no relationship to previous learning surely diminishes reading's appeal.

Examples of Reading Lessons

A reading lesson is usually a segment of a larger unit dealing with a complete story, part of a story, a particular skill or set of skills, or the use of certain skills and abilities for special purposes. Following are three sample lessons derived from a commercially produced teacher's guide to a basal reader, a lesson that is representative of the content of several skill development programs currently on the market, and a noncommercial reading strategy lesson.

1.   *A Story-centered Basal Lesson*

This lesson involves the story "Freddie Found a Frog" from *Pets and Promises*, a second-level reader in the basal series *Reading Basics Plus: A Sequential Skills Program* that is highly specific and skill-oriented.[14]

      a.   Vocabulary: Print the words *found, afternoon, yard,* and *lily pad* on the board. Ask the children to read the target words; then

---

14. Dolores R. Amato et al., *Reading Basics Plus* (New York: Harper and Row, 1976).

to read related words (e. g., *found–round*); and then ask them to use the target word in a sentence. Help them to understand compounding (*afternoon*) and meaning relationships (a pad is the leaf of a floating water lily). The lesson also includes discussion of two other categories of vocabulary.

b.   Sound and letter relations: Review sound-letter correspondences for final consonant digraph [sh] sh, initial clusters [kw] qu, [pl] pl, [sw] sw, and initial, medial, and final vowels. Present final consonant digraph [th] th by writing *bath* on the board and asking someone to read it. Underline letters that represent the target sound and print other words containing the same sound on the board for children to read. Finally, assign a workbook page on final consonant digraphs.

c.   Sentence building and analysis: Print contractions on the board. Ask students to read them and write what they stand for (e. g., *couldn't-could not*). Ask them to identify pronoun antecedents in sentences that appear on the board. Assign a workbook page on contractions.

d.   Reading the selection: Have pupils read the story title and examine the pictures. Ask questions requiring students to predict story content. After they state their predictions, have them read silently to confirm the predictions.

e.   Comprehending the selection: The program gives twelve questions to use in discussing the story.

f.   Oral reading: Have pupils tell the story orally then ask for volunteers to give a dramatic reading.

g.   Workbook: Assign three workbook pages on figurative language, detail, and generalization.

h.   Practice and extension: Read to the children a trade book selected from the bibliography provided. Suggested follow-up activities focus on empathy, onomatopoeia, and nonverbal communication. Review activities, more workbook activities, exercises from duplicating masters, challenge activities, and a bibliography of library materials conclude the lesson.

2.   *A Skill-centered Lesson*

The purpose of this lesson is to teach the prefix *re-*. The lesson is not from any particular source, although the skill development programs in basal reading series have similar lessons. The steps in the lesson are as follows:

a.   Remind the children that earlier they had to write letters over again in preparation for taking them home to their parents. Ask for another way to say *wrote again*. The children suggest *rewrote*.

b.   Ask for another way to say "We *addressed* our envelopes *again*." If the children have difficulty, tell them the word is *readdressed*.

    c.   Write *rewrote* and *readdressed* on the board and ask the children what they mean. Add *wrote over again* and *addressed over again* to the board.

    d.   Write the following words on the board: *retell, return, reappear, reappoint, rearrange.* Ask the children for their meanings and write them beside the words.

    e.   Ask the children the meaning of *re.* They respond *again* or *over again.* Ask them if they know what kind of syllable *re* is. If no one knows, tell them and write *prefix* on the board.

    f.   Ask the children for other words beginning with the prefix *re.* Their suggestions might include *rebuild, recall, refill, replace, restate, resell,* and *retype.*

    g.   Ask for sentences using the words *retold, redirect,* and *reorganize,* which have been added to the children's list. Discuss the meaning of *re* as an addition to each word.

    h.   Ask the children to write five sentences using any five words from the list on the board.

3.   *A Reading Strategy Lesson*

Non-English graphic units (e. g., "Carol said, 'Vamanos, we really must hurry.' ") and "eye" dialect (e. g., "zee sveet babee") are disconcerting to some readers. Authors sometimes use them to indicate or emphasize the social class or national origin of their characters. When children first encounter "eye" dialect or foreign phrases, teachers should help them to understand these usages by asking questions like "How does the author let you know that the word or phrase is not like others in the story?" or "What cues do you see in the word or phrase that tell you it isn't English?" Comic strips provide a rich resource for such study, as do some children's trade books. An example is Mabel Leigh Hunt's *Little Girl with Seven Names,* which makes the point that it is not as important to be able to pronounce Milissa Louisa Amanda Miranda Cynthia Jane Farlow as it is to know that a particular language unit is a name and that the reader's task is to search for information about the person being named.[15] As they read, they must continually ask themselves "What will happen next?" (predict) and "Did it make sense?" (confirm).

These sample lessons show small segments of the overall process of teaching reading and give an idea of the kinds of resources that are available. They do not illustrate every type of lesson that might be effective with a given class or situation.

---

15. Yetta M. Goodman, "Strategies for Comprehension," in *Findings of Research on Miscue Analysis: Classroom Implications,* edited by P. D. Allen and D. J. Watson (Urbana, Ill.: National Council of Teachers of English and ERIC Clearinghouse on Reading and Communication Skills, 1976), pp. 97–98.

MATERIALS FOR READING INSTRUCTION

Programs designed to meet the objectives of reading instruction must be broadly conceived with respect to instructional materials as well as organization and teaching procedures. A never-to-be-forgotten fact is that the basic materials for reading are books, and an effective reading program cannot have too many.

Basal Readers and Other Books

The principal materials of instruction in the majority of reading programs are the basal readers, series of books structured for use in a developmental sequence. Designed to introduce and teach a basic vocabulary and present reading skills in an organized manner, they also aim to develop and maintain children's interest in learning to read and using reading. Basal reading programs vary in terms of content and readability level, skills to be taught and sequence of introduction, recommended teaching procedures, and supplemental materials. Most basal programs include workbooks, teacher's guidebooks, test materials, supplemental reading books, charts, audiotapes, and so on. Recently developed series stress somewhat less vocabulary control and provide considerably more supplemental materials than earlier basal programs did.

Because all reading programs should extend considerably beyond the books and supplementary materials in the basal program, many other books must be available for students' use. An individualized reading program, in particular, requires a library of books. The "self-selection" feature simply will not function unless readers have access to many books that vary in difficulty and cover a wide range of subjects. Early advocates of self-selection instruction stated that a classroom should have a minimum of ten trade books per child (suitable to ability and interest),[16] which certainly is a minimal number unless the books are rotated, although newspapers and reference works would round out the selection somewhat. In fact, self-selection programs, like basal programs, require dictionaries, appropriate textbooks in all curriculum areas, encyclopedias, and other books to supplement textbooks.

Other Commercial Materials

The following examples of supplemental materials are useful in reading instruction. Furnishing a complete listing would be impossible because the amount of new materials that appear each year is quite large.[17]

---

16. Shelley Umans, *New Trends in Reading Instruction* (New York: Teachers College, Columbia University, 1963), p. 100.

17. Listings of such materials often appear in reading methods books. Spache and Spache, for example, list materials and briefly describe them at the ends of most chapters.

1. *Reading Skill Builders:* Supplemental readers at eight reading levels. The new series includes audio-cassettes to accompany the workbook-type readers (available from Reader's Digest Services).
2. *EDL Study Skills Libraries:* A total of twenty-one kits (three for each grade level from third through seventh, Educational Development Laboratories).
3. *SRA Reading Laboratories:* Kits of graded reading selections and self-corrective exercises for speed, comprehension, and listening for grades 1–6 (Science Research Associates).
4. *Careers: A Supplemental Reading Program:* Story folders on careers plus sound filmstrips and cassettes (Harcourt Brace Jovanovich).
5. *Study Cards:* Three sets of forty-eight cards for maintaining or extending skills such as getting the main idea, using context cues, seeing relationships, doing critical thinking, and so on (Scott, Foresman and Co.).
6. *Power Reading:* Three kits to diagnose and prescribe (BFA Educational Media).
7. *Barnell Loft Specific Skills Series:* Books for levels 1–6 that focus on comprehension skills (Barnell Loft).
8. *Ginn Word Enrichment Program:* A series of workbooks for developing phonics and structural analysis skills; cassettes available with some (Ginn and Co.).
9. *Mini-systems Programs for Individualized Instruction:* 100 mini-systems for beginning reading skills, each of which includes a cassette lesson, teacher's guide, and activity sheets (D. C. Heath and Co.).
10. *Patterns, Sounds, and Meaning:* Word analysis workbooks for four levels; cassettes introduce skills, give directions, and provide feedback (Allyn and Bacon).
11. *Building Word Power:* Programmed booklets for vocabulary development and word identification (Charles E. Merrill).
12. *Reading:* Sets of color strips that treat phonics, structural analysis, comprehension, dictionary, and study skills (Pacific Productions).
13. *Audio Reading Progress Laboratory:* Twenty-six lessons at each of three levels (primary, intermediate, junior high) designed to provide individualized instruction in word analysis and comprehension skills; includes progress books, audiotapes, and teacher's guide (Educational Progress Corp.).
14. *Califone Audio Reader Program:* Grades 1–6; includes tapes, story cards, manual and key to quizzes (Califone).
15. *Readwell Essays:* Sound filmstrips to build comprehension skills of upper-grade pupils (Herbert M. Elkins Co.).
16. *Reading Attainment System:* Two kits of reading selections and skill cards (Grolier Educational Corp.).
17. *Mission: Read:* Four kits that are multiethnic in approach and con-

tent; each kit has twenty stories and skill exercises (Singer/Random House).

18. *Target Reading Skills Program:* Six audiotaped self-instructional kits; primarily on audio and visual discrimination, structural analysis and phonics skills (Addison-Wesley).

Many other publications describe activities, games, and materials that teachers can make. Representative of these are the following:

- Darrow, Helen F., and Allen, R. Van. *Independent Activities for Creative Learning.* New York: Teachers College Press, Columbia University, 1961.
- Kaplan, Sandra; Kaplan, Jo Ann B.; Madsen, Sheila K.; and Taylor, Bette K. *Change for Children: Ideas and Activities for Individualizing Learning.* Pacific Palisades, Calif.: Goodyear Publishing Co.
- Mueser, Anne Marie; Russell, David H.; and Karp, Etta E. *Reading Aids Through the Grades,* 2d rev. ed. New York: Teachers College Press, Columbia University, 1975.
- Spache, Evelyn B. *Reading Activities for Child Involvement.* Boston: Allyn and Bacon, 1976.
- Spache, George D. *Good Reading for Poor Readers.* Champaign, Ill.: Garrard Publishing Co., 1974.
- *Spice.* Stevensville, Mich.: Educational Services.
- Wagner, Guy; and Hosier, Max. *Reading Games: Strengthening Reading Skills with Instructional Games.* Darien, Conn.: Teachers Publishing Corp., 1960.

Additional Materials

In general, materials prepared by teachers are of secondary importance only to books in any reading program. Teacher-made materials include experience stories and charts, parallel stories (written by the teacher and using the same vocabulary as the story in the reader), worksheets for duplicating, word and phrase cards, games, study exercises, and various objects for building reading interests—bulletin boards, displays, etc.

Teachers often find that having children write and illustrate materials is quite effective. At the middle and upper grade levels these materials may take the form of a class newspaper or yearbook. Many of the materials suggested above—charts, games, bulletin boards, etc.—may be made by children or by the teacher and the children working together.

Some child-prepared materials may present difficulties in preparation unless the teacher can enlist the aid of someone to help with typing, although certainly not all such materials must be typed.

Many teachers have children in the primary grades prepare picture dictionaries. In the middle grades vocabulary books may be prepared.

Other materials necessary for effective instruction include the chalkboard, bulletin boards, pocket charts (to hold word and phrase cards), charts, and flannelboards. In addition, television and films on many subjects can be used for building backgrounds and interests and possibly for direct instruction.

EVALUATION IN READING INSTRUCTION

The principal means of evaluating a child's reading performance is daily observation by an alert and well-informed teacher. Nevertheless, the teacher must have more objective ways of measuring skill development and comparing a child's performance with other children of corresponding abilities, backgrounds, and instructional experiences. Planning and implementing an instructional reading program that fits the needs of individual children requires measuring and appraising skills and abilities at particular times and intervals and in particular areas of concern. A teacher evaluates growth in reading abilities and skills by:

1. Observing a pupil's reading.
2. Administering informal tests, inventories, and checklists of material in readers and similar textbook materials.

3.   Giving standardized reading achievement tests.
4.   Examining a pupil's work in other subject areas and records of his or her reading.

Teacher Assessment and Diagnosis

Because observation is the process teachers use most often to evaluate academic growth, the procedure should be as systematic as possible. Thus, a record of the information gained through observation is essential. Record keeping need not be elaborate or complicated. Simple, regularly written notes about a child's progress in reading are often sufficient. A checklist that calls for assessment of a student's achievement in reading for details, main ideas, and so on, and/or a record of word recognition problems further simplifies record keeping. Although the subject of checklists will come up in a number of other chapters, it is worth pointing out here that teachers must use them with some regularity in order to remain aware of the learning that has taken place.

Another assessment procedure is to have children read selections from basal readers (other than those used in the instructional program) of different difficulty levels. This may be a silent reading followed by a series of questions to determine how well the children comprehended the selection. If the focus of the evaluation is word identification and language understanding, the teacher can ask students to read the selection aloud while he or she marks their errors (mispronunciations, omissions, substitutions, insertions, repetitions, and inversions of word order) on a duplicate copy. From both oral and silent reading a teacher can reasonably determine the levels of difficulty at which a child can read with understanding.[18]

In order to avoid confusing the pupil in a direct teacher-pupil assessment situation and in order to assess a child's strength of commitment to a search for meaning, Taylor recommends completing the following checklist while listening to a tape of a child reading orally without assistance.[19]

  I.   *Is she trying to make sense of it at all?*
        A.   If so, *to what degree?*
              1.   How many sentences still *make sense* in the total context the way she read them?   ☐
              2.   How many sentences still make sense just as a single sentence?   ☐
              3.   What percentage do these two figures represent of the total number of sentences in the story?   ☐

        TOTAL   ☐

---

18. Reading methodology textbooks frequently describe this procedure, which is known as the informal reading inventory.

19. JoEllyn Taylor, "Making Sense: The Basic Skill in Reading," *Language Arts* 54 (September 1977): 670–71. Copyright © 1977 by the National Council of Teachers of English. Reprinted by permission of the publisher and the author.

      B.   In what *ways* is she striving for meaning?

         1.   Self-correcting ☐

         2.   Logical substituting ☐

         3.   Using her own dialect ☐

         4.   Indicating dissatisfaction with nonsense ☐

  II.   *Is she appearing to settle for nonsense?*

      A.   If so, *to what degree?*

         1.   How many sentences (as she read them) do not make sense? ☐

         2.   What percentage do they represent? (or simply subtract the combined figure in IA.3 from 100 percent) ☐

      B.   In what *ways* is she arriving at nonsense?

         1.   Substituting words that don't make sense ☐

         2.   Making critical omissions ☐

         3.   Pausing so long that she forgets what she has already read ☐

         4.   Other ☐

Other assessment tools include library or book-use records, anecdotal records, progress charts, interviews, and autobiographies. The anecdotal records can be simple notes that a teacher makes from time to time about a pupil's reading. Teachers can maximize the accuracy and usefulness of any assessment procedure by structuring or systematizing it and quantifying what they observe.

Information gained by these assessment procedures is not an adequate basis for reading diagnosis. For diagnostic purposes, teachers need as much quantitative and descriptive information as they can obtain about a child's reading and reading-related behavior. Test results alone do not supply it.

Measurement of Reading Readiness

As we have pointed out, reading readiness is an important factor not only at the first-grade level, when formal instruction in reading usually begins, but also throughout a child's progress from one level of performance to the next during the elementary years. We can define readiness as the maturity or ability necessary to learn a new skill or reach a higher goal successfully. The idea that pupils should have adequate preparation for learning situations in which teachers expect them to perform is a long-accepted principle of teaching that is unique neither to beginning reading instruction nor to any other aspect of reading instruction.

Readiness for a reading task depends on many factors. Among them are intelligence, the ability to perceive written and oral symbols accurately, physical health and vigor, background of experience, an understanding and ability to use language, emotional and social stability, and interest in reading and learning. Equal or comparable development of each of these factors is not vital to success in every new reading task, but sufficient development in most areas is necessary. To appraise a child's development of readiness characteristics, a teacher can use formal and informal methods.

Marie Clay considers three language concepts crucial to success in reading: (1) understanding that print can be turned into speech to provide a message; (2) knowledge that pictures can aid in understanding the printed message; and (3) realization that print must be as sensible as spoken language.[20] Successful readers can integrate these language concepts with three concepts about print: (1) print moves from left to right; (2) a word is surrounded by spaces; and (3) the concepts of word and letter are not the same. In addition, Clay believes that children acquire this knowledge through interaction with books and print, not through instructional isolation of skills for mastery. Based on Clay's findings, McDonell and Osburn constructed this example of an informal readiness checklist:[21]

MESSAGE—EXPECTS MEANING (D)

ATTENDS TO VISUAL CUES (A)   *USES INTUITIVE KNOWLEDGE OF LANGUAGE (B)*

_____ left-right progression (a)   _____ invents story to go with pictures (f)
_____ concept of word-space-word (b)   _____ begins to use book talk (g)
_____ concept of letter (c)   _____ begins to use picture cues as
_____ voice-print match (d)   guide (h)
_____ some word recognition   _____ uses memory and pictures (not
        within context (e)   necessarily exact words) (i)

BEGINS INTEGRATION OF VISUAL AND LANGUAGE CUES (C)

_____ begins to read sentences word by word (j)
_____ can search for cues (k)
_____ self-correction develops (l)

20. Marie Clay, *The Patterning of Complex Behavior* (Auckland, N. Z.: Heinemann Educational Books, 1972).

21. Gloria M. McDonell and E. Bess Osburn, "New Thoughts About Reading Readiness," *Language Arts* 55 (January 1978): 27–29. Copyright © 1978 by the National Council of Teachers of English. Reprinted by permission of the publisher and the authors.

A.   Does the child attend to the visual cues of print?
   • If I am reading a story, can the child tell me where to start and where to go next? (a)
   • Is the child able to point to words as I read them, thereby demonstrating knowledge of directional patterns of print? (d)
   • Does the child understand the concept of words and letters? Can he/she circle a word and letter in the book? (b and c) To eliminate the good guesser, this ability should be demonstrated several times.

B.   Does the child use his/her intuitive knowledge of language?
   • Can the child look at a picture book and invent a story to go with the pictures? (f)
   • Does the invented story, when the teacher begins to write it down, indicate the child is using a more formalized language that approximates the language used in books (book talk) rather than an informal conversational style? (g)
   • Does the child recognize that the print and the pictures are related? (h)
   • Can the child "read the words" of a memorized text such as a nursery rhyme, even though the spoken words are not completely accurate matches for the print? Is this recall stimulated or changed by the pictures? (i)

C.   Is the child beginning to show signs of integrating the visual and language cues?
   • Is he/she beginning to read single sentences word by word, pointing to each word with a finger while reading? (j)
   • Can the child use all the cues available to a reader: the predictability of language, word order, a beginning sound, and an appropriateness to context while reading? (k)
   • Does he/she stop and correct, without prompting, when a visual-vocal mismatch occurs? (l)

D.   Does the child expect meaning from print?
   • Does he/she demonstrate that a message is expected by relating a sensible story?

Standardized readiness tests focus in a formal way on specific skills and abilities that implicitly are critical to success in beginning reading. These instruments measure children's performance in all or most of the following areas: visual discrimination, auditory discrimination, word meanings and concepts, listening comprehension, visual-motor coordination, rate in learning words, number concepts, and word-picture relationships. The tests briefly described below are among the better known readiness tests.

   • *The Harrison–Stroud Reading Readiness Test:*[22] Typical test in which teacher gives directions orally. Measures pupil's ability to: (1) use symbols, (2) make visual discriminations, (3) use context, (4) make auditory discriminations, and (5) use context and auditory clues.

---

22. Lucille Harrison and James B. Stroud, *The Harrison–Stroud Reading Readiness Test* (Boston: Houghton Mifflin Co.).

- *Gates–MacGinitie Readiness Skills Test:*[23] Eight subtests survey word recognition, auditory blending of word parts, visual-motor coordination in completing letters, letter recognition, ability to follow directions, visual discrimination of words, auditory discrimination, and listening comprehension.
- *Metropolitan Readiness Test:*[24] Measures (1) general reading readiness in several areas, (2) number readiness, and (3) total readiness.
- *Lee–Clark Reading Readiness Test:*[25] Measures (1) discrimination of letters, (2) selection of pictures from verbal descriptions, and (3) discrimination of printed word forms.

Standardized Reading Tests

Most standardized achievement tests are group tests that enable a teacher to compare in an approximate way each child's performance to a norming sample of children. Standardized reading tests are not diagnostic tests, nor do they accurately measure the functional reading levels of the children tested. They do perform a useful function in the broad sense of reading evaluation, but we should not depend on them (unfortunately, many school systems do) as guides to the development of goals for the reading instructional program or as measures of the reading abilities of individual children.

School administrators and teachers do need to check regularly the general achievement level of their students against national norms. In making this comparison, however, they must take into account local instructional objectives, the school population, and the nature of the program materials. Also, they must keep in mind that a norm is an average and that as many of the norming pupils were below the norm as were above it.[26]

The standardized tests described below, in general, are fairly popular, are new, or are recent revisions.

- *Gates–MacGinitie Reading Tests:*[27] Available in six separate forms (for various levels); measure vocabulary, comprehension, and speed and accuracy of reading.

---

23. Arthur I. Gates and W. H. MacGinitie, *Gates–MacGinitie Readiness Skills Test* (New York: Harcourt Brace Jovanovich).

24. Gertrude Hildreth and N. Griffiths, *Metropolitan Readiness Test* (New York: Harcourt Brace Jovanovich).

25. J. Murray Lee and Willis W. Clark, *Lee–Clark Reading Readiness Test* (Los Angeles: California Test Bureau).

26. The article "Reading Testing for Reading Evaluation" by Walter R. Hill is an excellent discussion of testing in the reading program. See William E. Blanton, Roger Farr, and J. Jaap Tuinman, eds., *Measuring Reading Performance* (Newark, Del.: International Reading Association, 1974).

27. Published by Teachers College Press, Columbia University.

- *Nelson–Lohmann Reading Test:*[28] A paragraph test for grades 4–8 using multiple-choice questions to measure the pupil's ability to comprehend the main idea, word meanings from context, and details.
- *S. R. A. Achievement Series:*[29] Test batteries for various areas of the curriculum with corresponding reading subtests.
- *Iowa Tests of Basic Skills:*[30] Available in three alternate forms for grades 3–9, the tests provide eleven scores in these areas: vocabulary, reading comprehension, language skills, work-study skills, and arithmetic skills.
- *Gray Oral Reading Test:*[31] A series of thirteen paragraphs of increasing reading difficulty for children to read orally as examiner marks errors on another copy (the concept and procedure are identical to the informal reading inventory described in the preceding section).

Evaluation of Instructional Programs

Various evaluative measures of pupils' reading performance provide teachers with information on the effectiveness of their instructional programs. As stated earlier, a reading program (and all other parts of the curriculum) should have an underlying philosophy about how children learn, what they should be taught, and what instructional procedures the teacher should follow. Teachers need to review their programs periodically by comparing them to criteria that reflect the bases and principles for effective reading programs outlined in this book. The following rating scale, devised by Aaron, provides a model for teachers and administrators to follow in developing an instrument suitable for a particular instructional program.[32]

Rating scale for program's or teacher's attention to "the basics of reading"

Directions: Selected characteristics of a reading program that are considered to be basic are listed below. Items 1–5 deal with how reading is taught whereas numbers 6–10 focus on what is taught or developed. Indicate by circling the appropriate number the extent to which your program (for an individual teacher or an entire school) gives attention to each characteristic. Use the following ratings:

1–Almost always	3–Sometimes	5–Undecided
2–Most of the time	4–Seldom or never	6–Not applicable

28. Published by Educational Test Bureau, Educational Publishers, Inc.
29. Published by Science Research Associates.
30. Published by Houghton Mifflin Company.
31. Published by the Bobbs-Merrill Co., Inc.
32. Ira E. Aaron, "Rating Scale for Program's or Teacher's Attention to 'The Basics of Reading.' "

1. Aims reading instruction toward the achievement of specific goals and objectives. 1 2 3 4 5 6
    a. Has clear understanding of goals and objectives in reading. 1 2 3 4 5 6
    b. Views instructional tasks in terms of pupil behaviors. 1 2 3 4 5 6
    c. Adapts objectives to individual children. 1 2 3 4 5 6
2. Adapts reading instruction to the individual achievement levels, abilities, and needs of all children. 1 2 3 4 5 6
    a. Determines reading levels by means of informal procedures. 1 2 3 4 5 6
    b. Knows (or uses a guide for) a sequence for teaching skills. 1 2 3 4 5 6
    c. Organizes in order to adapt to instructional levels. 1 2 3 4 5 6
    d. Knows strengths and weaknesses of ability measures and uses that knowledge in interpreting results of such tests. 1 2 3 4 5 6
3. Merges materials and equipment into a total program. 1 2 3 4 5 6
    a. Is thoroughly familiar with any core materials used in program. 1 2 3 4 5 6
    b. Knows many children's books. 1 2 3 4 5 6
    c. Integrates materials and equipment into a whole. 1 2 3 4 5 6
4. Evaluates progress in reading in terms of instructional goals and objectives. 1 2 3 4 5 6
    a. Matches evaluative techniques and instruments to program goals and objectives. 1 2 3 4 5 6
    b. Knows how to administer, score, and interpret standardized test results. 1 2 3 4 5 6
    c. Is thoroughly familiar with what tests being used measure and what they do not measure. 1 2 3 4 5 6
    d. Uses a variety of sources for decisions made about pupil progress. 1 2 3 4 5 6
5. Organizes the classroom for effective management of reading instruction. 1 2 3 4 5 6
    a. Works with children individually and in groups. 1 2 3 4 5 6
    b. Uses various kinds of grouping (skill, research, and interest) in reading instruction. 1 2 3 4 5 6
    c. Manages pupil movement easily and smoothly. 1 2 3 4 5 6
    d. Gathers needed materials in advance of instruction. 1 2 3 4 5 6
6. Gives adequate attention to word recognition instruction. 1 2 3 4 5 6
    a. Develops a well-planned and systematic program of word recognition instruction. 1 2 3 4 5 6
    b. Teaches a variety of word attack skills: use of context, word structure, phonics, dictionary use. 1 2 3 4 5 6
    c. Adapts phonics instruction to the children being taught. 1 2 3 4 5 6
    d. Teaches word recognition skills thoroughly as means to the ends of comprehension and appreciation. 1 2 3 4 5 6

7. Gives adequate attention to comprehension skill instruction.   1 2 3 4 5 6
    a. Develops a well-planned and systematic program of comprehension skill instruction.   1 2 3 4 5 6
    b. Emphasizes comprehension as the major goal of reading instruction.   1 2 3 4 5 6
    c. Includes instruction aimed toward the development of word meanings and "thinking" skills.   1 2 3 4 5 6
8. Gives adequate attention to reading study skills.   1 2 3 4 5 6
    a. Develops a well-planned and systematic program of reading-study skills instruction.   1 2 3 4 5 6
    b. Teaches students to locate information in single and multiple sources.   1 2 3 4 5 6
    c. Teaches students to organize information from single and multiple sources.   1 2 3 4 5 6
    d. Teaches students to evaluate information.   1 2 3 4 5 6
    e. Teaches students to be flexible, independent readers.   1 2 3 4 5 6
9. Teaches the special vocabulary and reading skills in each subject taught.   1 2 3 4 5 6
    a. Helps students to use basal skills in each content area.   1 2 3 4 5 6
    b. Teaches special vocabulary of subject.   1 2 3 4 5 6
    c. Builds concept background for reading.   1 2 3 4 5 6
    d. Teaches students how to read materials in the subject.   1 2 3 4 5 6
    e. Teaches special reading skills of the subject.   1 2 3 4 5 6
    f. Teaches symbols and abbreviations of the subject.   1 2 3 4 5 6
10. Leads students toward enjoyment of reading.   1 2 3 4 5 6
    a. Makes children's books readily available in the classrooms and library.   1 2 3 4 5 6
    b. Reads prose and poetry selections frequently to children.   1 2 3 4 5 6
    c. Schedules time for children to read with a minimum of teacher supervision.   1 2 3 4 5 6
    d. Shows children that the teacher enjoys reading.   1 2 3 4 5 6
    e. Knows "typical" interests of children and specific interests of those children being taught.   1 2 3 4 5 6

EXERCISES FOR THOUGHT AND ACTION

1. Make an independent inquiry into reading for a special population (e. g., visually handicapped children, black children, children for whom English is not the native language, children who read before they started school). Find out what materials are available for the group you choose.
2. Examine the diagnostic and evaluative suggestions of several basal reading programs. Locate examples of checklists and other recommended informal devices.

3. Design a practice exercise in finding the main idea, selecting details, determining organization, or summarizing a reading selection.

4. Plan a reading activity that you could direct for a group of children at a particular grade level. State specific objectives and detail the procedures you would use.

5. What is wrong with calling any single approach to reading a "linguistic approach"?

6. Examine materials for reading instruction that in some way alter printed symbols (e. g., Words in Color, Unifon, i/t/a).

7. Explain why most elementary teachers might rely heavily on basal reading series and commercial kits. If possible, interview elementary teachers and use their comments to support your answer.

8. Select two standardized reading tests and compare:
    a. Content
    b. Quality of pupil directions
    c. Ease of administration
    d. Ease of scoring
    e. Ease of score interpretation
    f. Standardization procedures

9. Select a scored reading profile of one child based on a standardized reading test. Using the information the profile provides, describe that particular child's reading performance. What doesn't the profile tell you? What instructional recommendations does this profile allow you to make?

10. Write a critique of one reading lesson from a basal series and corresponding teacher's manual suggestions. What would you add or delete? Why? Include in the critique the substitutions you would make (e. g., alternative questions or activities).

11. Become acquainted with the services of the National Council of Teachers of English and the International Reading Association. Obtain catalogs of their current publications. Attend conferences in your area. Examine *Language Arts* (NCTE) and *The Reading Teacher* (IRA), both of which publish reading-related articles.

12. Plan a lesson or lesson series consistent with the characteristics of the language experience approach.

13. Observe a child reading orally. Describe the performance and note errors, attitude, and observable behaviors that provide clues for the future instruction of that child.

SELECTED REFERENCES

Allen, P. David, and Watson, Dorothy J. *Findings of Research in Miscue Analysis.* Urbana, Ill.: National Council of Teachers of English and ERIC/Reading and Communication Skills, 1976.

Allen, Roach. *Learning Experiences in Communication.* Boston: Houghton Mifflin, 1976.

Allen, Roach, and Allen, Claryce. *Learning Experience Activities*. Boston: Houghton Mifflin Co., 1976.

Ashton-Warner, Sylvia. *Spearpoint, Teacher in America*. New York: Alfred A. Knopf, 1972.

Ashton-Warner, Sylvia. *Teacher*. New York: Simon and Schuster, 1963.

Berger, Allen, and Bean, Rita, eds. *School Reading Programs: Criteria for Excellence*. Pittsburgh: University of Pittsburgh, 1976.

Ehri, Linnea; Bannon, Roderick W.; and Feldman, Jeffrey M. *The Recognition of Words*. Newark, Del.: International Reading Association, 1978.

Farr, Roger, and Anastasiow, Nicholas. *Tests of Reading Readiness and Achievement: A Review and Evaluation*. Newark, Del.: International Reading Association, 1969.

Goodman, Kenneth S. *Miscue Analysis: Applications to Reading Instruction*. Urbana, Ill.: National Council of Teachers of English and ERIC/Reading and Communication Skills, 1973.

Hall, Mary Anne. *The Language Experience Approach for Teaching Reading: A Research Perspective*, 2d ed. Urbana, Ill.: ERIC Clearinghouse on Reading and Communication Skills, 1978.

Hall, Mary Anne. *Teaching Reading as a Language Experience*. Columbus, O.: Charles E. Merrill Publishing Co., 1970.

Heilman, Arthur W. *Principles and Practices of Teaching Reading*, 4th ed. Columbus, O.: Charles E. Merrill Publishing Co., 1977.

Hodges, R. E., and Rudorf, E. H., eds. *Language and Learning to Read: What Teachers Should Know About Language*. Boston: Houghton Mifflin Co., 1972.

Hunt, Lyman C., Jr., ed. *The Individualized Reading Program: A Guide for Classroom Teaching*, Proceedings of the Eleventh Annual Convention of the International Reading Association, vol. II, pt. 3. Newark, Del.: International Reading Association, 1967.

McCracken, Robert A., and McCracken, Marlene J. *Reading Is Only the Tiger's Tail*. San Rafael, Calif.: Leswing Press, 1977.

Quandt, Ivan J. *Teaching Reading: A Human Process*. Chicago: Rand McNally Publishing Co., 1977.

Spache, George D., and Spache, Evelyn B. *Reading in the Elementary School*, 4th ed. Boston: Allyn and Bacon, 1977.

Stauffer, Russell G. *Directing Reading Maturity as a Cognitive Process*. New York: Harper and Row, 1969.

III

PRODUCING LANGUAGE

Teachers agree that at least four elements should be present to make a communicative situation. The pupil ought to have facts or ideas to express, a reason for saying or writing them, enough linguistic ability to speak or write understandingly, and a person or persons to hear him or to read what he writes. —*Wilmer K. Trauger,* Language Arts in Elementary Schools

Learning to express one's thoughts is an important aspect of growth. An inability to speak and write effectively is a lifetime handicap. A substantial foundation for these necessary skills must be built in the elementary school. Furthermore, as we have already stated, a child's capacity for self-expression through language affects his or her ability to read well and to listen skillfully.

Children must learn skills and have many experiences in order to speak and write with assurance and ability. They come to school, however, with considerable speaking and perhaps even print background. The instructional program in the elementary school must provide ample opportunities for natural and purposeful oral communication to occur, aid children in learning skills for particular speaking occasions, and build their confidence in voicing their thoughts. Writing, an ability that the school has almost complete responsibility for developing, requires an equal amount of attention to opportunities, forms and occasions, and confidence. In addition, handwriting and spelling must receive instructional attention. Thus, four of the seven chapters in this part deal exclusively with written expression.

10

Skills and Abilities Important to Both Oral and Written Language

Let's search for ways of helping boys and girls write and speak more maturely, more logically, more interestingly.—Edgar Dale, National Conference on Research in English meeting, 27 November 1964

Writing and speaking are the expressive areas of the language arts. Speaking, oral language, is basic and writing is the graphic representation of language. Obviously, writing and speaking are quite different. But to use either, and to grow in ability to use both, an individual must have some common skills and abilities, including the ability to choose appropriate words and organize them for effective expression, the accumulation of a large storehouse of functional vocabulary, and knowledge of where to find information relevant to expression.

In the first part of this chapter, we will discuss the teaching of language usage. Many of the suggestions relate to our discussions of grammar and linguistics in Chapter 2, the learner in Chapter 3, and the teaching suggestions in Chapter 4. Next we will consider organization of expression and improvement of sentences—a consideration that also relates to the earlier chapters as well as to Chapters 11–14. In addition, the discussion of vocabulary growth is especially relevant to Chapter 9. The implication of these relationships is that not only are speaking and writing inseparable, but the skills and abilities common to both cannot be separated from the skills and abilities important to listening and reading.

A FUNCTIONAL APPROACH TO TEACHING ENGLISH USAGE

Current social acceptability is the principal criterion for what is labeled "standard" usage. In other words, we can justify only a small part of this usage by any historically grounded evidence or logical principle. Language usage is largely a personal matter. Each of us uses language to express thinking, but the effective user of language recognizes that the choice of language for any communicative act depends on the purpose of the communication, the intended meaning, and the desired effect.

Grammar and Teaching Usage

The principal problem in teaching acceptable usage is not the various forms children's speech may take—some of which differ considerably from what is *generally* socially acceptable—but the persistent reliance on the teaching of grammar. Although we discussed this issue in Chapter 2, the false assumptions that are so common ("This *new* grammar will produce the long-sought results") require further attention here. With respect to reliance on grammar as a means for changing pronoun usage, Pooley states, "This fallacy arises from the assumption . . . that a variant pronoun use (*'him* and *me* went home') is 'corrected by' teaching the declension of the pronoun."[1] We could make a similar case against the assumption that verb conjugation can change usage, that learning rules for the formation of the comparative and superlative will affect a child's choice of adjective forms, and that learning many words ending with *-ly* helps a child to use adverbs properly.

The solution to the problem of establishing an acceptable usage form does not lie in "authority"—knowledge of grammar and application of rules. Rather, it lies in genuine and purposeful communication, in meaningful practice, and in awareness of what one is saying, whether it differs from the acceptable form, and how acceptable form is necessary in many language situations for communication to be most effective.

However, teachers and pupils alike should recognize that there are dialect differences and levels of language usage and that both word choice and sentences should be suitable for the occasion of use. Teachers sometimes become too pedantic about language expression. They need to be aware that effective language is

---

1. Robert C. Pooley, *The Teaching of English Usage.* (Urbana, Ill.: National Council of Teachers of English, 1974), p. 180.

often the comfortable, clear, idiomatic, forceful type of expression used in the informal situations of life, in school and out of school. They should also recognize that even words that are generally labeled "nonstandard" are appropriate for some situations. On the other hand, teachers must recognize that they would be shortchanging children if they did not try to give them the security of language usage appropriate to their aspirations and potential.

Teacher Analysis of Usage Problems

In Chapter 2 we identified usages that commonly need teaching attention in elementary schools, but it is not possible to dictate which items of usage to teach at particular levels and in a specific classroom. Textbooks provide exercises and activities on specific usage items—and some of the activities are useful—but teachers should use them only if the children (or a single child) have problems with these items—and then only if they are the grossest deviations from the local standard. Teachers should survey the children's oral and written usage to determine specific instructional emphases. An example of a survey record form, shown below, shows how one teacher recorded in a compact and specific manner usage items needing teaching attention.

Another example, shown on p. 269, focuses on previously selected items and provides an easy means of noting improvement.

Teachers should regularly update surveys of instructional needs. Some prefer to keep running anecdotal records in a notebook containing a page for each child. The initial survey of a class may reveal that many items of usage need instructional attention, but a teacher should not attempt to change all of them. Thus, until surveys show that improvement has occurred for selected items, keeping records only for those usages simplifies the process considerably.

	verb forms	pronouns	redundancy	double negatives	illiteracies
John	he done	her & me	this here	don't have no	youse hisn
Harvey	they knowed brung	they's	this here		
Lucille	she don't				
Peggy	has took				onct
MaryAnn			John he		
Douglas	has took	it's			
Cynthia					

Usage survey for October

	Harry	Chas	Harriett	Jo	Betty	Roy	Doris	Tom	Gus	Henry	Sally	Alma	Bob
we was	✓			✓	✓				✓	✓			
have saw	✓	✓		✓		✓	✓			✓	✓		
me and	✓			✓		✓							
brung		✓						✓					
haven't no			✓										
he don't	✓												
hisself	✓												

In addition, many usage items that ordinarily require instructional emphasis in the elementary school appear on standardized language and general achievement tests. These tests, of course, do not measure a child's spoken usage. The selected usage items for testing also may be unrealistic, particularly in that it may fail to include the gross kinds of nonstandard usages that many teachers encounter. Furthermore the number of test items generally is so small that, although the test may permit comparisons of different classes, it provides little help in diagnosing an individual pupil's needs.

The Role of Habit

Teachers are generally aware that dialects are ingrained; children's usage habits persist from year to year in spite of efforts to change them. Moreover, the least acceptable habits tend to be the most difficult to eradicate. Several reasons have been suggested for this problem:

1. The habits that a child acquires in the five or six years of life, prior to starting school, are firmly fixed.
2. These habits tend to be strengthened even after coming to school because the child usually continues to live in the same environment.
3. The child whose usage habits may be most in need of change is likely not to be interested in changing them because doing so may mean alienation from the home.
4. The school generally does not provide enough active language situations for real exercise of acceptable usage.
5. Many of the usage lessons taught in the school are ineffectively motivated and taught.

In addition to these reasons, and perhaps even more important, is the emphasis the school typically gives to changing usage through written drill, although inappropriate usages may be more prevalent in children's speaking than in their writing. The objective of eliminating undesirable usage habits and substituting more desirable ones may be unrealistic because the school can do little to change the influences of a child's environment outside the school. Nevertheless, the school—and every teacher—can do something about instruction-related reasons for the persistence of undesirable usage habits. Teachers can also attempt to make children sensitive to the appropriateness of language for particular purposes and in specific situations so that they will recognize that their nonstandard dialect *is* appropriate in some situations and settings.

A teacher can also provide active language situations to promote genuine exercise of desirable habits. Every teacher should understand, as Blair has pointed out, that "the chief cause of deficiency in oral and written expression is probably *lack of experience and practice in using correct form.*"[2] He further states that evidence from the field of psychology indicates that pupils *learn to do what they do.* If they learn a rule of grammar, they will be able to repeat that rule but not necessarily be able to apply it in their speaking and writing. Transfer of training takes place only between elements and situations that are approximately identical.[3] If pupils are to speak and write in a manner that is appropriate for a range of social situations, they must practice in approximately the same situations.

Every teacher must recognize, too, that applying the remedy to the exact fault is a basic instructional principle. Thus it is imperative to identify the usages of individual children that depart from acceptable language. Surveying and recording along the lines suggested in the preceding section should provide the necessary information.

Basic Instructional Procedures

A teacher who recognizes the role of habit in a child's usage, the importance of using language for genuine communication purposes, and the need for a direct, systematic attack on the usage items selected for instructional emphasis can achieve measurable success by following the steps described here.[4]

The first step is to appraise the usage problems of each individual in the class by completing checklists and cataloging written usages. Upon completion of

---

2. Glenn Myers Blair, *Diagnostic and Remedial Teaching* (New York: Macmillan Co., 1956), p. 343.

3. Ibid., p. 355.

4. A number of linguists and others interested in language usage in schools hold that many "errors" and "deviations" do not need the type of instruction suggested here. Labov states that "In cold fact, the number of differences between most nonstandard dialects (especially those of middle-class speakers) and standard English are relatively few. In one way or another, most students have gradually learned to approximate the teacher's style, more or less. More important, their dialects have not obviously interfered with the learning of reading and writing to any serious degree." (William Labov, *The Study of Nonstandard English*. Champaign, Ill.: National Council of Teachers of English, 1970, p. 4.).

this survey, compare deviations from standard usage to lists like the ones in Chapter 2 to determine which items require instructional attention.

Step two is to select the most frequent and grossest departures from accept- ability for consistent attack. After selecting them, reveal them to the children (how they look and how they sound) along with the reasons for their selection. From this time on, strive to eliminate deviation from acceptable forms, but always keep in mind that the overriding concern is *what* is said or written rather than how it is done. This effort calls for diligence, genuine rapport with the children, and many opportunities for the children to practice proper usage in natural communication. Practice opportunities should involve both oral and written expression and should appeal to the children.

Informing parents of usages that are under attack and asking for their cooperation may be helpful in changing undesirable usage habits. A group con- ference, PTA meeting, or letter is appropriate for this purpose. Pupils may also write letters to their parents explaining their goals with respect to learning usage. Be careful, however, not to single out as undesirable usages commonly heard in the community that residents do not regard as "errors."

The children themselves should have as much responsibility for improve- ment as possible. One way of involving them is to ask them to make individual lists of troublesome items and individual charts of usages that they have mastered.

An essential part of the process of teaching good usage is building interest in words and expressions and imparting a sense of enjoyment of the fitness of prop- erly used words (see the vocabulary section of this chapter).

Perhaps the most vital ingredient in a program to develop acceptable usage habits is motivation. Pupils must be stimulated to want to use English effectively, or little benefit will accrue from teaching efforts. Utilize every possible device to relate the activities of the classroom to the basic goals for each pupil. A child must feel that improving his or her English usage will have personal benefit. Children must be convinced that their communication is more effective when they use English that suits a particular occasion and that most people vary their usages but do use standard English most of the time. In short, over a period of time children must gain the point of view that an inability to use standard English will be a handicap to them. Of course, efforts to develop these attitudes and to motivate pupils should accommodate each pupil's individuality.

Usage Practice

The most effective kind of usage practice is "normal and natural use of language for a purpose recognized by the pupil."[5] Traditionally, however, the favored ap- proach is to assign written exercises requiring the pupil to choose between accept-

---

5. Pooley, p. 181.

able and unacceptable usage. Such practice requires repeated performance of similar exercises (usually the variations are minor). Some people call it practice; others would say that it is drill. Regardless of what it is called, it has little to recommend it.

More recently, oral drills have replaced written ones out of recognition that the habits established in speech are more apt to transfer to writing than vice versa. Too, successful application of the audiolingual approach in teaching foreign languages has encouraged teachers to adapt it for changing usage habits.

Some types of practice are very intensive and require forceful repetition of standard English expressions as well as strict adherence to the usages taught.[6] Other structured practice activities that are less intensive and less drill-like in the traditional sense are more popular.[7] They present expressions for children to hear and to repeat, but their approach is less formal and more flexible with regard to deviations during nonpractice time in the school day. These programs require children to listen to and repeat patterns of standard usage such as this one:[8]

- *She carry me home.*
- She takes me home.
- He
- John
- Mrs. Rock ⟩ takes me home.
- The teacher
- Mother
- You take me home.
- They ⟩ take me home.
- The ladies

Some linguists prefer exercises that more totally recognize the systematic nature of a dialect and focus on the points at which the phonology and grammar of that dialect conflict with the phonology and grammar of standard English.[9] This example illustrates their approach:[10]

---

6. Carl Bereiter and Siegfried Engelmann, *Teaching Disadvantaged Children in the Preschool* (Englewood Cliffs, N. J.: Prentice-Hall, 1966).

7. For example, see Marjorie B. Smiley, "Gateway English: Teaching English to Disadvantaged Students," *English Journal* 54 (April 1965): 265–74; Charlotte K. Brooks, "Some Approaches to Teaching Standard English as a Second Language," *Elementary English* 42 (November 1964): 723–33.

8. *Language Patterns for the Culturally Disadvantaged*. Mimeographed (Edison Park Elementary School, Miami, Fla., 1965–66), p. 11.

9. Kenneth R. Johnson, "Should Black Children Learn Standard English," in *Social and Educational Insights into Teaching Standard English to Speakers of Other Dialects; Viewpoints*, edited by Maurice L. Imhoff (Indianapolis: School of Education, Indiana University, March 1971), p. 98.

10. William R. Slager, "Effecting Dialect Change Through Oral Drill," *English Journal* 56 (November 1967): 1166–76.

Repetition

Teacher	Class or pupil
Dick lives on a farm.	Dick lives on a farm.
He doesn't live in Fairfield.	He doesn't live in Fairfield.

Substitution.

Teacher	Class or Pupil
The Scotts don't live on a farm.	The Scotts don't live on a farm.
Mr. and Mrs. Scott_____.	Mr. and Mrs. Scott don't live on a farm.
Tom Scott _____.	Tom Scott doesn't live on a farm

Completion.

She's doing the same thing she
    always does.
She's reading _____.

Transformation

1. Change the affirmative to a negative: → He lives on a farm.
   He doesn't live on a farm.
2. Change the statement to a yes-no question: → He lives on a farm.
   Does he live on a farm?
3. Change the statement to a *wh* question → He lives on a farm.
   Where does he live?
4. Add a tag question: He lives on a farm, → doesn't he?

Apparently the effectiveness of oral practice of this kind varies, possibly because of differences in materials and procedures. These exercises may be worth trying, however, depending on the rapport between teacher and pupils and the teacher's understanding of students' problems. Following these guidelines may improve their effectiveness:

1. Practice exercises are most effective when pupils feel a genuine need for their use.
2. Children must clearly understand both the purpose of any practice activity and the accompanying explanatory material.
3. The content of practice exercises should be familiar to the children whenever possible. For example, a recent field trip or some seasonal interest might be a good subject.
4. The value of practice comes from repetition of the desired usage; therefore, an exercise must contain some repetition.
5. Practice sessions should be short and each should stress a specific usage.
6. The time of day devoted to usage practice should vary.

7.   Teachers can individualize practice by working with single pupils or with small groups of students who have the same usage problems.
8.   Students should concentrate on a limited number of usage items until they have achieved some degree of success.

RHETORICAL SKILL DEVELOPMENT

Perhaps the greatest weakness of language arts programs in elementary schools is the lack of attention given to the rhetorical skills of expression. Webster defines rhetoric as "the art of expressive speech or discourse; . . . the study of principles and rules of composition formulated by ancient critics (as Aristotle and Quintilian) and interpreted by classical scholars for application to discourse in the vernacular." Thus, rhetoric along with grammar and logic made up the "trivium" of medieval days. Rhetoric fell into disrepute because it emphasized nomenclature and form rather than content, but there is evidence that it is undergoing a rebirth.[11] The new rhetoric includes writing as well as speaking, and exposition and evocative and creative writing as well as argumentation and persuasion. Additionally, it requires attention to content selection, to organization and style, to sentence construction, and to consideration of the reader or audience.

Organization of Expression

Children must learn that the best way to present an idea or thought clearly is to organize expression around a central point and present information in orderly and interesting sequence. The problem of organization is inherent in composition. Although composition requires other skills and abilities, organization is fundamental, and is needed in the construction of sentences, paragraphs, and extended discourse. No expression—oral or written—is effective unless it is well organized, unless it has been properly composed.

When children begin to recognize relationships they are learning to organize. Telling a story in proper sequence, putting together a puzzle, making a list of things seen on a field trip, and making an outline are all organizational activities. Children must incorporate organizational ability as part of the thinking process before they can become skillful in arranging ideas or information in written or spoken expression.

Above all, communication must be direct. In oral communication, the speaker must limit the scope of a discussion, the content of an announcement, or the theme of a report, and relate the ideas and thoughts expressed to the desired point. Another feature of good organization is presentation of material in the

_____

11. J. N. Hook, Paul H. Jacobs, and Raymond D. Crisp. *What Every English Teacher Should Know* (Urbana, Ill: National Council of Teachers of English, 1970), p. 33.

most effective sequence. For example, the logical sequence in which to discuss a series of events may be chronological, or if a causal relationship exists between the facts or ideas being conveyed, the speaker might present them in cause-and-effect order.

Mature organization flows from the ability to outline, but children should first learn to organize ideas before being exposed to the mechanics of outlining. In other words, children should learn early to make lists, to classify, and to organize. From this experience, skills in outlining and more formal organizing will develop quite naturally.

Sequence of ideas within a sentence. We cannot give a set formula for the presentation of ideas within a sentence. Many dull and uninteresting sentences result from always arranging them in subject-predicate fashion. Actually, almost any word or phrase can begin or end a sentence as long as the resulting sentence makes sense and expresses the intended idea fully and clearly. Simple sentences take on interest when their beginnings vary. Teachers should encourage children to transpose an appositive to the beginning of a sentence, to place a word or phrase modifier at the beginning, and to use increasingly complex and compound-complex sentences. Of course, we do not expect them to learn these terms or receive direct instruction on their use, rather that they become aware of these and other natural ways to make their sentences interesting, varied, and meaningful.

Organizing paragraphs. Organizing relatively short pieces of discourse—the paragraph in written expression or the oral expression of comparable content—is usually the best starting point for teaching organization of all expression. Basically, children need to learn to tell about one subject or topic and to arrange everything they want to say or write about that topic in an order that accomplishes the purpose of the communication.[12] In fact, this skill is not as difficult to teach as many people think, particularly if it receives somewhat consistent attention. It is also helpful if children in the primary grades learn to write single-sentence paragraphs first and paragraphs of two and three sentences later. This sequence should help them to master the idea of beginning a new paragraph when they want to introduce a new idea. Applying this knowledge to their reading, children will come to recognize that a paragraph has a main idea, or that sentences are like the branches of a tree: they all lead to the trunk, or main idea. One curriculum guide suggests the following:[13]

---

12. This recommendation does not mean that the teaching should stress topic sentences, as many paragraphs do not have topic sentences. Braddock has reported that "fewer than half of all paragraphs in essays [a total of 889 paragraphs in 25 essays studied] have even explicit topic sentences, to say nothing of simple topic sentences" (Richard Braddock, "The Frequency and Placement of Topic Sentences in Paragraphs," *Research in the Teaching of English* 8 (Winter 1974): 299).

13. *English Language Arts: Composition, K–12* (Albany: University of the State of New York/State Education Department, 1969), p. 49.

- The snow was very deep.
- The car got stuck.
- The snowplow had not yet cleared our street.
- Father drove the car out of the driveway.

Have the children rearrange the sentences in a more effective order.
Lead the children to understand the cause-and-effect patterns involved.

This guide points out that children need to learn that they can arrange a composition, and usually a paragraph, by chronology, cause and effect, classification, and comparison and contrast, and by leading up to a generalization or supporting one.

Points to remember in teaching good paragraphing include the following:

1. Emphasize the function of the paragraph as an aid to clarity of expression.
2. Stress the importance of putting sentences in logical or sequential order.
3. Inspect and analyze each pupil's writing for improved sentence sequence.
4. Encourage children to watch for ways in which professional writers move skillfully from topic to topic and use paragraphs in their writing.
5. Demonstrate to children that the beginning sentence should be interesting enough to get the reader's attention and should lead into the theme of the paragraph.

Poorly organized written or oral discourse of any length is the product of poor thinking. If the purpose of the communication is not clear, not explicit, or too diffuse, the expression of it wanders and lacks order. Thus, all activities that help children to think clearly about what they want to say and why are appropriate. Particularly helpful are activities that emphasize outlining. (Chapters 11–14 suggest other such activities.)

Outlining.   From the time children first learn to write independently, teachers can help them jot down their ideas and organize them in sequence. This is the beginning of outlining and may be as simple as:

- I went to the park.
- I saw the animals.
- I had a balloon and ice cream.
- I came home on a bus.

Outlining should be taught for specific purposes. In other words, making an outline should aid in completion of another activity. So that the children will grasp this idea, the teacher should stress spending a minimum of time to produce a good outline. The children's first outlines should be a group effort in which they generate the outline orally and the teacher writes it down. After creating composite outlines together, the children can copy them individually as needed. Activities in which children can work together to organize facts and prepare an outline include: (1) dictating a story that the teacher writes on a chart, then cutting the story into strips, and arranging the sentences in outline form; (2) listing events that happened on an excursion in the order in which they occurred; and (3) outlining a process in either logical or chronological order.

The teacher should always stress that any task worth doing is worth planning in advance and that outlining is a valuable way of planning many activities, even those that do not involve language expression. The time to introduce outlining is when something the children are expressing could be improved by it, usually when they begin writing group compositions. After introducing the concept, the teacher will find it necessary to review the procedure frequently. Nevertheless, practice should always occur in the context of actual communication. Of course, outlining instruction is much more meaningful and acceptable to children who know how to organize their own thinking, planning, and recording and thus will be able to appreciate fully this organization tool.

Sentence construction.   Teachers should avoid defining a sentence as a group of words that expresses a whole or complete thought. Rather, children should learn to think of a sentence as a device for expressing an idea. The definition is irrelevant if students understand that the purpose of a sentence is to express an idea in a way that is clear and exact. In fact, a substantial number of children generally speak in sentences. Thus they have considerable knowledge of the grammar of the language, although, of course, they do not know the grammatical terminology, nor can they express grammatical rules.[14]

By providing many opportunities for expression and carefully guiding them, the teacher can help children who use sentence fragments to better understand sentences. These children, as well as the ones who initially have greater control of language, will discover very early that a sentence always has at least a subject and a verb, either expressed or implied. They learn that one word or several words—present or implied—make the group of words state something. They also learn that another word or several words are present or implied about which something is stated. They come to realize, too, that sometimes other elements must be present or implied to express the idea with clarity and precision and that the inclusion in a sentence of too many elements could make a statement unclear.

Effective sentence construction corresponds closely to children's fluency with the language. Fluency depends on the size and depth of their vocabularies, which, in turn, is attributable to the experiences they have had. The most common faults in sentence construction that occur in the elementary school are discussed in the following paragraphs.

Omissions. Children's thinking sometimes runs ahead of their writing and speaking. Consequently they often omit vital points from their sentences. In addition, children tend to forget about their reader or listener, or they assume that what they have omitted is known by everyone, and so they might leave out parts of the sentence necessary for complete understanding. For example, the words *the wind blew* may express a complete thought, but they do not include elements necessary to the development of the essential idea. *The cold wind blew the snow into deep drifts* may better express the intended thought. A student who limits the expression to *the wind blew* might have given no thought to necessary details. Or he or she might simply have neglected to fill in the details for the reader or listener.

Loose "ands". The word *and* is a conjunction, which is used to connect words, phrases, and clauses. Overuse of *and* or *but* or any conjunction, a common practice of young children, detracts from effective sentence structure. A conjunction should be used to connect words, phrases, and clauses of *equal* importance; it is inappropriate to use it to tie together a series of simple sentences, as young children commonly do. The otherwise interesting little story that follows illustrates this improper usage:

> Yesterday was my birthday and I was eight years old and my mother and father gave me an electric train and we had a birthday cake.

All sentences need not be simple ones, but children who have a tendency to string simple sentences together with conjunctions should learn to express only one idea

---

14. Walter D. Loban, *The Language of Elementary School Children* (Champaign, Ill.: National Council of Teachers of English, 1963).

at a time in a sentence until they have firmly grasped the idea of sentence construction. This problem of loose "ands" is just one of the obstacles to good sentence structure, but it often is a major one.

Run-ons. A common error in sentence structure is the expression of a series of more or less rambling and complete statements unseparated by adequate pauses or by proper punctuation and capitalization. For example: "He went to the store Bill did too bought candy." This type of error is quite common in the early elementary grades and decreases as children get older if the curriculum focuses on purposeful language expression.

Unnecessary words. Another common fault is the use of primers or launchers (*well, see, you know*, etc.),[15] which contribute nothing to meaning and do not function as transition elements. A related mistake that children often make is the repetition of words in speech, a habit that is sometimes regarded as stuttering but is more often simply an attempt to clarify thinking and to find the right words.

Misplaced sentence elements. Very often the location of modifiers and antecedents in a sentence is critical to clarity of meaning. All of us have been confused by ambiguity in sentences like: "John told Harry that the postman had brought a letter for him." Misplaced modifiers can be amusing as well as confusing, as in the sentence, "John said that the letter had been brought by the postman which he found in the mailbox"; a reader could not help but envision the postman's head bobbing incongruously from the letter slot of a mailbox. Sentences like "He counted three beautiful paintings coming down the stairs" and "She dropped the letter she was carrying to her mother in the mud" intrigue pupils because of their humorous aspects and may lead to a serious consideration of word order. Children need to learn that whether a sentence is in natural or inverted order, whether it begins with its subject or with a modifying clause or phrase, its meaning is clearer if modifiers adjoin the words they modify (or come as close as possible to them) and if pronoun placement leaves no doubt about proper antecedents.

Sentence sense.   Certainly children must develop a degree of sentence mastery before they can express ideas and feelings effectively and meaningfully in either written or oral form. It is a common criticism that far too many pupils pass through the entire language program without gaining a clear conception of what a sentence is. Many of these pupils could recite the definition of a sentence memorized from a textbook, but the oral and written structures they create stand as proof that their understanding of the elements that make up a sentence or that determine sentence quality is either extremely vague or nonexistent. They are unable to construct good clear sentences of their own or to examine and edit their sentences critically. There are no shortcuts to becoming skilled in sentence con-

---

15. The many young adults who cannot utter a sentence without saying "you know," provide evidence of teachers' inattention to this fault—or at least of unsuccessful efforts to change it.

struction. Constant and conscious teaching and learning on the part of the teacher and the pupil are the keys. The pupil must learn that sentences must make sense—that is, that they cannot be vague or incomplete and that they cannot try to tell so much as to confuse or destroy meaning. By focusing on the development of sentence sense teachers should be able to eliminate most sentence construction errors. The following suggestions should be helpful to most pupils:

1. Provide children with ample opportunity for oral composition, especially in the primary grades.
2. Encourage pupils in their oral expression to form habits of using sentences that make sense and are clear and concise.
3. Begin by emphasizing one-sentence statements to make the child understand that a sentence must tell one thing and only one thing.
4. From the one-sentence composition move to the two- and three-sentence composition as sentence skill develops.
5. Continually expose pupils to good sentences read by a good oral reader. This generally means the teacher should read well-written materials frequently to the children in a voice that portrays "sentence feeling."
6. Encourage pupils to do considerable group composing, dictating of letters, and other forms of written expression in the early grades.
7. Provide exercises in which each child tells one thing about some personal experience, such as an excursion, a project, or a picture.
8. Make frequent use of dictation exercises that require punctuation and capitalization.
9. Encourage children to answer questions in sentence form.
10. Provide exercises that require pupils to distinguish between fragments and sentences.
11. Insist that pupils proofread their own writing.
12. Provide exercises for making sentences out of nonsentence groups of words.
13. Use matching exercises consisting of short lists of complete subjects to be matched with lists of complete predicates.
14. Provide exercises for breaking up run-on sentences into correct sentences.
15. Develop the sentence concept through the use of contrast. The teacher could write two different versions of stories told by children to illustrate good and poor sentence sense. The class should compare, discuss, and evaluate the two compositions and reconstruct the improper version.
16. Provide exercises requiring children to organize sentence elements according to their proper relationships.

17. Give careful explanations of the various types of incorrect sentences and illustrate each.
18. Make certain that children are able to recognize verbs (really the core of every sentence) around which all the other words are grouped as subject or predicate modifiers. Next see that they learn to find the subject of a verb and understand how a verb and subject form the framework of a sentence. Then pupils can advance to the study of words that modify the subject and verb.

In particular, teachers should help children relate the sentence sense they produce in their speech to their written expression. Although a child may include unnecessary words, use "and" excessively, and ramble a great deal when speaking, he or she is likely to pause between sentences to separate them. A teacher could ask a child who has written run-on constructions to read the result and point out to the child that the junctures (pauses) used do not coincide with the punctuation and capitalization. Often the first reading by the child will not reflect an accurate rendition of the run-on sentences in the writing, but if the teacher asks for a rereading after calling attention to the drop in voice, the child will begin to be more aware of sentences in oral expression. Alternatively, the teacher may choose to read a faulty passage exactly as it is written and ask the writer to suggest editorial changes. A tape recorder can assist children in comparing oral with written language, and teacher with child readings.

Interest and Variety in Expression

Interesting content and words and varied sentence construction are tools for building interest, accuracy, and appeal into expression. To persuade children of this fact a teacher might present a literature excerpt to initiate a discussion of why some characters seem to come alive, how the piece creates a mood, how an interesting beginning invites further reading, and what role action has in creating interest. Children may select stories that they think are interesting and list factors that they believe make them so. The teacher will have to help them get started, because most children will make general statements ("It was funny" or "I liked the dog") rather than identifying specific factors. Children could even compile criteria associated with high interest and then apply them to their own oral and written expression.

Many factors affect interest and appeal of expression, even if the expression is only a single sentence. In general, the most effective way to enhance the appeal of a composition is to provide a rich content base from which writing may grow and to encourage children to share their own direct or indirect experiences. On the basis of a child's background, the teacher can guide the selection of the topic and the content that will result in expression that is both interesting and appropriate.

Word choice is important to interest and appeal, as well as to accuracy of meaning. In all expression, the use of concrete words and phrases improves both interest and meaning. One curriculum guide includes the following activities for developing sentences based on concrete words and ideas.[16]

> Present to the child a series of pictures of story characters whose facial expressions indicate feelings of happiness, sadness, or surprise. Have the children suggest exact words which describe the expressions, such as: *laughing, crying, smiling, surprised*.
>   Have the children write a sentence, using one of the words and describing the expression, such as:
>
>> The man is surprised.
>> The girl is crying.
>
>   Now have the children write a sentence which describes the expression in more detail, such as:
>
>> The man's mouth is open in surprise.
>> Tears are coming down the girl's face.

By comparing materials with the children the teacher can demonstrate how concreteness stimulates interest. Exercises that call for listing words in order of their definiteness or concreteness are helpful, too, as is the use of a dictionary to determine the exact meaning of a word. Teachers should stress the exact meanings of synonyms so that students will learn to use the one that expresses the desired meaning most definitely and concretely. Of course, the most effective means of developing skill in expressing thoughts and ideas concretely is by actually constructing sentences and paragraphs and by critical editing and revision.

Expression also becomes more interesting if it contains examples, illustrations, and figures of speech. That children recognize the effectiveness of these additions early is evident in their creation of drawings to accompany their writing. Teachers should not discourage this practice but they should help students to discover that a "word picture" can serve the same purpose. For instance, the child who is writing a letter to his or her grandmother and wants to tell her that the family puppy is getting fat should be encouraged to write something like this: "Our puppy is getting fatter every day and now is fatter than Grandpa's red pig."

A figure of speech that is particularly helpful in making a talk or composition interesting is the *simile*, a comparison or likeness introduced by words like *as* or *like*. Similes that are themselves interesting and readily understandable enrich the meaning of communication, and children should learn to use this device to add interest and meaning to oral and written expression.

These suggestions for teaching similes, examples, and figurative expressions illustrate the kind of procedures teachers can use to encourage variety and interest in expression:

---

16. *English Language Arts, Experimental Material: Composition Section* (Albany: University of the State of New York/State Education Department, 1965), p. 12.

1.   Encourage children to list interesting comparisons they encounter in their reading, in assembly programs, in television and radio programs, and at home and to share them with other members of the class.
2.   Encourage children to watch for opportunities to use examples, figures of speech, and unusual comparisons in written and oral expression.
3.   Have the children maintain a column on the bulletin board similar to *Reader's Digest* "Patter."
4.   Have the children practice completing sentences like the following with the most interesting phrase: The boat rocked as _____.

Variety in sentence structure also enlivens communication. Of course, children come to school with knowledge of word order in English; that is, through their experience with language they have discovered the language system. Presented with the following frames for inserting the missing words, they would have no difficulty choosing nouns for them.

- I saw _____.
- He hasn't any _____.
- The _____ was interesting.

Likewise, they should have no difficulty correctly inserting verbs into these frames:

- You _____ quickly.
- He _____ it.

Or inserting adjectives into this sentence:

- The _____ boy is very _____.

Most children have this knowledge; most children also understand that some parts of sentences cannot be moved, while other parts can. For example, "Bob hit the ball hard" cannot become "The ball hard Bob hit." Of course, the same words can be written "Bob hit the hard ball," just as "They looked up eagerly" can be changed to "Eagerly, they looked up" or "They eagerly looked up."

Some textbooks supply exercises for children to change the word order in sentences. One book for the fourth grade includes the following exercise:[17]

Change the word order in the following sentences without changing the meanings. Write the new sentences you make.

_____

17. John S. Hand et al., *Exploring in English: Experiences in Language* (Chicago: Laidlaw Brothers Publishers, 1972), p. 27.

1.   Slowly the plane moved toward the takeoff point.
2.   Bob sat down quickly.
3.   I wrote a poem yesterday.

The children would be expected to write:

1.   The plane moved slowly toward the takeoff point.
      The plane moved toward the takeoff point slowly.
2.   Quickly Bob sat down.
      Bob quickly sat down.
3.   Yesterday I wrote a poem

More common in textbooks are exercises requiring students to arrange a group of words in sentence order. Although this activity may have some value, it makes poor use of knowledge that children already have. Often children do not receive enough instruction and practice in saying the same thing different ways; for example:

- I saw the fishing boat leaving the harbor as I came down to the dock.
- As I came down to the dock, I saw the fishing boat leaving the harbor.
- The fishing boat was leaving the harbor as I came down to the dock.

Children can learn to vary expression also by experimenting with language through the following:

1.   Substituting nouns for other nouns in sentences
2.   Replacing verbs in sentences with more vivid ones
3.   Replacing adjectives in sentences with more descriptive ones or ones which more accurately modify the nouns
4.   Changing the positions of movables in sentences
5.   Adding words, phrases, or clauses to the subjects of sentences
6.   Modifying the predicates of sentences by adding words, phrases, or clauses

A simple way to get children to practice these techniques is to write words on individual tagboard cards and place them in the chalkboard tray or hang them on a string stretched across the front of the room. The children can then move the words themselves to change word order and expand and transform sentences. New words can be written on blank cards as they are needed. For example, the sentence "Men in the jungle hunt" can be expanded to "Men in the jungle hunt with primitive weapons" and to "Men in the jungle hunt their daily food with primitive weapons." Similarly, this method allows children to make transformations by focusing their attention on interest and variety without learning or using grammatical terminology. For example, "Bill bought a bicycle" may become the passive "A bicycle was bought by Bill," the negative "Bill did not buy a bicycle," or the exclamatory "What a bicycle Bill bought!"

THE IMPORTANCE OF VOCABULARY

By the time the average child enters school, he or she has acquired a considerable understanding of a large number of words; current estimates of the number range from 3000 to 17,000.[18] The levels of their understanding vary, however. Most of us "understand" some words well enough to make sense of them when we hear them or read them but not well enough to use them ourselves. Elementary schoolchildren also frequently "understand" one meaning of a word when they hear or read it but do not understand the same word when they hear or read it in a context in which the meaning is different.[19] Too, if children are unsure about the pronunciation of a word, they generally will avoid using it in their speech. The same is true of spelling in their writing. At all times, the school must emphasize understanding by teaching the proper use of words. Promoting the growth of writing, speaking, reading, and listening vocabularies is a most important function of the language program in every classroom.

Role of Experience in Vocabulary Building

The best way to add breadth and depth to a child's vocabulary is to provide a variety of opportunities for new and interesting experiences. For example, many kindergarten or first-grade children will benefit from a visit to a farm. This experience might add the following words and many more to their vocabularies:

milking machine	crop
tractor	harvest
barn	cattle
silo	orchard
pasture	well
manger	flock
grain	irrigate

All areas of the curriculum lend themselves to many kinds of direct experience. In all cases, these experiences should afford opportunities for vocabulary enrichment, as do the following activities, which are particularly suitable for the primary grades.

---

18. Albert J. Harris, *How to Increase Reading Ability*, 5th ed. (New York: David McKay Co., 1970), p. 392.

19. Edgar Dale and Joseph O'Rourke, *The Living Word Vocabulary* (Chicago: Field Enterprises Educational Corp., 1976).

1.   Manipulative activities that involve handling various materials, tools, and equipment; learning new names and understanding directions; discussing plans and results
2.   Social experiences within the classroom, such as "show and tell," the daily news period, committee work that calls for planning and discussing, free conversation periods, and general class discussion
3.   Development of the children's social responsibility for receiving and greeting guests, extending courtesies, and helping one another
4.   Development of children's interest in the natural environment and in community activities by means of field trips that entail preliminary discussion of plans, training in observation, and eventual discussion of the total experience
5.   Observation and handling of specimens and articles brought into the classroom in connection with science or social studies
6.   Establishment of a class science museum or hobby displays that involve classification, organization, and production of appropriate labels
7.   Encouragement of children's interest in and increased curiosity about words

Unquestionably, many school activities hold possibilities for vocabulary growth, but without special attention, this growth might not occur. A summary report of vocabulary research says:[20]

> . . . studies on teaching vocabulary have shown that some teaching effort causes students to learn vocabulary more successfully than does no teaching effort, that any attention to vocabulary development is better than none . . . it is possible to note accumulating evidence to dispel the widely held notion that having students "read, read, read" is a satisfactory method for teaching vocabulary.

Too often a real or vicarious experience brings children into contact with new words and ideas without clarifying meanings. For example, children might describe the classroom gerbil as "a little brown animal," but with teacher guidance, they might call it "a tiny, tawny-furred rodent, whose fur feels like silk."

Vocabulary Growth Through Reading

The practicality of teaching some words through actual experiences is limited, and one of the best methods for overcoming this limitation is to read extensively.

---

20. Walter T. Petty, Curtis P. Herold, and Earline Stoll, *The State of Knowledge About the Teaching of Vocabulary* (Urbana, Ill.: National Council of Teachers of English, 1968), p. 84.

One language authority describes reading as a means of developing vocabulary in this way:[21]

- Reading, reading, reading. The more the children read the more meanings they learn.
- Reading things one is interested in
- Reading easy things for fun
- Reading anything and everything that adds to the value of the things one is do- ing or studying
- Reading to build new interests
- Reading newspapers, magazines, books, catalogs—anything that adds interest to living

Reading as a means of vocabulary development depends, of course, on the guidance given, the pupils' skill in reading, their interest in reading, and their skill in deriving meaning from the context. Guidance by the teacher is instrumen- tal in vocabulary building and requires attention to Deighton's "principles of con- text operation":[22]

- Context reveals the meaning of unfamiliar words only infrequently.
- Context generally reveals only one of the meanings of an unfamiliar word.
- Context seldom clarifies the whole of any meaning.
- Vocabulary growth through context revelation is a gradual matter.

In addition, what the context reveals to readers depends on their previous ex- periences, the clarity of the relationship between unknown words and the context that reveals their meanings, and the physical proximity of the context to the un- familiar words.

Thus teachers need to do much more than provide time for children to read (although having time to read is important, too) if they expect children to strengthen their vocabularies this way. Guidance in choosing reading materials is necessary so that children will understand what they read and will build upon their prior experience. Children also must have the teacher's help in learning to use the dictionary with many reading activities and to use all the clues to meaning that the context of the material contains. Such clues include examples that may explain unknown words, restatements that are really definitions, and modifying clauses or phrases that reveal meaning. In addition to picking up clues to the meanings of words and phrases, children need to learn to make inferences, to "read between the lines." Teachers should give direct attention to particular categories of words; for example, they can teach children the meanings of (1)

---

21. Ruth G. Strickland, *The Language Arts in the Elementary School* (Boston: D. C. Heath and Co., 3d ed., 1969), p. 250.

22. Lee C. Deighton, *Vocabulary Development in the Classroom* (New York: Teachers College Press, 1959), p. 3. Copyright © 1959 by Teachers College, Columbia University.

words often used figuratively, such as *eye, face, hill, river;* (2) judgment words, such as *fine, great, heavy, long;* (3) relationship words, such as *across, over, under, still, among;* (4) indefinite words, such as *some, several, most, much;* and (5) common idioms, such as *clear up, hold out, make do, bring down.* With proper teacher guidance children can reinforce their vocabularies each time they read and gain confidence and a sense of mastery in using words that they recognize and understand but have hesitated to use in their own expression.

Some children read fluently but without discrimination or feeling. Teachers can help these pupils to notice words or phrases that are particularly well chosen and appropriate. Properly stimulated, pupils will discover and think about the feelings that various words arouse and become aware of the difference between vivid and colorless expression in their reading.

Vocabulary-building Activities

In addition to reading, these activities will develop a consciousness of the meanings and uses of words:

1. List on the board and on charts new words encountered in classroom activities, in reading, and in experiences outside of school. Then the class should discuss these words and examples of their use.
2. Keep individual lists of new words that pupils like and want to use. This should not be an assignment of so many words a day or anything of the sort that becomes drudgery, but something a child wants to do because of interest in the words.
3. Make charts of "quiet" words, or perhaps "sound," "sad," "musical," or "sports" words. Other possibilities are charts of words to use in place of commonly overworked words and words for special occasions or special interests, such as football games, space travel, and camping trips.[23]
4. Find words and phrases that suggest images, such as "dancing leaves," "a pacing tiger," and "a shining beach."
5. Build words from root words by adding various prefixes and suffixes. For example, the root word *port* takes many prefixes and suffixes, including: *report, transport, portable, portage, porter, reporter, export.*
6. Look for alliteration and rhyme in posters and slogans, and for picturesque and descriptive phrases, in other forms of reading matter.
7. Suggest ideas and topics for written compositions and oral reports that will bring forth new words and new uses of familiar words. The following examples may serve this purpose:

---

23. Marguerite P. Archer reported that one class found 104 words to use instead of *said.* "Building Vocabulary with a Fourth Grade Class," *Elementary English* 37 (November 1960): 447–48.

- • The Freshness of Spring
- • Across the Nation by Jet Airliner
- • Sounds at Night
- • What I Saw in the Park
- • What a Duck Sees While Flying South

8. Play word games such as Scrabble, rearrange letters of a word to make new words, change the suffix of a word, find a word that begins with the letter that ends the preceding word, and so on.

9. Find words whose meanings have shifted or that have taken on new meanings, for example: *junk, phone, splurge, stage, capsule, pad, bird, clean* (in space jargon).

10. Have vocabulary-building campaigns, in which students are responsible for learning a new word each day, a word of the week, or new words from social studies.

Use of New Words and New Meanings

Basic to vocabulary development is using new words and new meanings, for only by using words will children genuinely come to understand them. A language program that focuses on real communication activities like the ones suggested throughout this book will provide the opportunities for achieving this goal and avert the need for artificial methods. The following report, for example, shows real understanding of the meaning of a new word:

> Ronnie shared his prized guinea pigs with the class. The children watched the little animals eagerly as they gnawed and nibbled. They held them close to feel the soft warm bodies. They listened to the characteristic "conversation" of the guinea pigs. They heard the scratching and digging of tiny claws.
>
> When the young guinea pigs were born and were less than an hour old, excited voices called, "See how tiny his claws are!" "Feel the soft velvety fur." "The babies are really miniature guinea pigs, aren't they?"
>
> This last comment came from Joe, who had been working on a miniature adobe house and had been fascinated by the new word *miniature*. He was eager to experiment with it in many situations.[24]

Because many words have several connotations, it is necessary for children to learn to use words accurately in order to convey the intended meaning. Words act as a bridge for understanding between them and their reader or listener, and therefore, they must learn to choose their words precisely. At the kindergarten and first-grade levels, the teacher may begin by teaching the correct names of

24. *Arts and Skills of Communication for Democracy's Children*, vol. 2 (San Bernardino, Calif.: San Bernardino County Schools, n.d.), p. 234.

familiar objects, such as parts of the body or school equipment. This practice of systematically introducing new words should continue at every grade level.

Children should also understand that some words have similar but not identical meanings and therefore require careful selection. For example, one teacher asked a class to express more clearly the sentence "He ate much too quickly." Some of the results were:[25]

- He gobbled his food like a young turkey who hadn't been taught his manners.
- He gulped whole pieces of bread. They almost choked him.
- He swallowed so fast, the milk just wouldn't go down and he had to wait to catch a little breath.

Instruction in Using Sources of Information

Skill in using the library and its materials as well as other sources of information is of great importance to both oral and written expression, especially for children in the middle grades whose environment is rapidly expanding. They are encountering many new facts and practices and they need to be correct and specific about information. Although young children also need library experiences, it is essential that older children learn the specific skills that will enable them to take full advantage of this valuable resource.

Underlying instruction in the proper use of different sources of information are several noteworthy principles. The teacher should:

1. Accommodate differences in pupil's abilities, interests, and needs through individual and small-group instruction and with instructional materials of varying levels of difficulty.
2. Deal with individuals or small groups on the basis of common needs.
3. Be sure that pupils understand the purpose of the instruction. They need to know exactly what technique they are to learn and how it will contribute to effective independent study and research.
4. Lead the pupils to acquire feelings of responsibility for understanding what they study. Discourage rote repetition of words not fully understood, a practice that leads to verbalism or answering in the words in the book.

The library.   The nature and type of library instruction depends on the extent of available library facilities in the school and the community, and the

<hr/>

25. *Developing Children's Power of Self-expression Through Writing* (New York: Board of Education of the City of New York), pp. 79–80.

degree of familiarity the children already have with libraries. Nevertheless, elementary school children should learn that:

- Books are arranged in the library in a systematic fashion (either the Dewey Decimal or Library of Congress classification) and that this system is an aid to library users.
- The card catalog is an index of all books in the library, arranged by name of the author, title of the book, and subject.
- Nonfiction books are shelved numerically within each category from left to right.
- Fiction is arranged alphabetically according to the authors' last names.
- Filmstrips, records, picture files, atlases, and other resources are in special areas.

In addition, children need to know how to check out and return books to the library; use the card catalog to locate books; use dictionaries, encyclopedias, atlases, and similar reference sources; use special reference sources such as the *Reader's Guide*; make use of bibliographies; and—one of the most important skills of all—take accurate notes.

Care and appreciation in handling books develop as a result of direct instruction, supervised practice, and good example. Speaking softly, walking quietly, and asking the librarian for help when necessary all make a library a good place to work. Teachers should also teach young children to handle books only when their hands are clean and to turn pages carefully. Insistence that older children also follow these practices is not out of order.

Because the card catalog is the fundamental guide to materials in a library, teachers should give particular instructional attention to:

1. The purpose, contents, and value of the card catalog
2. The meaning of the letters on the drawers
3. Skill in finding a word in an alphabetical list
4. Skill in using guide cards
5. The meaning of each piece of printed matter on each of the following types of cards: (a) the author card, (b) the title card, (c) the subject card, and (d) the analytic card
6. The meaning and use of *see* and *see also* on cards

In teaching children to use the library, an elementary teacher may seek help from a trained librarian. Following library instruction, children should always receive assignments that require them to use newly acquired skills.

The dictionary.   Words intrigue most people and it is natural for children to like dictionaries because they contain interesting information about so many words. Children also seem to have an affinity for names and pictures of objects arranged in alphabetical order. Indeed, the dictionary is such a basic source of information that if it were possible to teach the use of only one reference source, that reference should be the dictionary.

Skill in using a dictionary develops slowly and requires the guidance of sympathetic and wise teachers over a period of years. Although every teacher a child encounters is responsible for teaching dictionary usage, its introductory teaching requires special care. Instruction in dictionary skills can begin as early as they will help a child achieve greater independence in oral or written expression or reading. Now that picture dictionaries are widely available, children may begin to learn many skills in the primary grades. First graders can learn beginning alphabetizing, the use of a dictionary to find spellings and word meanings, and the importance of the dictionary as a source of new and interesting words, as well as most of the dictionary skills listed below.

Each child should have a dictionary, especially after the primary years. In addition, each intermediate grade classroom should have other dictionaries available, including an unabridged one. Above all, children should not have to go to another room, look on a closet shelf, move a pile of books, or ask the teacher's permission to use a dictionary.

Often children learn dictionary skills only in connection with the reading program as a means for checking pronunciations and clarifying meanings. Such training will not necessarily enable them to use the dictionary effectively to clarify their own expression. Using the dictionary as an aid to expression requires deliberate, definite, and specific instruction for this purpose. What follows is a list of dictionary skills that children should learn and an approximate sequence for introducing them.[26]

1. Learning the names of letters and being able to recognize both lower and upper case forms of each
2. Learning the alphabetical, consecutive arrangement of letters
3. Learning the location of letters in the alphabet in relation to each other
4. Finding words beginning with certain letters in any alphabetical arrangement
5. Arranging words alphabetically; with different first letters; with the same beginning letter
6. Appreciating the dictionary as a tool and interesting source of much information
7. Understanding that the dictionary is built on alphabetical order by first, second, third letters, and so on, of words

---

26. Adapted from listing in Iowa Elementary Teachers Handbook, vol. 2, *Reading* (Des Moines: Iowa State Department of Public Instruction, 1944), pp. 170–74.

8. Familiarity with relative position of letter sections: *d*'s come in first third of the dictionary, *y*'s in final third, and so on
9. Using guide words to determine which page and column contain the word
10. Understanding that words are listed by root forms
11. Using the dictionary to find the correct spelling of a word
12. Using diacritical markings, key words, and accent marks as pronunciation aids
13. Learning the meaning and the use of respelling to show pronunciation
14. Learning the meaning and the use of syllabication
15. Using the definition best suited to a context
16. Determining the correct use of homonyms
17. Understanding dictionary abbreviations
18. Using synonyms and antonyms to clarify meaning
19. Learning how to find related forms, irregular plurals, and irregular verb forms
20. Using cross-references to find additional information
21. Understanding the significance of word derivation, prefixes, suffixes, and so on
22. Learning about special features of the dictionary; for example, a table of measures or an atlas

Alphabetizing. Many children acquire some knowledge of the alphabet even before they come to school. Beginning schoolchildren soon learn the letters in their names, if they did not know them prior to coming to school. Children learn the letters and their order in the alphabet as they learn to write and read. But learning the alphabet involves more than simply memorizing the order of the letters in a mechanical, sing-song fashion. It means instantly knowing the approximate place of any letter in the alphabet and which letters immediately precede and follow it. Some suggestions for teaching these skills are as follows:

1. At various times throughout the day ask questions that call for remembering the position of letters. Questions such as these are appropriate:
   Which letter is before *i*, after *i*; before *y*, after *y*?
   Is *f* near the first or the last of the alphabet?
2. Ask children to turn to words beginning with certain letters in a telephone directory, glossary, or dictionary.
3. Point to or name a letter and ask the children to say the alphabet forward or backward to some other letter.
4. Have children arrange lists of words alphabetically. The first lists should be those in which each word begins with a different letter. Later exercises could require alphabetizing based on the third or fourth letters of words.

5.   Ask children to make alphabetical lists of their names, names of cities, or names of objects, at first only according to the first letter.
6.   Ask children to alphabetize words that begin with the same letter.
7.   Give children time to explore dictionaries for themselves.
8.   Ask children to divide the dictionary into thirds and learn which letters are in each third.
9.   Have children practice opening the dictionary to certain letters.
10. Give children practice exercises such as, "If you are looking for *j* and open the dictionary to *h*, which way should you turn to find *j*?"

Guide words. After children have become acquainted with the dictionary and have developed considerable skill in alphabetizing, they are ready to learn to use the guide words that appear at the top of each page in the dictionary. To teach them the meaning of guide words the teacher can ask questions like: "Do any words come after the right-hand word?" Children must see that in order to use the guide words efficiently they must thoroughly understand alphabetical order so that they can tell quickly whether the word they are seeking appears before or after the guide word. The following sample activities should be helpful in teaching about guide words:[27]

Directions: Notice the two words at the top of each page in your dictionary. The one on the left side is the same as the first word on the page. The word on the right is the same as the word which appears last on the page. These words are called *guide words*. Turn to a page in your dictionary and read the guide words. Look up the word *insect*. Between what two guide words is it?

Directions: You may read the words below when studying about *airplanes*. Each word in the list is in your dictionary. Find each of the words and write the two guide words on that page.

Word	First Guide Word	Second Guide Word
propeller		
hangar		
aviation		
airdrome		
wing		
beacon		
ceiling		
goggles		
parachute		

Directions: The line below represents page 472 in a certain dictionary. *Nest* and *new* are the guide words on the page. Underline words in the following list which would be found on this page of the dictionary:

---

27. Iowa Elementary Teachers Handbook, pp. 173–74.

nest	472	*new*
lake		nerve
net		nail
neutral		nettle
neglect		next
nesting		
nestling		

Other dictionary skills. Middle-grade and upper-grade children frequently turn to the dictionary for help in pronouncing words. These children need to learn to use pronouncing keys and diacritical marks and to understand syllabication and accent marks. In fact, the only point of teaching diacritical marks is to aid pupils with pronunciation. Thus teachers should introduce these skills in situations that call for their use.

Finding meanings of words is another area in which children need help. In most instances, a child looks up a word not merely to learn the meaning, but also to determine the meaning in a particular context or to use the word in a particular way. The following is a sample activity for teaching this skill:

Directions: The dictionary often lists several meanings for one word. The use of the word in the sentence tells you which one you need. In front of each sentence below put the number of the meaning that fits that sentence. Write four other sentences and use the word in each of the four meanings.

Sup-port.' (su-port'), v.1. To hold up; to keep from sinking or falling; as pillars support the porch roof. 2. To bear. 3. To take sides with; to back up; as, to support a candidate. 4. To provide with food, clothing, shelter, etc.; as, he supports his mother.

1.   He could not *support* the suspense any longer.
2.   Many people must *support* candidates to get them elected to office.
3.   She helped to *support* her family by working after school.
4.   The shelf was *supported* by braces.

Other reference sources.   Using encyclopedias, atlases, almanacs, biographical dictionaries, and other, similar reference sources exercises many of the skills necessary for effective use of a card catalog or dictionary. In addition, using most reference books requires skill in skimming (determining the general content of a passage) as well as the related skill of scanning (locating specific information within a broad discussion of a topic). These skills should be learned in the reading program and reinforced in the context of reference usage as means for getting information and ideas.

Because children use books as sources of information as well as sources of pleasure, knowing how to use the table of contents, the index, and the glossary is another valuable skill for them to learn. At the time children begin reading, they can learn to use the table of contents. Teachers should give assignments that require consulting the table of contents or the index rather than simply giving page numbers. Many children's books contain glossaries of new words that appear in the stories or lessons. Like the dictionary, a glossary is a key to the pronunciation and meanings of the new words in that book. In doing research, children should be able to find and use a glossary when they encounter a word that is unfamiliar to them.

Teachers should introduce the index as a tool for doing research in a book; that is, pupils should learn to use the index as a means of locating information on a given topic. In addition, they should learn to prepare an index for written records, reports, or summaries of their own creation. Specifically, these skills and information concerning index usage should be part of the language arts curriculum:

1. The difference between topics and subtopics
2. What the different punctuation marks in the index mean
3. By what key an index shows page numbers of maps, graphs, tables, or diagrams
4. The use and significance of the key or direction at the beginning or end of the index
5. Different types of subtopic arrangement
6. How to identify the pages of the most important discussions on a particular topic
7. Whether or not an index denotes pronunciation
8. How to use more than one topic if necessary to find the desired information

EXERCISES FOR THOUGHT AND ACTION

1. Evaluate the program suggested in this chapter for teaching usage. Consider its applicability to all children, regardless of dialect differences. If you would make changes, tell why.
2. Compile a list, in priority order, of the usage needs of one child. Design an oral practice exercise for a selected usage item based on the guidelines in this chapter.
3. Develop a list of ways to add interest to oral and written expression that you would hope to elicit from children during a lesson. Convert the list into a checklist that would be useful for pupil self-evaluation.
4. Plan a series of practice exercises asking children to separate sentence fragments from sentences. Explain the rationale for your design.
5. Develop a game that you could play with a child who lacks sentence sense. You may base the rules on common games like Old Maid, Bingo, Concentration, or any board game.

6. Develop and report on a series of exercises designed to teach organization of expression to a particular group of children.

7. Report how one language textbook series teaches organization of expression. You will need to examine books (teacher's editions) at several levels to get a picture of the overall progression.

8. Make a brief visit to an elementary school classroom and tabulate the usages that you think the instruction program should attack. Explain the reasons for your selection.

9. Listen to the oral language of several children in a classroom. Based on your observations, predict the character of each child's writing. Test your predictions by examining writing samples and/or consulting with the teacher.

10. Design a vocabulary-building campaign for your own or a hypothetical class. Compare your idea with those of your peers. Which is the most original and potentially most effective?

11. Develop a teaching and/or resource unit for a group of intermediate-grade children on figures of speech that relates to their own writing.

12. Develop a series of exercises designed to give pupils at a selected level practice in alphabetizing, using an index, or using guide words in a dictionary.

13. Plan a lesson that requires children to research information in an encyclopedia. If you choose to plan for an upper-grade level, your lesson should require them to use more than one encyclopedia.

14. Select a fourth-, fifth-, or sixth-grade textbook in any subject area and build a unit lesson plan around it that requires children to use the library to obtain additional information. Be sure to plan for differences in library experiences and abilities.

15. What would you teach elementary school children about the denotation and connotation of words? Briefly tell how you would accomplish this objective.

16. Some small school libraries may not classify books according to the Library of Congress or Dewey Decimal system. What would you teach pupils attending such schools about using a library?

SELECTED REFERENCES

Blair, Glenn Myers. *Diagnostic and Remedial Teaching.* New York: Macmillan, 1956.

California Association of School Librarians. *Library Skills.* Belmont, Calif.: Fearon Publishers, 1973.

Dale, Edgar, and O'Rourke, Joseph. *Techniques of Teaching Vocabulary.* Palo Alto, Calif.: Field Educational Publications, 1971.

Deighton, Lee C. *Vocabulary Development in the Classroom.* New York: Teachers College, Columbia University, 1959.

Holstrop, R. W. *Education Inside the Library Media Center.* Hamden, Conn.: Shoe String Press, 1973.

Imhoof, Maurice L., ed. "Social and Educational Insights into Teaching Standard English to Speakers of Other Dialects," *Viewpoints* (bulletin of the School of Education, Indiana University) 47 (March 1971).

Karlin, Robert. *Teaching Elementary Reading.* New York: Harcourt Brace Jovanovich, 1971.

Mott, Carolyn, and Baisden, Leo B. *The Children's Book on How to Use Books and Libraries*, 3rd ed. New York: Charles Scribner's Sons, 1968.

Petty, Walter T.; Petty, Dorothy C.; and Becking, Marjorie F. *Experiences in Language: Tools and Techniques for Language Arts Methods.* Boston: Allyn and Bacon, 1973.

Pooley, Robert C. *The Teaching of English Usage.* Urbana, Ill.: National Council of Teachers of English, 1974.

Shankman, Florence, and Kranyik, Robert. *How to Teach Reference and Research Skills.* New York: Teachers Practical Press, 1964.

11

Focus on Oral Creativity

Learning to read and write . . . should not be made a sudden transition. These activities should be preceded, accompanied and followed by talk. —*John Dixon*, Growth Through English

Virtually all children possess the ability to speak, to express needs and feelings orally, and to explore an expanding world before they come to school. When they manipulate language to interpret their environments, they are exercising a creative power that is uniquely human. Thus, their effort to "make sense" out of the world develops both creative and language powers. Yet this natural process only barely taps strong creative urges and infinite language potential. Continued discovery and exploration are necessary if a child's creativity is to flourish and language ability is to grow.

SPEECH IN SCHOOL

Many teachers provide opportunities for children to talk, for they recognize how language power develops as well as what the practical and personal needs of children are. But the traditional cliché "the good classroom is a quiet classroom" provides a convenient rationalization for less-informed teachers who are content to live with tradition.

Every teacher has a responsibility to develop each child's linguistic and creative potential as fully as possible. Hence, at the very heart of language arts programs must be a willingness to take complete advantage of the many daily opportunities for oral expression. In practical terms, this principle means simply that oral language should be a primary concern in every classroom. Children must have freedom to express themselves, to "talk out" their ideas and feelings, and to receive encouragement in oral expression rather than restriction.

Teachers must recognize that the child who lacks maturity in oral expression is not ready to tackle reading and writing tasks, which require even greater language maturity. Finally, teachers who capitalize on the interrelationships discussed in Chapter 10 in all teaching endeavors can maximize the learning transfer potential of each child in all language skills.

Speech and Children's Development

Recognition of the importance of oral language ability in other language arts areas is increasing. As Loban has pointed out:[1]

> Teachers have begun to note that outstanding readers and writers among their pupils also have a way with words when they speak—an observation not discredited by an exceptional child who compensates for spoken inarticulateness by increased reading and writing skill. Power with speech usually belongs to those who have a healthy self-respect and are well rounded in all of the arts of language.

The relationship between oral language and other aspects of growth and development also is undeniable. Children's oral expression, although it does not always reflect their language development accurately, is influenced by and influences their motor, cognitive, and emotional development. Research has shown that:[2]

> The capacity to articulate is paced by growth; the tendency to vocalize can be encouraged by social reinforcement; the acquisition of language and the development of syntax is uniquely a personal bio-social experience; speech development is significantly interrelated with the growth of intelligence and the emergence of personality; communication difficulties can become emotional difficulties. In every instance the interdependence of social and development factors is essential in assisting the child to develop language and speech.

---

1. Walter Loban, "Oral Language and Learning," in *Oral Language and Reading*, edited by James Walden (Urbana, Ill.: National Council of Teachers of English, 1969), pp. 101–02.

2. Gerald M. Phillips et al., *The Development of Oral Communication in the Classroom* (Indianapolis: Bobbs-Merrill Co., 1970), p. 52.

The strong relationship between oral expression and children's personal and social development is particularly significant to school programs and their objectives.[3]

> While research evidence appears not to be available to support the viewpoint that language ability directly affects the personality and social development of every person, adequate substantiation of the interrelatedness of language ability, environmental and physical and inter-personal factors, personality, and several behavioral tendencies such as the expression of anxiety has been shown.

Certainly, many teachers have noticed that personality differences among children affect oral language activities. An aggressive child might assume a great deal of classroom leadership and monopolize speaking activities. Perhaps the child's assurance in speaking fostered the aggressive behavior, or possibly an aggressive personality provides the speech confidence. On the other hand, a shy, retiring personality could be due to language immaturity; or it may be that a particular child's shyness has undermined confidence in speaking. Of course, these characteristics do not always go together. The cause and effect relationships are not clear, but they are strongly suspected to apply to speech. Children's speech often seems to reflect their anxieties, the most obvious example being stuttering.

In handicapped children the degree of individual development especially influences oral language abilities. Research indicates that children who suffer hearing loss, articulatory difficulty, parental rejection, or environmental

---

3. Walter T. Petty and Roberta J. Starkey, "Oral Language and Personal Social Development," *Research in Oral Language*, edited by Walter T. Petty (Urbana, Ill.: National Council of Teachers of English, 1967), p. 7.

deprivation tend to use oral language less effectively than children without such handicaps.[4]

Teachers must know and respect the personalities of all children in their classrooms. They must foster the development of speaking ability in the shy child, teach the overly aggressive child to respect the rights of others, attempt to reduce the anxieties of the insecure child, and try to help handicapped children compensate for their disabilities. Every teacher should take note of children's special interests and abilities and build upon them in developing a program of oral language instruction.

Classroom Environment and Speech

Every classroom is an environment that has the potential for fostering or hindering both children's creativity and oral language development. An environment has many components, as we pointed out in previous chapters. In the classroom, the environment essentially is comprised of the different personalities, characteristics, and experiences of the teacher and the pupils. Yet the essence of an environment is its atmosphere; it is how the teacher and children view one another, communicate with one another, and empathize with one another. An environment that fosters creativity and language growth expresses this characteristic in goodwill, respect, friendliness, open communication, and honest freedom.

Responsibility for the classroom environment belongs chiefly to the teacher, even though interaction among teacher and pupils is an integral part of its creation. The teacher must insure that interaction is not one-sided. In other words, if a child says something or produces something, the teacher must react to it. If the teacher's reaction is a "chopping off," the child will likely respond either by withdrawing or rebelling. Certainly the teacher can stymie creativity in any curricular area and at any time of day by making any of the following remarks:[5]

Don't be silly.	We've tried that before.
Let's be serious.	That's not part of your assignment.
That's ridiculous.	That's childish.
Let's be practical.	It won't work.
You should know better.	Don't be so sloppy.
What's the matter with you?	

On the other hand, many children need a teacher's help in finding ideas and relating words to them, in voicing feelings, and in sticking to tasks. What children need, as Trauger has said, is a "calm, steady interest."[6]

---

4. Ibid., p. 3.

5. Joseph S. Renzulli and Carolyn M. Callahan, *New Directions in Creativity* (New York: Harper and Row, Publishers, 1973), p. 11.

6. Wilmer K. Trauger, *Language Arts in Elementary Schools* (New York: McGraw-Hill Book Co., 1963), p. 253.

In many instances the teacher serves as a model for pupils. Some research evidence indicates that young children tend to imitate a teacher's speech mannerisms, but it is doubtful that they learn basic language patterns merely from listening to a teacher.[7] Nevertheless, the teacher who gives warm and encouraging counsel, who shows a democratic pattern of leadership, and who provides organized and stimulating guidance is enhancing pupils' self-confidence and their willingness to participate in oral language activities. Willingness to participate is the first step in all classroom learning, and self-confidence is essential for effective speaking.

Peers are also a major influence on a child's actions and speech; beyond the primary grades peer pressure is a greater motivational force than the teacher's authority. Although the body of research on the effects of peer speech on a child's basic language patterns and on articulation and pronunciation is small, the available evidence supports the general feeling of teachers that the effects are likely to be negative in the sense of improving speech.[8] Teachers and parents know that most children adopt the idiom of the school group. More importantly, however, children acquire their aspirations and values from their peer group. Just as the relationship of the teacher to the class group can provide support and foster willingness to participate, peers can influence a child's attitude toward speaking and improving skills.

As the research suggests, teachers should evaluate their own voices and ways of speaking. They should also evaluate their personal relationships with the children and the possible effects that they have on the children's use of oral language.

A teacher should attempt to build upon peer influences on a child's speech. How successful this effort will be hinges largely on the rapport between the teacher and class and on the degree to which the program accommodates students' creative abilities and genuine communicative needs.

CREATIVITY IN LANGUAGE EXPRESSION

Creative behavior appears to be a peculiarly human characteristic that is independent of basic drives but fills a need for satisfaction in discovery and exploration.[9] As a uniquely human trait, it is related to other human traits, of which language is perhaps the most human. In many ways creativity may be synonymous with the human potential. Lowenfeld stated, "I believe that one of

---

7. Frank B. May, "The Effects of Environment on Oral Language Development," *Research in Oral Language*, p. 30.

8. Evidence is reviewed in Thomas P. Carter, "Cultural Content for Linguistically Different Learners," *Research Bases for Oral Language Instruction*, edited by Thomas D. Horn (Urbana, Ill.: National Council of Teachers of English for the National Conference on Research in English, 1971), pp 36–49.

9. Jack Getzels and George F. Madaus, "Creativity," *Encyclopedia of Educational Research*, 4th ed., edited by Robert L. Ebel (New York: Macmillan Co., 1969), p. 268.

the outstanding differences between man and animal is that man intentionally creates and the animal does not. That implies that every individual is a potential creator."[10] Young children show evidence of this creative potential through interaction with their environments, particularly as they interpret what they have learned by experimenting with language. Teachers can encourage continued experimentation, which is necessary for the extension of children's creativity and further development of language ability.

Definitions of Creativity

Definitions of creativity abound. Torrance says that we may define creativity in terms of a process, a product, a personality, or an environmental condition, but he chooses to define it as "the process of sensing problems or gaps in information, forming ideas or hypotheses, testing and modifying these hypotheses, and communicating the results."[11] On the other hand, Smith describes creativity as the "sinking down [of] taps into our past experiences and putting these selected experiences together into new patterns, new ideas or new products."[12] Rogers also has defined it as a process: the "emergence in action of a novel relational product, growing out of the uniqueness of the individual on the one hand, and the materials, events, people, or circumstances of his life on the other."[13]

In other definitions, creativity becomes the contribution of something of an original nature, the opposite of conformity, the placement of isolated experiences and ideas in new combinations or patterns, a departure from the main track, and the adaptation of ideas and information to one's needs. Concepts associated with curiosity, imagination, discovery, innovation, and invention usually also find their way into descriptions of creative products and processes.

Everyone expects creativity to be part of the fields of literature, music, painting, sculpture, and dance and readily accepts it in these activities. But creativity exists in many activities that we do not always recognize as requiring imagination, needing innovation, or calling for discovery. Usually we think of the activities of the store clerk as being largely routine. Yet the store clerk may very well produce a new sales approach or a new method of displaying a product that represents genuine creativity. In mathematics, new thinking stems from a markedly different point of view. Max Beberman is quoted as saying that

10. Viktor Lowenfeld, "Basic Aspects of Creative Teaching," *Creativity and Psychological Health* (New York: Syracuse University Press, 1961), p. 130.
11. E. Paul Torrance, *What Research Says to the Teacher: Creativity* (Washington, D.C.: National Education Association, 1963), p. 4.
12. James A. Smith, *Setting Conditions for Creative Teaching in the Elementary School* (Boston: Allyn and Bacon, 1966), p. 4.
13. Carl Rogers, "Toward a Theory of Creativity," *Creativity and Its Cultivation*, edited by Harold H. Anderson (New York: Harper and Brothers, 1959), p. 71.

"mathematics is as creative as music, painting or sculpture."[14] In this age of nuclear power and man-made satellites and their potential for good or evil, we must recognize and nurture all forms of creativity no less in language expression than in other areas of mental and physical activity.

Some persons maintain that creative expression must be spontaneous. Although a considerable amount of expression is spontaneous, much of it is not particularly creative. For example, a spontaneous answer given in response to a question may be merely a parroting of someone else's words. A spontaneous expression of thanks for a present or a favor may lack sparkle and imagination. On the other hand, much creative expression is a product of careful and lengthy preparation. Even the creation of a rhyme may be a spontaneous act or the result of considerable thought.

Spontaneous is a close relative of *voluntary*, a word we often hear in connection with creative expression. Again, a relationship is evident: much creative expression is voluntary. But if we could rely solely on voluntary action to produce creative language expression it would be unnecessary to devote effort to fostering it or to emphasize the importance of an "intake" of experience in the teaching of language expression.

Some people hold the point of view that expression that is creative generally does not have utility and that expression for a practical or utilitarian purpose cannot be creative. They would not classify writing a letter as a creative process or the result a creative product because it has practical value. Likewise, they would not consider an oral report containing information of interest and benefit to an audience to be creative. In contrast, some people hold that whatever individuals do, say, or write in their own ways is creative. Considered from this point of view, all expression is creative, whether or not it has utility, as long as it is not merely a repetition of what someone else has said or written. And in the final analysis, of course, all expression can be utilitarian, even if the only result is an emotional release for the expressor.

Teachers have a strong tendency to separate writing activities into "creative" and "practical" (see Chapter 13) and sometimes to divide oral activities similarly. But creative expression does not necessarily lack utility and purpose. In fact, the point of view taken in this book is that any expression that is the individual's own is creative and that all language expression should represent the individual. It should show the thinking and feelings—the individuality—of the expressor.

Fostering Creativity in the Classroom

Children's creativity is an outgrowth of their natural curiosity—process of testing, questioning, and exploring. No matter how conducive to creativity the classroom

---

14. Helen Rowan, "The Wonderful World of Why," *Saturday Review*, 2 November 1957, p. 42.

environment is, however, no one can expect children to be creative immediately. Teachers must recognize and accommodate each child's individuality. Marksberry suggests that the creative process consists of four definite stages or periods:[15]

1. Preparation
2. Incubation
3. Insight, illumination, or inspiration
4. Verification, elaboration, perfecting, and evaluation

Too often we expect children to be in the perfecting stage, or at least in the inspirational one.

Creativity of expression hinges on many factors, including an abundance of ideas and thoughts, which, in turn, require a rich background of meaningful, vital experiences on which to draw. Earlier in the book and in this chapter, we stressed the importance of the classroom environment, the key role of the teacher, and the need to use language. These are essential ingredients of any language arts program, for they enable children to stretch their skills as much as possible and they help the teacher to elicit the children's best efforts.

TALK IN THE CLASSROOM

Children talk with one another naturally and informally if they are permitted to do so. They talk about themselves, their friends, what they have done, what their fathers and mothers have said, and what they are thinking. They talk among themselves as they come into the classroom, as they hang up their coats, and as they go to their seats. Language growth is occurring all this time, personalities are developing, and creative expression is taking place.

Although classroom activities must follow a plan and be orderly and purposeful, they need not rule out talking. In fact, just the opposite is true. Activity plans should include opportunities for both informal talk and more structured oral communication.

Most preschool, kindergarten, and primary teachers understand the need to plan talking situations. They provide materials that foster talk: a tub of water or a sandbox in which to play, objects to manipulate, and items to smell, taste, or feel. They provide time to observe and to have new experiences. The goal of all these activities is to promote talk and so to further language growth and the development of each child.

Unfortunately, once children leave the primary grades, opportunities to talk may become less prevalent, and even in the primary grades talk can become too

---

15. Mary Lee Marksberry, *Foundation of Creativity* (New York: Harper and Row, Publishers, 1963), pp. 17–21.

formal or routine. The familiar "show and tell," which Lucy in the *Peanuts* comic strip calls "Bring and Lie," may not serve the intended purpose because it frequently allows only a few children to talk daily, their talk is often unnatural, and little listening and exchange results. As we will see later in this chapter, however, better planning can alleviate these faults.

It is a basic rule that much classroom talk should involve the teacher, who listens and responds. Teachers who recognize the importance of verbal interaction give it full attention.

Although a good deal of classroom talk should be informal and unstructured—the kind of social exchange that adults have—other, equally informal talk should have specific purposes: deciding an issue, making plans, exchanging information, or discussing ideas. Frequently overlooked are the opportunities for purposeful talk in small group settings rather than among the entire class. Nevertheless, both small group discussions and discussions involving the entire class provide practice in a wide range of talk-related skills, including assertion, inquiry explanation, and exploration. These sessions establish a foundation for the more explicit and formal settings for talk that individuals encounter both as children and as adults (see Chapter 12). Though this informal, purposeful talk requires no detailed structuring, it does require the rapport we have discussed. It also requires that children be listening and internally planning responses or re-joinders. It requires participation.

CREATIVE DRAMATICS

A prime source of oral participatory experience is creative drama. Children delight in pretending. Young children seem spontaneously to create "let's pretend" games starring themselves, and they perform them for their own pleasure. In these games they enjoy expressing their ideas and feelings, as often in what they say as in what they do. Older children usually do more planning and structuring, but with encouragement, they will retain interest in informality.

Creative dramatics takes a variety of forms. Examples are the expression of feelings through rhythmic activities and unstructured dramatic play, pantomime and puppetry, and play production involving scripts and props.

Values of Creative Dramatics

Most teachers recognize that creative dramatics is a valuable and enjoyable activity for children. Research evidence supports this observation. Stewig reports that studies indicate that dramatics causes growth in the following areas: vocabulary; paralinguistic elements of pitch, stress, and juncture; syntactic maturity; fluency; the ability to retell a story; and nonverbal aspects of language, such as pantomime.[16] In addition, he cites studies of the beneficial effects of participation in creative dramatics on reading and creativity. Other authors have also described the values of creative dramatics; many of these sources are given in Hoetker's *Dramatics and the Teaching of Literature.*[17]

Basically, creative dramatics fosters creativity in language, thinking, uses of the voice, and body movement. "Playing" someone else gives children a chance to use their imaginations to choose words and actions that convey ideas and feelings to other players and/or an audience. Children's natural desire to express themselves as another person, animal, idea, or object leads them to experiment with tone, rate of speaking, use of gestures, and body stance in an effort to create a believable idea, mood, or character.

In the realm of personal and social growth, creative dramatics may give the

---

16. John Warren Stewig, "What Do We Really Know About Creative Drama?" in *Creative Dramatics in the Language Arts Classroom*, edited by Patrick J. Finn and Walter T. Petty (Buffalo: Department of Elementary and Remedial Education, State University of New York at Buffalo, 1976), pp. 1–12.

17. James Hoetker, *Dramatics and the Teaching of Literature* (Urbana, Ill.: National Council of Teachers of English, 1969).

shy child confidence, teach the aggressive child to respect the rights of others, and convey to all children the importance of cooperation. Additionally, children seem to gain a better understanding of themselves and others through these activities.

Dramatic Play

Dramatic play is the beginning form of creative dramatics; it is the imaginative play of the young child who imitates life as he or she sees and feels it. Certainly, it is not a dramatic activity as most adults think of it; rather, it is a play activity. As suggested in Chapter 3, dramatic play is inherent in many children's activities. During dramatic play children express feelings and thoughts with spontaneity and natural enthusiasm. For example, a preschool child or a child in the primary grades sits in the cockpit of an airplane built of blocks or boxes. She is the pilot, and she talks as she thinks the pilot would talk. She does the things she thinks the pilot would do. Such activity broadens the child's ability to use language as she experiments with new words, new ideas, and new ways of talking and acting.

The toy industry has been capitalizing on the naturalness of dramatic play for years. The dazzling array of items in a toy store suggests a wide range of imaginative play activities. A teacher should also provide opportunities for dramatic play in the beginning school years. Every properly equipped kindergarten or primary classroom contains the necessary materials—building blocks of various sizes, empty boxes and cartons, tables, chairs, blankets, and so on. Children have marvelous imaginations, and to them a table with a blanket over it might be anything from a tent in a fever-ridden jungle to the cave of a hibernating bear. The teacher's primary role is to enter into the imaginary world, talk with the children about it, supply or amplify related ideas, and suggest vocabulary for discussing them. In this way, dramatic play can foster creativity, language growth, personality development, and social maturity.

Young children love the land of make-believe, where they play "house," "school," "office," and other games based on real life. Because much of children's emotional and social growth throughout the school years occurs through this form of creative experimentation and expression, dramatic play should continue, merging into other forms of creative dramatics to promote further growth.

Improvisational Drama

All drama should be creative, as Stewig points out,[18] and improvisation occurs in all dramatic activity. In this section, however, our concern is the drama that arises largely from children's activities and leads them to improvise—to plan and participate in a dramatic act. Planning is not extensive and will generally be spontaneous and quickly accomplished. One child may decide to be the greedy king in *Midas Touch* and another the pathetic daughter. Then they improvise by speaking and acting as they think these characters would. Usually the scene will be short and will cover just one event. The children's purpose is to pretend, to have fun, and to express feelings.

This spontaneity, or improvisation, in creative drama will occur if the story or poem or the object of the dramatization is simple and familiar. In such dramatizations, the children need encouragement and full freedom to act and talk the way they think the characters they are portraying would act and talk. Several children will cooperatively plan and test ways of talking and acting. This kind of preparation is necessary to maximize the activity's creative values.

The first stage of improvisation often derives from rhyming activities, and Mother Goose rhymes, in particular, lend themselves to dramatization. A rhyme to be dramatized should be familiar or the children should read it several times before attempting to improvise it. They should understand the sequence of events and the characters so that they need not ask questions. Children may need encouragement to use the words and actions that they think are appropriate.

Once the children have had experience dramatizing simple rhymes, they can dramatize stories that have more of a plot and more varied action. Stories like "Cinderella," "The Three Bears," and "Chicken Little" are suitable for the initial efforts of young children. Older children can dramatize more complex stories and parts of stories.

---

18. John Warren Stewig, *Exploring Language with Children* (Columbus, O.: Charles E. Merrill Publishing Co., 1974), p. 161.

Informal Drama

Teachers in the intermediate and upper grades who want to extend improvisation by having children create scripts and express ideas dramatically face a major problem if the pupils have little experience in dramatic play and improvisation. The introduction of dramatization through charades, action songs, and choral speaking will help to break down any reserve and will build interest in other dramatic activities. Motivation in these activities can come from the rhythm of chant, song, or verse. With enough of this kind of experience in which a real mood of enjoyment exists, even reluctant pupils will become ready for the more formal dramatizations.

Dramatizing well-known stories is a good way to introduce children to drama that goes beyond improvisation because the formality of a script will be minimal. In addition, most audiences will know these stories, and audiences become important when creative dramatics moves beyond the dramatic play and improvisation stages (sometimes even in those stages the children "play" to an audience). For elementary school productions, the audience may be a group of children within the class, the rest of the class, or a neighboring class. Perhaps the best reason for having an audience is to elicit constructive criticism for the players. Growth in self-expression can result from peer answers to questions like the following:

- What did you notice that was especially good?
- Why was it so good?
- What could the players do next time to make the playing even better?

In informal drama the teacher should not serve as director, as might be the case in a more formal presentation. Rather the teacher should show interest and provide friendly guidance; encourage the development of ideas, spontaneous dialogue and fluid action; and foster group and individual solutions to problems.

The following suggestions should be useful to a teacher who wants to extend interest and activity in informal drama:

1. Material that is thoroughly familiar to the children should be the source of dramatizations. The teacher will want to discuss with children the characters in the dramatization: how each character feels about each other one; why this feeling exists; how each character looks, walks, talks, and so on; the content of each scene; what the dramatization is saying; and what the setting is.

2. The children should plan and produce minimal costumes, props, and scenery when these are absolutely essential. Making simple costumes and props offers an opportunity to develop responsibility, ingenuity, and special talents and to draw out the shy child.

3.   When the children thoroughly understand the proposed dramatization, the teacher should cast the drama with volunteers; repeating the dramatization several times will give eager children the opportunity to take several roles. Emphasize the way a child creates a character. The characters' actions should reflect an understanding of the dramatization and the characters' parts in it. The words and actions should come from the actors.

Planned dramatization should in no way interfere with the continuation of the creative, spontaneous dramatic activities of earlier years. Teachers should encourage all creative endeavors, but they can channel many of them into planned dramatizations. With careful planning, teachers can capitalize on the creativity of many children and guide them through activities that may give them greater satisfaction than their spontaneous efforts.

Opportunities for Dramatization

Aside from scripts and stories, including those written by the children themselves, many situations are suitable for dramatization. Examples are: introducing people, answering telephone calls properly, eating different kinds of food, delivering a message, entertaining visitors, going on a shopping tour, holding a club meeting, extending greetings or saying good-bye, and giving directions.

Pupils can plan skits of their own to dramatize. Appropriate topics for dramatization are happenings in the community, news events, and the like. Or children might choose one of the following ideas for dramatization:

1.   One child asks directions to a location; another child gives the directions.
2.   A family discusses a TV program.
3.   An auto is stuck in a snow drift and a crowd gathers to help.
4.   A mother and young child are in a supermarket; the child knocks over the cereal display.

Many social situations provide good skit content. A few examples are:

1.   How to ask for a job
2.   How to sell tickets for a benefit party
3.   How to present a gift
4.   How to introduce a stranger

Historical events are good subjects for dramatization. Reading about the events can lead to impromptu speaking and action or to dramatizations written by the children. Appropriate topics are:

1. Men around a campfire at Valley Forge
2. The Boston Tea Party
3. A night on the Oregon Trail
4. A stopover on the Underground Railroad

Children may also dramatize situations suggested by the teacher or by the entire class. For example, children in the middle grades could dramatize these situations:

1. You are waiting for your friends to pick you up to go to the park. You think you hear a car stop in front of the house. You rush to the window and are disappointed when it is not your friends.
2. You are walking barefoot on some pebbles that are hot from the sun. Quickly you move to some cool grass. Then you walk on the hot sand until, finally, you can put your feet into cold water.
3. You are walking to school and see smoke on a roof. Soon you see a spark of fire. You run to the door and let the person who lives inside know about it.
4. You see some shoes in a store window that you would like to try on. You go into the store and try them on.
5. You are a cautious person. You never take chances. You meet someone who is adventurous. With a friend, act out what happens and what is said.

Many situations and ideas are suitable for dramatization and all of them bring forth creativity, but the major focus in the classroom should be the dramatization of children's literature. Folk tales, short stories, incidents from novels, and fairy tales all afford opportunities for creative drama and thus add to the understanding, values, and attitudes otherwise gained from literature.

> Books become more real to children as they identify with the characters through creative dramatics. . . . Children play out the story as they "believe" in the roles they assume. The teacher's major concern is with the process and values of the children involved. . . . The value of creative drama lies in the process of playing.[19]

An important part of the "process" in informal drama is the discussion that precedes the actual dramatization. At this point creativity occurs as children talk about how individual characters might behave; what kinds of gestures, mannerisms, and vocabulary would make them both interesting and believable; how time and setting might influence actions; and so on. Evaluation, too, has a vital role, particularly if the actors and the audience can discuss dramatization con-

---

19. Charlotte S. Huck, *Children's Literature in the Elementary School*, 3rd ed. (New York: Holt, Rinehart and Winston, 1976), pp. 664–65.

structively by pointing out strengths and searching together for ways to improve future productions.

PANTOMIME

Pantomime is silent dramatization. It provides a way to share a story, describe a situation or action, or express a feeling or idea without speaking. In pantomime the performer moves eyes, hands, face, legs, and entire body in order to convey an idea or message.

Pantomime is very much like dramatic play, for when children imitate their fathers and mothers ironing or driving a car, often they do so without talking. Young children do much pantomiming quite naturally and without urging. They pretend to drive a golf ball, mow the lawn, and do carpentry—if these are activities they have seen their parents perform. Thus, schoolchildren usually do not react to pantomime as something new.

Introduction of pantomime.   Opportunities for introducing pantomime often occur naturally.[20]

> One first grade teacher, for instance, noted a little girl vigorously "sweeping out the kitchen" the day after she had told them the story of Cinderella. Quietly she called the attention of the other girls and boys and asked, "Does Sue remind you of someone in a story I have told you?" Their response came in a chorus of "Cinderella! She is Cinderella!" The teacher continued: "Who can show us something else that Cinderella did? Just show us. Don't talk." From that point on, pantomime became a favorite form of creative expression.

A simple exercise for introducing pantomime involves asking children to show with action what they most enjoy doing. Possibly the teacher will have to lead the way by pantomiming and asking the children to guess what he or she was trying to show.

Another way to begin is to ask all the children to interpret an action or feeling. Speaking of "Let's Pretend Play," Hennings suggests that children pretend they are:[21]

> rubber bands stretching back and forth or masses of clay being flattened out;
> balls rolling on the ground, bouncing up and down, hurling through the air;
> kits flying on the breeze;
> animals: snakes, horses, kangaroos, tigers, seagulls, hermit crabs;

---

20. Henry A. Bamman, Mildred A. Dawson, and Robert J. Whitehead, *Oral Interpretation of Children's Literature* (Dubuque, Iowa: Wm. C. Brown Co., 1964), p. 81

21. Dorothy Grant Hennings, *Communication in Action* (Chicago: Rand McNally College Publishing Co., 1978), p. 147.

machines: helicopters with propellers in action, windmills on a breezy day, a jackhammer tearing up the street;
natural phenomena: waves rolling toward shore, wind gusting, snowflakes floating to earth, clouds bouncing.

Easier subjects might be a rag doll, a robot, a dish of Jell-o, a monster, a tree on a windy day, and a flopping fish. These are only suggestions; every class of children will have more and better ones.

Values of pantomime.   Pantomime activities develop sense awareness; that is, through pantomime, children can show how something tastes, feels, smells, or looks. For example, a child may pantomime putting a foot into a tub of ice water, biting into an apple with a worm in it, beginning to eat an egg mistakenly sprinkled with sugar rather than salt, or smelling and tasting sour milk.

After children have begun to pantomime and to enjoy it, they will be ready to do pantomime that is completely original. To begin, the teacher might list pantomime situations suggested by the children and ask each child to choose one, think of a way to do the pantomime, and then present it so that the class can guess the subject of the pantomime.

Older boys and girls also enjoy pantomime, particularly a game approach (variously called Charades, Who Am I? and Secret) that requires guessing what action is being pantomimed. The object is not to fool the audience but to convey the action or idea effectively, and the teacher must make this point clear. It is also a good idea for the teacher to know in advance which pantomime a child is going to give.

Following are some situations that children can pantomime. They should suggest many other possibilities. The obviously simple ideas are the ones to begin with.[22]

1.   Throwing a ball
2.   Pulling a wagon
3.   Drinking water
4.   Picking flowers
5.   Putting on a coat
6.   Tying a shoelace
7.   Washing dishes
8.   Eating a banana
9.   Setting the table
10.   Two children giving a dog a bath
11.   An angry man chasing a dog from his lawn
12.   Two people talking on the telephone

---

22. Adapted from listings in Bamman et al., p. 85; and *Curriculum Guide for the Language Arts, Kindergarten–Grade 6* (Darien, Conn.: Darien Public Schools, 1971), pp. 43–45.

13. Someone getting into a cold swimming pool
14. Aladdin seeing the genie for the first time
15. Standing in a supermarket with a box of broken eggs at your feet
16. Pushing a child in a swing
17. Rip Van Winkle awakening from his sleep
18. Homer Price trying to stop the doughnut machine
19. William Tell shooting the apple off his son's head
20. A police officer helping a duck family across the street
21. Tom Sawyer and his friends whitewashing the fence

Children need encouragement and help in adding creative touches to pantomime. For instance, several boys might easily and recognizably pantomime the actions of Tom Sawyer as he whitewashes the fence and then "sells" the job to his friends, but can they also show how Tom feels about the job before his friends appear, what each boy trades for the privilege of whitewashing, and the change in Tom's attitude after others have taken up his job. What is the police officer's reaction upon seeing the duck family approach the intersection, and how does he or she indicate that these are ducks rather than people and that there are more than one of them? Is the child setting the table or washing dishes doing the task willingly or reluctantly, and what might happen if he or she breaks a dish, either accidentally or intentionally? Discussing such questions beforehand will cause children to think of ways to make their pantomimes original and interesting.

PUPPETRY

Possibly no activity in an elementary school classroom can stimulate oral language expression more effectively than puppetry. Many shy children find it easier to project their ideas and character interpretations through a puppet actor. It is easier to stage some dramatizations with puppets than with the children themselves, especially when the stories are about animal figures, folklore characters, and "talking" inanimate objects.

Also puppetry gives children an emotional outlet. For the very imaginative child puppets are an excellent vehicle of self-expression. And many children use puppets as friends who can both listen and talk.

Types of Puppets

The variety of puppets includes *stick puppets*, which are made of cardboard and fastened to long sticks; *shadow puppets*, which are blank stick puppets with holes in the faces for eyes; and *hand puppets*, which are made from solid, three-dimensional materials, such as paper bags, socks, and papier-mâché.

A stick puppet is easiest to make. To construct one, a child or teacher draws

the outline of a figure on cardboard and attaches it to a stick. Hand puppets also are easy to make. The simplest one is a paper bag with a face drawn on it. Papier-mâché or cloth are other suitable materials for making puppets.[23] Every puppet should have a definite "personality."

A *marionette* is a string-controlled doll with head, body, legs, and arms that the puppeteer works from above. Upper-grade children enjoy making these figures and planning performances for them. The skilled storyteller can use marionettes for visual effects.

Using puppets and marionettes calls forth much creativity on the part of children. Much of the dialogue is spontaneous and this is to be preferred over a written script.

Use of Puppets

There are two general ways to use puppetry. One is to choose or create a story or situation to dramatize and then make puppets for it. The other is to create one or more puppets, get acquainted with them, and then find or develop something to dramatize.

Any story or event suitable for dramatization is appropriate for puppetry—providing, of course, that the stage does not become so crowded that it becomes difficult to maneuver the puppets. Generally no more than about five

---

23. See the following publications for information about puppet construction and use: John Bodor, *Creating and Presenting Hand Puppets* (New York: Reinhold Publishing Corp, 1967); Marjorie H. Batchelder and Virginia L. Comer, *Puppets and Plays: A Creative Approach* (New York: Harper, 1956); T. Tichner, *Folk Plays for Puppets You Can Make* (Nashville, Tenn.: Abingdon Press, 1959); Shari Lewis, *The Shari Lewis Puppet Book* (Secaucus, N.J.: Citadel Press, 1958).

puppeteers can work on a story at a time. The settings should be simple. In fact, simplicity is one of the keys to success. The stage may be fashioned out of anything available—a box, two chairs, a desk, and so on.

The subject of a puppet dramatization should be something that the children like. From dramatizing literature selections children can move on to writing original puppet shows. Individually or as a group, they can create puppet plays based on incidents in history or current events, on health practices that come up in class discussions, on social events, and on imaginative stories written for fun.

Chiefly, puppetry should encourage children to use their imaginations in creating puppets, settings, and dialogue to express their ideas in original ways. It is important also for children to make their own puppets. A teacher may demonstrate, guide, and encourage, but every puppet ought to be a child's creation. By providing only guidance, a teacher can ensure that all of the children's puppets will be different in some way. Some types of puppets are obviously more difficult to make than others, so the teacher must take into account the age and experience of children when making suggestions.

There should be a logical reason for constructing and using puppets. Having children spend several days making puppets to use for a language expression activity that lasts only a short time is not good planning. Nor is it a good use of time.

An excellent use of puppets, particularly hand puppets, is to help tell a story; many storytellers consider a puppet an integral part of themselves when they tell stories. Teachers may also use puppets to get children's attention and to teach certain skills. For example, stick puppets representing punctuation marks—Rollo Period, Slim Exclamation, etc.—have appeal and may help to convey ideas effectively. A puppet also might lead choral speaking, give rules for a game, or be the "authority" on classroom manners.

CHORAL SPEAKING

The principal purpose of choral speaking as an expressional activity is the enjoyment of the participants. Sometimes called choral reading or verse speaking or verse choirs, it is an excellent way for children to become acquainted with and to enjoy poetry, as well as to develop their speaking skills. Oral interpretation also requires creativity, and the readings themselves could be the children's own creations. In addition, choral speaking might give children insight into the importance of stress, pitch, and juncture and teach them new vocabulary. A final but very important effect could be to free children from inhibitions about speaking before an audience.

Choral Speaking Instruction

A teacher may have little success with choral speaking unless the children have had extensive experience listening to oral presentations of selected prose and poetry. Children whose teachers have read or recited selections for them, particularly in the lower grades, may have been encouraged to join in reciting lines of poetry that they heard frequently. Teachers can readily lead these children into choral speaking. In general, the first selections they read should be nursery rhymes that they know well.

As children develop and gain experience saying rhymes with the teacher, they can help the teacher plan choral speaking activities. Poetry chosen for group reading may have a particular cadence or rhythm or simply be fun to do. Choral speaking involves much interpretation, and teachers should encourage children to decide whether a line should be said rapidly or slowly, whether their voices should be soft or loud, and so on. They should experiment with different ways of presenting each selection, although perfection in performance is neither the expectation nor the goal. The primary value lies with the process, the involvement, and the pleasure the activity brings to participants and audience alike. To make the most of this experience, Kean and Personke suggest that teachers observe these guidelines in planning choral speaking activities:[24]

1. Choral verse should be for fun.
2. Choral reading should occur often for its own sake.
3. Choral reading requires a leader, not a teacher.
4. Selection of poetry should be by children.
5. Interpretation is the province of the children.

---

24. John M. Kean and Carl Personke, *The Language Arts, Teaching and Learning in the Elementary School* (New York: St. Martin's Press, 1976), pp. 125–26.

Choral speaking is appropriate for children of all ages. It teaches them to listen, to remember, and to interpret words and word patterns. And it provides an opportunity to learn to modulate the voice—an important first step in developing good speaking habits. Between the third- and sixth-grade levels children become interested in choral speaking on themes of adventure or mystery. Teachers can use this interest to direct improvement of diction, voice quality, vocabulary, and understanding of meaning.

Arrangements for Choral Speaking

Having made a selection for choral speaking, the teacher and children must arrange it for performance, just as someone must interpret a musical selection for performance by an orchestra or a chorus. Some poems readily suggest an arrangement; others require discussion and experimentation.

When arranging a selection for presentation by very young children whose voices are developing, the teacher should not attempt to group pupils according to voice quality. As children mature and as they learn to enjoy a poem thoroughly, they will often suggest some voice grouping themselves. Elementary school voices may be divided either into light and heavy groups or into light, heavy, and medium groups. Every teacher quickly comes to know the children's voices and should have little difficulty grouping them for the most effective speaking.

After trying out and discussing various interpretations of a poem and working out articulation and pronunciation, teacher and children together should decide what arrangement is the most suitable. Types of choral speaking arrangements are the following:[25]

- *Refrain:* A soloist reads the narrative and the class joins in refrain.
- *Two-part or antiphonal:* Two groups alternate speaking (light versus heavy voices, boys versus girls, and so on). Question-and-answer poetry or poems of contrasting moods are suitable for this arrangement.
- *Line-a-child or sequential:* A number of individuals interpret one or two lines apiece and the reading builds to a climax, for which unison voices are often effective.
- *Unison:* All voices speak all lines as one.

Sources of choral speaking selections are numerous. Whitehead suggests "Clocks" (author unknown), "Hickory, Dickory, Dock," and "The Mysterious Cat" (Vachel Lindsey) for refrain; "The Barnyard" (Maude Burham) and "Jump

---

25. Robert Whitehead, *Children's Literature: Strategies of Teaching* © 1968, pp. 122–23. Reprinted by permission of Prentice-Hall, Inc., Englewood Cliffs, New Jersey.

or Jiggle" (Evelyn Beyer) for line-a-child; "Puppy and I" (A. A. Milne) and "Laughter" (author unknown) for antiphonal; and "A Kitten" (Eleanor Farjeon), "The Bells" (Edgar Allan Poe), and many Mother Goose rhymes for unison speaking. These are only a few suggestions; other sources are basal readers, children's literature texts, and books of poetry. The number and types of selections appropriate for choral speaking are limitless. Of course, selections should appeal to the children, the content should fit their level, and the rhythm should be simple.

Although well-motivated children might decide to write poems for the class to recite, usually the words they speak are not their own. The principal values of choral speaking, therefore, are similar to those obtained from participating in plays that someone else has written: the children come to understand how intonation, gesture, volume, and speed of speaking affect understanding and emotional response. With guidance, they learn also that the sounds of words and the way a writer or speaker puts them together may add to or detract from meaning and total effect. Combined with vocabulary study and instruction in individual speaking, choral speaking should help children to become more effective and creative in both oral and written expression.

STORYTELLING

Storytelling is an ancient art that once was almost universal. Today few people are good storytellers, a fact that reflects the demands of modern life. The ability to tell stories develops through use, but unfortunately because books and radio and TV programs are readily available, children have little time to listen to stories except in school and even less time to learn to tell stories themselves. Consequently, the storyteller has only a very limited time to practice the art.

Yet not all is lost. Some parents still tell stories to their children. Many public libraries have weekly story hours, and camp and recreation leaders usually tell stories. Too, some teachers recognize the importance of storytelling and help to keep the tradition alive.

The discussion that follows presents storytelling both as an art that teachers should practice and as an art that children should learn. Children are interested in storytelling as members of an audience; a story is something they like to hear. But all of us, children included, also enjoy telling stories. We want to tell a story that we have heard or read. Many like to tell stories they have created.

The Experience Story

As Ramon Ross says, "Stories swarm around us, seeking our attention."[26] Thus everyone may become a storyteller. And we all do tell stories, even though

---

26. Ramon R. Ross, *Storyteller* (Columbus, O.: Charles E. Merrill Publishing Co., 1972), p. 57.

sometimes we consider them to be mere incidents or just gossip. But a story is a systematic account of a happening—something that has a setting, a plot or purpose, characters, and meaning. Many stories are, or at least begin as, remembrances imprinted on the memory or events that caught and stirred the emotions at the time they occurred.

Telling personal stories occurs in school in the primary grades during show and tell and sharing times, but storytelling experience should not end there, and the quality of delivery should improve in time. Teachers should encourage children at every grade level to relate experiences that will interest their peers while observing the suggestions made here.

Ross suggests that telling experience stories entails several stages of preparation: finding the experience to tell, giving the story a time and place, choosing details that bring characters to life, cutting and shaping the original incident to make a better story, writing the story as it is to be told, and practicing the telling.[27] Teaching children to complete these steps requires considerable teacher guidance, but the task is by no means impossible. Asking a child to identify his or her most meaningful experiences is the starting point. After receiving thoughtful responses to this question, the teacher should ask questions that cause the children to think about time, place, and characters. The next series of questions should help the pupil clarify, give more details about the people (what they were like and what they did), link incidents and develop threads of commonality, and attach words to the plot and action.

The Teacher as Storyteller

To teach storytelling to children successfully, a teacher must have a real love of stories and some ability to tell them. The teacher is the model, and if he or she takes pleasure in telling and listening to stories, the children will acquire this feeling. The skills necessary for telling a good story are the same for all persons; therefore, children will learn from what a teacher does as well as feels. Particularly, the teacher can show much about the use of the voice. Pitch and quality of tone, the suitability of voice volume for different parts of a story, breath control, and rhythmic speaking are all skills that are best learned by example.

Good storytellers keep eye contact with their audiences in order to awaken and hold interest. Likewise, the teacher should show proper use of the hands to emphasize parts of a story.

Preparation is also part of storytelling. Even if a teacher has told the same story many times, he or she should review it mentally to be sure of details and sequence. A good aide is to keep a card or set of cards noting important details of the setting, a list of characters, and a brief sketch of the plot of each story, and review these notes quickly before each telling so that the story will be fresh in mind.

---

27. Ibid., pp. 66–72.

The following questions may be useful in deciding whether or not to tell a particular story:[28]

1. Does the story personally excite you, the storyteller? Is it one that really should be shared with others?
2. Is it a tale that you can tell effectively? Consider whether the content and the mood of the story are compatible with your personality.
3. Does the story genuinely lend itself to telling? Or would it be better to read it orally?
4. Will the tale appeal to the age group to which the listeners belong?
5. Is the length of the story suitable for the audience? Is it too long for young children or too short for those in the middle and upper grades?

Positive answers to these questions, in addition to thorough preparation, will make storytelling a delightful and rewarding experience for both teller and listener.

Selection of Stories to Tell

Needless to say, the story a storyteller chooses to present is a significant element of the storytelling experience. The whole world is a source of stories, so how does a storyteller choose a good story from the vast array of literature and personal experiences? Ruth Tooze has spelled out some generally accepted criteria for choosing.[29] A summary of these standards follows:

1. The story must have a good plot with something of interest to resolve. The development of the plot must be easy to follow.
2. The characters must be believable. They must be genuine and lifelike. They may be imaginary or fantastical, but they must also be logical and relevant.
3. The background of the story must be authentic. The place, the time, and the setting must give validity to the story.
4. The mood of the story must make it ring true.
5. The style of the language of the story must be appropriate. The words and the way they are put together should be natural, appropriate to the pace of the story, and helpful in conveying the mood.

Tooze and other storytellers add one other criterion to this list: the story must be personally absorbing and involving. The teller must search for a story that interacts with his or her personality, experiences, and views about the universe and mankind for maximum impact on the listener.

---

28. Adapted from Dewey W. Chambers, *Literature for Children: Storytelling and Creative Drama* (Dubuque, Iowa: William C. Brown Co., 1970), p. 16.
29. Ruth Tooze, *Storytelling* (Englewood Cliffs, N.J.: Prentice-Hall, 1959), pp. 50–78.

Many stories are suitable for telling. Whitehead lists the following story-telling fare for different age groups:[30]

> *Preschool through kindergarten.* For this age group the stories must be short and to the point. Stories should be of familiar things: animals, children, home, machines, people, toys. Humorous and nonsense story poems, jingles, Mother Goose rhymes, and the accumulative tales are especially apt choices. Typical stories would include those in The Three Series: "The Three Billy Goats Gruff," "The Three Little Pigs," "The Three Bears," and the "Adventure of Three Little Rabbits." Others: "Little Red Riding Hood," "Henny Penny," and "The Teeny Tiny Woman."
>
> *Ages 6 to 10.* Animal tales, stories of child life in other lands, and the ancient and modern fairy tales are types of stories that appeal to this group. Among the many tales to be recommended we would include, "The Elves and the Shoemaker," "Rumpelstiltskin," "Slovenly Peter," "The Steadfast Tin Soldier," "Hansel and Gretel," "The Sleeping Beauty," "The Bremen Town Musicians," and "Jack and the Beanstalk."
>
> *Ages 11 to 14.* Children in this stage of development demand true stories, tales of adult life, hero tales, and stories that teach something about personal ideals. These children want stories of adventure, too. The thirteen-year-old and fourteen-year-old youngsters seek out the myths, legends, and epics, along with those stories of a biographical and historical nature that teach patriotism and service to country. Tales for telling to this group would include "The Story of Aladdin," "How Thor Found His Hammer," tales of Robin Hood and King Arthur, "Pecos Bill," "Paul Bunyan," and various tales about sports heroes.

Additional suggestions appear in many of the references given at the end of the chapter.

Teachers should encourage children to be constantly on the lookout for stories to tell. Many excellent stories about Halloween, Thanksgiving, Rosh Hashanah, Christmas, and other holidays and special occasions are included in magazines. Stories from supplemental readers are another source of material for children. It is generally a good idea for the teacher to help pupils evaluate the worth and appropriateness of a story they are planning to present to the class. Sometimes a student committee can assist the teacher with this screening process.

Storytelling Techniques

There are many ways to tell stories. Successful storytellers have their own ways of telling their favorite stories. Some even vary their methods to fit different types of stories. Similarly, no single way of teaching storytelling seems best. Some of the following general suggestions may be helpful to the teacher and the class in planning a story hour.

---

30. Robert Whitehead, *Children's Literature: Strategies of Teaching* © 1968, pp. 103–104. Reprinted by permission of Prentice-Hall, Inc.

1. The practice of relating the story closely to the experiences of the audience is a sound and widely heeded principle. In order to tell a story well, the storyteller must have full knowledge of the events, situations, and content of the story.

2. The general atmosphere in which the story is told should be free of outside distractions, the room should be quiet and the audience should be comfortably at ease. Storytelling will be a thoroughly enjoyable experience—one in which all pressures and cares are laid aside—if a calm air of informality prevails in the room. Usually the children will prefer to sit in a circle, perhaps on the floor, grouped closely around the storyteller. Children enjoy watching the storyteller, and a good storyteller likes to be able to look directly at the audience.

3. Because the pleasure of a storytelling experience depends completely on masterful presentation, the importance of careful preparation cannot be overemphasized. The storyteller must know the story well enough to be able to see every detail in the mind's eye. The storyteller must sense the mood of the story and plan ways to convey that feeling to the audience. The words used must be well chosen. Sometimes the words will be the storyteller's, and other times they will be the words of characters in the story.

4. Realistic standards and friendly criticism should be part of every storytelling experience, but they should never be so exacting as to mar the pleasure of the occasion. Standards are valuable reminders for the storyteller, but they must be attainable. Criticism should be friendly and sensible. The prime objective is to develop successful storytellers and to foster a willingness to tell stories. Finding too much fault with a child is a poor way to encourage further efforts.

5. As is the case with all other language abilities, mastering storytelling skills requires repeated practice in lifelike activities.

Finally, teacher and children should formulate brief storytelling guidelines. One typical set of guidelines is as follows:[31]

1. Speak clearly.
2. Speak so all can hear.
3. Do not string sentences together with "and-uhs" or "so's."
4. Stand still.
5. Look at your audience.
6. Use colorful words.
7. Have a good beginning and ending.
8. Talk naturally.
9. *Be interested* in your story!

---

31. Ibid., p. 107. Reprinted

Flannelboards and Other Storytelling Aids

To add variety to storytelling the storyteller may use a flannelboard, puppets, pictures, and other objects. These aids help storytellers to remember the story, establish rapport with the audience, and gain confidence in their storytelling ability. Nevertheless, the use of aids should not interfere with the story. For example, a storyteller usually cannot manipulate more than one puppet and should use one only if he or she can do it well and if it adds to the story. Generally, the puppet becomes the storyteller or a special member of the audience.

A flannelboard permits the storyteller to show more than one character and to show a simple setting in addition to characters in a story. Ross suggests that the story "The Tiger, the Brahman, and the Jackal" lends itself to presentation on flannelboard because it has a limited number of characters and objects, all of which are easy to make.[32] Of course, for other stories, the teller might have to show only some of the characters or objects in order not to detract from the focus of the story. It is best to show only familiar characters or objects, such as an animal, a tree, or a house.

A storyteller who plans to use a flannelboard should number the cutouts, test them to be sure they will adhere to the flannelboard, and arrange them, face down and numbers up, where they will be easy to reach. A cutout should be placed on the flannelboard the first time the storyteller mentions it in the story. So

---

32. Ross, p. 120.

that the board does not become cluttered, the storyteller should remove them as soon as they are no longer needed to move the story along.

Storytelling may provide the best single means for helping children to develop both skill in oral expression and the creativity to make that expression unique and effective. The effective storyteller must use skills of organization, placement of events in proper sequence, selection of supporting details, clear enunciation, and so on. But personality and ingenuity come into play in selecting a story to tell, planning audiovisual aids, working out characterizations, choosing vocabulary and gestures to use, and experimenting with volume, tone, phrasing, and so on. This is not to say that storytelling should be the only activity in the oral language program, but certainly in the early grades it is a principal one—especially if experience stories, show and tell activities, and the telling of jokes are part of it.

More Storytelling Suggestions

Although the primary purpose of storytelling is enjoyment, teachers can inconspicuously inject other oral language goals into the experience without spoiling the fun. By listening to the teacher tell a story and then telling it themselves, children learn how to put ideas in sequence, how to compose sentences, and how to emphasize meaning with the voice. Children who have had frequent opportunities for listening to and telling stories are better able to appreciate storytelling techniques than are children who have had no such experience.

Storytelling activities in a classroom primarily should involve either the teacher or one of the pupils telling a story to the group. Nevertheless, improvement in storytelling from one occasion to the next should be a class goal. Generally, improvement starts with the teacher and pupils together deciding what areas need improvement and then working on these needs cooperatively and appraising success. If these procedures do not satisfactorily accomplish the purpose, special activities or other kinds of lessons might be necessary. For example, telling stories in small groups rather than in the total classroom setting might give the best practice in particular storytelling techniques—gesturing, for example—and it facilitates making plans for the next storytelling experience, telling jokes and anecdotes, and working on new standards.

Teachers should take advantage of children's spontaneity, encourage them to tell stories, and develop their storytelling ability. Certainly children like to tell stories that they have heard, and doing so teaches them good storytelling techniques, but children have a natural desire to tell their own stories, to recount their own experiences, and to embellish stories they have heard. Teachers should encourage all these tendencies because they often lead to a child's most creative efforts.

Creative forms of storytelling that children enjoy, in addition to description of personal experiences, include: telling chain stories, in which the teacher or one pupil starts a story and after a time stops and asks someone else to continue; making up an ending for a story heard or read only in part; and developing a story based on a title or a briefly described setting.

EXERCISES FOR THOUGHT AND ACTION

1. Observe a group of children in a kindergarten or first grade who are participating in dramatic play. Describe to the class what you observed and what value you believe the experience had for the children.

2. If you are teaching, assess as objectively as possible the degree of creativity your classroom environment fosters. Do children's ideas abound or is the class teacher dominated? Does the classroom belong to the entire group or is it predominantly yours? Cite evidence to support your answer.

3. Prepare to tell a story to a particular audience (i. e., children of a particular age or adults). Plan to use either a puppet or a flannelboard you have created. Be prepared to recount any problems you encountered.

4. Locate and read a book on creative dramatics, pantomime, or storytelling. Summarize its contents in writing for the class and make an evaluative statement about it.

5. Make a file of poems suitable for the several categories of choral speaking activities—refrain, antiphonal, line-a-child, unison, and voice-parts speaking—for a specific grade level.

6. Sometimes poetry that teachers choose for choral speaking does not coincide with selections children might make. Look up Ann Terry's study *Children's Poetry Preferences* (National Council of Teachers of English, 1974) and select six poems that you think would be appropriate for choral speaking. State the reasons for your selections.

7. Suppose the children in your fifth-grade class have never pantomimed. How would you arouse their interest in pantomime and how would you begin guiding it?

8. Begin to compile a file of stories appropriate for oral presentation to children. Follow the suggestions in this chapter in organizing the file.

9. In addition to those suggested in this chapter, what oral language situations or activities might provide opportunities for creative language expression? What are the conditions that make these opportunities?

10. Are choral speaking programs appropriate for the entire school or for parents? Why?

11. This chapter made no mention of evaluating children in the oral expressional activities discussed (except in the use of standards and guidelines). Would you advocate evaluating children's expression in these activities? Why? If you favor evaluation, how would you do it?

12. Teachers sometimes do not use choral speaking in their classes because they have never participated in choral speaking themselves. Plan a choral speaking activity for your classmates and engage your colleagues in choral speaking.

SELECTED REFERENCES

Bamman, Henry A.; Dawson, Mildred A.; and Whitehead, Robert J. *Oral Interpretation of Children's Literature*. Dubuque, Iowa: William C. Brown Co., 1964.

Bauer, Caroline Feller. *Handbook for Storytellers*. Chicago: American Library Association, 1977.

Donoghue, Mildred R. *The Child and the English Language Arts*. 2nd ed. Dubuque, Iowa: William C. Brown Co., 1975.

Duke, Charles R. *Creative Dramatics and English Teaching*. Urbana, Ill.: National Council of Teachers of English, 1974.

Gillies, Emily. *Creative Dramatics for All Children*. Washington, D.C.: Association for Childhood Education International, 1973.

Henry, Mable Wright, ed. *Creative Experiences in Oral Language*. Urbana, Ill.: National Council of Teachers of English, 1967.

McIntyre, Barbara M. *Creative Drama in the Elementary School*. Itasca, Ill.: F. E. Peacock Publishers, 1974.

Pierini, Mary Paul Frances. *Creative Dramatics: Guide for Educators*. New York: Herder and Herder, 1971.

Possien, Wilma. *They All Need to Talk*. New York: Appleton-Century-Crofts, 1969.

Ross, Ramon R. *Storyteller*. Columbus, O.: Charles E. Merrill Publishing Co., 1972.

Sawyer, Ruth. *The Way of the Storyteller*. New York: Viking Press, 1962.

Stewig, John Warren. *Exploring Language with Children*. Columbus, O: Charles E. Merrill Publishing Co., 1974.

Tooze, Ruth. *Storytelling*. Englewood Cliffs, N. J.: Prentice-Hall, 1959.

Whitehead, Robert. *Children's Literature: Strategies of Teaching*. Englewood Cliffs, N. J.: Prentice-Hall, 1968.

12

Oral Expression: Attention to Skills

School should be a place where children talk at least as much as out-side, for fostering speech is the business of the language classroom.
—James Moffett, A Student-centered Language Arts Curriculum

The fact that children come to school with the ability to talk—although with varying degrees of effectiveness—does not rule out the need for instruction in speech skills. Helping children to speak well should be a major objective of every teacher. As pointed out in Chapter 11, the more opportunities children have to talk, the more creative their use of language will be. Not all oral language activities should be unstructured or unplanned, however. Planning specific types of speaking situations is a necessity. Additionally, structured activities help children learn to articulate language sounds properly—to enunciate clearly and pronounce words in acceptable ways—and provide a means of working on speech difficulties or disorders. Furthermore, planned speech situations allow the teacher and students to focus on the kinds of expression dictated by significant social occasions.

SPEECH SKILL DEVELOPMENT

Speaking effectiveness and ease results only from constant practice in lifelike situations. But in learning to speak effectively and confidently, many children need more than simply the opportunity to talk: "the oral proficiency of children will be enhanced by instructional programs which offer specific practice in articulation, voice control, usage, and other elements of oral expression."[1]

Teachers can help children develop speech skills and the motivation to use them by constantly setting good examples. Also, the instructional program should recognize that children are individuals. In other words, it should reflect awareness that some children need little instruction in speech skills, that some "problems" are developmental stages or dialect variations, and that some children may require instruction by a speech specialist.

Speech Problems

While few children have serious speech problems, virtually all children (as well as adults) could improve their speaking skills. Too, speech problems vary in seriousness. Actually, the number of children in any school who have what may be called speech disorders that require extensive training by specialists may be small, but teachers must be able to spot children in this minority. In addition, the speech of a greater number of children borders on the unintelligible and these students also need special instruction from the teacher.

Estimates of the percentage of children who have speech disorders vary considerably. One speech textbook estimates that 5 percent do;[2] another puts the figure at approximately 10 percent.[3] The authors of the latter book add that "Only about 15 percent of the disorders have any structural bases, and only about 25 percent could be called involved, complicated, or difficult to correct. In other words, the majority are of the bad-habit type, resulting from imitation of poor models, or induced generally by carelessness, laziness, or indifference."[4]

Speech disorders are described or categorized several ways. One way is by cause: environmental, psychological, and physical. Anderson and Hayes classify them by symptoms or characteristics: (1) voice disorders—malfunctioning of the sound-producing mechanism; (2) articulatory, or pronunciation and enunciation disorders; (3) linguistic, or language disorders; and (4) disorders of speech rhythm.[5]

Voice disorders affect quality, pitch, and intensity (too little or too much carrying power). Children with articulation disorders, which are by far the most

---

1. Frank B. May, "The Effects of Environment on Oral Language Development," in *Research in Oral Language*, edited by Walter T. Petty (Champaign, Ill.: National Council of Teachers of English, 1967), p. 36.

2. Alan W. Huckleberry and Edward S. Strother, *Speech Education for the Elementary Teacher* (Boston: Allyn and Bacon, 1966), p. 94.

3. Virgil A. Anderson and Hayes A. Newby, *Improving the Child's Speech*, 2d ed. (New York: Oxford University Press, 1973), p. 8.

4. Anderson and Newby, p. 16.

5. Ibid., p. 23.

common speech disorders, cannot form sounds (enunciate) clearly or do not produce sounds (pronounce) correctly according to some standard.[6] An injury or abnormal development in the association areas of the brain is the basis for disorders that involve formulating, expressing, or understanding language. The principal and most severe disorder of rhythm is stuttering, which is characterized by abnormal repetition of sounds or words and blocks in speech. Normal shyness, hesitations, and irregular rhythm patterns in speech should not be confused with stuttering, just as many reading "problems" or laborious writing or speaking behaviors should not be identified as aphasia traceable to brain injury or abnormal development.

As already mentioned, speech problems or disorders vary in seriousness. Furthermore, not all speech that deviates from the norm is symptomatic of a speech problem. Sometimes children's muscles and nervous systems are not sufficiently developed for them to speak words that contain certain consonant blends (*desks, asked, fists, wasps*). Children who make reversals—"aminal" for *animal*—have retained some baby talk, or simply mispronounce words. Baby talk and reversals may become speech problems if they continue after a child has been in school a year or so. Likewise, failure to enunciate blends or to pronounce words correctly will become a major problem if it persists. Examples of the articulation difficulties young children may have are these:[7]

---

6. Jon Eisenson and Mardel Ogilvie, *Speech Correction in the Schools*, 2d ed. (New York: Macmillan Co., 1963) state that approximately 75 percent of "the speech defects in a school population are articulatory defects" (p. 5).

7. Louise Binder Scott and J. J. Thompson, "Good Speech," *The Instructor*, (February 1958), pp. 59–62.

332

1. *w* for *r*—wabbit for rabbit
2. *y* or *w* for *l*—yamp or wamp for lamp
3. *th* (voiceless) for *s*—Tham for Sam
4. *th* (voiced) for *z*—thoo for zoo
5. *d* for *g*—doat for goat; dough for go
6. *t* for *k*—tum for come; tea for key
7. *f* for *th* (voiceless)—fank for thank
8. *b* for *v*—balentine for valentine
9. *t* or *ch* for *sh*—too or chew for shoe
10. *sh* for *ch*—shoe for chew
11. *w* for *wh*—watt for what
12. *l* or *w* for *y*—less or wess for yes
13. omission of initial sounds—es for yes

It is sometimes difficult to differentiate between pronunciations that are common to a dialect and articulation problems. The expressions below are examples of ones that a teacher needs to listen to closely, because they are expressions that may be misunderstood if they are not articulated clearly.

did you	gave them	how are you
don't you	gave him	how do you do
why don't you	give me	would you
what did you	give her	let me
didn't you	came to meet you	let him
did he	could have	let her
she may have	shouldn't have	

Teachers should not regard pronunciation differences based on acceptable speech in a particular geographical area as careless and slurred speech. But differences in speech among educated persons are not as numerous as they are among persons with less education. No educated person from one state or area in this country should have difficulty understanding an educated person from a different area.

Teaching Principles and Practices

A study performed some years ago showed that elementary school teachers with no orientation to speech disorders were unable to locate speech-defective children with more than 60 percent accuracy.[8] Although today's teachers may have

---

8. C. F. Diehl and C. D. Stinnett, "Efficiency of Teacher Referrals in a School Testing Program," *Journal of Speech and Hearing Disorders* 24 (February 1959): 35–36.

greater awareness and knowledge of speech problems, the danger exists that some children who need corrective speech training are not being identified by classroom teachers. Of course, the number of speech therapists employed in school districts has increased and so has the number of screening programs (although they are generally not repeated every year). Despite these advances, therapists depend on teachers to make referrals. It is imperative, therefore, for every teacher to be alert for possible problems and to use available resources to sharpen their perception. These resources include books, journal articles, and pamphlets, as well as people (the speech therapist, nurse, psychologist, or physician). The school principal is also a source for securing materials and services.

There are several principles which all teachers should observe in connection with speech instruction:

1. Teachers should continually strive to be good speech models for children.
2. There should be a program for the continuing development of each child's oral skills.
3. Children should be informally screened each year for speech problems. Having young children pronounce a group of words that includes all of the phonemes is one simple screening procedure. Older children can read sentences that include all of the language sounds (see the subsequent evaluation section in this chapter for other suggestions).
4. Seek advice from speech therapists before attacking serious speech problems. Cooperate with the therapist in implementing corrective programs.
5. Teach the skills that directly relate to children's real difficulties.
6. Instruction should begin as soon as possible after the discovery of a problem.
7. Work on the problems of individual children rather than on a given sound that is supposed to be a problem for every child in the class.
8. Speech instruction should instill in children the realization that good speech is important in all oral expression and not just during instruction sessions. An integrated, ongoing oral language program will best accomplish this goal.

If a speech therapist is not available, or if the response to a request for assistance is slow in coming, teachers can attack an articulation problem directly as follows:

1. Illustrate and demonstrate for the child how to make the sound correctly.
2. Form the sound clearly while the child observes the action of the lips and tongue.

3. Have the pupil examine his or her imitative attempts by use of a mirror.

4. Follow this procedure in practice exercises that require the child to:
   a. Repeat the sound several times
   b. Speak syllables that include the sound
   c. Speak short sentences in which the sound is used with some repetition, including sentences containing words of high social utility that children actually use in their own expression
   d. Utilize exercises that facilitate breathing and using lips and tongue

Attention to Voice Quality

To be able to speak most effectively children must develop a clear voice tone, a speaking tempo that facilitates understanding of what they say, the ability to pitch the voice appropriately for different situations, and the ability to adjust voice volume for various settings.

Some children always seem to speak too loudly, while others seem to speak in a whisper. Many children do not know how to adjust their voices to the size of the room. Some children speak in a monotonous tone; others pitch all their speaking in a shrill one. Some voices are resonant, pleasant, and clear; others are nasal, breathy, hoarse, or thin. Some children speak so rapidly that they obscure the meaning of the communication; others speak too slowly, but the result is the same.

The tone and quality of a child's voice may depend as heavily on mental and emotional attitudes as on physical factors. A child who speaks freely and without fear and hesitancy generally has a voice which shows satisfactory quality and control.[9] When normal children are embarrassed or emotionally upset, however, they sometimes speak in shrill or monotonous tones. Thus, as suggested earlier, the emotional climate for speech practice should be free from tension. In an atmosphere that invites spontaneous expression, children are likely to use the appropriate intonation for the activity. Except for children who have speech difficulties of a physical nature, spontaneous speech is seldom of poor quality.

Children generally do not realize that their voices may interfere with communication. Therefore, recording their voices so that they can hear how they sound is a good way to help them realize how they sound to others. An additional way for a teacher to help children become aware that they are talking too loudly, too harshly, or in an unpleasant voice is simply to say, "Keep your voice down," or "Speak softly this time." Spoken in an encouraging tone and accompanied by a

---

9. Edith B. Mallory and Virginia R. Miller, "A Possible Basis for the Association of Voice Characteristics and Personality Traits," *Speech Monographs* 25 (November 1958): 296–304.

warm and friendly smile, such a remark will not make a child self-conscious or discourage fluency of expression.

Another solution is to have the class establish standards for a speaking situation and to include suggestions about voice tone. The teacher may interject the idea of voice quality by playing parts of several spoken recordings (not necessarily of children in the class). Then he or she could ask the children these questions:

1.   Which of your classmates did you enjoy listening to?
2.   Why do you suppose you like that voice?
3.   Can you name someone whose voice you especially like?

After discussing the answers, the class could consider what they could do to make their speaking voices more pleasant. Their recommendations should be listed on the board or on a chart to become the standards for the next speaking situation of a similar type. The next speaking occasion should occur as soon as possible so that the standards and the discussion of them will be fresh in everyone's minds. At the end of this next activity class members should evaluate themselves in terms of the standards they have established and determine whether they need to add to or take away items from the list. The new standards will serve as an evaluative tool for the next speaking activity.

Still another way to make children aware of the way they speak is to challenge them to find a "sound-alike" twin among their classmates within a specified time (e.g., three minutes). Be sure they understand that "twin" does not mean really identical but similar. "Pretend" situations, such as announcing the arrival of a plane in a crowded terminal, are also useful. Of course, these situations need not all involve speaking above competing sounds. Some may require low volume but distinct speaking, as in asking a librarian a question.

As stated in Chapter 11, children whose voice quality needs improvement can profit enormously from participation in choral speaking. Children will put forth much effort to modulate their voices and control pitch, tempo, and volume to blend with the voices around them.

Activities for Improving Speech Production

Relaxation exercises may help a child whose speech shows tenseness and great emotional involvement. Examples of such exercises include dropping completely relaxed into a chair, dropping the head and letting the arms dangle, shaking the hands and arms, and rotating the head slowly. Breathing exercises—taking short quick breaths, inhaling deeply, exhaling slowly, etc.—also may be beneficial.

Tongue exercises that call for stretching the tongue out and up and down and inside the lips while watching oneself in a mirror may relieve articulation difficulties. Likewise, saying various rhymes and sets of words containing a problem sound is sometimes useful. Using such exercises requires care, however, because many children simply outgrow articulation and enunciation difficulties, and giving undue attention to them can make a child reluctant to talk.

One curriculum guide suggests combining words from the spelling list, basic and supplementary readers, and content-area textbooks to make tongue-twisting sentences:[10]

> "Arthur and Kenneth had a birthday party on Thursday. Theodore used a toothbrush to clean his teeth."

The same curriculum guide also suggests keeping a class list of unacceptable pronunciations and practicing the correct pronunciations; demonstrating the appropriate voice pitch for a story character; and saying phrases that show anger, boredom, surprise, fear, and so on.

Another guide suggests that yawning, panting, "blowing out the vowel sounds, and the teacher producing sounds correctly and incorrectly will help remedy nasal speech."[11] These exercises might reduce enunciation and articulation problems as well as those related to speech volume and rate.

Finally, children may practice using high pitch to convey excitement, nervousness, or gaiety and low pitch to express mystery or reverence. Story characters or made-up situations are good source materials for the demonstration of these emotions.

Annoying Mannerisms

Even though elementary school teachers are not responsible for developing accomplished public speakers, they do have a responsibility for trying to eliminate mannerisms that detract from effective communication. Furthermore, it is necessary for both pupils and teachers to recognize that speech is often visible as well as audible, that it is almost impossible for anyone to speak without somehow moving the body, and that body movements should be natural and in harmony with the speaking activity. Undesirable physical mannerisms include fidgeting; head jerking; hand twisting; eye blinking; any twitching of mouth, face, or body; a constant and inconsistent changing of facial expression or an unchanging facial expression; and, generally, any exaggerated physical movement.

Basic to the elimination of most annoying mannerisms is the development of a receptive and positive climate in the classroom. Without this kind of support a child's self-consciousness, the basis for most distracting physical movements, will persist. A child cannot stop certain muscular movements at the teacher's urging.

---

10. *Curriculum Guide for the Language Arts, Grades 4, 5, 6* (Chicago: Board of Education, 1964), p. 96.

11. *Toward Better Speech*, Curriculum Bulletin, 1952–53 Series, no. 5 (New York: Board of Education, 1953), pp. 33–34.

Nervous movements are expressions of an emotional state, although many mannerisms often become habitual and outlast the cause of their development. In such cases, substituting a positive mannerism usually helps. Physical activities may eliminate problems that stem from lack of coordination. Particularly helpful in ridding children of undesirable mannerisms during speech activities are rhythmic games, pantomime, creative dramatics, play memorization, puppet and shadow plays, monologues, dialogues, imitations, and demonstrations.

Audience Sensitivity

Obviously oral communication is not a one-way street. People talk because they have something to say *to someone.* There must be an audience, but every speaker must have something to say that an audience—even if only one person—is interested in hearing. Furthermore, the speaker must deliver the message in such a way as to provoke an audience response. Children should become aware of their double responsibility in oral language situations: as speakers to be conscious of the audience at all times and sensitive to their feelings, and as listeners to be attentive, courteous, and ready to react to what they hear.

We gauge the effectiveness of any speaking activity by the reaction of the audience; the principal responsibility for this reaction is the speaker's. An audience tends to recognize immediately the degree of the speaker's sincerity, the depth and extent of the speaker's knowledge, and the thought that has gone into what is being said and how it is being said. Children especially are born critics and, consciously or not, sometimes judge a speaker even before he or she has uttered a word. Although they may not express their critical thoughts verbally, their body language gives away their inner feelings (bright, smiling face; attentive posture; noticeably inert posture; constant talking; etc.).

A speaker who is sensitive to his or her audience prepares the presentation in advance to appeal to the special interests of that audience. With such consideration last-minute adjustments in the content or its organization will usually not be needed. Basic also to audience sensitivity is looking at them while talking, speaking clearly and distinctly, and speaking at the appropriate volume for the situation and setting.

Teaching children to plan for an audience is an important task. Since much speaking is spontaneous, the planning needed in most situations should not be very formal. Simply talking with children about a possible speaking activity is a planning step, as is discussing an activity just completed. In fact, planning should begin with evaluation of a past experience. From this evaluation should come attention in the next speaking activity to the content and organization of what is to be said, the speech skills, aids to speaking such as notes and visual effects, and what the audience may be expecting to hear.

All speakers, whether children or adults, hope for audiences that understand what is being said and that react to it—hopefully, from the speaker's stand-

their abilities to the maximum. A program of instruction based on the following principles should accomplish this goal:

1. Conversation is a two-way process between a listener and a speaker, who exchange ideas in turn.
2. Conversation involves listening to the contributions of others and reacting to them.
3. Conversation is not random talk but involves real interaction about a subject of mutual interest.
4. Courtesy should prevail in the behavior of the participants, even though the conversation may be very informal.
5. Good conversationalists have a responsibility to themselves and others to be truthful and considerate in their remarks.
6. Good conversationalists at all times attempt to avoid aggressive or argumentative attitudes. After all, conversation is a friendly discussion, not a verbal battle.

In a program based on these principles, the teacher should convey to children the value of being informed on suitable topics and of discovering sources of interesting material. They should learn also to be enthusiastic, to use vocabulary that is varied as well as appropriate to the topic and the situation, and to avoid distracting mannerisms. And they need to learn the proprieties associated with conversation: when and where it is appropriate *not* to talk, how to change the subject tactfully, how to suit topics to situations and people, how to follow an introduction with remarks that put everyone at ease, and how to be a good listener.

Observing courtesies in conversation requires special emphasis. Among those deserving attention, in addition to the ones already mentioned, are avoiding unpleasant topics, being too personal, futile arguments, using unfamiliar language, and repeating needlessly.

Because conversation is a more spontaneous activity than most other oral language activities, the teacher should exploit it. Throughout the school day many topics arouse pupil interest and stimulate the desire to communicate ideas and thoughts to others. Most of these topics relate to purposeful activities of the classroom program, so conversing about them is natural. Therefore teachers should refrain from discouraging relevant conversation and, indeed, should capitalize on it to develop children's conversational skills. If regular activities do not furnish opportunities to teach these skills, it may be necessary to plan lessons for this purpose.

Initially, in either the spontaneous conversational situation or the planned approach, attention should center on the content of the discussion. For example, if a group of children is conversing about the lunch choices in the cafeteria, focus first on the accuracy of what the children are saying and its relevance to the major topic. As the conversation progresses, however, attention may shift to the best ways of carrying on a conversation. The teacher may ask if any of the pupils have noted that some contributions are better than others and if they know why this is so. As appropriate, given the children's ages, the teacher may interject observations for discussion and notation on the board or on a chart. By limiting the number of points discussed and recording only the key ones, the teacher can avoid overwhelming children with technicalities about conversational skill. Of course, it is best not to formalize the analysis of a conversation too much or to analyze conversations too frequently. Children quickly learn to assess the strengths and weaknesses of their conversations when they have many opportunities and genuine encouragement to converse.

Children have so many interesting experiences both in and out of school that a teacher should never be at a loss to find opportunities for teaching and practicing conversational skills. Sometimes, however, teachers overlook opportunities or fail to examine them carefully enough to determine whether conversing about a particular topic is purposeful. Purposeful conversations may develop while children are planning class activities or responding to them. Children will converse about what they want to see at the museum, what games to play at a party, and where they might find materials for their social studies projects. Someone may point out a picture in a book or bring an item from a newspaper that generates spontaneous conversation. And hobbies, games, and TV programs all can become the focus of a class conversation, as can behavior (working on a committee, looking after a class pet, and so on).

Conversation is an activity of some intimacy and such intimacy is difficult to achieve in a formal physical setting. A shy child may find it much easier to talk in a conversational group of four or five children than from the isolation of a seat in a traditional classroom physical setting. Seating a small group in such a way that children face one another makes it possible to talk in a low voice and the physical closeness of the speakers and listeners provides security. Even a small group may need the leadership of a self-confident child, however, to keep the conversation rolling and to urge the participation of all members of the group.

Discussion

Undoubtedly, discussion between teachers and pupils and among pupils is the oral language activity that occurs most frequently in the classroom. Through discussion, children gain information, learn to deal with facts and problems, and develop the ability to express themselves effectively. Discussion not only occupies a key position in the school program but also has a prominent place in adult activities. In a group that has a common interest that requires planning, a solution, or agreement, discussion will develop naturally.

Discussion differs from conversation in that it has a more purposeful goal. This goal is generally understood and, in school situations, has been agreed upon by both teacher and pupils. In the lower grades, the goal is perhaps less apparent to the pupils than to the teacher, but it is still present.

The guiding principles and courtesies of discussion are much the same as the ones applied in conversation. Because discussion has a more definite goal, however, the emphasis should be slightly different. Pupils must remember to be courteous listeners and speakers—that is, they must remember to allow others to speak, to respect the opinions of others, and to speak so that all may hear—but they must also learn specific skills for discussion. The most important of these is staying on the topic and working toward a suitable conclusion. A related skill is the ability to make concise and worthwhile contributions, in the form of either statements or questions. We can contribute to a discussion only after listening to and thinking about what others have said, and then we must be able to support arguments with facts, to distinguish between fact and opinion, and to know the difference between relevant and irrelevant material, or our contribution will not be worthwhile. In a discussion, facts take precedence over emotion.

Children must clearly recognize the need to be somewhat informed in order to contribute to a discussion. Thus, they must also appreciate the need for preparation. For many discussion situations to be effective, children must use reference sources and conduct other research. In addition, a teacher often needs to help children relate their individual experiences to the topic.

The more talkative children in the class should not dominate the discussion. In order to prevent a few children from monopolizing every discussion, the teacher may want to keep a "participation index" showing the distribution of children's contributions.[14] A participation index is simply a tabulation of the number of times each child contributes to a discussion. Teachers who want to focus on the quality as well as the frequency of participation may delegate one or more pupils to keep the index, which could serve as an additional device for relating the discussion to previously established standards.

Discussional activities also make children aware of the importance of cooperation. Solving or clarifying a discussion problem requires the participation of all. Discussion implies reaching a better understanding of a problem or solving it. It implies tolerance and good sportsmanship.

Leadership training is part of the instructional program in discussion. Many, but not all, children in a classroom need practice in the skills that a discussion leader must possess. Leaders must know how to open a discussion, how to draw out thinking and information through skillful questioning, how to summarize main points, and how to handle sharp differences of opinion in a tactful manner. To teach these skills, the teacher must serve as a model, discuss how to use them, and possibly refer to appropriate sections of a language textbook. In

---

14. Dorothy G. Petersen and Velma D. Hayden, *Teaching and Learning in the Elementary School* (New York: Appleton-Century-Crofts, 1961), p. 121.

pupil-led discussions, the teacher should remain in the background as much as possible and provide guidance only as necessary.

Many everyday classroom situations provide opportunities for teaching discussion skills. Representative situations or problems are:

1. The program for Schools Week
2. How to raise money to buy a record player for the classroom
3. How best to organize the art show
4. What makes a movie good
5. Classroom housekeeping
6. A book everyone in the group has read
7. An experience shared by all
8. How to converse, use the telephone, etc.
9. How different people talk
10. What a fifth-grade pupil should know about the Constitution

The following is one teacher's report on a class discussion:[15]

When the boys and girls in our third-grade class returned to the room after the lunch hour some were quite indignant because one of the boys had thrown a rock at another. Since we are very particular at our school about rock throwing, the children know it is something they shouldn't do.

I asked the accused if he really had thrown the rock. He said he had because the other boy had said a certain area on the playground belonged to him and no one else could walk there. Some of the children thought that was funny and laughed. I asked what seemed funny and they replied that the playground belonged to all and no one person could claim part of it as his alone.

This seemed a good opportunity to discuss property and belongings. One child said, "That is just like saying that the school cafeteria belongs to only one person and no one else could eat there." I asked if children should share their lunches just because they shared the cafeteria. They promptly replied that that was different. That each should eat his own lunch because a lunch is meant for only one child.

We continued our discussion by naming a number of objects, buildings, and other things, and deciding whether each was something which might be used by only one or should be shared by a number of people.

Later we talked about places where it would be proper and safe to throw rocks. One boy said that his father and he sometimes spent an hour or so throwing rocks into a river near their home. We agreed that it would be good exercise and training to throw rocks under some conditions.

Reporting

Oral reporting is an important activity in the middle and upper grades. An outgrowth of the show and tell activities of the primary grades, oral reporting in-

---

15. Reported by Mrs. G. W. McCready, Sonora, Calif.

cludes speeches or talks organized in advance of presentation and given to convince or inform. It is more than the reading of a written report, but it does not have the characteristics of the rather formal speeches emphasized in secondary school speech classes, particularly those of a traditional nature. In the elementary school oral reporting should have a genuine communicative purpose. Thus, it may take many forms: reviewing books and television programs, summarizing a science experiment, explaining a log or other written record, explaining how to do something, and providing information about a social studies topic. Individual and group trips, play or concert attendance, current events, class government activities, experiments and research, and many other school situations provide raw material for oral reports.

Oral reporting instruction should give specific attention to selecting and organizing information and to the actual presentation of the report. Particular points for a teacher to keep in mind in teaching reporting are the following:

1. Encouraging children to condense information from sources
2. Not allowing the direct copying of materials without crediting the source
3. Basing reporting activities on the needs of the individual and the group
4. Assigning topics according to individual interests
5. Stressing the importance of good beginnings and endings
6. Supervising note taking occasionally
7. Training pupils to give full credit for the ideas, materials, and quotations they use in reports
8. Evaluating reports individually and as a group
9. Using reporting activities to discover individual pupil weaknesses in usage, organization of ideas, voice control, and other oral skills

Even though many reports are and should be quite informal, children need to learn definite steps to follow in preparing a report. In every case, communication should be the purpose of the report and good form should enhance its effectiveness. Pupils usually should follow these steps:

1. Make a list of questions that the subject of the report suggests.
2. Consult reference sources and make notes that help to answer these questions.
3. Look over notes and determine the organization of the report. First divide the report into main divisions and then prepare a complete outline that arranges details in the proper sequence. For many reports the outline may be short and simple. In fact, throughout most of the elementary grades the teacher should stress the importance of a simple outline.
4. Think about the length of time required for giving the report; reorganize or cut the outline if necessary.

5.   Give particular attention to ways to begin and end the report with interesting statements.

What makes a good oral report is an appropriate topic for class discussion. From an exchange of ideas among pupils, major points of agreement might emerge and these might be worth recording. One class agreed on these requirements, which were written on a chart:

1.   Choose a topic.
2.   Find books and materials.
3.   Select the information for the report.
4.   Organize the information.
5.   Make notes to use.

To add content or interest to an oral report, the speaker can use a variety of techniques and materials. For example, pictures or cutouts on a flannelboard may help to show the organization of the report, to enhance the verbal description, or to minimize the self-consciousness of the reporter. For similar effects, diagrams, charts, chalkboard drawings, or an outline might be appropriate. Having a partner is also useful. The partner might pantomime what the reporter is describing, hold up charts or pictures, or otherwise assist. Providing charts, displays, and so on, for the audience to see prior to the report arouses interest in what the reporter has to say.

Telephoning

Talking on the telephone is a common activity for most of us. How effective these communications are is debatable, as is the wisdom of teaching telephoning in school. Some persons believe that because most children begin using the telephone at home at an early age, the school need not teach its use. Others contend that some instruction in the use of the telephone is necessary. Certainly many adults and some children use the telephone skillfully; others antagonize callers and telephone operators alike.

Telephone instruction should emphasize attitudes and abilities important in everyday life. Children should learn how to formulate messages, inquiries, orders, and other detailed information as concisely as possible before making a call. They should learn to identify themselves and the reason for the call clearly and courteously. As in face-to-face conversation, they should speak graciously and they should know how to end a telephone call politely. They should learn other courtesies related to using the telephone: the importance of returning calls, taking messages for others, avoiding placing calls at times inconvenient to the person called or monopolizing his or her time, and the necessity of asking permission to use someone else's telephone. And they should learn to consider whether or not others might wish to use the same phone.

In addition to the above social objectives, distinct speech, a well-modulated tone of voice, brevity, and pointedness are desirable language objectives. Specific telephoning techniques to learn include using the directory to find numbers, reaching the operator, dialing a number, making emergency or special service calls, and placing long-distance calls.

Most of the actual situations involving the use of the telephone arise outside of school. In fact, many schools place definite restrictions on the use of the school telephones. More often than not a teaching situation involving the use of the telephone at school is a dramatized or imaginary situation, depending on the maturity of the pupils.

Language textbooks may include telephoning activities. For example, a fourth-grade textbook suggests the following:[16]

Choose a partner and act out these telephone conversations.

1. Mrs. Rothwell, your mother's friend, telephones. Your mother is at a neighbor's house. Mrs. Rothwell wants to borrow your mother's drill. She needs it right away.
    Talk to Mrs. Rothwell; then call your mother and give the message to her.
2. Your grandfather calls. You are the only one at home. He is expecting all of you for dinner on Friday at 6:00. He won't have time to go to the bakery and would like you to bring dessert.
    Talk to your grandfather, and then give the message to your mother or father.

In the primary grades, learning about telephoning provides a meaningful opportunity to teach the courtesies of "please," "thank you," taking turns, and listening; self-confidence and spontaneity of expression; and creativeness in oral expression. In the middle and upper grades, telephone instruction provides an opportunity to teach additional courtesies of conversation; the informational or research skills of alphabetizing and locating specific services or products through the Yellow Pages of the telephone directory; a calm reaction in emergencies that require calling the police, the fire department, or a hospital; and the speech skills of articulation, enunciation, pronunciation, pleasing voice, and correct word usage.

Interviewing

Increasingly oral language programs are giving some attention to interviewing as an activity that occasionally enters into the lives of both children and adults. Social studies and science stress interviewing as a method of procuring information; the interview has a prominent place in television news and information programs; interviewing and its variations, such as the panel presentation, are used in club programs. Not only does interviewing call for the use of many speaking and social skills, but it also emphasizes careful listening. Forty years ago, Broening

16. *Language for Meaning* 4 (Boston: Houghton Mifflin Co., 1978), p. 86.

advised starting a direct program of instruction in interview techniques in the school:[17]

> The interview has become a very useful technique with the present-day emphasis on the students' having actual contact with the activities about them . . . .
>
> Are we helping our students to ask important, direct questions, so that they can bring back the information desired? Are we stressing the necessity of quoting statements exactly as they were made? Are we insisting on courtesy at all times? Are we teaching students how to make a tactful and pleasing entree and introduction to the person being interviewed?

Many opportunities occur for children to conduct interviews. For example, they may interview a teacher who has taken a trip or has a special interest or hobby; they may interview a new child about his or her former home; they may interview parents who have special fields of interest, hobbies, or professions; they may interview school personnel about their work, or community workers such as the grocer, mailman, and fireman. The following guidelines warrant particular attention and practice:

1. Preplan the interview; research the topic and the person to be interviewed.
2. Allow the individual who arranged the interview to introduce the subject and close the interview.
3. Avoid trite opening statements like "Our teacher wants us to . . ." and "I have to . . . ."
4. Stick to the topic of the interview.
5. Develop sensitivity regarding the amount of time the interview is taking.
6. Create a feeling about when an interview should end.
7. Learn to make appointments at appropriate times.

Some people will be able to come to the classroom for an interview, but some will not. If the interviewer must travel to the interview, extra planning will be necessary. For such an interview it might be appropriate to make a sound or video recording, and the interviewer might have to learn to use recording equipment. Or, possibly, the interview could take place over the telephone with a loudspeaker hookup. In planning an interview, the interviewer should give careful thought to how the information gained from the interview will be utilized.

---

17. Angela M. Broening et al., *Conducting Experiences in English* (New York: Appleton-Century-Crofts, 1939), p. 128.

Meeting Participation

Classroom activities offer daily opportunities for children to learn orderly procedure. Many classrooms have class organizations or clubs and most pupils participate in organizations outside of school. Children enjoy taking part in organizations and their meetings, and their participation can help them develop desirable attitudes and understandings as well as provide opportunities to develop and practice speaking skills. Meetings of organized groups vary in formality (and orderliness!), so children should know something about meeting etiquette. In spite of this obvious need, children's language textbooks seldom include the procedures for effectively conducting and participating in meetings. Even recently published school curriculum guides fail to stress teaching meeting procedures. An older guide suggests that children should learn the following:[18]

Rules governing parliamentary procedure

1. The chairman calls the meeting to order.
2. The secretary reads the minutes of the previous meeting.
3. The chairman asks for corrections or additions to the minutes. After corrections or additions have been made, the minutes are then accepted.
4. The chairman calls for business to come before the meeting.
5. The group proceeds with the business of the day. (See making and voting on motions.)
6. The meeting is adjourned.

Making and voting on motions

1. The member who wants to make a motion rises and addresses the chairman by saying, "Mister (or Madam) Chairman."
2. The chairman recognizes the member be repeating his name.
3. The member proposes the motion by saying, "Mister Chairman, I move that. . . ."
4. Another member seconds the motion by stating, "I second the motion." (All motions must be seconded before they can be discussed or voted upon.)
5. After the motion has been seconded it is stated in full by the chairman as follows, "It has been moved and seconded that. . . ."
6. The chairman calls for discussion.
7. The chairman calls for a vote by saying, "All in favor say 'Aye.' Those opposed say 'No.'"
8. The chairman announces the result of the vote by saying, "The motion has been carried" or "The motion has been lost."

---

18. *Toward Better Speech*, p. 77.

If the teacher considers these parliamentary procedures to be too formal, he or she should discuss with the children various ways of conducting meetings and appropriate rules of behavior. Actually, even when a set of procedures is available for a particular group, it is a good idea to discuss their appropriateness to the organization and its meetings. From this discussion children should learn the value of rules in saving group time and energy. A wall chart or a mimeographed guide may be the outgrowth of the discussion.

Needless to say, the teacher should know parliamentary procedure thoroughly in order to teach it or to teach habits of orderly procedure in group activities. The form of the procedure should suit the age and ability level of the children, but the instructor should strive for progressive skill development and a degree of proficiency that will be useful to the child throughout school and adult life.

Announcements, Directions, and Explanations

Both children and adults frequently need to make announcements and give directions and explanations. School announcements concern lost and found articles, school programs, exhibitions, and parties. Often children give directions for playing games or for performing some classroom task. They explain how they found a particular item or fact in a book. Outside of school, children make announcements at scout meetings, club meetings, and parties. They give directions to one another during play, and they explain their hobbies to anyone who will listen. Adults are called upon to make announcements at social gatherings and public meetings, to give directions to motorists, and to make explanations to employees or employers as part of their work.

The skills and abilities necessary for making announcements and for giving directions and explanations are similar to the ones required in other oral language situations. The speaker must give complete information relative to who, what, when, where, and how in words carefully chosen for the situation. Generally, a limited amount of time is available for communication to occur, so the speaker must express the information concisely and clearly.

Teachers can best teach children how to make announcements and give directions and explanations in real situations. Children can make announcements about programs, events, exhibitions, games, lost and found articles, rules, and other subjects to their own classmates, to other classes, in assemblies, and to neighborhood adult groups. Making announcements at school club meetings is good experience, and often one or more youngsters may be called upon to make announcements or to act as master of ceremonies at school or club programs.

Social Amenities

Everyone should know how to extend and receive greetings, how to make introductions, how to give and accept compliments, how to show courtesy to others when speaking or listening to them, and how to apologize for breaches in social conduct. Most children recognize the importance of this etiquette, but sometimes they require outside motivation. One way to stimulate interest in social conventions is to discuss customs of other people, periods, and places. For example, pupils are interested in the ways people in different parts of the world greet each other.

1. French, Austrian, and some other European men kiss each other's cheeks.
2. In many European countries, men greet ladies by kissing their hands.
3. Japanese clasp their own hands and bow several times.
4. The Bakuba tribe in Zaire say "hello" and "goodby" by clapping their hands.
5. In this country, it was once proper for girls to curtsy and boys to bow when greeted by another person.

Acting as a host or hostess to classroom visitors is a common task in school. The room host and hostess may introduce themselves to the guests and, in turn, introduce the visitors to others in the room. With careful teacher guidance, performance of this duty helps children become aware of the uses and value of socially accepted forms of courtesy.

After extensive discussion and practice, children must become accustomed to observing the conventions that govern making and responding to introductions. The most effective time to teach children how to make introductions is just prior to a real occasion when they need to use the skills. The upcoming event provides immediate and effective motivation for learning. Discussing the skills is helpful, but it does not give children experience and assurance. If numerous real situations do not occur, children should dramatize imaginary social situations that require repeated exercise of these skills so that they learn to use them with ease and confidence.

The following general rules for making introductions apply to boys and girls alike. Most have no difficulty learning to perform each type of introduction with complete assurance.

1. Speak each person's name plainly to avoid embarrassment to either one. It is not improper for either person to ask to hear names again if he or she did not understand them at the time of the introduction.
2. In introducing two persons who are complete strangers, the person making the introduction should tactfully add some remark that might start a conversation.
3. An individual introducing himself or herself to another should be certain to tell his or her name and add some personal, identifying remark.
4. Introducing a relative requires mentioning his or her last name at some point during the introduction.

5. One of the following formulas will help children to master the form of introduction:

    _____, this is _____.

    _____, I'd like you to meet _____.

The following rules indicate which person to name first:

1. When introducing a man and a woman (or a boy and a girl), give the name of the woman or girl first.
2. When introducing an older and a younger person, mention the name of the older person first. If those being introduced are nearly the same age, either name may be given first.
3. When introducing an individual to your class or club meeting, mention the class or group first.

As suggested, many occasions naturally require children to make and to respond to introductions. They might want to introduce friends and parents to the teacher and to class members. Hosts and hostesses are often in demand, too. Sometimes one class may visit another and practice extending greetings and making introduction. Children may usher at school events. Other special occasions, such as class parties, call for many social skills. Children may also practice courtesies in out-of-school activities by replying correctly to greetings on the street, responding to introductions at church, and greeting people and introducing themselves while collecting for the paper drive, selling Scout cookies, and so on. Children especially need to learn courtesy for older persons. Also, giving an apology in a gracious manner and receiving a compliment or congratulations simply and sincerely are difficult for many of us to do. Occasions that require performing these duties do occur rather frequently, however, and learning to do them properly and easily should be a goal of the language program.

Teachers themselves sometimes forget to practice many of the courtesies. Particularly in this area of the language program, the most effective teaching "method" is to "practice what you preach." A potential reference on courtesies and the social conventions, as well as concrete hints and techniques for developing these skills, is the teacher's manual of an elementary school language textbook.

EVALUATION OF ORAL EXPRESSION

In spite of the importance of oral expression, no standardized evaluative instruments for appraising speech production skills or the total expressional product are available. Reasons for the lack of measuring instruments include the intangibility of speech and the difficulty in identifying norms or standards for most types of speaking situations.

Although standardized instruments are not available, teachers and pupils can evaluate expression informally. For example, tape recorders are useful in appraising the speech of individual children and the products of both individual and group expression. Additionally, some language textbooks suggest informal methods of evaluation and diagnosis. In the following sections we will discuss the use of these and other evaluative tools.

Detection of Speech Disorders

Producing speech sounds requires extremely accurate coordination of all of the mental, physical, and emotional aspects of the speech mechanism. Thus, only a specialist should try to diagnose speech production problems. The function of the classroom teacher is to observe students and refer any showing noticeable speech difficulties to trained clinicians for examination and treatment. Eisenson and Ogilvie prepared the following guide to help teachers identify speech disorders.[19] They suggest that a preponderance of "yes" answers to these questions for a particular pupil signals the need to consult a speech specialist.

Analysis of speech defects

Articulatory Defects. Does the child substitute one sound for another? Does he omit sounds? Does he distort sounds? Is he very hard to understand?

Stuttering. Is the child disturbed by his dysfluency? Does he repeat sounds or syllables or words more than his classmates? Is his speech decidedly arhythmical? Does he block frequently? Does he have difficulty in getting his words out?

Vocal Difficulties. Is the child's voice noticeably unpleasant in quality? Is his pitch higher or lower than most of his classmates? Is his voice monotonous? Is his voice light and thin? Is his voice husky? Is his voice too loud? Is his voice too weak? Is his voice difficult to hear in class?

Cleft Palate Speech. Is there an obvious cleft of the teeth ridge or palate? Is his voice excessively nasal? Are his *p, b, t, d, k,* and *g* inaccurate? Are some of his other consonants distorted?

Cerebral Palsy Speech. Does the child have obvious tremors of the musculature phonation and breathing? Is his speech slow, jerky, and labored? Is his rhythm of speech abnormal?

Delayed Speech. Is his speech markedly retarded in relation to his classmates? Does he omit and substitute sounds substantially more than his classmates? Does he use shorter and simpler sentences than his classmates? Does he use fewer phrases and prepositions than his classmates?

Language Impairment. Is the child's comprehension of language markedly retarded? Does he seem to be inconsistent in his ability to understand and his ability to

---

19. Reprinted with permission of the Macmillan Publishing Co., from *Speech Correction in the Schools*, 2d ed., by Jon Eisenson and Mordel Ogilvie, pp. 10–12. Copyright © 1957, 1963, by Macmillan Publishing Co., Inc.

use language? Is the profile of his linguistic abilities uneven? (For example, can he read much better than he can spell?) Is he surprisingly good in arithmetic and yet quite poor in either reading or writing?

Speech Defect Due to Impaired Hearing. Does the child have frequent earaches and colds? Does he have running ears? Does he omit sounds or substitute one sound for another? Does he distort sounds? Does he speak too loudly? Does he speak too softly? Does he frequently ask you to repeat what you have said? Does he turn his head to one side as you speak? Does he make unusual mistakes in the spelling words you dictate? Does he misinterpret your questions or instructions frequently? Does he do better when given written instruction than when given oral instructions? Does he seem more intelligent than his work indicates?

As this set of questions shows, many observable speech defects are largely the consequence of habit. Conditions that reflect habits rather than physical or emotional problems are subject to instruction by the classroom teacher. Particularly, the teacher can provide retraining and can give a feeling of acceptance and security to the child with these habits.

Further Diagnostic Aids

The following chart lists possible causes of many speech problems and suggests remedial treatment. A teacher who does not have access to a speech clinician or who cannot procure a clinician's services immediately will find these suggestions helpful.

Diagnostic and remedial speech chart

Observable speech disorder	Possible causes	Suggested remedial treatment
1. Baby talk	Immaturity; home example; low mentality; defective hearing; inability to discriminate sounds accurately.	Set correct example and encourage home to do likewise; check hearing and discrimination; provide secure classroom environment.
2. Lisping	Malformation of teeth or jaws; loss of front teeth; hearing deficiency; immaturity.	Arrange for physical examination; teach formation of sounds; give breathing exercises.
3. Poor articulation	Carelessness; home background; defective hearing; inadequate knowledge of sounds.	Set correct example; give training exercises in making sounds; motivate class to set high standards

Diagnostic and remedial speech chart (continued)

Observable speech disorder	Possible causes	Suggested remedial treatment
		in articulation; listen to recording of speech.
4. Excess nasality	Poor breathing habits; physical defects; home example.	Arrange for physical examination; give breathing exercises (panting, yawning, etc.), auditory discrimination exercises, exercises requiring blowing.
5. Breathiness	Emotional tension; improper breathing.	Give emotional security; prescribe deep-breathing exercises; check causes of excessive tension; arrange for choral speaking.
6. Stuttering	Physical defects; emotional problem.	Give security; avoid ridicule; arrange for physical examination; arrange for choral speaking.
7. Stammering	Feelings of inferiority; physical defects.	Give encouragement and security; encourage participation in group activities; focus on the thought rather than on manner of speech.
8. High pitch	Self-consciousness; insecurity; fatigue; faulty hearing and sound discrimination.	Prescribe adequate rest; give security; listen to recorded voice; do reading exercises.
9. Stridency	Poor social adjustment; home conditions; hearing defect; emotional problems.	Give security; listen to recorded voice; arrange for dramatization with need for soft voice or choral speaking.
10. Low pitch	Physical defects; fatigue; emotional problems.	Arrange for medical examination; provide practice in articulation and nonsense verse; provide security.

Appraisal of Oral Language Performance

All evaluation should be based on objectives. In evaluations of oral language performance these should be the skills, attitudes, and abilities that the program of instruction has sought to develop. The list of functional objectives that follows is
not exhaustive, but it provides a framework for identification of other objectives
and development of appraisal procedures.

1. To converse with classmates and adults easily and courteously
2. To participate in discussions, sticking to the point and respecting the opinions of others
3. To organize information and report it effectively
4. To plan an interview and carry it through courteously and effectively
5. To use the telephone competently
6. To conduct a meeting by means of parliamentary procedures
7. To give clear directions, explanations, and announcements orally
8. To tell a story or personal experience effectively and interestingly
9. To greet others properly in various social situations
10. To participate in choral speaking
11. To make use of parliamentary procedures as a member of a group
12. To take part in a dramatic activity

In extending this framework reference should be made to the specific objectives stated for the various oral language activities identified in this chapter and
in Chapter 11, as well as related standards and guidelines. The listed objectives,
combined with specific objectives for a particular type of speaking situation, provide a good basis for evaluative checklists and records of pupils' progress.

The following checklist for discussion appraisal comes from a curriculum
bulletin.[20] The format is appropriate for other speech activities, too.

1. *For the group*
   a. Was the problem suitable for class discussion?
   b. Was the problem stated clearly?
   c. Were all the terms defined?
   d. Was the topic of interest to all?
   e. Did the members display attitudes of sincerity and cooperation by listen-
      ing attentively, keeping to the point under discussion, requesting further
      information or clarification of information presented, permitting all
      members to participate?
   f. Were all members qualified to discuss the problem intelligently on the
      basis of indirect and direct preparation?
   g. Were the important issues discussed?
   h. Did the discussion promote a better understanding of the problem and of
      the members of the group?

---

20. *Toward Better Speech,* pp. 81–82.

      i.   Were the voices audible and of good quality?

      j.   Were the speech patterns acceptable? Did they permit free and easy exchange of ideas?

      k.   Were the thoughts well organized and expressed in a convincing and concise manner?

      l.   Was the discussion worthwhile in proportion to the amount and quality of information gained and the time consumed?

2.   *For the discussion leader*

      a.   Did the leader guide the discussion wisely?

      b.   Did he encourage all members to participate?

      c.   Did he discourage individuals or small groups from monopolizing the discussion?

      d.   Did he keep the discussion on the point at issue?

      e.   Did he keep the discussion moving forward by raising a new issue as soon as the one under discussion seemed to have been handled adequately?

      f.   Did he focus attention on the important points by the use of a running summary?

      g.   Did he summarize at the close of the discussion period?

In using checklists teachers should keep records for each child on an individual card in order to have a means for making further individual diagnosis and for showing evidence of progress over a period of time.

Self-evaluation by Pupils

Self-evaluation based on standards that children set themselves should be an important part of the evaluation. For example, a class might adopt a list of "rules" for giving an oral report similar to the following one and use it as the basis for judging the effectiveness of their reports.

1.   Have an interesting topic.
2.   Start with a good opening sentence.
3.   Look at the audience.
4.   Make your voice loud enough to be heard.
5.   Organize your report carefully.
6.   Stick to the topic.
7.   Use good sentences.
8.   Have a good closing.

Teachers also should practice self-evaluation. Questions such as the following will help a teacher appraise the oral language program:[21]

---

21. George C. Bolz, "Promoting Oral Expression," *National Elementary Principal* 42 (April 1963): 41–43.

1.   Do I recognize the need for children to practice oral expression?
2.   Do I consistently provide opportunities for children to communicate orally?
3.   Am I willing to work with children where I find them—willing to work patiently and understandingly with a shy child?
4.   How can I improve my own skills in oral expression? Do I set a good example in my speech—enunciating clearly, speaking comfortably and easily, organizing my thoughts logically?
5.   Do I listen to children? Do I give them my complete attention? Do I respond fully to their questions and comments?

Finally, teachers can check students' self-evaluation by using a checklist that corresponds to the one they have developed. Examples of dual evaluation checklists for individual speaking situations appear in *Children and Oral Language*.[22]

EXERCISES FOR THOUGHT AND ACTION

1.   Record the exchange of several children in a natural communicative situation. Evaluate their speech to determine teaching needs. How can you decide what their greatest needs are? Do you need additional evidence?
2.   For a particular grade level, devise a chart of standards for a specific oral language activity.
3.   Obtain from the telephone company materials for teaching telephone skills. Plan a lesson using these materials.
4.   Interview and, if possible, observe a speech therapist in a local school. Learn what kinds of speech problems the therapist encounters, how he or she locates children with speech problems, and what kinds of remedial programs the therapist recommends. Ask also for suggestions that might be useful to elementary school classroom teachers.
5.   Suggest steps to make pupils more directly aware of the need for sensitivity to the audience in various speaking activities.
6.   Assuming you are a teacher, what should you do for a child who stutters? Justify your answer.
7.   Prepare a one-page letter or bulletin for parents suggesting ways for them to foster the development of their children's speech. Include cautions for the overanxious parent. You must select a particular age level because suggestions will vary considerably with the maturity levels of children.
8.   Survey a group of elementary school teachers to find out which of the special situations for developing oral language skills described in this

22. Helen K. Mackintosh, 1964.

chapter they use. If they do not take advantage of all of the situations described here, attempt to determine why.

9. A good source of information about speech in the classroom is *The Speech Teacher*, a publication of the Speech Association of America. Read three articles in the journal that relate to the discussion in this chapter. Report on them to the class.

10. Plan a bulletin board display that will contribute to the development of abilities in one of the special situations described in this chapter. Also explain how you would involve children either in making the bulletin board or in using it in a speaking activity.

11. Devise a pupil self-evaluation checklist that covers speaking skills and products.

12. Tape-record your own spontaneous speech and/or oral reading. Analyze volume, clarity, speed, pronunciation, intonation, and so on. Then set personal speaking goals.

13. Listen to someone you consider to be a good speaker (on radio, television, or live). What qualities make him or her effective? How would you use this procedure of identifying and analyzing a positive speaking model with children to establish a list of speaking standards? Describe your plan in detail.

14. Begin a collection of literature appropriate for choral speaking by children at the level that particularly interests you; your collection probably will include more poetry than other literary forms. Index your selections for easy reference.

15. Examine a current language arts textbook for children at the level that interests you. How much attention does it devote to speaking? How comprehensive, balanced, and sound is the treatment? Do the same for a curriculum guide.

SELECTED REFERENCES

Anastasiow, Nicholas. *Oral Language: Expression of Thought*. Newark, Del.: International Reading Association, 1971.

Anderson, Virgil A., and Newby, Hayes A. *Improving the Child's Speech*. 2d ed. New York: Oxford University Press, 1973.

Blake, James N. *Speech Education Activities for Children*. Springfield, Ill.: Charles C. Thomas, 1970.

Book, Cassandra, and Galvin, Kathleen. *Instruction in and About Small Group Discussion*. Urbana, Ill.: ERIC/Reading and Communication Skills and Speech Communication Association, 1975.

Carlson, Ruth K. *Speaking Aids Through the Grades*. New York: Columbia University Press, 1973.

Dixon, John. *Growth Through English*. Reading, England: National Association for the Teaching of English, 1975.

Donoghue, Mildred R. *The Child and the English Language Arts.* 2d ed. Dubuque, Iowa: William C. Brown Co., 1975.

Eisenson, Jon, and Ogilvie, Mardel. *Speech Correction in the Schools.* 2d ed. New York: Macmillan Co., 1969.

Huckleberry, Alan W., and Strother, Edward S. *Speech Education for the Elementary Teacher.* Boston: Allyn and Bacon, 1966.

Klein, Marvin. *Talk in the Language Arts Classroom.* Urbana, Ill.: ERIC/Reading and Communication Skills and National Council of Teachers of English, 1977.

Mackintosh, Helen K., ed. *Children and Oral Language.* Washington, D.C.: Association for Childhood Education International, 1964.

Mowrer, Donald. "Speech Problems: What You Should Do and Shouldn't Do," *Learning,* January 1978, pp. 34–37.

Munkres, Alberta. *Helping Children in Oral Communication.* New York: Teacher's College, Columbia University, 1959.

Pennington, R. C., and Pennington, James E. *For the Parents of a Child Whose Speech Is Delayed.* Englewood Cliffs, N.J.: Prentice-Hall, 1965.

Petty, Walter T., ed. *Research in Oral Language.* Champaign, Ill.: National Council of Teachers of English, 1967.

Petty, Walter T.; Petty, Dorothy C.; and Becking, Marjorie F. *Experiences in Language: Tools and Techniques for Language Arts Methods.* 2d ed. Boston: Allyn and Bacon, 1976.

Phillips, Gerald M., et al. *The Development of Oral Communication in the Classroom.* Indianapolis: Bobbs-Merrill Co., 1970.

Rasmussen, Carrie. *Speech Methods in the Elementary School.* New York: Ronald Press, 1962.

Van Riper, Charles. *Speech Correction: Principles and Methods.* 4th ed. Englewood Cliffs, N.J.: Prentice-Hall, 1963.

13

Effective Written Expression:
The Foundation

To write well it is first necessary to have something to say. —*Stephen Leacock*

Writing is "an important medium for self-expression, for communication, and for the discovery of meaning—its need increased rather than decreased by the development of new media for mass communication."[1] Yet in recent years, many have questioned the ability of children, youth, and adults to write satisfactorily. The media—particularly the press—have enumerated the increasing numbers of college and university "bonehead" English and remedial writing courses, reported on the establishment by many states of minimum writing competency standards for high school graduation, and quoted findings by the National Assessment of Educational Progress concerning how well students and young adults write.[2]

Although many persons and groups have concluded that writing ability has

---

1. National Council of Teachers of English Commission on Composition, "Composition: A Position Statement," *Elementary English* 52 (February 1975): 194.

2. The National Assessment of Educational Progress (Education Commission of the States, 1860 Lincoln Street, Suite 700, Denver, Colo. 80203) from time to time issues reports.

declined, others deny it.[3] Still others make a case that writing quality has re-mained constant as the need for better writing has increased.[4] Perhaps this latter point of view is generally true; however, the evidence is strong that substantial numbers of adults do not write well in such "practical" areas as letter writing, writing directions, and completing forms.[5] Thus, the necessity for emphasizing writing instruction in elementary schools seems undeniable.

Here and in Chapter 14, we will describe the writing process, identify situa-tions in which writing instruction is appropriate and the form writing products should take, and suggest the kind of teaching that is necessary. We will also discuss creativity in written expression, which is so vital in the development of children. But teaching children to write effectively takes more than these chapters alone can explain. The ability to write well is an elusive goal. The preceding chapters on language learning, approaches to the organization of in-struction, listening—in fact, all of the previous chapters as well as all that follow—bear on the teaching of writing, because all language activities are related. So suspend final judgment on what the teaching of written expression in-volves until you have read the entire book.

THE PROCESS OF WRITING

Writing is the mental and physical act of forming letters and words. But it is much more than that. It is putting words into sentences and sentences into paragraphs, spelling words correctly, punctuating and capitalizing in customary ways, and observing conventions in written forms—and more. Writing is a pro-cess of expressing thoughts and feelings, of thinking, and of shaping experiences.

Writing Is Composing

Writing, like speaking, is a thinking process of the highest order. Writing requires putting words and larger units into a pattern or arrangement for the purpose of expression. The arrangement is composition, and its effectiveness depends on the thinking that went into it.

Effective composition consists of a number of elements that reflect the quality of the writer's thinking, and these warrant instructional attention. We mention them here to stress the point that whatever the form of written expres-sion—essay, letter, story, or report—it will genuinely communicate only if these

---

3. George H. Douglas, "Is Literacy Really Declining?" *Educational Record* 57 (1977): 140–48.

4. Richard Lloyd-Jones, "Is There a Crisis in Writing Skills?" *Today's Education* 64 (January–February 1975): 63–64.

5. J. Stanley Ahmann, "A Report on National Assessment in Seven Learning Areas," *Today's Education* 64 (January–February 1975): 63–64.

elements are discernible. Later in this chapter and in Chapter 14, we will discuss each one in detail. Here, then, are the elements of effective composition:

1. A clear-cut, controlling purpose
2. Content details relevant to this controlling purpose
3. Systematic arrangement of content (e.g., order of importance, spatial relationships, cause and effect, time sequence, general to specific, or concrete to abstract)
4. Use of comparison and contrast, valid evidence and generalization, and formal and informal language style as appropriate to content and audience
5. Clear sentence constructions
6. Varied sentence structures

This list does not include experience, observation and research, and the selection and recording of ideas and information, all of which are crucial elements in composing. We will discuss these skills and abilities in this chapter, as well as ways to motivate children to express themselves by writing.

What Children Do in Writing

Considerable research has been done in recent years to determine what writers do while they write. Almost all of this research has identified three phases in a single writing act:[6] prewriting, writing, and postwriting.

The *prewriting* phase includes discussion of the proposed writing—the theme or topic, ideas and related words, feelings and thoughts. It also takes in environmental stimuli and any form of "rehearsing" for writing.[7] In fact, a writer may bring all of his or her experiences to bear on the composing act in this prewriting phase, providing there is both time and encouragement to do so.

The prewriting phase may *not* include some activities that teachers tend to stress. For example, children rarely make outlines on a spontaneous basis. After observing and interviewing thirty boys and thirty girls randomly selected from a group of 230 fifth-grade children, Sawkins reported that they seldom preplanned stories completely and they made virtually no use of notes and outlines.[8] She did find, though, that children tend to consider aspects of content before they begin

6. See, for example, Donald H. Graves, "An Examination of the Writing Processes of Seven Year Old Children," *Research in the Teaching of English* 9 (Winter 1975): 231.

7. Graves found that seven-year-old children "rehearsed" writing by participating at home in family discussions and, just prior to the writing act, by making drawings of what they intended to write about.

8. Margaret W. Sawkins, *The Oral Responses of Selected Fifth-grade Children to Questions Concerning Their Written Expression* (Ph.D. dissertation, State University of New York at Buffalo, 1970).

"What are you drawing?"
"I don't know. It isn't finished yet."

The Family Circus by Bil Keane. Reprinted Courtesy of The Register and Tribune Syndicate, Inc.

writing and that the more capable writers gave more time to this step than the less capable writers did. But even better writers do not begin writing with a complete composition in mind. This result supports the contention that the act of writing aids in discovering meaning, that "when the writer writes he discovers what he has to say."[9]

The *writing* phase includes pausing and rereading as the writing is occurring, interaction with others (further discussion), consulting resources (looking up word meanings or spellings, for example), talking to oneself (sometimes aloud), and reformulating the ideas and organization of the composition. All but the latter of these is observable, and a teacher should note these behaviors and attempt to relate them to the child's thinking and, in turn, to the strengths and weaknesses of the compositional product. Sawkins emphasizes the importance of this effort:[10]

9. Donald M. Murray, *A Writer Teaches Writing: A Practical Method of Teaching Composition.* Boston: Houghton Mifflin Co., 1968, p. 9.

10. Margaret W. Sawkins, "What Children Say About Their Writing," in *The Writing Processes of Students*, edited by Walter T. Petty and Patrick Finn, (Buffalo: Department of Elementary and Remedial Education, State University of New York at Buffalo, 1975), p. 48.

"Children need a teacher who provides help while writing is taking place rather than giving criticism and correction after first drafts and returning the writing for correction or revision."

The *postwriting* phase encompasses all behaviors that follow the actual writing act and may include the writer's solicitation of approval from others, proofreading, contemplating of the product, and finally, its disposition. Ideally, the postwriting phase involves repeating some behaviors from the composing phase until contemplation and approval signal that the product is satisfactory. For, as Murray has written, "all effective writers know writing is rewriting."[11]

Thinking and Feeling

One writer says, "It's all in the mind, waiting to find its way to paper."[12] Certainly this statement is true, as is another cliché: "what children think, they can say." But sorting out and organizing one's thoughts, which writing especially demands, is no easy process. Nor is it a process that all children can perform in the same way or equally well. Nor does it take place only before the act of writing begins. As researchers have found, thought is an important component of the prewriting phase; thinking generates ideas about the content and form of the proposed piece of writing. But both content and form continue to develop as the writer writes. If sufficient thought has gone into the ideas and feelings that appear on paper first, the act of writing should spawn even more ideas and uncover more feelings that will move the composition toward completion.

Although thinking about one's own writing is relatively easy to talk about and to describe, it is a difficult and complex process to engage in. Everyone who tries to write needs help translating and organizing his or her thinking, and this is especially true of the inexperienced writer, the child in the elementary school. Thus teachers must help children with their thinking. The teacher who simply plunges children into a writing act, even if external stimuli are ample, "without giving them help in translating their inner potential to the surface in writing"[13] is asking too much of them and is likely retarding their development as effective writers.

EXPRESSION OF INDIVIDUALITY THROUGH WRITING

Teachers rightly want to foster children's uniqueness and tend to have greater interest in developing originality in writing than in encouraging creativity in oral

---

11. Murray, p. 11.

12. Jack Perron, "Beginning Writing: It's All in the Mind," *Language Arts* 53 (September 1976): 653.

13. Perron, p. 653.

expression. Virtually the entire writing program in some classrooms focuses on the writing of "creative" stories, rhymes, and poems; but writing that is imaginative should be good writing and good expression above all. All writing should develop through the same process. Sloppy and careless writing is nothing but that; it reflects sloppy and careless thinking.

Definitions of Creative Writing

Although stories and poetry tend to show more evidence of creativity, almost all writing is creative if it reflects the special individuality of the writer. Nevertheless, there are about as many different definitions of creative writing as there are authors defining it. One textbook lists the following synonyms for creative writing: "personal writing, writing for fun, expressive writing, free writing."[14] Another says that "when we add a heart and mind to writing . . . it becomes creative."[15] Still another emphasizes "the spontaneous outpouring of the child's imagination."[16] Other statements tend to deemphasize spontaneity in the sense of writing done quickly, without planning or revision. Most suggest that creative writing shows imagination and the personal involvement of the writer.

One curriculum guide says that creative writing is also labeled "personal" or "imaginative" and that it may be characterized as follows:[17]

1. It draws upon imaginative and/or emotional resources of the student.
2. The structure of the writing is not dictated by the teacher, though guidance may be given. Individual responses tend to take different forms.
3. This writing provides an avenue for the student's self-expression of reactions and responses, an expression necessary to the growing awareness of himself as an individual.

A particularly well-formulated definition comes from Jean Ullyette's interesting booklet *Guidelines for Creative Writing*. She says that creative writing "is the child's response to the world around him . . . [the] putting of his thoughts on paper in the form of a story, article, poem, letter, or play . . . [with the emphasis always] on freedom of expression."[18]

---

14. Itis M. Tiedt and Sidney W. Tiedt, *Contemporary English in the Elementary School*, 2d ed. (Englewood Cliffs, N.J.: Prentice Hall, 1975), p. 169.

15. James A. Smith, *Adventure in Communication: Language Arts Methods* (Boston: Allyn and Bacon, 1972), p. 329.

16. Lillian M. Logan, Virgil G. Logan, and Leona Paterson, *Creative Communication: Teaching the Language Arts* (Toronto: McGraw-Hill Ryerson, 1972), p. 201.

17. *Selecting, Organizing, and Expressing Ideas*. Elementary Composition Curriculum Guide. (Lakewood Center, Wash.: Clover Park School District, 1967), p. 8.

18. Jean M. Ullyette, *Guidelines for Creative Writing* (Dansville, N.Y.: Instructor Publications, 1968), p. 5.

Creative Writing Objectives

Any statement of purpose covering the encouragement or development of creativity in writing also defines the types of writing done. Again, the primary objective of all language expression is clear communication of thoughts with enough emotion and feeling to make the expression effective. The major purpose of creative writing is no different. The key to creative writing is involvement, personalization, and imagination, and these factors point to two other significant benefits inherent in creative writing:

1.   Creative expression serves as a release for pressures and tensions that build up in most of us. From time to time we become confused about external conditions and their possible effects on our lives. At such times, releasing our thoughts through language expression may provide satisfaction and a sense of relief. The attempt to meet, explain, and justify these external conditions and effects, if only to ourselves, is likely to be creative, individual, and original. In general, people who suppress their feelings are often unhappy and their personalities may be underdeveloped. So personal growth and well-being alone may be justification for regular writing, perhaps in a personal diary, because it gives us a chance to unload.

2.   Creative expression of a truly imaginative nature produces fun and adventure. We all derive real pleasure and satisfaction from doing something new and original. Self-expression bolsters the ego and sense of self-worth, with pleasure resulting from achievement and inventiveness.

Children's writing often demonstrates these advantages. For example, one child's beginning sentence, "My sister is dumb," set the tone for his story about sibling rivalry at home. Nancy's poem was just for fun, and she glowed after receiving the praise of her third-grade classmates.

> Tabby is our mother cat,
> She's going to have a litter.
> With all those kittens at her side
> She'll need a baby sitter.

Bill was equally appreciative that his sixth-grade classmates thought these paragraphs from a letter to a pen pal in Ohio were "sure good":

> We have an ambitious class. Everyone has a Pen Pal and we write every week. Getting letters is the most fun, but telling about things is fun, too. Here's what happened yesterday.

Jim brought a snake to school! It was only a little garter snake but some of the kids screamed and wouldn't get close. Jim put it in a cage we have but it got out. That's when the fun started. It took about an hour to find it. It was under our notebooks in the cabinet. Jim had to turn it loose outside after that.

Content and Correctness

Children who can write and speak imaginatively will want to use acceptable language and proper form. Indeed, children who do not have some confidence in their ability to use appropriate language are not likely to express their thoughts and feelings in writing. Children who have difficulty producing legible handwriting, lack confidence in spelling and punctuation, or have little knowledge of the form of a particular piece of writing will repress self-expression and what they produce will not reflect their individuality.

Some authorities on language arts instruction assert that teaching sentence construction, usage, and mechanical skills stifles creativity. Certainly these elements alone do not make masterpieces out of letters, poetry, announcements, or any other form of language expression. Form and correctness are not the ultimate goals of expression. On the other hand, form and content are so interwoven in normal expression that it is impossible to separate one from the other completely or to say that one is so important that we can disregard the other. Content deserves primary emphasis always, but not exclusive emphasis.

Initially when most of us try to put ideas and feelings into written form, we pay more attention to getting the substance of our thinking on paper rather than to spelling, punctuation, subject-verb agreement, and so forth. Later, usually during the postwriting stage, we correct errors and rewrite as necessary. Almost automatically, we emphasize content but not without regard for accuracy, mechanics, and matters of convention. To disregard these is to sanction practices that later must be unlearned.

Thus, elementary schoolchildren who are just learning to write must learn the practice of first giving attention to content and then to form or correctness. Teachers who write are aware that even mature writers give priority to expressing their ideas and expect to polish their form at a later time. To expect the simultaneous production of worthy ideas in a final form is unreasonable for both developing and experienced writers. Refinement of writing during the final composing stage can be facilitated by teacher identification of individual skill needs as revealed in the compositions and direct teaching until application of the skill is a matter of habit.

EXPERIENCE AND WRITING

By the time they start school, all children have had many experiences, and their horizons continue to broaden throughout the elementary school years. They learn from these experiences and form their own ideas from them, ideas about which they will talk and write if properly encouraged and taught.

The Role of Experience in Writing

Most of us would be appalled if we were called upon to write a report with the title "Gas Dynamics." Even after considerable reading, we probably would be unable to write a paper that would either interest a reader or satisfy ourselves. In the first place, we would probably have difficulty finding information on a topic so far removed from our experience. And many of us would have little interest in the topic, as reflected by our lack of knowledge about it.

In evaluating the role of experience in children's expression we must go back for a moment to our discussion of how children learn language. Language is a set of symbols that represent concepts or ideas, and their meaning may differ from one person to another. A meaning that is shared by two or more individuals reflects common elements in their experiences. In developing language children learn symbols and their related concepts and ideas from other people in their environment. A child does not learn language—the words and the larger units—if there is no occasion in the environment to use it. In other words, children do not learn concepts that have no relation to their environment. Children's knowledge derives from their experiences.

The experiential background of each child is different, though children of the same neighborhood and the same social and economic classes may have had similar experiences. Thus, the experiential value of a school activity for a particular child is very difficult to determine. Our best guess generally is that the interests children show are clues to their experiential backgrounds, and our best procedure is to extend these interests as far as possible.

Children at all age and grade levels have many interests and, therefore, have much they can write about. Nevertheless, the school must extend their experience. Even if a child comes to school with fluency and spontaneity of expression or if the school develops these abilities early, unless he or she has opportunities to acquire new knowledge to relate to previous experience, these skills could lapse. The words below, certainly as true today as when they were written, should be read frequently by every teacher, every textbook writer, and every other person propounding what the curriculum in the elementary school should be.[19]

> The further the child progresses in the elementary school, the greater is the danger that his language period may degenerate into one of exercise-doing, learning words in columns out of context, or studying language forms divorced from the use he is mak-

---

19. Cora V. Smith, "Growth in Language Power as Related to Child Development," *Teaching Language in the Elementary School.* The Forty-third Yearbook of the National Society for the Study of Education, pt. 2 (Chicago: University of Chicago Press, 1944), p. 59.

ing of language the rest of the day. Special care, therefore, needs to be exercised to continue the kind of rich program of well-motivated enterprises common in the lower grades in order that the growth of language may continue in relationship to the development of meaning and that the challenge of a social purpose may motivate expression. Then the needed remedial drill and positive instruction in word knowledge and linguistic forms may be related directly to the problems which confront the pupil in his daily use of language.

There is no defensible reason for the degeneration suggested to occur—even though it commonly does. As children mature they have wider interests, more to talk about. Teachers simply need to take advantage of these interests and their related motivation so that children's use of language will continue to grow in relationship to the development of meaning and so that the challenge of a social purpose will motivate expression. Any necessary instruction in word knowledge and linguistic forms should relate directly to the problems that confront pupils daily.

Because experience is the basis of expression, all writing is limited by the impression, or the "input" received. For example, after a discussion of the shape of the earth one group of fourth-grade children wrote down their observations. One child wrote:

> The earth is round and full of bumps. The cars and buses have a hard time on the hills.

This expression was the natural observation of a child who lived in a rugged section of the country, where transportation over steep roads was the only lifeline to the rest of the world.

In another fourth-grade class, the children discussed places in the West they had visited. They looked at pictures, films, and filmstrips of mountains, deserts, and rivers, and read about the places that seemed the most interesting. After these experiences one child wrote:

> I saw a canyon narrow and deep,
> With colors dull and bright.
> I heard the water rush and leap.
> What a wondrous sound and sight.

Children must have abundant and continuous opportunities for gaining ideas and impressions, for relating these to previous experiences, and for learning the words to describe new experiences.

Fostering imaginative and vivid writing requires more than activities and opportunities for experience. For example, teachers must help children learn to use new words. Furthermore, as Mauree Applegate has suggested, "If you want your children to write . . . , you must take plenty of time to appreciate the little things that happen every day."[20] Many children—and some teachers—are unobservant and may not note the significance of apparently commonplace details in their lives. They may fail to notice the intricacies of the dew-covered spider web in the plant by the schoolyard fence, the design formed by the shadows of the flag pole and the oak tree on the corner, and the eager expression of the puppy waiting for supper. A teacher must constantly encourage children to be observant and to appreciate what they observe. As David McCord has said,

> If you're going to write poetry of any kind, you have to be what Thomas Hardy calls a noticer. You have to notice *little* things. After you have met and evaluated a person, you should remember this and that about him that another will have missed. This is what Sherlock Holmes did. You must learn to observe minutiae. I don't know how else to express it. I can't tell you how to train yourself in that. You just have to be—or become—perpetually curious. You must perpetually want to know why something works and why this happens and that doesn't happen.[21]

The best way to instill this curiosity in children is to build flexibility into the daily schedule and to take time to discuss the details of observations and experiences. Talking about sights, sounds, and events deserves particular emphasis. Certainly, we all see, hear, taste, and feel, but sometimes our impressions of these experiences remain vague. Discussing experiences helps to expand and intensify impressions, providing the exchange is thought provoking and related to other experiences. The teacher who calls the class's attention to a flight of geese in the gray October sky has been observant and has shown the children something to watch for during that time of the year. To extend the experience the teacher might start a list of things of beauty and interest that appear in the sky, including:

1. A streaking, falling star
2. A floating, drifting balloon
3. A swooping swallow
4. The trail of a jet plane
5. A chugging, blinking helicopter
6. A circling hawk
7. Darting sea gulls
8. A kite straining on a string
9. Churning storm clouds

---

20. Mauree Applegate, *Helping Children Write* (Evanston, Ill.: Row, Peterson and Co., 1954), p. 17.

21. David McCord, "Poetry, Children, and the Encounter Between the Two," *Language Arts* 55 (March 1978): 385.

Or the same observation could provide the beginning of a verse or a story. It may bring forth an expression like fourth-grade Susan's "Clouds":

> I like to see the clouds
> Floating all around.
> Often they smile,
> Sometimes they frown.

Experiences need not be firsthand to be inspiring. Sometimes vicarious experiences spark creativity as readily as experiences in which the child has actually participated. Reading, looking at pictures, listening to music or speech, and watching other people and things may all lead to creative expression. The key is not participation but relating the experience to the individual and to his or her thoughts, ideas, and impressions. Writing comes forth as a reaction to experiences.

The Role of Literature

Vapid language expression often is a consequence of having read little. Reading good literature to children and encouraging them to read—avenues that every teacher can and should follow—is immensely rewarding to both the teacher and the children. Hearing and reading good language expression enables children unconsciously to learn to think, awakens ideas, and gives impetus to expression. As we stressed in Chapter 5, literature gives pleasure, excitement, and access to our heritage, as well as a framework for interpreting the world. It challenges the imagination and enriches experiences; both elements are essential for effective writing.

A child must want to read and must have the skills necessary to satisfy this desire. Imparting the desire and teaching the skills to each child are the principal purposes of the school reading program. To fulfill these goals requires ready access to an abundance of books and other reading materials. Also necessary is the kind of teacher guidance that stimulates interest, relates what is read to the children's experiences, fosters personality growth through reading, and, if necessary, directs readers to literature that inspires creative expression.

Whether or not a pupil reads is the basic test of the effectiveness of reading instruction. Students will not read unless reading engenders feelings and evokes an emotional or thoughtful response. Therefore, a discerning teacher will allow children sufficient time to become aware of their reactions. This is one way for a teacher to encourage children to read for satisfaction, for feeling, and for development of a desire to express.

The Role of Words

One writer has called attention to the need in expression for words that "sparkle and spin." Her contention is that words can add brightness, vitality, and gleaming appeal to our writing. Skillfully chosen words can do for expression what a spider's painstaking work does for its web.[22] Language expression is dependent on words, but children do not automatically grasp the uses of words in such a way that they will always choose the most suitable ones to express the meaning they intend to convey. Frequently, in order for creative and effective writing to result from a particular experience, the experience must be translated or expanded through the use of language, that is, through words. The effort it takes to build interest in words—in what they denote and connote, in careful selection and use, and in their intrinsic appeal—will generate expression that truly shows "sparkle and spin."

As shown in Chapters 10 and 11, many activities both appeal to children and lead to accurate use of words and to better expression. These exercises illustrate the possibilities.

1. Complete the following comparison phrases and sentences.
   a. The wind howled like _____
   b. As soft as _____
   c. As smooth as _____
   d. He ran like a _____
   e. As green as _____
2. Make a list of substitutes for "tired" words.
   a. *Said:* called, urged, shouted, began, exclaimed, replied, giggled
   b. *Funny:* amusing, odd, laughable, strange
   c. *Real:* quite, actual, genuine
   d. *Nice:* pleasing, considerate, appealing, well-mannered
3. Find adjectives for lists of nouns, such as the following:
   a. *Happy* song
   b. *Curving* sidewalk
   c. *Steep* hill
   d. *Swaying* trees
   d. *Lazy* dog
   f. *Polished* desk
4. Find words that a particular person or group would use often (for example, an astronaut, a tennis player, an automobile salesman, a fisherman, a pioneer going overland to California).
5. Before asking children to write stories, have them list words and phrases appropriate for particular settings.
   a. *Jungle:* humid, filtered sunlight, chattering, rotting leaves
   b. *Christmas:* holly, sooty chimney, tinkling bells, tinsel, symmetrical tree, bitter wind

---

22. Ruth Kearney Carlson, "Sparkling and Spinning Words," *Elementary English* 51 (January 1974): 15.

        c.   *Spring:* popping crocuses, delicate leaves, lashing rain, bursting blossoms

6.   Make lists of different kinds of words.
        a.   *Color:* chartreuse, amber, violet
        b.   *Quiet:* soft, tinkle, hush, whisper
        c.   *Noisy:* roar, bang, clatter, thunder
        d.   *Weather:* rainy, foggy, drizzle, humid, changeable

It is important to recognize that providing experiences or even building interest in words does not automatically result in vocabulary development. Teachers must also give direct, conscious attention to the meanings of words for particular uses.

MOTIVATION TO WRITE

Children cannot learn to write effectively, to improve their writing, unless the learning process involves their interests, their experiences, and their sense of satisfaction or value in writing. Certainly they will put words on paper, but often they will do only what they sense is necessary to "get by." They will not compose; they will not write from thought, from eagerness, or from desire unless the instructional program recognizes their individuality and motivates them to express themselves. In other words, writing derives from a need and a purpose that the child recognizes.

Stimulation of a Desire to Write

It is easy to stimulate normal children to write if there is an apparent, meaningful purpose for the writing. Children will write when they have something to say, when they feel that someone will read and appreciate or learn from what they have written, or when writing provides emotional and intellectual support. For instance, a child will write a report readily enough if others in the class need the information for a social studies project. Another child will gladly keep a record, and do it as effectively as possible, if someone will actually need it for future reference. Still another child will write a summary of a science experiment if he or she enjoyed working on it and knows that his or her parents will see it.

Teachers can prepare students for writing assignments by initiating oral discussions relating the assignment to the activities of the class. They can guide the discussion with questions like these: "Do we know everything we should about life in an Indian village before we show the fifth-graders about it?" "Should different children see what they can find out about Indian cooking, shelter, and ceremonies in the village?" "Judy, you visited the reservation at Tama last year; what do you remember about the ceremonies?" "Do you suppose you could write down what you remember and perhaps find others and prepare a report each of us could read?"

The key to teaching writing is purposeful communication. Sometimes it is necessary to convince children that they have as much to write about as they have to talk about. Through careful guidance and planning, a successful teacher helps them recognize the need. Consider, for example, the many types of writing that one child might do in a single day:

1. Record temperature and other weather conditions on a chart
2. Enter the plans for the day in the class log book
3. Label the spaces for various items in the storage cabinet
4. Take notes from reference books for a social studies report
5. Compose a party invitation to send to the adjoining classroom
6. Answer questions about a reading assignment
7. Outline the main ideas and related details of a science experiment
8. Make a bibliography of references used for a report
9. List the properties needed to dramatize a story the class read
10. Write questions for a bulletin board display
11. Make notes on homework assignments
12. Record new vocabulary words in a notebook
13. Write a description of a person whose identity others in the class will have to guess
14. Write a story based on a recently seen television program

Individualism in Writing

We have repeatedly stated that when children come to school they have a foundation for growth in using language. This foundation includes the ingredients essential for growth in written expression, namely, "a background of experiences, the ability to make associations and discriminations, a vocabulary through which either literally or metaphorically [they] can express a wide range of meanings, a knowledge of the syntax of the language, and the ability to use all of these in simple oral compositions. We as teachers must take [them] from there."[23]

The experiences of children differ as do their levels of maturity. We should not expect all children in a classroom to write about the same theme, to be motivated equally by external stimuli, or to exhibit the same behaviors as they write. According to Graves's research, there are generally two distinctive types of writers: *reactive* and *reflective*.[24] Children identified as reactive show erratic

---

23. Mary J. Tingle, "Teaching Composition in the Elementary School," *Elementary English* 47 (January 1970): 72.

24. See footnote 6 and Janet Emig, *The Composing Processes of Twelfth Graders* (Urbana, Ill.: National Council of Teachers of English, 1971).

problem-solving strategies in their composing: using overt language to accompany prewriting and writing, proofreading at the word unit level, rarely contemplating or reviewing their products, and showing no sense of audience. The reflective writers do little rehearsal before writing, use little overt language, periodically reread what they have written, and show a growing sense of audience. Graves indicates, however, that all children exhibit characteristics of both types in varying degrees and that they can emerge under different writing conditions.

Children's Internal Motivation

As we have suggested, children have "built-in" motivation to write. A recent research report identifies inherent "allies" to teaching as (1) self-competency, (2) modeling, (3) personal acceptance, and (4) peer status.[25]

Children want to feel competent at whatever they do. They want to write effectively, just as they want to play a game well. This is self-realization and all of us have it. But assignments that are too difficult or of the "everybody-has-to-do-it" type can destroy or submerge this motivating force. Teachers must foster this sense of self-realization by giving careful attention to each child's needs, abilities, and experiences.

Children also emulate models with whom they identify. In writing, the model may be an adult whom the child admires and who writes or it may be a literary one. Teachers who write and share their products with children can become important models. A teacher's behavior while writing (which should not differ markedly from that expected of and natural to the children) and the relevancy of the writing produced to the time, age, place, and culture of the class are indicative of his or her effectiveness as a model.

An example of the use of a literary model appears in the research report edited by Lundsteen.[26] The purpose of the assignment was to have a group of children describe a place in a way that would suggest a feeling. For a model, the children received a description of the interior of the barn from *Charlotte's Web* (Dell, 1967, p. 13). After a stilted attempt with some unfamiliar material, the children in the project selected their own classroom as the subject of the group composition and produced the following description based on their own experience:

> The school room was very large and old. It smelled of chalk dust and children's clothes. It often had a quiet smell—as if nothing bad could happen in school. It smelled of pencil lead, ink, paste, water-color paints, and crayons. Whenever it rain-

---

25. Sara W. Lundsteen, ed., *Help for the Teacher of Written Composition: New Directions in Research* (Urbana, Ill.: National Conference on Research in English and ERIC Clearinghouse on Reading and Communication Skills, 1976), p. 29.
    26. Ibid., p. 31.

ed or snowed, the wet coats and boots in the dressing room smelled like a skunk. When the children walked into the room, it smelled like potato chips, candy, nuts, and pumpkin seeds. Most of the time it smelled like smoke and dust. The dust came from the windows; the smoke came from the chimneys.

Related to the motivational element of self-realization is the fact that "children want to be respected, loved, understood, forgiven, and accepted as they are at the moment."[27] Acceptance, of course, is important in all aspects of the school curriculum. Teachers can readily communicate nonacceptance to children by being too critical and/or disinterested in their writing attempts.

Finally, children want to be liked and respected by their classmates. In writing, as in other aspects of the curriculum, a teacher needs to build attitudes that cause children to want to do well in the activity. Lacking such attitudes, children may seek peer approval through behavior contrary to what the teacher is seeking to develop.

BASIC TEACHING RESPONSIBILITIES

The greatest impetus for children's writing comes from classroom conditions that foster openness, thinking, freedom of expression, and opportunities to have and react to many new experiences. But a teacher has many additional responsibilities to fulfill in order to develop fully each child's potential as a writer. In this section, we will discuss the basic areas requiring special teaching effort; later in this chapter and in subsequent chapters we will consider others.

The Classroom Environment

Before discussing particular procedures, we must consider the environment in which the children function daily. The measure of opportunities for writing, showing creativity, and thinking depends on the atmosphere in the classroom. Teachers should make every effort to see that each child feels relaxed, takes an interest in the activities, and finds acceptance as an important member of the group. Therefore the classroom climate should respect each child's personality, including idiosyncracies that might impede adjustment to the school and to other children. It must also be a climate that recognizes and respects the effects on a child of the environment outside school.

Some instructional programs schedule writing, particularly "creative writing," on Friday afternoon! If this is "the time," the classroom climate is likely to be directed toward "everything in its place" rather than upon the factors necessary for effective writing. Thus, the most important ingredient in classroom

---

27. Lundsteen, p. 32.

environment is the teacher. The values, the attitudes, the way the teacher operates (in other words, the personality of the teacher) largely determine how free a child feels to write imaginatively, to express knowledge and feelings, to try something new, and to seek help in organizing thoughts and using words.

As suggested earlier, other personnel in the school contribute to the environment, and so do physical materials in the classroom. Little creative stimulation comes from a classroom that does not have many shelves of colorful and interesting books. Dynamic and thought-provoking wall decorations and displays, an abundance of materials for science and social studies, attractive furnishings, and other lively and decorative touches all noticeably help to make the classroom a stimulating place. A classroom environment that is attractive to the adult eye, however, will not necessarily draw forth a child's expression. Children are highly sensitive to sham or pretense. In an air of honest freedom children will sense willingness and encouragement to participate. They must feel that they have a share in designing the physical environment. They must feel that the classroom is theirs.

Planning and Guiding

Whether or not we have said so explicitly, one major reason that children's writing may not be as effective and satisfying as the teacher or the children themselves desire is that they receive too little direction and guidance before, during, and after writing. Another reason is that they frequently lack knowledge about various forms of writing (see Chapter 14). These explanations, together with discouragement of oral expression, too little time for thought, and meager vocabulary, are supportable by research evidence and the opinions of observers.[28]

Writing activities require preplanning. The environmental setting reflects planning, but beyond that, teachers must set objectives for individual children. Applegate says that "most of the stimulation of our three-dimensional classrooms is lost without special direction before the writing starts."[29] Ullyette calls attention to the necessity to plan a daily writing time, space for a child to write undisturbed, and the availability of materials.[30] According to these and other writers, teacher guidance, praise, and constructive criticism are crucial to writing development. One curriculum guide states, "Opening the way to creative writing is not enough. The teacher must respond to the children's work with encouragement, sincere appreciation, and inspiration."[31] Another says, "Without help in thought organization, without help in recognizing an appropriate vocabulary

28. Lester S. Golub, "How American Children Learn to Write," *The Elementary School Journal* 74 (January 1974): 237–47.

29. Mauree Applegate, "After All, Mrs. Murphy—," in *When Children Write*, edited by Constance Carr (Washington Association for Childhood Education International, 1955), p. 25.

30. Ullyette, p. 14.

31. *Creative Writing*, Curriculum Bulletins 33–36s (Indianapolis Public Schools, 1965), p. 46.

range, even the child who wants to write can be truly lost and wandering among the countless possibilities and immensities of the English language, and will perhaps not have the satisfaction of crystallizing his thoughts for clear expression."[32]

The following is an account of the preparation for a writing activity in a fourth-grade classroom. It suggests the planning that has occurred and illustrates the prewriting discussion, attention to individual words, thought organization, and encouragement of creativity.

1. The group was shown a picture of a costumed girl, standing next to a white picket fence and holding a jack-o-lantern lit by a candle. The picture was mounted on a piece of tag board with these questions written under it:

    What time of the year is it?
    What is the girl going to do?
    Have you ever seen a jack-o-lantern like this?
    What do you suppose this girl's name is?
    If we could look down the street, what else might we see?

2. This was followed by asking other questions about what might be heard on Halloween, what might be smelled, how people feel, what they say and do, and so on. As these were answered and, as the discussion continued, the teacher began listing words and expressions on the board.

3. The teacher then asked the children if they could classify the words and expressions that were written. After further discussion the children decided on the classification as shown below.

What we hear	What we see	What we smell	What we taste	What we feel
laughter	goblins	candy	candy	scared
strange noise	orange pumpkins	apples	apples	funny
shouts	spooks	burning leaves	cookies	cold air
happy talking	blinking lights	candles burning	cider	leaves falling
footsteps running	leaves		licorice	happy
	shadows			
	other children			

32. Oregon ASCD *Curriculum Bulletin*, no. 318 (Salem, Ore.: Oregon Association for Supervision and Curriculum Development, August 1973), p. 2.

4. The teacher then suggested that each child try to add other words and to think of adjectives, adverbs, and verbs to accompany the words on the chart (not referring to the parts of speech by names, however, but only by examples such as *buoyant* shouts, running *haltingly*, *glimpsed* a flitting shadow).

5. Finally the teacher suggested that the children write stories about Halloween, making them as vivid and realistic to a reader as possible, and perhaps writing of imagined experiences rather than relating in detail things that had happened to them on Halloween.

Of course, this procedure may produce some stories containing only words listed by the group or based on suggestions made by other children during the discussion. Such behavior rarely persists, however, for most children quickly gain the confidence and skills to improvise. They will eventually write stories that are truly their own. The goal of this kind of teacher guidance is to motivate pupils and to teach them to think before writing. With adequate and continuous input, this procedure stimulates writing on countless topics; and it is especially useful early in the school year.

Preliminary Class Discussions

Probably the greatest deterrent to creative, communicative expression that pleases pupils and teachers is writing without adequate preparation. Premature efforts could reflect insufficient planning by the teacher, the children, or both. Suggesting and providing the opportunity to write a report, a story, or a poem without also discussing the information the children have, their thinking and feelings, the possibilities for organization and form, and similar concerns will not bring forth their best thinking or writing.

Talking about writing means discussing pertinent ideas immediately preceding a writing assignment—the sounds a train makes, how people feel during a fog, possible explanations for the fact that the baby in a picture is crying, what the sky looks like just before a thunderstorm—but it also means discussing new ideas daily, discouraging the use of vague words, listening and reacting to sounds, providing both free and planned talking situations. Above all, it means taking the time to really talk, to actually exchange thoughts, and to pursue ideas in some depth.

Sensitivity to Words

Talking with the class will lead to the introduction of new words, new meanings, differences in pronunciation, and appropriate word usage. It will lead to writing words on the board, to talking about them, to using the dictionary. Children enjoy words that rhyme, new words, and words that are particularly expressive. They like to "collect" words for bulletin boards, for notebooks, or for use in writing assignments. For instance, when a group of third graders encountered the word "dashed" in a story, the teacher seized the opportunity to discuss words that "can tell about how people moved." The children suggested the following and with some success dramatized their meanings: *skipped, darted, scampered, trotted, limped, charged.* The teacher added *leaped, glided, slid, coasted,* and *ambled,* and the class discussed them as well.

Another teacher, who taught a fifth-grade class, took advantage of a similar situation to teach word meaning and appreciation of the language. The children had read the expression "at the foot of the hill" in a social studies text, and although they generally understood the meaning, one child mentioned that the names of parts of the body are often used in descriptions. This comment led to a discussion of figurative language and these expressions:

face of the cliff	brow of the hill	arm of the law
eye of the storm	heart of America	leg of the journey

Similar discussions might focus on relationship words, such as *over, above, near, among, down;* judgment words, such as *cold, bad, beautiful, best, deep, good, great;* indefinite words, such as *few, many, any, some, several;* and definite words, such as *all, always, certain, every,* and *sure.*

The more able children tend to find figures of speech fascinating. Simile, metaphor, onomatopoeia, alliteration, personification, and imagery all have tremendous appeal. Even young children like to attempt to spell words that imitate the sounds they describe (onomatopoeia)—(e.g., *buzz, hiss, boom,* and *clang*). Children may experiment with such words by sounding the noises of a dentist's drill, the wind rustling through leaves on a tree, a horse's trot, radio static, and the like.[33]

Until high school, teachers often ignore alliteration. Given explanation and encouragement, however, younger students will write such combinations as:[34]

A butterfly can fly, flap, flutter, flop, flitter, flick, float, flip-flop, and floop in a loop.

Words in patterns also make interesting word-play activity.[35]

Drippity, drippity, drippity—
—Plop
Drippity, drippity, drippity—
—Plop
Drippity, drippity, drippity—
—Plop
That's the song of a
DROP

---

33. Dorothy Grant Hennings and Barbara M. Grant, *Content and Craft, Written Expression in the Elementary School* (Englewood Cliffs, N.J.: Prentice-Hall, 1973), p. 175.

34. Walter T. Petty and Mary Bowen Hall, *Slithery Snakes and Other Aids to Children's Writing* (New York: Appleton-Century-Crofts, 1967), p. 68.

35. Hennings and Grant, *Written Expression in the Language Arts,* 2d ed. (New York: Teachers College Press, in press), p. 176. Used by permission of the authors.

Teachers can develop knowledge of words and sensitivity to their use in many ways, including the following:

1. Notice and bring to the classroom colorful phrases and apt words, such as *walking in the moss-silenced forest, a car snarling away from a curb,* and *the wind churning and ladling the snow.*
2. Have the pupils try defining common objects, such as *a window, a ball,* and *a piece of chalk.*
3. Put etymology "teasers" on the board. Some to try are: Which is more, a million or a myriad? Who were the first glamour girls? How are a dentist and a dandelion alike? What is the relationship of noise, an upset stomach, and a ship?
4. Have discussions about the appropriateness of terms for different circumstances. For example, when would a person hop? Crawl? Skip?[36]
5. On the bulletin board illustrate word families (*port, portage, portable, import,* etc.), words for particular days (February 14—*heart, heartache, hearten, heartily, heartsick,* etc.) words with prefixes (*uninterrupted, reread*) or suffixes (*invitingly, stubbornness*).
6. Take trips for the sole purpose of "collecting" words, or have pupils bring to class words heard on TV, on the school bus, or at a shopping center.
7. Interest the children in foreign words that have come into our language with little or no change in spelling and meaning (*sombrero, chocolate, opera, petite,* etc.).

Literature-based Experiences

Certainly a teacher should provide many types of literary experiences for children, including reading aloud and telling stories, having children orally read and tell stories, and, of course, fostering their personal reading. Not all reading will lead to talking and writing, but particular kinds of expression demand that the speaker or writer have read or heard expression of the same kind. In other words, if children are to write "tall tales," they should have heard or read many, just as writing poetry requires a background in poetry and the ability to write a description comes from having heard or read good descriptions.

Although literary experiences alone may inspire some children to write, most children need the teacher's guidance. Specific assignments can help to meet this need, but other types of guidance are also necessary. One author suggests that:[37]

---

36. *A Curriculum in Written Composition, K–3* (English Curriculum Study Center, University of Georgia, 1968), p. 39.
37. Jean M. Ullyette, *Guidelines for Creative Writing* (Dansville, N.Y.: Instructor Publications, 1968), p. 8.

Pupils in primary and middle grades can learn much by noticing how the authors of their favorite books start and end stories. Older children should begin to notice how authors develop plots and build characters. Read parts of stories aloud, and help the children discuss techniques used by the author to catch and hold the reader's interest. Here are some methods for beginning stories.

Describe the time, place, or circumstances affecting the story to be unfolded.
Begin with questions to be answered later.
Describe the main characters through conversation or action.
Tell some incident or action related to the present or past, and then weave the story forward or back as required.

Another teaching guide focuses on individual variation in expression and suggests that after reading *The Bears on Hemlock Mountain* children might try one of several types of writing:[38]

1. Newspaper account of Jonathan's experience
2. Letter written by Jonathan to Aunt Emma (Jonathan tries to avoid frightening her)
3. Letter written by Jonathan to Uncle James (Jonathan might brag)
4. New chapter told in third person
5. Expository writing with research on pioneer days
6. Imaginative writing (another adventure of Jonathan)
7. Descriptive writing (how Jonathan viewed the mountain in the morning)

Beginning Expression

Teachers should not hesitate to begin writing activities because the children lack experience with various forms of writing. Writing begets more writing. Get children writing and build upon that foundation.

This section contains ideas for stimulating children's written expression. Most aim to encourage imaginative thinking, but some should foster the writing of descriptions, letters, reports, and so on (all of which Chapter 14 discusses further).

Group expression.   In previous chapters of this book, we described the role of cooperatively written statements and stories in developing children's language skills. Captions for pictures, signs on science collections, memoranda, greetings for cards, letters to be sent home, and experience stories of many types are some of the projects already suggested for group expression with the teacher as the

---

38. *Language Arts, Grades 3, 4, and 5* (Wilmette Public Schools, District 39, Wilmette, Ill., May 1970), p. 11.

scribe. Primarily, however, the context in which these suggestions were made has been the development of writing prior to learning to spell and write. Group composition need not be limited to fulfilling this need, for the group writing of a story, a poem, a summary, or a description is appropriate at any elementary grade level and, in fact, is a desirable prelude to individual creative expression.

One fifth-grade teacher made it a group project to describe the class hamster. Small groups of students each contributed a descriptive sentence, which the teacher wrote on a transparency. Occasionally the teacher asked questions to clarify sentence construction. After all the sentences had been written, the children discussed whether they were in the most desirable order and what changes should be made. They decided to alter the sequence slightly and also made minor changes in wording. Then the teacher put the description on a chart and the class discussed why it was a good description. This composition was appropriate for the particular group of children at the time, but in general, group compositions should strive to convey pupil feeling and personal reactions rather than factual content. Of course, a description requires facts, but had the children composed a story about what the hamster thought of various happenings, personal feeling and imagination would have flowed into their sentences.

In addition to being a desirable procedure for initiating creative expression, group composition has particular advantages for teaching some skills and attitudes. For example, it impresses on children the value of thinking about an idea before putting it in writing. Also, the talking that the group does before agreeing upon the best sentence shows the value of discussion. Another advantage of group composition is that it allows teachers to show that a writer can correct or improve spelling, margins, and illegible handwriting after completing the original draft. If the teacher makes such corrections naturally, students will learn that it is an integral part of the writing process. This is the time to show that proofreading for mechanical errors alone is insufficient; emphasis on group reading for organization, appeal, clarity, and so on illustrates another natural and regular part of all writing. It is also less threatening to criticize typical faults in expression without having to direct this criticism at particular pupils and their personal efforts.

During group composition teachers can present models for various kinds of writing products without specifically identifying them as models or instructing students to regard group products as models. The teacher may also use group effort to show children that it is permissible to use some words or expressions that they may have hesitated to use and that expression should show feelings and thoughts without pretense and unrealistic language forms.

Writing topics.   The way that teachers most commonly try to encourage children to write with imagination and personal involvement is simply to assign a topic. Quite often this procedure is the *least* successful means of motivating good writing, in part because not all pupils are likely to be interested in the same topic and assigned topics rarely stimulate the pupils' thinking. A good topic is one that does not constrain; one that children can easily relate to what they know. The following topics illustrate the countless number suggested in the professional literature:

- Looking Down from a Skyscraper
- The Robot Who Cried
- The Biggest Boy on Our Block
- What Robins Say to Sparrows
- Getting up Early in the Morning
- My Sister's Boyfriend (Brother's Girlfriend)
- When I was a Jack-o'-lantern
- Walking Barefoot in the Mud
- My Life as a Dollar Bill
- Billy Learns to Ski
- The Biggest Fish in the Bowl
- Around the World in Eighty Days
- A Runaway Raft
- A Rendezvous in Space
- Between the Goal Posts
- Substitute Teachers
- The Life of an Apple Seed
- Soup Again?
- How I Slipped and Fell
- A Bulldozer on a Rampage
- The Way I Feel First Thing in the Morning

It is a good idea to list topics on the board or on a chart where they will be available to the children. Also, keeping topics in a card file or in folders with accompanying pictures is useful. Children frequently like to add their suggestions to the list.

Composition frameworks.   A method of inspiring writing that is similar to topic suggestion is to provide a setting, or framework, from which the children can develop a title and composition. The following are examples of settings:

1.   You are a large oak tree on the corner of the school grounds. You have been standing there for many years—since before the school was built. Write about some of the things you have seen and heard.
2.   You are among a group of people going overland by covered wagons to California in the 1850s. Write about what happened on one day of the trip.
3.   You have just received a message from a friend telling you that you can have half interest in his motorcycle.
4.   You heard on television that someone reported seeing a creature with three wings. No pictures were available. What do you suppose it looked like?

5.   What does the name Winslow Treadwell or Neville Shurtliff make you think of? Can you write a story about one of these characters?[39]

6.   You wake up suddenly in the middle of the night. Everything is quiet except for a distant honking, honking of an automobile horn. Describe what you think about.

7.   The puppy ran outside when the garage door was opened. He ran down the street. What do you suppose his adventures were?

8.   There were five people at the table, but places had been set for six. No one said a word about the extra plate, but a knock at the door caused all five to look up. Then they heard running. What do you think happened next?

9.   Christmas is a time for fun, for giving and receiving presents, for secrets and crunching snow. It is a time for the sight of a glittering tree and the smell of mince pies and turkey. Write a Christmas story that will really make us think it is Christmas. Try to do it by describing sights, sounds, smells, and tastes.

Story beginnings.   Children may enjoy making up stories from appealing beginnings. One way to start stories is to ask a group to invent an opening and allow each child to finish the story any way he or she wants. Often magazines for teachers and children's magazines contain story beginnings that the teacher may modify for maturity levels. And teachers, of course, can invent story beginnings themselves. The ones that follow have been used with children and illustrate beginnings of different lengths.

1.   The lamp on the table wobbled as the door slammed. It continued to wobble as Sue dashed across the room.

2.   At the back of the yard a large black and white cat crept carefully along the top of the fence.

3.   I could hear the sound of water. It was louder than the gentle rushing sound of the stream as it poured over the rocks; it sounded like a waterfall. "But there is no waterfall here," I thought. "What could it be?" I looked carefully upstream and started threading my way through the hanging branches and the tall grass.

4.   The air was crisp and cold, the sky pale, and even Mr. Smith didn't seem to be awake. Shivering and yawning, I looked down the street. I spied Bill hurrying round the corner with his hands jammed deep into his pockets. Under one arm was his pole and under the other was a crumpled paper sack. I put my sack down and started around the house to the garage.

5.   The fire had raged all night. The announcer on TV said that it was

---

39. Adapted from R. E. Myers and E. Paul Torrance, *Invitations to Thinking and Doing* (Boston: Ginn and Co., 1964), p. 39.

spreading to the east. One picture showed animals running—a fox, rabbits, chipmunks and squirrels, and even a deer. I knew that Pokey could run fast, but he was so friendly he might not start running in time. With the fire moving east there wasn't any reason to worry anyway.

6. Jim just stood there. His legs refused to move. Sweat broke out on his forehead.

7. Tracy and Beth burst into the classroom. Together they shouted . . .

8. "This one may throw you, Jerry," the old man said as he handed over the reins of the pinto.

9. We could smell the dinner cooking. Michael was setting the table. It was a pleasant time of day. What was keeping Rosemary? It was time to eat.

10. Usually we have fun at Grandmother's. We go to the park and see all the animals. We play with the toys from the attic. We have good things to eat, especially cookies and candy that Grandmother makes. This time, though, I knew things would be different.

As Mary and I got off the bus, Grandfather came hurrying up as always but he didn't pick Mary or me up and swing us about as he usually did. He wasn't even smiling. He kissed us and then said, "Children, your grandmother is in the hospital. She isn't seriously ill but she'll have to stay there several weeks. I don't know how we'll get along without her."

11. I pounded and pounded but the door wouldn't open.

12. The wagon master gave the signal and the wagons began circling. I rode faster trying to keep up. Then I heard shooting and the men began to shout.

13. There was a slight flutter as the ship settled. Peering through the thick glass, the captain ordered the ladder lowered. This was it! Who would be the first down? Since I was only in the fifth grade, I hoped it would be me. I held my breath waiting for the captain's next words. I looked at Dick. He was watching the captain, too.

Stories about objects, pictures, situations. Showing children a picture and suggesting that they write a story about it is a common teaching practice. It may yield writing, but it has the disadvantage, as do some of the suggestions in the preceding sections, of causing children to look outside of themselves for things to write about rather than to think about their own experiences and to recognize story topics in their everyday activities. The key to overcoming this disadvantage is to relate the picture, the object, the framework or situation, or the story beginning to the children's experiences by extensive oral presentation.

Not all people have the same reaction to an object or a picture or to participating in an activity, such as a field trip. Creativity would not be possible if they did. What children write about a picture or an object or some experience need not be related specifically to the subject used to stimulate writing. What each child produces will reflect his or her own personality, ideas, and experience.

Teachers can use objects in several ways to inspire written expression. Showing a picture to a group is one of them. Another example, which comes from a curriculum guide suggests showing children different pictures of a football game and asking them what is happening in each picture.[40] The views recommended are:

- An aerial view of the location
- An aerial view of the stadium
- A view of one of the goalposts
- A view of the referee signaling a touchdown

Children should have the opportunity to think and talk about a picture before writing about it. For example, they should describe what is happening in the picture, characterize the people in it, decide what events might have led up to the scene, suggest ways to express the feelings and actions it conveys, and list words that might be good to use in writing about it.

Additional ideas.   Among the additional resources a teacher can use to initiate creative expression are these:

1. Objects can be as varied as a bent shovel, a battered suitcase, an oddly shaped rock, a kite, a ragged shirt, two left shoes, an old school textbook, an alarm clock, and so on.
2. Pictures can be varied, but they should evoke feelings. Pictures of animals and people are the most desirable, especially if they show action or expression.
3. A field trip or other situation is an appropriate source of topics. Talking about the sounds heard on the trip will be more successful than talking about the entire trip and will usually stimulate more personal expression.
4. Films and filmstrips arouse pupils' interest and foster thought. Showing a film without the sound, for instance, will bring forth many ideas. Running only part of a film is a good way to stimulate interest in writing about what happens next.
5. A newspaper story can become the basis for retelling, for writing a letter to someone mentioned in the story, for writing a "follow-up" or for remaking into an imaginative news story of local interest.
6. To bring the senses into expression, present to the class pickles, different cloth textures, objects hidden from sight in a bag, flowers and spices that have different odors, and so on.

---

40. *Language Arts*, p. 11.

Commercial materials.   The concern for fostering children's creativity has led to the development of many commercial materials. Generally, these materials incorporate the methods suggested in this chapter, although they rely much more on instantaneous, unaided stimulation of thought and imagination than we advocate. Photographs, drawings, filmstrips, films, tapes, objects, and reading materials all are available commercially. The newer materials usually include more than one type. The quantity of these materials and the widespread advertising by their producers make it unnecessary to list examples here. We do want to emphasize, though, that although commercial materials may be useful to teachers, particularly as time-savers, they are only teaching aids. Using them successfully depends on a rich language and experience base. And it requires that teachers have clearly in mind what they hope to accomplish with them, know the capabilities of the children in their classes and provide for the inevitable differences, and know how to supplement the materials and follow up the gains they effect in children's writing.

MORE TEACHING PROCEDURES

Teachers need to set aside time to help children to construct clear and varied sentences. This is often a neglected part of the teaching of writing. Of course, many of the teaching practices discussed in Chapter 10 apply here, but it is appropriate to discuss these procedures specifically as they relate to writing.

Growth in Sentence Structure

Differences in the structure of sentences written by elementary school children and those written by secondary school students are obvious. Teachers and other adults would say that the older students' writing shows more "maturity." Research, primarily studies based on Hunt's work, support this observation.[41] Hunt examined 1000-word samples of writing by students in grades 4, 8, and 12 and the writing of adults who published in *The Atlantic* and *Harpers*. To measure maturity, he introduced the "T-unit," a "main clause plus any subordinated clause or nonclausal structure that is attached to or embedded in it."[42] He found that there was a developmental progression and that the best index of syntactic maturity is T-unit length. The second best is clause length; third best is clauses per T-unit.

---

41. Kellog W. Hunt, *Grammatical Structures Written at Three Grade Levels* (Urbana, Ill.: National Council of Teachers of English, 1965). See also Roy C. O'Donnell, W. J. Griffin, and R. C. Norris, *Syntax of Kindergarten and Elementary School Children: A Transformation Analysis* (Urbana, Ill.: National Council of Teachers of English, 1967).

42. Frank O'Hare, *Sentence Combining: Improving Student Writing Without Formal Grammar Instruction* (Urbana, Ill.: National Council of Teachers of English, 1973), p. 21.

Subsequent research focused on the rate of syntactic growth.[43] Essentially, researchers sought to promote syntactic growth through sentence-combining "problems." They provided children with a series of exercise materials, each of which illustrated a sentence-combining technique and followed with practice activities using that technique. This research showed that students who worked through the exercises wrote significantly more and longer clauses than did their counterparts who did not do the exercises. Furthermore, the students who completed the sentence-combining activities seemed to write compositions "that were significantly better in over-all quality."[44]

Sentence-combining research has involved mostly students in high school or the upper grades (e.g., O'Hare used seventh graders). Extensive use of sentence-combining exercises, particularly in the elementary school, may make the instruction program more formal and the content less relevant to the interests and activities of children than is necessary to successfully teach children to write more mature and varied sentences (see Chapter 10).

Sentence-combining Activities

The following exercises illustrate sentence-combining:[45]

> A.   One day a girl walked into the cafeteria.
> B.   The girl was little.
>   Combined: One day a little girl walked into the cafeteria.

> A.   Alex was lonely.
> B.   Alex was hungry.
> C.   Alex was tired.
>   Combined: Alex was lonely, hungry, and tired.

Sentences can get progressively more complex.

> A.   The gas station attendant stumbled out of his shack.
> B.   He was an emaciated-looking fellow.
> C.   He had white hair and skin the color of an old saddle.
> D.   He stood scowling at us.
> E.   His chin was thrust forward.
> F.   His eyes were blazing.
>   Combined: The gas station attendant, an emaciated-looking fellow with white hair and skin the color of an old saddle, stumbled out of his shack and stood scowling at us, with his chin thrust forward, his eyes blazing.

---

43. Ibid., p. 35. The principal study in this area of research is O'Hare's, but others have obtained the same results with slightly different methods. For example, see Warren E. Combs, "Sentence-combining Practice: Do Gains in Judgments of Writing 'Quality' Persist?" *Journal of Educational Research* 70 (July–August 1977): 318–21.

44. O'Hare, p. 68.

45. Thomas D. Horn and Elaine Fowler, "Written Language—Skills Are Important," *Instructor* 58 (February, 1974): 51. Copyright © February 1974 by The Instructor Publications, Inc., used by permission.

Sentence-combining lessons might be something like this:

Can you write these two sentences as one sentence? Use the word *and*.

- Claire wanted a kitten.
- Shirley wanted a hamster.

Did you remember to use a comma?
Check your sentence by looking at the model below. It shows how two simple sentences can be combined.

- The turtle walked slowly.
- The rabbit raced past him.
- The turtle walked slowly, and the rabbit raced past him.

Use this model to combine these pairs of sentences.

1. The fox fell into the well.
   The goat jumped into the well.
2. The dog was hungry.
   The cat wanted to play.
3. One chair was large.
   Another chair reclined.

Compare the sentences you wrote with those written by classmates. Did you remember punctuation?

To go beyond the drill-like approach, however, provision should be made for children to depart from the model-following pattern.

There are other ways to use *and* in combining sentences. Combine these two sentences.

- The skunk fought the terrier.
- The porcupine fought the terrier.

Did you combine them this way?

- The skunk and the porcupine fought the terrier.

Or, maybe you added another word besides *and*.

- Both the skunk and the porcupine fought the terrier.

Can you think of other ways to combine the sentences? You can change words or the way they are arranged but don't change the meaning.

Sentence-building activities also should include exercises that focus on changing meaning, usually by extending it or making it more precise. For example, ask the children to describe what they "see" or what comes to mind when they hear or see this sentence: "The dog ran along the fence." Ask what kind of dog it was, what kind of fence it was, where the fence was, and whether the dog was running fast. Ask the children to write a sentence that conveys the images brought to mind specifically and clearly. One child might write, "The Labrador ran along the red-wood fence." Another might write, "A large spotted mongrel paced back and forth along the picket fence." You can extend this process by having the children rearrange the words in the sentence: "Pacing along a picket fence was a large, spotted mongrel" or "The mongrel, large and spotted, paced along the fence."

The context of all sentence-building activities should be classroom activities and the children's interests. Consequently, teachers must devise them themselves. These activities stem from the notion that power in written expression grows from active manipulation of language rather than from studying about language as an abstract system.

EXERCISES FOR THOUGHT AND ACTION

1.   Select a writing topic, framework, or story beginning from this chapter and write a plan adapting it for use with a group of children at a particular grade level.

2.   Observe the behavior of two children of the same age while they are writing. Contrast the processes they employ and the results. Compare your observations with the research reports described in this chapter.

3.   Examine the following passages.[46] Which was written by a fourth grader? An eighth grader? A twelfth grader? Why did you decide as you did?

> I had to take my little brother to a haunted house last night. It was dumb, but he got scared by this phony flying bat and some sheet that was supposed to be a ghost. Then there was this ugly old woman who called herself a witch. She was standing over this pot mumbling junk and stirring some soup stuff.

> I went into a haunted house that was so far out you had to see it to believe it! As soon as I got inside, a screeching bat came flying out at me. And a ghost came up out of the floor—like real—and scared the daylights out of me! Then there was a crazy lady in the corner, a witch I'm sure, stirring some bubbly goo in a great huge pot. It was all just too much for your mind!

---

46. Perron, p. 652.

I visited a house and it was haunted and I saw a bat and it was
—— flying and a ghost and I saw a witch and her pot.

4. Write something yourself—a report, essay, or description of a person
    or object and make notes about the steps you follow and the order in
    which you do them throughout the writing process—prewriting,
    writing, and postwriting stages. What did you learn about the task of
    writing? How will your awareness affect the way you teach writing to
    children?
5. Develop a file of topics, statements, and ideas that might stimulate
    children to write. Make the file one that children can use indepen-
    dently of a teacher's guidance.
6. Write a letter to the editor stating your position on whether the
    writing skills of America's children are declining.
7. Design a group-writing experience based on the children's book of
    your choice.
8. Find out how other textbook authors define creative writing. Do they
    distinguish between the "practical" and the "creative"? How and
    why? Do you believe any writing can be "uncreative?"
9. Begin a file of pictures that might be useful in motivating writing. Be
    sure to include some action pictures, pictures of single individuals or
    objects, pictures that convey mood, and so on. For each of the pic-
    tures, jot down a list of questions that would be appropriate for discus-
    sion prior to writing. Make a list of writing topics suggested by the
    pictures.
10. Collect quotations from various writers on the issue of "content and
    correctness."
11. Survey a classroom as objectively as possible to determine the degree of
    freedom of expression fostered by the environment. Do children's ideas
    abound or have they been suppressed? Is the classroom primarily the
    teacher's rather than that of the teacher and the children?
12. Make a list of factors that could cause children not to write as well as
    most teachers and parents hope. You might think about specific class-
    rooms and groups of children as well as influences discussed in this
    chapter as you make your list.
13. This story (source unknown) is entitled "The Chicken." Read it and
    decide whether it is well written. Study it and then rewrite it in a bet-
    ter way. What major changes did you make? Don't leave out any im-
    portant parts.

A man lived in a farmhouse. He was old. He lived alone. The house was small. The
house was on a mountain. The mountain was high. The house was on the top. He
grew vegetables. He grew grain. He ate the vegetables. He ate the grain. One day he
was pulling weeds. He saw something. A chicken was eating his grain. The grain was
new. He caught the chicken. He put her in a pen. The pen was under his window. He

planned something. He would eat the chicken for breakfast. The next morning came. It was early. A sound woke the man. He looked out the window. He saw the chicken. He saw an egg. The chicken cackled. The man thought something. He would eat the egg for breakfast. He fed the chicken a cup of his grain. The chicken talked to him. He talked to the chicken. Time passed. He thought something. He could feed the chicken more. He could feed her two cups of grain. He could feed her in the morning. He could feed her at night. Maybe she would lay two eggs every morning. He fed the chicken more grain. She got fat. She got lazy. She slept all the time. She laid no eggs. The man got angry. He blamed the chicken. He killed her. He ate her for breakfast. He had no chicken. He had no eggs. He talked to no one. No one talked to him.

SELECTED REFERENCES

Applegate, Mauree. *Freeing Children to Write*. New York: Harper and Row, 1963.

Burrows, Alvina Treut, et al. *They All Want to Write*, 3rd ed. New York: Holt, Rinehart and Winston, 1964.

Carlson, Ruth Kearney. *Sparkling Words: Two Hundred and Twenty-five Practical and Creative Writing Ideas*. Geneva, Ill.: Paladin House, 1973.

Hennings, Dorothy Grant. *Words, Sounds and Thoughts*. New York: Citation Press/Scholastic, 1977.

Hennings, Dorothy Grant, and Grant, Barbara M. *Content and Craft*. Englewood Cliffs, N.J.: Prentice-Hall, 1973.

King, Martha L.; Emans, Robert; and Cianciolo, Patricia J., eds. *The Language Arts in the Elementary School: A Forum for Focus*. Urbana, Ill.: National Council of Teachers of English, 1973.

Lundsteen, Sara W., ed. *Help for the Teacher of Written Composition: New Directions in Research*. Urbana, Ill.: National Conference on Research in English/ERIC Clearinghouse on Reading and Communication Skills, 1978.

McPherson, Elisabeth. "Composition," in *The Teaching of English*, pt. I, edited by James R. Squire. Chicago: National Society for the Study of Education, 1977.

Mellon, John C. *National Assessment and the Teaching of English*. Urbana, Ill.: National Council of Teachers of English, 1975.

Petty, Walter T., and Bowen, Mary. *Slithery Snakes and Other Aids to Children's Writing*. New York: Appleton-Century-Crofts, 1967.

Petty, Walter T., and Finn, Patrick J., eds. *The Writing Processes of Students*. Buffalo: State University of New York, 1975.

Trauger, Wilmer K. *Language Arts in Elementary Schools*. New York: McGraw-Hill Book Co., 1963.

Ullyette, Jean M. *Guidelines for Creative Writing*. Dansville, N.Y.: Instructor Publications, 1968.

14

Fostering Growth in Writing

The ability to write is not a gift, it is a skill.—Donald M. Murray, A Writer Teaches Writing

Learning to write effectively takes time, encouragement, and teaching. In Chapter 13 we discussed what children do when they write, as well as the teachers' responsibility for providing a congenial classroom environment, planning, providing experiences, and getting writing started, and gave specific suggestions for improving sentences. In this chapter we will make additional teaching suggestions, discuss types of writing, discuss mechanics and conventions, and suggest evaluation techniques.

TEACHERS AND CHILDREN—AND WRITING

An effective writing program hinges on the rapport between the teacher and the children that causes all to have enthusiasm for writing. Developing the rapport and enthusiasm is largely the responsibility of the teacher and essentially calls for the teacher to participate actively in the program rather than merely assign writing, monitor to be sure that each child does his or her own work, and mark papers. Murray has identified seven skills that he believes a writing teacher must have in order to participate most effectively.[1] A successful writing teacher, in Murray's view, listens, coaches, diagnoses, displays flexibility, writes with students, hones creativity with discipline, and keeps at a distance from the process. He stresses the need to be understanding but argues that it is necessary also to have standards, to be sincere and honest, and to get out from behind a desk and face students individually—"to be encouraging to one and discouraging to another, to lead one student, drive another, support a third."[2] He writes about the need to spot the most critical problem in each student's writing and to address it instructionally. In addition, some teachers may resist the idea of writing themselves, but they must do it to show students that they, too, have trouble writing, that they struggle with organization and word choice, and that they might not know how to spell a word they want to use.

Skills like the ones Murray describes also are identified by other writers. For example, a long-time leader in the field of teaching children to write, Alvina Treut Burrows, stresses "points" that teachers should observe.[3] In stating these points, she emphasizes that they derive both from research and from the beliefs of nationally known leaders in language arts teaching. Paraphrased, they are:

1. Written composition should develop out of much and varied oral expression.
2. A stimulating environment is necessary to inspire thinking and creativity.
3. Motivation to communicate comes from within.
4. Children's literature can contribute greatly to children's development in writing and speaking.
5. Different audiences help to shape the style and content of writing.
6. Children's writing efforts will be more successful if they receive positive feedback.
7. First drafts of the writing attempts of adults or children are messy and contain errors.
8. It is better to guide children's writing improvement by having them read it aloud rather than having it corrected.
9. Development in writing occurs in irregular spurts.
10. Developing powers of observation is essential to the writing process.[4]
11. In supportive environments, children develop individual styles and creativity in writing as they mature.

---

1. Donald M. Murray, *A Writer Teaches Writing: A Practical Method of Teaching Composition*. Boston: Houghton Mifflin Co., 1968, pp. 15–25.

2. Ibid., p. 17.

3. Alvina Treut Burrows, "Research into Practice," in *Help for the Teacher of Written Composition: New Directions in Research*, edited by Sara W. Lundsteen (Urbana, Ill.: National Conference on Research in English/ERIC Clearinghouse on Reading and Communication Skills, 1976), pp. 1–6.

4. See George Hillocks, Jr., *Observing and Writing* (Urbana, Ill.: National Council of Teachers of English, 1975).

12. The substance of composition comes from a child's creative problem-solving ability.

Closely related, supplementary guidelines (some of which reemphasize discussion in Chapter 13) derive from the same research findings and reflect the same point of view. Elementary school teachers should observe these guidelines in teaching written expression:[5]

1. The writing of each child is worthy of respect. In effect, respecting a child's writing shows respect for the child.
2. Children will write if there are many opportunities to write purposefully in a supportive environment. The supportive environment should include opportunities for many experiences, audiences for much of the writing, appropriate help in getting started, guidance during and following the writing, and time for talking about, as well as for doing, the writing.
3. Teachers should recognize children's desire for occasional privacy in their writing; that is, a child should not be forced to "turn in," read, or display a piece of writing if he or she wants to keep it private. Respecting a child's privacy is easy if the teacher encourages self-motivated writing in addition to assigning writing. Much of what children write independently they will share with the teacher and classmates.
4. Ideas, originality, precision, and vividness of language should be valued above competence in spelling, sentence construction, and conventions.
5. Group composing of various types of writing encourages creativity and thinking and also teaches writing skills.
6. Children should evaluate and edit their own writing, although constructive peer criticism—channeled toward understanding and clarity—should be encouraged.
7. Teacher comments on expression and conventions should stress what the child has done well and can build upon in future writing. The comments should be specific rather than general and, preferably, offered orally; written comments attached to the child's paper should be few in number.

---

5. These guidelines, in part, derive from statements in H. Alan Robinson and Alvina Treut Burrows, "Criteria for Excellence in Teaching the Language Arts," *Teacher Effectiveness in Elementary Language Arts: A Progress Report* (Urbana, Ill.: National Conference on Research in English/ERIC Clearinghouse on Reading and Communication Skills, 1974), pp. 79–80; Elizabeth A. Thorn, *Teaching the Language Arts* (Toronto: Gage Educational Publishing, 1974), Chapter 13; and Walter T. Petty, Dorothy C. Petty, and Marjorie F. Becking (*Experiences in Language: Tools and Techniques for Language Arts Methods*, 2d ed. (Boston: Allyn and Bacon, 1976), Chapter 2.

PREPARATION FOR AND IMPROVEMENT IN WRITING

Children frequently write less effectively than they might because they lack the skill to gain and retain the information they need for the writing, to organize their thoughts and the information they do have, and to improve their first writing efforts. Teachers must direct substantial teaching effort to the acquisition of these skills. In the following sections and in Chapter 10 we discuss ways of teaching these skills.

Notetaking

In the primary grades teachers should begin to provide activities that will enable children to determine the main idea, select supporting facts or details, and plan a sequence for relating their thoughts. For example, children can suggest several titles for pictures, and choose the most appropriate. They can also make charts of classroom duties and plans, dictate the main idea and details of trips and other experiences, and draw pictures to show what they learned by listening or observing.

Group activities are useful also for showing children more directly how to take notes. First the teacher can assign a short selection containing information about something the children are interested in. After they have read it, the teacher can ask each of them to come to the board and write statements describing what they learned. Then class members can compare statements and write a composite, adding what they believe is necessary, and choosing the order in which the statements should appear. The same kind of activity can follow a film or television viewing.

Finding answers to specific questions helps children learn to make notes rather than writing down all that they read or hear. Of course, they should compare the results to standards or "rules" for notetaking developed by the group.

In the middle and upper grades, when the children prepare a greater number of reports and use reference materials, more refined and more inclusive standards are essential:[6]

1. Skim. Glance through the article to see whether it contains information that is important to the report.
2. Write down the name of the book, author's name, and page numbers on which the information is found. For encyclopedias, write the name of the encyclopedia, volume number, subject heading, and page numbers.
3. Write down only the important facts or the particular information you are looking for. Use your own words: *do not copy.*
4. If you do wish to use the author's words for some particular reason, use quotation marks and *write down the exact page number.*

---

6. Petty, Petty, and Becking, p. 414.

5.   Check names, dates, and figures for accuracy.
6.   Skim once more to see if you have missed anything important.

Also remind children to avoid writing extraneous material, material that does not relate to the subject of the report. Peer evaluation will help to prevent this mistake.

Outlining

Our principal discussion of outlining appears in Chapter 10 because it is a study aid as well as a preliminary step in composing oral and written expression. Outlines help to organize what we read, work that we will do, a story that we plan to tell, or a report that we will present to a group. Children in the primary grades can begin to learn about outlining in various areas of instruction by learning to classify and organize. For example, kindergarten children might dictate lists of items like the following for the teacher to write on the blackboard:

Fruits	*Vegetables*
oranges	lettuce
apples	carrots
grapes	potatoes

Young children can make simple outlines of a story to be told or dramatized, a forthcoming or past trip, materials needed for a project, and so on. In the intermediate grades these outlines should contain more detail.

The basis for outlining is clear thinking. Understanding what is important and how to organize it are the elements of all good composition. Although outline form should be taught, the emphasis should always be on organization—order and relationships—rather than on proper indentation and use of uppercase and lowercase letters, Roman and Arabic numerals, and the like. On the other hand, children must appreciate the significance of such details in providing organization and showing relationships.

Outlining instruction should have a context; teachers should not present outlining as an isolated skill. A good way to begin is for the teacher and the pupils to outline something they all have read. Next they might prepare an outline for a report combining information from several sources. One of the best early outline topics is a story that the pupils know well so that they will have a good understanding of the sequence. Many stories are written in a way that makes it easy to distinguish the major and minor topics. The purpose of such an outline might be to dramatize the story for another class. Children could repeat this procedure every year until they have mastered the skill of outlining.

The point to stress is that most activities worth doing are worth planning, and the teacher will have to illustrate this point to the children. One way is for them to write a story twice, once with and once without an outline, and then to compare and evaluate the results. An alternative is to write a report with and without an outline.

Outlines may take a topical or a sentence form. Undoubtedly younger children find the sentence form easier to follow. The teacher should point out that a period must end each sentence, as in all other written work. Children should also learn to use one form consistently within the same outline. Several forms of outlining are acceptable, but some major principles apply to all types:

1. The outline should have an introductory and a concluding topic or sentence.
2. Each major topic should be of comparable importance and should relate directly to the subject of the outline.
3. If a topic is divisible, there must be at least two subtopics.
4. Numbering, lettering, indenting, capitalizing, and punctuation should follow a single style throughout the outline.
5. No punctuation is required after the topics unless they are sentences.

The following is a general guide for either a topical or a sentence outline carrying two main topics with subtopics. Indenting subtopics clarifies their subordinate value.

I. First main topic
   A. First subtopic
   B. Second subtopic
II. Second main topic
   A. First subtopic
   B. Second subtopic

Self-editing and Proofreading

Too many teachers do not include proofreading and self-editing or revising in writing instruction. As indicated in Chapter 13, some children will never read what they write, whereas others will reread only part of what they have written. Even the child who does proofread might scarcely know what to do next. As for self-editing, pupils who do it are generally the ones whose teachers persistently encourage them to practice it.

From the beginning of instruction in written expression, children should be encouraged to depend on themselves to improve the expression and to find and correct their errors. They should learn to examine carefully what they have written in terms of idea selection or information, effectiveness of organization, clarity of expression, and courtesy to the readers, which includes legible writing, correct spelling, necessary punctuation, and acceptable usage.

In a situation that genuinely calls for expression it is relatively simple to instill in children the desire to write well. This attitude generally develops through reference to standards that the class establishes and later to standards each child sets for himself or herself. For example, a child might develop these criteria for self-editing:

1. Does my title tell what the story is about?
2. Do I have a good beginning?
3. Does my story reach a high point or climax?
4. Do all the parts of the story fit together?

Some simple proofreading skills should be taught even before children begin to write. Kindergarten teachers can demonstrate that they are proofreading a chart or a board story. In the first and second grades, teachers should expect children—and give them time—to read over what they have written, to check that they capitalized the first words of sentences, and to make certain there is a period at the end of each sentence. It is not enough for the teacher to say, "Proofread what you have written," for this admonition is meaningless to young children and ineffective with older ones who have had no instruction in proofreading. In the early stages of teaching proofreading, the teacher and children together can develop standards or lists of appraisal questions to serve as proofreading guides. As children progress through the grades, however, they should be encouraged to develop their proofreading and editing criteria. Depending on the teacher to always lead them through an evaluation of their work is almost as harmful as depending on the teacher to make the corrections. Therefore, in spite of the fact that teachers must give guidance in proofreading, they should try to develop the children's self-reliance.

Class or individually developed proofreading criteria at first should include only one or two guidelines. Later additions might include more details regarding organization, form, and mechanics. The first set of group-designed criteria should include questions like these:

1. Have I written sentences?
2. Have I capitalized the first word of every sentence?
3. Have I put a period at the end of each sentence?

Subsequent criteria might include questions like these:

1. Have I indented the first word of each paragraph?
2. Have I left margins?
3. Does each paragraph tell about one topic?
4. Does each sentence in a paragraph tell something about the topic?
5. Does each sentence begin and end correctly?

Directions for proofreading usually appear in elementary language arts textbooks. The criteria vary in comprehensiveness and thus require teacher adaptation and extension. One example follows:[7]

1. Find and correct mistakes in capital letters.
2. Find and correct mistakes in punctuation.
3. Find and correct mistakes in spelling.
4. Find and correct mistakes in using word forms.
5. Find and correct mistakes in sentences that are run together.
6. Find word groups that are not sentences and add words to make sentences.

One reference suggests that "by the fourth grade, children can function as independent editors quite successfully if they have a gradual introduction to editing procedures."[8] But the same source also points out that "the teacher who asks her students to work as editors without giving them any general pointers about how to proceed may find that they do not know where to begin."[9] A subsequent section in this chapter considers the role of self-editing further.

TYPES OF WRITING

A vital writing program presupposes that the total program of a classroom is meaningful and challenging. Where ideas abound, expression flows freely, and "assignments" are irrelevant. Writing can originate in science class, on a social studies field trip, in the need to establish rules for a game, during the development of an imaginative story, in the reading pupils do, and in numerous other genuine situations. This type of writing need not be haphazard and unplanned. Rather, frequent and careful planning will maximize children's skill learning and enable them to improve their work progressively. This section emphasizes the variety of opportunities that make it possible for children to write for meaningful purposes.

Experience Stories

Simply by writing stories and records of experiences that an individual child or a group of children dictate, a teacher can develop many writing skills. This activity is particularly important at the beginning grade levels, before children have

---

7. *Language for Meaning*, Book 3 (Boston: Houghton Mifflin Co., 1978), p. 71.
8. Dorothy Grant Hennings and Barbara M. Grant, *Content and Craft* (Englewood Cliffs, N.J.: Prentice-Hall, 1973) p. 151.
9. Ibid., p. 150.

learned handwriting skills, but later it also frees them from undue concern with mechanical elements and conventions so that they can focus on composition—what is said.

Children of all ages are eager to talk about their experiences, and frequently they will want to keep a record of them, particularly of group experiences. Some records may be temporary, for instance, the "news" of the day written on the board. Ordinarily, however, it is appropriate to write experience stories and accounts on newsprint or chart paper if the experience was one that the class or a group from the class shared. The experiences of individual children can be written on ordinary-size paper, although frequently the individual experience of an elementary school child should be written on newsprint larger than $8\frac{1}{2} \times 11$ inches so there is room to draw a picture relating to the story. Sometimes, of course, the picture is drawn before the story is dictated.

Even in the first experience stories, mechanical skills should receive instructional attention. Perhaps instruction may be limited initially to pointing out that the first words of sentences are capitalized and that sentences require end punctuation. Later the teacher should ask the child or the group where the title belongs, what words should be capitalized, and so on. The primary focus of these discussions, however, should be on organization, sequence, sentence construction, word choice, and ways to make a story better. The teacher should raise questions about how to start the story, the subject of the story, the sequence of ideas or events, and so on to guide the discussion.[10]

Letter Writing

Letter writing is a major written language activity and one that should receive considerable instructional emphasis in the elementary school. The different types of letters that children should learn to write include personal letters (invitations and replies and expressions of sympathy, regret, thanks, apology, congratulations, and friendship) and business letters dealing with requests, orders, applications, and complaints. Special letter-writing skills are necessary for composing business and personal telegrams, writing postcards, and addressing cards and envelopes.

Letter writing is most effectively taught as an integral part of an ongoing classroom activity. Children must know that in certain situations letter writing is necessary and understand the importance of content, form, and courtesies before they can master the art of letter writing. Teachers must be alert for opportunities that require the writing of real letters. Commonly occurring occasions that call for writing letters include:

---

10. A helpful reference is Virgil E. Herrick and Marcella Nerbovig, *Using Experience Charts with Children* (Columbus, O.: Charles E. Merrill Publishing Co., 1964).

Invitations

1. To friends or parents to visit the classroom
2. To another class or school to come to a play day
3. To the principal or supervisor to observe an activity

Replies

1. Of acceptance to an invitation from another class or a parent
2. Of regret at not being able to come to a program

Sympathy

1. To a sick classmate or teacher
2. To a teacher or family of a classmate after a death or accident

Greetings

1. To the principal, teachers, and classmates on birthdays or holidays
2. To friends on special occasions

Friendly letters and postcards

1. To children in another classroom or school
2. To a former classmate
3. To last year's teacher
4. To a student in another country

Thank-you notes

1. To someone who spoke to the class
2. To friends and relatives who gave presents at Christmas
3. To another class for the use of some books or to a parent who loaned materials
4. To the principal for some special favor

Requests

1. To a company or individual for information
2. To a shopkeeper for materials
3. For permission to visit someone's business or home
4. To the principal for permission to take a trip
5. To the school custodian for doing some task in the room
6. To the luncheon cook for the addition of a special item to the menu

Orders

1. To a business for class supplies
2. For a magazine subscription

Applications

1. For a position on the school paper
2. For a job in the school office
3. For summer work or an after-school job
4. For membership in a club

Complaints

1. About an article in a newspaper
2. About a practice on the playground

These are a few suggestions. Language textbooks sometimes provide other suggestions and the alert teacher will think of many more. The important point is that many occasions that are appropriate for letter writing occur naturally in a classroom bustling with activity.

It is imperative that all children acquire proper habits and attitudes regarding letter writing. Generally, these qualities develop through informal discussion and the teacher's wise use of real situations to generate letter-writing activities. For instance, answering questions raised in a letter from someone else, inquiring about matters that concern the reader, not writing letters in anger (or at least not mailing them right away) and rereading letters before mailing them are all habits that children should learn. Answering letters promptly, replying to invitations, and expressing sympathy appropriately are also fundamental.

In addition, children need to learn certain mechanical aspects of letter writing. These include:

1. The fact that a letter has several parts, that each part has a purpose, and an appropriate place on the page
2. The capitalization and punctuation that each part requires
3. The writing materials appropriate to the purpose and type of letter
4. The proper ways to fold letters

Finally, children need to develop a sensitivity to situations in which they should write a letter, the appropriateness of various salutations and closings, and techniques to make a letter interesting or informative.

Content.   Teachers of the lower grades should spend considerable time discussing with pupils the purpose of letters, in general, and specifically, the purpose of a particular letter that they are planning to write. Periodic repetition of this practice should occur throughout the middle and upper grades. Obviously, what children learn about the purposes of letters depends on the situations that call for writing them. The children must discover that in order to extend an interesting activity in which they are engaged, they must write a letter to obtain information or material. They must understand that in a different situation courtesy demands a letter of thanks or sympathy.

A discussion of letter writing should focus on the content and amount of detail necessary to achieve the writer's purpose. If the purpose of a letter is to order material, the writer should specify the amount needed and the use that will be made of free materials. The letter should also indicate when it is needed and to whom it should be sent. These details should be organized into a logical sequence; in beginning letter writing they should be listed and organized on the board. The teacher will need to emphasize the importance of beginning and ending sentences. Particularly for writing friendly letters, children should learn to phrase their thoughts in interesting and vivid ways.

Form.   Children learn good letter-writing form by seeing and studying good models. Most textbooks contain samples of different types of letters, but unfortunately a letter printed in a textbook does not resemble the original letter in many respects. Although the content may appear verbatim and in script, the size of the page, widths of margins, lengths of lines, size of the writing, and spacing between the lines all depend on the specifications of the textbook publisher rather than on standards of correctly written letters. As a supplement to or perhaps an antidote for these textbook models, the teacher and the class should develop correct forms of the several types of letters using content dictated by the children. After the class has accepted each form, they should consider the size, shape, and color of paper suitable for the type of letter the model represents. The teacher should then obtain the proper paper and each child should produce a teacher-approved copy of the model letter for personal use. Then they might prepare similar models for envelopes. Once the children have properly folded and inserted the model letters in the model envelopes, they can attach them to textbook or notebook covers for convenient reference.

In addition to making their own models, pupils should see letters secured from business concerns, professional persons, and friends. These actual letters may differ greatly from the textbook models, and the pupils should be aware of this fact. Nevertheless, all letters have much in common in terms of heading, inside address, salutation, closing, and signature. Their placement on the page may vary and not all letter writers use the indentations shown in the textbook but the elements will all be there.

Typewritten letters of both the business and the friendly varieties should receive greater instructional attention than most textbooks suggest, because more and more children are learning to use typewriters in elementary school. Even though letter-writing instruction may emphasize the utilitarian purpose of writing letters, it should not overlook the possibilities for creative letter writing. In fact, humor, vividness of expression, and attention to reader interests increase clarity and effectiveness. The child who wrote the following exercised originality and showed feeling but did so with courtesy and good form.

> Dear Aunt Phyllis,
>
> We had fun while you were here, and I hope you will be back soon.
>
> My favorite time was the trip to the zoo. The monkeys were really funny. You made funny faces too.
>
> Going out to eat was great! I liked the big hamburgers with everything. I could eat a hundred!
>
> Thanks a lot.
>
> Love,
> John

Reports

Report writing is important at every elementary grade level for it provides a good foundation for much of the writing children do in the upper grades. Usually, experience accounts are the first reports that children write. In addition, teachers can assign group or individual reports describing a completed unit of work or giving directions for doing something. In the second and third grades, children should be doing some of the report and summary work themselves. Children in the intermediate grades are capable of writing summaries of an increasing number of paragraphs, recommendations of books to read, reports on excursions taken or projects developed, and directions relative to classroom trips and activities.

The objectives for the various grade levels should resemble these:

Primary level

1.   To learn to make accurate observations and note essentials clearly and in order

2. To see the value of concrete experiences as a means of learning
3. To learn the importance of definite, descriptive language
4. To begin to express observations in written form either with pictures or with symbols
5. To learn habits of persistence in observation and reporting

Intermediate level

1. To learn the importance of planning for reporting
2. To learn to organize for a particular purpose
3. To learn to use a few key words that will aid in recalling data
4. To be able to use related materials to stimulate interest
5. To learn to select only appropriate material and to do so accurately
6. To develop the habit of noting the source of material and giving credit for its use
7. To refine previous objectives

Upper level

1. To acquire skill in taking notes while reading, listening, or observing
2. To prepare reports of increasing length
3. To continue to refine and extend all previous objectives

Children have many occasions to report facts and experiences to their fellow pupils. Essentially the purpose is to convey information, but a report also can convey something of the writer and his or her feelings. The fourth grader who wrote, "Why We Celebrate Lincoln's Birthday" could have copied the information directly from the encyclopedia and presented it to the class in much the same language as the encyclopedia used. Instead, the report demonstrates a creative approach, as this introductory paragraph illustrates:

> Every time I lie by the fire and read, I think that one of America's greatest presidents did just that. That man was Abraham Lincoln. He hated slavery, but he wanted to keep the states together. He said that "someday this country will be friends again." If you take this country and cut it into two pieces you will no longer have one country but two half-countries. Try to join each half to another country. It would not stay on. So the halves will have to join together again.

Each year students should practice defining and limiting the scope of a report, organizing a report, using various sources to gain information, and giving attention to the form and appearance of a report. As for other language activities, the class should devise standards for report preparation. The following guidelines exemplify what the class might come up with:

Writing a report

1. Organize your report carefully and make it interesting.
2. Write the title on the top line and in the center of the page.
3. Capitalize the first word and each important word in the title.
4. Skip a line after the title.
5. Leave margins on each page.
6. Write legibly.
7. Use correct spelling and punctuation.

News Articles

A special form of reporting is the news article. An alert class will see all kinds of opportunities for writing articles to publish in a class or school newspaper, in the district-sponsored newspaper, or even in the local newspaper, where Karin's article appeared.

> On November 10th, a wild deer decided to be educated in the Howe Avenue Elementary School shortly before 9:00 A.M.
> A couple of teachers, a janitor, and several children saw the deer.
> One boy tried to catch the deer and has a torn shirt and a bruised side to prove it.
> Much to the school's regret, the deer got away through the south gate after running across the playground.

Children love to discover and report events around the school, the neighborhood, and the community. Actually, various writing forms are appropriate for the class or school newspaper, including news accounts, letters to the editor, editorials, features, reviews, jokes, and poetry. Having to make decisions about what to include in a class newspaper and what the placement should be also calls organizational skills into play. A special advantage of a class newspaper is that the wide range of possible kinds of writing accommodates the writing abilities and interests of all of the children in the class.

Records

Throughout their elementary school years children need to keep different kinds of records, including records or minutes of club and class meetings. Activities that lend themselves to record writing include:

1. Making a yearbook record of class and individual experiences and information learned

2. Compiling special-topic books, such as *Learning About Iron and Steel* and *Pioneers Travel West*, which may include a variety of records
3. Listing standards for oral reporting
4. Meetings of the class historical society for which minutes must be kept
5. Listing new words learned in different subject areas, their meanings, and usage
6. Writing points to remember about a film the class has seen
7. Writing the daily news on the chalkboard
8. Writing recipes for things made for social studies or science, such as "How We Made Butter" or "Making a Tin-can Telephone"

Elementary school children have a particular interest in nature and in science. It is not difficult to motivate them to keep records on topics like the following:[11]

1. The time the sun sets during different seasons of the year
2. When the birds go south and return north
3. The dates of planting and appearance of flowers and different crops
4. Changes in the amount of water in streams and ponds and the causes thereof
5. The action of wind vane, thermometer, barometer, and compass
6. Weather calendars
7. The changing position of the stars
8. Relation of community industries to soil, climate, and waterways
9. Habits of wild animals and pets
10. How animals and plants adapt to their surroundings
11. Height and weight records and their relation to nutrition, sleep, and exercise

Record keeping offers an excellent opportunity for instruction in written composition, as well as in the basic value of the records themselves. The records children keep should be accurate, definite, and written in their own words so the children can understand and use them. With careful instruction in record keeping children should come to appreciate language and its broad usefulness better.

Announcements and Notices

Writing announcements gives children the chance to be both practical and creative. For instance, one youngster who had a bicycle to sell wrote this creative announcement:

---

11. *The Language Arts: A Handbook for Teachers in Elementary Schools.* (Bureau of Elementary Curriculum Development, New York State Education Department, 1957), p. 26.

> For Sale: The fastest bike in the West! Reduced for the Spring Red Sale. Only $25 if you zoom in fast. It is red, has a chiquita banana seat, 5 speeds, and dual brakes. Demonstration rides at 223 Poinsetta Drive after school. Don't be late. Buy! Then get home fast!

Included in this category of writing opportunities are concise, short phrases or statements that present information accurately, attractively, and completely for the purpose of the communication. Opportunities for such writing are numerous: labels, poster and chart titles, signs, newspaper or bulletin board notices, and so on. Instruction should highlight clear, accurate, and purposeful statements and give special attention to neatness and essential details. Prior to writing labels, signs, and notices, the class should consider what wording to use as well as where it would be appropriate to post or display them. Having children practice giving directions, making announcements, or orally suggesting titles, labels, and the wording of signs is another necessary preliminary step. One useful activity that naturally appeals to children is looking for notices, signs, and labels in stores, along the streets and highways, and in school. Rewriting some of the weakest of these in class can be fun and educational.

Form Completion

As adults, we frequently must fill in forms to provide information requested on a test booklet, a driver's license application, an order blank, and so on. Many times in day-to-day school activities children also have to complete forms. These occasions are suitable for language instruction. If they are to fill in forms accurately and completely, children must approach the task with an informed attitude. In particular, they must (1) realize the necessity of completing a form accurately and neatly; (2) realize the necessity of following directions completely and precisely; (3) give information in the manner specified; (4) strive to furnish *all* the information called for; and (5) try to make the completed work look attractive.

School situations that sometimes involve filling in forms include the following:

Writing a money order

1. To a company for pictures to use in booklets
2. To a nursery for seeds for a school garden
3. To a manufacturing company for material to use in social science
4. To a publishing company to subscribe to a class magazine

Information blanks

1. Questionnaire regarding personal history or health
2. Enrollment card

3.   Library loan card
4.   Call slip for books at the library
5.   The heading of a standardized test
6.   An application blank for membership in a magazine club
7.   A book plate for textbooks

Forms concerned with banking

1.   A deposit slip for a school savings account
2.   An application card for a bank account in the school savings organization
3.   A withdrawal slip

Mail-order forms

1.   A subscription blank
2.   A coupon for samples or free booklets advertised in a magazine
3.   An order for reference books

Skill at filling in forms with accuracy and neatness derives principally from practice. In the primary grades, some children need oral practice answering these and similar questions: "What is your name?" "How old are you?" "How old will you be on your next birthday?" Later the teacher may expand this sort of exercise into a game in which children test their knowledge of the personal history they might have to supply on, say, a standardized test blank. Of course, this activity should relate to a specific need, but in order to give this skill sufficient attention the teacher might have to stimulate interest by preparing different types of forms for the children to complete. One teacher suggests using this procedure to teach the skills necessary to complete forms:

1.   Introduce by pointing out a situation in school in which filling in a form is necessary, such as a request for material, an absence excuse, or a test blank. Discuss these and related questions:
     a.   What kinds of forms are there and how are they used? Why are they used?
     b.   What do we need to know to fill out a form correctly? Are there any special words we need to know the meanings of?
2.   Have the children bring to class as many forms as they can find. Discuss them and practice filling them out. The teacher might need to bring in forms that the children won't locate. Discussion should emphasize the purpose of the forms and the need for legibility and accuracy.
3.   Have the children construct a form, for example, to gather information about who will need a ride to a picnic, who can provide a ride, what type of food each will bring, which games they want to play, and so on.

Reviews, Biographies, and Essays

As suggested earlier, children can write newspaper reviews and editorials, which really are a form of the essay. They might review a book or story (instead of the traditional book report) or even movies and television programs. Children need to learn that a review is a teaser in the form of the reader's or viewer's reaction and not a detailed account of "what happened." By examining reviews in children's magazines and such journals as *Language Arts* and *The Horn Book*, the children will learn the difference between the book reports that they are familiar with and a review.

Children can write biographies of members of their families or of friends that they know well. To prepare for the writing they might interview the persons about whom they plan to write and other people who can provide information about them. In addition, children might make up biographies for characters in stories and even personify "characters" such as a clapboard house, a spreading elm, or an almond-eyed cat.

The word *essay* has fallen into disuse, and yet many forms of writing are really essays. Even a personal letter is a loosely organized essay, as are many personal accounts. In a more formal sense, "essay" is an apt term for a type of writing that stimulates children's most creative thinking and best expression of feelings. One advantage of the essay is that children have had experience with it in their writing of personal accounts in the primary grades. In the writing program its importance comes from the need for the children to organize their thinking both before and during the writing process and at the same time to infuse the composition with creativity and personal involvement.

Stories

Story writing is a major form of expression for elementary school children. As suggested in Chapter 13, teachers can inspire story writing in many ways. For example, after one first-grade teacher read a poem about owls, the children drew pictures based on the poem and recounted the essence of the poem to each other. Then the class decided that they would all like to write one child's version of the poem:

> Two baby owls were sitting in a tree. They could not see in the daytime. They decided they should go home and go to bed.

In another first-grade class, Garry wrote this story after the teacher's friend spoke to the class about penguins with the help of Willie, the marionette penguin.

> Willie is a penguin.
> He likes water.
> He likes fish.
> He danced for us.

Third grader Wayne used a question format for his story.[12]

The floor

Does the floor ever get tired of getting stepped on? Does the floor ever get tired of being washed? Does the floor like to get marks on it? Do you think the floor should get up and walk away?

John, age eight, showed his maturity and his developing story-writing ability in his story about a volcano.[13]

One calm day in the jungle far away there was a village, and the village was very small.

Behind the village was a volcano, and the villagers did not know that the volcano was a volcano. The reason they did not know that the volcano was a volcano was because the volcano had not erupted for eight hundred years.

Days went by and after a while the volcano began to shake and then to throw hot rocks and lava down the volcano side.

It was a sad time for the people. They ran for their lives, leaving all behind but what they could grab up on the run.

Days later, after the eruption had stopped, the villagers returned. They found that the only two huts left were the one on the hill and the one in the tree.

David, a sixth grader, demonstrates real imaginative power in his story of the origin of wind.

One day the Spirit of the Moon was walking along. He came to a large cave, and started to enter it. All of a sudden he felt that he had to sneeze! He went, "Ah, ah, ah-choo" right into the cave. The back force of the sneeze was so great that when repelled it knocked over Moon Spirit.

He was so angry that he called the force a bad name! "Wind!" he yelled.

The Indians too, were afraid and brought him presents. Since the wind came from the north they called it the North Wind.

As children's story-writing skill increases, they can concentrate on improvement of organization, characterization, and story beginnings. For example, children might consider these questions in evaluating their stories:

1. Does your story have an interest-catching beginning?
2. Will your reader clearly recognize the characters, the setting, and the sequence?
3. Does your story reach a high point or climax?

---

12. From *The Spark*, Starpoint Central School, Lockport, New York, 1967, p. 51.
13. *Guiding Growth in Written Expression* (Los Angeles: Los Angeles County Schools, June 1956), p. 122.

4.   Is there an adequate explanation of how the problem in the story was solved?
5.   Do all the parts fit together at the end in a way that will satisfy a reader?

To help children learn to focus on the plot of a story and to develop it, suggest they write a five-sentence outline. For example:

1.   Mother and I were sitting in the kitchen after dinner one quiet evening.
2.   Suddenly we heard a scratching noise.
3.   Mother screamed and jumped up on a chair as a gray mouse darted across the floor.
4.   I stood there and laughed at the funny sight while Mother recovered from her terror.
5.   I imagine the mouse was more frightened than Mother was.

One group of children began noting how stories begin and developed the following list. The result was that their stories began to vary from the standard "once upon a time" type. They said that stories might begin with:

1.   Conversation to set the stage for action
2.   The end of the story, followed by the beginning
3.   The middle of the story, followed by the actual beginning
4.   A descriptive sketch of the chief character or characters
5.   A paragraph summarizing the story
6.   A description
7.   A statement of time, place, or circumstance
8.   A question

Poetry and Rhymes

Generally children like to write poetry and simple rhymes, but they cannot do it successfully unless they have been exposed to much poetry. Mauree Applegate tells the story of the forgetful gardener who plowed and cultivated a plot of ground but forgot to plant any seeds. Even though he was forgetful, she says, some seeds that fell from parent plants did spring up. She applies this analogy to the classroom and notes that "Reading poetry to the children, appreciating things together, giving the daily invitation to write, having a quiet hour each week, and providing a poetry drawer will grow more and better poetry." Furthermore, she adds, "one cannot travel to the stars in a wheelbarrow, or speak of his journey there in the words of the field."[14]

14. Mauree Applegate, *Helping Children Write* (Evanston, Ill.: Row, Peterson and Co., 1954), pp. 29, 31.

Selecting poetry to read to children requires care, as we discussed in Chapter 5. If children are overwhelmed by poetry—fail to understand or appreciate it—they may tend to copy rather than create their own. Reading poetry written by other children often helps encourage them to express their own thoughts and feelings. For most poetry and verse writing, teachers need to draw children away from a preoccupation with rhyming and toward awareness of the thought. The expression of feelings and use of vivid imagery also command emphasis. Despite the fact that writing poetry and verse is a highly individual act, teachers can be enormously helpful to budding poets, as subsequent examples from a number of different classes and schools illustrate.

A discussion of spring sights, sounds, and feelings by one teacher and her class brought forth the phrases "a brisk wind, driving rain, exploring flowers, and the peeping sun," which inspired one pupil to write:

> The brisk March wind blows
> Spring ever nearer and nearer
> The brisk March wind blows
> The shadows from the peeping sun.
> Spring is near, ever nearer.
> Make sure you're ready to play and run.

Another wrote:

> Hang onto your hat; hold it tight!
> The driving rain is after it.
> Hold onto your hat; hold it tight.
> Or the gulping wind will get it!

A second-grade class had been studying the circus and had seen the animals and the crowds and excitement of the circus when it was in town. It was the main topic of conversation at school, and Arnold wrote:

> When circus time is here,
> People come from far and near
> To see the animals dance and play—
> It makes their lives so bright and gay.

A fifth-grade class enjoyed hearing their teacher read "City Rain" by Rachel Field and then talking about other sights visible in the streets of the city during a rain storm. Following this experience, Evelyn wrote:

> The wind blows,
> Leaves fall,
> Red, yellow and brown.
> The rain,
> From a gray sky,
> Plasters them
> To the wet ground.

Children like to learn about poetic forms. Teachers may introduce them during poetry reading (see Chapter 5) but will usually have to reintroduce them when preparing children to write poetry. Keep in mind, however, that the idea is more important than the form. The form of a poem is only an aid to expressing content.

A good way to introduce form is to provide the first line of a couplet and ask the children to supply the second line.

> Leaves are falling to the ground
> With a gentle, rustling sound

> Leaves are falling to the ground
> Stirring squirrels who bound and bound

> Leaves are falling to the ground
> Gently, gently without a sound.

Children also like to write triplets, quatrains, limericks, and other verse forms. The cinquain structure, for example, appeals to most children: the first line is one word, the title; the second line is two words that describe the title; the third line has three words, which express action; the fourth line consists of four words, which express feeling; and the fifth line has one word, a synonym for the title. After the fourth-grade class had written cinquains together, Billy wrote this one:

> Puppy
> Warm, sleepy
> Wobbling and sniffing
> Lost without a mother
> Doggy.

Some children will do very little poetry or verse writing regardless of the amount of poetry they hear or read and the encouragement they receive. They should not be forced to write, but the teacher should keep the door open for them to try when they want to. Sometimes simple observation will elicit words and phrases from even the most reticent poet and lead to an almost spontaneous writing of verse. A straight and sharp icicle, the activities in an ant hill or a hive of bees, the drip of a leaky faucet, and so forth, would all surely start a flow of words.

Other Forms of Writing

Again, practically every situation or activity in the elementary school provides opportunities for writing, and many of these opportunities may call for forms other than the ones we have discussed. For example, one teacher secured some creative and thought-provoking ideas from his sixth-grade children by having them write their interpretations of adages like these: "The best place to find a helping hand is at the end of your own arm"; "The best way to climb a mountain is to begin at the bottom"; and "A mind is like a parachute; it is useful only when open."

The same teacher developed much interest in writing copy for advertisements of imaginary products. Leonard wrote:

> Ladies and gentlemen! I am from the Milky Way. There is plenty to eat, if you know what I mean! Our delicious product is the Really-Big Bar.
>
> Look at all those kids eating our Really-Big Bar.
>
> If you want one, go out to the store and buy our Really-Big Bar! After that it will become yours. Aren't you glad? You will find that its luscious chocolate, creamy vanilla filling, and brown crisp almonds are what makes the Really-Big Bar the best.
>
> Take a tip from me, it's great!

Written description often brings forth considerable creativity. Skill in observation is instrumental in discovering what something or someone looks like. And this skill must extend beneath the surface. One teacher reported that when one class discussed Abraham Lincoln, the children mentioned his homely appearance but beautiful expression and the personal qualities that this expression showed. Following this discussion, she instructed the class, "Write about someone you know, someone you admire, and describe how he appears and how he is. You don't need to say who it is—just give a careful description." In response, Jim wrote:[15]

> I admire an elderly person who knows how to fish like the greatest of fishermen and hunts like the greatest of huntsmen. He can do almost anything! He is a tall, well-built man with silverish black hair and a rough tan face. He has built a cabin as a vacation home for all of his relatives. He accepts what I can do and what I can't. This man is my rehtafdnarg.[16]

Children also like to keep journals recording their own activities or imaginary ones about historical or fictional persons. Other possible activities include writing radio or television scripts, autobiographies, and directions.

CONVENTIONS IN WRITING

The conventions in writing include capitalization, punctuation, and manuscript form (the arrangement of writing on a page). Many judgments about a piece of writing stem from—or at least are affected by—the correctness or acceptability of these writing conventions. In addition, spelling ability (see Chapter 15) and

---

15. *Oregon ASCD Curriculum Bulletin*, 1973, p. 35.
16. Note the child's creative disguise for the word *grandfather*.

handwriting legibility (Chapter 16) give rise to favorable or unfavorable reader impressions.

Manuscript Form

A neat and attractive paper, whether it is a letter, a report, an announcement, or a story, implies courtesy to the reader and helps to increase the effectiveness of the expression. Because schools are interested in developing children's individuality, some teachers let pupils present written expression without regard to custom, neatness, and other factors that show consideration for the reader. Nevertheless, in working out guidelines for producing a neat and acceptable paper, the teacher and class should not disregard individuality. Children generally like to understand what people expect of them, and later in their school careers and in adulthood they will certainly appreciate having been obliged to learn how to prepare neat and attractive papers.

There are no set rules for manuscript form. One generally accepted guideline is to leave margins at the top and bottom and on each side of the paper, but the recommended width of these margins varies with the person prescribing the form. To avoid needless confusion, some schools have adopted specific guidelines for use within the system.

An excellent practice is to compile a school handbook on form, style, and usage for the use of teachers and pupils. Publishing a handbook, however, does not mean that pupils cannot help set their own standards. The handbook can serve as a guide to the development of classroom standards. When compiling a handbook, school personnel might consider including the following manuscript format guidelines:

Kindergarten

1. The teacher should call the children's attention to material that involves form, for example, the attractiveness of neat work, margins in books and newspapers, titles of stories, attractive arrangements of work on paper

Grade 1

1. Margin at left and right
2. Spacing at top and bottom of page
3. Writing done carefully and on one side of the paper only

Grade 2

1. All grade-one guidelines
2. First word of a paragraph indented

3.   Second line of paragraph brought back to the margin
4.   Correct placement of name and date

Grade 3

1.   All guidelines given for lower grades
2.   Spacing between title and body of a composition
3.   No crowding at end of line

Grades 4, 5, and 6

1.   All guidelines listed for lower grades
2.   Use of paper appropriate for the writing occasion

Few curriculum guides mention this type of detail, although some suggest adopting a standard form. It is also fairly common for both guides and textbooks to suggest a standard for heading papers:[17]

Write heading according to school policy:

Name	P.S.
Date	Class

Other items that a teacher might need to teach include avoiding capitalization of words in the body of material for the purpose of emphasis, not putting periods after titles of stories and reports, and avoiding excessive abbreviation.

Of course, every teacher must try not to suppress children's creativity or retard their willingness to express themselves, but establishing standards need not suppress or retard. Therefore, it is advisable for teachers and supervisors within a school system to formulate standards of manuscript form and appearance, such as position of name and date on the paper, placement of the title of a report and other written material, preferred size and type of paper, use of one or both sides of the paper, and width of top, bottom, and side margins.[18] Within the limits of the schoolwide criteria, teachers and pupils should address matters of manuscript appearance in the standards they establish for their own written work. Once they have helped to set standards, children should be expected to observe them in their written work. This requirement is likely to have a more positive effect on the development of the child's personality and writing than the "anything goes" policy of some teachers.

17. *Handbook for Language Arts.* Curriculum Bulletin, 1965–66 Series, no. 8 (Board of Education of the City of New York, 1966), p. 287.
18. These guidelines should not conflict with matters of manuscript form suggested by the language textbooks in use.

Punctuation

Errors in punctuation are the most common type of error in writing. Studies of the writing of elementary and secondary school children and of adults show that errors in punctuation persist through all educational levels. In general, these studies indicate that either proficiency in punctuation is difficult to acquire or the schools do not teach it well.[19] Perhaps the greatest cause of punctuation errors is that too little attention is given to the punctuation items of greatest social importance and too much effort is wasted teaching items of little importance.

Some educational literature relates punctuation to intonations in speech.[20] Certainly punctuation at the end of a sentence is a major clue to the reading intonation pattern. Some punctuation items signal the need for a change in pitch as well as indicating junctures. For example, an oral reading of the sentence "The two girls in the first row are close friends" will not sound the same as "The two girls, in the first row, are close friends." But it is a fallacy to assume that any pause or change in pitch requires a punctuation mark. Thus, teaching children to punctuate sentences according to speech signals can be misleading. On the other hand, relating punctuation items to intonation patterns of speech is helpful to both oral and silent reading because they are often clues to meaning.

It may be useful to teach children that punctuation links sentences and parts of sentences and words, separates sentences and parts of sentences, encloses parts of sentences, and indicates omissions. Attaching particular punctuation marks to each purpose probably is an oversimplification, but one curriculum guide identifies the linking marks as the semicolon, colon, dash, and hyphen and the separating items as the period, question mark, exclamation point, and comma.[21] Omissions are said to be shown by the apostrophe and the dash, although the dash is also an enclosing item when it is paired, as are commas, parentheses, and quotation marks.

The following list suggests which punctuation items should receive instructional attention at different grade levels in elementary school. The listing should not be held too rigidly because punctuation needs vary and each item should be taught as the need occurs.

Grade 1

1. Period at the end of a sentence that tells something
2. Period after numbers in any kind of list

---

19. Robert R. Odom, "Growth of a Language Skill: Punctuation," *California Journal of Educational Research* 15 (1964): 12–47.

20. For example, see Mary E. Fowler, *Teaching Language, Composition, and Literature* (New York: McGraw-Hill Book Co., 1965), p. 200; Paul C. Burns and Alberta L. Lowe, *The Language Arts in Childhood Education* (Chicago: Rand McNally and Co., 1966), pp. 183–85.

21. *Selecting, Organizing, and Expressing Ideas.* Clover Park School District No. 400, Lakewood Center, Wash., 1967, p. 18A.

Grade 2

1. Items listed for grade one
2. Question mark at the close of a question
3. Comma after salutation of a friendly note or letter
4. Comma after closing of a friendly note or letter
5. Comma between the day of the month and the year
6. Comma between name of city and state

Grade 3

1. Items listed for grades one and two
2. Period after abbreviations
3. Period after an initial
4. Use of an apostrophe in common contractions, such as *isn't* and *aren't*
5. Commas in a list

Grade 4

1. All items listed for previous grades
2. Apostrophe to show possession
3. Hyphen separating parts of a word divided at end of a line
4. Period following a command
5. Exclamation point at the end of a word or group of words that makes an exclamation
6. Comma setting off an appositive
7. Colon after the salutation of a business letter
8. Quotation marks before and after a direct quotation
9. Comma between explanatory words and a quotation
10. Period after numerals and letters in outlines

Grade 5

1. All items listed for previous grades
2. Colon in writing time
3. Quotation marks around the title of an article, the chapter of a book, and the title of a poem or story
4. Underlining the title of a book

Grade 6

1. All items listed for previous grades
2. Comma to set off nouns in direct address
3. Hyphen in compound numbers
4. Colon to set off a list
5. Commas to set off transitional/parenthetical expressions (e.g., *yes, no, of course, however*)

Capitalization

Capitalization is another mechanical element of written language about which considerable evidence has accumulated concerning children's needs at different grade levels.[22] Researchers have identified these needs by examining examples of spontaneous and assigned writing and then graded the difficulty of particular capitalization skills. Many courses of study and textbooks in language list quite definite grade requirements in the area of capitalization. Such listings are useful guides, but within a classroom there will be considerable variation in capitalization proficiency, as there is in other skills and abilities. Therefore, a child should have mastered items of capitalization generally recommended for instruction in grades two and three before being required to learn items listed for grades five and six (this principle also applies in all other matters of form and convention).

The following list of minimal capitalization skills by grades is suggestive only, but it does take into account what children need to know in order to write and indicates the relative difficulty of the items.

Grade 1

1. The first word of a sentence
2. The child's first and last names
3. The name of the teacher, school, town, and street
4. The word "I"

Grade 2

1. Items listed for grade one
2. The date
3. First and important words in titles of books read
4. Proper names used in children's writing
5. Titles of compositions
6. Names of titles: "Mr." "Mrs.," "Miss," and "Ms."

Grade 3

1. Items listed for grades one and two
2. Proper names: month, day, common holidays
3. First word in a line of verse
4. First and important words in titles of stories and poems
5. First word in salutation of informal note, such as "Dear"
6. First word in closing of informal note, such as "Yours" or "Your friend"

---

22. Robert R. Odom, "Sequence and Grade Placement of Capitalization Skills," *Elementary English* 38 (February 1961): 118–21.

Grade 4

1. Items listed for lower grades
2. Names of cities and states
3. Names of organizations to which children belong, such as Cub Scouts, Grade Four, and so on
4. "Mother," "Father," and so on, used in place of a name
5. Local geographical names

Grade 5

1. All items listed for lower grades
2. Names of streets
3. Names of all places and persons, countries, oceans, and so on
4. Capitalization in outlining
5. Titles used with names, such as President Lincoln
6. Commercial trade names

Grade 6

1. All items listed for lower grades
2. Names for the Deity and the Bible
3. First word of a quoted sentence
4. Proper adjectives indicating race, nationality, and so on
5. Abbreviations of proper nouns and titles

In addition to teaching the proper use of capital letters, children should learn not to capitalize unnecessarily and, in particular, not to capitalize words for emphasis.

Teaching Capitalization and Punctuation

Whatever the children's competence level in using punctuation and capitalization, the most effective teaching occurs—as it does for all skill teaching—as the need to use these skills arises. The more children write, the greater the need for practice in punctuation and capitalization. In the kindergarten and first grade, children need to know to capitalize their first names. When they make a weather calendar they need to know that the names of the months and the days of the week are capitalized. With the help of the teacher, children will notice when they read what they have written that difficulties in understanding arise unless some capital letters and punctuation marks are present. One course of study effectively expresses the functions of punctuation in this way:[23]

---

23. *Using Language* (Wilmington, Del.: Division of Elementary Education, Wilmington Public Schools, 1955), p. 121.

Children soon learn that punctuation marks act as traffic signals to help them on their way. The best learning for the use of these comes from having the child read his own work and find the places where they are needed for clarity. Periods, commas, question marks can be introduced when the need to use them arises. When added practice is needed, make that practice meaningful to the children.

Following the initial discovery of need by the children, the next step is the presentation of a model. If a report contains many errors in punctuation and capitalization, the teacher might rewrite the material on the board or a chart, using correct punctuation and capitalization. This procedure emphasizes that teachers themselves must use punctuation and capitalization carefully.

Children need to develop habits of punctuation and capitalization. Because they ordinarily do not know how to write before coming to school, the school must take the responsibility for forming habits of acceptable use of these mechanics. Emphasizing as few punctuation items and capitalization rules as possible will aid in motivating children to develop good habits. Much of the practice should derive from writing for genuine communication purposes, although occasional individual or small group drill on troublesome items is appropriate.

Language textbooks usually do not provide enough practice exercises to establish punctuation and capitalization habits. Many of them address more than one item at a time (for example, selection of a conjunction and use of commas or use of commas in series and direct address). Therefore it is up to the classroom teacher to construct practice exercises, a procedure that is preferable anyway because the teacher can relate them directly to the children's writing and class activities and tailor them to the specific needs of individual children.

The following suggestions for developing capitalization and punctuation skills should prove useful:

1. Observe all written work carefully, note errors made, and perhaps tabulate the types of errors. Use observations as the basis for further teaching and review.
2. Provide many proofreading experiences that emphasize the types of situations that seem difficult for pupils to handle.
3. Insist that pupils critically edit and proofread whatever they write.
4. Use dictation exercises that call for certain skills as well as avoidance of excessive punctuation and capitalization.
5. Give children practice exercises that require using capitals or punctuation.
6. Help children to compile personal lists of words that they frequently fail to capitalize or that they capitalize erroneously. Introduce or review rules covering these situations and provide appropriate practice exercises.
7. Have pupils edit their own or other pupils' papers with special attention to capitalization. Sometimes this task can be done individually; at other times the child should work with a group.

8. Emphasize careful use of capitals and punctuation in all written work. Continually stress good form in writing.
9. Have pupils check their own writing after a dictation exercise. Emphasize self-diagnosis of difficulties.
10. Stress the relationship of sentence structure to punctuation and of both to clarity and smoothness of expression.
11. Give special attention to handwriting if that is the cause of some capitalization faults.
12. Give short diagnostic tests on the major capitalization and punctuation items on a frequent basis. Have pupils check their own work.
13. Make all practice periods short and relate them to specific needs. For example, use a five-minute individualized drill period near the close of the day to work on errors observed during the day.

SKILLS IN USING BOOKS FOR WRITING

Alphabetizing and indexing are essential aids to elementary schoolchildren both for their reading and for preparing their own writing. Crediting sources used in gathering information for written expression is another basic point to be mastered in elementary school; thus children need to learn skills in footnoting and in using and preparing bibliographies. In this section we will discuss all these skills; related teaching suggestions also appear in other sections of this book.

Alphabetizing and indexing.   As discussed in Chapter 10, the best way to learn alphabetical order and its uses is to practice putting letters and words in alphabetical order and using materials that require mastery of the alphabet to find particular information. In addition, children need to know how to use tables of contents, indexes, and paragraph headings. Instruction in these skills requires a meaningful context. When children put together a book of pictures they have collected or stories they have written, for example, they should compile a table of contents and perhaps an index. In order to answer questions or prepare reports, children will need to use reference sources. In such activities lies the basis for teaching the skills of alphabetizing and indexing. Both reading and English or language textbooks suggest activities for teaching these skills; for example:[24]

Follow these steps to gather information for your report.

1. Locate four or five sources that contain information about your topic. If possible, find both books and magazine articles. Do not use more than two encyclopedias. Make a list of the sources you find.
2. Make a list of three or four questions about your topic that you want to explore.
3. Read the information and take notes. Be sure your notes help you answer the questions you listed.

24. John S. Hand et al., *Progress in English* (Chicago: Laidlaw Brothers, 1972), p. 163.

Another example, this one for the fourth-grade level, gives practice in alphabetical order by using an index:[25]

These words are listed in the index. Can you put them in alphabetical order? Look at the second letter of each word.

Accent mark	Alphabetical order	Address
Apostrophe	Abbreviations	*And* fault

Teachers can easily devise these types of exercises and others that necessitate using locational skills and they will have to, because such exercises do not appear in sufficient numbers in textbooks to establish the pupils' skills. Furthermore, the ones in textbooks are not likely to relate as closely as is desirable to the activities of a particular classroom.

Bibliographies.   Children should learn to make and use bibliographies as soon as they encounter books that contain them. They should learn acceptable bibliographical form for listing references in their social studies, science, and other reports. A systematic program may incorporate the following form, to be introduced as the need arises and combined with practice activities so that children will learn it.

1.   Give completely and accurately all necessary information, such as author's name, title page numbers, and date of copyright.
2.   Use alphabetical order whenever suitable.
3.   Write the author's surname first and put a comma after it.
4.   Underline all titles of books or magazines.
5.   Develop habits of absolute accuracy on references and forms.

A suggested bibliography for the middle grades is the following:

Author, A. B., *Bibliography Form.*

For the upper grades and junior high school, the following form is acceptable:

Books

Author, A. B., *Bibliography Form as Practiced by the Publishers.* Boston: Hale University Press, 1962.

Magazine articles

Author, A. B., "The Standardization of Bibliography Forms." *School Review*, 26:348–357, July, 1935.

---

25. Mildred A. Dawson et al., *Language for Daily Use*, Level Orange, New Harbrace Ed. (New York: Harcourt Brace Jovanovich, 1973), p. 109.

Footnoting.   Teachers of the lower elementary grades can begin to instruct children to give credit in their writing for ideas and information obtained from others. Many children develop a vague feeling that there is something wrong about using someone else's ideas, so they copy material and try to hide the fact without realizing that the only thing wrong with this practice is hiding it. None of us, children included, can possibly be fully knowledgeable about all subjects. In fact, most people have few completely original ideas. We learn many things from others, and after a time we cannot identify the actual source of the idea or information. When we do know the source, however, we should identify it, and this rule should be stressed to children at an early age.

In large part, how well children develop the habit of properly quoting others and acknowledging words and ideas depends on the concern shown by the teacher and the instructional emphasis it receives. The teacher should have pupils practice these skills and provide for proper acknowledgment in their note-taking and information-gathering activities. No elaborate footnoting forms are necessary. At first students need to specify only the author, title, and page numbers for a source. Later they can learn to include the publisher and date of publication. Most language textbooks discuss footnoting and give models.

WRITING EVALUATION

The evaluation of both writing products and the writing process is an activity that some teachers avoid. Yet evaluation is an inherent part of any teaching; and certainly anyone who observes children in the act of writing will note that they evaluate their own and their classmates' writing. Too often writing evaluation means marking papers and grading them or putting grades on report cards. Too often, too, it means a score on a test that becomes a basis for comparison with an earlier effort or with other children.

Evaluation, of course, means more than merely assigning a grade; it is more than comparing one pupil with others or marking a pupil's paper. In a writing program, evaluation should also take in appraising the program itself and the teaching procedures and materials. It should include measurement of the general quality of writing, as well as the quality of each pupil's efforts, and assessment of pupils' growth over time and from one writing activity to another.[26]

Evaluators of Writing

Teachers, parents, and the children themselves all should evaluate written expression. Although each group plays an important evaluative role, self-evaluation

---

26. Walter T. Petty and Mary Bowen, *Slithery Snakes and Other Aids to Children's Writing* (New York: Appleton-Century-Crofts, 1967), pp. 81–82.

by children is fundamental to effective assessment. Assuming that the purpose of education is to make children capable of independent and thoughtful action, much of the evaluation of their work ought to come from them, rather than from the teacher. When children have succeeded in composing a sequence of ideas, they should be able to evaluate the effectiveness of their products.

A small child might unknowingly judge effectiveness by saying, "That's the way I want to say it." In a few years the same child might say, "I have trouble sticking to one main idea in a paragraph, so this time I jotted down all the things I wanted to say first. Then I took everything that's part of the main idea and put them all together. I'm better now on sticking to telling one thing. Maybe next I'll work on going from one idea to another." Both comments are evaluations.[27]

A teacher's evaluation of writing must intertwine with the evaluation of what is going on in the classroom throughout each school day. Teachers should ask themselves questions like these:[28]

1. Have the boys and girls "who could not write" found that they could?
2. Are the children aware that planning helps in creative writing?
3. Am I having enough individual conferences to point out strengths and weaknesses in ways that promote progress?
4. Do I take notes on pupil work that are useful in direct teaching lessons?
5. Do I search for something to praise in all papers, including the poorest ones?
6. Am I concerned more with errors and mechanical details than with ideas that will promote growth in creative writing?

Of course, there are no easy answers to these questions. Certainly teachers must ask their own questions and supply their own answers.

An accumulation of evidence points to a number of factors that may cause children's interest in writing and their actual writing ability to be less than is generally anticipated or at least hoped for. These factors, which every teacher should consider in evaluating the writing program, include the following:

1. Lack of adequate direction and guidance during the planning stage and while children are writing
2. Fear of teacher disapproval on the part of pupils
3. Suppression of oral expression of thoughts
4. Meager vocabularies
5. Ignorance of form

---

27. Adapted from *Selecting, Organizing, and Expressing Ideas.* Clover Park School District No. 400, Lakewood Center, Wash., 1967, p. 16.

28. Adapted from Jean M. Ullyette, *Guidelines for Creative Writing* (Dansville, N.Y.: Instructor Publications, 1968), pp. 42–43.

6. Deficiency of input of ideas and information
7. Failure to recognize the role of an audience for writing
8. Too little knowledge of composing—putting together a sequence of thoughts
9. Blocking writing by expecting children to do it without time for thought and possibly discussion

Evaluation by the teacher should be ongoing. It should be a continuous questioning and reflecting process. Any time children are writing and any time their writing products are examined, evaluation by the teacher should be taking place.

Whether teachers like it or not, parents evaluate virtually everything that goes on in school. They frequently are critical of creative writing because they have a strong orientation to correct spelling, neat handwriting, and "proper" usage. Thus, the wise teacher brings parents into the program by explaining objectives and suggesting how parents can help. In particular, teachers should urge parents to read their children's writing, praise it honestly, and talk *with* (not *to*) their children about their work. Of course, parents justifiably want to see improvement in their children's spelling, "mechanics," and compositional skills and also to see evidence of increased creativity.

Evaluating Objectively

Many commercial tests purport to measure overall writing ability and/or relevant skills and knowledge. The validity of such tests is open to serious questioning. As a recent publication states:[29]

> What actually is included in commercially available tests that is purported to measure "writing ability"? Usually tests consist almost entirely of items concerned with sentence structure, word meaning, and mechanics. They never attempt to cope with a student's ability to select a subject, pursue a specific intention, and effectively address a particular audience. Occasionally, however, a test will include items which relate to a student's ability to judge the organization and substantive details of a piece of writing—even though, of course, the writing is not the student's and the prospective readers are usually not identified.

Truly, however, the possibilities for objective evaluation of pupil achievement and growth in written expression are much greater than they are in oral expression—a natural enough conclusion, considering that the written product endures for examination. As the foregoing quotation points out, the difficulty lies in

---

29. Richard Braddock, "Evaluation of Writing Tests," in *Reviews of Selected Published Tests in English* edited by Alfred H. Grommon (Urbana, Ill.: National Council of Teachers of English, 1976), p. 120.

separating knowledge about grammar, usage, and social convention from ability to use that knowledge in writing. Furthermore, decisions about what is good writing, or even what is "normal" at various age levels, are not all that easy to make. Such limitations, however, do not preclude evaluation of most writing or make it impossible to achieve some objectivity in evaluation. The performance or behavioral objective movement in education that has become popular in recent years, if viewed sensibly, suggests the need for objectives that can be clearly understood. Thus, whether a child has learned to fill in a form properly can be judged. Likewise the ability to write a footnote correctly can be measured. If a letter was to address a specific purpose, the extent of the writer's success can be determined. Of course, for some kinds of writing, different people would render different judgments. Nevertheless, few people would argue against stating objectives as clearly and specifically as possible. Lack of specificity always clouds evaluation.

The failure of standardized instruments to measure writing ability adequately has led to repeated attempts to objectify or even standardize appraisal procedures.[30] In other words, ways have been sought to supply teachers with examples of various levels of writing ability in order to keep teachers' judgments consistent for all writing samples. These attempts have resulted in rating criteria and scales. The weights that the rating criteria assign to organization, style, ideas, mechanics, and so on, reflect beliefs about what is "good writing." Weights of various elements of writing also are evident in the scales, in the examples of writing chosen, and the rank given them.

The following standards from a curriculum guide represent an attempt to objectify evaluation by having the teacher look for the same features in each writing product.[31] Although this particular example does not show the weights of each category, generally they would be Content, 30 points; Organization, 20 points; Style, 20 points; Command of Standard English, 15 points; and Appearance, 15 points.

    A.   Content
        1.   Relevant to the writer, to the reader, to the assignment
        2.   Worth of the communication to the writer and to the reader
        3.   Adequacy of coverage or treatment
        4.   Freshness and originality
        5.   Sincerity
        6.   Validity and supporting evidence or development
        7.   Interest to the writer, to the reader
        8.   Clarity of intention on the part of the writer and as perceived by the reader

---

30. Paul B. Diederich, *Measuring Growth in English* (Urbana, Ill.: National Council of Teachers of English, 1974).

31. *Handbook for English Language Arts, Speech and Composition, Grades 5–12.* Bureau of Curriculum Development, Board of Education, City of New York, 1971, pp. 210–11.

B.   Organization
   1.   Logic in order of arrangement
   2.   Psychological soundness in presentation
   3.   Coherence
   4.   Smoothness of transitions
   5.   Unity
C.   Style
   1.   Appropriateness to purpose and situation
   2.   Revelation of the writer's personality
   3.   Imagination, originality, creativity in patterns of thought and expression
   4.   Appeal to reader's interest
   5.   Vividness of language
   6.   Variety in sentence structure and language
D.   Command of standard English
   1.   Soundness of sentence structure
   2.   Standard usage and grammatical relationships
   3.   Correct spelling
   4.   Standard punctuation and capitalization
E.   Appearance
   1.   Legibility
   2.   Neatness
   3.   Standard format, as in business letters

The curriculum guide in which this checklist originally appeared suggests that teachers modify the criteria to suit their students' needs and perhaps eliminate some of them for certain types of writing.

This is good advice because writing varies from one form to another and, more important, children's backgrounds and needs differ in the many elementary school settings that we tend to generalize about. Increasingly schools and school districts are developing scales and evaluative criteria based on the performance of their own children. One of the best examples of this practice is one district's model based on "actual analysis of children's writing on each grade level, grades 1–6. Writing samples were grouped into performance levels, and a descriptive analysis was made of the characteristics of the papers in each level."[32] These characteristics became criteria for evaluation and were revised as they were used. For each grade the district developed several levels of criteria, which were stated so that teachers could judge the quality of each paper.[33]

Greater effort to design valid and reliable evaluation methods is necessary both to supplement or replace measures from the typical standardized instruments and to overcome the shortcomings of teacher judgments about writing;

32. "What Research and Evaluation Tells Us About Teaching Written Expression in the Elementary School" (Mimeographed), p. 7 (sent to the senior author by Roger A. McCaig, Director of Research and Development, Grosse Pointe Public School System, Grosse Pointe, Mich.).

33. A complete description of the criteria is available in booklet form from the Department of Instruction, Grosse Pointe Public School System (389 St. Clair Avenue, Grosse Pointe, Mich. 48230).

a teacher may judge a piece of writing differently at different times and in different settings, and several teachers judging a piece of writing at one time are likely to disagree. As one specialist put it: "Teachers who have never graded a set of papers that have previously been graded by another teacher seldom realize how commonly and seriously teachers disagree in their judgments of writing ability."[34]

Evaluating Specific Writing Skills and Products

Evaluation of any writing is largely an appraisal of the quality of the product in terms of its purpose. From the beginning of instruction in written expression, teachers should encourage self-evaluation by pupils, perhaps by providing each child with models, when possible and appropriate, for guidance and comparison. Self-evaluation checklists, such as those suggested earlier are also helpful. Here, for example, are specific points to check in evaluating a business letter.

1. Is my letter brief, courteous, and to the point?
2. Is all of my spelling correct?
3. Have I positioned the heading correctly?
4. Do I have the inside address correctly placed?
5. Did I use a suitable greeting for a business letter?
6. Did I use a suitable closing?
7. Did I sign my letter?
8. Is the paper I used suitable for a business letter?

Students can and should make their own checklists. They will need guidance from time to time in deciding what to look for and what questions to ask themselves and to make sure that they are actually applying their own criteria.

Examples of scales or other checklists that a group of teachers might design for their own use in writing evaluation follow. The first example is from the Carlson Scale, which is designed to measure "original elements of children's stories" and *not* to evaluate all qualities.[35]

Unusual Beginning—Beginning used which appears with statistical infrequency in stories written by children at this grade level.

Unusual Dialogue—Dialogue is used with unusual facility; child sometimes speaks to animals in plausible manner.

---

34. Diederick, p. 5.

35. Ruth Kearney Carlson, *Sparkling Words: Two Hundred and Twenty-five Practical and Creative Writing Ideas*, (Geneva, Ill.: Paladin House, 1973), p. 224. Available from the National Council of Teachers of English, Urbana, Ill.

0	Ordinary traditional beginning. "Once upon a time" or "Once"		0	No dialogue or conversation.
1	Fairly usual type of beginning. "One day, one night, one afternoon, one evening." "It happened this way."		1	One or two words of dialogue or conversation. "'Yes,' she said."
3	Unusual beginning. "Judy was nine years old. She had blue eyes, red freckles, and golden curls." "When I was on my vacation last summer, I had the time of my life."		3	Some dialogue is used which causes the story to progress. "Bill said, 'What are we going to have for dinner?'" "Mother replied, 'Cream puffs.'"
5	Beginning which appears rarely. "Do you believe in ghosts? Well, I didn't until this happened." "The slow, lumbering mule cart came to a stop on a turn of the bumpy road." "Clank, bang, crash, bang! I finished."		5	Dialogue is used naturally and does not seem to be forced or artificial. "But mother fish said, 'Now Joe, you are too young, you will swallow a fish hook and be fried and eaten,' 'Mother knows best, pooh!' said little Joe as he swam off." "I saw Mr. Chipmunk and said, 'Hi, Mr. Chipmunk.'"

The next example is part of a scale developed at the University of Pittsburgh.[36]

A.	Fulfillment of purpose	Scoring standard	Maximum points	Assessment
1.	Main idea, or theme, is clear.	(0) muddled, (1) clear, (2) very clear	(2)	_____
2.	Six relevant events develop the theme.	(1) ea. of 6 relevant (−1) ea. of 6 irrelevant	(6)	_____
3.	Content conveys definite feeling (amusing, relaxing, frightening, astonishing, confiding, mysterious.)	(0) indefinite (1) moderate (2) very strong	(2)	_____

B.	Organization	Scoring standard	Maximum points	Assessment
1.	The title fits the story.	(0) does not fit (1) fits adequately (2) fits, triggers strong interest	(2)	_____

---

36. Used with the permission of Professor H. W. Sartain and Mrs. Linda Benedict.

B. *Organization*	*Scoring standard*	*Maximum points*	*Assessment*
2. Story begins with action or mood appeal.	(0) no appeal (1) appeal or action	(1)	_____
3. A separate paragraph is formed for each different event or idea.	(1/2) ea. of 4 correct (−1/2) ea. of 4 missing	(2)	_____
4. Sentences are stated in understandable sequence.	(1/2) ea. of 4 in order (−1/2) ea. of 4 out of order	(2)	_____
5. Events lead to a satisfying ending or surprise.	(0) unsatisfying (1) satisfying (2) surprise	(2)	_____

The final example is a portion of a scale that has had only limited use but suggests an effort to evaluate more than originality.[37]

A. Is there an overall impression of literary flavor and vitality?

1   Total work lacks style and fails to elicit responses in reader.

3   Figurative language is attempted but total work lacks individuality and flavor, and fails to elicit strong emotional reactions in reader.

5   Highly individualistic in thoughts, in structures, and/or in use of figurative language—similes, metaphors, descriptive words, phrases. Harmonious effect sparks deep emotional reactions in reader.

B. Is there a main train of thought?

1   There is a main train of thought.

3   The main train of thought is evident throughout.

5   The main train of thought elicits feelings throughout.

Evaluating Papers and Grading

Evaluation is a major part of the total teaching process, a part from which the teacher learns what needs teaching attention and what knowledge, skills, and abilities the pupils possess. Responding to papers is also a part of teaching, though too often it becomes an exercise in fault finding. Assigning grades, however, is different from evaluation. The purpose of assigning grades is reporting—first to

37. Developed by Dr. Juanita Russell and Mrs. Marion Cross and used with their permission.

pupils and later to the school system and to parents. This section contains some suggestions on how to respond to papers and assign grades.

Marking errors.   Covering a paper with marks indicating errors is of little value to anyone. Pupils do not learn from seeing their errors marked in this manner and information of a specific nature concerning those things needing further attention may be lost to both teacher and student. A teacher should call the pupils' attention only to the grossest errors and simultaneously note them for follow-up instruction.

Marking good points.   The red pencil is a favorite teacher weapon, but the sight of red marks usually causes pupils to destroy their papers or at least conceal them from classmates. To overcome this problem use the red pencil to call attention to commendable aspects of the writing—a good choice of words, an apt expression, a neat margin, well-organized thought, and so on. It is even better to avoid defacing the paper altogether by commenting on an attached slip of paper or at least to use light erasable pencil.

Using the positive approach.   Everything that every child writes has some quality to praise. A better-formed letter, fewer erasures, greater promptness in turning a project in, and so on can be the focus of the response if those are the only qualities that are sincerely commendable.

Providing reasons.   Letter grades and numerical scores are cold and empty symbols. They say little. Adults do not give a novel a "B" or a "C"; we say it was a good book or not as good as the last one we read. The teacher should supplement grades with specific oral and written comments.

Knowing the child.   Evaluation of a child's writing should concentrate on teaching the child to write better. This goal is attainable only if the child desires improvement. Holding frequent personal conferences with pupils to discuss specific writing is helpful.

Because a particular letter or number grade means different things to different persons and because it has little specific value for teaching, avoid unrequired grading. This recommendation does not mean that evaluation procedures should diminish; teachers, in fact, should use them much more often than they usually do. Teachers should ask themselves if they are more interested in teaching—actually evaluating and analyzing the progress of each pupil's work—or in accumulating rows of marks in a book.

Further Evaluative and Diagnostic Suggestions

Evaluation permits teachers to diagnose problems requiring further teaching. It facilitates identification of specific strengths to capitalize on in later writing, as well as discussion of weaknesses for corrective instruction.

The child's composition that follows illustrates how a teacher might comment on the child's writing and suggest areas for improvement. This particular writer should receive praise for her interesting beginning and her ability to communicate strong feeling. Coherence (e.g., "And she liked to go to the bakery.") and the need for better-developed detail might be the subject of a brief, informal teacher-pupil conference. The teacher's anecdotal records would indicate the need for future instruction in proofreading for inconsistencies in spelling, capitalization, and punctuation.

> Tad went into the guest room even tho he knew he had no reason to bee in there. All he wanted was sum fancy wrapping paper. . . . . to wrap a scarf for his mother. He opened up the closet door and looked _____! there must be wrappin paper in here he said to himself. he did see something else too and he pretended that he din't see it because he was shur it was for him. And she liked to go to the bakery. And Tad pretended from that Day to This day that he didn't see ɪᴛ in the closet. Can you guess what tad was going to get for christmas.

The teacher's written comments to the child—clipped to the paper—were these:

> Your story captured my interest from the beginning, and it steadily built suspense. I will guess that Tad is getting a baseball bat.
>   Could you give me more clues so I can make a better guess? (Is the bakery a hint?) Also, does your story have a title?
>
> Mr. Jones

EXERCISES FOR THOUGHT AND ACTION

1. Describe the kind of classroom where much assigned and unassigned writing occurs, where children like themselves, like to write, and think they *can* write. Describe the teacher of this class.
2. Write a letter to a nonwriting teacher telling him or her that you feel only a writer can teach writing well. Include the reasons for your belief.
3. Consult at least two language arts textbooks for the intermediate grades to learn whether and how they teach outlining skills. How would you supplement the material provided?
4. In the story about Tad in this chapter, what clues do you see that indicate the author needs to work on proofreading (as opposed to spelling instruction on the words *be, some,* and so on, or capitalization instruction on the first words in sentences, for example)? What "mistakes" do you suspect the author would be prompted to correct by herself if you said, "Kay, I'd like to hear you read this story to me"?
5. Begin within your general teaching file a collection of examples of good business letters, friendly letters, thank-you notes, applications, complaints, reports, records, notices, forms, and so on.

6. Plan a lesson for a small group of children at a specific grade level that requires them to use their imaginations in writing something other than a story or poem (for example, a cartoon caption, dialogue for a cartoon strip, graffiti).
7. Describe a strategy using a prose passage similar to the one below to elicit from children a list of criteria with which to evaluate their own descriptive writing.

> Barnaby is a basset hound eleven weeks old. My wife says he looks as if he were put together with parts left over from various discontinued dogs. He has sad, dissipated-looking eyes. His ears are floppy and enormous: he trips over them when he tries to run, and when he eats they have to be put up with clothespins. His paws, especially his front paws, are much too big, and the silky fur on his legs is pleated. When he tries to run there is a wonderful lack of communication between his front and his back; he runs with his front legs and bounds with his back legs and wriggles excitedly in between, so that one or other of his paws is sliding out from under him. Barnaby is a charmer.[38]

8. As a group project, read and compile a bibliography of children's trade books that contain haiku (e.g., Richard Lewis's *In a Spring Garden*), limericks, cinquain, free verse, and other poetry forms. Describe a strategy you could use to get children to *state* the characteristics of a verse form after they have heard many good examples.
9. Compile a bibliography of published children's writing, including books (e.g., Richard Lewis's *Miracles*) and periodicals (e.g., *Stone Soup*).
10. Plan a lesson in which the objective is to make clear to children that punctuation has a purpose, that it can make a big difference in meaning. To illustrate:

   Pair 1: Private. No swimming allowed.
   Private? No! Swimming allowed.
   Pair 2: Mr. Jones, the secretary, is an hour late.
   Mr. Jones, the secretary is an hour late.
   Pair 3: A smart dog knows it's master.
   A smart dog knows its master.
   Pair 4: The show ended happily.
   The show ended, happily.

11. Plan an elementary class project (e.g., the making of a book) that would give children the opportunity to learn and apply skills in indexing, compiling tables of contents, footnoting, and making bibliographies.
12. In actual practice, you should bring to bear all of the information you know about a child in formulating your response to a piece of his or her writing (e.g., whether this sample appears to represent a best, worst, or typical ef-

38. Donald Barr, *Who Pushed Humpty Dumpty* (New York: Atheneum, 1971), p. 86.

fort would govern the nature of your reaction and your mutual plan for improvement). Nevertheless, pretend you have received this piece of writing:

A smart pet

Ponies are my favorites because they are smarter than any other pets. One day I had an experience that showed why I think so. As we were eating dinner, we heard a pounding outside. As my family looked, we saw our pony, running around the yard. My father got a rope and ran after him. He ran and ran for ten minutes, but it was no use, he could not catch him. Panting, my father stopped.

Five minutes later the pony stopped, and went into the barn. All he wanted was to exercise his legs a little.

Now we let him loose and he goes in by himself. I think this is proof enough that a pony is a smart pet.[39]

Describe in detail the form of your response (e.g., written feedback, oral feedback, or both; the form it will take; anecdotal records for future reference).

13. Find evidence of the personal element of punctuation. Do you think that if you asked ten professional writers to punctuate a 500-word passage each would do it the same way? What items of punctuation seem fixed? Which ones seem to allow for individualization?

14. In groups of two or three, look at a class set of compositions. Formulate evaluation criteria and rank them according to quality. To what extent do you agree among and within groups? Test the reliability of your process by reranking the compositions two weeks later.

15. Further analyze the set of papers in Activity 14. What recurring problems in content and form would justify planning small-group instruction? Who (or what paper numbers) would attend each of the proposed group lessons? Determine the single most apparent need of each writer.

16. Make a list of situations or activities occurring in the elementary school that would offer opportunities for writing. Try to think of situations and activities different from those given in this chapter. Describe the types of writing that might occur.

17. Describe how you would teach outlining at a particular grade level.

SELECTED REFERENCES

Arnstein, Flora J. *Children Write Poetry: A Creative Approach.* New York: Dover Publications, 1967.

Braddock, Richard; Lloyd-Jones, Richard; and Schoer, Lowell. *Research in Written Composition.* Urbana, Ill.: National Council of Teachers of English, 1963.

---

39. Adapted from *Evaluating Written Composition in the Elementary and Secondary School* (Baltimore: Baltimore County Public Schools, 1967), p. 31.

Burrows, Alvina T. *What Research Says to the Teacher: Teaching Composition.* Rev. ed. Washington, D.C.: National Education Association, 1966.

Cooper, Charles R., and Odell, Lee, eds. *Evaluating Writing: Describing, Measuring, Judging.* Urbana, Ill.: National Council of Teachers of English, 1977.

Corbin, Richard. *The Teaching of Writing in Our Schools.* New York: Macmillan Co., 1966.

Fagan, William T.; Cooper, Charles R.; and Jensen, Julie M. *Measures for Research and Evaluation in the English Language Arts.* Urbana, Ill.: ERIC Clearinghouse on Reading and Communication Skills and National Council of Teachers of English, 1975.

Lundsteen, Sara W. *Children Learn to Communicate.* Englewood Cliffs, N.J.: Prentice-Hall, 1976.

Smith, E. Brooks; Goodman, Kenneth S.; and Meredith, Robert. *Language and Thinking in School.* 2d ed. New York: Holt, Rinehart and Winston, 1976.

Thorn, Elizabeth A. *Teaching the Language Arts: Speaking, Listening, Reading, Writing.* Toronto: Gage Educational Publishing, 1974.

Wolsch, Robert A. *Poetic Composition Through the Grades: A Language Sensitivity Program.* New York: Teachers College Press, 1970.

15

The Spelling Program

The ultimate goal in spelling instruction . . . is to enable students to spell correctly the words needed both in and outside school, in their present student status and later as literate adults. —Thomas D. Horn, "Spelling," in Encyclopedia of Educational Research

It is not ususual to hear someone say, "I never could spell." Sometimes the speaker goes on to say that "content is more important than mechanics" and that "oral communication is replacing writing and reading anyway." Interestingly, though, when such remarks appear in written expression no words are misspelled.

Certainly spelling correctly is not as important as content, to name just one basic element of written expression. But we know that content is unintelligible if the graphic symbols lack no meaning because words are misspelled. Occasional misspellings by adults usually present few problems, although most of us can cite instances when a person has been judged on the basis of spelling faults. Hanna and his colleagues point out that "The ability to acquire and use the skills basic to written communication is a requisite in modern society, and indeed it is to some extent basic to all forms of human communication."[1] Educational romantics and "establishment" critics notwithstanding, most teachers and parents agree with this assessment.

---

1. Paul R. Hanna, Richard E. Hodges, and Jean S. Hanna, *Spelling: Structure and Strategies* (Boston: Houghton Mifflin Co., 1971), p. 3.

In the first section of this chapter we will consider the place of spelling in the school curriculum—the goals of the program, the words taught, spelling attitudes and habits, and the relationships of spelling to other areas of the language arts. Next we will look at the type of instructional program a teacher should follow, major issues in spelling instruction, and spelling measurement and diagnostic instruments and procedures.

SPELLING IN THE SCHOOL CURRICULUM

In most schools the instructional program in spelling centers on a textbook or a workbook. In some cases the teacher supplements the instruction suggested in these materials. In a few schools the spelling program (largely the selection of words to learn) is based on the children's daily work. Regardless of the materials or the basis for the selection of the words, however, spelling instruction in too many schools is limited and inadequate.[2] The reasons for poor instruction include a lack of understanding of what should be taught and why, faulty instructional procedures, and a failure to integrate spelling with all written work.

Goals of the Program

The basic goal of spelling instruction is to teach children to spell correctly all of the words they write. Although there is general agreement on this goal, spelling authorities have different ideas about how teachers should achieve it. Some say that children should learn to associate letters with sounds so that they develop a general spelling ability.[3] Others say that such associations may be misleading and that spelling instruction should focus on the most commonly written words, along with certain attitudes and habits that encourage children to learn to spell words not included in formal instruction.[4] Both points of view (which we will discuss further later in the chapter) set the general pattern for the spelling program, but they must be expressed in specific objectives if they are to lead to effective instruction. The objectives of every spelling program should be stated in terms of attitudes, skills or abilities, and desirable habits, as shown here:

Attitudes:

Each child should
1. Recognize the necessity for correct spelling in effective communication
2. Show a desire to spell all words correctly
3. Believe that spelling correctly is something he or she can accomplish

---

2. Daniel J. Dieterich, "Diserroneosospellingitis or the Fine (Language) Art of Spelling." *Elementary English* 49 (February 1972): 246.

3. Hanna et al., p. 245.

4. Thomas D. Horn, "Spelling," in *Encyclopedia of Educational Research*, 4th ed., edited by Robert L. Ebel (New York: Macmillan Co., 1969), pp. 1282–99.

Skills and abilities:

Each child should be able to
1. Recognize all the letters of the alphabet in capital and lowercase forms in both printed and handwritten materials
2. Write all the letters of the alphabet in a legible manner in both capital and lowercase forms
3. Alphabetize words
4. Hear words accurately as they are spoken
5. Pronounce words clearly and accurately
6. See printed words accurately
7. Group and connect the letters of a word properly
8. Use punctuation elements that are necessary for spelling
9. Use a dictionary, including diacritical markings and guide words
10. Pronounce unfamiliar words properly
11. Use knowledge of sound and symbol relationships
12. Use knowledge of orthographic patterns that recur in language
13. Use the most effective spelling rules
14. Use effective procedures in learning to spell new words

Habits:

Each child should habitually
1. Proofread all writing carefully
2. Use reliable sources to find the spellings of unknown words
3. Follow a specific study procedure in learning to spell new words

Children should participate in setting objectives, although their involvement will not at once produce a listing of objectives as comprehensive as the one just presented. Gradually, however, teachers can bring children to consider what they need to learn and to evaluate themselves in terms of the objectives they set.

A Basic Vocabulary

Research has established that we write 3000 to 4000 words so frequently that every child should learn to spell them.[5] School personnel should regard this list as the "security segment" of the curriculum, the core of the spelling program. Other words that relate directly to writing needs and frequently misspelled words may lengthen the basic list. As one curriculum guide points out, however, additions to the basic list should be made carefully.[6] Words related to subject matter topics (in social studies, for instance) often have only temporary utility. Rather than adding such words to a basic spelling list, it is preferable to teach children to try to spell all words correctly by checking their spelling with textbooks and the dictionary. Also, rather than teaching them formally, teachers can write temporarily useful words on the chalkboard or on charts so that they are at hand when children need them for their writing.

Most commercial spelling programs provide in their books a list of basic words for the elementary grades. Usually these lists reflect research on the most frequently written words. Some books suggest additional words to use in efforts to teach generalizations about sound representations and structural patterns.

The words that make up the spelling program require careful selection, but equally important is emphasizing correct spelling in all writing activities as well as the supplemental spelling skills of proofreading, using the dictionary, and learning to apply spelling generalizations. And teachers must remember to adjust the list of spelling words to fit the needs and abilities of learners. Adjustments should reflect the relative importance of the words in the basic list for a specific grade level or for the school. Teachers should turn to spelling reports for help in modifying basic spelling lists and not attempt to decide subjectively the importance or suitability of a particular word.[7]

---

5. Horn, p. 1285.
6. *Guidelines to Spelling Instruction*, Curriculum Bulletin 2–71–16 (Houston, Tex.: Northeast Houston Independent School District, n.d.), p. 3.
7. Probably the easiest source for a teacher to use, and the one most likely to be available, is Harry A. Greene, *The New Iowa Spelling Scale* (Iowa City: University of Iowa, 1954). The most comprehensive report on word frequency is the list of 86,741 words presented in rank order in John B. Carroll, Peter Davies, and Barry Richman, *Word Frequency Book* (Boston: Houghton Mifflin Co., 1971). This list was assembled from textbooks, however, rather than from the writing of either children or adults generally. The classic studies are Ernest Horn, *A Basic Writing Vocabulary* (Iowa City: University of Iowa, 1926) and Henry D. Rinsland, *A Basic Vocabulary of Elementary School Children* (New York: Macmillan Co., 1945).

Attitudes Toward Spelling

Being a good speller is not simply a matter of being able to spell a basic core of words correctly or even to spell many words. Certainly it is more than making a perfect score on a spelling test. The good speller recognizes the importance of correct spelling, endeavors to spell each word correctly, and knows where to find out how to spell unknown words. The good speller is aware that correct spelling enhances the quality of written expression. In other words, the good speller has an attitude conducive to learning both through direct instruction and by incidental means.

To develop favorable attitudes toward spelling, teachers must regard spelling as something that really matters. They should endeavor to spell correctly all words that they write and to use a dictionary openly when in doubt about a spelling. Also, they should show children that the words in spelling lessons are words that they consistently use in writing and need to spell correctly. Simple tabulations of the children's own writing and that of their parents and friends will make this point clear.

Each child should develop a specific and efficient method of learning to spell a word and **should be required to study only those words that spelling tests and actual writing situations indicate that he or she is unable to spell.** Asking pupils to study words they already know is a major deterrent to the development of favorable attitudes.

The teacher should require a high standard of neatness and accuracy in all writing that is to be read by others. Teachers and pupils should cooperatively develop these standards and consistently observe them. Developing standards will encourage a spirit of mutual pride and cooperation in spelling achievement. To further this spirit, teachers should allow children to help one another study and proofread for spelling errors and to give encouragement to those who have difficulty spelling correctly.

Teachers should attack any negative attitudes as soon as they spot them by encouraging and stimulating the children's efforts. Instead of finding fault, a teacher should determine the cause of specific spelling difficulties. Praising the class's accomplishments and helping individual pupils to see their own progress also helps to stamp out negative attitudes. The pupils themselves might keep records of their progress so that they can measure their achievement against earlier performance.

Good Spelling Habits

A good attitude toward spelling is basic, but merely desiring to spell correctly will accomplish little unless a child has established certain habits, including:

1. *Showing concern about the spelling of all words written:* Children should ask themselves "Is this word spelled correctly?" and "Am I

sure?" This habit is established by the development and maintenance of standards in written work and regular attention to proofreading.

2.   *Checking the spelling of all words written about which there is doubt as to the correctness of their spelling:* They may look for unknown words in books, ask the teacher, or, after mastering skill in the use of a picture or regular dictionary, consult it.

3.   *Using a specific procedure for learning the spelling of new words:* The procedure may vary from child to child (as we will discuss later), but the particular steps a child follows should be thoroughly known by that child.

Spelling and the Other Language Arts

We have long known that a close relationship binds spelling and reading. The correlation between reading and spelling test scores has been reported, for example, to be .48, .51, .61, and .63.[8] We must be careful not to misinterpret these numbers, however, for the act of meeting a new word in reading does not automatically mean that the reader will learn to spell it. Words must crop up frequently in reading matter for this process to occur. Still one study showed that 63 of the 222 most frequently misspelled words are among the 1000 words that appear most frequently in reading material.[9] Thus, although there is a good deal of transfer of learning between spelling and reading, teaching spelling through reading activities probably interferes with the process of getting meaning from print and, further, is not an effective way to teach spelling. Additionally and in contrast to the opinions of some, little evidence suggests that spelling instruction promotes growth in reading.[10] It is particularly important to remember, too, that spelling is an encoding act whereas reading is a decoding one. Gaining meaning from graphic symbols involves a set of clues that differ completely from the ones available to the speller who is attempting to write a word.

It is a common belief that speed and legibility of handwriting affect spelling achievement. Certainly in spelling test situations in which time is a factor—and it often should be to prevent the development of poor listening habits—a faster writer obviously has an advantage over a slower one. It is equally obvious that the reader must consider an illegible word to be incorrectly spelled. Writing activities that give some emphasis to speed will aid spelling instruction by helping pupils to write with greater facility. In addition, pupil self-evaluation will improve legibility. Most commercial spelling materials provide for some hand-

---

8. Horn, p. 1289.

9. James A. Fitzgerald, *A Basic Life Spelling Vocabulary* (Milwaukee, Wis.: Bruce Publishing Co., 1951).

10. Albert J. Harris, *How to Increase Reading Ability*, 5th ed. (New York: David McKay Co., 1970), p. 344.

writing instruction and practice, and most handwriting programs provide for writing practice with frequently used words. Although there is some controversy about the relationship between handwriting form and spelling achievement, apparently no differences in achievement are attributable to the use of manuscript or cursive form or to the time at which children switched from manuscript to cursive.[11]

Speech problems also can affect spelling achievement: with ease and consistency of pronunciation and articulation comes a positive change in spelling ability.[12] Again, however, a program which seeks to foster the mutual development of language skills, although this goal is desirable, will not take the place of direct instruction in each area. This warning does not mean that instruction in spelling or any other language skill should take place in a meaningless and rigid environment. Systematic instruction does not prevent a teacher from capitalizing on the interrelationships of the language arts in designing the total curriculum.

The Instructional Program

The teaching of spelling may seem like a relatively simple task in comparison to instruction in, say, social studies and science. Nevertheless, repeated expressions of concern, complaint, and frustration indicate that achieving the desired instructional results is not a simple matter. Explanations for ineffectiveness in spelling instruction vary, but the authors of this book believe that inadequate and improper instruction is due to the failure to apply the knowledge gained from past research. One source sums up the instructional problem as follows:[13]

> Research pertaining to spelling instruction is neither new nor is it lacking in quantity. The greatest concern today is the apparent lack of application of the research evidence now available. The actual procedures followed in the teaching of spelling throughout Canada and the United States appear to be heavily influenced by the commercial materials used. Unfortunately many of the commercial spelling materials are not always based on the latest research findings. Furthermore it is often difficult or even impossible to incorporate good teaching techniques into textbooks, workbooks, or other packaged materials. To ensure that proper techniques are being utilized in the classroom, the teacher must be aware of the research evidence. It takes a knowledgeable teacher to select methods and materials discriminately and to use them effectively.

---

11. Lois Ann Bader, "The Effects of Manuscript-cursive Combinations of Instructional Treatments on Spelling Achievement" (Ph. D. dissertation, University of Maryland, 1970). See also June M. McOmber, "A Study of the Relationship Between Handwriting Form and Spelling Performance of Intermediate Grade Pupils Using Manuscript and Cursive Handwriting" (Ph. D. dissertation, Utah State University, 1970).

12. Jon Eisenson and Mardel Ogilvie, *Speech Correction in the Schools* (New York: Macmillan Co., 1963), p. 200.

13. Ves Thomas, *Teaching Spelling* (Toronto: Gage Educational Publishing, 1974), p. 55.

Of course, research has not yet turned up answers to all instructional questions, and in some cases interpretations of research findings differ. A thorough critique of this research by Sherwin indicates, however, that many of the instructional practices suggested in the literature are sound.[14] But according to a report by Fitzsimmons, over 50 percent of teachers either did not know of or did not support the research findings concerning time allotted for spelling, studying hard spots in words, taking spelling words from curricular areas, and teaching by phonics rules.[15] Virtually all other practices established by research were unknown to at least 25 percent of the teachers sampled.

The Problem of Spelling

Of course, no instructional procedures can ever alleviate frustrations traceable to the complex and illogical nature of the spelling of our language. But excessive concern with the hybrid nature of the English language, with the fact that it is studded with words lifted in whole or in part from other languages, or with the lag in changes in spelling compared to changes in pronunciation will not solve instructional problems.[16] It is highly unlikely that it will ever be possible to change spelling to conform to pronunciation, and some authorities argue that congruence is not desirable anyway.[17] Nor does it seem possible to alleviate fully frustrations caused by inconsistent sound-letter relationships by teaching numerous generalizations about how sounds are represented. The effect of this approach is merely to substitute one source of frustration for another—although some persons writing about spelling instruction dispute this conclusion.

Instilling confidence largely eliminates frustration. Teachers can build children's self-confidence by (1) making sure that each child has a definite and efficient method of learning, (2) teaching words that are necessary for the children's writing, (3) making certain each child recognizes his or her progress in learning new words, (4) making spelling instruction meaningful and interesting, and (5) developing in each child an interest in language and a desire to spell and use words correctly.

In particular, teachers should attempt to develop *a spelling consciousness* or the ability to know whether a word is spelled correctly and, if there is doubt, to check it. Spelling consciousness is not a new concept, but as Valmont pointed out,

14. Stephen Sherwin, *Four Problems in Teaching English: A Critique of Research* (Scranton, Pa.: International Textbook Co., 1969), pp. 29–108.

15. Robert J. Fitzsimmons, "A Study of the Attitudes of a Representative Population of Iowa Elementary Teachers Toward Spelling Theory and Practice" (Ph. D. dissertation, University of Iowa, 1971).

16. Jean S. Hanna and Paul R. Hanna, "Spelling as a School Subject: A Brief History," *National Elementary Principal* 38 (May 1959): 9.

17. William J. Stevens, "Obstacles to Spelling Reform," *English Journal*, 54 (February 1965): 85–90.

it is a neglected one.[18] Valmont suggests that spelling consciousness relates "to intelligence, overall academic achievement, and abilities such as visual discrimination, a functional knowledge of phonics, and correctness in using homonyms."[19] Some of these elements are amenable to instruction: phonics as it relates to encoding rather than decoding, skill in visual discrimination, and knowledge of homonyms. Probably, though, spelling consciousness develops primarily from teacher example, insistence upon proofreading, and genuine knowledge of how to use a dictionary.

An Instructional Plan

Spelling programs in elementary schools range from the informal and incidental to those that set aside time for specific instruction. The majority fall into the latter category, possibly because teachers are observing the research evidence related to the value of direct and systematic instruction, but more likely tradition is the major guiding influence.[20] We must remember, however, that systematic instruction does not mean that learning to spell cannot be correlated with other parts of the school program or that individual differences must be ignored. In fact, good plans accommodate differences and relegate systematic study to appropriate times during the school day.

Most often teachers set aside a certain time for spelling lessons. They follow the spelling book's recommendations of what words to teach and what teaching procedures to follow. Most teachers use one of two general plans: the *test-study* plan or the *study-test* plan. Sherwin says, "the evidence is fairly consistently in favor of test-study. The poorer studies are the ones on the other, study-test, side."[21] In the test-study plan, the teacher tests the pupils first to determine the words that each pupil cannot spell. Thus, pupils who know how to spell all or many of the words in the spelling lesson will not lose interest and the teacher will not waste instructional time. This plan of spelling instruction consists of these features:

1. A preliminary term or monthly test determines the general level of spelling achievement of the individuals within the class.
2. A test on each weekly (or other instructional period) assignment precedes instruction on that assignment. Sometimes, before the test the teacher pronounces each word as the pupils look carefully at it. Then

18. William J. Valmont, "The Effects of Searching for Spelling Errors on Spelling Consciousness and Achievement" (Ph. D. dissertation, University of Delaware, 1969).

19. William J. Valmont, "Spelling Consciousness: A Long Neglected Area," *Elementary English* 49 (December 1972): 1221.

20. T. Horn, p. 1295.

21. Sherwin, p. 107.

the pupils pronounce the words. A problem with the pronunciation or meaning of a word is a signal to drop the word from spelling study because the children will not use words in their writing that they are unable to say or understand.

3. The words each pupil misspells on this pretest become his or her study list.

4. In learning to spell each word, the child's particular needs are met through using methods developed by the group and in individual conferences with the teacher.

5. A mid-lesson test determines progress since the pretest. A final weekly or lesson test shows the total progress made during the lesson and identifies words for later review.

6. Each child keeps a personal record of spelling achievement on a chart or similar device.

7. Any words that a child misspells on the final test he or she records in a special review word list.

8. Children study the words in their review lists in the same manner as they studied them in their original presentation.

9. At regular intervals, the teacher tests each child's progress in learning the review words until he or she has mastered all of these words.

10. A final term or monthly test measures the progress made since the administration of the first test.

The major distinction between the test-study plan and the study-test plan is that the study-test plan does not include a pretest. The pupils begin to study the words in the first step. Thus all words in a lesson become the study list for all pupils, whether or not they need to study them. Also, the study-test plan usually involves only two tests—a mid-lesson test and a final one.

Some teachers are reluctant to use the test-study plan because they are uncertain about what to do with pupils who misspell few or no words on the pretest. How can they keep these pupils busy without asking them to complete the study exercises and activities pertaining to all of the words in the lesson? What the teachers fail to recognize is that "the exercises are merely 'busy work' for those students who already know the spelling of those words."[22] Actually, as we shall see, there are many alternative activities for pupils who know the words.

The Spelling Lesson

Commercial spelling textbooks and workbooks sometimes present new words in context or with particular attention to symbol or sound patterns rather than in a list. Research has shown, however, that the most efficient and economical

---

22. Thomas, p. 59.

method of presentation is in list form. The intent of presentation in sentences or some more extended context is to call attention to the meanings of the words, but words selected for utility in writing will likely be words that the children have encountered in their reading, use in their speech, and perhaps have written. Thus, any kind of contextual presentation may be a waste of the pupils' time. Similarly, undue attention to patterns can distract from the purpose of learning to spell the words, because the patterns themselves might be rather obvious.

Extraneous activities in spelling lessons distract from the principal objectives. If a teacher plans and presents lessons to meet the objectives presented in an earlier section, they will require less time than typically is the case. In fact, spelling research indicates that spelling lessons should take up no more than seventy-five minutes per week.[23] If pupils have the desired attitude and if the teacher unleashes a spirited attack on the lesson, learning new words could take up as little as sixty minutes per week. Certainly efficient procedures and positive attitudes and habits prevent dawdling and loss of interest.

A typical weekly spelling program, which takes into account research evidence regarding instruction, would have these features:

First day

1. Administering the pretest on the words in the lesson (see the form of test on p. 469)
2. Checking the tests; pupils check their own
3. Making individual study lists of words misspelled
4. Teacher discussion with the group or individual pupils, as necessary, of word meanings and use, unusual spellings, application of spelling rules, or etymological matters that are appropriate and of interest

Second day

1. Visual and auditory study by pupils of structural and phonemic elements related to words they misspelled
2. Study of words on individual spelling lists

Third day

1. Administering a test (usually including all words in the lesson as a means of insuring that guessing did not account for some correct spelling on the pretest)
2. Checking the test; again pupils check their own
3. Studying the words misspelled

---

23. Walter T. Petty, "Handwriting and Spelling: Their Current Status in the Language Arts Curriculum," in *Research on Handwriting and Spelling*, edited by Thomas D. Horn (National Conference on Research in English, 1966), p. 2.

Fourth day

1. Continuing individual practice in visual-aural analysis of misspelled words
·2. Learning new meanings for listed words
3. Extending word knowledge through practice in use of linguistic principles
4. Studying words misspelled on the third-day test

Fifth day

1. Administering the final test
2. Checking the tests; still pupils check their own
3. Writing words in a review list
4. Marking achievement on a progress chart

In addition, the spelling lessons may provide diagnostic data and activities in handwriting, practice in using the dictionary, and vocabulary building.

Study Steps

Modern spelling programs incorporate the findings of research that favor presenting to children the steps involved in learning to spell a word. The steps involve visual, auditory, and kinesthetic imagery as well as emphasis on recall. Most children need to follow all the steps, although the best spellers will learn the words primarily by visual imagery and, thus, quite rapidly. The poorer spellers need extra help and encouragement in learning the steps; teachers might individualize the steps by adding extra ones to help less competent spellers say the words properly or gain better auditory or kinesthetic impressions. Teachers should particularly encourage poor spellers to use systematic study steps and to concentrate on the ones that require recall, because recalling is the principal ability needed to spell words correctly in actual writing.

In spite of the fact that most spelling books list learning steps and suggest that pupils refer to them often, optimally the teacher and children should devise their own steps and use them without reference to the book. Teachers can guide children to think about how to study a word, and after some discussion, the children will be able to state the necessary steps themselves. A chart recording the children's statement can be hung someplace in the room where all can readily refer to it. As they acquire experience studying words, the children may want to modify or revise their statement from time to time. The teacher should encourage amendments if they have omitted any of the generally recommended steps or if local conditions or individual problems seem to warrant change. In addition, it is a good idea for the children to determine individually whether the steps listed by the class are the ones they should follow or whether some modification would help them study better.

Following is a model of how to study the spelling of a word that can serve as a guide for any class in the development of a statement of steps.

1. Look at the word carefully and pronounce it correctly. If you are not sure of the pronunciation, look it up in the dictionary or ask someone who is sure to know. Say the word slowly, naturally, and clearly, and look at the word while it is being said.
2. Cover the word or close your eyes, pronounce the word, and think about how it looks. Try to visualize just the way the word is written as you repeat the letter sequence to yourself.
3. Look at the word again to be sure that you said it and spelled it correctly. If you did not, start over with the first step.
4. Cover the word and then write it, thinking carefully how the word looks. Check the accuracy of your spelling. If you misspelled the word, begin again with the first step.
5. If you spelled the word correctly, write it again without looking either at the book or at your previous attempts. Again, check your accuracy.

The Lesson Test

Outside the classroom words are seldom spelled orally or written in list or column form. Normally a writer must choose words and write them without thinking too much about the correctness of their spelling. Some educators therefore favor teaching and testing spelling words in contextual form, that is, presenting words to be learned or tested in connected discourse—sentences and paragraphs. Advocates of this practice contend that it provides training in handwriting, punctuation, capitalization, and the form or appearance of a manuscript, as well as making spelling more natural. Limited use of this sort of procedure is advisable, however. Experimental evidence favors a column or list presentation and testing of the words.[24] Besides, the list approach is less time consuming and children learn the other skills that the contextual approach allegedly teaches along with spelling more effectively by focusing on one of them at a time. Ernest Horn summarized the evidence on the question of how best to present spelling words as follows:[25]

> Written tests are to be preferred to oral tests . . . Recall tests are superior to and more difficult than recognition tests. The evidence indicates that the most valid and economical test [in spelling] is the modified recall form, in which the person giving the test pronounces each word, uses it in an oral sentence and pronounces it again. The word is then written by the student.

---

24. Sherwin, p. 107.
25. Ernest Horn, "Spelling," in *Encyclopedia of Educational Research*, 3rd ed., edited by Chester W. Harris (New York: Macmillan Co., 1960), p. 1340.

Nevertheless, the instructional program in spelling certainly should not ignore the pupil's need to spell words in context in all writing activities. Perhaps, then, a combination of list study and testing and context dictation activities may provide the most effective teaching.

Correcting spelling tests is a key part of spelling instruction. In the first place, tests are learning activities as well as a means of measuring spelling achievement. Evaluating the results should be the pupils' responsibility, and each child should evaluate and correct his or her own paper. Ernest Horn stated that "when corrected by the pupils and the results properly utilized, the test is the most fruitful single learning activity per unit of time that has yet been devised."[26] Subsequent research has confirmed the efficacy of this procedure.[27]

So that children will derive the greatest educational benefit from the testing process, the teacher should show them how testing identifies the words they need to learn to spell, how it is a learning procedure in that it calls their attention to the way they have misspelled a word and what they need to do to spell it correctly, and how it forces them to recall either the actual spelling of the word or associations that help them remember how to spell it. As stated previously, pupils should correct all their own tests and record their own scores; occasional rechecking by the teacher will encourage them to check their work carefully.

Individual Needs and Abilities

A successful spelling program should accommodate individual pupils' needs and challenge each according to his or her ability. This goal is not as difficult as many instructors think. Pupils should study only those words that they need to use in personal written communication but cannot spell. Thus, if a child can correctly spell carefully chosen words on a pretest, he or she need not study them. To avoid frustrating a child who has great difficulty with spelling, the teacher should reduce the number of words he or she is responsible for learning. This kind of adjustment also fosters a positive attitude toward spelling and teaches a study procedure.

The teacher can group children for spelling instruction as for reading and mathematics instruction. The first step in constituting groups should be the administration of a quarterly, semester, or yearly pretest of twenty-five to seventy-five words (depending on the abilities of the children to handle the mechanics of writing). The words on this test should be a random selection from the words to

26. Ernest Horn, *What Research Says to the Teacher: Teaching Spelling* (Washington, D.C.: National Education Association, 1954), p. 17.

27. Robert W. Ash, "A Comparison of Various Procedures for Using the Corrected Test as an Instructional Device in Fifth Grade Spelling" (Ph. D. dissertation, University of Minnesota, 1970).

be taught for the particular quarter, semester, or year. Children who misspell none or very few of these words may comprise one group, those who misspell 10 to 50 percent a second group, and children who misspell more than 50 percent of the words a third group.

The first two groups may take a test for each lesson on all the words in a lesson, although the teacher may add some carefully selected enrichment words to the list for the first group. For the third group, the test should include one-half or fewer of the lesson words. The actual number should be sufficient to challenge but not so great as to frustrate these pupils.

To test groups of pupils on different numbers of words a teacher can use several procedures. One possibility is to give the enrichment words to the first group and then give the regular lesson words to the first and second groups. The third group might begin when the teacher reaches their words during the testing procedure. Another possibility is to treat each group separately and test one group at a time while the other groups work independently. A third method involves pronouncing all the test words with the first group writing each word, the second group every other word, and the third group every third word. Or the teacher can administer the test to all in the following manner: "Group 1, *hygiene*—A good hygiene practice is to brush one's teeth after every meal—*hygiene*. Group 2, *during*—Be quiet during the test—*during*. Group 3, *idea*—I have no idea where he is—*idea*."

Activities for the High Spelling Achiever

A good spelling program includes enrichment activities for children who learn spelling words easily and who make few spelling mistakes in writing. Fundamentally such pupils should have a great deal of independence in choosing how to spend their time. Perhaps they will want to read or pursue a research interest. Some teachers, though, feel that during spelling lessons every child should be doing something related to spelling. One such activity would set the good speller to finding the origins of new words, such as *radar, jeep, videotape, astronaut*, or *backlash*, or to looking up the histories of *desperado, digit, festival, vocation*, and so on. In fact, studying the history of the language, the borrowing of words from other languages, spelling changes, and the acceptance of new words into the language are all activities that should appeal to children.

The good spellers may also be interested in making charts of interesting synonyms and antonyms, of useful contractions and abbreviations, of usages found in newspapers and books that illustrate compounding or particular meanings, and of substitutes for such overworked words as *awful, funny, scared, pretty, good, glad*, and *got*. Word games such as Scrabble and anagrams are another spelling-related activity. In addition some children enjoy working crossword puzzles and creating their own word puzzles.

Help for the Slow Speller

The child who has difficulty learning and retaining the spelling of words often has problems in other areas of the language arts. For teachers the problem is not insurmountable, however; consideration of the child's frustrations should lead to the conclusion that the child "may best be accommodated through attention to relevant factors conditioning spelling ability, such as particular disabilities, and by a reduction in the number of words to be studied."[28] In teaching the slow speller, the teacher should focus on readiness factors, even though the child may be outside the normal beginning stages of spelling instruction, and on building favorable attitudes and good study habits. These suggestions are especially applicable:

1. Emphasize the importance of the words the student is to learn. Teach a minimum list and make certain that the words on it are as useful as possible.

2. Teach no more words than the pupil can successfully learn to spell. Success is a motivating influence and the poor speller has probably had much experience with failure in learning to spell the words in the weekly lessons. Difficulty in spelling a word does not necessarily depend on its length or on the frequency or infrequency of its use. For assistance in determining the difficulty children have with common words and in selecting the words that they might learn to spell successfully, the teacher should turn to a source like *The New Iowa Spelling Scale*[29] which cites the results of hundreds of actual spelling attempts by children.

3. Give more than the usual amount of time to oral discussion of the words to be learned. In addition to making certain the children know the meanings of the words, ask questions about structural aspects of the words. For example, ask what word begins with a particular letter, which word has a vowel sound like one in another word, or which word has two specific letters together.

4. Pay particular attention to pronunciation. Make certain the pupil can pronounce each word properly and naturally. Provide listening lessons that test perception and discrimination skill.

5. Provide exercises to strengthen visual perception and discrimination. Activities like inserting missing letters in words, substituting letters to make new words, putting syllables together into words, fitting words into outlined word shapes, and categorizing words according to some structural element are useful.

28. T. Horn, p. 1288.
29. Greene, *The New Iowa Spelling Scale*.

6. Strengthen pupils' images of words by having them trace the forms with their index finger as you write them on the board.
7. Note bad study habits. Show how the habit is harmful and may prevent success in spelling.
8. Check and perhaps modify the child's method of individual study. Study at the board may facilitate teacher observation of learning techniques.
9. Provide a wide variety of writing activities that necessitate using the words learned.

Practices to Avoid

Some of the practices that teachers follow in spelling instruction are undesirable. For one thing, teachers should probably not waste time calling attention to possible hard spots in words. Many identifiable hard spots exist, but a more positive approach is advisable. Instead, encourage children to look carefully at a word as it is pronounced and take note of its structure, the sequence of letters, and the letter representations given to sounds, rather than watching for a possible stumbling block.

The practice of writing words in the air has doubtful value. Not only does it take time, but it also fails to give children a realistic image of the word. Supposedly, this practice gives a kinesthetic impression of the word, but the result is questionable, for the arm and hand movements are generally not the same as in writing a word. A kinesthetic impression is useful to a few very poor spellers but this process does not provide it. To create a tactile-kinesthetic impression, have children make finger-tip impressions in sand or on the chalkboard.

Avoid requiring children to write repeatedly words without intervening attempts at recall. Spelling is a *recall* act, and copying a word five, ten, or even more times encourages poor habits and attitudes.

The teacher should avoid condemning children for asking how to spell a word. Of course, it is acceptable to discourage the habit a few children develop of always asking, particularly for spellings of words they have had in their spelling lessons. Generally, asking how to spell a word is an expression of the desire to spell correctly and should lead to using the dictionary and other sources of spelling information. When a teacher does spell a word for a child, he or she should write it on a slip of paper or on the chalkboard, rather than spelling it orally. The teacher should always endeavor to get the child to look at the word and thus gain a visual impression. In many classrooms, requested word spellings become additions to a child's own dictionary, where they will be available for future reference.

The teacher must recognize the folly of forcing children to study or write spelling words as a form of punishment. This practice will certainly not aid the spelling program, and its value as a punishment is doubtful.

SPECIAL ISSUES IN SPELLING INSTRUCTION

There are several noteworthy issues regarding the planning of spelling programs. The first and principal one of these "centers on the regularity—or lack of it—of the English language. What is the nature of the phoneme-grapheme relationship in English?"[30] Or put another way, it "centers on the question of whether competency in spelling can be obtained through a general use of spelling generalizations [rules] or not."[31] This is not a new issue. Reports by Turner in 1912 and Archer in 1930 showed generally negative results from rule teaching, whereas Lester in 1917 and Watson in 1926 reported positive results.[32] Current opinion probably corresponds to Sherwin's conclusion that, "After examining the studies and weighing their methodological virtues and defects, it appears that rules offer limited help in the teaching of spelling."[33] Nevertheless, some spelling researchers today emphasize the learning of sound-to-letter generalizations and, particularly, patterns of sound-to-symbol correspondence.

Linguistics and Spelling

Before the advent of interest in linguistics, the regularity and irregularity of sound and written symbol correspondence generally came under the heading of "phonics." Thus, after studying a 3000-word vocabulary, Hanna and Moore reported that "Nearly three-fourths of the vowel phonemes are spelled by their regular representations from about 57 per cent to about 99 per cent of the times they occur."[34] Based on the study of a larger list of words, Horn asserted that "The sound of long *a* (a) . . . was found 1,237 times, with 601 exceptions to the commonest spelling; the sound of *k* was found 2,613 times, with 932 exceptions; and the sound of *s* in *sick*, 3,846 times, with 1,278 exceptions."[35] These studies and the conclusions of the investigators clearly have implications for classroom instruction. On the one hand, the study by Hanna and Moore led them to suggest that the degree of "regularity" is great enough to warrant "grouping words about a phonemic family for a week's lesson and teaching the pupil inductively to *hear* the phoneme, then to *write* that phoneme with alphabetical letter or letters."[36] Horn, on the other hand, stated, "One is hardly justified in calling spellings

30. Caryl Rivers, "Spelling: Its tyme to Du Somthing." *Learning* 3 (November 1974): 76.

31. Albert H. Yee, "The Generalization Controversy on Spelling Instruction," *Elementary English* 43 (February 1966): 154.

32. Ibid., p. 155

33. Sherwin, p. 106.

34. Paul R. Hanna and J. T. Moore, "Spelling—from Spoken Word to Written Symbol," *Elementary School Journal*, (February 1953): 329–37.

35. Ernest Horn, "Phonetics and Spelling," *Elementary School Journal*, (May 1957), 424–32.

36. Hanna and Hanna, p. 16.

'regular' or in teaching the commonest spellings as principles or generalizations when the exceptions are numbered not merely by the score but by hundreds."[37]

More recently, researchers at Stanford University conducted extensive studies involving computerized analysis of a vocabulary of 17,000 words. They reported:[38]

> The great majority of individual phonemes of oral American-English are indeed consistently represented in writing by particular graphemic options when the main components of the phonological structure underlying the orthography are taken into consideration. Without regard to their occurrences in respective positions in syllables, consonant phonemes collectively were represented by an equal number of graphemic options over 80 per cent of the time in the selected list of words.

For the second phase of this study, the investigators devised an algorithm of several hundred rules for spelling the 17,000 words. This programming took into account the following characteristics: "(1) the simple phoneme-grapheme relationships, (2) the effect of position of a phoneme in a syllable, and (3) the effect of syllabic stress upon choice of graphemic option."[39] They included a fourth factor, identified as "internal constraints"—such as a particular phoneme following another in a word. This computerized spelling showed that 49 percent of the words were spelled correctly, 37.2 percent with only one error, 11.4 per cent with two errors, and 2.3 per cent with three or more errors. The researchers concluded that "even a limited knowledge of the phonological relationships between the sounds and the letters of the orthography can provide the power to spell literally thousands of words."[40]

Certainly the findings of the Stanford study may have applications in spelling instruction, particularly as they call attention to some patterns, but as Fries and others pointed out, spelling patterns (that is, the consistency of sound and symbol relationships) to which *readers* must respond are different from spelling patterns that writers must produce.[41] In addition, analysis of how a phoneme is represented in writing usually does not recognize dialect differences in speech, that the same individual varies his or her pronunciation of many words depending on the context (e.g., *and* in snow and ice, head and arm, man and beast, rod and gun), and that decisions as to which graphic symbols represent specific sounds in a word call for a great deal of subjective judgment.[42]

37. E. Horn, "Phonetics and Spelling," p. 430.

38. Paul R. Hanna et al., "Linguistic Cues for Spelling Improvement," Report to U.S. Office of Education on Project Number 1991 for the period January 2, 1963 to December 31, 1964 (mimeographed), p. 4.

39. Richard E. Hodges and E. Hugh Rudorf, "Searching Linguistics for the Teaching of Spelling," *Research on Handwriting and Spelling*, edited by Thomas D. Horn (Champaign, Ill.: National Conference on Research in English, 1965), p. 34.

40. Ibid., p. 532.

41. Charles C. Fries, *Linguistics and Reading* (New York: Holt, Rinehart and Winston, 1963), p. 170.

42. Walter T. Petty, "Research Critiques—II," *Elementary English* 42 (May 1965): 584–87.

The success of actually teaching children to see linguistic principles that may aid them in spelling has scarcely been tested, even though a good many commercial spelling materials profess to have selected words that teach generalizations. Maier developed a procedure for analyzing spelling programs with respect to linguistic variables, and using it showed that the programs studied overlook many linguistic characteristics.[43] In general, however, few studies have actually sought to determine the effectiveness of teaching sound-symbol correspondences. One of the few that did reported that the "use of generalizations for spelling instruction appears to be less useful than test-study methods."[44] But this study has come under criticism. Personke, for example, stated that he found major fault with the "method used to teach the generalization."[45]

The analysis by Plessas of the issue perceptively points out the difference between using grapheme-phoneme relationships in reading and using them in spelling.[46] He suggests that proper and thoughtful attention to the amount of stress given to teaching generalizations "may prevent the phonemic cues in reading from becoming graphic miscues in spelling."[47]

A good example of Plessas's point comes from Personke's study of the use of nonsense words to test generalizing ability in spelling.[48] The generalizations he tested included:

1. Before *a*, *o*, and *u*, or a consonant, *g* has the hard sound. Before *e*, *i*, or *y*, *g* has the soft sound of *j*.
2. The *c* spells the soft sound of *s* before *e*, *i*, or *y*. Before any other letter, *c* spells the hard sound of *k*.

These are useful generalizations for deciding how to pronounce words beginning with *g* or *c*, but how do they help children spell *jar*, *jewel*, *sight*, *kayak*, and so on? We could raise similar questions about the other "generalizations."

The value of even more sophisticated statements of generalizations also is questionable. For example, "final /k/ is usually spelled *ck* in a stressed syllable (smock), but *c* in an unstressed syllable (plastic)."[49] How many children would recognize *-tic* as unstressed? The same authors suggest using such words as *pick*,

43. Julius C. Maier, "Analyzing Linguistic Characteristics of Spelling Programs" (Ph. D. dissertation, State University of New York at Buffalo, 1973).

44. Albert H. Yee, "Is the Phonetic Generalization Hypothesis in Spelling Valid?" *Journal of Experimental Education* 37 (Summer 1969): 91.

45. Carl Personke, "Generalization and Spelling: Boon or Bust?" in *A Forum for Focus*, edited by Martha L. King, Robert Emans, and Patricia J. Cianciolo (Urbana, Ill.: National Council of Teachers of English, 1973), pp. 148–57.

46. Gus P. Plessas, "Cues or Miscues in Spelling," in King et al., pp. 159–64.

47. Ibid., p. 164.

48. Carl Personke, "The Use of Nonsense Words to Test Generalization Ability in Spelling," *Elementary English*, December 1972, pp. 1233–37.

49. Hanna, Hodges, and Hanna, p. 187.

rock, pack, and *truck* in their "level 1" program to teach the generalization that the /k/ "may be spelled *ck* in final position."[50] Although this is a valid generalization, how appropriate is this instruction when the more commonly written *make* is left until "level 2"?[51]

Statements by certain linguists and others regarding "regularity" and "system" in orthography also demand thoughtful examination. For example, saying that "all the vowel letters can represent both full vowels and schwa without sacrificing regularity" does not tell what generalizations might be taught or when—or even if any need to be taught.[52] Knowing the facts about our language system—at the verbalizing and conscious level—historically has never made any difference in how most persons use language.

On the other hand, children do make generalizations, in the same manner in which all of us have learned to transfer spelling knowledge of some words to new words that we encounter. Many spelling programs also teach children to apply these generalizations cautiously, but most adults learned to do the same in spelling programs that lacked great emphasis on spelling patterns. Of course, for years teachers and programs have taught children to note sound and symbol relationships by teaching word "families," suffix addition, compound word building, analysis of words into syllables, and the influence of context (as in choice among homonyms). Too, spelling authorities have long stressed the importance of careful pronunciation and the need for sight, sound, and taction to fix images of words. The crucial aspect of teaching a program suggested by linguistic findings, however, is in determining which generalizations are actually helpful and how these may be learned by children efficiently and economically of their time so that they are aided in spelling correctly the words they write.

The Teaching of Rules

How much emphasis to put on spelling rules, of course, depends somewhat on the view that we accept regarding the regularity of sound representation. True, the inductive development of some understanding of the degree and kinds of grapheme-phoneme correspondence can impart a generalized understanding and need not extend to the teaching of formally stated rules. On the other hand, numerous contemporary spelling generalizations are little different from the formalized rules presented in some textbooks about twenty years ago. Teaching rules to which there are many exceptions, particularly with respect to the words children most often need to spell, has proven to have little value. The rules listed below, however, have few exceptions and thus are of practical value.

---

50. Ibid., p. 142.

51. *Word Frequency Book,* by John B. Carroll et al., gives these frequencies: *pick* 459, *rock* 925, *pack* 197, *truck* 410, and *make* 8333.

52. Fred Brengelman, "Roundtable Review," *Research in the Teaching of English* 5 (Fall 1971): 220.

1. Words ending in silent *e* usually drop the final *e* before the addition of suffixes beginning with a vowel, but they keep the final *e* before the addition of suffixes beginning with a consonant (*make—making; time—timely*).
2. Words ending in a consonant and *y* change the *y* to *i* before adding all suffixes except those beginning with *i*. The *y* is not changed to *i* when adding suffixes to words ending in a vowel and *y*, or when adding a suffix beginning with *i* (*busy—busily; carry—carrying; stay—stayed; enjoy—enjoying*).
3. One-syllable words and words accented on the last syllable, if they end in a single consonant preceded by a single vowel, double the final consonant when adding a suffix beginning with a vowel (*run—running; begin—beginning*).
4. The letter *q* is always followed by *u* in common English words (*quite; quart*).
5. English words do not end with *v* (*believe; give*).
6. Proper nouns and most adjectives formed from proper nouns should begin with capital letters (*France; French*).

One generalization that is often taught in reading and writing activities or in spelling is that compounding does not change the spelling of the words that make up the compound. Another is that the spelling of prefixes and suffixes does not change from one base word to another. Also, children should learn how to form plurals and use the apostrophe in contractions and in showing possession.

Rules should be taught inductively; that is, a rule should be developed from examination of words to which it applies. The teacher should focus on only one rule at a time, including exceptions. A systematic review of the rules taught is recommended. Of course, teaching emphasis should be on application rather than rote memorization of spelling rules.

Bright children tend to generalize rather easily, but a slow-learning child will usually have difficulty and will tend to try to learn the statement rather than its application. It may be much more satisfactory to teach this child to spell the words he or she most needs for writing than to use time presenting words to which an abstract rule applies.

Spelling Readiness

As a result of linguistic studies of the graphic representations of the words in our language, interest in teaching children to perceive sounds accurately and to discriminate among similar ones has surged. In preparing children to learn to read and write, educators have all but ignored skills of auditory discrimination. Children need to learn about rhyming, and they need to develop the capacity to discriminate among beginning and ending consonant and vowel sounds in words, to associate sounds and letters, and to recognize and identify letters.

Certainly the readiness concept is as important in spelling as in any other educational endeavor, as many teachers have recognized in the past. The time and effort teachers spend determining children's readiness will provide dividends throughout their school years. A child who cannot tell that *ball* and *tall* do not look alike or begin with the same sound, that *him* and *men* do not rhyme, and that *mouse* begins with the letter *m* is not going to succeed in spelling; neither, of course, is he or she ready for formal reading instruction.

Activities that help to develop readiness for beginning spelling instruction include the following:

1. Show pictures of two or more objects that have names beginning with the same sound, and ask the children to identify the ones with the same beginning sounds. For example, show pictures of a *bear*, a *baby*, a *ball*, and a *lion*.
2. Do the same for ending sounds, for example, *sled*, *bread*, *bed*, and *cap*.
3. Pronounce words and ask the children to hold up their hands when pairs of words begin with the same sound (or have the same end or internal sound, e.g., *big—boy*, *fill—ball*, *live—give*).
4. Pronounce pairs of words and ask the children whether they rhyme.
5. Ask children to give other words which begin with the same sound as objects that you name (or end with the same sound, and so on).
6. Pronounce a key word followed by several other words and ask the children to hold up their hands for each one that begins (or ends, etc.) with the same sound as the key word, for example, *soft—dot*, *sit*, *sing*, *bought*, *fan*, *song*.
7. Give a lot of practice in careful and accurate pronunciation by having the children name many objects, identify pictures, think of words that relate to other words the teacher or they have mentioned, and—most important—actually talk about subjects that interest them.
8. Have the children match pictures with letters that begin their names.
9. Do the same for ending or medial sounds and the letters that represent them. Caution must accompany these activities because the letters representing some final sounds are obvious (as in *men*, *bad*, *top*), but other representations are less clear (e.g., *sing*, *cake*, *ball*).
10. Have children think of words that begin with the same letter and then pronounce these words to compare beginning letters and sounds.
11. Vary the preceding exercise by asking for consonant clusters rather than single consonants.
12. Practice visual perception and discrimination by finding like and different objects, words, and word elements.

Naturally, readiness for spelling differs among individuals. When children enter kindergarten and first grade, they have not developed equally in ability to express themselves orally. They also listen with varying degrees of effectiveness.

Spelling Games

Some spelling authorities advocate the use of spelling games and others criticize this idea. Some of these games may have merit and we must evaluate their value individually in terms of the following questions. What is the game's potential for upgrading an individual's spelling ability? Does it simulate demands that the real world makes on spellers? Does the game actively involve all pupils? Is unfair or unrealistic competition a part of the game? Games that meet these and other criteria can help to stimulate and maintain students' interest. The games listed here are representative of the kind described abundantly in the professional literature.

1. One child begins by saying, "Who can spell the word that means (for example) more than one shoe?" One child goes to the board and writes it, while the other children write it at their seats. If the spelling on the board is correct, the speller asks the next question.
2. One child begins by saying, "I am thinking of a word that begins with *gl*" (or some other letter or combination of letters). Children who think they know the answer raise their hands. One child is called on to write the word on the board. If the spelling is correct, this child thinks of the next word.
3. One child starts the game by writing a base word on the board, such as *write*. The child then asks the other members of the group to spell as many new words as possible that have this word as their base (e.g., *writing, writer*). The child who gives the most words writes the next base word on the board.
4. Write a number of words to which the endings *ed*, *er*, and *ing* can be added and see who can add the most words to the list.
5. Divide the group into pairs. One child begins the game by writing a word and asking a partner to spell a word that begins with the last letter of the first word. If the child's partner cannot think of a word or misspells the one attempted, he or she scores a point.

Spelling Demons

Authors of journal articles often identify and list spelling "demons," the words that children most frequently misspell in written expression. And school systems commonly recommend that teachers give special teaching and review attention to the words on these lists. We will combine many of these words into lists of words that represent similar problems as an aid to teaching them more successfully.

Phoneme-grapheme irregularity. Many common words include the representation of one or more sounds by a letter (or letters) that is atypical for that particular sound. These words require direct teaching, particular attention to forming visual impressions, and frequent review. In addition, teaching them requires informing children of the limitations of generalizations about sound and symbol correspondence as well as the benefits that may result from knowing the generalizations. Commonly written words that fall into this category include the following:

ache	birthday	friend	thought
across	build	guess	tonight
afraid	color	heard	very
again	could	mother	wait
already	cousin	one	want
among	dead	school	were
any	decide	sure	when
beautiful	does	the	women
because	doesn't	they	you
believe	enough		

Homonym problems. Many frequently and persistently misspelled words are homonyms. Among these words, too, are some that contain atypical letter representations, as do the words in the previous list. Learning these words successfully requires that the pupils clearly understand their meanings, know the meaning and spelling of the word that has the same pronunciation, and form visual images of the words for recall. The homonyms most frequently misspelled include:

there	hear	for	write	know
their	here	four	right	no
they're	buy	our	piece	some
two	by	hour	peace	sum
to	would	your		
too	wood	you're		

Failure to apply rules. Application of the six rules stated earlier in this chapter and an understanding of compounding, capitalization, and the use of the apostrophe can reduce children's spelling errors. The most persistently misspelled words in this category are the following:

coming	its	Sunday
didn't	it's	that's
don't	getting	tried
I'll	sometimes	truly
I'm	studying	writing

Other causes.   Improper pronunciation is another common cause of spelling errors. The following words are often misspelled, typically as a result of improper pronunciation: *and, going, third, today, Saturday, pretty, hundred, kept, been, library, children.* Of course, silent letters are a major source of spelling difficulty. Problems with the spelling of words containing silent letters (and about half of the words in the dictionary include "silent" letters) are related to words characterized by phoneme-grapheme irregularity. Pupils must look closely at these words, identify specifically the letter representations of the sounds, and associate the generalizations that they have learned in reading that are helpful in determining pronunciations. Words with silent letters that are persistently misspelled include: *February, Christmas, time, have, fine, like, are, safe, half.*

DIAGNOSIS AND TESTING IN SPELLING

Aside from being able to do well on weekly spelling tests, the good speller recognizes the social importance of correct spelling in written work, makes a special effort to spell correctly, and knows how to find and/or learn to spell new words. Children do not learn spelling; they learn to spell specific words. Their ability to learn these words depends, in part, on attitudes, skills, and habits discussed earlier, but spelling ability also involves mental capacity, the ability to develop a visual image, the ability to relate sounds and symbols properly, and the ability to memorize.

Detection of Spelling Learning Problems

Informal and regular observation will indicate if a child's learning efforts during spelling lessons and actual spelling attempts in meaningful writing require special attention. Additional diagnostic procedures include the following.

1. *General capacity:* Group and/or individual intelligence tests or available results from such tests give measures of general learning capacity.
2. *Attitude toward spelling:* Previous records in spelling and scores on a series of carefully constructed spelling tests will reveal children's attitudes.
3. *Reading ability:* Silent reading comprehension tests that emphasize vocabulary and meaning will establish a child's reading ability. Oral reading tests also can reveal superficial speech defects, as well as difficulties in pronunciation and enunciation.
4. *Handwriting, legibility, and speed:* Handwriting difficulties arise through slow and faulty letter formation. Previous school records on handwriting, as well as speed and quality ratings on standardized scales, are useful diagnostic tools.

5. *Visual defects:* Observation and school-administered tests of vision will turn up possible visual defects. Apparent deficiencies justify immediate medical examination.
6. *Auditory defects:* Observation and informal tests will suggest when a medical examination is necessary.
7. *School attendance:* Records secured for diagnostic purposes should include a complete school history of attendance.
8. *Speech defects and maturity:* Speech problems will be evident in class activities. If needed, a speech specialist can provide supplemental speech data.
9. *General health:* General health information is available from school medical or nursing service data.
10. *Personality characteristics:* Observing a student's industry, aggressiveness, independence, attentiveness, exactness, and so on may provide clues to the reasons for a child's spelling problems.

One of the most encouraging approaches to the identification of the causes of spelling difficulties seems to be careful observation and examination of children's work habits. The failure of pupils to learn and utilize sound methods of learning to spell new or difficult words is a major cause of poor achievement in spelling. Certainly, the child is not always to blame for this failure. Frequently children do not know how to study, and as discussed earlier, ineffective teaching procedures may be responsible for poor study habits. Usually, general observation alone reveals whether or not a child systematically attacks the learning of new or difficult words. Does the child concentrate on the word, try to visualize it, and so on, as the study steps suggest?

Misspelling is also a consequence of writing words to correspond to the way they sound. Improper pronunciation by the pupil is more likely to result in misspellings than is mispronunciation by the teacher either in teaching or in testing. Imperfect hearing or improper pronunciation or enunciation of the words by peers thus becomes a contributing cause. It is imperative therefore that children form habits of correct pronunciation and enunciation.

The relationship between spelling ability and visual perception, discrimination, and memory is strong. Therefore, if pupils transpose the order of letters, double the wrong letter, substitute an incorrect letter, or insert or omit silent letters, they need practice in visualizing words and recalling them. By keeping a simple checklist of the kinds of errors a child makes, a teacher can generally see what type of instruction the child needs.

Tests of auditory discrimination are relatively easy to devise. For example, a teacher might ask the children to record the letter representing the first sound in *jump*, or the last sound in *sat*.[53] Another approach is to pronounce pairs of words (*tag—rag, bag—bat*) and ask pupils whether they begin with the same sound,

---

53. Wayne Otto and Richard A. McMenemy, *Corrective and Remedial Teaching* (Boston: Houghton Mifflin Co., 1966), p. 218.

have the same medial sound, and so on. Teachers should administer informal tests of auditory perception and discrimination to one pupil at a time.

Asking individual pupils to pronounce words will aid in determining whether they have speech problems that could affect their spelling ability. Take care, however, to separate speech problems from dialect differences in pronunciation.

The lack of a spelling conscience or a critical sensitivity to correct spelling is a typical cause of poor spelling in normal written expression. Children must develop pride in spelling ability and a sensitivity toward spelling errors to the point that they carry over into all of the normal writing activities in school and life.

In summary, the main differences between the good speller and the less competent one are (1) the study technique each uses, (2) individual mental and personality characteristics, and (3) the emphasis each gives to the subject. Of course, the teacher and the spelling materials used strongly affect these factors.

Spelling Tests

The nature of spelling ability makes it extremely difficult to construct valid spelling tests. In the first place, the words tested should come from the list of words taught. This constraint places a burden on a standardized test maker because the words in specific lessons vary considerably from classroom to classroom, to say nothing of the grade-level variances in commercial spelling materials.[54] In the second place, the form of the spelling test should resemble an actual spelling situation as closely as possible; actual spelling requires recalling a spelling or association of sounds and letters, so asking a child to choose the correct spelling from several spellings of a word does not test the right skill. Thus, the most useful way to measure spelling achievement is to construct tests for a specific class, assuming the teacher can do it properly.

Spelling tests must cover words that children write or will need to write often. Although it is several years old, *The New Iowa Spelling Scale* is a valuable list of socially evaluated and difficulty-rated words.[55] The 5507 words comprising this list were screened from eight different vocabulary sources. The directions that accompany the scale explain how to use it to construct spelling tests that will provide valid and reliable measures of spelling ability.

Common sense dictates that the words included in any spelling test should not be too difficult for the group taking the test. Theoretical considerations suggest that test words ranging in difficulty from 14 to 86 percent standard scale accuracy, with a mean of 50 percent, tend to give a distribution of scores approx-

54. See Douglas F. Dickerson, "Misleadings vs. Actualities in Spelling," *American School Board Journal* 120 (February 1950): 33–34.

55. Greene, *The New Iowa Spelling Scale.*

imating the normal frequency curve, in which pupil scores fall closely around the mean.[56]

The principle of sampling that is commonly applied in testing applies equally well in spelling. How many words will give reliable results depends largely on the purpose the test is to serve. For a survey of the status of spelling in an entire school system, a list of twenty-five carefully selected words may be sufficient. But measuring the spelling ability of individual children requires a much larger list of words. Fifty words may be adequate for use with one class.

Earlier in this chapter we looked at the recommended form for a spelling test. Following is a description of how a teacher might prepare and administer this type of spelling test.

Let us assume that a fourth-grade teacher has checked the words that appear in the prescribed spelling textbook against the vocabulary of *The New Iowa Spelling Scale*. This comparison reveals that children in this grade spell the following words with the accuracy shown next to each.

List A				List B			
grade	67	month	50	luck	67	inch	50
floor	57	army	48	miles	57	copy	48
able	56	evening	45	unlike	56	fighting	45
track	54	gloves	40	party	54	meetings	40
boots	50	office	35	mails	52	program	35

In an actual situation, the spelling tests undoubtedly would include a larger number than shown here. But these lists do illustrate how two parallel and approximately equal word lists could be developed. The sample dictation list that follows includes the words in list A. Beginning fourth graders probably would spell approximately 50 percent of them accurately prior to studying them.

Directions: Write the following words as I read them to you. First you will hear a word, then a sentence in which the word is used, and then the word. Do not begin writing until you have heard the sentence and the word repeated. *Write only the word.* Do not write the sentence. Be careful of your writing and your spelling.

1. grade   I am in the fourth grade this year.   grade
2. floor   The floor of the room was covered with mud.   floor
3. able   Jim was able to work the puzzle.   able

---

56. Through this discussion, *spelling difficulty* should be understood to be best represented by the percent of times a word is misspelled in a given grade without regard to or without information about previous opportunities the pupils may have had to learn the words. The quality, as defined here, is really "persistence of error" and should not be confused with "learning difficulty" as such.

4.	track	A broken rail on the track caused the wreck.	track
5.	boots	How did you get your boots so muddy?	boots
6.	month	School started a month ago today.	month
7.	army	My brother was in the army two years.	army
8.	evening	Every evening Father reads me a story.	evening
9.	gloves	You may wear your gloves to school today.	gloves
10.	office	My sister works in an office in the city.	office

The rate of dictation of spelling words depends on the writing ability of the children. The proper dictation rate for spelling lists is easy to determine by observing the children at work.[57]

Of the standardized tests that have value, the best ones are the subtests of achievement test batteries.[58] These tests permit a teacher to compare the spelling achievement in different schools or classrooms, but they do have the serious shortcomings enumerated earlier because they usually call for some kind of recognition of the correctness or incorrectness of spelling. For example, the test might ask the child to indicate a spelling as incorrect among several different words or groups of letters that appear to be words, or to mark words "right" or "wrong." Even if we accepted recognition of the correct spelling as evidence of spelling ability, these tests offer little assistance in determining the spelling needs of specific children.

EXERCISES FOR THOUGHT AND ACTION

1. Develop a lesson with the objective of helping children to recognize the need for standardized spelling and to value it in their own work. (You may want to take a historical perspective: Have people always spelled words the same way?)
2. What techniques do you use to recall the spelling of a word when you want to write it? Do you, for example, write the word several different ways to see which one "looks right"? Do you look it up in the dictionary? Do you try to remember a rule? (Which rules do you know?)
3. Compare three books from different commercial spelling series directed at the grade level that most interests you. Evaluate them in terms of (a) the source of the words, (b) the generalizations taught, (c) activities for motivating children, and (d) the criteria for good teaching practices suggested in this chapter.
4. Choose a spelling generalization that has few exceptions, one that children can grasp. What questions would you ask to lead the children to induce the generalization and to apply it to unknown words?

---

57. Experience has shown that good testing procedures, including a proper rate of dictation, result in improved achievement—and do not instill poor listening habits.

58. For example, *Iowa Tests of Basic Skills* (Boston: Houghton Mifflin Co.), *Metropolitan Achievement Tests* (New York: Harcourt, Brace and World), and *Stanford Achievement Tests* (New York: Harcourt, Brace and World).

5. A child joins your class at mid-year. Describe the data you will collect—and your methods for collecting it—in order to determine that child's spelling needs.

6. List at least five principles around which you will design your spelling program. Make certain that these principles derive from research evidence, such as that outlined in this chapter.

7. Make a file of spelling games that fit the criteria stated in this chapter. Discuss the sources that contained several good ideas and include them in a bibliography.

8. Teachers can learn much from an analysis of the types of spelling errors children make. What would you deduce about the spelling needs of three children who spell penny "pinny," "peny," and "beni"?

9. Dictate the following words to a group of your peers: Antarctica, satellite, fluorescent, silhouette, poinsettia, desiccated. Spell the words orally while peers make corrections. Tally the number of people who can spell six, five, four, three, two, and one of them correctly. Retest immediately. Self-correct. Tally the results. Repeat the process. Retest a week later. Discuss the efficiency and effectiveness of this teaching procedure.

10. Interest in reforming spelling instruction is long-standing and persists today. George Bernard Shaw came up with a proposal for simplifying the relationship between sounds and their written symbols that rekindled some interest several years ago.

A drim kum tru[59]

If he had not tried to rush it, George Bernard Shaw might have succeeded in giving the English-speaking peoples a phonetic alphabet. Says the Smithsonian Torch, a slim house organ put out by the Smithsonian Institution for the museum set: "We are in complete accord with Bernard Shaw's campaign for a simplified alphabet. But instead of immediate drastic legislation, we advocate a modified plan.

"In 1957, for example, we would urge the substituting of 'S' for soft 'C.' Sertainly students in all sites of the land would be reseptive to this.

"In 1958, the hard 'C' would be replased by 'K' since both letters are pronounsed identikally. Not only would this klarify the konfusion in the minds of spellers, but typewriters and linotypes kould all be built with one less letter and all the manpower and materials previously devoted to making the 'C's' kould be used to raise the national standard of living.

"In the subsequent blaze of publisity it would be announced the the troublesome 'PH' would henseforth be written 'F.' This would make words like 'fonograf' 20 persent shorter in print.

"By 1959, the publik interest in a fonetik alfabet kan be expekted to have reatshed a point where more radikal prosedures are indikated. We would urge at that

59. Reprinted by permission from TIME, The Weekly Newsmagazine; Copyright Time Inc. 1957.

time the elimination of al double leters whitsh have always ben a nuisanse and desided deterent to akurate speling.

"We would al agre that the horible mes of silent 'E's' in our language is disgrasful. Therefore, in 1961, we kould drop thes and kontinu to read and writ merily along as though we wer in an atomik ag of edukation. Sins by this tim it would be four years sins anywun had used the leter 'C', we would then sugest substituting 'C' for 'Th.'

"Kontinuing cis proses year after year, we would eventuali hav a reali sensibl writen languag. By 1975, wi ventyur tu sa cer wud bi no mor uv ces teribly trublsum difikultis. Even Mr. Shaw, we, beliv, sud bi hapi in ce noleg cat his drims finali kam tru."

Do you ever simplify spellings? In what situations? Do you think there will ever be large-scale formal changes in spelling? Divide the class in half, prepare arguments, and debate the issue.

11. Investigate and report on the research relating auditory defects to spelling ability.

12. Following the suggestions in this chapter, construct a spelling test for a class of children at a particular grade level.

SELECTED REFERENCES

Bennett, D. M. *New Methods and Materials in Spelling.* Hawthorn, Australia: Australian Council for Educational Research, 1967.

Boyd, Gertrude A., and Talbert, F. Gene. *Spelling in the Elementary School.* Columbus, O.: Charles E. Merrill Publishing Co., 1971.

Greene, Harry A. *The New Iowa Spelling Scale.* Iowa City: Bureau of Educational Research and Service, University of Iowa, 1955.

Hanna, Paul R.; Hodges, Richard E.; and Hanna, Jean S. *Spelling: Structure and Strategies.* Boston: Houghton Mifflin Co., 1971.

Horn, Ernest. *What Research Says to the Teacher: Teaching Spelling.* Washington, D.C.: National Education Association, 1967.

Personke, Carl, and Yee, Albert H. *Comprehensive Spelling Instruction.* Scranton, Pa.: Intext Educational Publishers, 1971.

Sherwin, J. Stephen. *Four Problems in Teaching English: A Critique of Research.* Scranton, Pa: International Textbook Co., 1969.

Thomas, Ves. *Teaching Spelling, Canadian Word Lists and Instructional Techniques.* Toronto: Gage Educational Publishing, 1974.

Venezky, Richard L. "Linguistics and Spelling." In *Linguistics in School Programs*, pt. 2, edited by Albert H. Marckwardt. Chicago: University of Chicago Press, 1970.

16

Teaching and Maintaining Handwriting Skills

Handwriting appears to be a highly complex skill. Such difficulties as are encountered in perfecting this skill may be due in part to the complex neuromuscular coordination that is known to be an essential aspect of handwriting, in part to the presence or absence of the desire or incentive to write legibly, and in part to the role handwriting plays in the activities and occupation of the individual.—Elaine M. Templin, New Horizons for Research in Handwriting

Handwriting has long been a part of the school curriculum, but in many schools today it receives minimal attention: "Teachers appear to neglect it more than any other subject in the elementary curriculum."[1] Virtually no one wants to return to the kind of handwriting instruction of earlier years, particularly to the "muscle-training" drills of push-pull, making ovals, and the like, or to teaching a formal system—Spencerian, Roman, Palmer. Nevertheless, handwriting is a necessary skill, one that the school has an obligation to teach.[2] This chapter describes a

---

1. Albert H. Yee and Carl Personke, "Teaching Handwriting: Why and How," *Instructor*, (November 1967): p. 126.
2. According to Patrick Groff, "The Future of Legibility," *Elementary English* 52 (February 1975): 205, five language-arts methods textbooks for teachers "make no explanation at all of how it [handwriting] should be taught."

473

handwriting program for elementary schools and includes specific teaching and learning activities, major issues of concern in handwriting instruction, and the role of diagnosis in effective programs.

HANDWRITING TODAY

Typewriting has become so important to nearly everyone that some teachers believe handwriting does not deserve much attention. In addition to the typewriter, the tape recorder and the computer record information that at one time would have had to be preserved in handwritten form. Certainly the use of these instruments has affected the quality and amount of instructional attention handwriting receives. We must recognize, however, that these instruments are not yet available to everyone all the time and the typewriter, at least, is not yet pocket-sized.[3]

Why Teach Handwriting?

It is common knowledge that hours of time and a great deal of money are lost while people in various jobs attempt to decipher handwriting. The possibility of reducing these costs is a major incentive for teaching handwriting.[4] An additional justification is evidence that adults still use handwriting in many activities.[5] In school, the need for handwriting is obvious. Many authorities believe that poor handwriting "limits academic expression, inhibits spontaneous productivity, and affects communication."[6] One study of teacher ratings of handwritten compositions by elementary schoolchildren indicates that the quality of handwriting influenced judgments about the compositions.[7] This research simply confirms findings of earlier studies that noncontent factors affect the grading of students' papers.

---

3. Frances Goforth and C. W. Hunnicutt, "A New Slant on the Second R," *Today's Education* 59 (February 1970): 45.

4. Recent reports of such costs are not available, but Robert O'Brien (*Saturday Review*, 18 July 1959) estimated that United States businesses lose about $1 million per week because of scrambled orders, lost time, missent deliveries, and other consequences of bad handwriting. Perhaps efforts to encourage printing have reduced this cost, but we are not convinced that it has.

5. Elaine M. Templin, "The Legibility of Adult Manuscript, Cursive, or Manuscript-Cursive Handwriting Styles" in *New Horizons for Research in Handwriting*, edited by Virgil E. Herrick (Madison: University of Wisconsin Press, 1963), pp. 185–200.

6. John I. Arena, ed., *Building Handwriting Skills in Dyslexic Children* (San Rafael, Calif.: Academic Therapy Publications, 1970), p. iii.

7. Lynda R. Markham, "Influences of Handwriting Quality on Teacher Evaluation of Written Work," *American Educational Research Journal* 13 (Fall 1976): 277–83.

Handwriting in Schools

In 1960 96 percent of the schools responding to a nationwide survey reported that they taught handwriting, with typically five periods per week given to its instruction in the primary grades.[8] About the same time, a survey covering four midwestern states showed that 70 percent of 680 school systems had formal handwriting programs, and 59 percent of them offered a minimum of fifty minutes per week of handwriting instruction.[9] Although no one has made a comparative survey recently, undoubtedly most schools would attest to having handwriting programs. The extent to which teachers actually maintain the programs their curriculum directors and administrators say exist is less certain.

Tradition, public opinion, and current trends influence handwriting programs, as do commercial handwriting materials. The surveys just mentioned revealed that handwriting programs were tied largely to commercial materials, and as many as sixteen commercial programs were in use at that time. Far fewer are in use today, and probably most of these can be found in the third grade and below.

THE INSTRUCTIONAL PROGRAM

For a number of years the trend in handwriting programs has been toward functionalism; that is, the instruction in handwriting takes place as much as possible

8. Virgil E. Herrick and Nora Okada, "The Present Scene: Practices in the Teaching of Handwriting in the United States—1960," in *New Horizons for Research in Handwriting*, edited by Virgil E. Herrick (Madison: University of Wisconsin Press, 1963), pp. 17–38.

9. Fred M. King, "Handwriting Practices in Our Schools Today," *Elementary English* 38 (November 1961): 483–86.

in the context of other areas of the curriculum that require writing. Nevertheless, the better programs do not treat handwriting instruction incidentally, for children must learn fundamental handwriting skills before they can reach their potential in writing activities, and effective writing demands maintaining these skills.

Objectives of Handwriting Instruction

The major reason for teaching handwriting is that it is an instrument of communication. Handwriting is the principal tool of written expression. Therefore it must be legible. The major objective of handwriting instruction, then, is legibility.[10]

Considering this objective, a teacher should strive mainly to have pupils produce copy that is sufficiently legible to communicate their intended meaning and should avoid meaningless handwriting drills. Misapplication of the principle of use and need results from neglecting sound procedures in instruction. Principally overlooked is the fact that handwriting is a developmental process that encompasses more than just a few years of the child's total period of growth. Simply permitting children to write as the need arises does not constitute handwriting instruction, nor is it responsible to teach handwriting once and drop it from the instructional program. The ability to write legibly at a reasonable speed is attainable and sustainable only with constant and meaningful practice. Thus, the handwriting program should seek to:

1. Encourage pupils to use writing as a means to achieve effective expression.
2. Help each child to discover how skill in handwriting aids expression.
3. Encourage all pupils to strive for neatness and legibility with moderate speed in their writing activities.
4. Establish practice periods, as appropriate, at all grade levels.
5. Analyze the handwriting of individual pupils and formulate goals and instructional procedures to upgrade performance.
6. Develop in each pupil a sense of personal pride and self-appraisal and a desire for self-improvement.
7. Encourage those postures, uses of writing tools, and other factors that facilitate the production of legible handwriting.

These objectives largely aim to develop in pupils attitudes that will aid them in learning and maintaining the fundamental skills. In addition, the qualities of good writing require these specific skills: legibility, acceptable appearance, and

---

10. Here legibility means that no word would be misread in the context in which it is written because of the formation of the letters, their sizes, spaces between them, and so on.

reasonable ease and speed. Legibility results from proper letter formation, adequate word and letter spacing, uniform slant, satisfactory alignment of letters and words, and proper letter size. An acceptable or pleasing appearance comes from an absence of smudges and erasures, suitable arrangement of the writing, and evenness of the pressure applied to the writing instrument. Of course, writing with ease and speed results, to a considerable extent, from development of legibility and appearance. Other contributing factors are posture, freedom of movement, and writing rhythm.

Attitude

As is true of other skills, the teaching of handwriting is most effective when both the teacher and the children have attitudes that favor its learning. All must value handwriting as a skill, one that is necessary for effective expression and one that must be learned. The teacher can help instill this attitude by setting a good example, that is, by forming letters correctly and neatly, showing good posture while writing at the desk or at the chalkboard, writing smoothly and rhythmically, and holding the pen, pencil, or chalk correctly.

Children will learn that handwriting is important if they recognize that when their own writing is unreadable, their attempt to communicate has failed. The development of favorable attitudes presupposes certain learning conditions. As stated some years ago, children learn to write best when the following factors are present:[11]

1. They write something that is meaningful to them and have definite ideas they want to convey.
2. They have considerable liberty in making handwriting adjustments.
3. They advance to each new step in the writing process without too great an expenditure of time and effort as they show readiness to succeed in it.
4. They have a strong personal incentive to improve their writing.
5. They are physically comfortable, emotionally secure, and have the proper materials with which to work.
6. They receive thorough teaching as they need it and ample opportunity to practice under continuous supervision.
7. They progress at their own rate of speed, and instructional procedures are individualized.
8. They are encouraged to evaluate their own progress in terms of their previous achievements and present needs.

---

11. *Practices and Problems in Handwriting*, Educational Research Bulletin of Bureau of Reference and Statistics No. 9 (New York: Board of Education of the City of New York, September 1947), p. 22.

Readiness for Writing

The consideration commonly given to readiness for beginning reading instruction is also necessary for handwriting. Children whose muscular coordination shows that they are not yet ready to make letter forms need many readiness experiences. A variety of body coordination exercises, especially rhythmic ones, are necessary and beneficial for most children entering school. The teacher should gradually build a sense of rhythm and balance in the child. In addition, each child needs to explore, feel, taste, touch, and see many things during the readiness process. These activities help in developing ability to see differences between letters, to note how they are made, to follow directions, to make the movements that beginning handwriting entails, to hold the writing instrument easily and properly, and to feel secure and positively motivated when instruction begins.

Specifically, readiness for handwriting instruction is shown by:

1. Facility in using crayons, scissors, brushes, and pencils in a variety of activities
2. Ability to copy simple shapes
3. Established hand dominance
4. Interest in writing and reading messages

The need to build readiness for handwriting, as for reading, continues throughout a child's handwriting development. For instance, not all children are ready for narrow-lined paper at the same time; thus making only one kind of paper available does not take into consideration children's readiness.

Beginning Handwriting Instruction

Virtually all schools teach a form of manuscript writing in the primary grades. The reasons for doing so are the following:

1. Manuscript writing has only two movements—a straight line and a circle (or a partial one).
2. It more closely resembles the print that children encounter in reading.
3. It is easier for a child to see and correct faults in letter formation.
4. It is more legible.
5. It permits a slight rest period between letters.

The primary teacher (usually first grade) has the obligations of teaching the children how to make the letters, correcting undesirable habits, and motivating and building proper attitudes. Commercial programs provide guidance in this effort. As good commercial programs recommend, beginning instruction does not mean starting the children in copying activities in a workbook.

Beginning handwriting attempts should be characterized by large, free strokes, usually at the chalkboard or on large sheets of paper affixed to an easel. From this stage, children may progress to writing on large sheets of paper (guided by folds in the paper rather than lines) and then to 12″ × 18″ newsprint, which, when folded several times (the long way of the paper), guides letter placement. Still later they can go to 1″-ruled paper, and in grade two the often-recommended paper will have ¾″ to ½″ lines.

In the first stages of instruction chalk and crayons are typically the principal writing instruments. The first pencils should not be bulky and cumbersome (remember that children have used pencils at home), but the lead should be as wide and as soft as possible so that the letters the children write will be easy to see.

In the beginning stages of instruction, children also need to have before them (and not only up at the board) models of the letters. The first models also should show the order and direction of the movements involved in making the letters. Later children can get assistance by looking at models of the letters of the alphabet (both lowercase and uppercase) and the arabic numerals above the chalkboard or on a bulletin board.

Handwriting instruction requires teacher supervision, especially when children are learning letter formation. Otherwise, incorrect practices may become rather firmly established. Individualized handwriting instruction is also important from the beginning. Children need to learn to evaluate their work independently, correct their errors, and practice forms that they specifically and individually need to practice.

Cursive Writing Introduction

Most schools teach both manuscript and cursive forms of writing. Generally children learn cursive in the third grade, but some children make the transition to cursive in the second grade and others in the fourth. The most desirable practice is to introduce cursive handwriting to each child as he or she shows readiness, rather than as the children reach a certain grade level. Readiness to learn the cursive form includes the ability to write in a legible manuscript form from memory and with little or no difficulty, the ability to read cursive writing, and a desire to learn it.

The practices employed in teaching cursive form vary, a fact that commercial materials reflect. Some introduce the cursive form as something new and different from manuscript. Others emphasize making a transition by slanting the manuscript letters and later connecting them. These materials illustrate how the slanted and connected manuscript letters resemble or differ from the new cursive forms. Unless a teacher has experience with and knowledge about a particular procedure, it is wise to seek the guidance of a commercial (or perhaps a district or state) program.

Initially children should continue to use manuscript writing for compositional work, spelling lessons, and the like. The teacher should closely supervise beginning efforts in cursive writing.

Neither research evidence nor modern practice hold children to a particular form of handwriting (e.g.,   versus   ). Instead they indicate that each child should be allowed to develop an individual style. Teachers should put little effort toward having each child make letters according to particular models and by specific movements. Nevertheless, a child does need to be taught letter forms and how to connect letters and make the necessary movements economically. In addition, studies of handwriting quality point out that most poor handwriting shows primarily a lack of uniformity necessary for legibility.[12]

After children have mastered the cursive forms, the major instructional focus should be on skill maintenance. The subject of the following section and a later section on diagnosis is maintenance of handwriting skills.

A Handwriting Lesson Plan

As we have seen, most schools purchase commercial materials for use in handwriting lessons. Usually these materials contain practice exercises and suggestions for their use, but they may not be flexible enough to accommodate fully the specific needs of individual children. Some school districts provide supplemental

---

12. Leslie Quant, "Factors Affecting the Legibility of Handwriting," *Journal of Experimental Education* 14 (1946): 297–316.

instructional help in the form of curriculum guides. The following lesson was adapted from one such guide to illustrate one way to tailor a handwriting lesson to individuals in a total class setting.[13] It also focuses upon a common handwriting problem—relative sizes of letters.

Suggested Approach

To achieve good writing you need to remember only four different letter heights.

- *Loop letters* and *capitals* are almost a space tall.
- *Intermediate letters* (d, p, t) are ⅔ of a space tall.
- *Small letters* (a, c, e, etc.) are ⅓ of a space tall.
- *Lower loop letters* go half a space below the line (f, p, g, etc.)

Let's check the writing we did for Lesson VII. Using the two sentences, we will draw a line that touches the top of the *capitals* and *loop letter*. A ruler will help us to do this easily. Do the same thing with the *intermediate letters*. Now draw a line along the top of the *small letters*. Check to see if all capital and loop letters touch their line. Check the other letters to see if they touch their lines. How well did you do?

Excellent——— Good——— Fair——— Poor——— .

Put the correct heading on your paper, and then write each of the following words twice:

little   baby   all   bill   kick   hall

Use your ruler to check the height of the loop letters. Then write:

did   tied   pit   tipped   test   top

Use your ruler to check the intermediate letters. Then write:

am   or   seem   mice   saw   size   was

Use your ruler to check the small letters. Then write this sentence carefully to check all four sizes: Everyone expected that the judges would quickly decide to award the beautiful prize for excellent work to Mary.

Now use the check sheet on the sentence you just wrote. How well did you do?

	Excellent	*Good*	*Fair*	*Poor*
Loop letters:	———	———	———	———
Intermediate:	-———	———	———	———
Small letters:	———	———	———	———
Lower letters:	———	———	———	———

---

13. Nathan J. Naiman, *A Handwriting Blitz for Grades Five and Six* (San Diego: San Diego City Schools, 1964), p. 8.

Look at all the writing you did today. What is the one main thing you need to work on to improve? Check it.

Slant of writing	———
Size of letters	———
Finish strokes	———
Letter formation	———

Of course, this lesson is somewhat lacking in functionalism, but it also presents possibilities for grouping pupils for specific aspects of handwriting practice. For example, the teacher might group a class as follows:

Group 1: Children needing further development of coordination. These children might work on the formation of the letters of the lesson.

Group 2: Children needing practice upon relative size of letters and letter slant. These children might work on writing words with various-sized letters.

Group 3: Children who form letters well but need practice in writing smoothly. These children might practice by writing sentences.

Group 4: Children who write smoothly and relatively easily, with well-formed letters, but should write more rapidly. This group may practice writing sentences, timing their efforts without sacrificing quality.

Suggestions for Handwriting Practice

In addition to (or instead of) using guides and textbook materials, teachers could use practical writing situations as the basis of instruction. Under the teacher's guidance, handwriting would receive emphasis together with other writing goals. The following are the principles that should guide handwriting practice:

1. Regular practice periods are necessary; practice should be appropriate to individual needs.
2. Practice periods should be frequent but of short duration.
3. The teacher should keep checklist notations of individual needs.
4. Writing periods should follow periods of quiet activity rather than periods of strenuous movement.
5. Whenever possible, practice should grow out of needs that arise in purposeful writing situations.
6. Children should learn to evaluate their own performance.
7. Teachers should collect and analyze samples of children's writing at regular intervals.
8. Each child's handwriting should be displayed on the bulletin board sometime during the semester.

Motivational Activities

Writing for genuine communication purposes is the best motivation for children to learn to write well, but some extra activities may be useful. The following examples aim to provide practice and build interest.

1. Spelling words may suggest writing exercises, for many spelling errors are actually handwriting errors.

2. Research activities can give practice in writing proper names. For example, from source materials such as the *World Almanac* or an encyclopedia, the children might list the ten largest cities in the United States, the ten largest cities in the world, the five highest mountains, the longest rivers, or other items that have meaning in social studies.

3. Occasionally show pupils' papers on an overhead projector (with their permission). Discuss the good qualities of each paper and ways in which the writer could improve the handwriting and the appearance of the paper. Encourage children to refer in their critiques to standards they have established.

4. To help children with spacing, turn lined paper sideways and have them write one letter for each space.

5. Good handwriting is not only writing legibly, but also writing quickly and easily. Tape-record a paragraph or two, speaking slowly but evenly and paying strict attention to the number of words per minute. Place the tape in a listening center to be played and copied. Ask each child to critique the product. Another day, dictate another recording at a slightly faster speed.

6. Occasionally the teacher might request letters of application for classroom "jobs." Selection for the jobs may depend, in part, on the neatness of the application and the appearance of the handwriting. To ensure a more objective selection, ask "applicants" to use fictitious names. Class officers or a committee appointed for the occasion might make the choice.

7. Elicit from children statements about the points they should think about after they have examined their own handwriting: slant, uniformity, size, roundness, spacing, and closed letters. Check on one point each week and assign practice as needed. "Before" and "after" handwriting samples kept in a folder will show what improvement a child has made.

8. Have pupils make a poster of good handwriting with pockets in which to insert their daily writing activities, evaluating the handwriting as they file. The pockets may be labeled "Much Improved," "Improved," "Try Harder," and so on.

9. Have children make individual mailboxes for their desks in which other pupils may place daily notes. Legible notes are read and filed in

a pupil folder; illegible notes go to the dead letter office, where a committee of pupils studies (and reports) weaknesses of the writing.

Setting aside part of the classroom specifically for children to use in diagnosing their handwriting and practicing improving it provides motivation. This "center" should include folders of each child's writing, evaluation charts, scales, checklist forms, charts for recording progress, and diagnostic aids (we will discuss these later in this chapter). Activity cards should also be available for handwriting practice.

Still another successful motivational activity is the study of ancient forms of handwriting and contemporary systems that differ from ours. The ideographic systems of the Chinese and Japanese are particularly intriguing, as are braille and stenographic shorthand. Some children, too, might be interested in the study of different typefaces[14] and the use of different script styles to connote special meanings, as in advertising.

Some "Dos" and "Don'ts"

Like other elements of the language arts program, handwriting instruction suffers from the use by some teachers of ill-advised practices as well as from the absence of some desirable practices. A short list of "dos" and "don'ts" follows.

1. Do not make children write until they are fatigued. The quality of handwriting declines rapidly when the writer becomes tired.
2. As with "writing" spelling words in the air, extended production of letter forms in such a manner accomplishes little.
3. Do not assign copywork as a means of keeping children busy or as a form of punishment. Motivation to write well will disappear and the children will likely practice faulty forms.
4. Handwriting instruction, including individualized maintenance instruction in the middle and upper grades should take place on a regular schedule. Daily instruction is not necessary at some levels, but teachers should set aside a short time for regular instruction, perhaps once or twice weekly, for those who need it.
5. Do not drill children on abstract forms. Children should practice letter forms, not push-pulls, ovals, circles, and so on.
6. Do not rush children to learn handwriting forms because doing so creates tension.

---

14. Various activities and references are described in John Warren Stewig, *Exploring Language with Children* (Columbus, O.: Charles E. Merrill Publishing Co., 1974), pp. 262–70.

Parents' Participation

Parents exert a great influence on children's attitudes toward handwriting instruction. Parents should be aware of the nature of handwriting instruction in the school at each level. Teachers can send home copies of the forms of letters—both manuscript and cursive—along with a description of how the letters are formed. Not surprisingly, parents who have taught their children block printing at home sometimes create problems over the teaching of manuscript style. They may not regard manuscript as actual writing or understand the why and how of the transition to cursive.

A teacher can keep parents informed by holding group conferences for them and sending them letters (perhaps written by the children) explaining areas of confusion. As one curriculum guide suggests, parents can reinforce the school's handwriting instruction if they:[15]

> Realize that, in order to write well, children need a clean, smooth writing surface in a well lighted place and suitable writing materials—well sharpened pencils, free flowing pens, smooth paper.
>
> Encourage the use at home of the style of writing children are learning and using at school.
>
> Give opportunities at home for children to write telephone messages, shopping lists, thank-you notes or other communications in which clear, easily-read writing is important. Help children to understand that legible handwriting is a courtesy to the reader and a source of personal satisfaction in a job well done.

ISSUES AND SPECIAL PROBLEMS

Research on handwriting problems has been minimal since the early 1960s. For example, a 1978 review of language arts research reported in *Language Arts* cited only three studies related to handwriting instruction.[16] The same review cites 105 studies related to reading. Lack of research concern reflects widespread inattention to handwriting teaching. It is not due to any accumulation of evidence that all handwriting issues have been settled. In fact, in 1961 Horn noted twenty-one questions about handwriting that since then have received only minimal attention.[17] In the following sections we will consider several major issues and questions related to handwriting instruction.

---

15. Reprinted from *Teaching Handwriting* (New York: Board of Education of the City of New York, 1961), pp. 34–35.

16. William D. Sheldon et al., "A Summary of Research Studies Relating to Language Arts in Elementary Education: 1976," *Language Arts* 55 (January 1978): 65–101.

17. Ernest Horn, "Questions for Research on Handwriting," *The Elementary School Journal* 62 (March 1962): 304–12.

Handedness and the Left-handed Child

Left-handed writers seem to be a perennial classroom concern of many teachers. Much of this concern stems from a lack of understanding of how to help the left-handed child adjust to performing a skill for which most people use the right hand and for which most instructional material is designed to be used. In addition, there is still some confusion among teachers as to whether to transform a left-handed writer into a right-handed one.

The first thing to realize is that no one is entirely left-handed or entirely right-handed. Freeman stated that "by the usual test five or six percent of the children are found to prefer the left hand over the right or to be more skillful in using it."[18] A smaller percentage are ambidextrous; that is, they do not favor either hand. The rest, 90 percent or more, are right-handed. Of those who are classified as either right-handed or left-handed, some have a stronger preference than others for using one hand. The range of preference extends all the way from extreme right-handedness, ambidexterity, and mild degrees of left-handedness to extreme left-handedness.

Freeman further pointed out:

> There has been some dispute among psychologists as to whether right-handedness or left-handedness is inborn or is learned by imitation or precept. The burden of evidence is that it is inborn. This is indicated by the fact that preference appears very early, that the superiority of one hand or the other is frequently great and that there exists a small group who are more skillful with the left hand, contrary to all examples of teaching.

Most authorities agree that hand dominance is fairly well established by the time children reach school age. They recommend training the child who is dominantly left-handed to use the left hand for writing rather than to conform to the right-handed pattern. Of course, some children come to school with a wavering dominance. For these few children educators recommend encouragement to use the right hand, because we live in a largely right-handed world. Before doing so, however, a teacher should make certain that dominance has not been established by administering tests such as throwing, putting pegs in holes, locking and unlocking a padlock, and cutting with scissors.

The left-handed pupil encounters daily a world of right-handed people, including (usually) a right-handed teacher. Unable to imitate the teacher as right-handed classmates do, this pupil feels different, perhaps peculiar. The teacher must be aware of this possible lack of self-confidence and be prepared to provide for particular needs.

Left-handed children, like their right-handed counterparts, will learn to

---

18. Frank N. Freeman, *Solving Handwriting Needs* (Columbus, O.: Zaner-Bloser Co., 1960), p. 24.

write with ease, legibility, and speed under favorable conditions. Drummond's suggestions of a number of years ago are still applicable:[19]

> Provide lots of writing on the chalkboard. It is practically impossible to use the upside-down style at the board.
>
> Make sure the paper is properly placed on the desk. For manuscript, paper should be square with the desk. For cursive, the bottom right corner should be pointed at the body. It is hard to write in the upside-down position if paper is placed properly. Also, less hand smearing occurs.
>
> Permit lefties to continue manuscript writing indefinitely. Their writing is almost always more legible before they learn to write cursive than afterwards. As the left-handed children begin to change to cursive, though, watch the placement of the paper like a hawk.
>
> Encourage children to hold pencils or pens so that the top of the writing instrument is pointing over the shoulder of the same arm.
>
> Encourage lefties to develop a writing slant which feels natural and good. The slant will, undoubtedly, be a bit backhand compared to generally accepted handwriting styles because it is natural that way. A *consistent* slant makes writing legible, and a lefty is not likely to be consistent using a slant which is natural for right-handers.
>
> Furnish lefties with pencils which have slightly harder lead than that used by right handers. Harder lead will not smear as easily, thus providing less reason for twisting the wrist so that the hand is in the upside-down position.
>
> When ink is used, be sure that all lefties have a good non-skip ballpoint pen which has a high quality non-smear cartridge.
>
> Encourage lefties to learn to type. Most classrooms should have typewriters to encourage children to write creatively. With lefties, the need for typewriters is even greater.

Posture and Movement

Undoubtedly one of the most important *physical factors* affecting handwriting quality is the writing surface and the writer's position with respect to it. The most desirable position permits the writer to sit comfortably with both feet touching the floor and both arms resting in a relaxed position on the writing surface. Opinions differ greatly about the optimum position of the writing arm, angle of the hand and wrist, and arm and finger movements. There is general agreement that the angle that the paper makes with the body should be such that the wrist of the writing arm is perpendicular to the line of writing. Most handwriting teachers advise holding the writing instrument lightly, with the forefinger nearer the point than the thumb and both at least one inch above the writing point.

---

19. Harold Drummond, "Suggestions for the 'Lefties,'" *The National Elementary Principal* 38 (February 1959): 15. Copyright © 1959, National Association of Elementary School Principals. All rights reserved.

Paper and Arm Positions for the Left-handed Writer[a]

A   *Reverse of right-handed position. Arm axis is 90° with paper ruling. Slant strokes are directed downward and outward (leftward). Slant is generally forward and uniform.*

B   *Paper is turned more to the right (clockwise) than the reverse of right-handed placement. Arm axis angle with paper ruling is greater than 90°. Slant motion is a sideward (leftward) push of the writing arm. Slant is uniformly forward.*

C   *Extreme turning of the paper. Paper ruling is 90° (plus or minus 5°) with the front edge of the desk. Slant motion is a sideward (leftward and upward) push of the writing arm. Slant is generally forward and uniform.*

The positions for writing with the left hand shown above are reported in the study as the most efficient adjustments to take into account (1) quality, (2) rate, (3) freedom from smearing, and (4) posture. Of these three, B was rated the most desirable, A the second most desirable, and C the third, among some fifteen positions found being used by left-handed writers.

[a] E. A. Enstrom, "The Relative Efficiency of the Various Approaches to Writing with the Left Hand," *Journal of Educational Research* 55 (August 1962): 573–77.

They also agree, in general, that rapid and legible writing is the result of the smooth coordination of whole arm, forearm, wrist, and finger movements.

Rhythm in Writing

Legible letter formation develops through practice in forming and connecting the letters, comparison of the results of this practice with acceptable models, and the establishment of rhythmic movements in writing. Smoothness of movement also relates to speed of writing, and both are highly correlated with maturity. Whether it is advantageous to encourage rhythmic writing has been a subject of debate for some time, but most schools have discontinued the use of rhythmical exercises set to music or counting. Years ago, Hildreth said: "The employment of rhythmical aids is increasingly discounted. The length of time taken to write down different letters of the alphabet in any form varies with letters. The use of a uniform rhythmical count for all children fails to recognize the needs of individual children."[20]

---

20. Gertrude Hildreth, *Learning the Three R's* (Minneapolis: Educational Publishers, 1947), p. 604.

Paper Positions for Writing

The relaxed angle of the forearm across the desk and the maximum convenience of the forearm and fingers to the paper decides the position of the paper. Usually the angle of the bottom of the paper with the edge of the writing surface should be 30 degrees.

For manuscript writing the paper is usually perpendicular to the edge of the desk. Some authorities suggest an angle of about 10 degrees.

Several years later, however, Myers said, "the point and purpose of counting [may] have been lost to many teachers of handwriting. It seems quite clear that guidance in finding the rhythmical movement for each letter is needed. Once the timing of the different parts of a letter is worked out, some counting to regulate the repetition of the rhythm of the letter can be used to encourage speed or rate of writing."[21]

Andersen probably represents current opinion that evidence concerning rhythm in handwriting is unclear.[22] After reviewing the research, he concluded that the lack of a common definition of rhythm and clear data regarding its role points to the need for further clarification of its instructional application. The Hildreth and Myers statements reflect differences in definitions, but each probably contains an element of truth. Certainly we should not expect all children to write at the same rate (rhythmic count), but every child should write with a smoothness that implies a rhythm.

---

21. Emma Myers, "A General Review of Handwriting Instruction" (Ph. D. dissertation, State University of Iowa, 1954).

22. Dan W. Andersen, "Handwriting Research: Movement and Quality," *Elementary English* 42 (January 1965): 48.

The Manuscript-Cursive Issue

Questions concerning the relative values of teaching manuscript and cursive forms of handwriting have persisted since the introduction of manuscript form over fifty years ago. The principal issues are these: can manuscript writing be done as rapidly as cursive writing and when should the change from manuscript form to cursive form take place?

Most schools have accepted the practice of teaching manuscript writing for the child's initial writing experiences, but the extension of manuscript form as the only or principal means of writing throughout the grades and high school is still a topic of considerable debate. A few schools continue to teach manuscript writing throughout the grades and give no instruction in cursive writing. Others continue to use manuscript style after introducing cursive. The number of school systems following either of these practices at this time is small, however.

Although manuscript handwriting generally is easier to learn and easier to read, arguments against its continued use as the major writing form are that it is slower to produce than cursive writing and that the general public considers it to be printing rather than writing. Increasing evidence suggests, however, that manuscript may be written as rapidly as cursive.[23] One researcher reported a study that found "in all cases manuscript writing was as fast as cursive writing, and in some instances faster. In every case the legibility of the manuscript papers was far superior."[24] Studies have shown, too, that manuscript writing seems to favor the development of fluency of expression in the primary grades. Because fluency of language expression is a major goal of the language program, extending the use of manuscript form, particularly into the third and fourth grades, has become a major element of the current controversy.

Groff believes that there is no point in changing from manuscript to cursive and that justification for changing is based largely on opinions rather than on facts derived from research. He adds that "no research evidence available suggests that children like cursive handwriting better than manuscript or that cursive is preferred for written material of greater length or of better literary quality. There is substantial evidence that contradicts the notion that cursive handwriting is easier to learn, easier to write, and that errors made in cursive are easier to correct."[25]

Nevertheless, tradition is a major controlling factor in all school practices and cannot be minimized—handwriting instruction is no exception. Therefore school handwriting programs will continue generally to provide a transition from manuscript to cursive form. *When* the transition should occur definitely remains

---

23. Arthur Dale Jackson, "A Comparison of Speed and Legibility of Manuscript and Cursive Handwriting of Intermediate Grade Pupils" (Ph. D. dissertation, University of Arizona, 1970).
24. Patrick J. Groff, "From Manuscript to Cursive—Why?" *The Elementary School Journal* 61 (November 1960): 97–101.
25. Ibid., p. 100.

an issue. In the past, attempts to settle this issue were based on surveys of current practice, in other words, tabulations of what schools do and what educators who have conducted handwriting research recommend. As poor a source for guidance as these efforts were, decisions are even less objectively based now. Despite an inadequate research base, however, we can make some logical judgments. For example, it is surely shortsighted for any school system, classroom, or commercial handwriting materials to suggest that a transition should be made during a specific semester, particularly by all children. Forcing a second writing system upon a child who has not yet achieved a legible style with the first is clearly unwise. Also, confronting children with a new form of writing at a time when they are intent on expressing their ideas and using their imagination is shortsighted. On the other hand, as most second-grade and even first-grade teachers know, many children do want to learn "real writing" and others can do so without great difficulty or loss of writing interest.

Opinion is growing that reasonable mastery of both styles of handwriting is essential for developing optimum skill to meet a variety of written communication needs. Considering the volume of information that the school curriculum includes and the increasing number of skills children need to know, however, we might wonder whether children have time to learn and to maintain two sets of skills for the singular purpose of expressing oneself in written form. And the fact that the majority of children now learn to use a typewriter means that they could conceivably be learning three forms of writing. Perhaps educators need to ignore pressures to include everything in the school curriculum, to firmly establish a position on this issue, and to hold to it regardless of tradition or other pressure.

EVALUATION AND DIAGNOSIS

Because the primary objective of handwriting instruction is the development of skills necessary for writing legibly with speed and ease, evaluation of the *instructional program* requires measuring the quality and speed of children's writing. In addition, if each child is to attain reasonable legibility, plus speed and ease of handwriting production, the program must give considerable attention to diagnostic and corrective activities.

Quality and Rate Measurement

A teacher can determine the quality of a pupil's handwriting by comparing specimens with samples of established or known value. At one time, teachers compared samples of the child's writing with the copy-book model. Naturally this procedure encouraged children to imitate the shapes and sizes of the letters—and to some extent the shading of the letters that had been included largely for decorative purposes. Under these conditions, quality and rate were not the main

---

Specimen 3—Medium for Grade 5

Similar cursive handwriting may be marked 75. The standard
speed for this grade is about 60 letters per minute.

*I live in America. It is good
to live where you have freedom
to work and play. As an
American, I support my country
and what it stands for.*

Specimen 5—Poor for Grade 5

Similar cursive handwriting may be marked 65, and writing
poorer than this may be evaluated accordingly.

*My name stands for
me. I want to write it
well.*

Specimen 2—Good for Grade 1

Similar manuscript writing may be given a mark of 80.

We love our flag,
red, white, and blue.

---

objectives of writing instruction or measurement. With the appearance of scales
for the evaluation of handwriting, instructional emphasis moved toward functionalism in terms of legibility and writing rate.

It is true, however, that handwriting scales are not in general use. Probably
a fair estimate is that only 10 to 20 percent of schools use a scale in evaluating
children's handwriting and, thus, their instructional programs. Of the schools
that use them, some use scales developed within school systems (a satisfactory
practice if the scales have been prepared properly) and others use the ones that
accompany achievement tests.[26] Andersen reported that the Freeman (Zaner-
Bloser) scale is the one most commonly used and the West and Ayres scales are
also in use.[27]

Handwriting scales definitely have a place in instruction for the purpose of
evaluating the legibility and speed of children's writing. Some kind of standard or

---

26. The *California Achievement Test*, for example.
27. Andersen, p. 51.

norm is always useful in evaluation. The fact that a scale does not take into account each pupil's stylistic inclinations does not mean that it does not provide a measure of quality and rate.

The *Guiding Growth in Handwriting Evaluation Scales* provide five specimens of handwriting for each grade level and suggest rating samples "good," "medium," or "fair."[28] The scale for each grade level suggests a numerical score for each of the five specimens. Several specimens from the scales are reproduced on p. 492. They undoubtedly show the general quality of handwriting nationally in a more accurate way than older scales.

The nature of the scale and the way in which it is used make it difficult to secure objective and highly accurate ratings of handwriting samples, but research shows that after a training period spent in study of the scale samples, other evaluator's scores, and directed practice with samples of known quality, the average teacher can learn to rate handwriting samples with sufficient accuracy and objectivity for survey use.[29]

The accuracy of handwriting rate scores depends largely on the care with which the samples are collected. Rate of writing may be expressed either in seconds per letter or in letters per minute, but the latter is the form most commonly used. To obtain the rate score, you count the total number of letters written by each child and divide this number by the number of minutes allowed for the writing.

According to the *Guiding Growth in Handwriting Scale*, different grade levels should be able to achieve the rates in words per minute shown below. The rate norms for grades one and two apply to manuscript form, the others to cursive.

Grade	1	2	3	4	5	6	7
Rate	25	30	45	50	60	67	74

Directions with this scale suggest that the teacher write the sentences to be evaluated on the board, that the children be permitted to practice writing them several times, and that the score period be two minutes long.

Diagnostic Charts

Teachers may develop their own methods of identifying individual handwriting needs or consult published materials like the *Handwriting Faults and How to*

---

28. *Guiding Growth in Handwriting Scale*. Columbus, O.: Zaner-Bloser Company. Specimens shown are adapted from the 1974 edition.

29. Leonard S. Feldt, "Reliability of Measures of Handwriting Quality," *Journal of Educational Psychology* 53 (December 1962): 288–92.

| How to test legibility: | Make a letter finder by cutting a hole a little larger than the letter in a piece of cardboard. Place the hole of this finder over each letter in turn and mark the letters which are illegible. Have the pupils practice these letters separately, then write the word again and test as before. |

ieligible   *ieligible*

| How to test slant: | Draw slanting lines through the letters and mark all letters which are off slant. If the slant is too great, the paper is tilted too much. If the writing is too vertical, the paper is too upright, and if the slant is backward, the paper is tilted the wrong direction. |

correct   incorrect

slant   *slant*

| How to test for spacing: | Draw parallel lines between letters (see diagram). Place the paper in front of you and mark all letters and words which are unevenly spaced. |

correct   incorrect

spacing   *s pacing*

| How to test alignment: | Alignment and size are closely integrated and should be studied together. Use a ruler (a diagnostic ruler is best) and draw a base line touching as many of the letters as possible. Also draw a line along the tops of the small letters. Mark the letters above or below these lines. |

correct   incorrect

alignment   *alignment*

| How to test size of letters: | Draw lines along the tops of the letters. Remember the minimum letters *i, u, v,* etc. are ¼ space high; *d, t, p* are ½ space; capitals and *l, h, k, b, d,* are ¾ high. All the lower loop letters extend ½ space below the line. |

Comparative size of letters

| How to test for quality of line: | Make a letter finder by cutting a hole a little larger than the letter in a piece of cardboard. Place the hole of this finder over each letter in turn and mark the letters which are illegible due to the quality of line. Have pupils practice these letters from their writing books separately until the letters are perfectly legible. Then have them write the whole word again and test as before. |

494

Correct Them Chart.[30] The purpose of this chart and other commercially available ones is to reveal whether or not a child's handwriting specimen violates one or more of the following essential qualities: (1) uniformity of slant, (2) uniformity of alignment, (3) quality of line, (4) letter formation, and (5) spacing. Three levels of quality (excellent, mediocre, and poor) are shown for each trait.

In addition to illustrating these qualities, the chart suggests how to test a child's handwriting copy for each quality. The chart is particularly helpful because it enables both the teacher and the pupil to discover specific handwriting weaknesses and recommends ways to overcome them.[31]

A particular value of diagnostic charts is that pupils become interested in using them. Many children appreciate a scientific approach to solving their problems and are motivated by it.

Other Diagnostic Suggestions

The fact that only 7 percent of the schools that participated in one survey had a planned program for diagnosis and remediation of handwriting difficulties supports the contention made several times in this chapter that handwriting instruction generally is inadequate.[32] The evidence is simply overwhelming that a diagnosis of individual handwriting needs and handwriting faults should be the basis of handwriting instruction. Ignoring problems and failing to take remedial measures compounds the difficulties.

Recent studies of handwriting illegibilities show that the problem centers on a small number of letters. Horton reported that the letter r accounted for 12 percent of the illegibilities and that r plus h, l, k, p, or z accounted for 30 percent of all illegibilities.[33] The tabulation that follows is an adaptation of the findings of an early study of causes of illegibilities.[34]

Important types of letter malformations

a made like *u*	*d* made like *cl*
a made like *o*	*e* closed
c made like *e*	*g* made like *y*
c made like *i*	*h* made like *li*

---

30. Zaner-Bloser, *Handwriting Faults and How to Correct Them* (Columbus, O.: Zaner-Bloser Co.).

31. Examples from *Guiding Growth in Handwriting Scales* (Columbus, O.: Zaner-Bloser Co.). Specimens are adapted from the 1974 edition.

32. Dan W. Andersen, p. 123.

33. Lowell W. Horton, "Illegibilities in the Cursive Handwriting of Sixth Graders," *Elementary School Journal* 70 (May 1970): 446–50.

34. L. C. Pressey and S. L. Pressey, "Analyses of Three Thousand Illegibilities in the Handwriting of Children and Adults," *Educational Research Bulletin* 6 (28 September 1927): 270–73.

i made like *c*	*o* made like *a*
i with dot right	*r* made like *i*
i with dot left	*r* made like *s*
l made like uncrossed *t*	*r* made like *n*
m made like *w*	*s* indistinct
n made like *u*	*s* made like *r*
n made like *v*	*t* made like *l*

The following list itemizes seven of the most common defects in writing and possible contributing causes. It should provide additional diagnostic and remedial assistance.[35]

Defect	*Causes*
1. Too much slant	a. Writing arm too near body
	b. Thumb too stiff
	c. Point of nib too far from fingers
	d. Paper in wrong position
	e. Stroke in wrong direction
2. Writing too straight	a. Arm too far from body
	b. Fingers too near nib
	c. Index finger alone guiding pen
	d. Incorrect position of paper
3. Writing too heavy	a. Index finger pressing too heavily
	b. Using wrong type of pen
	c. Pen too small in diameter
4. Writing too light	a. Pen held too obliquely or too straight
	b. Pen too large in diameter
5. Writing too angular	a. Thumb too stiff
	b. Pen too lightly held
	c. Movement too slow
6. Writing too irregular	a. Lack of freedom of movement
	b. Movement of hand too slow
	c. Pen gripping
	d. Incorrect or uncomfortable position
7. Spacing too wide	a. Pen progresses too fast to right
	b. Excessive sweeping lateral movement

---

35. These factors—slant, spacing, etc.—can be assessed with a checklist that a teacher can construct. See Elizabeth G. Allen and Jone P. Wright, "Personalizing Handwriting Instruction," *The Elementary School Journal* 74 (April 1974): 426. A checklist could also include a record of the legibility of individual letters.

In addition to handwriting charts that illustrate levels of quality and therefore suggest particular needs, teachers should use overhead projectors and other such devices to show children's handwriting for group appraisal and comment. Pupils can also project their own papers. Enlargement of their writing can help them to spot their own errors.

Pupil Evaluation of Handwriting

Teachers must master a variety of handwriting diagnostic techniques, including those that involve the use of product scales and charts, in order to tailor instruction to individual needs. Nevertheless, the role of the child in this process of upgrading the quality of handwriting is critical.

Characteristics of legible handwriting, for example, need not derive from the teacher or from a text. Children can view specimens and generate descriptions of "good" handwriting. To illustrate, children might examine one of the two sentence pairs shown on p. 498, depending on their level of development. They will readily see that sentence one in each pair is "easier to read." Asking them to think about what makes number one easier to read, the teacher can encourage children with a series of probing questions to develop a list of the qualities of legible handwriting that is similar to this one:

1. The letters "sit on the line." (They are aligned.)
2. There is even spacing between letters and between words.
3. The letters all slant the same way. (They are parallel.)
4. Each word ends in the middle of the space. (Ending strokes are important.)
5. Closed letters are closed and round letters are round.

After establishing criteria of legibility, children can apply their standards to an analysis of their own handwriting. Working in pairs might facilitate the production of a list of personal handwriting goals, stated in order of priority. The first of these goals might become the focus of one week's practice. At the end of the week the child evaluates the handwriting specimens that he or she has collected in a folder to determine how much progress is evident. The following week the child might emphasize goal two while continuing to maintain and reinforce goal one. The process should be cumulative.

This technique is fundamentally different from one in which the children and teacher alike use a commercially produced scale for evaluation efforts. Allowing children to evaluate growth toward legibility by comparing present and past writing specimens acknowledges the developmental nature of the process; in other words, it reflects the recognition that legibility depends on muscular control, calm nerves, adequate vision, hand-eye coordination, and other factors. The

1. The brown fox jumped over the lazy dog.

2. The brown fox jumpedover the lazy dog.

1. The brown fox jumped over the lazy dog.

2. The brown fox jumped over the lazy dog.

specimens that comprise a commercial product scale may be based on actual children's writing, but they may not correspond to the reality of an individual child or even a particular group. Teachers should not frustrate conscientious pupils by stressing unrealistic goals that they might reach if they work harder.

A second method for getting children to devise criteria for defining legible writing is to have them examine the range of writing samples that abound in their environment. Newspaper and magazine advertisements are a prime source of a variety of writing forms used for diverse purposes. An illustration is shown below.

As in every school subject, corrective work in handwriting can be effective only if the teacher works with each child on an individual basis after making a careful individual diagnosis. With far too few exceptions, programs for handwriting instruction have been and are incomplete. Many do not include skill maintenance, individual diagnosis and correction, and measurement of the success with which the instructional goals are being met.

DO YOU WANT TO PLAY CHOO-CHOO?

Then we'll be ready with cruise wear.

Teacher: "What do these say?" "Did you have trouble reading either one?"

Children: "No."

Teacher: (Optional review of legibility characteristics.) "Which style do you think would be best for your everyday use?"

Children: "The second."

Teacher: "Why?"

Children: "It would take forever to make those first letters." "My hand would get sore."

Teacher: "What, then, would you say about handwriting that is good?"

Children: "It's easy to read." (legible) "It's quick and easy to do." (produced fluently and efficiently)

EXERCISES FOR THOUGHT AND ACTION

1. Handwriting is said to evolve from art. What clues might you get about children's "readiness to write" by looking at their scribbles (including their ability to copy the shapes that compose their first names)? What kinds of experiences could you provide which would encourage a readiness for writing?

2. Think of the situations in which you are instructed, "Please print." What are they? In what situations are you required to produce cursive writing? (Do not mention "signing your name" because the courts have ruled that manuscript signatures are legal because they show individuality). Do you have any predictions about the future use of cursive writing in schools and society?

3. Plan a lesson with the objective of illustrating to children the value of legible handwriting. You might utilize a resource similar to this one.[36]

forum

Read by the Decision-Makers of Texas

The costs of poor penmanship

Can you write legibly? This is a question seldom asked today, and the subject is one which is receiving less and less attention. The art of penmanship is dying because many persons regard instruction in the art of writing as a waste of time.

This complacency, or indifference, to neat handwriting is costing the U.S. many millions of dollars each year. One estimate pushes the cost to $70 million.

Many handwriting complaints come from insurance executives, who say that badly written policy forms turned in by their salesmen cost them money. Even banks, where accuracy is of prime importance, have trouble with illegibility.

Not only educators but the public as well should take up the battle against handwriting illiteracy. Perhaps if each businessman were to take the time to figure what illegible handwriting is costing him, there would be an awakening in the business world.

And if each consumer realized that the cost of this sloppiness was included in the price of the articles he buys, perhaps he, too, would react.

---

36. Reprinted with the permission of the *Austin American-Statesman*. Copyright © 1979. All rights reserved.

4. Be a good model. Self-analyze your writing. Practice on chalkboard and paper. (Note: you can practice chalkboard writing at home by taping newspaper want ads horizontally on a wall. Felt-tip pen simulates chalk, one ad column a half space, and two ad columns a full space.)

5. Examine several commercial handwriting systems and describe differences in the forms of letters, order of strokes, and the sequence in which forms are taught.

6. Over a period of weeks, collect written materials that you receive—envelopes, letters, notes—and rank them according to legibility. Then examine the best and poorest for specific features to improve.

7. Report to the class on books about the writing systems of languages other than English, shorthand systems, and the history of writing suitable for use with elementary school children.

8. What would you do for a new child in your fifth-grade classroom who formed letters differently from the way prescribed by your handwriting program? Would you force the child to change styles? Why or why not?

9. Use a handwriting scale or diagnostic chart and evaluate your own handwriting. Did you learn anything about the legibility of your writing?

10. Describe specific practices you would follow in teaching a left-handed child.

11. Present to the class several of the procedures that commercial handwriting systems suggest using to make a transition from the manuscript to the cursive form of handwriting.

12. There is some argument in favor of teaching only a combination of manuscript and cursive forms (often called an italic style). Find out all you can about this proposal.

13. Observe a group of children while they are writing and note the relationship between posture and the legibility and rate of their writing.

14. Suggest additions to the list of motivational activities that appeared in this chapter. Identify your sources.

SELECTED REFERENCES

Andersen, Dan W. *What Research Says to the Teacher: Teaching Handwriting.* Washington, D. C.: National Education Association, 1968.

Askov, E.; Otto, W.; and Askov, W. "A Decade of Research in Handwriting: Progress and Prospect," *Journal of Educational Research* 64 (1970): 99–111.

Burns, Paul C., and Broman, Betty L. *The Language Arts in Childhood Education,* 3rd ed. Chicago: Rand McNally College Publishing Co., 1975.

Feldt, Leonard S. "The Reliability of Measuring Handwriting Ability," *Journal of Educational Psychology* 53 (December 1962): 288–92.

Freeman, Frank N. "On Italic Handwriting," *Elementary School Journal* 60 (February 1960): 258–64.

Gray, William S. *The Teaching of Reading and Writing: An International Survey.* New York: Columbia University Press, 1956.

Groff, Patrick J. "From Manuscript to Cursive—Why?" *Elementary School Journal* 61 (November 1960): 55–62.

Herrick, Virgil E. *Comparison of Practices in Handwriting Advocated by Nineteen Commercial Systems of Handwriting Instruction*. Madison: University of Wisconsin Press, 1960.

Herrick, Virgil E., ed. *New Horizons for Research in Handwriting*. Madison: University of Wisconsin Press, 1963.

Horn, Thomas D., ed. *Research on Handwriting and Spelling*. Champaign, Ill.: National Conference on Research in English and the National Council of Teachers of English, 1966.

Myers, Emma H. *The Why and Hows of Teaching Handwriting*. Columbus, O.: Zaner-Bloser Co., 1963.

Otto, Wayne, and Andersen, Dan W. "Handwriting." In *Encyclopedia of Educational Research*, 4th ed., edited by Robert L. Ebel. New York: Macmillan Co., 1969.

Stewig, John Warren. *Exploring Language with Children*. Columbus, O.: Charles E. Merrill Publishing Co., 1974.

INDEX

DATE DUE

MAR 2 1 1995			

Demco, Inc. 38-293